XRA

HITLER'S VIENNA

ALSO BY BRIGITTE HAMANN

The Reluctant Empress: A Biography of Empress Elisabeth of Austria

Hitler's Vienna

A DICTATOR'S APPRENTICESHIP

BRIGITTE HAMANN
Translated from the German by Thomas Thornton

New York   Oxford
Oxford University Press
1999

Oxford University Press

Oxford   New York

Athens   Auckland   Bangkok   Bogotá   Buenos Aires
Calcutta   Cape Town   Chennai   Dar es Salaam   Delhi   Florence
Hong Kong   Istanbul   Karachi   Kuala Lumpur   Madrid
Melbourne   Mexico City   Mumbai   Nairobi   Paris   São Paulo
Singapore   Taipei   Tokyo   Toronto   Warsaw

and associated companies in
Berlin   Ibadan

Copyright © 1999 by Brigitte Hamann

Published by Oxford University Press, Inc.,
198 Madison Avenue, New York, New York 10016

Oxford is a registered trademark of Oxford University Press

Library of Congress Cataloging-in-Publication Data
Hamann, Brigitte.
[Hitlers Wien. English]
Hitler's Vienna : a dictator's apprenticeship / Brigitte Hamann.
p.   cm.
Includes bibliographical references and index.
ISBN 0–19–512537–1
1. Hitler, Adolf, 1889–1945—Childhood and youth.   2. Hitler,
Adolf, 1889–1945—Homes and haunts—Austria—Vienna.   3. Heads of
state—Germany—Biography.   4. Vienna (Austria)—Intellectual life.
5. Vienna (Austria)—Politics and government.   I. Title.
DD247.H5H281913   1999   943.6'13051'092—dc21   [B]   98–33886

1 3 5 7 9 8 6 4 2

Printed in the United States of America
on acid-free paper

CONTENTS

PREFACE

This book is an attempt at a cultural and social history of Vienna in the years before World War I from the point of view of a young, single handyman from the provinces: Adolf Hitler. At the same time it is a biography of this young man, up until his move to Munich at the age of twenty-four. I have connected these two topics in order to illustrate how profoundly Vienna influenced Hitler.

Hitler's Vienna is not the artistic-intellectual "fin-de-siècle Vienna"—that is to say, the Vienna that has long since turned into a lifeless cliché—we associate with Sigmund Freud, Gustav Mahler, Arthur Schnitzler, and Ludwig Wittgenstein. Hitler's Vienna is the Vienna of the "little" people, who viewed Viennese modernity with incomprehension and rejected it as "degenerate," too disconnected from the people, too international, too "Jewish," too libertine. It is the Vienna of the disadvantaged, of those who were living in *Männerheime* (men's hostels), typically men full of fear and susceptible to obscure theories, particularly ideas that despite their misery made them feel to be part of an elite, to be "better than" other people after all. To these men, being "better" in this multinational "Babylon of races" meant belonging to the "noble German people" rather than being a Slav or a Jew.

In order to come to a closer understanding of this specific image of Vienna, I picked up cues found in Hitler's *Mein Kampf* as well as in his monologues and stories about Vienna. (Passages from these sources are quoted in italics throughout the text that follows.) Whenever possible, I identify and portray the Viennese personages Hitler mentioned, placing particular emphasis on describing the young Hitler's multifaceted relationships with Jews. In view of Hitler's virtual addiction to newspapers, I quote mainly from those newspapers that influenced him—not from the famous intellectual journals but from those of the Schönerians, the German Radicals, and Christian Social Party members. I give particular consideration to the local papers in the districts where Hitler lived, partly because I want to give an impression of the very peculiar language of these sources, which has so far been largely ignored.

The main problem of a biography of the young Hitler lies in the meagerness of the sources. This lack is due to Hitler's efforts to remove all traces of his years in Linz and Vienna. The only source for his biography was supposed to be *Mein Kampf*, in other words, his version of his life in hindsight. Because any biography of Hitler depends on a critical appraisal of the source materials, a comprehensive critique of these sources is a major concern of this book.

During the years of my research for this book I received a great deal of help for which I want to express my thanks, above all to the librarians in the archives and collections I consulted. I am particularly indebted to two eyewitnesses: Professor Marie Jahoda in Sussex for her stories about her uncle Rudolf Jahoda's house, which the young Hitler visited; and Marianne Koppler, the daughter of Hitler's friend Rudolf Häusler, who enabled me to introduce this man, virtually unknown in the literature, in this book.

HITLER'S VIENNA

1
From the Provinces to the Capital

The Dream of Linz

One of the last photographs of Adolf Hitler depicts him shortly before his suicide as he sits in the bunker of his Chancellery. While the Red Army advanced into the ruins of Berlin outside, he pondered a pompous architectural model of the Upper Austrian provincial capital of Linz, the gigantic buildings illuminated by a sophisticated arrangement of spotlights: Linz in the morning sun, at midday, at sunset glow, and at night. "No matter at what time, whether during the day or at night, whenever he had the opportunity during those weeks, he was sitting in front of this model," the architect Hermann Giesler reported, saying that Hitler stared at it as if at "a promised land into which we would gain entrance."[1]

Visitors to whom he showed the model, often at the most unusual hours of the night, were confused and horrified: the man who had reduced Europe to ashes and ruins had clearly lost his sense of reality and hardly noticed how many people were still dying in these last weeks, in his name, and according to his will, as he continued to refuse to capitulate and end the horror.

Hitler dreamed of Linz, his hometown, which he had appointed "the Führer's sister city" and had wanted to make the Greater German Reich's

cultural capital, the "most beautiful city on the Danube," the "metropolis," the petrified glorification of his person and his policies: *Linz owes everything it has and is yet to obtain to the Reich. Therefore this city must become the carrier of the idea of the Reich. Every building in Linz should have the inscription "Gift from the German Reich."*[2]

On the left bank of the Danube, in Urfahr, opposite the old part of town, a party and administration center had been planned with an assembly area for 100,000 and grounds for celebrations accommodating 30,000 people, an exposition area with a Bismarck monument, and a technical university. According to the plan, a "district center"—with a new city hall, the Reich governor's house, the district and party center, and the Linz community center—was to be built around a national commemorative site: Hitler's parents' tomb, with its steeple, visible from far away, whose chimes were to play—albeit *not every day*—a motif from Anton Bruckner's *Romantic Symphony*.[3] This steeple was planned to be higher than that of Vienna's Saint Stephen's Cathedral. Thus, Hitler said, he was making up for an old injustice; for, to the Linzers' vexation, during the construction of the neogothic Linz cathedral, Vienna had reduced the height of the steeple *so that the Stephen's Tower would remain the highest steeple in the country*.[4] A monument "to the foundation of the Greater German Empire" was to be built too, along with a large stadium. Hitler told the Upper Danube district director, August Eigruber: *The stones for this will be shipped by the Mauthausen concentration camp*.[5]

On the opposite side of the Danube, in Alt-Linz—the old part of town—a boulevard was to be built under arcades, "wider than the Ring Boulevard in Vienna."[6] A hotel was to be constructed for more than two thousand guests, with a direct subway connection to the train station; there were also to be built the most modern hospitals and schools, among them an "Adolf Hitler School," a district music school, and a Reich Motor Flying School for the Luftwaffe. There were projects for model settlements for workers and artists, two homes for SS and SA invalids, new streets, and an access road to the autobahn. In order to make Linz rich, Hitler advanced industrialization, bringing steel and chemical factories to Linz. Transforming the farm town into an industrial city was almost the only thing that was actually realized. The "Hermann Göring Factory" still exists as the Voest factory.[7]

The planned cultural center was to have metropolitan proportions, in particular the Linz art museum, which Hitler mentioned in his last will the day before his death: *I collected the paintings in the collections I have bought over the years, never for private purposes, but always exclusively for enlarging a gallery in my hometown of Linz on the Danube. It would be my most fervent wish for this legacy to be realized.*[8]

In fact, money for this project was always available, even when there was a shortage of foreign currency during the war. From April 1943 to March 1944 alone Hitler purchased 881 works of art, among them 395 Dutch pieces from the seventeenth and eighteenth centuries. By the end of June 1944 the museum had cost 92.6 million reichsmark.[9] Goebbels wrote in his diary, "Linz costs us a lot of money. But it means so much to the Führer. And it probably is good too to support Linz as a cultural competitor to Vienna."[10] For, as Hitler remarked emphatically, *I won't give Vienna a pfennig, and the Reich won't give it anything either.*[11]

The most distinguished pieces for the Linz museum were requisitioned from private galleries, museums, and churches in the parts of Europe Hitler's army had occupied—for example, the Veit Stoss Altar in Cracow or the Van Eyck Altar in the cathedral of Ghent. Hitler derived particular satisfaction from transferring holdings from Vienna, for example from such "un-German" Viennese collections as those of Baron Nathaniel Rothschild. The formerly imperial Art History Museum also gave pieces to Linz, which, as Hitler remarked in 1942, *his dear Viennese didn't like at all; his dear Viennese, whom he knows so well after all, were so stodgy that when he was looking at some of the requisitioned Rembrandts, they tried to let him know in their genial way that all genuine paintings should really remain in Vienna, but that they would be glad to let galleries in Linz or Innsbruck have paintings by anonymous masters.* When he decided differently, it hit the Viennese *between the eyes.*[12]

Hitler planned to spend his retirement on Mount Frein above the old part of town in a building modeled after an upper Austrian farm. *I* climbed these rocks when I was young. On this hilltop, looking over the Danube, I daydreamed. This is where I want to live when I'm old.[13] And: I won't take anyone along except Miss Braun; Miss Braun and my dog.[14]

Albert Speer—after 1945, to be sure—ironically characterized Hitler's exaggerated love for Vienna as a "provincial mentality," adding that Hitler "always remained one of the small-town people, an insecure stranger in the large metropolises. While he was almost obsessively thinking and planning in huge proportions, it was in a town like Linz, where he had gone to school and where everything was on a manageable scale, that he felt at home socially." The nature of this love, Speer claimed, was "one of escape."[15]

Yet the point here is a lot more than the contrast between province and capital: it is the nationally homogenous, "German" Linz on the one side and multinational Vienna on the other. Furthermore, Hitler experienced the rural character of the provincial town as honest and rooted in the soil compared to the sophisticated, intellectual, and self-confident metropolis. Thus Goebbels, functioning as his master's mouthpiece, remarked after a visit to Linz: "Genuine German men. Not Viennese scoundrels."[16]

From a biographical perspective, Linz represented for Hitler the backdrop for an orderly, clean, petit-bourgeois time of his youth, which he spent with his beloved mother, whereas Vienna was witness to lonely, unsuccessful, and wretched years. However, most important from a political angle was Hitler's goal to dethrone the Hapsburg empire's old capital and to subjugate it to the German capital of Berlin. Vienna, he said, exuded *a huge, even gigantic fluidum*. Therefore it was *a tremendous task to break Vienna's cultural preponderance in the Alpine and Danube districts*.[17]

Complicated Family Relations

Linz, Upper Austria's rural capital, episcopal see, and educational center, situated in a bright landscape on the right bank of the Danube, had almost 68,000 inhabitants at the time of Hitler's youth, and thus—after Vienna, Prague, Trieste, Lemberg, Graz, Brünn, Cracaw, Pilsen, and Czernowitz— was the tenth largest city in Cisleithania, as the western part of the Dual Monarchy was called.[18]

Although he called it his "hometown," Hitler lived in Linz only a short while, from ages sixteen to eighteen, 1905 until February 1908. Until then, his life as the son of Austrian customs officer Alois Hitler had been unsteady. The border town of Braunau on the Inn, where he was born on April 20, 1889, and which he left when he was three years old, did not gain any significance until later, when Hitler could interpret it as *fate: For this little town lies on the boundary between two German states which we of the younger generation at least have made it our life work to reunite by every means at our disposal.*[19]

Family relations were complicated. Adolf was the product of his father's third marriage, to Klara née Pölzl, who was twenty-three years her husband's junior. Adolf, his mother's fourth child, was the first one to survive. In the household were also two half-siblings from the father's second marriage, Alois Jr., born in 1882, and Angela, born in 1883. In addition, there was "Haniaunt," Johanna Pölzl, Mother's hunchbacked and apparently feebleminded sister, who helped with the household chores.[20]

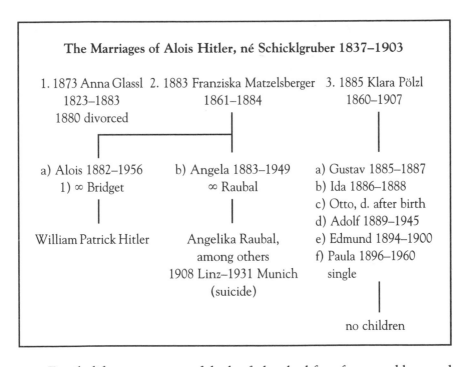

The Marriages of Alois Hitler, né Schicklgruber 1837–1903

1. 1873 Anna Glassl	2. 1883 Franziska Matzelsberger	3. 1885 Klara Pölzl
1823–1883	1861–1884	1860–1907
1880 divorced		

a) Alois 1882–1956	b) Angela 1883–1949	a) Gustav 1885–1887
1) ∞ Bridget	∞ Raubal	b) Ida 1886–1888
		c) Otto, d. after birth
		d) Adolf 1889–1945
William Patrick Hitler	Angelika Raubal,	e) Edmund 1894–1900
	among others	f) Paula 1896–1960
	1908 Linz–1931 Munich	single
	(suicide)	
		no children

Family life was not peaceful: the father had fits of rage and battered his oldest son, Alois, who in turn was jealous of Adolf, pampered by his young mother. The half-brother remarked about Adolf, "He was spoiled from early in the morning until late at night, and the stepchildren had to listen to endless stories about how wonderful Adolf was." But Adolf, too, was beaten by his father. According to Alois Jr., once Alois was even afraid he had killed Adolf.[21]

Between 1892 and 1895 Alois went to work in Passau, on the

German side of the border, during which time the three- to six-year-old boy acquired his peculiar Bavarian accent: *The German of my youth was the dialect of Lower Bavaria; I could neither forget it nor learn the Viennese jargon.*[22]

In 1895 the fifty-eight-year-old Alois Hitler retired after forty years of service. He bought a remote estate in the hamlet of Hafeld in the community of Fischlham near Lambach in Upper Austria to try to make a living as a farmer and beekeeper. His son recalled in 1942: *Bee stings were as normal as anything at home. Mother often took forty-five, fifty stings out of my old man when he returned from emptying the honeycombs.* His father, he said, had protected himself against the bees only by smoking.[23]

After a fierce fight with his father, fourteen-year-old Alois Jr. left the home in Hafeld and was disinherited. Thirteen-year-old Angela, Adolf, and Edmund, born in 1894, remained at home. In 1896, Paula, the youngest child of the family, was born.

In May 1895, six-year-old Adolf entered the one-room village school of Fischlham, which had one class. From the small antechamber, Hitler recalled, *I used to listen, while I was in the lowest grade, to what the pupils of the second grade were doing, and later on, the pupils of the third and fourth grades. Thank God I left there. Otherwise I would have had to go to the last grade for two or three years.*[24]

Because the rundown farm could not be managed on a civil servant's pension and Alois's abilities as a farmer were insufficient, he sold the estate in 1897. The family moved into temporary quarters in the town of Lambach. Now the eight-year-old entered grade school in Lambach and for a short time also joined the Benedictine boys' choir school. There, he said, he had an *excellent opportunity to intoxicate myself with the solemn splendor of the brilliant church festivals.*[25] What with all his criticism of the church, even later Hitler would praise it for *wonderfully exercising* man's *natural need . . . for something supernatural.* It had, he said, known how *to work on people with its mystical cult, its large sublime cathedrals, with blessed music, solemn rites, and incense.*[26]

The Hitler family was not pious. Only Klara went to Sunday mass regularly. The anticlerical father kept his distance and at most accompanied his family to services on holidays and on the emperor's birthday, August 18. For that was the only opportunity where he could don and display his civil servant's uniform, which the rest of the year hung in the closet unused.[27]

At the end of 1898 the family moved to the village of Leonding, south of Linz, where for 7,700 kronen Alois Hitler acquired a small house next to the cemetery.[28] In 1938 Goebbels said about his visit to this place,

Hitler attending grade school in Leonding

which had become "the entire German people's place of honor," "Quite tiny and primitive. I am led to the room which was his realm. Small and low-ceilinged. This is where he designed plans and dreamed of the future. Then there's the kitchen, where his good mother used to cook. Behind that the garden, where little Adolf picked apples and pears at night. . . . So this is where a genius developed. I'm beginning to feel quite sublime and solemn."[29]

The nine-year-old entered the village school in Leonding, where he was a *happy rogue*[30] and saw himself as *a young scamp: Even as a boy I was no "pacifist," and all attempts to educate me in this direction came to nothing.*[31] One of his schoolmates from Leonding, later Abbot Balduin of Wilhering, recalled, and by no means unkindly: "Playing war, always nothing but playing war, even we kids found that boring after a while, but he always found some children, particularly among the younger ones, who would play with him."[32] Otherwise, young Hitler practiced his "favorite sport": shooting at rats with his handgun in the cemetery next to his parents' house.[33]

Around 1900 the Boer War, when the southern African Boer republics tried to fight off their English conquerors, excited many Austrians. The German nationalists firmly endorsed, even enthusiastically welcomed, "David's fight against Goliath," the "poor farmers' freedom fight" against British imperialism. Signatures and money were collected in support of the Boers. Boer marches and Boer songs were composed. Boer hats, herrings, and sausages—still popular in Vienna—became fashionable.[34]

For young Hitler, the Boer War was bonafide *summer lightning: Every day I waited impatiently for the newspapers and devoured dispatches and news reports, happy at the privilege of witnessing this heroic struggle even at a distance.*[35] The boys now preferred the game "Boers against the English,"

Klara Hitler, née Pölzl   Alois Hitler, né Schicklgruber

with no one wanting to be an Englishman and everybody wanting to be a Boer. As late as 1923 Hitler would say, *On the side of the Boers, the just will to liberty, on the side of England, greed for money and diamonds.*[36]

In 1900 six-year-old brother Edmund died in Leonding of the measles, and eleven-year-old Adolf was left the only son of the family. The difficulties with his father began to increase. Hitler's schoolmates described him as "hardly an engaging person, neither in his external appearance nor in his character."[37] "Old Mr. Alois demanded absolute obedience. Frequently he put two fingers in his mouth, let out a piercing whistle, and Adolf, no matter where he may have been, would quickly rush to his father. . . . He often berated him, and Adolf suffered greatly from his father's harshness. Adolf liked to read, but the old man was a spendthrift and didn't hand out any money for books." Alois Hitler's only book is said to have been a volume on the Franco-Prussian War of 1870–71: "Adolf liked looking at the pictures in that book and was a Bismarck enthusiast."[38] In *Mein Kampf*, however, Hitler himself mentions his *father's library.*[39]

All witnesses portray Klara Hitler as a calm, loving mother and good housewife. A female fellow pupil from Leonding who passed the Hitlers' house daily remembers (after 1945, to be sure) that when little Paula left for school, Klara would always walk her "to the fence door and gave her a kiss; I noticed that because that was not what typically happened to us farm girls, but I liked it a lot, I almost envied Paula a little."[40]

Alois determined that his son should become a civil servant. After

Adolf had had five years of grade school, in fall of 1900 Alois sent him to high school (*Realschule*, a lower-level *Gymnasium*) in Linz, an hour's walk from Leonding. The eleven-year-old, who every day had to switch from the roughness of country life to the strictness of the small-town school, could not adapt and did not do well. In his first year he earned 'unsatisfactory' marks in math and natural history and was kept back. In addition, according to school records, every year he received a reprimand, alternately in general conduct and homework. Still, his tuition was waived, which indicates that his family was indigent.[41]

In 1924, the well-meaning French teacher Dr. Huemer said of his former pupil, "He was decidedly gifted, if one-sided, but had difficulty controlling his temper. He was considered intractable and willful, always had to be right and easily flew off the handle, and he clearly found it difficult to accommodate himself to the limits of a school." He demanded "unconditional subordination from his schoolmates," had enjoyed "the role of the leader," and apparently had been "influenced by Karl May stories and tales about Red Indians."[42]

Later, Hitler would frequently enjoy talking about his favorite author, Karl May: *I read him by candlelight and with a large magnifying glass at moonlight.* He thanked May for *introducing me to geography.*[43] In 1943 he proudly showed his companions the Hotel Roter Krebs in Linz, where the revered writer stayed in 1901 for a length of time.[44]

Young Hitler made no effort at advancing in school. According to a schoolmate, Klara frequently had to go to school "to check on him."[45] In *Mein Kampf* Hitler states that he deliberately did not apply himself in school so that he would not have to become a civil servant. Later he would criticize those parents who prematurely determine their children's careers, *and then, if something goes wrong, start talking about their prodigal or ill-bred son.* His father had *dragged* him at the age of thirteen *into Linz's main customs office, a genuine state cage where those old men had sat on top of one another, like monkeys.* Thus he had *learned to deplore thoroughly the career of a civil servant.*[46]

His relationship with his father was coming to a head. His sister Paula remembered; "every night Adolf got a thrashing because he came home late."[47] Hitler summarized that period as follows: *I was forced into opposition for the first time in my life. Hard and determined as father might be in putting through plans and purposes once conceived, his son was just as persistent and recalcitrant in rejecting an idea which appealed to him not at all, or in any case very little.*[48]

Among friends, Hitler would later paint a negative picture of his father. An entry in Goebbels's diary reads; "Hitler suffered almost the same youth as I did. Father, a domestic tyrant, mother, a source of kindness and love."[49] Supposedly Hitler was to tell his lawyer Hans Frank that even as a ten- to twelve-year-old he had to take his drunk father home from the bar: *That was the most horrible shame I have ever felt. Oh, Frank, I know what a devil alcohol is! It really was—via my father—the worst enemy of my youth.*[50]

Having retired, Alois Hitler had nothing to do and distracted himself by going to bars every day. Frequently he met with the farmer Josef Mayrhofer, with whom he worked for the German nationalists.[51] This might have been one of the "table societies," those tiny party factions among the circle of family and friends that some German nationalist parties entertained. Mayrhofer said of Hitler senior; "He was a curmudgeonly, taciturn old man, a smart libertine, and like all libertines in those days, a staunch German-National, a Pan-German, but still, strangely enough, loyal to the Emperor."[52]

In Upper Austria at that time, it was the governing Deutsche Volkspartei (DVP, German People's Party) that was libertine, German-national, and loyal to the emperor. Grown out of the circle around the extremist German nationalist Georg Schönerer, it had a moderate German-national platform and accepted Jews as members. There is no reason to believe that Hitler misstated the truth in *Mein Kampf* when he said about his father that he had viewed anti-Semitism as *cultural backwardness* and that he had adopted *more or less cosmopolitan views . . . despite his pronounced national sentiments.*[53]

Politics at School

The atmosphere at the Linz high school was politically turbulent. Together, "clericalists" and Hapsburg loyalists fought against libertines and German nationalists. Pupils eagerly collected and displayed their colors: while the high school students loyal to the emperor collected black-and-yellow ribbons and badges, photographs of the imperial family, and coffee cups depicting Empress Elizabeth and Emperor Franz Josef, the German nationalists collected devotional objects such as Bismarck busts made of plaster, beer mugs with inscriptions of heroic maxims about Germany's past, and, above all, ribbons, pencils, and pins with the "greater German" colors of 1848: black, red, and gold. In *Mein Kampf* Hitler states that he too took part *in the struggle of nationalities in old Austria. Collections were taken for the* Südmark [i.e., Austria viewed as part of the Greater German Empire] *and the school association; we emphasized our convictions by wearing cornflowers* [the emblem of Austria's Pan-Germans] *and red, black, and gold colors; "Heil" was our greeting, and instead of the imperial anthem we sang "Deutschland über Alles," despite warnings and punishments.*[54]

The German-national associations Deutscher Schulverein (German School Association) and Südmark (South Mark) sold "defense treasury coupons" to finance the "protection against the Czechization" and the "preservation and spreading of Germandom." The profits from these collections were used to finance German kindergartens and schools in mixed-language areas. The South Mark mainly supported German farmers in linguistic enclaves and also bought land for new settlements. These collections, which involved the entire population, were very popular—and probably served as the model for the National Socialists' "Winter Relief."

Cornflowers, the "Heil" greeting, and the colors black, red, and gold belonged to the Pan-Germans, those extreme German nationalists under the leadership of Schönerer who fought for German Austria's *Anschluss* (annexation) to the German Reich. Thus in their German nationalism the high-school students were more radical than their teachers, who, as civil servants, had to remain loyal to the emperor.

Most teachers at the high school were German-national in outlook. They incited the youths' enthusiasm "for fighting for German soil at the border to Bohemia"—and, according to a schoolmate, did so doubtless "with pedagogic intent: You have to study diligently lest we in Austria lose our leading role and so that you can prove yourselves in the national struggle!"[55] Hitler reported something similar about his favorite teacher, Dr. Leopold Poetsch: *He used our budding nationalistic fanaticism as a means of educating us, frequently appealing to our sense of national honor. By this alone he was able to discipline us little ruffians more easily than would have been possible by any other means.*[56]

Poetsch was Hitler's teacher from first through third grade (1901–04) in geography, and in second and third grade in history. He also ran the school library, where Hitler checked out his books. As a special privilege, Hitler was allowed to bring his teacher maps, which put him in particularly close contact with him.[57] Aside from his service at the school, Poetsch was a sought-after official speaker. He spoke at German-national associations, but also on the occasion of the emperor's anniversary in 1908.[58] Thus he was, like Hitler's father, simultaneously German-national and a Hapsburg loyalist, which was in line with his chosen party: in 1905 he joined the Linz city council as a representative of the German People's Party.

Poetsch gave popular slide lectures entitled "Images of German History." In them he strongly emphasized the Germanic era and the time of the early German emperors—that is to say, before the Hapsburgs—and proceeded to pinpoint the Germans' "national awakening" up until the Franco-Prussian War: "Since the great days of the magnificent German victories of the years 1870–71 we have become increasingly conscious of our Germanic identity and now thumb more ardently through the books of German myths, legends, and history."[59]

In the Hapsburg monarchy, the "Sedan celebrations" in commemoration of Prussia's victory over France* were officially prohibited. The students celebrated clandestinely, invariably ending with the "Wacht am Rhein" (Guard on the Rhine), the Prussian-German battle song against the "archenemy" France and the German nationalists' anthem. In his speech after the Anschluss in March 1938 Hitler mentioned another song of his youth: *When these soldiers marched in, I again heard a song of my youth. Once upon a time I sang it so often with a heart full of belief, that proud battle song: "Das Volk steht auf, der Sturm bricht los" (The people are rising up, the storm is breaking loose). And it was indeed the uprising of a people and the breaking loose of a storm.*[60]

The students' actions against "black-yellow" teacher of religion Schwarz also clearly had a pan-German twist. Later Hitler would relate with unabashed pride how during religious instruction he had spread pencils before him with the greater German colors black, red, and gold. The teacher said, *"You will immediately get rid of these pencils with those disgusting colors!" "Huh!" said the whole class. "Those are the national ideals!" "You needn't have any national ideals in your hearts but only one ideal, and that is our fatherland and our house of Hapsburg. He who isn't for the house of Hapsburg isn't for the Church, and he who isn't for the Church, is not for God. Sit down, Hitler!"* According to Hitler, there had been a *generally revolutionary atmosphere*[61] at school, an assessment other former schoolmates confirmed.

Another example: When Linz's students were supposed to cheer Emperor Franz Josef during his annual ride to his summer vacation in Ischl, their teacher found it necessary to advise them: "You have to yell 'Hoch!' I don't want anyone to yell 'Heil!' "[62] "Heil" was the greeting of the German nationalists, "Hoch" (up) the shout for the house of Hapsburg.

Later Hitler liked to emphasize that on account of their experiences

---

*On September 1, 1870, Prussia defeated the French army, taking Napoleon III prisoner. Three days later the Third Republic was proclaimed in France. Austria remained neutral throughout the German-Franco War, which resulted in France losing its hegemony in Europe to the newly formed "Second German Reich" governed by Emperor William I and Chancellor Bismarck. (*Translator's note*) in the multinational empire, the German-Austrians had developed a much more alert and progressive form of nationalism than had the "Reich Germans," even early on, when they still attended school: *In this way the child received political training in a period when as a rule the subject of a so-called national state knew little more of his nationality than its language.* At the age of fifteen, Hitler reported, he had already realized the distinction *between dynastic "patriotism" and folkish "nationalism."*[63] At any rate, even at that early age he clearly joined the camp of the radical "folkish nationalists," rejecting the multinational state as did the Schönererians. On this important issue he thus distinguished himself from his father and his favorite teacher, Poetsch.

It is understandable, then, that Poetsch was annoyed when he, the Austrian patriot, discovered that in *Mein Kampf* he received high praise as a teacher but at the same time was denounced as an enemy of Austria: *For who could have studied German history under such a teacher without becoming an enemy of the state which, through its ruling house, exerted so disastrous an influence on the destinies of the nation? And who could retain a loyalty to a dynasty that . . . betrayed the needs of the German people again and again for shameless private advantage?*[64]

When in 1936 some teachers in Linz sent their now famous pupil photos to remind him of them, and they asked Poetsch to join them, he refused, arguing "that he did not agree with Hitler in his defamation of Austria; he had sworn an official oath for Austria."[65] However, "the Führer's beloved teacher" could no longer protect himself from a national funeral.

Jews and Czechs in Linz

The high school in Linz apparently had a good reputation, for almost one-third of its students came from out of town. Fifty pupils were from Lower Austria, including Vienna; twenty-one from Salzburg, Tyrol, Styria, and Carinthia; another twenty-one from Bohemia, Moravia, and Silesia; two apiece from Galicia and Hungary; seven from the German Reich; and one each from Italy, France, and Bosnia.

One of the Viennese students, from 1903 until his graduation in 1906, was Ludwig Wittgenstein, the son of the industrialist Karl Wittgenstein. He was only a few days Hitler's junior but, instructed by private tutors, was two grades ahead of him. Hitler is bound to have at least laid eyes on Wittgenstein, for in Linz the latter was a conspicuously bizarre fellow: he spoke an unusually pure High German, albeit with a slight stutter, wore very elegant clothes, and was highly sensitive and extremely unsociable. It was one of his idiosyncracies to use the formal form of address with his schoolmates and to demand that they too—with the exception of a single friend—address him formally, with "*Sie*" and "Herr Ludwig." He did not love school—his first impression, recorded in his notebook, was "Crap"—and he was frequently absent and had an average record. When he went to Berlin in 1906 to attend university, his spelling was scarcely better than Hitler's.[66]

As Hitler's schoolmates would later affirm,[67] pupils of Jewish descent, like Wittgenstein, had no trouble at the high school in Linz, especially not if, like Wittgenstein, they participated in religious instruction as Catholics. According to statistics, at that time only 17 pupils in the school were Jewish, next to 323 Catholics, 19 Protestants, and a visiting Bosnian student who was Greek Orthodox.[68]

Indeed, anti-Semitism can hardly have played a major role, and Hitler's statement in Mein Kampf is probably correct: *At the Realschule, to be sure, I did meet one Jewish boy who was treated by all of us with caution . . . but neither I nor the others had any thoughts on the matter.* Only at the age of fourteen or fifteen had he encountered the word Jew with more frequency, *partly in connection with political discussions.*[69]

Around 1900 only 1,102 Jews lived in all of Upper Austria, 587 of them in Linz—in other words, less than one percent of the city's population—and 184 in Urfahr. The numbers for 1910 were 1,215 in Upper Austria, 608 in Linz, 172 in Urfahr.[70] The Linz Jews for the most part came from Fürth in Bavaria or from Bohemia and were assimilated into the rest of society. Most of the 224 Jewish heads of household living in Linz at the time were merchants, professionals, or manufacturers.[71] Some were esteemed as patrons and held honorary federal posts; April 7, 1907, the Upper Austrian governor gave Rabbi Moriz Friedmann the Franz Josef Medal in appreciation of Friedmann's twenty-five years as a member of the Austrian district school board.[72]

The number of Jews in Linz, then, stayed approximately the same and Eastern Jews did not immigrate into the little provincial city. In the meantime, more and more Czechs came to town. Most of them were seasonal workers who were not included in official statistics. In any case, the "fight against Slavization," and thus against the Czechs, dominated the almost uniformly German-speaking town far more than anti-Semitism against the German-speaking Jews. In the twenty years before 1914 the "Czech question" was the main topic for discussion in the Linz City Council as well as the Linz newspapers—and the schools.

The Linz newspapers fanned the native Linzers' fear of over-alienation, of losing their jobs on account of cheap competition, of "selling out" their native soil, and of a soaring crime rate. According to the pan-German *Linzer Fliegende*, Linz's main square had long been a "reservoir" of "Czech boys": "Every night you can see a number of Czechs on the asphalt pavement—who speak Czech rather loudly and march up and down in tight circles. That way they simply want to prove that they have already conquered downtown Linz."[73]

The "defense battle against advancing Slavdom" was a "central topic" among students, according to a former classmate of Hitler: "To be sure, we didn't look at the Slavs as an inferior ethnic group, but we fought against the curtailing of our rights."[74] Frequently, we are told, there was some wrangling between young "Slavic" and "Germanic" men. Another schoolmate stated, "The competition between the languages and the frictions in Parliament made a great impression on us pupils. We were totally against the Czechs and the ethnic Babel."[75]

Hitler was to tell Albert Speer that almost all his Linz schoolmates had rejected "Czech immigration to German Austria." He hadn't recognized the "danger of Jewry" until he was in Vienna.[76] And in Munich in 1929 he said, *I lived my youth enmeshed in the border struggle for German language, culture, and thought, of which the great majority of the German people had no idea during peacetime. Even when I was thirteen, that fight incessantly pushed itself on us, and it was fought in every high school class.*[77]

Yet the Linz *Realschule* did not really have a nationality problem: of 359 pupils in the academic year 1902–03, 357 named German as their mother tongue, and only two Czech.[78] It was not much different at the other schools of higher education in Linz: the Czech inhabitants of Linz were almost exclusively railroad workers who could not afford to send their children to advanced schools, or seasonal workers whose children lived in Bohemia.

Hitler was fourteen when in 1903 a language fight broke out in Linz: when the bishop permitted a Czech sermon in a Linz church, the city council requested in a unanimous, urgent motion "to cancel the Czech service, which has been misused for Czech demonstrations," and at the same time advised all Linz businessmen in the future only to hire "German assistants and apprentices."[79] In March 1904 German national pupils and students broke up a concert by Czech violinist Jan Kubelík. Thus the national question continued to be pushed into the foreground.

The question of whether someone was "Germanic" or "Slavic" played an important role even among the high-school students of Linz. According to a statement by his schoolmate Josef Keplinger, young Hitler diligently studied the alleged differences between races. One day he apparently told Keplinger, "You are not Germanic, you have dark eyes and dark hair!" Another time he is said to have divided his classmates at the entrance of their classroom into two groups left and right, "Aryans and Non-Aryans," according to purely external characteristics.[80] What group the dark-haired Hitler joined we do not know.

Alois's Death

On January 3, 1903, at 10 A.M., sixty-five-year-old Alois Hitler suddenly died of pulmonary bleeding.[81] He was sitting in a tavern at the time.

The obituary in the Linz *Tagespost* described him as "a thoroughly progressive man" and a "true friend of the free school," an allusion to the deceased's anticlerical tendencies, his involvement in the association "Free School," and an argument he had had with the local priest. Socially—in other words, in the tavern—he had "always [been] happy, of a downright youthful joyfulness even," and also "a friend of song." Plus: "Even though a rough word may have escaped his lips once in a while, a good heart was hiding behind a rough exterior."[82] This discreet way of putting things seems to indicate that he was cheerful in the bar but tough at home. Hitler's future guardian Josef Mayrhofer confirms this: "In the bar he always had to be right and had a quick temper. . . . At home he was strict, not a gentle man; his wife didn't have an easy life."[83]

At least the thirteen-year-old boy must have felt relief at his tyrannical father's death. Hitler was to tell his secretary a great deal "about his mother's love," which he returned. " 'I didn't love my father,' he used to say, 'but I was all the more afraid of him. He had tantrums and immediately became physically violent. My poor mother would always be very scared for me.' "[84]

Still, there was no improvement in school. On account of continued bad grades, Hitler was asked to leave the Linz high school in 1904. Yet his mother was not ready to give up and sent him to the next closest *Realschule*, to Steyr, an industrial town with a population of 17,600, where he lived with a couple who boarded him. This was a great financial sacrifice for the civil servant's widow. She sold the house in Leonding and moved to Linz, to the third floor of a house at 31 Humboldtstrasse.

The separation from his mother was very hard on the fifteen-year-old. Goebbels would note: "The Führer talks about his childhood. . . . And how he was longing and pining away when his mother sent him to Steyr. And almost became ill over it. . . . And how he still hates Steyr as a city to this day."[85]

While the Hitlers lived in Steyr, the Russo-Japanese War broke out. Hitler would later say that his class was divided into two camps; the

Fifteen-year-old Hitler, drawn by his Steyr
classmate Sturmlechner

"Slavs" had been for Russia, and the others for Japan: *When during the Russo-Japanese War the news of Russia's defeat arrived, the Czech boys in my class cried, while we others cheered.*[86] Even then Hitler, just like the German nationalists in Linz, suspected schoolchildren of harboring pan-Slavic convictions.

At Whitsuntide 1904 the pubescent Hitler, who still did not want to study, was confirmed at the Linz cathedral. His godfather would later say, "Among all my candidates, there was not one who was as gruff and obstinate as this one, you had to climb inside him for every word." The boy had not appreciated his confirmation present, a prayerbook. Neither had the expensive ride from Linz to Leonding in a carriage excited him: "I had the impression that he found the whole confirmation disgusting." In Leonding a "pack of boys" was already waiting for him, and he "quickly took off." The godfather's wife added, "They behaved like Red Indians."[87]

To be sure, such conduct was not unusual for a fifteen-year-old. In 1942 Hitler would say in retrospect, *At thirteen, fourteen, fifteen, I no longer believed in anything, certainly none of my friends still believed in the so-called communion, only a few totally stupid honor students! Except, at the time I thought everything should be blown up.*[88]

With three unsatisfactory grades—in German, math, and stenography—Hitler was again kept back. *This idiot of a professor spoiled the German language for me, this bungling, pathetic gnome: I would never be able to write a proper letter! Imagine! With a D minus from that buffoon, I never could have become a technician.*[89]

In this situation, he would write, *suddenly an illness* came to his help, *my serious lung ailment,* which ultimately decided *the eternal domestic quar-*

rel.[90] He was allowed to abandon his career at school and return home to his mother.

According to relatives, the sick boy let himself be pampered by his mother during the following summer in Waldviertel, having her bring him a big mug of warm milk every morning. He lived like a recluse, avoiding almost all contact with his various cousins.[91]

This alleged serious illness must have been a temporary indisposition; otherwise the new family doctor, Dr. Eduard Bloch from Linz, would have known about it. After checking his files, the doctor later maintained that he treated the boy only for minor ailments, colds, or tonsilitis, and that Hitler had been neither robust nor sickly. He certainly did not have any serious illness whatsoever, let alone a lung disease.[92]

Dr. Bloch, a Jew, was born in Frauenburg in Southern Bohemia in 1872. After attending school in Prague he served as an army doctor and from 1899 on was stationed in Linz, where he settled after his discharge. In 1901 he opened his office in the baroque house at 12 Landstrasse, where he also lived with his family: his wife Emilie, née Kafka, and their daughter Trude, born in 1903. According to Linz's future mayor Ernst Koref, Dr. Bloch was held "in high regard, particularly among the lower and indigent social classes. It was generally known that even at any time at night he was willing to call on patients. He used to go on his visits in his hansom, wearing a conspicuously broad-brimmed hat."[93]

As an old man in American exile, Dr. Bloch published his memoirs, in which he painted a remarkably positive picture of young Hitler, saying he had been neither a ruffian nor untidy nor fresh: "This simply is not true. As a youth he was quiet, well-mannered, and neatly dressed." He had patiently waited in the waiting room until it was his turn, then, like every well-behaved fourteen- or fifteen-year-old boy, made a bow, and always thanked the doctor politely. Like the other boys in Linz he had worn short *lederhosen* and a green woolen hat with a feather, he had been tall and pale and looked older than he was: "His eyes—inherited from his mother—were large, melancholy and thoughtful. To a very large extent this boy lived within himself. What dreams he dreamed I do not know."

The boy's most striking feature was his love for his mother: "While he was not a 'mother's boy' in the usual sense, I have never witnessed a closer attachment." This love had been mutual: "Klara Hitler adored her son. . . . She allowed him his own way wherever possible." For example, she admired his watercolor paintings and drawings and supported his artistic ambitions in opposition to his father; "at what cost to herself one may guess." However, the doctor expressly denies the claim that Hitler's love for his mother was pathological.

According to Dr. Bloch, the family's financial resources were scarce. He mentions that Klara Hitler had not even indulged in "the smallest extravagance" and lived extremely modestly and frugally.[94] We have some data on the Hitlers' family budget: Klara Hitler's widow's pension amounted to 100 kronen per month, plus 40 kronen in federal aid for Adolf's and Paula's education. The sale of the house in Leonding yielded 10,000 kronen, minus mortgage, taxes, expenses, and the inheritance for Adolf and Paula—frozen until their twenty-fourth birthdays—of 652 kronen each.[95]

At 4 percent interest, the remaining approximately 5,500 kronen may have netted some 220 kronen annually. In addition, Klara was permitted to dispose of the interest for Adolf's and Paula's inheritance up to their eighteenth year, which yielded another 52 kronen per annum. However, the interest total of no more than 23 kronen per month did not cover the current rent. The family of four, who now no longer even had the Leonding fruit and vegetable garden at its disposal, had to live very modestly, particularly because around 1905 inflation had become noticeable and Klara had fallen ill. Even if "Haniaunt" contributed to the family's expenses, from then on Klara Hitler had to fall back on her savings. Even though their apartment was small, she acquired an additional boarder, twelve-year-old Wilhelm Hagemüller, the Leonding baker's son, who on schooldays ate lunch with the family.

Sixteen-year-old Adolf, by now "the only man" in the family, acted just as if he were a son of a better family. He had his own room, the cabinet—which means that the three women shared the only remaining room and the kitchen. He spent his days taking walks, with nightly entertainments, reading, and drawing. Thus in *Mein Kampf* he pays tribute to the two ensuing years in Linz as *the happiest days of my life*, which *seemed to me almost a dream*. He says he had lived as his *mother's darling* in *the hollowness of comfortable life* and on a *soft downy bed*.[96] After the unpleasant period in Steyr he now enjoyed the attractions of the provincial capital. At fifteen or sixteen, he would say in 1942, he went *to all the wax works and everywhere it said, Adults Only*.[97]

During that time the young man began to devour newspapers. There was a large number of papers in Linz, among them offshoots of the large Viennese party organs that brought such Viennese topics to Linz as anti-Semitism. For example, the Christian-Social *Linzer Post* advocated the slogan "Don't buy from Jews" and commented: "If money supply is cut off from the Jews, then they themselves have to retreat and Austria will be rid of the disgusting lice infestation." "The Jews" were portrayed as seducers of girls, as a danger to the state, and as Socialists, for "always and everywhere the fellow tribesmen of these workers' tormentors are the tried leaders of Social Democracy."[98]

The *Linzer Fliegenden*, on the other hand, subtitled "Völkisches Witzblattl" (folkish joke journal), propagated ethnic anti-Semitism in the manner of the pan-Germans. The journal was anticlerical, rejected the multinational state, and made propaganda against the Hungarians (the "Huns"), the Czechs, and the Jews. There was a great deal of publicity for the *Alldeutsches Tagblatt*, whose writers, including Guido von List and Jörg Lanz von Liebenfels, were quoted frequently.

The paper distributed pan-German brochures, including the speeches of Schönerer, and "Jew coupons"—sheets of forty couponlike stamps at ten heller each with more or less fabricated anti-Semitic utterances by famous people, such as Helmuth Count of Moltke: "The Jews form a state within the state; following their own laws, they know how to bypass those of the country"; or even Tacitus: "The Jews are the abomination of the human race. Everything that to us is sacrosanct, is contemptible to them; while they are permitted to do anything that is an outrage to us. They are the lowliest of all peoples (*deterrima gens*)."[99] When these sayings reappeared on doors and windows of Jewish shops in Linz, Linz's Austrian Israelite Union retaliated on October 16, 1907, by pressing criminal charges.[100]

One of the readers of the *Linzer Fliegenden* is said to have been young Hitler.[101] Even at that early age he had fallen under the influence of the pan-Germans, whose main enemy were the Social Democrats.

In a 1929 speech Hitler would brag about being one of the early fighters against the "Reds": *When I was a boy, I wore the black, red, and gold badge and, like innumerable of my early friends, was seriously beaten up by Marxists. They tore up the black, red, and gold flag and kicked it in the mud.*[102]

Theatre and First Love

In Linz young Hitler discovered his love for the theatre. Linz's regional theatre performed operas, operettas, and plays from the typical repertoire for the educated—from Mozart's *Magic Flute* to Strauss operettas and comedies of manners. Standing room only, in the third gallery, cost just fifty heller, hardly more than a ticket for a concert by the army orchestra or the extremely popular movies.[103]

In 1905, the hundredth anniversary of Schiller's death, the German nationalists celebrated their "freedom poet." In the regional theatre Schiller's plays were at the center of the program, above all, *William Tell.* Krackowizer wrote on May 4, 1905: "Anniversary celebrations wherever German hearts are beating." The most popular official speaker was Leopold Poetsch.

Wagner's oeuvre was also being cultivated, for Linz's music director August Göllerich was old enough to have known the maestro personally. Among the regional theatre's repertoire was *Lohengrin* and, since January 3, 1905, also the early opera *Rienzi,* which received particular notice as the town's gymnastics club took part in the famous "sword dance."[104]

Later, Klara Hitler's boarder Hagmüller would relate that young Hitler frequented the regional theatre and even outlined plans for its reconstruction. According to Hagmüller, Hitler preferred Wagner operas and Schiller plays and liked to sing "Du Schwan zieh hin" from *Lohengrin* while walking back and forth in his room.[105] When in 1938 an emissary of the NSDAP archive collected biographical material on the "Führer" in Linz, he learned much to his amazement that "funnily enough" Hitler's favorite actors in Linz—that is to say, his Wagner and Schiller heroes— were "almost exclusively Jews."[106]

In 1905, in the regional theatre's standing room, Hitler met August (Gustl) Kubizek, who was almost the same age. They became friends. Kubizek worked as an upholsterer's apprentice in his father's shop; his father was happy that Gustl had such a well-behaved and polite friend as Adolf.[107] Hitler profited from Kubizek's excellent training in music. The two shared their enthusiasm for Wagner. In his memoirs, Kubizek describes in detail the outstanding impression *Rienzi, der letzte der Tribunen* (Rienzi, the last of the tribunes) made on young Hitler.[108] The pompous work required a large orchestra with a great deal of brass and drums, and contained thrilling scenes with large crowds; the endings of its acts were overpowering, and it was full of roaring shouts of "Heil."

In the fourteenth century Cola di Rienzi rose from being the son of a Roman bartender to the people's tribune, unifying splintered Italy into a powerful republic after a classical model, but he was subsequently toppled by the people and died during an uprising. In the nineteenth century, the age of national unification, his story was romantically glorified in a much-read novel by Edward George Bulwer-Lytton. During the preliminaries of the revolution of 1848 young Richard Wagner also tried his hand at this national material. For him Rienzi was the hero who saved and liberated the people, in Wagner's words, an "extreme enthusiast who like a flashing beam of light appeared among a people that had sunk low and was degenerated but which he believed he was called upon to enlighten and lift up high."[109]

After the opera, Kubizek later wrote, sixteen-year-old Hitler walked with him in a "totally transported state" to Linz's Frein Mountain until the early hours of the morning. "In grand, infectious images he outlined to me the future of the German people." Kubizek quoted at length verses that had "touched (their) hearts," such as when Rienzi sings, *doch wählet ihr zum Schützer mich / der Rechte, die dem Volk erkannt, / so blickt auf eure Ahnen hin: / Und nennt mich euren Volkstribun!*" (and if you choose me as your protector of the people's rights, look at your ancestors and call me your people's tribune!) The masses reply, "Rienzi, Heil! Heil, people's tribune!"

Later it was important to Hitler to be looked on as Rienzi reincarnate. Among the Kubizek family his alleged statement, "I want to become a people's tribune," was passed on.[110] The spirited *Rienzi* overture became the secret anthem of the Third Reich, well known as the introduction to the Nuremberg party conventions.

According to Kubizek, sixteen-year-old Hitler was a puny, pale, serious young man, always simply, but neatly and properly attired: "Adolf made much of polite conduct and strict, proper form."[111] With his only suit, pepper-and-salt with perfect creases he wore white shirts ironed by his mother and black kid gloves,[112] as well as a special touch, a little black ebony cane and sometimes even a top hat, an outfit like a college student's. Kubizek wrote: "Since Linz didn't have a university, the young people of all classes and strata of society all the more eagerly emulated students' customs."[113]

Young Hitler's manner of speaking, Kubizek noted, was "very choice." In other words, contrary to those around him, he did not speak a dialect but High German. In addition, he had a "well-developed sense of performing." The young man displayed his desire to be the center of attention by being given to talking much and persistently, always in the form of monologues. He did not permit anyone to contradict him. "Sometimes, when he became entirely lost in his fantasies, I got the suspicion that everything he said was nothing but an exercise in oratory."[114]

Kubizek was surprised that his friend avoided all contact with his former schoolmates. Once, he reported, they ran into a former classmate of Hitler on the promenade in Linz. To the question, "How are you?" Hitler only brusquely replied "that that was none of his business, just as Adolf himself couldn't care less what the other one was up to."[115]

It was probably in the spring of 1906 that the seventeen-year-old first fell in love. To be sure, the blonde Linz beauty of higher standing, two years his senior, never noticed her shy admirer, who watched her from afar as she walked in the Linz main street with her mother. Stefanie had already graduated and then been to Munich and Geneva for professional training, and was now back in her hometown of Linz.[116] She had many admirers, a fact Hitler jealously observed during the strolls, particularly if they were officers. He called them "lazybones" and got flustered about their social standing, "but particularly about the opportunities these airheads had with the ladies." According to Kubizek, Hitler only lived for "that woman . . . who possessed all of his passionate affection, without being aware of it." And: "He envisions Stefanie as his wife, he is building the house in which she lives with him, surrounds it with a magnificent park," and so on.[117] Yet according to Kubizek he did not exchange a single word with this "being in his dream world."

First Time in Vienna

Even though his guardian urged him to alleviate some of the burden in his mother's household, Hitler did not accept any jobs nor start an apprenticeship. Instead, he announced his desire to become an artist, an aspiration his mother supported. She even paid for a trip to Vienna so he could go to the imperial art gallery, an unusual and expensive undertaking for the son of a civil servant's widow. In May 1906, after a six-hour trip on an accommodation train, the seventeen-year-old arrived in the imperial capital and residence for the first time.

The size, the tumult, and the brightness of the metropolis impressed and confused anyone arriving from the provinces. Nowhere in the Austrian-Hungarian monarchy was traffic as heavy as it was in Vienna. In 1907 1,458 automobiles, more than half the total number registered in the whole empire, were in the capital. They caused 354 accidents per year, even with a speed limit of fifteen miles per hour in the city. More important still were horsedrawn carriages: there were 997 hansoms drawn by two horses, 1,754 one-horse carriages, and 1,101 cabs, which altogether caused 982 accidents.[118]

The ten inner districts were already electrified, so in the streets there were no longer any gas lights. The Westbahnhof—the western station, where trains arrived from Linz—was illuminated by electric lights too. Electrification of tenement buildings was progressing rapidly: in 1908, in nonofficial buildings alone, there already were 176 arc lamps and 657,625 incandescent lamps[119]—one incandescent lamp per person. Linz, on the other hand, had only six electric arc lamps on the main square and one on the bridge between Linz and Urfahr; otherwise it had only gas and kerosene lamps.[120]

We do not know where in Vienna Hitler lived. That he found lodgings with his godfather Johann Prinz, as is frequently claimed, does not seem possible. In a document from 1885, Mr. and Mrs. Prinz are mentioned as "a married couple, the husband being a swimming pool attendant at the Sofienbad, Vienna," living in the Third District, 28 Löwengasse.[121] That they were still at that address in 1906 is not documented, and there is no other information about this either. According to Kubizek, Hitler never visited relatives; "even later this never came up during conversation."[122]

Hitler's first visit to Vienna, he later says in *Mein Kampf*, triggered his enthusiasm for the architecture of the Ring Boulevard. *The purpose of my trip was to study the picture gallery in the Court Museum, but I had eyes for scarcely anything but the museum itself. From morning until late at night, I ran from one object of interest to another, but it was always the buildings that held my primary interest. For hours I could stand in front of the Opera, for hours I could gaze at the Parliament; the whole Ring Boulevard seemed to me like an enchantment out of* The Thousand-and-One Nights.[123]

The only sources concerning this first trip to Vienna are four picture postcards to Kubizek. They are the earliest known autographs of Hitler to date.[124]

Not even the post office stamps reveal how long the trip lasted. (In *Mein Kampf* Hitler suggests two weeks.[125]) One card, postmarked May 7, 1906, contains a three-part view of the Karlsplatz, where Hitler marked the music club building with an X: to indicate the place of the conservatory school, which Kubizek dreamed of attending one day. The card reads: *Sending you this card, I must at the same time apologize to you for not having written sooner. So I did arrive all right and now walk around busily. Tomorrow I will go to the opera to hear* Tristan, *the day after tomorrow the* Flying Dutchman, *etc. Even though I like everything fine I am still looking forward to being back in Linz. Today to the City Theatre. With best regards, Your friend Adolf Hitler.* The seventeen-year-old, having been taught by his mother to be polite, does not forget to ask Kubizek to give his regards to his parents.

What Hitler mentioned matches perfectly with the program: on Tuesday, May 8, 1906, there was a performance of *Tristan*, from seven to eleven-thirty, with Erik Schmedes as Tristan, Anna von Mildenburg as Isolde, and Richard Mayr as King Marke. On Wednesday, May 9, *The*

Flying Dutchman was scheduled. On May 7, 1906, the City Theatre performed a rural farce by Ludwig Anzengruber.[126] The other postcards depict views of the outside and inside of the Opera and Parliament.

At any rate, on at least two evenings the young man experienced the ultimate of contemporary Wagner interpretation at the Court Opera: the Wagnerian "total work of art," constructed by court opera director Gustav Mahler and his stage director Alfred Roller and "cleared" of tradition. What is most important is this: for the first time in his life, young Hitler witnessed Gustav Mahler as a Wagner conductor—in the May 8 performance of *Tristan*.[127]

After this first sojourn in Vienna, the capital attracted the young man like a magnet. Kubizek observed; "In his thoughts he frequently was no longer in Linz but was already living right in the center of Vienna."[128] But even if the provincial town may have become too small for him, it still offered quite a few attractions: on May 26, 1906, the Buffalo Bill circus show performed a spectacle entitled "Wild West," involving eight hundred performers in costumes, among them a hundred American Indians, plus five hundred horses. On June 7 the young people in Linz marveled at 150 luxury cars and their noble "gentleman drivers," who were making a stop in Linz during their race. On September 28 the performances by the American cinema group The Royal Video started in the Volksfesthalle (people's party hall), and according to Krackowizer performances were "jam-packed every day, netting a fortune."[129]

On October 13 the State Theatre for the first time performed the greatest music hit of the era, Franz Léhar's *Merry Widow*. Via gramophones the tunes spread ad nauseam into cafés and bars. Hitler remained faithful to this favorite operetta of his until the end: in 1943–44, at the Wolf Entrenchment in East Prussia, he was not listening to Wagner, but "never anything but the *Merry Widow*," as an earwitness reported with a moan.[130]

From October 1906 on Hitler took piano lessons with Kubizek's teacher for no less than five kronen a month. He did not get very far. The teacher visibly cringed when in 1938 he was supposed to tell the NSDAP's main archive his memories of the "Führer": "As far as the lessons are concerned, he was never distracted, and—as for other conversations—before or after the lessons—rather reserved. . . . In short, at the time I wouldn't have had the slightest idea as to what a great statesman was taking lessons with me."[131]

In January 1907, when his life was about to take a turn, Hitler decided to discontinue his lessons: on January 14, 1907, Klara Hitler, who

Main staircase at the Vienna Court Opera

was in excruciating pain, consulted with the family physician, Dr. Bloch. He detected a breast tumor and advised an operation, which was performed four days later, at the Hospital of the Sisters of Mercy in Linz. Because she had no health insurance, such a hospital stay posed an enormous financial burden, particularly because the daily rate was set at five kronen instead of the usual two. In addition, there were various other invoices, such as the surgeon's bill. For the twenty-day stay (January 17 to February 5), the hospital charged one hundred kronen, which, according to the bill, was paid by "the son," who at the time was seventeen years old.[132] Furthermore, Klara needed aftercare by the family doctor, Bloch, and this was getting more and more costly. Apparently seventeen-year-old Hitler made the necessary decisions by himself. His eleven-year-old sister Paula was too young, and his married half-sister Angela Raubal was no longer part of the common household. Besides, she was only Klara's stepdaughter. "Haniaunt" was not up to such tasks and kept so much in the background that neither Dr. Bloch nor Kubizek mentioned her.

It was the spring of the first national elections since the introduction of the general, direct, and equal suffrage for men. Krackowizer wrote on May 2 1907: "Those interested get extremely excited during national elections: fliers, assemblies, etc. galore." The right to vote invigorated the Social Democrats, who were now serious competitors against the Nationals and Clericals. They gained all of Linz's three parliamentary mandates. It is certainly possible that Hitler's hatred for the "Reds" goes back in part to this bitter and, in the end, lost election campaign of what had been Linz's main parties—fought and lost especially by the German People's Party (DVP).

After a brief recuperation period, forty-six-year-old Klara Hitler had difficulty climbing the stairs to the third floor. In early May 1907 the family moved to the small town of Urfahr across the Danube, to 46 Hauptstrasse. Financial difficulties may have been a factor too. In any case, Urfahr, which was not incorporated into Linz until 1917, was said to be particularly cheap, for one thing because of its agrarian markets, but also because it was free of the consumption tax that made all goods more expensive in Linz. According to Kubizek, even before that time Hitler had done the family's major shopping in Urfahr.

After only two weeks, the family moved once again, this time to nearby 9 Blütenstrasse in Urfahr. At fifty kronen, rent on the first floor of this nice, even elegant house was very high for Urfahr,[133] amounting to almost half of Klara's widow's pension, which was certainly more than the family could afford. Thus it continued to be necessary to tap the small capital acquired from the sale of the house. Klara, who was seriously ill, lived another few comfortable months there.

According to Dr. Bloch, the apartment had three small rooms. The windows offered a magnificent view of Mount Pöstling. "My predominant impression of the simple furnished apartment was its cleanliness. It glistened; not a speck of dust on the chairs or tables, not a stray fleck of mud on the scrubbed floor, not a smudge on the panes in the windows. Frau Hitler was a superb housekeeper."

The house belonged to the widow of a district court judge, Magdalena Hanisch, who lived in an adjoining apartment on the first floor and showed great concern for Klara Hitler. In the house also lived a retired postmaster with his wife, a retired professor, and (apparently in the basement rooms) two day laborers.[134]

According to Dr. Bloch's cash book,[135] Klara Hitler visited his office on July 3 and did not return until September 2. It is not clear whether the doctor's office was closed during the summer—in which case, however, he would have noted the name of his substitute, Dr. Kren—or if the patient had left once more for Waldviertel with her family to recuperate there. Considering travel conditions at the time, the ride was relatively comfortable; the train went from Linz to Gmünd, and from there a pair of oxen took the family to Klara's parent's house in the village of Spital near Weitra.

The First Exam at the Academy

Despite his guardian's objections, Hitler managed to persuade his mother to let him attend the Academy of Visual Arts in Vienna from the fall of 1907 on. In early September he left Linz, *keeping before my eyes the image of my father, who had started out as the child of a village shoemaker, and risen by his own efforts to be a government official.*[136]

Before his departure he bid farewell to Stefanie, who later had difficulty remembering what happened: "Once I received a letter from someone telling me he was now attending the Art Academy, but I should wait for him, he was going to return and marry me. I don't remember what else the letter said, and neither, whether and how it was signed. At the time I just didn't have a clue as to whom I should attribute the letter to."[137] In 1908 Stefanie Rabatsch became engaged to a captain from the Hessian command that was stationed in Linz.[138] Only decades later did she learn who the unknown admirer was.

In Vienna Hitler looked for a sublet, which was not all that hard to find: in the poorer districts almost all leaseholders sublet rooms and beds so they could pay their own rent. Posted on the buildings' doors were scraps of paper advertising the rooms available.

In the back premises of the house at 31 Stumpergasse in Mariahilf, second staircase, basement, door number seventeen,[139] he moved into a small bedroom of approximately one hundred square feet for ten kronen a month. His landlady was a single woman, Maria Zakreys, a tailor and typical representative of Vienna's "Babylon of peoples": she was Czech, had immigrated from Policka in Bohemia, and spoke German only with difficulty. Hitler remarked to Kubizek on August 17, 1908: *Zakreys probably has a hard time with writing (she speaks German so badly).*

The incorrect information that Maria Zakreys was Polish goes back to Kubizek, who on account of her accent concluded that "she must be from Stanislau or Neutitschein," at the same time, however, describing her accent as "Bohemianizing"—German with a Czech twang—and mentioning relatives from Moravia. Neutitschein is in Moravia, but Stanislau is in Galicia—and Zakrey was from neither one of those places, her name, furthermore, being of Czech origin: *zakreys* is the imperative of *zakrýt se*, to cover oneself.[140] According to Kubizek, at forty-nine years of age Maria Zakreys had the appearance of "a shriveled, little old woman."[141] Because she herself had to pay between 320 and 491 kronen annually for rent for her small apartment[142]—living room, kitchen, and bedroom—Hitler's rent was extremely low.

The district of Mariahilf was overbuilt with tall apartment houses that were all from the turn of the century, a time of heavy industrialization and immigration. Like most others, the house at 31 Stumpergasse consisted of a more striking part that faced the street, and a very narrow, dark back of the house with small apartments, uniformly consisting of living room, kitchen, and bedroom, with hardly more than three hundred square feet each, lined up in a row along a large hallway with the watering places—called *Bassena*—and toilets, which were all shared.

In the front part of the house was the library of the Saint Vincent Book Club. With more than eleven thousand books it was about twice as large as the main library of the Sixth District. Borrowing privileges were two kronen a year or two heller per book.[143]

A few houses farther down, at 17 Stumpergasse, were the editorial offices of the *Alldeutsches Tagblatt* (Pan-German Daily). The paper endorsed Schönerer's program and fought for German-Austria's Anschluss to the German Reich, for German to become the national language in Cisleithania, and for the "Away from Rome" movement. It also supported the interests of all Germans in non-German areas, in particular those of the German Moravians. News and reports were interpreted exclusively with a pan-German slant and contained only little actual information. Above all, the paper served as the basis for a political discussion among all pan-German sympathizers. The printer of this daily, Kalmus & Co., was at 7 Stumpergasse. As usual, there were glass boxes containing the latest issues. Thus the *Alldeutsches Tagblatt* was probably the first Viennese newspaper that Hitler read on a daily basis.

In the business district, Mariahilf, any kind of shopping could be done quickly and cheaply. There were restaurants and cafés nearby. The tram passed through the nearby Mariahilfer Strasse toward downtown. Because a ticket at the daily rate was no less than twelve heller—fourteen heller after 1909—the young man walked instead, and within not quite ten minutes of his residence reached the pompous historical building of the Academy of Visual Arts, one of Theophil Hansen's principal works. Right by the entrance one passes the splendid main auditorium, which, with its Parthenon imitation frieze on the walls, leaves the impression of an ancient temple. The ceiling fresco painting is by Anselm Feuerbach, whose work excited Hitler.

Like the building, the professors' college was modeled in the spirit of the Ring Boulevard era. In art, historical painting was still the dominating style and genre. Female students were not admitted, inasmuch as they were alleged to bring down the students' overall level by virtue of their dilettantism. In short: the Academy, which, in Oskar Kokoschka's words, people attended "clad in velvet robe and beret" in order "to be considered artists," was a refuge for conservatives.[144] ("Superruffian" Kokoschka, three years Hitler's senior, attended the Academy's modern counterpart, the School of Arts and Crafts.) The national makeup of the student body was uncommonly homogeneous for the Dual Monarchy: 245 of the 274 students during the fall semester 1907–8 were German-speaking.[145]

The examination procedure then was hardly different from today: the decision whether a candidate qualifies for even taking the exam is based on the works submitted. In early September 1907 Hitler was one of 112 candidates who would take the admission test: he *set out with a pile of drawings, convinced that it would be child's play to pass the examination.*[146] He passed this first part of the test and was admitted to the drawing exam. Like other candidates, before the decisive examination Hitler took lessons in the private and expensive Rudolf Panholzer Drawing and Painting School in Hietzing. The school was not opened until 1906 and had two teachers and approximately twenty permanent students, among them young women too. In preparation for the examination, individual tutoring was offered as well.[147]

The academy's drawing exam was administered under supervision on October 1 and 2, 1907, in two separate groups, lasting three hours each in the morning and in the afternoon. Eight "composition tasks" had to be carried out from one group of themes each, such as "(1) Expulsion from Paradise (2) Hunting (3) Spring (4) Construction Workers (5) Death (6) Rain."[148]

This time Hitler's works did not meet the requirements. The "Classification List of the General Painting School 1905–1911" contains the entry: "Adolf Hitler, b. in Braunau on the Inn, Upper Austria on 20 April 1889, German, Catholic senior official of the Dual Monarchy (father), few heads," and the result: "Drawing exam unsatisfactory."[149] Of 113 candidates who showed up, only 28 were accepted into the painting school, which approximately equals today's admissions percentage.

The decision was made by the faculty: professors Rudolf Bacher, Franz Rumpler, Heinrich Lefler, and Kasimir Pochwalski, but above all, the directors of the two painting schools, Christian Griepenkerl and Alois Delug, and, as the faculty's speaker, Siegmund l'Allemand. Most of them had gained their reputations working on the interior decoration of the buildings on the Ring Boulevard. Only the director of the second painting school, Delug, was one of the Modernists; along with Gustav Klimt and Alfred Roller, he was a founding member of the artists' association "Secession." Delug was forever in the midst of argument with his colleagues, and his involvement in the academy was limited. Neither in 1907 nor in 1908 was he in Vienna during examination time: he had declared that he could not accept anyone into his class and had retired to his native South Tyrol for vacation.[150] Thus the other director, the old professor Griepenkerl from northern Germany, carried particular weight. He, rather than one of those "Moderns" whom Hitler so despised, had the final say regarding the result of the examination. Speculations tracing Hitler's anti-Semitism back to his rejection by Jewish Academy professors[151] are entirely unfounded: not one of the responsible men during the examination was Jewish. L'Allemand, whose name might lead one to think he was, was from a Protestant, probably Huguenot, family in Hanau, Hesse.[152]

Downcast, I left von Hansen's magnificent building on the Schillerplatz, for the first time in my young life at odds with myself.[153] To be sure, some of those who failed gained artistic recognition even without studying at the Academy; for example, Robin Christian Andersen, who like Hitler had failed the drawing exam in 1907, became dean of the Academy from 1946 to 1948.[154] Later Hitler also liked to refer to the respected Feuerbach, *who, ten years after he was rejected as untalented, was celebrated and honored by the very same academy.*[155]

Hitler would from then on bicker against professors ("projesters"), universities and art academies in particular, *for the professors teaching there were either artists who could not make it in the struggle of real life, or they were accomplished artists but could sacrifice at most two hours of their day to their work at the academy, or looked upon that work purely as an occupation for their old age.*[156]

Klara's Death

Soon after his defeat Hitler returned to Linz because, as Paula Hitler will state later on, Klara Hitler's condition had taken a dramatic turn for the worse and she wanted to "have [her son] at home."[157] Kubizek remarked about the patient, "The joy about the son's return and his devoted care for her transfigured the somber, worn-out face." On October 22, 1907, there was a meeting at Dr. Bloch's office, where the family learned that Klara's condition was hopeless. From October 28 on, Klara Hitler was confined to bed.[158]

According to Kubizek, eighteen-year-old Hitler took care of his mother "in the most affectionate manner." "I had never before noticed this loving, sympathetic affection in him." There had been "a unique harmony of souls between mother and son."[159] The sickbed was in the only room that could be heated, the kitchen, and the son rearranged the furniture so he could put in a sofa for himself as well: this way he was there for his mother day and night. In Kubizek's words: "There was an atmosphere of relieved, almost serene, contentment about the dying woman."

These statements are consistent with the reports by Dr. Bloch, who from November 6 on called on his patient every day. On that date Klara Hitler received morphine for the first time and her first treatment with iodoform.[160] During this form of treatment, typical of the time and extremely painful, cloths containing iodoform were put on the open wound to "burn it out," which resulted in excruciating thirst and the simultaneous inability to swallow. Although Klara suffered these pains without complaint, Dr. Bloch reports that they seemed "to torture" the son, who expressed to the doctor his appreciation for his alleviating the pain with morphine.[161]

Klara Hitler was worried: Paula was only eleven years old, and stepdaughter Angela was about to give birth to her second child. But most important, "Most of her thoughts were for her son," Dr. Bloch writes. Independently of him, Kubizek reports, "Adolf was heading straight toward the unknown. This thought torments his mother incessantly."[162]

On December 21, 1907, forty-seven-year-old Klara Hitler died. Dr. Bloch, who filled out the death certificate, writes: "Adolf, his face showing the weariness of a sleepless night, sat beside his mother. In order to preserve a last impression, he had sketched her as she lay on her deathbed."

The body was put upon a bier in the apartment. Two days later, on an extremely foggy and wet day,[163] it was accompanied by the family and a few friends to church, where it was consecrated. The hearse, which took

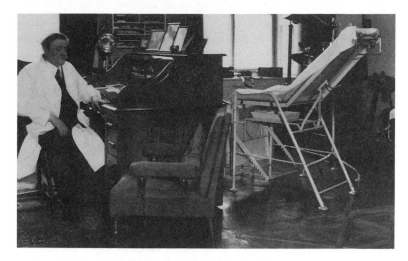

Dr. Eduard Bloch, shortly before closing his office in 1908

the coffin to Leonding from there, was followed only by two one-horse carriages. In the first one were Paula and Adolf, who, according to Kubizek, wore black gloves and a top hat with his mourning clothes; in the second one were the very pregnant Angela Raubal and her husband.[164] Around noon Klara Hitler was buried next to her husband at the cemetery of Leonding, which bordered on her former house.[165] Hitler stresses in *Mein Kampf* what significance he attributed to that day, when he compares it in its riveting impact to Germany's capitulation in 1918: *Since the day when I had stood at my mother's grave, I had not wept.*[166]

A few bills concerning the funeral still exist: the undertaker charged 369.90 kronen, including transportation and burial,[167] with the heavy, polished coffin with metal ingots costing 110 kronen, for Klara Hitler's modest means a gigantic sum of money. Just as with his choice of the high-priced class of care at the hospital, the son picked what was most expensive.

On December 24 the family called on Dr. Bloch to express their gratitude. He remembers, "In the practice of my profession it is natural that I should have witnessed many scenes such as this one [the family grieving their deceased mother], yet none of them left me with quite the same impression. In all my career I have never seen anyone so prostrate with grief as Adolf Hitler."

The son paid Dr. Bloch's invoice of three hundred kronen. Because this was obviously a flat fee, Dr. Bloch's cashbook does not clearly tell how much of it was allocated to wages and how much to medicine and bandages. Since the last partial invoice of November 1907, forty-six house calls were reported, almost every time with the expensive iodoform treatment. Thus, including drugs and bandages, each house call totaled approximately seven kronen, a very low amount if one considers that the district physician supervising the soldering of the coffin charged twenty kronen for this not very time-consuming service alone, and his colleague in Leonding twenty-eight kronen.[168] Speculations to the effect that false, overly expensive, and unnecessarily painful treatment by the Jewish doctor had triggered Hitler's hatred are entirely unfounded.[169]

Young Hitler clearly expressed his gratitude and reverence to the doctor with handmade gifts, for example, a large wall painting which, according to Bloch's daughter Trude Kren, "was lost in the course of time. My mother didn't like it."[170] For New Year's Day 1908 the doctor received a watercolor postcard depicting a Capuchin monk, presumably in the style of Hitler's favorite painter, Eduard von Grützner, that read, *My very best wishes for the New Year, With eternal gratitude, Yours, Adolf Hitler.* Against his habit, the doctor kept this card, as well as Hitler's first one of September 1907, which read, *From my trip to Vienna I am sending you my very best regards. With eternal gratitude, Your patient, Adolf Hitler,*[171] "as a memento of a good, exemplary son who so deeply loved and cared for his dear mother."[172] Apparently Dr. Bloch had a special fondness for the Hitler family.

When German units marched into Austria in 1938, the sixty-six-year-old doctor's life changed dramatically. His practice was closed on October 1, 1938. His daughter and son-in-law, Bloch's young colleague Dr. Franz Kren, fled overseas. Bloch himself had confidence in Hitler's sense of deep personal attachment. After all, in 1937 the "Führer" had asked Linzer Nazi party members about him and called him a "noble Jew." The doctor tried through a number of letters and several go-betweens to approach his former patient and to ask for his support. He was convinced, he wrote on November 16, 1938, that Hitler "has not forgotten his mother's doctor, whose professional conduct was always determined by ethical, never material, considerations; but I am also convinced that thousands of those who share my faith and, like me, are suffering so much torment of the soul, are governed by the same principles!"[173]

Hitler promptly responded to Bloch's request for help and placed him under the protection of the Gestapo, as Linz's only Jew: Dr. and Mrs. Bloch were allowed to remain in their home undisturbed until all the formalities regarding their emigration were settled. Without interference from the authorities they could sell their large, beautiful home for a fair price, and they were allowed to keep their money—extraordinary privileges at that time.

Despite this special treatment, the Anschluss was the most unfortunate turn ever in Dr. Bloch's life. After so many years of respect and comfort, he lost the basis of his existence, his friends, his house, and his homeland. In 1940 he and his wife emigrated to the United States. Because his medical degree was not recognized there, he could no longer practice his profession. In 1945 Dr. Bloch died a broken man in New York.

The Last Weeks in Linz

Some facts are known about the few weeks between the mother's funeral and young Hitler's departure from Linz in February. On January 4, 1908, Angela Raubal's child was born; she was named Angelika and later would become Hitler's "great love." On January 7, 1908, Hitler became a member of Linz's Museum Association for the steep annual fee of 8.40 Kronen; thus he became part of Linz's educated class and had free admission to the District Museum and its library. At the time the museum had the largest number of visitors since its opening: hundreds of people marveled at the "Discovery of Schwanenstadt," the entire collected household goods of a well-to-do citizen of the seventeenth century, including his clothes and everyday articles.

On January 18, 1908, the court's "inventory after death" took place in Urfahr. No property was listed,[174] which indicates that whatever money there was was distributed internally. An out-of-court settlement was important, because that was the only way a freezing of the inheritance of the children Adolf and Paula, who were still under age, could be prevented. Until their twenty-fourth birthdays, the paternal inheritance of 652 kronen each was in an officially frozen account anyway. Both children urgently needed money to live on, and the official orphan's pension of twenty-five kronen per month was not sufficient.

We can only guess at the amount of the inheritance. The proceeds from the sale of the house in Leonding of about 5,500 kronen in 1905 had most certainly dwindled down—on account of Angela's dowry, Adolf's expensive tuition in Steyr, his two trips to Vienna, three moves, and above all, Klara's long sickness and her funeral. In Klara's last year, inflation had seriously diminished the value of the pension of approximately 100 kronen per month. Krackowizer wrote on December 1, 1907, "Much inflation for weeks now. Rallies against this everywhere, debates in all corporations as well as in Parliament. A desolate situation for the 'little' people." On December 10 he noted "protest assemblies everywhere against general inflation"; on December 14, "Passive resistance of the postal workers in all of Austria"; on January 19, 1909, "Harvesters strike in Austria"; and so forth.[175]

By a conservative estimate, no more than 2,000 kronen could have been left as Adolf and Paula's inheritance, with half going to each. The maternal inheritance and the orphan's allowance combined were enough to live on in expensive Vienna for about one year without having to work. Therefore, Hitler's complaint in 1921 that his *total cash when I went to Vienna (was) approximately 80 kronen* cannot have been quite true.[176] That by 1907 he had become a "downright well-to-do man,"[177] as some historians would have it, is patently incorrect.

The newly orphaned art student encountered much sympathy in those weeks. His neighbor, postal worker Presemayer, offered to help him get a job at the post office, but the eighteen-year-old declined: he wanted to become "a great artist." "And when he then was told that the necessary monetary means and personal connections for that were lacking, he only gave the brief reply, 'Makart and Rubens too worked themselves up from impoverished conditions!' "[178]

The housewife in the house at Blütengasse, Magdalena Hanisch, had more sympathy for the ambitious young man. On February 4, 1908, she wrote a long letter to her friend Johanna Motloch, called "Muki," who lived in Vienna, asking her for a recommendation letter to Alfred Roller, the well-known stage and costume designer at the Court Opera, Gustav Mahler's closest associate and a professor at the School of Arts and Crafts. She wrote, "The son of one of my tenants is becoming a painter, has gone to school in Vienna since the fall, he wanted to attend the Austro-Hungarian Academy of Visual Arts, but was not accepted and went to a private institution instead (Panholzer I believe). He is a serious, ambitious young man, 19 years old, more mature and settled than his age indicates, nice and sensible, from a perfectly decent family. His mother died before Christmas, suffered from breast cancer, was only 46 years old, the widow of a higher-up official at the local main customs office; I liked the woman *very* much; she lived next to me on the first floor; her sister and her daughter, who is in high school, are keeping the apartment for the time being. The family's name is Hitler; the son, in whose behalf I'm asking your help, is called Adolf Hitler."

Young Hitler knew two of Roller's Wagner productions, *Tristan* and *Dutchman*. Mrs. Hanisch told her friend in Vienna: "We happened to talk about art and artists the other day, and among others, he mentioned that Professor Roller is a famous man among artists, not only in Vienna, but one could even say he has world renown, and that he reveres him in his works. Hitler had no idea that I am familiar with the name Roller, and when I told him that I used to know a brother of the famous Roller and asked him if it might be helpful to him in his endeavors if he received a recommendation to the director of the Court Opera's Scenery Department, the young man's eyes started glowing; he flushed crimson and said he would consider it the best luck he ever had if he could meet *that* man and got a recommendation to him! I would love to help the young man; he simply has no one who could put in a good word for him or help him by word and deed; he arrived in Vienna a complete stranger and alone, and had to go everywhere alone, without anyone giving him direction, to find entrance. He has the firm intention of learning something solid! So far as I have gotten to know him, he won't 'operate in low gear,' since he is focusing on a serious goal; I hope you won't waste your good offices on someone unworthy! Perhaps you'll do a good deed." The young man is still in Linz, she says, "but will return to Vienna in a few days. He is only waiting to get notice from the senior guardianship's office regarding the pension for himself & his sister."[179]

Johanna Motloch immediately wrote to Roller. And that busy, famous man replied by return mail, on February 6, 1908, with a three-page letter: "Dear Madam, I will be happy to oblige you. Do tell young Hitler to call on me and to bring some of his works so I can see how he is doing. I surely will advise him as best I can. He can meet me every day in my office at the Opera, entrance Kärntherstrasse, Principal Offices staircase, at 12:30 and at 6:30 P.M. Should I happen not to be in the office, the servant will call me by phone. It is rare that I am not around at those hours. Should Hitler be unfortunate enough to come at one of those times, he shouldn't let himself be discouraged and call again the following day."

"Muki" immediately forwarded Roller's letter to Mrs. Hanisch in Linz, who as early as February 8, 1908, wrote a thank-you note "for granting my request so promptly" and reported about how the letter was received: "You would have found your effort rewarded by seeing the happy face of the young man when I had him come over and told him that you had been so kind as to recommend him to Director Roller, that he may call on him! I gave him your card and let him read Director Roller's letter! You should have seen the boy. Slowly, word for word, as if he wanted to learn the letter by heart, as if absorbed in prayer, a happy smile on his face, that's how he read the letter, quietly, all to himself. Then he put it down with heartfelt gratitude. He asked me if he could write to you to express his thanks; I told him yes! . . . Even though the guardianship office still hasn't sent him notice, Hitler now no longer wants to wait here and plans to go to Vienna in a week after all. His guardian is a simple enough restaurant owner, a very decent man, but as far as I can tell, he doesn't quite know what's going on. He doesn't live here but in Leonding. The boy has to run all the errands usually done by a guardian. Enclosed I'm returning Director Roller's letter. When you see the gentleman, please say a sincere thank you for me for so kindly offering to receive and advise young Hitler even though he is so busy with his work. Not every young man is that fortunate, Hitler will know how to appreciate it!"

On February 10, 1908, Hitler composed his thank-you letter to Johanna Motloch in Vienna, endeavoring to write in beautiful handwriting on stationery with black borders, with almost correct spelling:

Dear Madam:

Herewith, dear Madam, my most sincere thanks for your good offices in obtaining for me admission to the great master of stage design, Prof. Roller. It probably was somewhat impertinent of me so completely to take advantage of your kindness dear Madam when you had to do this for a complete stranger. All the more I am asking you to accept my most sincere thanks for the action you took, which was so successful, as well as for the card you, dear Madam, were kind enough to pass on to me. I will immediately grasp this felicitous opportunity.

Once again, with heartfelt thanks, I am, with a handkiss,

Sincerly [sic] yours,

Adolf Hitler.

Urfahr, 10 Feb. 1909[180]

That same day Adolf and Paula Hitler applied for orphan's allowance at the Principal Revenue District Office. The law stipulated that orphans up to the age of twenty-four were entitled to receive one half of the maternal widow's pension, in this case fifty kronen—twenty-five each—per month, with the understanding that they would attend a school or university. The application was granted, and soon afterward, Hitler received his first payment in Vienna.[181]

Again the guardian urged the almost nineteen-year-old finally to get a job or start an apprenticeship in order to secure for his sister the full allowance of fifty kronen per month. That led to an argument, and in February 1908 Hitler left Linz in discord. He told Kubizek's mother "that he is tired of all the pestering and escaping them by fleeing to Vienna.

[handwritten letter signed Adolf Hitler]

He says he has a small amount of cash which will enable him to get by for a while; he wants to become an artist and prove to his Philistine relatives that he is right, not they."[182]

He persuaded his friend to follow him to Vienna soon to study music at the conservatory. In order to achieve that, Kubizek says, he had to summon up "great suggestive power in his speech" to "induce my parents to let their only son move to Vienna"—after all, aside from all financial sacrifices, they had to face the possibility of "losing with me forever the support for my at the time already sixty-one-year-old father's business."[183]

There is an indication in the household log of when Hitler left Linz: contrary to the order that will be kept strictly later on, from the first to the last of each month, the log does not start until February 12, 1908. The preceding pages have been torn out. This indicates that the previous "head of household" had left the house on that day or soon thereafter, taking all his accounting documents, including the pages of the log written by his mother, along with him. The other family papers, such as letters by his parents or Hitler's own letters, never turned up again either. Kubizek took his friend with his four heavy suitcases to the train station.

On February 19 Hitler wrote a postcard to Kubizek from Vienna: *Am already dying to get news about your arrival. Write soon and definitively so I can prepare everything for a welcome celebration. All of Vienna is already waiting. So come soon. Will of course pick you up.* And: *So as I said first you stay with me. We'll see what happens then. You can get a piano at the so-called "Dorotheum"* [the federal pawn shop] *for no more than about 50–60 fl[orins].* Postcript: *Again, please come soon!*[184]

For the time being "Haniaunt" stayed with Paula at Blütengasse. Yet because she was just as inept at running a household as the twelve-year-old girl, half-sister Angela Raubal now did the shopping and diligently recorded everything in the household log.[185]

They did not hear any news about their brother for a long time. In 1945, during an interview with the Americans, Paula said: "After Mother died, Adolf didn't return home." She had believed him dead. When in 1921 he stood in her doorway in Vienna, she had not even recognized him.[186]

Hitler's Ancestors in Waldviertel

The roots of the paternal and maternal side of Hitler's family reach north of Linz into the Lower Austrian district of Waldviertel, where all his traceable ancestors were from. Klara Hitler kept in close contact with her parents, who lived in the small town of Spital near Weitra, where she went every summer with her children.

The district of Waldviertel, situated near the border to Bohemia, with its harsh climate, bad soil, and lonely landscape of high pine forests, is still considered Austria's poorhouse. Aristocratic castles and rich manors give the highly romantic landscape its character, but the small farmers, the farm laborers, forest workers, workmen, and day laborers in poor villages were economically dependent on the clergy and the aristocracy and were barely able to make a living.

For centuries the border to Bohemia had been open and the population mixed. Many names of townships and families in Waldviertel are of Slavic origin. That the name Hitler, whose spelling has the variants Hiedler, Hittler, and Hüttler, may come from the Czech, is certainly possible too, but has always been eagerly denied by admirers of Hitler.[187] The most plausible interpretation is that the name comes from "Hütte" (cottage), in other words, that it means "Häusler," which is both an old term for miner and denotes someone who lives in a small house.[188] Thus among Hitler's known ancestors there is no one whose name indicates Czech origin.

Hitler's parents grew up in Spital, in houses directly across from each other. As a five-year-old foster child, Alois, born out of wedlock to forty-one-year-old Maria Anna Schicklgruber in Strones near Döllersheim in 1837, joined the household of farmer Johann Nepomuk Hiedler after the latter's older brother Johann Georg had married the child's mother. Johann Georg Hiedler was an unemployed miller's assistant who did not legitimize his wife's premarital child.

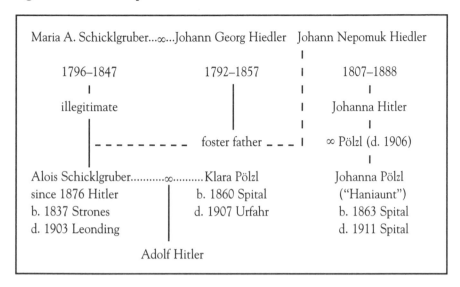

Maria Anna Schicklgruber died in 1847 at fifty, when her child was ten years of age, in the tiny village of Klein-Motten near Döllersheim, of "phthisis on account of dropsy of the chest."[189] Her husband, about whom little is known, died ten years later of apoplexy at sixty-five. He still lived in Spital, his hometown, but not with his brother.

Alois Schicklgruber grew up in Spital along with Johann Nepomuk Hiedler's three daughters, who were approximately the same age. At thirteen he left the Waldviertel district to find his fortune in the capital. In Vienna he first learned the trade of a cobbler, but his ambition urged him to strive for a loftier goal, and despite his lack of formal education he was rather successful in his quest: in 1855 he entered the Austrian Department of Financial Supervision, first becoming a border guard, and—exempt from military service on account of his profession—then advancing steadily: in 1864 he became a civil servant; in 1875, after various preliminary posts, a customs official in Braunau-on-the-Inn; in 1892, temporary chief customs official in Passau; and in 1894, chief customs official in Linz. In 1895, after the forty years of service required, he retired.[190]

Thirty-nine-year-old Alois Schicklgruber did not adopt the name Hitler until 1876. The change of name was entered in the parish register of Döllersheim, as an addendum to the 1837 certificate of baptism. Georg Hiedler, who had died nineteen years previously, was now entered as the child's father, which turned illegitimate Alois Schicklgruber into legiti-mate Alois Hitler—twenty-nine years after his mother's death. This un-usual procedure was carefully prepared and arranged by Johann Nepomuk Hiedler, at the time a sixty-nine-year-old widower and foster father.

Döllersheim's Rev. Zahnschirm was legally covered. He was pre-sented with an affidavit affirming legitimacy, which was signed by three witnesses and notarized on June 6, 1876, by the City of Weitra's notary public.[191] The witnesses, who were all from Spital, had declared under oath "that Georg Hitler, who died . . . on 5/6 January 1857 . . . said in their presence and repeatedly before his death that it was his last and unalterable will to have his son Aloys, conceived by him . . . and his former wife M. A. Schicklgruber . . . declared his own legitimate heir and to have him formally and legally legitimized."[192] These three witnesses now appeared with Johann Nepomuk Hiedler in Döllersheim and per-sonally confirmed their statement to the reverend. Whereupon the latter changed the entry in the parish registry—now with the spelling "Hitler."

Subsequently this official procedure of changing the name was ex-amined by the Lower Austrian governance and deemed lawful. According to an expert legal opinion, rendered later, legitimization could have been challenged only if someone had proven "that Aloys Hitler was not con-ceived by Georg Hitler"—which would have been difficult and, from a financial point of view, useless to boot: the man who was named the child's father had nothing to bequeath anyway.[193]

According to Kubizek, Adolf, born thirteen years later, was very happy about this change of names: "No step his 'old man' ever took satisfied him as completely as this one; for he found 'Schicklgruber' too coarse, too boorish, and also too complicated and awkward. 'Hiedler' he found too boring, too soft. But 'Hitler' sounded good and was easy to memorize."[194]

The reasons for undergoing this long procedure remain unclear. The fact is, six months after his foster father's death, in March 1889 newly named Alois Hitler bought a farm with land in the Waldviertel com-munity of Wörnhart (no. 9) near his hometown of Spital for 8,000 to 10,000 kronen.[195] If the money for the purchase were indeed from the inheritance from Johann Nepomuk, that does not necessarily mean that everything went to Alois. For in the meantime, the latter had gotten married for the third time—to Johann Nepomuk's granddaughter, Klara Pölzl. When he bought the house, she was in the last trimester of her pregnancy with Adolf.

We do not know if Hitler was informed about the intricacies of his family's history. All of his grandparents had already died before he was born. His father died when Adolf was thirteen. Thus Hitler's sister Paula's statements ring true: "I didn't hear anything about my father's family. It wasn't customary to pass on one's family history." And: "We considered only our maternal relatives real relatives. . . . I didn't know any of my father's relatives, so we, my sister Angela and I, frequently said, 'We don't know, but Father must have had relatives too.' "[196]

It is likely that Hitler never had to deal with his intricate family relations in Waldviertel until he was a politician: in 1932, to be more exact, when, during the election campaign, they were used to threaten him. His opponents acknowledged the sensible argument that a politician who placed such crucial significance on people's background could not but accept it if inquiries into his own history were made.

Immediately after the first vague hints were dropped in the press about compromising facts in Hitler's family tree, the prestigious and, when it came to business, smart Viennese genealogist Karl Friedrich von Frank offered Hitler his services on February 8, 1932: he said he already had a complete family tree of the Hitler family reaching back four generations—that is to say, to a row of eight ancestors—and that he could create an even more detailed family tree for three hundred marks. In a postscript he added, "You might be interested to learn that during my recent research I noticed that other independent research into your family background has been done at the behest of political authorities in Austria."[197]

Hitler retained Frank's services on February 29. The genealogist mailed his report as early as April 8, 1932, on the same day on which the headlines of late newspaper editions announced in huge block letters: "Hitler's Name Is Schücklgruber." In the article the young reporter Hans Bekessi, who later went by the name of Hans Habe, revealed the heretofore unknown history of Hitler's father's late change of name—a revelation that had a spectacular impact.[198] Tens of thousands of copies of the newspaper were hauled into Germany to affect the election campaign.

Frank had properly recorded the Schicklgruber story in his family chart and did not understand all the excitement, inasmuch as illegitimate births were not unusual and not even a handicap in rural areas. In his opinion, Maria Anna Schicklgruber and Georg Hiedler's eventual marriage had legitimized Hitler's father anyway. In May Frank presented his work in print.[199] Hitler thanked the scholar in a letter of June 25, 1932.[200]

Yet in the summer of 1932 there was an even far greater uproar in the press. First, on June 16, the *Neue Zürcher Zeitung* published a letter to the editor regarding the topic of "Hitler's Ancestors": the sender questioned Frank's opinion that "with the exception of the name Wallj [the family chart contained] only German names," and offered that "the family name Salomon, which comes up repeatedly," surely couldn't be "accepted without qualms as a German name. . . . At least, Adolf Hitler and his followers are not in the habit of simply accepting that name as a German name."[201] In the family tree that Frank published, there appears as a great-great-great-grandmother, as number forty-five, a Catholic Katharina Salomon from Nieder-Plöttbach, parish of Döllersheim, daughter of the Catholic farmer Johann Salomon in Nieder-Plöttbach. It was the appearance of this Jewish-sounding name that started speculations about Hitler's alleged Jewish background.

Yet here, of all places where the genealogist could have bungled, is where he apparently made a mistake: in point of fact, number forty-five in the family tree was not Katharina Salomon, but Maria Hamberger from Nieder-Plöttbach (1709–1761), whose father was Paul Hamberger from Nieder-Plöttbach (1680–1706). Frank corrected this mistake as early as August 30, 1932. Yet the print run containing the error had already been shipped.[202]

Now scores of reporters started searching for Hitler's alleged Jewish relatives. It was discovered that the name Hitler appeared among Jewish families in the small town of Polna in Moravia, in Poland, and that there was a Jewish merchant in the Leopoldstadt district who claimed to be a relative of Hitler via Polna. In Warsaw some Jewish families by the name of Hitler officially applied for a change of name, adverting to the anti-Semitic German politician.

The summer of 1933 brought new headlines. *Lidove Noviný* in Prague reported on July 6 that in Polna people were mentioning an Abraham Hitler from the eighteenth century as Hitler's ancestor. *Deutsche Freiheit* of Saarbrücken wrote on July 6, "The Jewish Hitler Family—with Sources." *Österreichisches Morgenblatt* wrote on July 13: "Brown Hitler* with His Yellow Spot." *Vorarlberger Wacht* wrote: "So he did have a Jewish grandmother after all—Mr. Hitler."[203]

In the meantime Bekessi had become an editor for the *Österreichisches Abendblatt* and published new revelations starting on July 12; for example, on July 14, 1933: "Awesome Traces of the Hitler Jews in Vienna," with photographs from Hitler graves in the Jewish section of Vienna's Central Cemetery and a cookbook by one Rosalie Hitler, written in Hebrew. On July 19 Bekessi's newspaper even printed the headline "Hitler's

---

*Brown was considered the color National Socialists' political color, after the uniforms of the SA. (*Translator's note*)

Jewishness Officially Confirmed!" This time the newspaper published the pedigree of a Jewish Hiedler family in Polna, with a Klara Hitler, born in 1821, married name Pölzl, Braunau, Austria. An alleged "official" statement was attached: "There is hardly a Jew who has such a beautiful family tree as Adolf Hitler."

To be sure, this Jewish Klara would have been no less than seventy-eight years old at the time of Hitler's birth, and the other details would not have fit Hitler's grandmother. In part of the article in smaller print the newspaper backed off, stating that this Jewish Klara was neither Hitler's mother nor grandmother, but a close relative of the grandmother—which was false as well.

This time it was fair game for Vienna's competing anti-Semitic newspaper, *Neue Abendzeitung*. On July 20 it promised, for its part, to reveal the "Truth about Hitler's Ancestry" and to refute the "myth of Polna": "It would have meant jubilation, would have beeen like shouting *Hosianna*, for all the Jews in the world, to have done in the man whose example and teachings have become the *greatest danger to their dream of global predominance*." What they were dealing with, the newspaper said, was the "most monstrous Talmudic pettifoggery of the century."

When Frank's corrected and extended family tree was published in 1933—without the name Salomon[204]—this was only viewed as an indication for a deliberate hushup. Soon afterward, writer Konrad Heiden picked up the story about the alleged Jewish grandmother from Polna in his Hitler biography, which was published in Zurich in 1936.[205] The myth became part of scholarly literature. Yet even though both reporters and genealogists set out to research the matter, nothing ever turned up except for names similar to those of Jewish families.

Hitler changed his genealogist: a large illustrated genealogical tree, put together by Rudolf Koppensteiner, appeared in Leipzig in 1937, to angry protests on the part of Frank. The new family researcher was from the Waldviertel district, was a distant relation to the Hitlers, and therefore had easier access to the documents, which had become too hot to handle. He did not mention the name Salomon either. And he, too, took it to be certain that it was illegitimate Alois Schicklgruber's father whom the mother later married, in other words, the miller's assistant Georg Hiedler. Thus Hitler had an unblemished "Aryan" pedigree.[206]

Astonishingly, neither genealogists nor journalists picked on the obvious weak spot in Hitler's family tree, his father Alois Schicklgruber, who was born out of wedlock and whose father uncertain.

After the Anschluss Waldviertel advanced to "the Führer's ancestral district" and paid homage to the Schicklgruber family's famous offspring by way of Hitler oaks and honorary citizenships. Even his ancestors were honored: the church square at Döllersheim was renamed Alois Hitler Place. The alleged—no longer even identifiable—houses in Strones in which Hitler's father and grandmother were born were spruced up as places of pilgrimage. Because graves of Hitler's ancestors could no longer be found at the cemetery of Döllersheim, "the Führer's grandmother"— Maria Anna Schicklgruber—received a belated honorary grave.[207]

Scores of journalists set out to look for heartrending stories about Hitler's ancestors. When the people in Waldviertel finally competed with one another on being related to the "Führer and Reich chancellor" and exhibited more or less fantastic family trees in all kinds of places, particularly in taverns, Hitler intervened in November 1938: "The Führer does not wish any family trees to be displayed which allegedly have anything to do with himself. Therefore the family trees now put up are to be removed immediately. As a precautionary measure, I furthermore advise you," the Lower Danube district leader told the district captain, "that persuant to the Führer's decision the display of memorial plaques meant to serve the memory of the Führer's ancestors or places where he stayed is prohibited."[208]

In contrast to his beloved Linz, Hitler did not grant Waldviertel any privileges. In September 1938 he even forbade the town of Döllersheim to issue a stamp with the addition "the Führer's native town."[209]

Yet as early as August 1938 troop-training grounds were established in the area around Döllersheim, Zwettl, and Allensteig—of all places!— with over sixty square miles, the largest of their kind in Western Europe.[210] People living there were transferred, and the villages, destroyed— including Strones, where Hitler's father and grandmother were born (thirty-nine houses), and Klein-Motten (ten houses), where Maria Anna Hiedler, née Schicklgruber, had died, and as late as 1942, Döllersheim (120 houses). This did not exactly attest to Hitler's piety regarding his "ancestral district" and fed rumors that he was embarrassed about his ancestors and wanted to extinguish traces. However, the Döllersheim parish register, the only source for the Schicklgruber's family history, was transferred to the closest parish, Rastenfeld, where it has survived intact to this day.[211]

Hitler did not want to hear anything about relatives: *I've got no idea about family history. In that area I'm an absolute dunce. Even when I was younger I didn't know I had relatives. I've only learned that since I became Reich chancellor. I am an entirely nonfamilial being, a non-clanning being by nature. That's not my cup of tea. I only belong to my folkish community.*[212]

Not until after 1945 did Hitler's personal attorney, Hans Frank, former governor general in Poland, make truly explosive material public: shortly before he was executed he wrote his memoirs—*Im Angesicht des Galgens* (Facing the gallows)—where he mentioned the following bona-fide scoop: at the end of 1930, he wrote, Hitler had shown him a letter, commenting that this was "a disgusting blackmail story of one of his most repulsive relatives, concerning his, Hitler's, ancestry." The relative had dropped hints to the effect that "in connection with certain remarks in the press one would be well advised not to broadcast certain circumstances of our family history." The point was that "Hitler had Jewish blood in his veins and therefore had scant credentials for being anti-Semitic."[213]

Frank claimed that after Hitler directed him to check confidentially into the matter, he found out "from all kinds of sources," which he did not want to divulge, the following: Before the child was born, Hitler's grandmother Schicklgruber had been a cook in Graz, in the household of a Jew by the name of Frankenberger; that she had become pregnant by the son of the house; and that for the next fourteen years she received child support payments for little Alois. There had been "a correspondence between these Frankenbergers and Hitler's grandmother, which went on for years, and whose basic thrust it was that everyone had tacitly acknowleged that Schicklgruber's illegitimate child was born under circumstances that obliged Frankenberger to pay child support." According to his own racial laws, Hitler thus would have been a "quarter Jew" and not been able to produce the necessary ticket into the Third Reich, the "proof of Aryan descent."

Frank was conspicuously ambiguous in leaving the impression that he did not find this theory implausible. It is with apparent deliberation that he made Hitler's denial sound so extremely feeble: Hitler, he said, knew "that his father wasn't the product of sexual intercourse between the Schicklgruber woman and the Graz Jew. He knew that from what his father and grandmother had told him." Yet his grandmother had died forty-two years before Hitler was born.

However—and at that point Frank came up with a confusing explanation, allegedly directly from Hitler—"the two had no money. The child support the Jew paid for years was a highly welcome supplement to meager poor household income. The Jew had been declared the child's father because he had money, and he did pay without going to court, probably because he feared the outcome of a trial and the publicity it would entail." In other words, Maria Anna Schicklgruber had only pretended that her mysterious employer's son was the father to make him pay—a popular excuse during the Nazi era, when one's "proof of Aryan descent" was in serious jeopardy because of an illegitimate birth and a Jewish father. With stories like this, Frank tried to explain Hitler's hatred of the Jews as the result of a condition he called "psychotic hatred of one's relatives due to a rebellion of one's blood."

To be sure, around 1830 there were no Jews living in Graz. After the expulsion of the Jewish community around 1500 under Maximilian I, the Styrian estates successfully blocked new Jewish settlements. Under Joseph II, in the late eighteenth century, Jews were again allowed to visit Graz, but only during the market season and for no longer than twenty-four hours at a time. Not until the passing of the basic laws of 1849 were Jews finally allowed to settle in Styria. From 1856 on Graz's Jewish community kept a community register.

Furthermore, during the period in question, in 1836–37, there was no family in Graz by the name of Frankenberger, not even a non-Jewish one. To be sure, there were families by the name of Schicklgruber, but neither a Maria Anna nor an Anna Maria.[214] The supposedly compromising correspondence never turned up, and no one ever mentioned it. Neither were there any indications ever for child-support payments to the child's mother, who after all gave the boy to her brother-in-law after she got married, lived in poverty, and died when Alois was ten. And, most important, there is not the slightest indication that Maria Anna Schicklgruber ever left Waldviertel. Accepting employment in faraway Graz would have constituted an extraordinary step, which certainly would not have remained unnoticed within the Waldviertel circle of relatives. Migrating workers from Waldviertel typically went to Vienna, which is sixty miles away, or Linz, which is even closer, but hardly to Graz, which is twice as far away, beyond the Semmering. This would have been particularly unusual for maids, who around 1830 traveled on foot.

When her son was born, dirt-poor Maria Anna Schicklgruber was already forty-one years of age—which was considered rather old in the nineteenth century—and surely not exactly what people could afford in some rich houses: a young, poor, and, considering the danger of infection, if possible innocent maid from the country who was supposed to introduce the son of the household to "love"—and who then would not be able to fend off the other members of the family either. Furthermore, Frank displayed such ignorance about Hitler's family relations that it is hard to believe Hitler was his source of information.

But now let us turn to Hitler's blackmailing relative, who supposedly was the reason for his desire to find out what happened. This must clearly be William Patrick Hitler, born in 1911, the son of an Irish mother and Hitler's half-brother Alois Jr. Shortly after the birth of the child, Alois disappeared—making his wife and child believe for years that he was dead—and remarried in Germany. In 1924 he was sentenced in court for bigamy.

When Hitler became famous, his poor Irish relatives, whom he did not know, saw their chance to make money and gave interviews to newspapers in England as "Hitler's relatives." Subsequently, in 1930, Hitler had nineteen-year-old Patrick, whom he had never met before, visit him in Munich, where he told him and his half-brother Alois that he forbade them to do things like that. He is supposed to have said that the family should not believe they could become famous at his expense: "You idiots!!" he was quoted to have shouted. "You're going to do me in! . . . How carefully I have always kept my private life and my personal affairs from the press! People must not know who I am. They must not know where I'm from and who my family is. Not even in my book did I allow one word to come out about these things, not one word! And then all of a sudden there's a nephew! A nephew! They will start investigating. They will sic snoopers on the tracks of our past." In a newspaper interview in 1939 Patrick Hitler even said that his uncle had started sobbing and in his anger shed tears.[215]

Later Hitler tried to deny that he was related to Alois, who had quite a criminal record. He said that Alois was not the son of his father but an orphan raised by the family. Yet Alois submitted the certificates of baptism as proof, according to which he was a premarital child of the second wife of Alois Hitler Sr., who had legitimized the boy.[216]

There was no getting rid of Patrick. After 1933, while unemployed, Patrick traveled to Berlin to ask his uncle for support. A hint at his father's certificate of baptism sufficed to make Hitler, who evidently interpreted this as blackmail, pay. He got Patrick a job and occasionally gave him money, but he left no doubt that he was not interested in familial relations.

After almost six years in Berlin, Patrick returned to England in January 1939, shedding any restraint he may have had before. Despite their thin content, his interviews created a sensation: "My Uncle Adolf," "Why I Hate My Uncle,"[217] and the like. In 1939 he and his mother emigrated to the United States, where he made a living going on lecture tours about his "Uncle Adolf." Patrick's mother Bridget Hitler, too, waged her "private war against the Hitler family" in the newspapers, increasingly so after the war started.[218]

None of these interviews ever mentioned an alleged Jewish grandfather. How much money Patrick and Bridget could have made with that story! In an interview with the Secret Service in New York in 1943 the nephew also vehemently denied that Hitler's godparents, Johann and

Johanna Prinz, had been Jewish, as had been claimed in a recently published book.[219] Neither did Bridget Hitler's posthumously published memoirs contain the slightest indication in the direction of any Jewish relations.[220]

The writer Franz Jetzinger illustrates how much manipulation went on in that area. He supported the Frankenberger theory by referring to an interview with Patrick Hitler in an issue of *Paris Soir* that was hard to come by—except, Jetzinger said, the nephew had mentioned the name "Frankenreiter" rather than Frankenberger.[221] This, however, is pure invention: neither Frankenberger nor Frankenreiter are mentioned, nor were any other allegedly Jewish grandfathers of Hitler.[222] Incidentally, investigations into the name "Frankenreiter" revealed that there was an impoverished Catholic butcher in Graz by that name. His son Franz, under suspicion of being Alois's father, was ten years old at the time.[223]

What needs to be pointed out is that the Frankenberger story has one single source: Hans Frank. In looking for a motive for his equivocal insinuations one cannot but suspect that the raging anti-Semite Frank even wanted to place the responsibility for an allegedly Jewish Hitler on the Jews, or at any rate rattle them by way of rumors.[224]

Kubizek and Jetzinger as Sources

Hitler's friend during his youth in Linz, August Kubizek, who was to be his roommate in Vienna for a few months, published his memoirs *Adolf Hitler: Mein Jugendfreund* (Adolf Hitler: The friend of my youth) in 1953. For lack of other eyewitness accounts, this book is the main source for an account of Hitler's early life and therefore needs to be examined critically.

First, some biographical data on Kubizek. After he lost contact with Hitler in July 1908, he continued studying music in Vienna and graduated in 1912. He was hired as second conductor at the city theater at Marburg on the Drau and worked there while the friend of his youth, Hitler, spent indigent years in the men's hostel, without any prospects for a better future. The outbreak of the war kept Kubizek from starting his new job at the city theater at Klagenfurt. On August 1, 1914, he married a violinist from Vienna and became a soldier. During the "Carpathian winter" in Galicia in 1915 he barely survived a serious infectious disease: "I had lost my strength forever." After the war he made do by becoming a private tutor and municipal secretary in Eferding near Linz, "where I organized the musical life of the small town."[225] When in the '20s he happened to recognize the friend of his youth as a political orator in a magazine, his response was one of pity: "I was very sorry that he had no more been able to follow through with his artistic career than I had. . . . Now he had to make a living as a speaker at assemblies. Tough job."[226]

When Hitler became Reich chancellor in 1933, Kubizek congratulated him in writing. In his response ("My dear Kubizek!") Hitler wrote, on August 4, 1933, *Once the time of my most difficult struggles is over, I would very much like to personally reawaken the memory of those most beautiful years of my life. Perhaps you could visit me.*[227] Yet Kubizek had neither the time nor the money for the trip and was probably too shy to boot.

The two former friends did not see each other again until April 9, 1938, for the first time in thirty years, at Linz's Hotel Weinzinger, one day before the referendum on the Anschluss that had already taken place. Hitler welcomed him by shouting, *Gustl!* but addressed him with *Sie*, the formal third-person pronoun. Standing at the window, they looked out on the Danube, and as in the old days, Hitler found the Danube Bridge irritating: *This ugly footbridge! It's still there. But not much longer, I'm telling you, Kubizek!*

Hitler wanted to know why Kubizek had not become a great conductor, asked about his family, his three sons—and immediately promised to finance their education.[228] In 1939 Hitler gave the modest local civil servant from Eferding "the most blissful hours of my earthly existence": he invited him to Bayreuth.[229] Kubizek attended four productions. On August 3, 1939, Hitler too arrived in Bayreuth and received Kubizek for a rather long private talk. As in the old days, they talked only about Richard Wagner, whose grave they went to see. Accompanied by the young Wieland Wagner, they visited Wahnfried, Wagner's house, where they looked at Wagner's grand piano. Finally Hitler introduced the friend of his youth to the mistress of Bayreuth, Winifred Wagner, and related to her the *Rienzi* experience of his youth, commenting on it momentously, *It began in that hour.*[230]

The two also met in Bayreuth in 1940, during the intermission of *Götterdämmerung*. After his victories over Poland and France Hitler was at the pinnacle of his power. Confronting the fifty-two-year-old friend of his youth, he seemed so pensive that Kubizek had the impression he was trying to "justify" himself. They then talked about old times. Hitler said: *Poor students, that's what we were. And we were hungry, God knows.* And so on. As in the old days, Kubizek patiently listened to everything.

Immediately after the opera Hitler left Bayreuth through a lane of cheering people. When he recognized Kubizek at the edge of the road, he stopped the fleet of cars, rode in his direction, shook his hand, and,

"Gustl" Kubizek, the friend of Hitler's youth

riding on, waved to him, which caused quite a stir. It was the last time the two saw each other.[231]

As "the friend of the Führer's youth," Kubizek now was a celebrity. He remained a local civil servant, managed the registrar's office, and dealt with all of the community's cultural affairs. He did not join the NSDAP—the Nazi party—until 1942, when he became "director of propaganda, director of the Central Cultural Office, and regional manager" of the leisure organization Kraft durch Freude (strength through joy), an apolitical position of little impact.[232] When Hitler's private secretary Martin Bormann directed him to write his memoirs of his and Hitler's youth together for the NSDAP's party archive, Kubizek received his only favor: in 1943 he got a special promotion to a higher wage group, the reason being that "Mr. Kubizek was a friend of Hitler during his youth," who was "busy writing his memoirs of the time he and the Führer spent together."[233] Kubizek's hopes of receiving a post as a professional musician through Hitler's help came to naught.

Kubizek found writing difficult: "this writing business is hard, it's not my cup of tea," particularly because he had "no peace whatever to collect my thoughts and was constantly interrupted by party traffic in the office."[234] To facilitate his work, he used a Vienna tour guide, copied its descriptions of Viennese tourist attractions, and reported which buildings young Hitler appreciated and which he did not. He also included anti-Semitic passages, for example, about their joint visit to the student cafeteria: "The cafeteria was teeming with Jews. You really felt like you had been transferred to Palestine, there was Yiddish everywhere, and males and females alike sported crooked noses."[235] Other-wise he mainly described in detail what he was well familiar with: the Wagner productions in Vienna and Hitler's musical plans, such as the Wieland opera: "In the life of my friend I was the musical collaborator and expert."[236] He doubtless admired his friend: "This man's creative power is inexhaustibly vast and all-encompassing too. I could really not tell in what area my friend wasn't completely well-versed even then."[237] This first manuscript has approximately 150 printed pages[238] and is credible as far as personal experiences are concerned, particularly in re-gard to music and the theater.

After the end of the war Kubizek was arrested on account of his personal relations with Hitler. He spent sixteen months in the Glasen-bach camp, where he was subjected to permanent—and futile—ques-tioning. His memoirs and Hitler's letters survived in a wall of his house in Eferding.

After his release in April 1947 Kubizek was unemployed and barely managed to make ends meet for his family. During that time of need he met the librarian of the Upper Austrian District Government, Dr. Franz Jetzinger, who was working on a book on Hitler and was trying to glean information from Kubizek.

Jetzinger, born in 1882, had formerly been a Catholic priest but was excommunicated in 1921. Between 1919 and February 1934 he was the Social Democratic representative in the Upper Austrian District Gov-ernment, and from 1932 on a member of the Upper Austrian District Government in Linz as district magistrate. In that function he got hold, in a roundabout way, of Hitler's military file, which he kept hidden in his attic. Kept under arrest in 1934 by the Dollfuss Government for five weeks, he rejoined the church in 1935 and became district librarian in Linz. In 1944 he was arrested by the Gestapo.[239] Hitler's military file, most eagerly searched for since 1938, remained hidden.

After 1945 Jetzinger planned to use this file as a foundation stone for a book on Hitler. He interviewed eyewitnesses, among them, Kubizek, who was hoping that Jetzinger would use his influence to help him retain his old position. Kubizek did a great deal of work for Jetzinger, wrote long answers to his questions, copied Hitler's letters and postcards, which were still entirely unknown to scholarship—and handed him the first draft of his memoirs.

Jetzinger, in turn, refreshed Kubizek's memory by asking him ques-tions, and, in the course of long conversations, told him details about his own archival research. Kubizek started to write his "own little book." He expanded on his old manuscript and now also used *Mein Kampf* as a reference. While working on his first draft, he asserted, he had a copy of the book but did not read it.[240]

Much to Jetzinger's surprise, Kubizek's memoir was published as early as 1953, under the title *Adolf Hitler: Friend of My Youth*. The approximately 150 pages had grown to 352. The writing is far more relaxed and readable than in the previous drafts, apparently having been thoroughly worked on by a skilled editor. The passages full of admiration for the "Führer" are missing, but still Kubizek leaves no doubt about his friendship with Hitler, just as he had stressed in a letter to Jetzinger: "I've only had one friend in my life: Adolf."[241] Yet as far as his statements regarding the time he had spent with Hitler were concerned, Kubizek changed almost nothing.

There were some stories he elaborated upon, such as the romance with Stefanie. Regarding dates he is not very reliable, and sometimes his memory deceives him. Some of his errors have entered into the record on Hitler, for example, the notion that his landlady in Vienna, Mrs. Zakreys, was Polish rather than Czech. Because he cited number 29—rather than the correct 31—as the house at Stumpergasse where Hitler lived, the wrong house continues to be photographed as Hitler's home to this day. Yet altogether, Kubizek is reliable. His book is a rich and unique source for Hitler's early years, not even counting the letters and postcards by young Hitler that it includes.

To be sure, Kubizek's statements about anti-Semitism are problematic. Although the book suppresses his own anti-Semitic attitude, young Hitler's racism is described at length in episodes not mentioned in the first draft of the manuscript. Thus Kubizek tells the story of young Hitler's allegedly denouncing to the police an Eastern Jewish peddler for begging, corroborating this with a quote from *Mein Kampf*.[242] He clearly tries to portray his friend as early on an anti-Semite who had led him astray: "Regarding the Jewish problem my friend and I had serious arguments even back in Vienna, because I certainly didn't share his radical views."[243]

Here Kubizek is clearly trying to promote himself. The Americans had questioned him exhaustively about his anti-Semitism, and now he is forced to maintain his line of defense. Thus he claims that Hitler had joined the Anti-Semitic League, filling out an application for him, Kubizek, as well, without his permission: "This was the high point of the kind of political violation which I had gradually gotten used to with him. I was all the more surprised since otherwise Adolf eagerly avoided joining any associations or organizations."[244]

However, before 1918 there was no Anti-Semitic League in Austro-Hungary. The Austrian anti-Semites were so at odds with one another, politically as well as ethnically, that an organization similar to the German Anti-Semitic League of 1884 never came about. Kubizek could have only joined the Austrian Anti-Semitic League, which was founded in 1919—and voluntarily at that, without Hitler's help. This issue is important because of all those early eyewitnesses who can be taken seriously, Kubizek is the only one to portray young Hitler as an anti-Semite, and precisely in this respect he is not trustworthy.

Kubizek's book was very successful and found one disdainful critic: Franz Jetzinger. His anger was understandable inasmuch as Kubizek published pictures and documents he had obtained from Jetzinger, for example, the photograph of Stefanie in Linz, and because he used information he had obtained from Jetzinger. Jetzinger's book, *Hitler's Jugend* (Hitler's youth), did not appear until three years later, in 1956. Jetzinger, who had not known Hitler personally, whose information was second-hand, and whose book does not constitute a primary source, found a few as yet unknown documents concerning a biography of young Hitler as well as eyewitnesses, for instance the boarder Hagmüller or schoolmates and neighbors of Hitler. Furthermore, he made a contribution to research by depositing copies of his documents in archives. We know Kubizek's first manuscript only through Jetzinger's copies.

Jetzinger's great weakness is his unfair polemics against the more successful Kubizek, from whose book he nonetheless quotes pages and pages. He erroneously accuses Kubizek of being of Czech origin, writes with contempt about the "grade school pupil of Kubizek's caliber," calls him "such a plain man,"[245] and so forth, and claims that virtually all of Kubizek's statements are false, saying that his book contains "at least ninety percent lies and fantastic fairy tales in the service of Hitler's glorification."[246]

That is clearly false. For Jetzinger also accuses his rival Kubizek of misstating facts that on second examination turn out to be entirely correct. For example, he considers it impossible for Hitler to have been a member of Linz's Museum Association,[247] and that Hitler had witnessed a rally during the time he and Kubizek spent in Vienna. Jetzinger details many such instances that are unimportant individually but, taken together, have unjustly shattered Kubizek's overall credibility.

Most historians have believed Jetzinger, not Kubizek. For Jetzinger, who was doubtless against Hitler and thus politically correct, deftly knew how to undermine the credibility of Kubizek, "Hitler's friend," and to make him politically untenable. And because Kubizek died in 1956, the year in which Jetzinger's book was published, he could not defend himself.[248]

Above all, two false statements by Jetzinger have had devastating consequences for historiography: one, that Hitler left his mother alone on her deathbed. That was more in line with the political atmosphere than was Kubizek's statement according to which Hitler had been a caring son—and Hitler's biographers were eager to accept it. However, Paula Hitler's and Dr. Bloch's statements prove unequivocally that Hitler was with his sick mother in Linz and that Kubizek's statements are true. Via Bradley F. Smith[249] the story about the uncaring, even cruel son entered the American literature on Hitler and inspired the psychiatrist Erich Fromm to his theory that Hitler suffered from "necrophily."[250] This "migrating mistake" is also common in the German literature on Hitler up to Joachim Fest.[251]

Jetzinger was the originator of yet another widespread myth by claiming that in reality Hitler was not poor, as he posited in *Mein Kampf* and as Kubizek confirmed, but was well to do. In order to corroborate this theory, he calculated the family income too highly and erroneously claimed that the paternal inheritance of 652 kronen was distributed after Hitler turned eighteen.

However, the guardianship court file of April 4, 1903, merely states that Klara Hitler was entitled to the interest of her underage children Adolf and Paula Hitler's inheritance claim until they turned eighteen,[252] in other words, that between the ages of eighteen and twenty-four the children were entitled only to receive interest. Pursuant to the legal statutes, their inheritance was frozen until they reached the age of twenty-four, and was distributed in May 1913. Thus as an eighteen-year-old he by no means refused his paternal inheritance, which is what Jetzinger criticized.[253]

Furthermore, without offering any proof, Jetzinger claimed that Johanna Pölzl had had a savings account worth some 3,800 kronen, which Hitler received. Jetzinger even made out that Hitler "deposited (the money) in a savings account," but had to concede: "Unfortunately I have not been able to prove black on white that Adolf was the heir."[254]

This threadbare claim, made mainly in order to accuse Kubizek of lying, was the foundation on which Werner Maser built his study of Hitler. He referred to an undated last will—which he had unearthed—of Hitler's great-aunt Walburga Rommeder, who had died in 1900 and made Hitler's grandmother Johanna Hiedler sole heir. Even if this will were documented, we still would not know whether it was ever enforced, what kind of inheritance it was, what happened to it after 1900, if any of it was still left in 1906, when Hitler's grandmother died, or who received it. Still, without offering any proof, Maser posited as a fact that Hitler received "very high amounts" from this inheritance, which made him "an utterly well-to-do man."[255] Thus the myth of a prosperous young Hitler was bandied about as an alleged historic fact.[256]

2

The Vienna of the Modern Era

The Austro-Hungarian Court Opera after the Mahler Era

Probably immediately upon his arrival in Vienna, at any rate some time
in February 1908, eighteen-year-old Hitler set out for the opera to introduce himself to Professor Alfred Roller. What happened then he would
later tell with surprising frankness to Vienna's district leader Eduard
Frauenfeld: Roller's letter in hand, he "went to the building once, then
he lost his courage and turned around. After some inner turmoil he overcame his shyness, started out a second time, went all the way to the
staircase, but no further. A third attempt failed as well." Some "person"
asked the shy young man what he wanted. "Muttering an excuse, he fled
and in order to find a way out of this constant agitation destroyed the
letter."[1]

Thus the chance to be discovered as an artist by Roller had evaporated. Young Hitler did not risk rejection and all his life could harbor the
illusion that he definitely would have received Roller's support if in February 1908 he had only had enough courage. *Without a recommendation
you didn't get anywhere in Austria. When I arrived in Vienna, I had a recommendation for Roller. I just didn't make use of it. If I had given it to him at
the time, he would have accepted me immediately. But I don't know if that*

Alfred Roller around 1910

would have been better for me: everything would have been much easier![2] Another time, he says, without mentioning Roller's name, *"How shy he had been during that time in Vienna, although he had been quite knowledgeable in the most different areas even then. He hadn't dared approach a great man any more than to talk in front of, say, five people."*[3]

Only many years later, on February 26, 1934, upon his invitation to the Chancellor's office, did Hitler, now Reich chancellor, meet the seventy-year-old, ill Professor Roller for the first time. According to the latter, Hitler talked about "his impressions in 1907 of my *Tristan* production in Vienna: *'In the second act, the tower to the left with the pale light.'* *'And then you also did Walküre. In the second act the steep slopes . . . and Rosenkavalier and other works by Strauss, Egyptian Helena, I believe, and whatever else you produced as well'."* Then, Roller recalls, Hitler laughingly talked about the episode "when he had wanted to show me his drawings and stage designs, had gotten himself a recommendation letter from a relative for that purpose . . . but at the last moment hadn't dared to call on me after all."[4]

On Hitler's recommendation, Roller staged *Parsifal* in Bayreuth in 1934. Richard Strauss conducted. During the opening Hitler sat next to Roller. And again he told the story "about the young student from Linz who so much would have liked to become an artist and didn't find the courage to knock on Professor Roller's door."[5]

Only a few days after Hitler's failed call on Roller, Hitler Linzer friend August Kubizek arrived in Vienna. His first impression of the accommodation at Stumpergasse was this: "I was struck by a nasty smell of kerosene. . . . Everything looked wretched and shabby." And: "From our abode we could see of the rest of the world only the bare, sooty back wall of the house in front. Only if you stepped right up to the window and looked straight up did you discover a small patch of the sky, but even that small piece was usually hung with smoke, dust, or fog."[6]

The very evening of his arrival Hitler took Kubizek, who was confused by the chaotic traffic and overtired, to the Ring Boulevard to show him the exterior of the Court Opera. Kubizek writes: "After the pitiful room at Stumpergasse, I now felt as if I had been transported to a different planet, the impression I had was so overwhelming."[7]

Despite their prolonged apartment hunting they could not find a suitable room to sublet because of Kubizek's rented grand piano. They thus came to an agreement with Mrs. Zakreys, who gave them the "large" room for twenty kronen a month. The two young men got settled; in the morning, Adolf stayed at home and slept late, while Kubizek, who passed the entrance exam on his first attempt, went to the conservatory. In the afternoon Hitler usually left the house, for during that time "Gustl" practiced the piano and the viola. At night Hitler kept his friend awake with monologues that lasted for hours.

In Vienna, too, the opera occupied the center of their interest. The work of Richard Wagner took up much room on the program: two to three times a year, the whole *Ring* was performed, as well as *Tristan and Isolde*, *Tannhäuser* with Leo Slezak in the title role,[8] *Der Meistersinger*, *Rienzi*, *Lohengrin*, and *The Flying Dutchman*. Kubizek reports that during their months together, from February to July 1908, they attended every Wagner performance at the Court Opera, saw *Lohengrin* and *Meistersinger* "at least ten times," and "of course" knew them by heart.[9] In 1935 Goebbels noted in his diary; "The Führer talks about the great singers in Vienna, particularly Slezak, whom he appreciated very much. That's where he first enjoyed music. Once again the old topic."[10] In Kubizek's words; "To him, listening to Wagner was not what one called going to the theater, but a chance to transport himself into that extraordinary state which he reached while listening to Richard Wagner's music, that self-forgetfulness, that soaring up into a mystical dreamland which he needed in order to bear the tremendous tensions in his volatile character."[11]

Kubizek reports that Hitler read everything available about the master "with a feverish heart," studying Wagner's work and biography "with incredible tenacity and determination . . . as if he could become part of his own being." "It could happen that Adolf . . . recited by heart a letter or a note by Richard Wagner or read to me one of his writings, for example, 'Kunstwerk der Zukunft' [The work of art of the future] or 'Die Kunst der Revolution' [The art of revolution]."[12] Wagner's weltanschauung and politics also become a model for young Hitler. *I was so poor during my years in Vienna that I could afford only the very best performances, which explains that I heard* Tristan *thirty or forty times back then alone, with the best cast, and also Verdi and a few others, but nothing else that was performed in addition to them.*[13]

Even though he lived extremely frugally, attending the opera so frequently in those first months in Vienna must have exceeded Hitler's financial means. A ticket in the standing room was two kronen, and special performances, such as a guest performance by Enrico Caruso or premieres, even four kronen. A standing-room ticket on the ground floor, beneath the emperor's box, with its excellent acoustics and perfect view, was highly sought after and could be obtained only after standing in line for hours. The standing room was divided by a bronze pole: one half was for civilians, the other for the military. Women and girls were not allowed, according to Kubizek, "a fact Adolf appreciated a great deal." Soldiers, who "attended the Court Opera less for the music than to enjoy the social event," had to pay only ten heller. "That would not cease to infuriate Adolf"—particularly because the military half of the standing room was usually only sparsely occupied, as opposed to the civilian part.[14]

According to Kubizek, Hitler did not at all like the cheaper places in the standing room on the third (1.60 kronen) and the fourth (1.20 kronen) galleries: for one thing, the acoustics and view were much worse than in the ground-floor standing room, and second—and above all—women were admitted there as well, which made Hitler feel uncomfortable.

To save money on the coat room, the two young men often went without hat and coat and freezed while waiting in line. Furthermore, they usually left the opera at 9:45 P.M. sharp so they could get to Stumpergasse before the building was locked at 10 P.M. and each save the twenty-heller superintendent's fee for letting them in.[15] Kubizek then had to play the concluding part of the opera, which they had missed, on his piano.

In 1907 Gustav Mahler resigned as director of the Austrian Court Opera after ten years of service. Unnerved by intrigues and anti-Semitism, he accepted an offer from the Metropolitan Opera in New York. Thus his alter ego Alfred Roller, a "modernist," was in a lonely position at the Court Opera in Vienna. In his letter to Johanna Matloch, Roller had also mentioned "the various discomforts naturally resulting from Mahler's resignation and the start of entirely new working conditions. . . . To be sure, Director von Weingarten is treating me with distinction, no doubt, but the pedantic bunch of civil servants frequently make life hard for me. Now, of course, is the roughest time."[16]

On February 25, 1908, Roller had his first production under Director Weingartner: *Tiefland* (Valley) by Eugen d'Albert. The work had had its first—and successful—performance the previous year in Berlin and could now be seen in Vienna for the first time. As to the libretto and music, the Viennese critics were reserved. They found the work's contrast between mountaintop and valley simplistic: "Above the snow line there are only virtuous, simple but pious people, yet down in the valley there are only sloth, the right of the masters, and contemptuous choruses." D'Albert's "cantilena is a little thin, his inventions tenuous by nature, and sparse to boot. Straightforward music, in part conventional, with a slight twist toward the ordinary. The cheerful scenes get their life from the operettalike touch, the tragic ones lack true elation." However, conductor Franz Schalk, the singers, and Roller as stage designer received praise: "In this incomparable performance and production the work grew, it literally got wings and had an extraordinary effect. And thus I gladly join in the cheers that erupted last night at the end," a critic said.[17]

It is very likely that Hitler attended that performance. Even as the Führer of the Greater German Reich, on October 27, 1938, during his official visit to the Vienna State Opera, he requested a performance of *Tiefland*. The conductor, Hans Knappertsbusch, and the players were surprised, inasmuch as they had counted on a request for Wagner rather than for that ancient Roller production from 1908. Professor Otto Strasser, who was present that night as a member of the philharmonic, told the author that Knappertsbusch had conducted this unpopular opera with ill humor and without acknowledging the special guest. Hitler's memories of the 1908 premiere with Schalk apparently outshined the repeat performance. It is possible that his criticism of the conductor was a result of that performance: "He said that listening to an opera with Knappertsbusch as conductor was a punishment."[18]

Under the new opera director, Felix von Weingartner, no less than twenty-one productions by Mahler/Roller remained in the Vienna Court Opera's repertoire, above all the works of Wagner. However, Weingartner tried to erase the traces of his unloved predecessor, fired many of those singers Mahler had preferred, and, to the applause of the anti-Semites, saw to it that Jews were no longer hired.

In June 1908, during a performance of *Walküre*, a melee broke out in the Court Opera's gallery. Wagnerians protested against massive cuts in the score and demanded that the opera be performed as written, just as during the Mahler era. The anti-Semites and numerous enemies of Mahler fought for Weingartner and the cuts. The *Alldeutsches Tagblatt* described the event in an article entitled "Jewish Insolence in the Court

Direktor Weingartner

Director Weingartner

Opera" as follows: "A number of crooked-nosed Wagnerians, their nice thick skulls (cat heads) delicately and charmingly bedecked with black negro wool (homo negroides), thought it was a good opportunity to indulge in boisterous demonstrations. The members of the orchestra, on the other hand, who revere Mr. Weingartner as a first-rate conductor and are happy finally to have got rid of that Jewish trickster Gustav Mahler, celebrated their director by getting up from their seats as one man and applauding him warmly."

Previously, the paper said, the performance of *Meistersinger* had been disrupted, "for the Negro-blooded have never liked the Germanic Wagner. But they reckoned without their host, for no sooner had one of those princes of darkness opened his jaws and bawled a little than he received a forceful box on his ear, delivered by a son of the Muses who had powerfully built up his strength on the fencing ground. For a few minutes brave students had a lot to do to leave their marks on all those Jewish faces and literally to throw the bones belonging to them out the door."[19]

Vienna's "high society" hardly made preparations to defend the unpopular Mahler. He had been too harsh as a director, adamantly rejected interventions, and been uncompromising in his artistic demands. He had turned the high-society forum for rendezvous into a temple of music theater, much to the dismay of those who did not go to the opera for the music.

Art requires serious concentration, young Hitler too remarked to his friend, upset about those *who go to the opera in order to be seen, who parade nice outfits and expensive jewelry and want to flirt or, if possible, make deals, and, before the performance is over, of course, amuse themselves by concluding their evening in a dance hall. . . . People of that sort don't belong into the Empire's foremost cultural institution, they should amuse themselves in a night club.*[20]

In the dispute over Mahler's concept of Wagner, the two young Wagnerians Hitler and Kubizek were clearly not on the side of the anti-Semites. Kubizek assures us that Hitler had had "the greatest admiration" for Mahler.[21] Even in the unpublished part of his memoirs, which were commissioned by the NSDAP, Kubizek says that Mahler "was probably a Jew too, but was still respected by Adolf Hitler, because Gustav Mahler concerned himself with the music dramas of Richard Wagner and produced them with a perfection that for its time literally shone."[22] With their admiration for Mahler and Roller, Hitler and Kubizek were on the side of the "crooked-nosed Mahlerians" and "Hebrews."

Despite all protests, however, the cut versions persevered even at the Opera in Vienna. In other houses they were the rule anyway. Winifred Wagner tells us that during a *Lohengrin* performance in Bayreuth in 1936, Hitler, who had been sitting next to her, became excited when the tenor surprised everyone by singing a passage in the story about the Grail that was usually cut.[23] Only those who knew the work well noticed that Hitler was entirely familiar with the uncut Wagner productions he saw during his period in Vienna.

Inspired by Roller, whom he revered from a distance, and perhaps still intending to call on him, Hitler familiarized himself with details about stage techniques during that time. According to Kubizek, he wrote plays and dramas about stories from German heroic myths and drew set and costume designs. The high point of these endeavors was the dogged attempt to "complete" the Germanic mythic play that Wagner had only outlined: *Wieland der Schmied* (Wieland the smith). In the myth, captured Wieland forges wings for himself to fly to freedom. Wagner's essay "The Work of Art of the Future" ends with the words: "O you one, magnificent people! You have written this poem, you yourself are Wieland; Forge your Wings and soar!"

According to Kubizek, nineteen-year-old Hitler had tackled not only text and stage design for *Wieland*, but also wanted to compose the music for it. He had wanted to prove to Kubizek "that even without attending the conservatory he was able musically to create the same as and even more than I could, for, he said, it was not the wisdom of the professors that counted but the ingenious idea."[24] Because Hitler neither had the slightest idea about harmonics nor was proficient in reading music, Kubizek had to write down his friend's "ideas" and—after Hitler had clumsily played them on the piano—then orchestrate them.

The obedient Kubizek would later euphemistically talk about the composition's "widely extended polyphony" and complain about Hit-

Adolf Hitler's sketch for a stage design for *Lohengrin*

ler's idiosyncrasies: in the end the score had been full of accidentals, and, furthermore, there was "a constant metric change of beat."[25] Hitler had worked "feverishly, as if an impatient opera director had given him much too close a deadline and was already tearing the manuscript out of his hands in installments."[26] The odd enterprise shows the obstinacy as well as presumptuousness of the young man, whose only musical education consisted of four months of not very successful piano lessons.

During these endeavors Hitler gained that knowledge with which he later astonished experts. Many a theater director was surprised at Hitler's "interest for revolving stages' diameter, trap door mechanisms, and particularly for the various lighting techniques. He knew all the electric control systems and was able to elaborate in detail on the right lighting for certain scenes." According to Albert Speer, even when he was Reich chancellor, Hitler still made stage-design drawings for Wagner operas and suggested them to his favorite stage manager, Benno von Arendt. These had been "cleanly executed" sketches, "colored with coloring pencils," for all the acts of *Tristan and Isolde*, and at another time sketches for every scene in *Ring of the Nibelungs*. "Full of satisfaction," Hitler had related at the dinner table how he had *sat over them for three weeks, night after night,* during a period in which he had a particularly full appointment calendar.[27]

The knowledge he gained in Vienna later clearly influenced the stage-productionlike Nuremberg party conventions and the most varied celebrations and hours of commemoration. Speer's "domes of light" were to continue Roller's "direction of light." The sea of red flags, the marching up during the roll of drums and music by Wagner, preferably in darkness, when it is easier to put an audience in a solemn, emotionally charged mood: all this was as if in a perfectly staged Wagner opera, with the Reich chancellor's entrance and speech as the big climax.

Aside from opera, Hitler had little interest in music. Sometimes Kubizek got free tickets at the conservatory for concerts in the Music Club's "Golden Room." There Hitler for the first time listened to the music—more precisely, the fourth, the "Romantic Symphony"—of his Upper Austrian compatriot Anton Bruckner, which was still rarely played at the time, and according to Kubizek was "intoxicated in every respect."[28] In later years Hitler would proudly mention Bruckner; for example, in 1942, after a performance of Symphony No. 7: *Everything, folk tunes from Upper Austria, none of them adopted literally, but still, piece by piece, slow regional waltzes and other tunes I've been familiar with since my youth. What that man made out of the primitive material! . . . You can imagine what a rough time that little farmer had when he arrived in Vienna, in that metropolitan, decadent society.*[29]

According to Kubizek, Hitler had no interest in non-German composers: "Neither Gounod, whose *Margarete* he called kitschy, nor Tchaikovsky or Smetana could impress him. . . . He only accepted the German masters. How frequently he told me he was proud to belong to a people that had produced such masters. What did he care about the others. Since he didn't want to approve of them, he also convinced himself that he didn't like their music."[30]

The only exceptions he made were Franz Liszt, as "Richard Wagner's protector," and Edvard Grieg, as the "Nordic Beethoven."[31] But he had no understanding of Beethoven, Mozart, or Gluck either, just as he did not in the least comprehend modern music—in which he was in agreement with most of his contemporaries.

The Architecture of the Ring Boulevard

Kubizek the musician leaves the impression that Hitler's thoughts in Vienna had mostly centered on opera, which they experienced together at night. What Hitler did during the day, his friend did not know exactly. He did not share Hitler's main interest, architecture, above all that of the Ring Boulevard. Even during his first visit to Vienna it had seemed to Hitler *like an enchantment out of* The Thousand-and-One Nights, and all his life he would rave about the Ring Boulevard being *the most beautiful line of streets that has ever been built on old entrenchments, with buildings that, to be sure, were designed in eclectic styles, but by idiosyncratic and good architects, and thus without any epigenous decadence.*[32]

The magnificent Ring Boulevard, a two-and-a-half-mile-long circle around downtown Vienna completed in 1865, represented the most important architectural change in Vienna since the Middle Ages. Until 1857, when Emperor Franz Josef ordered the city walls to be torn down, Vienna was a narrow, dark, overcrowded city, squeezed in between medieval walls. The surrounding suburbs were separated from the city by the Glacis, a broad, undeveloped, 1,400-feet-wide meadow that was used as a drill and parade ground, but also as a recreation area, and now provided the land for the new buildings.

Construction work had been almost completed around 1900, when downtown Vienna was joined with its suburbs. Vienna was now an expansive modern metropolis, with the Ring Boulevard an expression of imperial power—but at a time when that power had long since been waning. Hitler said in a speech in 1929 that the Ring Boulevard was based on the political idea *of giving the monarchy, which even at that time already was torn apart by destructive forces, a central force, a force of attraction, in a large, outstanding, magnificent center. . . . The little man who arrives in the big city, who arrives in the imperial capital, he shall have a sense of that's where the king, the sovereign, lives.*[33]

The street's greatest attractions were the public buildings in various historical styles: from Hellenism (Parliament) to Neo-Gothicism (Votive Church and City Hall) to Renaissance (Burgtheater, Court Opera, Stock Exchange, University). In between were the most elegant hotels of town, the mansions of the new financial and industrial nobility, the "Ring Boulevard Barons," and the rental mansions.

All his life Hitler would praise the Vienna Court Opera as the *most magnificent opera house in the world, with superb acoustics*, and he frequently told the story of the building's two unfortunate architects, Eduard van der Nüll and August Siccard von Siccardsburg. One committed suicide because he was hurt by unfair criticism, and the other died shortly afterward. Neither of them lived to see his glorious rehabilitation.[34] Hitler studied the neo-Gothic city hall and raved about the *magnificent building* of the Parliament, the main work of Danish architect Theophil Hansen: *A Hellenic miracle on German soil.*[35]

Hitler admired above all Gottfried Semper, the architect of the Burgtheater,[36] and copied his sketches for his own designs of a regional theater in Linz.[37] One can detect in Hitler's plans Semper's famous, grandiose stairway at the Burgtheater as well as the construction style of the Re-

Gottfried Semper's Burgtheater on Ring Boulevard

naissance, which Semper preferred. As late as 1940 Hitler planned to carry out Semper's old plan for a "Reich opera" in Berlin: *The most beautiful and best thing there can be.*[38]

Kubizek reports that Hitler would "get downright intoxicated" with these buildings, which he studied in detail: "Often he could look at such a building for hours, memorizing even totally minor details."[39] "At home he would then make drawings for me of the ground plans or the longitudinal sections, or he tried to tackle some interesting detail. He borrowed tomes that taught him about the history of the individual buildings. . . . I was always astonished at how well-informed he was about side gates, staircases, even about little-known doorways or back entrances. . . . Thus the Ring Boulevard became a living object of study to him where he could gauge his architectural knowledge and demonstrate his views."[40]

According to Kubizek, nineteen-year-old Hitler sourrounded himself "increasingly with technical literature," in particular with a volume on the history of architecture. He enjoyed "randomly opening up an illustrated page, covering the explanation underneath with his hand and telling me by heart what the illustration depicted, for example, the Cathedral of Chartres or the Palazzo Pitti in Florence. His memory was downright remarkable,"[41] as was his diligence: "One time Adolf would sit over his books for hours, another time he would write until the middle of the night, and yet another time the grand piano, the table, his bed and mine, even the whole floor, were covered with drawings."[42] According to Kubizek, his friend never designed "secular buildings or plants. . . . His imagination was always floating on higher planes, and when he made designs he never gave a thought to costs."[43]

Later on Hitler would regret having lost those early drawings: *these were the most precious things I owned, my cerebral property, which I never would have given away the way I gave away my paintings. . . . If today I am, for example, able to sketch with the greatest of ease the floor plan of a theater building on paper, I don't do that in a state of trance, after all. All that is nothing but the result of my studies back then.*[44]

Later on, witnesses would confirm how knowledgeable Hitler was. According to Speer, he could draw the Ring Boulevard and the adjoining districts with the large buildings true to scale and from memory.[45] Hitler was to tell the architect Hermann Giesler that when he was young he had also studied the large city plannings of Paris under Haussmann and of Munich under King Ludwig I.[46] Indeed, as eyewitnesses noticed with astonishment in 1940 in Paris, he had precise knowledge of the great buildings in Paris, in particular of the opera.[47]

How seriously Hitler was molded by Vienna also became evident when in 1942 he criticized some German monuments for their lack of artistic quality: they typically consisted of *potentates high on their horses with helmets and undulating plumes.* Of the six praiseworthy examples he mentioned, four were in Vienna—Emperor Frederick III's tomb in Saint Stephen's cathedral, the classicist monument of Joseph II as a horseman on Joseph Square, and two monuments among the group of buildings around the Heldenplatz: the group around Maria Theresia, erected in 1888 between the court museums, and Anton Fernkorn's monument of Prince Eugene on his horse.[48]

Kubizek was surprised to find that his friend did not seek the opportunity "to actually apply his knowledge or at least to participate in exercises in construction drawing in university classes. He was not at all interested in associating with people who shared his professional interest and in discussing problems of mutual concern."[49] Upon his friend's worried question whether he was really planning on mastering his studies with books alone, Hitler rebuked him: *You of course do need teachers, I can see that. For me they are not necessary.* He called his friend an *intellectual boarder* and *hanger-on who sits at other peoples' tables.*[50] Kubizek did not try to defend himself.

As with music, Hitler proceeded extremely selectively with architecture: when it came to the modern, functional style he was at a loss and, according to Kubizek, let only Otto Wagner's streetcar system pass as something that "answers its purpose."[51] Even though official Vienna still was built in the style of the Ring Boulevard, modern architects preferred a deliberate simplicity. Adolf Loos coined his much-quoted slogan "Ornaments are crimes" and called the architecture of the Ring Boulevard "an immoral act." In 1910, opposite the pompous dome of the new court castle at the Michaelerplatz, he built the house of a men's fashion parlor as a deliberate provocation that flustered the Viennese as "a monstrosity of a house" and as "a house without eyebrows." For it made do without the usual ornaments above the windows and had a smooth surface. Loos was thoroughly delighted with all the excitement and on December 11, 1911, to an overcrowded audience, gave a lecture entitled "A Monstrosity of a House."

Hitler's reaction to the house under dispute was idiosyncratic: when he drew the Michaelerplatz, he pretended the Loos House did not exist and copied a historic representation from the eighteenth century (see ill. p. 163).

Visual Arts

Even though he prepared for another exam at the Academy's painting school, and despite his veneration of Roller, Hitler entirely ignored contemporary art. Here too he turned toward old-fashioned styles. He loved Anselm Feuerbach, who emulated antiquity, Rudolf von Alt and his famous views of Vienna—and Eduard Grützner, the portrayer of happily imbibing monks: *Once as a young man I saw a Grützner in the window of an art store in Vienna. . . . I was so excited, I couldn't get enough looking at it. Somewhat coyly I entered the store and inquired about the price. Considering my circumstances, it was fantastically high, unaffordable! Would I at some point in my life be in a position where I would be able to buy a Grützner? I thought!* According to statements by photographer Heinrich Hoffmann, in later years Hitler would own some thirty Grützners.[52]

Most Viennese—from the emperor to the good burghers—also still paid homage to the "style of Makart": the furniture was "old German," the picture heroic-bathetic or idyllic-folkish, at any rate, concrete. According to Oskar Kokoschka, the bourgeois viewed art as a wall decoration, and the aristocrats "used it for the veneration of their ancestors, just as the Court employed a court photographer."[53] Hans Makart, who had died in 1884, was the dividing line between two directions. The moderns rejected him as bathetic, which annoyed Hitler, a fervent admirer of Makart, even when he was Reich chancellor: *In Vienna, almost everything that was wholesome was called kitsch by the filthy Jews. Makart's last paintings were no good, he had gone insane. That they rejected, whereas others only became valuable because they were insane!*[54] While a large exhibition in 1908 triggered a veritable Makart renaissance, the Viennese modernists tried to promote an understanding of modern art in the large-dimension "art show" under the direction of Gustav Klimt. Some three thousand people attended the opening at the exhibition grounds designed by Josef Hoffmann, the place of today's Concert Hall. In fifty-four divisions—plus artfully built gardens, yards, wells, a country house, a small cemetery, and a café with two terraces—they exhibited the works of sculptors, painters, goldsmiths, embroiderers, and glass artists. The "Viennese Workshop" also displayed beautifully shaped mass products, all kinds of household stuff, toys, dollhouses—one even had electric lights—picture books, the new reform fashion, posters, fabric patterns, and other items.

In the center of art were the new works from Klimt's "Golden Period": *Danae, The Kiss, Three Ages,* and erotic drawings. Twenty-two-year-old Kokoschka, a student at the School of Crafts and Design, upset viewers. Aside from his book *The Dreaming Boys* he exhibited a self portrait in the form of a bust with painted clay, entitled *Warrior*—mouth agape, as if he were screaming ferociously. Kokoschka wrote in his memoirs: "My exhibit space became the 'cabinet of horrors' for the Viennese spectators, my work the object of people's scorn. Every day pieces of chocolate or something else were in my bust's wide-open mouth, by which I assume girls expressed their additional scorn for the 'savage chief.' "[55] The newspapers bestowed high praise on the art exhibit's theater division, with stage and costume designs created by Roller. It is well possible that this made Hitler join the hundreds of thousands of visitors to the art exhibit. It would have been his first encounter with the artists of Viennese modernism.

The following year Kokoschka excited people with his play *Mörder, Hoffnung der Frauen* (Murderer, hope of women), a deliberate provocation he used "as a means against the lethargy typically experienced in the theater today." With torchlights, accompanied by rambling drumbeats and shrill whistle blows, young actors, their bodies coarsely painted and clad in rags, improvised a gory murder play. Spectators were revolted. Bosnian soldiers from the adjoining barracks sat on the wall around the art exhibit, ready "to intervene in the fake killing." Toward the end "the stamping, brawling, and fighting with the chairs . . . went dangerously far," and "finally the audience ended up getting into a scuffle with the soldiers."[56]

The provocation was followed by an assault in the press on the "degenerate artist," "terror of burghers," "spoiler of youth," the "prison plant." At the ministry's direction Kokoschka had to leave the School of Crafts and Design.

Viennese modernism loved what was exotic and strange, above all that which was primitive and unadulterated. It was enthusiastic about Gauguin paintings at the art show in 1909. When an Abyssinian village was shown at the Prater in 1910 and an Ashanti family exhibited the way it "really" lived, the Prater regulars were delighted at seeing "the blacks' " family life and the bodies of those half-naked attractions. So were the artists.

The modernists certainly meant all this as a protest against nationalistic and "clerical" narrowmindedness—and their antagonists angrily understood it that way too. They called the artists of Expressionism "degenerate" and liked to refer to Richard Wagner as their spiritual ancestor. In his essay "The Work of Art of the Future" Wagner had complained about the "frequent, restless change" of fashions and the inclusion of extra-European motifs and elements of style and argued that true art could flourish only after overcoming modernism. "True," national art, he said, was what would remain, and the "moderns" would always be but a temporary aberration.

His youthful experience with Viennese Expressionism may have helped to mold Hitler's disgust at modern art, which in 1942, for example, he called *nothing but crippled daubing.*[57] And at the 1935 party convention he said: *It is not the function of art to wallow in filth for filth's sake, to paint man only in the state of decay, to draw cretins as a symbol of becoming a mother and to portray crooked morons as models of virility.*[58]

Literature

Young Hitler remained a stranger to literature. That he—as Kubizek noted, full of admiration—read Goethe, Schiller, Dante, Lessing, and Stifter, is utterly doubtful, as is the claim that in Vienna he was "always surrounded" by Schopenhauer and Nietzsche.[59] However, it is possible, even likely, that Hitler knew a great number of quotations from the works of those masters, from which Kubizek deduced that Hitler read them diligently. The German-national newspapers were full of quotes by famous "German men" around that time. Particularly the pan-Germans loved corroborating their arguments by hard-to-check quotes, on stickers as well as postcards and calendars. With the aid of such quotes Hitler did not have to read a single book to make himself appear to be an expert in literature.

Even during Hitler's school years in Linz it was a matter of "German" honor to be familiar with Schiller's life and works, in particular *William Tell*, and always to be able to claim the Germans' right in a classical manner, for example, by quoting, "The nation is worth nothing that doesn't gladly put everything at stake for its honor." Or, "By virtue of owning it for a thousand years, the soil is ours!" Or, "He must expel who does not want to be expelled, / That is the point, and only strength will win."

What is left as a source of his literary education for Hitler were the novels printed in newspapers and the rare theater performances he attended. Kubizek relates that they went to the famous perfomance of *Faust II* together—it must have been the performance on April 25, 1908, at the Burgtheater with Josef Kainz as Mephisto and the very young Rosa Albach-Retty as Ariel.[60] There was such a tremendous rush that those buying standing room tickets had to stand in line as early as 8:00 A.M. After the box office opened at 5:00 P.M., the rush began, followed by the struggle for the best seats. The performance lasted until 1:30 A.M. Kubizek tells us that Hitler was "very moved" by the evening and talked about it long afterward.

According to Kubizek, Hitler had no appreciation for Henrik Ibsen, for whose eightieth birthday in March 1908 the Burgtheater produced an Ibsen cycle, nor did he care for any of the other modern writers. Yet the two certainly went to see one modern drama, largely, we may presume, so they could get upset about it: *Spring's Awakening* by Frank Wedekind, a scandal on account of its alleged pornography. The play, published in 1891, had its premiere in 1906 in a production by Max Reinhardt after a few arguments with the censorship bureau, which ordered, among other things, that the word "intercourse" be cut. Now it was scheduled as a guest performance in the Deutsches Volkstheater (German people's theater) in Vienna. Wedekind himself played the "Masked Gentleman."[61]

Wedekind was an artistic dividing line in Vienna as well as in Berlin. The puritans found him offensive. The young writers and artists, on the other hand, were enthusiastic; for example, the twenty-three-year-old composer Alban Berg, who later was to turn Wedekind's Lulu material into an opera, exclaimed, "Wedekind—the entirely new direction—the stress on sensual moments in modern works!!—...We have finally reached the conclusion that sensuality is not a weakness, not a giving in to one's own will, but a tremendous power we have inside us—the turning point of all being and thinking. (Yes: of all thinking!)"[62]

When it came to Wedekind, all Hitler could think of was "vices" and "threat of infection." The performance inspired him to take Kubizek to the Spittelberg district to demonstrate to him the evil of prostitution as a warning example.

As in all of Europe, in Vienna modernism was defined by its revolt against the prudishness of the all-too-bourgeois nineteenth century. The artists of Expressionism fought for the liberation from moral constraints, against a cloying idyll, for truth, enlightenment, and the exposing of social ills and ugly realities. In addition, they provoked the good burghers by practicing in actual life the moral independence and promiscuity they promoted in their works. In traditional, Catholic-conservative surroundings they made a point of being personally offensive.

In 1905 Schnitzler's *The Round* was censured as pornographic. In 1905 Sigmund Freud published his *Three Essays on the Theory of Sexuality*. In 1906 the novel *Young Törless* by twenty-six-year-old Robert Musil appeared, which portrayed the fatal connection between violence and sexuality in young people. Leopold von Sacher-Masoch published his erotic novels (e.g., *Venus in Furs*) in which male slaves let themselves be whipped by strong fur-clad women. The writer made sexual history through the term "masochism," which was derived from his name. Klimt and Schiele provoked audiences with their utterly uninhibited erotic pictures.

In 1905 Richard Strauss completed his opera *Salome*, based on Oscar Wilde's notorious play. For years Mahler had unsuccessfully tried to get the work premiered at the Court Opera, but it kept being banned "for religious and moral reasons" by the Court's censorship bureau.[63] Not until 1910 did the National Opera in Vienna, which was not subordinate to the court authorities, perform the scandalous work—which had meanwhile been premiered in Dresden—in a production by Roller. Salome, the prototype of the sensual, mankilling woman, quickly became a cult figure of modernism.

The pinnacle of public offense was the fashionable cult some literary figures made of prostitutes around 1900. For them, the whore was an embodiment of a sexuality that never exhausts itself. In his neverending battle against too-prude morals, Karl Kraus urgently pointed out the solidarity between artists and working girls.[64] Altenberg and many others emulated him. Klimt illustrated Lucian's *Dialogues of the Courtesans*.

Felix Salten not only wrote the extremely successful animal novel *Bambi*, which Walt Disney made world famous, but also the pornographic bestseller *Josefine Mutzenbacher: Die Lebensgeschichte einer wienerischen Dir-*

ne, von ihr selbst erzählt (Josefine Mutzenbacher: A Viennese whore's life story, told by herself). The book was unintentionally also a sociohistorical document: Josefine, having been raised in a large tenement building in the district of Ottakring, abused by the family's lodger when she was an infant, endured incest with brother and father and dozens of affairs with men from the beer seller to the catechist, cannot get enough sex and finally turns her rich experience into money. This story clearly tells a woman's sexual success story from a male point of view. It appears that Josefine does only what she loves most, what she was meant to do as a "real" woman. What the novel was not—as generally was not portrayed in Viennese modernism—was a depiction of prostitution, with its concomitant diseases, violence, the ordeal of children, and alcoholism.

The enemies of modernism angrily protested against this "culture of prostitutes" and the "prostitutionalization of art," and called for censorship. Schönerer's *Unverfälschte Deutsche Worte* (Unadulterated German words), for example, argued that people were "following every filthy wether like a herd of sheep . . . even if he walks through the worst puddles," and needed to be protected through censorship. "Clever seducers," he wrote, were "leading them step by step—quietly and not noticeably—astray." "No doubt the poisoning of the young generation and the abandoning of our national future" were an imminent danger.[65]

The Christian-Social camp sang a similar tune. The most prominent preacher around 1900, Father Heinrich Abel, raged against books and the theater as sources of immorality: "Girl, I beg you, refrain from reading novels, instead, I beg of you, take an embroidering needle into your hand and do some work for my poor people!" He even argued that Goethe corrupted men: "I alone personally knew four young men who were made immoral by reading *The Sorrows of Young Werther* and then shot themselves. I alone know four of them! O fathers, o mothers, watch over what your children are reading!"[66]

Science too, in particular medicine, tried to explore and describe the abysses of sexuality. The pioneer was the neurologist Professor Richard Krafft-Ebing with his *Psychopathia Sexualis*, which appeared in 1886 and during the following decades was expanded in one new edition after another: in ultimately 238 medical histories it described the most varied sexual "perversions" and declared them degenerations.[67] Finally Freud broke the last taboos when he published his theses about early infantile sexuality and thus destroyed the traditional image of the innocent and pure child. More than ever, science was considered an enemy of faith and the university a bastion of immorality and shamelessness.

These opposites were augmented by the ever-present battle between the different nationalities in Austro-Hungary. Around 1900 the German-national newspapers in Vienna were up in arms in countless reports of other ethnic groups' alleged advances against "German" culture; invariably they called for every German to assume the obligation to fight for "pure German art." This concerned not only "German works of art," but also "Germans in the arts," from conductors to women singers. The *Alldeutsches Tagblatt*, for example, protested against the National Opera, because a "full-blooded Czech" and "Czech agitator" had conducted *The Flying Dutchman* there. Furthermore, with the performance of Dvořák's *Rusalka* the director had proven his predilection for "Slavs and Jews." A "Czech colony" was threatening to develop there.[68] This in turn inspired the Czechs and Hungarians to use similar methods against Germans.

There can be no doubt about Hitler's position. Kubizek writes that he was "unconditionally devoted" to the German people: "He lived in that people alone. He knew nothing but that people."[69] In his sublet at Stumpergasse, Kubizek says, Hitler would grow agitated all night long: "He was again trying to erect the Reich of all Germans which put the 'guest peoples,' as he called them, in their proper place. Sometimes, when he expounded on that for too long, I fell asleep. As soon as he noticed that, he would shake me awake and yell at me, was I perhaps no longer interested in what he had to say? Then I should just go ahead and sleep, just as all those who had no national conscience were sleeping. But I forced myself to sit up straight and keep my eyes open."[70]

"Jewish Modernism"

As far back as in his essay "The Work of Art of the Future" Richard Wagner had used the term "Jewish modernism," calling it "something quite miserable and very dangerous, especially for us Germans." It would, he argued, continue to be destructive "until all original dispositions of its German contemporaries are entirely ruined."[71] And in his essay "Modern" he denounced the Jews' alleged predominance in the press and in publishing, which promoted immorality and licentiousness in modern art.

The accusations in Vienna around 1900 were quite similar. Modernism, the argument ran, was exclusively an expression of "Jewish taste"—*goût juif*—but not of honorable Catholic and "Aryan" citizens' tastes.[72] The *Alldeutsches Tagblatt* criticized "that whole dramaturgy, Jewish through and through, of taking one's clothes off . . . which would be impossible without well-formed breasts and legs."[73]

If the Christian-Socials judged modernism according to Catholic ethics, the pan-Germans got all excited about one of the main characteristics of progressive art, that of internationalism, against which they fought with the motto, "Art is not international, it is folkish."[74] "International" and "without morals or faith" were accusations anti-Semites used as codes for a certain group: the Jews. Viennese modernism was considered to be Jewish, and in the Vienna ruled by anti-Semitism the "fight against Jewry" was in the center of the cultural battle.

Strictly speaking, however, Viennese modernism was "Jewish" only with qualifications—one need only think of the many non-Jews, such as Gustav Klimt, Alfred Roller, Oskar Kokoschka, Alban Berg, Otto Wagner, Josef Hoffmann, Adolf Loos, and others. Yet the anti-Semites were examining the modern artists' ancestry until they discovered something that entitled them to reject the pertinent work of art as "Jewish." After the great success of Strauss's *Elektra* at the Court Opera, the *Alldeutsches Tagblatt* pointed out that librettist Hugo von Hofmannsthal's great-grandfather's name was Isaak Löw Hofmann and that he had been director of the Hebrew Cultural Community in Vienna. That clearly indicated "that hidden behind the enthusiasm for *Elektra*, to a not inconsiderable degree, is Jewish solidarity."[75]

To be sure, as far as the social pillars of modernism were concerned, the Jews' share of art and science in fin-de-siècle Vienna was relatively large: they were involved as builders, patrons, buyers, and as the audience that went to performances of modern plays and exhibitions, and listened to modern music. However, in Vienna the term *Jewish* designated more than being a member of the Jewish faith. It symbolized above all a libertine school of thought with an international direction that was neither clerical nor national—and that was not afraid of breaking out of tradition, daring something new, and violating taboos. Religious Jews were part of this circle, just as were longstanding converts, but also the "Jew slaves," that is to say, those who had Jewish friends, who worked with them, and who had similar thoughts.

One example for the close interconnection is the industrialist Karl Wittgenstein, the father of Ludwig, Hitler's schoolmate in Linz. As a patron, Karl Wittgenstein was involved in all the arts, from music— Johannes Brahms, Clara Schumann, Gustav Mahler, Bruno Walter, and Pablo Casals gave concerts in his mansion and always got his support— to the visual arts. For example, he financed the construction of the Secession's exhibition building. Josef Hoffmann built the Wittgensteins' summer residence Hochreith in Lower Austria, which the Vienna Workshop decorated in a uniform style, from the furniture to the chinaware to the paintings. Wittgenstein's daughter Margarete Stonborough had a portrait of herself made by Gustav Klimt and her apartment decorated by

Kolo Moser. The family was entirely assimilated, and there were so many mixed marriages that later, when "proof of Aryan descent" became necessary and everyone was forced to dabble in extended arithmetic, the Wittgenstein family was divided into two halves after one turned out to be a tad more "Aryan," and the other more Jewish.

When going to the opera, young Hitler, seriously disapproving of his *German bloodmates*, would notice that *Jewish youth is represented everywhere in the educational institutions . . . whether male or female, while there were hardly any Aryan youth.* According to Kubizek, he complained that the Viennese owned *the cultural scenes of their hometown only on the surface* and knew *their concert hall only by its name*, but *found all their happiness in the Prater, the tavern, and at the wine festival. This kind of people makes up the large herd of philistines and bar table heroes, which from the vantage point of tavern politics judge the well-being of the nation. . . . We must no longer accept the fact that even college students from the provinces have no idea about the works of art of their own blood and that they seek and find their greatest satisfaction in students' bars.*[76]

According to Kubizek, nineteen-year-old Hitler reflected on how the "Aryans' " obvious educational deficit and lack of interest in culture could be reduced. One of the solutions he suggested was the institution of a mobile "Reich symphony orchestra" for promoting music in the provinces and with students. He thought of everything: the orchestra, Kubizek reports, needs to travel *with its own cars*, independent of trains, the musicians needed uniform clothing—*but not the ugly dress coat or tux of today's orchestras*. If no room large enough were available, the local church should be used: *A symphony concert is a sacred hour, so the church's sacred character is not tainted in any way.* The mayor would have to take care of the organizational preparations. *Trained expert lecturers* should travel ahead of the orchestra and *elucidate the immortal works of German art to the people*, and the teachers should do the same thing for the students. Even the daily schedule was exactly planned: the first concert, consisting of chamber music, should take place in the morning, imediately upon arrival. In the afternoon there would be an orchestra concert for the pupils, and in the evening, the festival performance, *and immediately afterwards, departure.*

Kubizek was infected by his friend's zealousness, inquired about the statutes concerning the musicians' wages, calculated the costs of their uniforms and instruments, and even made provisions for establishing an orchestra archive. According to his calculations the costs of the enterprise were astronomical, but "in no wise did they deter my friend." Hitler, he tells us, had "such power of conviction in speech and presentation that no doubts whatever could arise."[77] The great aim was to win the culturally all-too-lazy "German people"—which consisted only of the Viennese, to be sure—over to classical German music in order to gain ground against the Jews.

The great liberal newspapers in Vienna generally supported and promoted Viennese modernism and offered intellectuals as well as artists a forum where they could reliably reach their audience. This resulted in the far-spread accusation that in reality "Jewish modernism" was no art at all but only artificially pushed by the "Jew press" with its business sense.

This politically overheated atmosphere in Vienna led to veritable press battles between the two large camps: the "Jewish press" on the one side and the "anti-Semitic press" on the other, the "wholesome opinion of the people" pitted against "Jewish modernism." Using the very lingo of the anti-Semitic press in Vienna, Hitler said as late as 1942: *By virtue of art reviews which one Jew scribbled about another, the people, which believes anything it reads black on white, was indoctrinated to a view of art which regards everything that is altogether kitsch as the latest artistic perfection.* Even during the time when he was attending the art academy, *scribblings making similar noise without sense had been lanced as the works of the "seekers."*[78]

In 1929 Hitler mentioned the campaign of the *Neue Freie Presse* and the *Neue Wiener Tagblatt* campaign for Bruno Walter, the conductor, as an example of the influence of the "Jewish" press. Thirty-six-year-old Bruno Walter—and Walter Schlesinger before him—conductor at the Vienna Court Opera and the most fervent pioneer of the work of Gustav Mahler, received an offer from Munich in 1912. Yet Vienna's liberal papers tried to keep him at the Court Opera. Hitler said: *No one looked at Mr. Bruno Walter as something special until then, but in the course of three weeks the name Bruno Walter was surrounded by a halo.* And: *Thus there was a synergy between the Jews of Vienna and Munich which gradually pushed the fourth-rate conductor Mr. Schlesinger from Vienna to the top.*[79]

Reich chancellor Hitler's wrath against "Jewish" art criticism finds expression in many of his utterances, for example: *This race simply has a tendency toward ridiculing everything that is beautiful, and it frequently does so by way of masterful satire. But behind that there is more: there is a tendency toward undermining and toward ridiculing authority.*[80] However, he also displayed a personal dislike of critics: *I cannot abide people whose only job is to criticize what others do.*[81] As Reich chancellor he prohibited all art criticism in the press and decreed that only "contemplations of art" and reports be allowed.[82]

Much of what Hitler said later is virtually identical with his anticultural utterances from his Viennese period, for example, when in *Mein*

Kampf he calls for a clearing away of *the filth of the moral plague of big-city "civilization" . . . ruthlessly and without wavering in the face of all the shouting and screaming that will naturally be let loose. . . . This cleansing of culture must be extended to nearly all fields. Theater, art, literature, cinema, press, posters, and window displays must be cleansed of all manifestations of our rotting world and placed in the service of a moral, political, and cultural idea. Public life must be freed from the stifling perfume of our modern eroticism.*[83]

The Term Degenerate

"Degenerate" (*entartet*) was a fashionable term in fin-de-siècle Vienna that was used in virtually all areas of life. It meant "strayed from one's kind" or "alienated from one's kind" and referred to behavior "inimical to one's nature." When women dared demand better education or even the right to vote, this was called "a degenerate women's emancipation fit," inasmuch as such desires were not in agreement with the role of women as nature allegedly intended. Viennese modernism's loose morals were called "moral degenerateness," and the art of Expressionism berated as "degenerate."

The term "degenerate" was not new but had been used in Classicism, albeit sparingly. Richard Wagner used it more frequently, both in his theoretical writings and in his libretti, in *Rienzi*, for example: the people that withdraws its loyalty to its leader and tribune is a "degenerate people."

The frequent usage of the word around 1900 suggests the popularity of the great doctrine of faith of that time, Darwin's theory of evolution. Following Charles Darwin, who died in 1882, *degeneration* means the abnormal devolution of plants and animals.[84] For example, everything that contradicted Darwin's law of progress and the permanent evolution toward a better state also was "degenerate."

Viennese modernism's turning toward the primitive was also termed "degenerate" as well, looked upon as a regression that defied nature. According to public opinion, however, art should evolve toward what was "beautiful" and "noble," toward an eternal and perfect art that would no longer undergo transformations. Modernism's appreciation of primitive art contradicted this alleged natural law, and was thus no longer viewed as progress or an independent form of art, but as "degeneration," a fashionable aberration, a sign of decay—at any rate, something that would soon be passed over anyway, as anything was that was sick.

In approximately this Darwinist sense Max Nordau, the physician and *Neue Freie Presse*'s correspondent in Paris, explained the word in his two-volume work *Entartung* (Degeneration), published in 1892–93 and reprinted several times, which made the term popular. Nordau especially called on French modernism to be in the service of progress according to Darwin's doctrine. Art, he said, should be uplifting and "wholesome." The artist should not glorify the ugly and sick like a "lunatic." Nordau wrote: "The degenerates babble and stammer instead of talking. They utter monosyllabic screams instead of constructing sentences that are grammatically and syntactically structured. They draw and paint like children who with useless hands dirty tables and walls. They make music like the yellow people in East Asia. The mix together all artistic genres."[85] Nordau argued, "We are now fully infected by a serious popular mental illness, a sort of black plague of degeneration and hysteria." "The fashionable aesthetic schools (are) a result of the mental illness of degenerates and hysterics," they "use the word 'freedom' when they pronounce their rotten egos their Gods and call it progress when they praise crime, deny morality, sanctify their drives, scorn science, and hold up aestheticizing idleness as the only purpose in life."[86]

According to Nordau, the degenerate artists and writers were "mentally disturbed." "Fashionable works" were but "written and painted deliriums."[87] This, he said, needed to be counteracted by "branding the leading degenerates and hysterics as sick, publicly revealing and denouncing the imitators as enemies of society, and cautioning the audience about these hangers-on's lies."[88]

To be sure, in his criticism Nordau, a German-speaking Jew hailing from Hungary and famous for several bestsellers, mainly wanted to point out the "degeneration" caused by "modern mysticism," the rule of feeling over mind, and the ignoring of the values of Enlightenment. And that was the point where he condemned the most prominent examples of that school of thought: Richard Wagner and Friedrich Nietzsche.

According to Nordau, Wagner was "filled with more degeneration than all other degenerates put together." He displayed "paranoia, megalomania, and mysticism." His works were ruled by a "shameless sensuality": "It is the love of the degenerates who in a sexual outburst become wild animals."[89] Wagner's mysticim, he argued, was "an expression of his inability to focus, to think clearly, and to master his emotions," and was based on a "weakening of the foremost centers of the brain." A "mystic" like Wagner was "the vermin antagonistic to society"[90] who violated the law of progress and of the evolution of humanity.

Nordau's book made the word *degenerate* fashionable but transformed its meaning in Vienna. It now was applied to the Jews and became an anti-

Semitic slogan that acquired a Darwinist twist; according to Darwin, the argument ran, it was also a sign of "degeneration" when animals and plants stopped procuring their own food and started to live as hangers-on at the expense of other creatures.

The theory of parasites played a significant role in the writings of Hans Goldzier, with whom Hitler was well familiar, and also in Guido von List, who said, "Those who, against God's will . . . merely want to enjoy what others have acquired and created, are a pest, degenerate, evil, and noxious human beings."[91] Otto Weininger, too, claimed that the Jews were unproductive and only trying to take advantage of Christianity's achievements for themselves—in other words, that they lived at the expense of the non-Jews.

In their periodical *Unverfälschte Deutsche Worte* the pan-Germans interpreted the term "degenerate" as follows: "Culturally, we have degeneration when the self is no longer aware of its root in the blood and soil of the people. Likewise, when a people's drive for self-preservation is lacking, and when a sense of working strange elements into one's own folkishness is lacking, we also have a form of degeneration; these instances make clear how appropriate it is to speak of degeneration, that is to say, of a lack of sense of one's own species."[92]

In 1909 pan-German newspapers in Vienna discussed a hierarchy of "racial esthetics" with reference to Darwin, assigning the modern, "degenerate" artist to the lowest level. A change, they argued, could occur only "by way of an appropriately long-lasting inbreeding" toward the improvement of the race and thus art.[93]

The products of a "degenerate afterculture" of the "modernists" should be banned, as well as "Jewish-contaminated" science: "otherwise we will be blown apart from inside. Everything that is sacrosanct to us, our people's customs, our ancestor's way," was in danger of becoming "Jewish-contaminated." And: "What does our land mean to him [the Jew], what our treasured native soil, steaming meadows, rustling trees? What else but glimmering gold that will yield more gold as interest."[94]

A sample from Schönerer's *Unverfälschte Deutsche Worte*, this time in reference to women's emancipation: "Generally speaking, nothing in degenerate creatures of that ilk can be salvaged any longer; neither persuasion nor medicine nor anything else is of any avail. One is well advised to leave them to perish. Only, we who are wholesome must be careful to protect ourselves from infection by these creatures who are rotten to the core."[95]

We can make out all these phrases in the outpourings of Hitler the politician as well. He used the term "degenerate" frequently in quite different contexts, for example, in 1941 at table in connection with bad nutrition; he also said, *A toad is a degenerate frog*; and finally, he called hunters *degenerate farmers*.[96]

In reference to art, he also used the term "degenerate" in the sense of primitive-backward and of being too unconnected with the people, for example in 1937: *The miserable, confused* artists of modernism created works *which maybe ten or twenty thousand years ago could have been made by someone from the Stone Age. They talk about how primitive art is, all the while totally forgetting that it is not the purpose of art to move backward from a people's developmental stage. . . . From now on we will wage a merciless cleansing war against the last remaining elements of our cultural disintegration.*[97]

3
The Imperial City

The Multinational Empire's Metropolis

What with all his dislike for Vienna, and in particular of the Viennese, Hitler would still praise this city's attraction as the center of a large empire for his entire life: *One thing of course,* Hitler said, *one can't create artificially; and that is the unusually intense intoxication which Vienna offered in past centuries, just as it does today, and which seems like a permanent Biedermeier. Because this intoxication, which you experience every time you walk through the pleasure grounds of Schönbrunn,* he said, *was unique.*[1] After the campaign in France, he remarked that Vienna even matched Paris.[2]

Vienna, the capital and imperial residence, reflected the Austro-Hungarian Dual Monarchy's great international significance. After all, taking into account the total population of almost 50 million around 1910, it was the second largest in Western Europe, behind the German empire with almost 65 million and ahead of Great Britain with Ireland (45 million), France (almost 40 million), Italy (34.7 million), and Spain (almost 20 million).

However, Hitler saw Vienna's significance less in its role as the Dual Monarchy's capital than in its historical significance, in Vienna's myth as a centuries-old residence of Roman-German emperors: *When I encoun-*

ter the leaders of other tribes in the Germanic realm, I am in a wonderful position by virtue of where I'm from: I can point out that through five centuries my homeland was a large, powerful empire with an imperial city.[3]

Aware of this city's pronounced self-confidence, which was based on history, Hitler tried not to allow any rivalry to develop between two capitals after 1938 and to use all available means to develop Berlin as the capital of the "Greater German Empire." That this was not an easy task, he realized as late as 1942: You can't blame someone from Vienna arriving in Berlin if in view of his own hometown's cityscape he finds Berlin disappointing, he said. Even to his own face people from Vienna once told him that Berlin was not really a capital; for, culturally, Vienna was superior anyway, and Berlin's cityscape couldn't compare with Vienna either. This remark, Hitler said, did have its merits, since there was hardly another city in Germany that held as many cultural treasures as Vienna. But proud Vienna had to step back behind Berlin: one of the Third Reich's most important tasks, he said, is to create in Berlin a truly representative capital. To begin with, even the train station and the Reich autobahns' ingresses needed to be such that even someone from Vienna would be overwhelmed by the impression: that's our capital![4]

After 1933 there was much construction in Berlin at great expense, but there were no investments in Vienna after 1938 for political reasons: Otherwise Vienna's cultural attraction will be too great. That would lead to an increase in political attraction, and that simply must not be. History has taught me that. There was no new construction in Vienna; the official reason was that it would have been a mistake to try to surpass the magnificent buildings . . . of the imperial residence.[5]

Thus the old imperial residence of Vienna was systematically sacked. Joseph Goebbels observed: "The Führer doesn't have any particularly great plans for Vienna. . . . On the contrary, Vienna has too much, and it might rather lose something than gain anything."[6] And: "The Führer stressed that even though Vienna is a city with over a million people, its role has to be reduced to one of a provincial city. . . . Besides, he said, Vienna used to always treat the Austrian provinces so badly that for that reason alone it shouldn't be given a leading role in the Reich, not even in Austria."[7] And as late as April 9, 1945, he noted: "The Führer certainly has figured out the Viennese correctly. They are a repulsive bunch, consisting of a mix between Poles, Czechs, Jews, and Germans." It was necessary to "keep a tighter rein" on them.[8]

Vienna was granted only renovation work: Vienna will start the war against the roaches and all the filth. The city needs to be cleaned up. That is the cultural task the Vienna of the twentieth century has to accomplish; it needn't do anything else. If it does that, it will be among the most beautiful *cities in the world.*[9] Hitler also included in this cultural task the "cleansing" of the nationally mixed population according to "folkish" criteria, that is to say, the battle against the "un-German" character of Vienna as the capital of a multiethnic empire with a centuries-old mix of Hapsburg peoples.

The Emperor

Every pupil in the Dual Monarchy, certainly including young Hitler in Linz, knew Emperor Franz Josef's title by heart and was as familiar with it as with the Lord's Prayer. This title expresses the centuries-old history and complexity of this multinational empire with conquests, inheritance, and money matches: "Francis Joseph I, Emperor of Austria by the grace of God, King of Hungary and Bohemia, of Dalmatia, Croatia, Slovenia, Galicia, Lodomeria, and Illyria; King of Jersalem, etc.; Arch Duke of Austria; Grand Duke of Toscana and Cracow; Duke of Lothringia, of Salzburg, Steyer, Carinthia, Crain, and Bukovina; Grand Duke of Transylvania; Margrave of Moravia; Duke of Upper and Lower Silesia, of Modena, Parma, Piacenza, and Guastalla, of Auschwitz and Zator, of Teschen, Friaul, Ragusa, and Zara; Princely Count of Hapsburg and Tyrol, of Kyburg, Görz, and Gradisca; Prince of Trient and Brixen; Margrave of Upper and Lower Lausitz and Istria; Count of Hohenembs, Feldkirch, Bregenz, Sonnenberg, etc.; Lord of Trieste, of Cattaro, and the Windy Mark; Great Duke of the Dukedom of Serbia, etc., etc."

Some of these titles had come to have merely historical significance, for example, that of "King of Jerusalem." Even the titles of Toscana, Lothringia, Silesia, and even the Swiss ancestral castles of Hapsburg and Kyburg were only remnants of long-lost Hapsburg property. Similarly, the impression the title leaves of a uniform Hapsburg empire is misleading. For since 1867—after the defeat at the hand of Prussia and the "settlement" with Hungary—the empire was divided in two and was called "Austro-Hungary." Since 1867, as king of Hungary, Emperor Franz Josef resided in Budapest, the Hungarian capital, several weeks a year, where he issued rules in Hungarian, clad in a Hungarian uniform, with Hungarian ministers and a Hungarian parliament.

After 1867 both parts of the empire went in more and more diverging directions. On one hand was strictly Magyar-dominated Hungary, ruled by a strong majority, with Hungarian as the national language; on the other hand was heterogenous, multilingual Cisleithania, split into many parts, with a parliament that was usually nonfunctional and governments that were unstable. Particularly after 1906, when universal and equal suf-

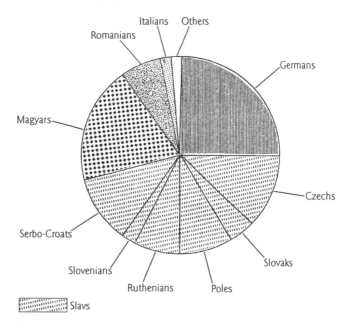

National shares in Austro-Hungary's total population in 1900

frage was established in Cisleithania but not in Transleithania, the two partners, who had equal rights, found it increasingly difficult, even almost impossible, to reach agreements on political issues.

Around 1910, the western half of the empire with its capital, Vienna, had 28.5 million people: almost 10 million Germans, almost 6.5 million Czechs, Moravians, and Slovaks, almost 5 million Poles, more than 3.5 million Ruthenians (Ukrainians), 1.25 million Slovenians, almost 800,000 Serbo-Croats, 770,000 Italians, 275,000 Romanians, almost 11,000 Magyars, plus some 500,000 foreigners, including Hungarians. There was no "Jewish" nation because the only criterion for being acknowledged as a nation was the everyday language used, and the Jews did not have a homogenous language. However, as a religious community and as citizens they had possessed full civil rights since 1867.

The old, widowed emperor was shrouded in the myth of the ruler who sacrificed himself, who worked indefatigably and did his duty, and who seemed to rule the countries he had inherited by strictly preserving the constitution but still adhering to the style of an aristocratic lord by primogeniture. People felt pity for him because of the heavy strokes of fate that had made him a lonely man: in 1898, his beloved "Angel-Sisi," Empress Elizabeth, was assassinated by an Italian anarchist in Geneva. The imperial couple's only son, highly talented Crown Prince Rudolf, committed suicide in Mayerling in 1889, when he was thirty years old, which caused a scandal. That he had killed himself along with a seventeen-year-old girl who was in love with him was the monarchy's best-kept secret. The disgrace of Mayerling weighed heavily on the Catholic House of Hapsburg and the crushed father.

According to Goebbels's diary, even as Reich chancellor Hitler liked to tell the usual stories about the lonely old man in the imperial castle: "Führer once again describes fragility of former Hapsburg Empire. . . . Emperor Franz Josef's simple, wistful character. The tragedy of Mayerling. Beautiful Empress Elizabeth."[10]

The sovereign's loneliness was enhanced by his anxious attempts to preserve the aura of his majesty even under the new conditions. At court the rules of protocol were observed more strictly than ever; the old upper nobility still held a position of power and formed the innermost circle around the emperor.

Since the days of old, the court's strict marriage laws required having a clear rank of high nobility, but not of any certain nationality. Thus the Cisleithanian aristocracy, as well as the high-ranking officials in the civil service and the military, had grown together into one supranational class that was anything but "German." Its members typically owned the estates they had inherited in non-German regions of the empire, and if they became active for any political party at all, they did so for their native homelands. In the national parliament, the Reichsrat, for example, Prince Andreas Lubomirski, Count Adalbert Dzieduszycki, Vladimir Ritter von Kozlovski-Bolesta, and Kasimir Knight of Obertynski represented Poland's conservatives; Count Franz Bellegarde, the Romanians; Aurel Knight of Onciul, the Libertine Romanians; Nikolai Knight of Vassilko, the Ruthenian-National Democrats; Count Yaroslav Thun-Hohenstein, the Czech Clericals; and Count Adalbert Sternberg appeared as a non-partisan, "wild" Czech.

As his empire's first aristocrat, Franz Josef was above all parties, did not personally mingle with nonaristocrats, and was not familiar with life outside the court conventions. He was looked on as a symbol, and almost only guarantor, of the empire that had begun to drift apart. True to the Hapsburgs' ideal, he tried to be a "just father to his peoples" and to treat all his subjects equally, no matter what nationality they were. He made everybody confident that even the poorest Ruthenian or Jew in Galicia could claim his right with the emperor personally if necessary. As long as this emperor was alive, the collapse of Austro-Hungary seemed inconceivable. "Surely you can't do that to the old man," was one of the standing expressions in the Dual Monarchy's public life.

Before 1918 the legal basis for the coexistence of the peoples of the empire's western half was clause nineteen of Cisleithania's national constitution of 1867: "All ethnic groups in the nation have equal rights, and each ethnic group has an inalienable right to preserve and cultivate its nationality and language." Emperor Franz Josef personally guaranteed strict adherence to this law.

Because the emperor considered himself the protector of equal rights for all nations and religions, patriotism was mainly triggered through him personally. Minorities that had been disadvantaged for centuries—for example, the Ruthenaians, Slovaks, and Slovenians—were grateful for having equal rights, and therefore were loyal to the state. The Jews particularly looked at strict constitutionality as a safe haven. Looking back, Stefan Zweig glorified pre-1918 Vienna: "Whoever lived and worked there felt free of narrowmindedness and prejudice. Nowhere was it easier to be a European, and I know that I owe it largely to this city . . . that early on I learned to love the concept of community as the loftiest idea I know."[11]

The idealizing view that a national economist such as Felix Somary passed on as the advice his father had given him is well known in many variants: "This empire is quite different from the rest of the world. Just imagine what would happen if the emperor and his government left for just one year—the various nations would be at each other all over the place. The government forms the fence which separates the zoo of wild animals from the outside world, and nowhere are there as many and dangerous political beasts as here at home."[12]

However, by no means did this patriotic view correspond to everyday reality, especially not in rural areas. There the old power structures of alleged "master" and "slaves" were still valid. To the degree that the authorities could intervene at all, they strictly tried to uphold equal rights in courts of law as well as in the administration. But those nationalities who for centuries had considered themselves to be the "leaders," did not accept the new equality, whether Poles were pitted against Ruthenians, Germans against Slavs, Italians against Slovenians, or other competing ethnic groups against this myth.

However, any opposition against the old, awe-inspiring monarch was useless, as Hitler also stressed in *Mein Kampf*: *In the last few years the state had been so bound up with the person of Franz Josef that the death of this old embodiment of the Empire was felt by the broad masses to be tantamount to the death of the Empire itself. Indeed, it was one of the craftiest artifices, particularly of the Slavic policy, to create the appearance that the Austrian state no longer owed its existence to anything but the miraculous and unique skill of this monarch; this flattery was all the more welcome in the Hofburg* [imperial castle], *since it corresponded not at all to the real merits of the Emperor.*[13]

And elsewhere he said: *Worst of all are the kings who have become old. If you touch one of them, everybody immediately starts yelling. Franz Josef certainly was a lot less intelligent than his successor, but a revolution against him, no way was that possible. He embodied an aura, even though there is no monarch who was beaten more than he was. He let everything happen and didn't do a thing.*[14]

Like probably everyone in Vienna at the time, young Hitler had a certain degree of interest in life at court, particularly in his first year, when he lived near Mariahilfer Strasse. There the old emperor passed in his car twice a day, in the morning from Schönbrunn to downtown to take care of government business, and back at night. There were always spectators in the street who waved to the monarch or simply stared at him as an attraction. Kubizek wrote: "When we saw the emperor, Adolf neither made a big deal about it nor talked about it, for he was not concerned with the emperor as a person but with the state he represented: the Dual Monarchy of Austro-Hungary."[15]

Hitler and Kubizek were, however, familiar with the imperial residence's attractions. For example, Kubizek reports that a few times they also went to hear the imperial court's orchestra to listen to the Sänger-knaben, the famous boy choir, like most tourists, and to take the opportunity to watch the famous changing of the guard at the castle.[16]

Hitler also witnessed the emperor's most spectacular public appearance, the procession on Corpus Christi Day. Aide-de-camp Albert von Margutti told the story how, early in the morning, the emperor went to Saint Stephen's in a state carriage drawn by six horses, "the arch dukes preceding him in state carriages drawn by four horses. . . . The wagons, made of glass and full of gold ornaments, the stallions' precious harnesses—magnificent Spanish-bred white horses—the coachmen, lackeys, and servants holding the horses in their gold-embroidered black rococo dresses, with white stockings, shoes with buckles, and wigs under the large tricorns and bicorns decorated with golden braids and ostrich feathers." Then followed reverences by the gorgeously and colorfully uniformed bodyguards in front of Saint Stephen's Cathedral.

After the service came the famous procession: first there were the members of the order of knighthood in their robes, the clerics, the cardinal-duke-archbishop with the monstrance underneath the portable canopy. Immediately behind this "heaven" strode the emperor as a humble Christian, bareheaded and holding a candle, followed by the arch-dukes, the aristocracy, the court's dignitaries, the mayor, the city council, and many others. According to Margutti, everything put together was "one of the most impressive attractions in the whole world."[17]

The young man from Linz was mainly impressed by the Arciere body-guards (called *Hartschiere* in Vienna) whose state uniforms consisted of silver helmets with tufts of white horsehair, gold-laced red dresses, white pants, and long black patent leather boots with tops.[18] As late as 1942, Hitler would relate: *Of course, if I post Hartschiere; when they were marching in front of the procession on Corpus Christi Day, everything was literally shaking—what a picture! They were so harmless, not even the revolution would hurt them.* His conclusion: *Mankind needs an idol. . . . Monarchy instituted something extremely useful: it artificially created the idol. All that fuss, the whole shebang, did make sense in a way.*[19]

Hitler also liked to describe how the carriages would drive up in front of the Court Opera: *What splendor when before dress performances the members of the imperial court, the archdukes in their uniform full of gold and the ladies with their precious jewels got out of the carriage!*[20] And: *The opera before the World War was beautiful! It too contained culture, incredible! The women with their diadems, splendor all over! . . . I had never seen the imperial box occupied. The emperor was not musical, I guess.*[21] (Which was true enough.) And at another occasion he mentioned *all that insanity of the hereditary monarchy, which needed all those pompous ceremonies to turn crowned ciphers at least into something after all.*[22]

The "Reich German" Princes Pay Their Respect

In 1908, the first year of Hitler's period in Vienna, the imperial myth was tended to as pompously as never before or after: Franz Josef, who had ascended the throne as an eighteen-year-old in 1848, the year of the revolution, celebrated sixty years of reign—a unique anniversary in the history of the Hapsburgs.

For a long time the weary, depressed emperor rejected any big, long anniversary celebrations. Yet their proponents listed important reasons: it would help trade and tourism and decrease unemployment. But above all, the festive mood, focusing on the old emperor and the fact that he would be paid his due respect, would strengthen patriotism and counteract the battle between the different nationalities.

Very late, not until March 11, 1908, the emperor reluctantly gave in to his advisers' arguments and approved celebrations and a parade. The latter was supposed to depict the history of the House of Hapsburg and give all the monarchy's peoples the chance to pay their respect to their emperor through deputations. The festivities were to be more

Emperor Franz Josef receives Kaiser William II at the train station

magnificent than those for the sixtieth anniversary of Queen Victoria's reign in 1897.

In order to comply with Franz Josef's express wish not to forget charity, what with all the festivities, frantic plans were hatched: every school in the monarchy, no matter how small, every orphanage and hospital, all barracks and offices, all department stores and rifle clubs prepared commemorative celebrations and collected donations for social institutions: homeless shelters, children's homes, orphanages and foundling hospitals, and—as a special sign of high regard for the enthusiastic hunter Franz Josef—even a home for sick hunters of all crown provinces.

In May the long line of foreign visitors congratulating the emperor began with a political sensation. In order to pay their respect to Franz Josef as the oldest German monarch, the German princes arrived in Vienna together, to wit: Kaiser William II, Prince Luitpold of Bavaria, the kings of Saxony and Württemberg, the grand dukes of Baden, Saxony-Weimar, Oldenburg, and Mecklenburg-Schwerin, the Duke of Anhalt, the Princes of Lippe and Schaumburg-Lippe, and—as the only nonaristocrat—the mayor of Hamburg as a representative of the Hanseatic cities, whose status as a commoner resulted in lesser honors. The grand duke of Hesse was missing, but this was considered an excused absence: at the time he was visiting the closely related family of the czar with the political mission to improve the climate between Germany and Russia.

In order to make this idea of his a reality, Kaiser William II had to go through extraordinary political troubles, for many princes were by no means enthusiastic about this concerted action. After all, the Austrian emperor was not a "German" prince in the sense of being a part of the German empire; as a multinational empire, the Dual Monarchy could hardly be called "German."

Political difficulties during the princes' visit were likely to arise in several areas, inasmuch as the wounds of Königgrätz still had not healed.* Despite their loyalty to the House of Hapsburg, many were wistfully look-ing toward the successful German empire, all the more so because the Slavs' influence in Cisleithania was increasing and surpassing that of the Germans. At the very least, the pan-Germans planned to announce their desire for an Anschluss with the German empire with black-red-gold flags, the greater German colors of 1848, and to pay their respect to "their" emperor: the prince of Hohenzollern, not the one of Haps-burg.

Emperor Franz Josef had a deep distrust of any kind of German na-tionalism in his empire. According to aide-de-camp Margutti, he held on to the view of "the Germans in Austria as the embodiment of 'Austri-anism' " and found any attempt by "his" Germans to get closer to Berlin utterly exasperating. "Even insignificant, harmless external signs in that direction could thoroughly annoy him." "With his hawk's eye" he invar-iably recognized black-red-gold flags immediately, "which would instantly cloud his good mood." "Whenever Germandom was displayed in such a manner, it would hit the emperor's Achilles' heel, for behind it he would invariably sense pan-Germanic tendencies."[23]

There was much excitement before the princes arrived to pay their respect so spectacularly. Large formations of soldiers prevented German-national rallies. Tens of thousands of people thronged the sides of the streets when William II, accompanied by the empress, two of their sons, and a convoy of fifty-four people, arrived in Vienna and started moving toward Schönbrunn. This was overly taxing on the police as well as on official protocol, especially because on the same day all the other princes were arriving from Germany, whose constant jealousies among each other were no secret.

In his address, forty-nine-year-old William II paid homage to the Austrian emperor as a model for "three generations of German princes"— thus, as if there had been no Königgrätz, including the Hapsburgs among the line of German princes as a matter of course. In this precarious situ-ation Franz Josef responded with utmost sensitivity. In his thank-you

---

*In 1866 Prussia's army won a decisive victory over Austria in the battle of Königgrätz in Bohemia during the "German War." (*Translator's note*)

speech he ignored the eminent visit's German-national aspect and constrained himself to the dynastic factor: he expressed his view of the eminent visit as "a festive demonstration of the monarchic principle . . . to which Germany owes its power and greatness." He then praised the value of the by now already thirty-year-old double alliance, happily expecting it "only to pursue peaceful goals." The exciting day ended with an evening celebration with military music and eight thousand singers in the park of Schönbrunn Castle. For security reasons the police closed the expansive park, which was usually open. The ten thousand guests, who had all been personally invited, were painstakingly checked.

Abroad—especially among the western powers, the Balkan nations, and Russia—this princely visit was viewed with suspicion. The Russian newspapers unanimously called the visit a "pan-Germanic demonstration" that "downright glaringly emphasizes Austro-Hungary's dependence on German politics." Lucien Wolf, the prominent British journalist, stressed the fact "that the idea of uniting the Hapsburg monarchy with the German Empire still hasn't died"—not in Vienna, to be precise. Berlin, on the other hand, was less interested in an Anschluss with Catholic German-Austria, Wolf wrote, and needed Austro-Hungary mainly as an ally against Russia.[24]

Everyone in Vienna was involved in the ferocious polemics of those days, and it is not to be assumed that young Hitler, of all people, stayed away from the controversy.

After the princes had paid their respect in such a spectacular fashion, more European monarchs appeared to congratulate the emperor, invariably with large convoys. They all were received with elaborate court ceremonies, the first one being the king of Sweden. During state receptions and dinners the monarchies' glorious future in general and that of the Dual Monarchy in particular was conjured up. The European monarchs, who were under pressure from democratic movements, moved closely together and gathered around their oldest and respectable member in Vienna.

Yet fermenting in the "audience" were need, discontentment, and national and political battles. On May 21, 1908, 82,000 Viennese pupils expressed their reverence for their emperor in the park in front of Schönbrunn, waving flower garlands and singing songs before hundreds of thousands of people. At the same time Liberal and German-national students were demonstrating before Vienna University for the "freedom of science" against Church, clericalism, and thus implicitly also against the House of Hapsburg. Because the police were on duty in Schönbrunn, the situation was dangerous, but could finally be mollified in a compromise à la Viennese. Yet the fear of a revolution remained.[25]

The Anniversary Parade as a Symbol of the Era

Even during its preparation stage, the parade, which was planned as a demonstration of harmony between peoples, illuminated virtually all the Dual Monarchy's problems and thus vividly illustrated the state the empire was in at the time of Hitler's years in Vienna, in other words, the impression it made on him in his very first year there.

At the start there were arguments about money. The giant project was supposed to finance itself through the sale of expensive gallery seats, a plan that soon proved to be an illusion. The Social Democrats in Vienna's city council voted against a subvention, arguing that the memory of the many sad events during Franz Josef's reign did "not give cause" for such an expensive celebration.[26] Yet opposition was to no avail.

In order to simplify the organization of the event—after all, there were only eighty-nine days left to prepare it—the committee secured the assistance of a few large companies. Among these businesses were Vienna's largest department store, Gerngross, a Jewish firm, against which the Christian-Socials protested: "the Jews" were only interested in the "profit" they could make from the parade, not in honoring the emperor.[27]

Then there were protests against the nobility's heavy representation in the parade. The committee defended itself, arguing that the nobility did not cost any money; on the contrary, many of the aristocrats, who were going to march on the Ring Boulevard clad in their ancestors' costumes, participated at their own expense, attired costumed groups, and contributed precious armaments and weapons from their collections, genuine old uniforms and splendid carriages, horses, and much more. But the nobility's disproportionately large presence was perceived as provocative.

As usual, the national conflicts presented the most dangerous threat. First the Hungarians announced that they would not participate in the "anniversary year." As far as they were concerned, it was not 1848 that counted as the beginning of Franz Josef's reign but 1867, when he acknowledged the Hungarian constitution and was crowned King of Hungary, thus "reconciliating" with the Hungarian nation. They pointed out that no official representative of Cisleithania had showed up in Hungary in 1907 at the forty-year anniversary of the coronation. In view of the ferocious arguments at the time, Franz Josef had even requested that he receive no official congratulations from abroad. On the day of the parade, the Budapest newspaper *Budapesti Hirlap* wished His Majesty "happiness, well-being, and blessing," but declared, "Still no one would like to participate in the Austrians' parade" because the Austrians were behaving "rudely, antagonistically, and contemptuously toward us."[28]

Then there were fights with the Czechs, triggered by a scheduled anniversary guest performance by the Czech National Theatre in Vienna of a Moravian and a Russian folk play and *Hamlet* in Czech. Mayor Lueger had the message delivered that the event was not in line "with the City of Vienna's German character" and predicted "large demonstrations and boisterous scenes." To applause from the Christian-Social and German-national press, the vice mayor affirmed that "Vienna was German and had to remain German, and a Czech theater group could not perform in a German city."[29]

Thereupon the Czechs canceled not only the performance but also their participation in the parade. The Czech members of Parliament announced that "if it was pointed out to the Czechs that they should regard Vienna as a city extremely hostile to them, it should be realized that from that moment on any Czech participating in any anniversary celebration or in anything arranged by those gentlemen who did not shy away from spitting in the face of art because it was Czech art, would have no character."[30] Greatly satisfied, the Christian-Social *Deutsches Volksblatt* jeered that in the future too, "any 'Viennese' who wants to enjoy the Czech *Hamlet* will have to make a trip to Prague."[31]

The parade gave the Czechs a legitimate reason to be angry anyway, for it represented Bohemia's history as the history of the vanquished. Rudolf von Hapsburg, who had conquered Austria in the thirteenth century in the battle against then-sovereign Ottokar Przemysl, was supposed to head the parade on horseback. The victor over the Bohemian king, who was extremely popular with the Czechs, was surrounded by thirty members of the oldest noble families, clad in knight's armor and sitting on battle horses bridled in medieval fashion, lances in their hands, in alphabetical order, from Auersperg to Zedtwitz—in other words, ostentatiously warlike.[32] The representation of the Thirty Years' War with the Catholic Hapsburgs' victory over Protestant Bohemia, too, tore open deep old wounds.

Then the Italians refused to join: they were annoyed that of all the historic parade's groups, it was the last one that celebrated Field Marshal Radetzky's heroic deeds—accompanied, of course, by the military band playing the Radetzky March, that victory march over the defeated Italian revolutionaries of 1848. Perhaps it was these controversies that Hitler meant when, trying to woo Italy as a future ally, he wrote in *Mein Kampf*,

In part the Austrian army's battle fame was built on successes which were bound to trigger the Italians' immortal hatred for all time. More than once I saw outbursts of the passionate contempt and bottomless hatred in Vienna with which the Italian was "devoted" to the Italian state. The House of Hapsburg had sinned for centuries *against Italian freedom and independence.*[33]

The Croats, finally, protested against slanderous passages in the printed festival program. Even though it said that the Croat was an excellent soldier, it also said, "He was especially talented in appropriating others' property. If, for example, pillaging was permitted on account of treason, his field pack would contain all sorts of things: scrap iron, women's clothes, wigs, even a grandfather's clock which was meant to be the soldier's pride in his native village." The celebration committee had to apologize and admit that this portrayal "seriously slandered" the Croats and violated historical truth. The Croats accepted the apology.[34] Yet the Hungarians', Czechs', and Italians' absence significantly lessened the parade's import.

In the meantime, bleachers had been constructed. Vienna was full of craftsmen, timber carriers, and the sound of hammers. Passers-by complained about the impediments to traffic and the wrecking of the city. It became more and more obvious to what degree the high bleachers virtually nailed downtown Vienna shut with planks. Fewer and fewer people wanted to have the parade, particularly when they began to realize that the gallery seats were prohibitively expensive and in between the huge wooden constructions there was hardly any room left for spectators in the streets.

There was tremendous organizational work to be done: 52,000 participants and collaborators had to be lodged in Vienna, fed, and attired, which alone cost some 78,000 kronen per diem. Because the hotel rooms were reserved for tourists, prices for private lodgings skyrocketed, going up to approximately twenty kronen per person per night[35]—which annoyed many out-of-towners. In addition, tens of thousands of horses were in town, not counting the numerous spans of oxen for the cannons and all kinds of contraptions, plus mules and other animals.

Just a few days before the parade something happened that the festival committee would later deplore as a "press campaign": almost all newspapers printed a notice according to which workers were allegedly planning to topple the bleachers. Committee President Hans Count Wilczek remarked: "That killed the parade. . . . The news went out to Munich, Berlin, Paris. They said, 'Don't go to Vienna! You will die!' And from that time on not one ticket could be sold any longer."[36]

There were thousands of gallery tickets that could not be sold, not even when they were offered for a fifth or a tenth of their original price. "In some places you could sit in the first row for a tip to the ticket salesman," the newspapers said, and a little later one could get tickets "like kisses during a charity bazaar." Finally, well-dressed people were approached on the Ring Boulevard and asked to take a seat on the bleachers for free so that they would not look so desolate.[37]

Fortunately for the organizers, June 12, 1908, was a beautiful sunny summer's day. The influx of people from the suburbs already began the night before. At 3:00 A.M. the ushers started working, and at 5:00 so did the military, which protected both sides of the eight-mile-long procession. Booths for drinking water and police, which had been put up just for that purpose, opened. The Voluntary Rescue Association was ready for people who got sick. Cars of the Association for the Protection of Animals prepared to provide for the animals in the parade. At fifty-yard intervals there were public toilets and refreshment stands. Men and women selling water, bread, postcards, and festival programs were busy. As were journalists: life behind the bleachers provided them with more colorful stories than did the parade itself.

For three hours the "peoples" paraded past their "hurrah emperor": twelve thousand participants, among them four thousand in historic and eight thousand in national costumes, plus horses, oxen, carriages of all kinds, and cannons. The historically made-up parade passed the historic Ring Boulevard buildings, which would have provided a perfect backdrop if they had not been almost invisible behind the high bleachers.

In a much admired posture, in a field marshal's uniform and a plumed hat, seventy-eight-year-old Franz Josef stood in the heat in front of the imperial tent by the Heldentor (heroes' gate). The tent was put up just for that purpose and was decorated with numerous flags so that the emperor could accept the respect paid him. Next to him were the honorary bleachers: to the left, the military, a sea of green plumed hats and field-gray uniforms. To the right, there was predominantly black: the high-ranking civilians sat there, according to protocol in dress coats and top hats. The ladies accompanying them wore elegant summer outfits in all kinds of colors.

In chronological order and in nineteen groups, the costumed history of the House of Hapsburg paraded through Vienna, mostly representations of military events, in the splendor of uniforms and old weapons: jousting knights from the days of Maximilian I, soldiers from the wars against the Turks, the veteran reserves of 1809 around Andreas Hofer with old cannons. Saleswomen from the Vienna Naschmarkt convincingly represented canteen women.

In the second division, eight thousand participants represented the present multinational empire in groups dressed in national garb, in the order of the crown provinces in the emperor's title: Lower and Upper Austria, Salzburg, Styria, Tyrol, Vorarlberg, Moravia, Bohemia, the German-language isle of Iglau, Silesia, Krain, Galicia, Bukovina, Cracow, Istria, Dalmatia. Each costume group paid its respect to the emperor in its people's mother tongue.[38]

The large German-language newspapers performed their patriotic duty and praised the parade as an expression of the empire's diversity and greatness, and as a sign of the "peoples' " love for their sovereign. The *Neuigkeits-Weltblatt*: "Wherever the eye can reach, it sees different colors, different national costumes, and different characters. And you can hear all national languages. All kinds of salutations blend together: 'Heil!', 'Grüass Gott!', 'Zivio!', 'Evviva!', 'Niech!', 'Treasca!', 'Zyje!', etc. One can tell that Cisleithania is a multilingual empire, an unequaled national mosaic."[39]

Yet the harmony among peoples was an illusion, inasmuch as the empire's largest non-German nationalities were absent. In addition, neither the multinational empire's national nor social groups were represented proportionately: only a few representatives of the rich provinces had arrived, but from the eastern and southeastern crown provinces more than twice as many had come as planned. From Galicia alone came two thousand people instead of a thousand, but from Lower Austria, only seventy to eighty came.[40]

The opportunity to visit the capital once in their lives had enticed especially the poorest people from the monarchy's most faraway regions. After all, the committee paid for transportation, board, lodging—mostly in tents and on straw mattresses—and in addition, gave three kronen to each participant. That was not enough for the well-to-do. The poorest, however, arrived in large numbers, particularly from Galicia and Bukovina.

To an extent heretofore unknown, the Viennese got to see these strange compatriots of theirs who, shy and helpless, moved around clumsily in the big city. They could not communicate and frequently were illiterate. The discrepancy in education and wealth in the huge empire was tremendous: 513,000 of the 730,000 people in Bukovina could neither read nor write. The illiteracy rate among the Ruthenians, Serbo-Croats, and Romanians was more than 60 percent, but among the Germans only 3.12, and among the Czechs no more than 2.38 percent.[41]

The strange compatriots also shocked Vienna. Even Karl Kraus said that they were homely, primitive, culturally retarded: "But if the different

Austrian nationalities look like the samples blocking our way in the streets of Vienna today, then, I believe, the unifying idea of ugliness might lead to a way of communicating."[42] The architect Adolf Loos wrote: "It is a disaster for a country if its people's culture spreads over such a long time period. . . . The parade included peoples who even during the migration of nations would have been considered backward. Fortunate is the country that doesn't have such stragglers and pillagers. Fortunate America!"[43]

Neither did the cartoonists want to miss out on the "savages," the "primitive people," resting assured of the applause of most Viennese. *Simplicissimus* published a full-page, colored, utterly defamatory caricature of members of the parade, veritable gangsters and ragged barbarians.[44]

The encounter with so many representatives of the "underdeveloped," "barbaric" peoples in the extremely elegant capital and imperial residence took place at a time that was deeply influenced by Darwin's theories and that believed in humankind's development from primitive ancient times to the "noble man" of the future as in a natural law. The different stages of development as determined by appearances, conduct, language, and cleanliness, resulted in the belief in man's inequality: "civilized" people considered themselves superior to "primitive" ones. In Vienna it was the Germans who looked upon themselves as the "noble people" as opposed to the "inferior" peoples of the monarchy.

The aftermath of the parade kept the public on the move for a long time. The first response was in Parliament, where Zionist representative Benno Straucher, expressed his protest against the discriminating portrayal of an Eastern Jew in the parade: he mentioned a man who had followed the group of the Turkish siege as a clown, making somersaults and earning horse laughs. He wore a caftan, a top hat, and a lovelock. Straucher said: "Without protection and defenseless, we Jews usually have to face persecution that frequently takes on virtually medieval but always well-nigh ugly forms." He indignantly rebuffed the interjection that the scene had been historic: "Excuse me, but that is not historical; at the time of the Turkish siege Jews didn't wear caftans and top hats." After all, the Jews also could have been portrayed in a positive manner. But his speech was lost in the noise of well-known interjections: the Jews, they said, had been spies and traitors of the fatherland throughout history.[45]

The pacifists also criticized the parade. Bertha von Suttner, winner of the Nobel Peace Prize in 1905, wrote to Alfred Hermann Fried, winner of the Nobel Peace Prize in 1911: "I am extremely annoyed at the parade. A raise-the-arms circus. Stone-blindness toward the modern spirit. Glorification of any imaginable savagery." Ten years previously she still had hoped "that the Emperor should take the opportunity the celebration offers to bring about a general European alliance, and that way, disarmament. At that time I still believed he would lend an ear to such ideas. Today I no longer believe that."[46] After all, even the Viennese gymnasts appeared in martial garb, as a "celebration of the Empire's youth, capable of bearing arms." The last group in the parade were the pupils of the boys' homes of the City of Vienna, who were militarily drilled: they marched in white uniforms in goosestep, to increased applause from the bleachers.

Then followed the discovery of a financial disaster, a deficit of approximately a million kronen. Many businessmen and craftsmen waited in vain for their money. Ultimately Government offices had to come up with the money, which was desperately needed elsewhere. A corruption trial in 1909 was the infamous finale of the enthralling parade.

All we know about Hitler in connection with the parade is his remark that legions of Gypsies from Hungary had worked as pickpockets. Still, that this gigantic spectacle thoroughly impressed him too is evidenced by the parades that he ordered as Reich chancellor in Munich in 1937, 1938, and 1939. At a time when historicizing parades were truly out of date, they were like miniature copies of the 1908 anniversary parade in Vienna. They, too, were instruments of political propaganda with the aim of strengthening patriotism. There, too, a history of heroes and warriors marched in the streets—except that now the costumed troops of Frederick II of Prussia marched next to the Wehrmacht, SA, and SS, instead of next to soldiers of the Turkish War, grandmasters, and military students.

The Viennese newspapers' bathetic-patriotic comments in 1908 were similar to those in Munich: "At issue was so frequently the defense of what was most precious! This Empire became what it is today in battle, a great community of peoples going their own ways and joined by the idea of a common fate."[47]

The Annexation of Bosnia and Herzegovina

The Dual Monarchy displayed its serious military prowess on October 5, 1908: in a surprise to the European powers, it annexed the Turkish provinces of Bosnia and Herzegovina. That area, with almost 19,800 square miles and fewer than two million people, dirt-poor and culturally as well as economically backward, had already been occupied and administrated by Austro-Hungarian troups for thirty years, since the Berlin Treaty of

1878. Formally, however, it was still under Turkish sovereignty, as agreed upon in the Berlin Treaty. Austro-Hungary now shook off Turkish rule and appropriated the country formally as well.

Diplomatic observers explained the sudden superpower policies as an attempt "to help the country get over its internal calamity by becoming very active in foreign policy in order to steer internal policy into a more promising direction."[48] To be sure, the real reason was indeed a patriotic one: annexing Bosnia and Herzegovina was meant to be an anniversary present to the old emperor. After all, in wars that had brought much loss, the empire had become smaller and smaller during Franz Josef's reign. In 1859 Lombardy was lost, and in 1866 Venetia's and Austria's predominant position in the German League. Now the empire finally was supposed to become larger again for a change, in a way that was erroneously deemed simple. The consequences of such a step on European politics were vastly underestimated, and preparation for the annexation was flawed on an international level. Even allied Germany was informed too late, and the czarist regime only in very vague terms.

The European superpowers were utterly surprised and irritated. After all, many crises had germinated in the pertinent area, Europe's much-quoted "weather angle," which now, through the Hapsburgs' advance, was thrown off balance, threatening the peace in Europe. England and Russia threatened to provide military aid to Turkey. This constituted an imminent threat of war.

The Balkans and its adjoining countries, particularly the Kingdom of Serbia, were alarmed. The latter considered itself to be the Southern Slavs' protecting power in the Balkans, in the long run aiming for a "Greater Serbian Empire" that obviously included Bosnia, Herzegovina, and other Hapsburg and Turkish Balkan provinces. Since 1906, when Vienna had placed an embargo on the import of meat from Serbia in the "War of Pigs" and thus ruined Serbia's economy, war had been in the air anyway. The rural population of Serbia—its vast majority—had thoroughly hated Austro-Hungary ever since. Indeed, Turkey's first reaction after the annexation was a trade embargo against the Dual Monarchy. Other Balkan nations followed suit, and Austro-Hungary's trade with the east was severely hurt.

A much-noted expert reported about the mood in Serbia: "In some villages even armed divisions of woman soldiers were formed. Seventy-year-old men as well as twelve- to fifteen-year-old boys applied for military service. A war between Serbia and Austro-Hungary would be horrible and so savage and gory that the whole world would tremble. It is said the Serbs are fanatics and ready for anything. They would have a lot of allies, entire scores of volunteers from Russia offer Serbia their services."[49] This pointed toward a sort of guerilla war on Bosnian soil by Serbia against Hapsburg's rule.

Domestically as well, the annexation crisis was dramatically coming to a head. The "peoples" were not at all as glad about the increase in power as Austro-Hungary's minister of the exterior Count Aehrenthal had imagined. On the contrary: the threat of war gave a tremendous boost to the nationalists, the Hungarians as well as the Czechs, the Italians, the Southern Slavs, of course, and the Germans, who once again exploited the slogan about the "Slavization of Austria." The *Alldeutsches Tagblatt* wrote, "This is not a German, but a Slavic conquest, which Germans certainly have no reason to support. . . . Any strengthening of Slavdom means a weakening of Germandom."[50] The newspaper argued that the population of Austro-Hungary did not need these dirt-poor provinces, that the annexation jeopardized peace in Europe and was advantageous only to the dynasty.[51]

In Parliament, the Social Democrats opposed the failed superpower policy through party speaker Karl Renner. For thirty years, he said, Austro-Hungary had administrated the two Balkan provinces on the basis of a European mandate that had been secured through the signatures of seven superpowers. Now, however, Austro-Hungary was threatening all of Europe with war, for nothing but a "mere title," in other words, the crown's sovereign right, "and we don't even know if it is our crown or Hungary's crown or that of some viceroy who first is supposed to be sent down there. . . . We are governing Bosnia on the basis of bayonets and, for the time being, only on the basis of a violation of law." The annexation, Renner argued, brought nothing but a burden on Austro-Hungary, and above all, the obligation "to defend (these two provinces) against any attack from outside or against internal upheavals." Mobilization costs and economic embargo would lead to unemployment and spell "disaster for thousands and thousands of families."[52] All parliamentary parties were angry at not having been informed about the annexation, let alone consulted.

During those hectic months there were national riots in Vienna anyway, for example, at the university between German and Zionist associations and between Italian and German students. Fights between Slovenians and Italians in Laibach resulted in two people dead and several injured. Fights also broke out between Germans and Czechs in Prague, constituting the most serious consequence of the national controversies in the anniversary year. The riots in Prague in the middle of the annexation crisis crossed over to other cities, such as Brünn, Teplitz, and Olmütz, and threatened to turn into an open rebellion. Barricades were erected, German businesses demolished, and police were attacked with rocks. There too, the revolt was compounded by foreign policy issues: black-and-yellow flags were torn with accompanying shouts of "Away with Austria!" and "Hail Serbia!" and thrown in the Moldau. There were rumors about Austrian Slavs conspiring with Russians and Serbs.

Appeals to exercise moderation were to no avail whatever. Because neither the police nor the cavalry could get a handle on the situation, martial law was finally established in Prague—on December 2, of all days. During this heightened state of emergency important personal liberties were suspended and the authorities could quickly try and sentence people who had committed violent acts in public. To be sure, martial law did put a forceful end to the riots, but it also increased the hatred among nationalities and Czech opposition to Vienna and the imperial family.

On December 10 the Serbs gave a requiem in Belgrade cathedral for the "victims of those fellow ethnic brothers who died for Slavic concerns in Prague and Laibach," as the German envoy in Belgrade reported to Berlin. A student delivered an address "full of sympathy for the oppressed Slavs in Austria and about the battle against the Germanic enemy, about the solidarity among all Slavs, and the like."[53]

In this atmosphere, on the mild and even springlike December 2, 1908, the eve of the sixtieth anniversary of Emperor Franz Josef's accession to the throne, the anniversary year had its finale with the bells ringing in all of Vienna's churches, a huge firework, and the City of Vienna being illuminated: the new Vienna of the Ring Boulevard and its magnificent buildings shone with electric light. In the competition about which building should be illuminated most effectively, the shining City Hall won.

Huge throngs of people moved from the surburbs toward downtown. In the early evening there was first some pushing and shoving, and then a panic broke out. Four people ended up dead, twenty-two seriously injured, and eighty-four lightly injured.[54] The anniversary year concluded with a day of mourning.

The strains of the anniversary celebration exhausted the emperor as well as his subjects. In Parliament Prague philosophy professor Tomás G. Masaryk voiced what many were thinking: "We have to reckon with the dynasty as one of Austria's forces. I do that. However, gentlemen, dynasty and monarchism do not mean byzantinism, and I have the feeling and am convinced that this foolery which keeps being performed, especially here in Vienna, really does harm to monarchism."[55]

*   *   *

On March 29, 1909, German Reich chancellor Bülow ended the annexation crisis by declaring in Parliament that the German Reich was determined "not to surrender any vital Austro-Hungarian interest." For the first time the expression "loyalty of the Nibelungs" was heard.[56] In order to consolidate the loyalty among allies, Emperor William II went to Vienna in May 1909 and was as enthusiastically cheered "as no other monarch before him," as the American envoy reported to Washington.[57]

Even though the annexation crisis ended without a disaster, it fundamentally changed European politics: since 1908 a prewar mood was in the air, and there was feverish armament for the great war for the Balkans, which was thought to be inevitable. Austro-Hungary's dependence on the German Reich was obvious. This also increased the non-German Austrian peoples' bitterness.

The anniversary year's intention to display the multiethnic state's political and military strength and the "peoples' love" for the dynasty turned into its opposite. Nationalism was increased rather than decreased, and those voices that perceived Austro-Hungary as outdated became louder. More and more nationalists began to view war as a solution and not only were ready to accept the collapse of the Hapsburg Empire but also desired it. This became palpable with the Czechs and Italians, and more and more so with the Southern Slavs, but also—if only within a tiny minority of the pan-Germans—with the Germans.

Hitler's View of the Hapsburgs

There can be no doubt about Hitler's dislike of the Hapsburg dynasty. Like the pan-Germans, even when he was still in high school he saw no future for the German-Austrians in Hapsburg's multiethnic empire but was hoping for an Anschluss to the German Reich in the near future, which first required that the multinational empire be shattered and the Hapsburg dynasty removed. That was also the reason why, like the Schönerians, he was in favor a starting a war soon and offering the Hapsburg state political and military support with the "loyalty of the Nibelungs."

In an essay—and frequently quite similarly elsewhere—he wrote in 1921: *Germany's sticking to this ragged Hapsburg state, come what may, was a crime for which the responsible leaders of German politics still should be hanged. . . . There can be a loyalty of the Nibelungs only toward one's own race.* The German Reich, he argued, had had *one single task: incorporating the ten million German-Austrians in the Empire and dethroning the Hapsburgs, that most miserable dynasty ever ruling over German lands.*[58] The double alliance had been *an absurdity*,[59] advantageous only to the Hapsburgs, but not the Germans in Austria. The Reich Germans had been *as though stricken with blindness, living next to a corpse, and in the symptoms of rottenness saw only the signs of "new" life.*[60] Berlin had failed to realize that *the internal conditions of this Empire were moving closer to disintegration by the hour.* As Hitler remarked later on, in order to realize how unsupportive the Dual Monarchy's non-German majority was of the double alliance, one only needed to pick up Prague newspapers: *There was nothing but bitter scorn and mockery for this "masterpiece of statecraft."*[61]

However, as long as he believed it was politically advantageous to him, as Reich chancellor he placed himself within the history of the House of Hapsburg. In doing so, he particularly liked to falsely attribute old Hapsburg's conquests to the Holy Roman Empire of the German Nation, certain that hardly anyone in his audience would really be able to differentiate between the two.

When in 1941 the German army conquered Belgrade, he joked *about his compatriots in Vienna asking over and over again whether we were going to give up Belgrade once again. "After having had to conquer it for the third time now,"* we should finally keep it![62] The two earlier conquests had been the one in 1717 by Prince Eugene I and the one in 1915 during the First World War. In his plans for the "Reich Fortress Belgrade" and a "Prince Eugene District" Hitler also placed himself within the tradition of Austrian history.

In 1942 he commended *the way of the Viennese to think historically,* alluding to Arthur Seyβ-Inquart, the Austrian Reich commissioner for the occupied Netherlands. "Concerning the future treatment of Belgium" Hitler had remarked, "without giving it much thought": *But it still was our province until 150 years ago.* (Since 1477, the Netherlands' Catholic part, Belgium, was part of the Hapsburgs' Burgundian heritage and was separated from it only on account of the French Revolution.[63])

More examples of this kind could be quoted. They indicate how much Hitler was still thinking along the lines of Austrian history. As Goebbels noted in 1943, he sometimes even had words of praise: "The Führer portrayed the man from the Ostmark as very talented in colonializing."[64]

Hitler said to Hans Frank, *You know, what you wrote about the old Austrian administration's principles concerning foreign areas is absolutely correct. The Austrian administration was the best in the world. The Austrian district captain was the monarch of his district. There was a genuine, paternal principle of leadership. After the war I will adopt it in that form for Germany.*[65] And at table in 1942 he said, *One day the Viennese will be proved right after all. In ten thousand cafés in Vienna the topic of Hungary is dealt with like this:*

The Berliners don't really know the Hungarians very well. Now that's an area right near us. We liberated them from the Turks. There won't be peace until we have liberated them again. Why aren't we taking them? The Slovaks too— yes, it's great that they are independent, but ultimately they belong to us! In that regard the Viennese will be more greater-German than anybody else. The sense of having a mission to accomplish stimulates them.[66]

Now it seemed to him that even the Hungarians, whom he hated so much while he lived in Vienna, were nostalgically seeking a joint German Reich: *today, when there is talk about the monarchy, the Hungarian is all of a sudden terribly moved. They still believe to this day that they are the tail end of the old German Empire's magnificence!*[67] To be sure: Hungary was never part of the "First" German Empire but only one of Hapsburg's crown provinces between 1526 and 1918—a difference for which Hitler had no use in this connection.

As Reich chancellor, Hitler never tired of attempting to legitimize his "Third Reich" by way of the Holy Roman Empire of German history. In 1935 in Nuremberg he let himself be presented with the gift of a copy of the German Reich sword, expressing his gratitude *for the symbol of the German Reich's strength.*[68] In 1938, by now "Führer of the Greater German Empire," he ordered that the old imperial insignia—the so-called crown of Charlemagne, imperial cross, orb, sword, Frederick II of Hohenstaufen's sacramental cloak, the holy lance, and other items, down to the coronation stockings—be transferred from Vienna's public treasury to Nuremberg.

This too was supposed to be justified with a reference to history. Since the days of old, the insignia were kept in the Free Reich City of Nuremberg and always sent to Aachen or Frankfurt for the coronations. They were not taken to Vienna, the Roman-German emperors' residence, until the Napoleonic era, so they would be protected from the French army. When the "first" imperial Reich was dissolved in 1806, the insignia stayed in Vienna as museum pieces.

Hitler adopted the idea of moving the imperial treasures from Vienna to Nuremberg from the pan-Germans of his years in Vienna as well. As early as 1906 they had provoked the Austrian government in Parliament with the motion to return the imperial treasures back to Nuremberg on the occasion of the hundredth anniversary of the dissolution of the Roman-German Reich.[69] This motion was instigated by pan-German author Harald Arjune Grävell von Jostenoode and his article "The Imperial Insignia Back to the Reich," published in Vienna in 1906 as part of the series of booklets *Ostara*, with which Hitler was well familiar.

In bathetic sentences, this article conjures up the magnificence of the former German Reich: "And once again the German Reich heralds shall ride into Vienna on horseback, accompanied by trumpet flourishes, to obtain the testaments to our glory. For they belong not to the periphery but in the center of the German people. In the old free Reich City of Nuremberg, where they used to be, they shall once again find their place." The result would be "an era of rapprochement and balance of all tribes," von Jostenoode wrote: "North and South will blend together to a greater German people." "Austria no longer, Prussia no more! / One noble Germany, inspiring awe! / The Hohenstaufens' heroic spirit will then return. . . . And once again our people will rule over Europe." Nuremberg, he wrote, would become "a sacred place of pilgrimage," "a center of pan-German statecraft." "Under the protection of the regained imperial crown and the blessing of the old sovereigns . . . all German tribes" would then annually assemble in Nuremberg "in order to discuss mutual affairs."[70]

In Hitler's understanding, the transference of the insignia to Nuremberg, the city of the party conventions, the old Reich's symbolic power, which he so praised in *Mein Kampf*—*The insignia of former imperial glory, preserved in Vienna, still seem to cast a magic spell; they stand as a pledge that these twofold destinies are eternally one*[71]—was transferred to the "new Reich" as well, which Hitler wanted to turn into a "Germanic Reich of the German Nation."[72] The insignia basically legitimized the "Third" Reich, but weakened Vienna, the former German imperial residence.

Days in March and the Heldenplatz

That the German army invaded Austria on March 12 and 13, 1938, of all dates, was not the result of precise planning. Yet, thoroughly familiar with Austria's history and mentality as he was, Hitler very deftly took political advantage of the date, its symbolism, and its historical significance.

On March 13, 1848—ninety years earlier—the revolution had started in Vienna as a national, liberal, and social rebellion against Metternich's rigid regime. At the time, black-gold-red flags were hoisted in Vienna as a sign of the pan-German, "greater German" movement of a unified German empire under Hapsburg leadership.

Many groups, the Democrats as well as the Nationals, viewed the history of 1848 as an obligation, particularly during Hitler's Vienna period. In a March 1908 article commemorating the sixtieth anniversary of the revolution, the *Alldeutsches Tagblatt* wrote that the start of the revolution was "a justified scream of a suppressed people, the rattling of chains by slaves who felt the fist of the police in their necks."[73]

The Social Democrats also celebrated March 13 as the day "on which Austria's working class for the first time entered the stage of history."[74] Every year they called on the workers to walk the traditional "walk to the graves of those killed in action in March" to Vienna's Central Cemetery, and this "walk" by tens of thousands of people was a demonstration for the values of 1848.

Around 1910, while he was in the Männerheim (men's hostel), young Hitler diligently studied the revolution of 1848, including its connection with his idols Richard Wagner and Gottfried Semper, who both had been revolutionaries in Dresden.[75] In 1938 he was keenly aware of the fact that in referring to the historic date of March 13 he was by no means speaking only to German nationalists directly, but also to those opposed to Austria's class system, in particular, the Social Democrats. Indeed, Austria's class system subscribed to many principles against which the revolutionaries of 1848 too had fought: the state was authoritarian, had eliminated Parliament as well as the Social Democratic opposition, used Catholicism as a political instrument, and was striving toward the restoration of the monarchy. The small republic of Austria was stricken with social poverty and extremely high unemployment.

In March 1938 Hitler also paid homage to the spirit of 1848 in Frankfurt, where the German emperors had been crowned, and in whose Paul's Church the pan-German representatives fought in vain for a "unified German fatherland" that included Austria and Prussia. In the Römer's (the city hall's) Imperial Hall, Frankfurt's mayor solemnly handed the "Führer of the Greater German Reich" a greeting from the Viennese, who were conscious of their German connection, to Frankfurt's parliament in 1848.

In his Frankfurt speech, Hitler went back two thousand years to Arminius* in order to illustrate the Germans' old longing for a greater German empire—which, incidentally, Linz's history teacher Leopold Poetsch used to do as well. Since the liberation wars, Hitler said, *millions of compatriots prayed to the Lord . . . for a unified Reich. Martyrs were killed for this longing.* Then he referred to the failed German unification movement of 1848, saying fate had blessed him: *We can now consider the work for which our ancestors fought and bled ninety years ago to be accomplished. It was based on the German people's longing for one Reich.* He put great emphasis on his claim to have annexed Austria to the German Reich *not*

---

*Hermann, chief of the Cherusci, a German national hero who organized a rebellion against Roman governor Varus and defeated three Roman legions at Teutoburg Forest in 9 A.D. (*Translator's note*) *in violation of the law, but as a restorer of the law*, and referred to both 1848 and the prohibition of the Anschluss in the Versailles Treaty of 1918.

The *Völkischer Beobachter*—the Nazi party's newspaper—reported, "Frankfurt, the city where the coronations used to take place, received him more enthusiastically than it ever received an emperor."[76]

However, March 13 was yet another important day of commemoration in Austrian history, the birthday of the "people's emperor" Franz Josef II, Maria Theresia's son and successor, who was additional link between that day and 1848: he became the patron of the March revolution of 1848, which started with a demonstration at Vienna's Josephplatz. The revolutionaries decorated their idol's monument with flower wreaths and black-red-gold flags, and sang German-national songs.

This emperor's late followers consisted of political camps which were not at all in agreement with each other—German Nationals, Liberals, as well as Jews and farmers. The German nationalists saw in him "Joseph the German," the "Germanicizor." He—and only he—had ruled the vastly different Austrian hereditary lands in a tight centralized manner and prevailed in making German the official language, which, after Joseph's death in 1790, the German nationalists unsuccessfully kept trying to reinstate until 1918.[77] Joseph turned the Hofburgtheater, which traditionally had produced French plays for the aristocracy, into a German national theater. He supported German rather than Italian operas, commissioning Wolfgang Amadeus Mozart to write *The Abduction from the Seraglio*. That in the eighteenth century all this certainly had no German-national origins but rather was due to the Age of Enlightenment made no difference around 1900 to the German nationals in their attempts to market this Hapsburg emperor.

Around 1900 the German-Bohemians used the cliché of "Joseph the German" in order to irritate the Czechs. They took donations to erect monuments of Franz Josef in mixed-language areas and near the borders with non-German crown provinces—most notably in the Sudeten district, but also in Waldviertel or in the area around Linz—and on anniversaries decorated them with black-red-gold flags rather than Hapsburg's black-yellow ones. Around 1900 there was such great demand for these monuments that they were manufactured in plants and made of cast-iron. Every "German Folk's Day"—for example, the one in Troppau in Lower Silesia in 1909—ended with rallies at the local Franz Josef monument. The emperor's remark, "I am proud to be a German," became a slogan on posters that were taken along during rallies. German-folkish almanacs contained pages and pages of sayings by the emperor, right next to those of Bismarck and Schönerer.

Yet the Liberals too revered Franz Josef II, particularly as a reformer who had eliminated the privileges of church and nobility and had relaxed censorship of the press. Protestants and Jews were grateful to him for the 1781 "patent of tolerance" for non-Catholics. The poor revered Franz Josef II as a "people's emperor" who had abolished serfdom, fought against corruption, and had an open ear even for the most destitute. He brought the Enlightenment to Austria, following Frederick II of Prussia, whom he fervently admired. According to general concensus, his vigorous reform policies prevented the outbreak of a revolution, which in France claimed his younger sister Marie Antoinette as a victim.

Everyone was familiar with the legend of Franz Josef II's plowing in the Moravian village of Slawikowitz and thus paying his respect to the agrarian class. Around 1900 the image of the plowing emperor was used by Georg Schönerer for propaganda in order to win over the farmers from the Clerical party to the pan-German camp. He generously paid for monuments of "Joseph, the friend of the farmers."

The cult around Franz Josef II flourished in the Hapsburg empire whenever times were rough, and was always a sign of criticism of whoever was ruling. During his reign, for example, every celebration of Franz Josef criticized the country's extremely close ties to the church, the political predominance of aristocracy, military, and church, as well as the fact that Hungarians and Czechs were favored over the Germans.

Even years later, when Hitler was already Reich chancellor, he would praise Franz Josef II as the only laudable exception among the otherwise hated Hapsburgs and consistently used the arguments that were generally employed in Vienna around 1910. Thus in 1941 he remarked with appreciation, *If Germany was spared the French Revolution, it was only because Frederick the Great and Josef II were around*[78]—yet another Viennese stereotypical slogan.

On March 15, 1938, the Heldenplatz (Heroes' Square) was the magnificent backdrop against which Hitler's first great rally took place in Vienna. One reason for the choice of place was because it was so large. But it also had a strong historical tradition, particularly for the German nationalists. The "heroes" to whom the name refers were the soldiers of the Napoleonic and Turkish wars, as well as the "unknown soldier," whose monument is inside the Heldentor (Heroes' Gate) to this day. The classicist Heldentor, erected in 1824 in remembrance of the Leipzig Battle of

The Heldenplatz on March 15, 1938, seen from the balcony of the New Hofburg; to the left, the classicist Heldentor; to the right in the back, Parliament

Nations, was the victory sign of liberation from Napoleonic rule and therefore was reminiscent of the time of early "pan-German" nationalism.

The Heldentor so clearly influenced Hitler's taste that it looks like a model for many neoclassicist buildings of the thirties. To be sure, the original is much smaller and more distinguished, not even to mention the inscription chiseled in the front, Emperor Franz Josef's motto, *Iustitia regnorum fundamentum*—"justice is the foundation of governments."

According to Kubizek, even young Hitler was very attracted to the Heldenplatz. As early as 1908 Hitler busily made drawings for expanding the square, because according to Kubizek he saw in the huge square a "virtually ideal solution for mass demonstrations," "not only because the half circle of buildings uniquely linked together the masses of people gathered there, but also because monumental sensations left a mark on every single person standing among the crowd of people, no matter where he turned."[79] There is no need to elaborate extensively on the young Hitler's Heldenplatz designs that Kubizek so minutely discusses. They did not originate in Hitler's head anyway. Clearly, he copied Gottfried Semper's old design for the imperial forum, which was never realized. At any rate, during his years in Vienna Hitler must have studied this concept assiduously.

For Hitler, the former Austrian, the Heldenplatz was no doubt an utterly familiar place when on March 15, 1938, he stood on the balcony of the Neue Hofburg, which was conceived by Semper, and proclaimed during the "demonstration for the liberation": *This country is German, and therefore, in this hour I can report to the German people the greatest accomplishment of my life. As Führer and Reich chancellor of the German nation and the Reich I am announcing to history my homeland's entrance into the German Reich.*[80]

He played the piano of historic symbolism like a virtuoso, using history to legitimize his rule and enthralling many Austrians conscious of their German connection. Very deliberately he stylized Emperor Franz Josef II, the Liberation Wars, 1848, and Bismarck into his predecessors, and himself into the one who was "fulfilling" German-national longings.

4
In Parliament

The Austro-Hungarian Parliament Since 1907

He was not yet twenty years old, Hitler wrote in *Mein Kampf,* when he *set foot for the first time in the magnificent building on the Franzensring,*[1] in other words, the Parliament building in Vienna, and to be more precise: the House of Representatives of the Austrian Reichsrat. This time, however, he was not interested in the building by Theophil Hansen, the architect he so admired, but in Parliament as a political institution.

Since 1907 Cisleithania's parliament, with 516 seats the largest in Europe, had been drawing public attention to itself, for it was the first time that representatives had been elected according to universal, direct, equal, and democratic suffrage. To be sure, women did not have the right to vote. Only men over twenty-four who could prove that they had been residents for at least one year in the town where they voted had that privilege. Thus Hitler was not allowed to vote while he lived in Vienna, for he left Austria in 1913, shortly after he turned twenty-four.

The old voting statutes, which were mainly based on the different tax brackets, had strongly discriminated against the poor classes and favored the well-to-do and the German-speaking bourgeoisie. Now that everyone was allowed to vote and votes counted equally, the parties representing the poorer classes won. The Christian-Socials, the party of the small businesspeople and craftsmen, won ninety-six seats as compared to their former twenty-five, and the Social Democrats eighty-six as compared to the ten in the previous election. The most extreme German-national and rather bourgeois party, however, the Pan-Germans, under Georg Schönerer's chairmanship, shrunk from twenty-two to three seats.

Of the approximately thirty parties and groups, none had an absolute majority. It is probably also remarkable that despite the great number of parties in the Reichstag there was not a single party that called itself "Austrian."

The parties and their number of seats in the Reichsrat in 1907 were:

- 96 Christian-Socials
- 86 Social Democrats
- 31 German People's Party, 21 German-Agrarians, 17 German-Progressives, 12 German-Radicals ("Wolfians"), 3 Pan-Germans ("Schönerians")
- 28 Czech-Agrarians, 18 Young Czechs, 17 Czech Conservatives, 7 Old Czechs, 2 Czech Progressives ("Realists"); 1 "nonaffiliated" Czech; and, the most radical group, 9 Czech National Socialists
- 25 Polish National Democrats, 17 Polish People's Party, 16 Polish Conservatives, and 12 Polish Center
- 4 Zionists and 1 Jewish Democrat
- 10 Italian Conservatives and 4 Italian Liberals
- 18 Slovenian Conservatives and 5 Slovenian Liberals
- 25 Ruthenian National Democrats and 4 Old Ruthenians
- 12 Croats; 5 Romanians; 2 Serbs; 1 Radical Russian
- 1 Free Socialist, 1 "Independent Socialist," 1 "Social Politician," 2 nonaffiliated members
- 2 seats vacant in 1907.[2]

The government was supported by the Polish Club, by Romanians, Italians, and various alternating German parties. The opposition was made up by the Social Democrats, the Czechs, Slovenians, the Pan-Germans, and others. In view of the precarious situation at home, most of the prime ministers, who were appointed by the emperor and dependent on the parliament, limited themselves to carrying on government affairs. They did not have a chance to push through their own political program anyway.

*   *   *

It is impossible to give an exact accounting of that parliament's national composition, because the population was frequently mixed and there were different criteria of nationality. According to the criterion that was typically applied in Austro-Hungary—that of one's everyday language determining one's nationality—Parliament was composed of the following nationalities: 233 Germans, 107 Czechs, 82 Poles, 33 Ruthenians, 24 Slovenians, 19 Italians, plus 13 Croats and 5 Romanians. Thus 233 German representatives faced a majority of 283 non-German representatives.[3]

It is unlikely that there has ever been a parliament as contentious as the Austrian Reichstag in the short period between 1907 and March 1914, when the House was closed. Not only were the different nationalities arguing with one another, but these nationalities were also in disagreement among themselves. The German parties had always been in disagreement with each other. The non-German parties argued together against the Germans, but they also were beset by internal disputes. Between Ruthenians (Ukrainians) there were even brawls in parliament. For although both Ruthenian factions were Russophile, one group sympathized with the czarist regime, and the other with the Hapsburgs.

An exception were the Poles, who tended to be united in their policies and to strengthen the state. Polish politicians were in agreement that as long as they could not attain their own state and their country remained divided, they got along best under Austrian rule. Their fellow Poles in Russia as well as in the German Reich were far worse off. The "Polish Club," consisting of almost all Polish parties represented in the Reichsrat, always provided several ministers.

Parliament's standing orders did not assuage the fight between nationalities; on the contrary, it exacerbated it on account of serious flaws. Because there was no national language, there could be no uniform language in Parliament. Each representative had the privilege of speaking in his native tongue. Ten languages were admitted: German, Czech, Polish, Ruthenian, Serbian, Croat, Slovenian, Italian, Romanian, and Russian. Yet there were no interpreters. There were limitations to boot: when in 1907 a Polish representative from Galicia tried to speak Russian, this was interpreted as sympathetic to pan-Slavism and immediately prohibited. On the other hand, Dimitri Markow, a "radical Russian" from Galicia, was allowed to give his speeches in Russian, because it was his mother tongue.[4]

Because things were so complicated, parliamentary procedures were sometimes argued about for days, which halted all actual work. The

German parties' motion to establish German as the language of parliamentary debate was rejected by the House's non-German majority. In a countermotion the latter requested that minutes of the speeches be taken in all languages admitted in parliament and that interpreters be employed.[5] The pertinent statute was not introduced until 1917, without any actual consequences.

German was indeed clearly preferred. The president of Parliament spoke German. The parliamentary stenographers took the minutes only in German. Urgent inquiries, which could be made in one's native tongue, had to be submitted in German translation. Non-German speeches were included in the minutes only if the speaker himself provided a written German translation.

Apart from the lack of a common language for debates, there was also no time limit for speeches. In additon, the statute determining that urgent motions always had to be given preference, afforded even the smallest parliamentary group the welcome opportunity to use minor, drawn-out motions to block parliamentary work for days and weeks.

Some non-German representatives took advantage of the lack of interpreters and of a time limit for speeches; because most of their colleagues could not understand them and minutes of their speeches were not taken because there were no non-German stenographers, it was difficult to have any control over whether a speech was really only about the motion under debate or if the only purpose was to gain time by reciting poems or by endless repetitions. That left the door wide open to filibusters and made expedited work impossible. The daily arguments in the mumbo-jumbo of ten languages turned the Austrian Reichsrat into an international spectacle.

An observer from Berlin noticed with astonishment that attending parliament was very popular with the Viennese. As far as he was concerned, the large number of parties represented in the Cisleithanian parliament made any serious work impossible anyway, and visits to the Reichsrat were "amusing" to the "natives": "there they can . . . attend an entertainment for free. The representatives personally 'jumping on' each other compensates the Viennese entirely for theater performances, which they would have to pay for after all if they wanted some entertainment. In Parliament they can have a grand time, 'by the grace of the representatives,' and what they get out of it also gives them enough material to amuse their good friends for many an evening in the tavern."[6]

The Viennese cracked jokes: the four *quadrigae* on the roof of the Parliament, who fly from one another in all four directions, were the symbol of the state drifting apart. When young Hitler mentioned this in

Mein Kampf[7] he was by no means telling his own joke but only repeating a commonplace in Vienna.

Hitler as a Visitor to Parliament

The House of Representatives had two galleries for visitors. The first tier was reserved for VIPs, the second gallery was open to anyone. Early in the morning free numbered tickets were distributed. August Kubizek was surprised at his friend's eagerness: "for it amazed me that Adolf was already that energetic and active at eight-thirty in the morning."[8] In *Mein Kampf* Hitler writes that *as a freedom-loving* man he had not at all been opposed to parliamentarianism at the time but rather had *admiration for the British Parliament* and *could not even conceive of any other possibility of government.*[9]

What he witnessed in Parliament in Vienna, however, did not coincide with this ideal image, he wrote. Even after a short while he became indignant about *the lamentable comedy* in the Reichsrat. He berated the content and form of the multilingual and incomprehensible debates. *A wild gesticulating mass screaming all at once in every different key, presided over by a good-natured old uncle who was striving in the sweat of his brow to revive the dignity of the House by violently ringing his bell and alternating gentle reproofs with grave admonitions. I couldn't help laughing.* Yet on another day Parliament was *changed beyond recognition* and almost completely empty: *Down below everybody was asleep.*

Still, the goings-on attracted him tremendously: *From now on, whenever time offered me the slightest opportunity, I went back and, with silence and attention, viewed whatever picture presented itself, listened to the speeches in so far as they were intelligible, studied the more or less intelligent faces of those chosen by the peoples of this woebegone state—and little by little formed my own ideas.*[10]

On occasion Hitler took his friend Kubizek along to the parliament. Not being interested in politics, "Gustl" did not understand the reason for these visits: "Once in a while I would ask Adolf what connection there were between the distant problems we encountered during our visits to the Parliament, for instance, and his studies. His reply would be, 'You can only build once the political foundation has been laid.' "[11]

Kubizek remembers, "Once, when Adolf had again forced me to go there with him . . . a Czech representative was making a filibuster that lasted hours. Adolf explained to me that that was a speech whose only purpose was to fill time and to prevent another representative from speaking. He said it didn't matter what the Czech was saying, he could say the same thing over and over again, only he mustn't stop. . . . Never did Adolf surprise me more than he did then. . . . But the way he was listening to this speech, which he couldn't understand anyway, tense all over inside, I could not comprehend him."[12]

Kubizek describes with amazement the representatives' screaming, rattling with their desk tops, and whistling: "and in the middle of this dreadful spectacle, German, Czech, Italian, and Polish curses—God knows how many languages there were—were flitting across the hall. I looked at Adolf. Was this not the ideal moment to leave? But what had happened to my friend? He had jumped up, his fingers clenched to fists, and his face was burning with excitement."[13]

In 1908 and 1909, when Hitler visited Parliament, there was a special aggressiveness in the Reichsrat on account of the hostilities during the anniversary year and the annexation crisis. The numerous national rows were taken from Parliament to Vienna and were further stirred up there, particularly the conflicts in Bohemia, but also in Laibach, where Slovenians protested against the planned establishment of an Italian university in Trieste.

What became most dangerous were the Czech National Socialists' filibusters, a revenge for the German Radicals and Pan-Germans previously having made the Bohemian District Parliament nonfunctional through filibusters. The majority of the House was unable to prevail against this minority's terror.

After martial law was established in Prague on December 2, 1908, Parliament finally turned into one madhouse. The president was making his introductory remarks, and already Czech National Socialists Vinzenz Lisy, Václav Fresl, and Frantisek Burival approached the president's platform in double march, blowing metal whistles and children's trumpets. They were followed by additional representatives whistling and yelling "Boo!" Representative Anton Hajn, equipped with a children's trumpet, was playing the assault march. Young-Czech representative Václav Choc said to the president: "That is the executioner!" And Lisy wanted to know: "Do you wish to transfer Prague's martial law to the Bohemian representatives in Vienna?"

The president was powerless. According to the *Kronenzeitung* he watched "the scene with binoculars and had the names of the members of the trumpet-and-whistle corps taken down. A—as word went in the House of Representatives—'list of whistlers' was put together rather than a list of speakers."[14]

Not even the old emperor himself was able to reconcile the warring parties for a short while: during the celebratory meeting for the sixty-year anniversary the Social Democrats, the German Nationals, the Pan-Germans, and the radical Czechs were absent, for very different reasons.

Franz Josef's hopes that universal suffrage would calm down the fighting among different national groups and politically stabilize the situation had long since evaporated. Disenchanted and irritated, he told the Hungarian prime minister, "If the representatives have nothing better to do than constantly argue about ethnic issues, they shall at least leave me alone!"[15] In his speech at the inauguration of the new Parliament he had still been moved and talked about the greatness of the moment, wishing that the representatives be directed by "the conciliating spirit of love for the common fatherland."[16]

In the spring of 1909 the draft of a language bill for the Bohemian provinces impassioned people. The government proposed a census-based compromise that on one hand pandered to the German-Bohemians by allowing for the national separation of their German-language areas, which they desired, particularly the "Sudeten areas," while on the other hand the Czechs were to be granted equal rights for both languages in all of Bohemia. However, the Czechs were strictly opposed to a census as the basis for a language bill and insisted on the enforcement of Bohemia's rights in all of Bohemia, as had been done in Hungary. That necessarily would have meant a bilingual solution, even in exclusively German-speaking areas in northern Bohemia.

Yet, although most Czech parties were willing to negotiate, when the bill was introduced on February 3, 1909, the Czech National Socialists responded with terror. Prime Minister Bienerth's reading of the draft was drowned by shouts of "Boo!" and all sorts of noises: the Czech National Socialists banged their desk tops, blew into trumpets and children's whistles, and rang pocket bells.

Tomás G. Masaryk of the Czech Liberals was the first speaker to approach the rostrum. There he stood until late afternoon without getting a chance to say anything. The radicals used new loud instruments, "rattles which were fastened to the desks and, by way of turning a crank, made a terrible noise. At the same time someone brought a kind of rattle into the building which makes a noise similar to the stage rain in the theater. Everything put together, with the children's trumpets and the stage rain, made such noise that the representatives and the visitors in the gallery had to hold their ears shut."[17] In the afternoon an even louder "foghorn-like" instrument was added. Masaryk, who always tried to get his compatriots in line on constructive work, did not have a chance to speak. An attempt by the Social Democrats and Christian-Socials to calm down the noisemakers ended in a brawl.

On February 4 a debate was possible for a short while. Masaryk rejected the bill in a calm, dispassionate manner, mentioning the situation of the Czechs in Vienna, and calling for a comprehensive solution: "If there is not enough courage to introduce in this House a general law for all the peoples in Austria, how can there be peace?" His suggestion: bilingualism throughout as an "ideal solution to the language issue."[18] That also would have meant a bilingual Lower Austria and Vienna—precisely what the Germans tried to prevent at all cost.

After a few more speeches the atmosphere was once again so heated up that the meeting had to be adjourned. On February 5 the attack started right after the debate was opened and could be heard even in the street, where a curious crowd gathered. A discussion was impossible.

The government then took a strong measure: it pronounced the meeting, and thus the House of Representatives, closed. The *Kronenzeitung* wrote: "Not one representative left the room, and everyone on the galleries waited breathlessly for what was going to happen next."[19] The tension led to fighting. To quote the *Prager Tagblatt*: "All of a sudden, during the enormous noise and wrangling, some Christian-Socials start singing the imperial anthem. The Czechs immediately respond to their singing with 'Kde domov muj?', and the Social Democrats, the 'Song of Work.' Rep. Iro, who is standing alone by his seat, also starts singing— 'Die Wacht am Rhein'; his clear voice drowns the singing of the other representatives."[20]

Closing down Parliament made all pending motions and drafts of bills obsolete, as well as the committees' work of the past months. The representatives lost their immunity, and the payment of their wages was discontinued. Everybody who had fought for universal suffrage and hoped that further democratization would improve matters was entirely at a loss, and angry. Pacifist Bertha von Suttner remarked with indignation, "Whistles, drums, fog horns, simultaneous singing by Czech, Reich German, and Austrian anthems, swinging fists, torn-off coat collars, bitten fingers, really, one has to blush with embarrassment. . . . It really is as if parliamentarianism was trying to commit suicide! Why are we everywhere safe from infernal rows and brawls, in the theater, in the hotel lobby, in the street—but not in the 'honorable House' where they make laws, laws for everybody except for themselves?"[21]

The Social Democrats, who after all had for decades fought for the establishment of this "people's parliament," tried to achieve a change of the standing orders. Representative Wilhelm Ellenbogen argued, "Democracy is not only a higher, but also a more complicated political in-stitution than an authoritarian monarchy, which is why it needs a kind of order that is planned more carefully." He said he saw no reason "why the Austrian Parliament has to be the most vulgar in the world. We Social Democrats truly don't need such rude manners" any more than "that disgusting, boyish yelling and screaming." Therefore he was in favor of increasing the presidency's power to exercise censorship.[22] However, changing the standing orders was not possible.

As far as their education and professions were concerned, those very same representatives were respectable men. Apart from 129 farmers there were sixty lawyers, twenty-two university professors and lecturers, thirty-eight clerics, fifty-four writers and newspaper editors, and a large number of civil servants.[23] As Christian-Social Prelate Joseph Schleicher wrote, personally they were "kind, pliant people . . . polite, considerate"—but only "outside of their periodic Reichsrat mania, their Representative's paranoia."[24] According to Schleicher, they were controlled by the radi-cals' terror, for example, the Czechs by the nine Czech National Social-ists. Schleicher said: "They turned into a nightmare that persecuted the Czechs, like the coachman who again and again urges the exhausted horses on to gallop."[25] The Germans, in turn, were controlled by the terror of the Pan-Germans and German-Radicals. Schleicher said that for ten, even twelve years "a sort of Huns' battle" was raging in Parliament.[26]

In order to get the Reichsrat back to work, the government threat-ened to apply emergency clause fourteen. Thus it would have been able to decree laws—for example, the urgently needed approval of a higher draft quota—without Parliament, that is to say, dictatorially. When the new parliamentary session opened in March 1909, its president virtually beseeched the parties to do their work. The draft bill was barely passed. The Czech parties voted against it, arguing that they were not willing "to provide the dung for Germanic world rule"—which the concerned German ambassador reported to Berlin.[27]

The threat of clause fourteen worked only for a little while. After long fights and futile negotiations the session was again suspended in July 1909. This time convening Parliament was impossible for months.

The assembly's inactivity also stopped social legislation, for example, bills on old-age and disability insurance—precisely at a time of the worst inflation, when there were hunger rallies in the streets. When the bill concerning the improvement of trade employees was protracted, the trade employees in Vienna held a protest rally. The postal employees, who were also waiting for bills to be passed, announced during a rally "that the people expect productive results from Parliament," and "that we are tired of the fighting between Germans and Slavs."[28] In October 1909 there were rallies for a functioning Parliament in all of Vienna's twenty-one districts.

When the Reichsrat reconvened after months, the Czech National Socialists made thirty-seven urgent motions on December 15, 1909, alone. This would have blocked any further business. Therefore the other parties decided to undermine the filibuster through interminable meetings. The representatives put up cots in Parliament and stocked food supplies. They arranged for shift work around the clock in order to intervene with the filibuster at any opportune moment. If need be, they were ready even to hold out through the Christmas holidays.

When the first speaker finished shortly before 2:00 A.M., he had set the filibuster record with thirteen hours. The debate about the second of thirty-seven urgent motions—on the breeding of government-owned horses—lasted from 7:00 A.M. until 8:30 P.M. In front of the Parliament building there was a rally against inflation. Shouts such as "Mass strike" and "Revolution" emanated from the crowd.

Czech-Radical Lisy continued with his filibuster in Parliament. The *Kronenzeitung* reported: "From time to time he takes a bite of a ham sandwich or a sip of cognac, without this interruption of his speech being noticed in the House. Here and there the speaker bangs on his desk to remind people that he is speaking." Then, while he was speaking, he looked through the latest newspaper. Thus one hour passed after another. "With the exception of Lisy, who still alternately eats, speaks, or drinks, only the president, the stenographers, and a page are present. The galleries are densely crowded, yet the visitors haven't gotten their money's worth. All of a sudden there is a loud shout of 'Boo!' in the hall, directed against Lisy, from the second gallery. This one shout is echoed, and for minutes, indignant, impetuous shouts are hurled from the gallery against the filibusters. 'Lazybones,' 'pickpockets,' 'bleeders' are the mildest expressions heaped on Lisy and his followers, who have quickly gathered around him again." The president orders the gallery to be vacated. "Even from the circuit around the gallery one can hear the bitter invectives against the Czech Agrarians."

Toward evening—Lisy had talked for six hours—an uproar started on the first gallery: "Down with the filibuster party!" "Chase them out of the House we have fought for with our blood!" "Band of thieves!" "Exit bleeders!" In the words of the *Kronenzeitung*: "All the while, the visitors on the gallery stomp their feet, others let out piercing whistles, up there the noise is dreadful, such as one has never heard before on the gallery." When finally this gallery too was vacated by force, the visitors started

Rally in front of the Parliament building, October 2, 1910

singing the "Song of Work," "and melody and words of the first stanza resound passionately throughout the House. When it has ended, one can see that the pages have to use force to remove the visitors. Some of them literally have to be carried out." At midnight the newspaperman has to hand in his report. Yet the meeting continues.

The *Reichspost* wrote on December 18: "Circulation in the House is getting increasingly insufferable, the air, heavy with steam and tobacco smoke mixed with dust, drags through the hallways. . . . Already, a disgusting heap of pieces of paper, dirt, and dust is gathering." More incomprehensible speeches. Again there are protests from the gallery, and again it is repeatedly vacated. The Czech-Radicals shout in unison, "Away from Vienna!"

Young-Czech Karel Kramar, of all people, who was considered a radical, saved the dangerous situation on that day: after consulting with the Social Democrats and Christian-Socials he grabbed the next urgent motion for changing the standing orders with a stunt. To the Czech National Socialists' surprise, he moved that the president of Parliament be authorized to prohibit for one year any misuse of the standing order and to suspend any noncompliant representative, for no more than three sessions. The motion was accepted by large majority, 331 to 72 votes. This ensured that Parliament would function for one year.

Parliamentary excesses continued as a permanent public offense, until in March 1914 Prime Minister Stürgkh finally enacted emergency clause fourteen and sent Parliament home because it was no longer functional. Again there were no attempts to reform the standing order. And thus the multiethnic empire entered World War I without Parliament having a say or sharing responsibility.

The Schönerians and the People's Parliament

The Pan-Germans had been the most aggressive of those opposed to the new voting rights bill, demanding that as a minimum prerequisite, German be established as the national language and the empire be restructured in order to ensure that there would be a German majority in Parliament. Now they considered themselves confirmed by the confusion in Parliament, which they interpreted as a logical consequence of the principles of equality and democracy.

The charge they leveled against the Government was "that the whole voting rights law reform was supported 'from above' only because it is intended to turn this state, created by Germans and governed by Germans for centuries, into a Slavic state, and to put a Slavic stamp on it."[29]

The more ungovernable the multiethnic empire turned out to be and the more paralyzed the People's Parliament became, the more insistently the Pan-Germans praised the Germans' erstwhile ability to lead the other, allegedly backward, ethnic groups, the "slave people." They claimed that during the period when the old suffrage still had given the Germans the majority, Parliament had still been functioning after all—which was an exaggeration, to be sure.

Pan-German representative Malik said in a speech, "Esteemed House! We are confronting a chaos such as Austria has never seen and experienced, and all that, gentlemen, after the universal remedy that was applied to this multilingual state, which was the Voting Rights Reform Bill and which was forced onto the decent and reasonable people in this Empire by the Court and the Government, in collaboration with the Social Democrats. The voting rights reform bill should have eliminated the ethnic quarrels line, hook and sinker, and now the gentlemen are in a jam. Just look and see how you get yourselves out of it!"[30]

We can read the identical arguments in Mein Kampf: *With the formation of a parliamentary representative body without the previous establishment and crystallization of a common state language, the cornerstone had been laid for the end of German domination of the monarchy. From this moment on the state itself was lost. All that followed was merely the historic liquidation of an empire. To follow this process of dissolution was as heartrending as it was instructive.*[31] And: *In parliament, for the moment, total collapse was averted by undignified submissiveness and acquiescence at every extortion, for which the German had to pay in the end.*[32] With the newly established suffrage *this country had sunk to the status of an un-German hodgepodge with a parliamentary government.*[33]

Reich chancellor Hitler, always trying to familiarize northern Germans with Austrian history, gave the following soliloquy in 1942: *The Austrian state . . . ! The different elements it combined—and still! The central force is bound to be destroyed if you introduce universal suffrage. . . . Until then, the German minority led the others so securely that you may not say, Only the English can accomplish that! No, we managed to do that as well.*[34]

Yet the reason for the multiethnic Parliament's failure was by no means the inadequacy of democracy and of the principle of equality, as the Pan-Germans boasted, but clearly the flawed parliamentary standing orders. It rendered the majority, which was willing to accomplish something, powerless and helpless against radical terrorist minorities, above all, the Czech National Socialists on one hand and the Pan-Germans on the other hand. Nowhere could young Hitler have studied the power of the terror of a few and the impotence of a large organization better than in Austria's Reichsrat in Vienna.

The Pan-German representatives' parliamentary speeches were always published in the party newspapers. The *Alldeutsches Tagblatt*, for example, printed a speech by Karl Iro under his title, "O Lord, Save Us from this Austrian Plague! Amen." Iro criticized "the new people's house" as a "fake constitutional bugaboo": "At any rate, the freedom fighters of 1848 wouldn't have dreamed that a democratic institution, for whose establishment they went to prison and gave their liberty, blood, and life, would be so distraught and dilapidated as it actually is today." He raised the specter "of complete Slavic predominance in Austria where the Germans would have to function as mere tax slaves."

The Pan-Germans, he said, were determined "to rigorously fight against the Austrian system which is inimical to Germans and . . . amidst this Austrian turbulence, for which we are not to blame but which owes its existence to a greedy marriage policy, to hold up the Pan-German idea until other, active times will realize them."[35]

The Pan-German papers had a small printrun and were distributed only among the innermost circle of party members and sympathizers. The public took hardly any notice of them, and the large Viennese newspapers mentioned them only to hold them to ridicule. Thus all the numerous urgent motions by the Pan-Germans evaporated in a puff, which only exacerbated this sectarian minority's aggressiveness.

In *Mein Kampf* Hitler is excited about the Viennese *Jewish press killing the Pan-German representatives with silence: But to speak of such a "forum" is really to cast pearls before the well-known domestic beasts. It is truly not worthwhile. . . . The Pan-German deputies could talk their throats hoarse: the effect was practically nil. The press either killed them with silence or mutilated their speeches in such a way that any coherence, and often even the sense, was twisted or entirely lost, and public opinion received a very poor picture of the aims of the new movement. What the various gentlemen said was quite unimportant; the important thing was what people read about them.*[36]

According to Hitler, the Pan-Germans would have been better off acting as a nonparliamentary opposition rather than sending their three deputies into Parliament—a question heatedly discussed after 1907: *Should (the movement's) members go into Parliament to destroy Parliament, in order to—as people used to say—"bore from within," or should they carry on the struggle from outside by attacking this institution? They went in, and they came out defeated.*[37]

Hitler saw the only positive element of democratic suffrage in its finalizing the end of the Hapsburg Empire: *The more the linguistic Babel corroded and disorganized parliament, the closer drew the inevitable hour of the disintegration of this Babylonian Empire, and with it the hour of freedom for my German-Austrian people. Only in this way could the Anschluss with the old mother country be restored.*[38] These entire passages could have been copied from the *Alldeutsches Tagblatt.*

The Example of the Gypsies

The degree to which the Pan-Germans influenced Reich chancellor Hitler's policy can be illustrated by the following example, which I am citing with care and deliberately without any comment. It illustrates the special way in which the Schönerians intended to solve the issue of the monarchy's non-German citizens, in this case, the Gypsies—and the way they worded their proposals in Parliament. It should be taken into consideration that they were far more moderate in the Reichsrat than in their "popular meetings" in the Bierhallen (huge beer saloons). The crudeness of their lines of argument also explains why all other parties avoided them.

In June 1908 the topic of a "Gypsy scourge" was all over Vienna's pan-German press. It had been triggered on June 5, 1908—one week before the anniversary parade—by the pan-German deputy Iro during an inquiry in Parliament. Iro requested drastic measures to "remove the Gypsy scourge." This was at the time when young Hitler still attended Parliament and lived at Stumpergasse, within shouting distance from the *Alldeutsches Tagblatt*'s editorial offices.

Iro called the Gypsies "one of the worst scourges for our farmers." "Gypsy broads" under indictment in Hungary, he said, had openly stated "that they made their living only by stealing." Their "sophisticated modus operandi" was astonishing. The Gypsies were also accountable for "many of the most horrible murders and robbery."

When in 1941 Hitler addressed the subject of the Gypsies in connection with the parade, he called them *the greatest scourge for the farmers.* He stated that in Gypsy villages in Hungary and Romania *there had been organized, almost institutionalized instruction in pickpocketing,* and *in 1908, for the sixtieth anniversary of Franz Josef's reign, thousands and thousands of those pickpockets came to Vienna, the police alone arrested three to four thousand of them.*[39] It is certain that in June 1908 Hitler occupied himself with this subject.

In the Reichsrat Iro proposed a sophisticated system for fighting this "scourge." The main difficulty, he said, was identifying the Gypsies. "Knowing their names is of tremendous value for the administration of justice, since upon his arrest, each Gypsy invariably pretends to have only one prior conviction at most. It is impossible to prove the contrary, precisely because his correct name is not known." Iro said that the various methods that had been applied were insufficient.

The Pan-Germans believed that "after being apprehended, each Gypsy should be marked in a manner that will make it possible to recognize him at any time. For example, a number could be tattooed on his right forearm, plus the name the Gypsy has given himself." Then "the numbers could be transmitted to the individual district courts, similarly to those of automobiles being transmitted (Decree of the Ministry of the Interior of 27 September 1905, R.G.Bl., No. 156, Sections 26 and 28) to the district administrators, who could then have them tattooed onto the Gypsies."

The Gypsies' "roaming about" could only be controlled by "settling them by force": "Of course, initially these Gypsy settlements would have to be supervised and, night after night, controlled by a constabulary patrol. After all, guards are also on duty in penitentiaries and correction facilities. The same measure should also be taken with regard to compulsory Gypsy settlements."

The Gypsies would have to be "treated as if they were put under police surveillance." "Children should be taken away" from those "who don't comply . . . for example, between their fifth and their sixth year. They could be sent to schools where they would have to be instructed in various crafts according to their disposition, not to be released until they are journeymen. These institutions would be some sort of correction facilities. All traveling trade licenses would have to be revoked from all Gypsies." And: "If their native homeland is unknown, strong young Gypsies aimlessly wandering about should also be sent to forced labor institutions."

For covering some damage they might have done, but also for feeding the children who were taken away from them, the Gypsies' property should be collected. Iro said: "To be sure, these are drastic measures, in particular, taking away their children." However, "More moderate measures appear to be entirely futile."[40]

The motion of the three Pan-Germans in Parliament was seconded by fifteen more deputies. Among them were some Czechs, a Ruthenian, and a Pole, who otherwise were the Pan-Germans' deadly enemies. Also among the supporters was an ordained priest, Isidor Zahradnik, one of the Czech-Agrarian deputies. As usual, the Pan-Germans' motion was rejected by the majority of the House.

We can roughly reconstruct how long Hitler continued his visits to the gallery in Parliament: It is certain—Kubizek testifies to that too—that during his first year in Vienna, in 1908, he was a frequent visitor. The Parliament building was only a few minutes' walk from his apartment at Stumpergasse. Hitler was still well dressed—after all, during that time he also often went to the opera—and he should have had no difficulty being admitted to the gallery.

Visits to Parliament were also possible from his next apartment, in the Fifteenth District, Felberstrasse, which was not far from Stumpergasse. In the fall of 1909 Hitler became homeless and, on account of his poor attire, was not likely to have dared go to Parliament. There are no documents indicating that he went to Parliament during his years at the men's hostel, which is unlikely anyway. Thus these visits were limited to the period between February 1908 and no later than summer 1909, which is in accord with what Hitler said in Mein Kampf: *A year of this tranquil observation sufficed totally to change or eliminate my former view of the nature of this institution. . . . By now I could no longer accept the parliament as such.* A few pages later he mentioned *two years' attendance at the Vienna parliament*, adding, *After that I never went back.*[41] Yet as a diligent newspaper reader he continued to be informed about the chaos in Parliament.

His opinion about parliamentarianism was not going to change for the rest of his life. The theory of parliamentarianism, *which at first sight seemed seductive to so many . . . none the less must be counted among the symptoms of human degeneration,* he wrote in Mein Kampf.[42] *There is no principle which, objectively considered, is as false as that of parliamentarianism.*[43] *Carry(ing) out the momentary will of the* majority, government *sinks from the heights of real government to the level of a beggar confronting the momentary majority.*[44] The ability of a statesman in modern democracy, he wrote, was only in *the art of making the brilliance of his projects intelligible to a herd of sheep and blockheads, and subsequently begging for their kind approval.*[45]

He called parliamentarians *a band of mentally dependent nonentities and dilettantes as limited as they are conceited and inflated, intellectual demimonde of the worst sort. . . . Measures of the gravest significance for the future of a whole state, yes, of a nation, are passed as though a game of* schafkopf *or* tarock*, which would certainly be better suited to their abilities, lay on the table before them and not the fate of a race.*[46]

The fact that later on the NSDAP was going to walk into Parliament on its way to power does not imply that its party chairman had changed his opinion. On the contrary, Hitler said that in 1928 he had not sent his twelve deputies *into the Reichstag so they could be functioning members, they only were directed to accelerate the end of parliamentarianism.*[47]

*Card games, the latter usually spelled "tarok." (*Translator's note*)

5

The Social Question

Separation from Kubizek

After the spring term, in early July 1908, August Kubizek went to Linz for the summer. The friends agreed to stay in Mrs. Zakreys's house, and Kubizek continued to pay his share of the rent. Hitler stayed in Vienna and by August had written no fewer than two rather lengthy letters and three postcards to Kubizek. He talked moodily about his life in Vienna with Mrs. Zakreys, the weather, the roaches, sent his regards to Kubizek's parents, and asked him to bring Krackowizer's Linz city guide.[1] *Am writing rather a lot, usually in the afternoons and at night,* he wrote, and grumbled about Linz's decision not to build a new provincial theater after all, for which he had been making designs for a long time.[2] In response to a card postmarked August 19 he mentions *Lohengrin, which I'm attending today.*[3] Nothing indicates an argument between the two friends.

Hitler also announced to Kubizek that he was making a trip to Waldviertel and mentioned tensions with his half-sister Angela Raubal: *Have no desire to go if my sister comes along.*[4] The two siblings were arguing about the orphan's allowance. For Angela Raubal demanded that her nineteen-year-old brother finally look for work and give up his share of the allowance for the benefit of his twelve-year-old sister Paula.

A look at the Hitler family's book of household expenses shows that the sister's worries were understandable. The book starts in February 1908, when after Mother's death and Adolf's departure the household consisted of only two people, twelve-year-old Paula and "Haniaunt." Apart from rent money of about fifty kronen, the two needed some sixty kronen per month for groceries, mainly flour, sugar, eggs, milk—which indicates frequent desserts—and cheap supplies of meat.[5]

Yet by then the nineteen-year-old too had money problems. Frequenting the opera so assiduously must have seriously diminished, if not exhausted, his funds. Part of the reason why he went to Waldviertel was apparently to look for a new source of income, namely "Haniaunt," who as usual was spending the summer there. A postcard congratulating Kubizek on his saint's day on August 28 with a view of Weitra Castle, Landgrave Fürstenberg's residence, is proof that he did make the trip.[6]

Hitler was successful with "Haniaunt." The 1908 book of the Linz household expenses contains an entry, unfortunately undated, by "Haniaunt," who was otherwise not given to writing: twice, and very conspicuously, she entered in her extremely awkward handwriting a loan to Adolf: "Adolf Hitler krone 924 loned Johana Pölzl" and "Adolf 924 kronen."[7] Hitler must have received this money—which was explicitly not meant as a present—in August 1908 in Waldviertel.

With this cushion, in September 1908 the nineteen-year-old again tried to take the entrance exam at the Academy, but this time was not even admitted to the "trial exam." Apparently there were a great number of building designs among his works, for during that year—and Kubizek confirms this—he studied architecture more than anything else. At any rate, the dean, Siegmund l'Allemand, allegedly asked him during a meeting, *what kind of an architectural school I had attended? . . . You clearly have a talent for architecture!* However, a high school diploma was required for attending the architectural school. The result of all these disappointments: *Thus I was resolved to continue as an autodidact.*[8]

On November 18, 1908, Hitler left his apartment at Mrs. Zakreys's without informing Kubizek or leaving his new address. The reason for his move is not clear. Yet Hitler by no means disappeared in the big city but, following regulations, registered on the same day with the police at 22 Felberstrasse, door number 16, with his landlady, Helene Riedl—this time as a "student." The apartment was not far from Stumpergasse, but a little bit farther away from downtown. Hitler would stay there until August 20, 1909. We do not know whether he had his own room or perhaps just a place to sleep.

When in November 1908 Kubizek returned to Vienna as planned

and found his friend gone, he was at a loss. The next time he was in Linz he inquired about the move of Angela Raubal, who received him coldly, saying "that my artistic endeavors were partly to blame for Adolf as a twenty-year-old still having no job and not making a living."[9] The bad blood between the siblings must have had something to do with the old quarrel about the orphan's allowance—and was also the likely reason for Hitler's playing hide-and-seek with Kubizek, who after all was the only connection to his relatives in Linz. That way Hitler also kept his sisters from finding out about his latest failure in the exam and from trying to collect his allowance. At any rate, Angela did not know where Adolf lived. She said that he had not written her again. Kubizek notes: "All of his relatives considered him a good-for-nothing who categorically shied away from any work that brought in money."[10]

The Great Inflation

There are no sources or eyewitnesses whatsoever for the year 1909 in Hitler's biography, and there is only one verifiable date: on March 4, 1909, after one year, he canceled in writing his membership for Linz's Museum Association, thus saving the annual membership dues of 8.40 kronen.[11]

Whether part of the reason for this glaring lack of sources for 1909 is that they were systematically destroyed later on—that is to say, whether there was something that was worth hushing up—cannot be established. There is no doubt that it was a difficult time for Hitler. Right at that time, when the money from his aunt was about to run out, he must have suffered those hardships he liked to expound on in the years to come. But—he later said—at least he had reason to feel grateful to that period *for drawing the mother's darling out of his soft downy bed and giving him "Dame Care" for a new mother; for hurling me, despite all resistance, into a world of misery and poverty, thus making me acquainted with those for whom I was later to fight.*[12] Ultimately, he said in a monologue in 1941, his sufferings in Vienna had *turned into the greatest blessing for the German nation.*[13]

No matter how frugally he may have lived, the money he borrowed from his aunt could not have lasted more than nine months. To be sure, government student loans were no more than 800 kronen annually either,[14] but it was impossible to live on that amount without jobs on the side, such as tutoring. The minimum subsistence level, for which no taxes were collected, was 1,200 kronen.

According to a public list, salaries for civil servants were as follows: in the lowest, the eleventh salary group (for example, office clerk, bridge supervisor, district veterinarian), 1,600 to 2,200 kronen. On 1,600 kronen, 13.50 kronen were deducted in annual taxes. In salary group ten (district doctor and teacher's trainer, for example) salaries were between 2,200 and 2,800 kronen, with taxes on the latter of 36 kronen. The highest salary in government service was paid to the prime minister: 24,000, kronen, of which 790 kronen were deducted in taxes.[15]

In other words, income tax was extremely low. The government collected the money it needed mainly in the form of consumption taxes. These were mercilessly imposed on the majority of the people at a time of frantic and constant military armament, which caused high inflation. A parliamentary inflation committee held meetings that brought no results. A "savings commission" was instituted, and all kinds of new taxes were introduced. Not only workers, but also low-ranking civil servants, who hardly got by, were forced into hunger and homelessness, particularly if they had several children. Inflation was increased by a failed customs policy, for in its farmers' interest Hungary kept import taxes for food supplies high and dictated prices, especially for meat, sugar, leather, and fatty products.

We may believe Kubizek when he reports that right after they arrived in Vienna, Hitler and he witnessed a rally by the unemployed.[16] It must have been the "spontaneous" demonstration—meaning it was not organized by the Social Democrats—in front of Parliament on February 26, 1908. Along toward noon the first shouts of "Boo!" were heard. A man screamed, "I'm hungry!," sat down on the tramway in front of Parliament, and was carried away by the police and taken into custody. The *Neues Wiener Abendblatt* reported, "The large crowd of people gathering around watched the incident with great agitation."[17]

In Kubizek's memory the event takes up much room: "All of a sudden the picture changed. The elegant stores were quickly closed and the gates drawn. The streetcar stopped. Policemen on foot and on horseback rushed toward the demonstrators. We were locked in among the spectators near the Parliament building and had a good view of the frantic goings-on. . . . Some men preceded the throng of demonstrators, carrying a large banner covering the entire width of the street. It had a single word written on it: 'Hunger!' "

Kubizek describes Hitler's response: "He took everything in so dispassionately and thoroughly as if all that was important to him—just like during his visits to Parliament—were to study the mise-en-scène of the whole event, the, as it were, technical execution of a rally. Much as he felt solidarity with the 'little people,' it didn't even occur to him to participate in the demonstration."

Kubizek continues: "More and more people were pressing forward. The whole Ring seemed to be filled with passionately excited people. . . . Red flags were carried along. Yet more so than even flags and slogans, the emaciated, extremely shabbily dressed figures and the visages of the passing men, marked by hunger and misery, indicated how serious the situation was. Embittered shouts and screams could be heard. Fists were clenched, full of anger. Those at the tip of the crowd had reached the square in front of Parliament and tried to make an assault on the building. Suddenly the mounted police, who had accompanied the demonstration, drew their sabers and started to strike at those standing next to them. The response was a shower of rocks. For an instant the situation was extremely critical. But then police reinforcements succeeded in breaking up the demonstrators and dispersing the crowd."[18]

Kubizek reports that Hitler did not talk about the event until evening. Although he sympathized with the demonstrators, he had rejected those "unequivocally . . . who organized rallies like that," that is to say, the Social Democrats: *Who is leading this suffering people? Not men who have experienced the hardships of the little man themselves, but ambitious, power hungry politicians, some of whom even foreigners to him, who enrich themselves with the misery of the masses.* "A fit of anger against these political profiteers concluded my friend's embittered indictment."[19]

This language not only matches Hitler's diatribes against Social Democracy in *Mein Kampf*, after which Kubizek may have modeled this passage, but is also in line with those of the Christian-Social as well as the Pan-German press, particularly the Pan-German pamphlet against Social Democracy, *Der Hammer* (The hammer), edited by Pan-German labor leader Franz Stein. The journal never tired of putting down the hunger rallies as a political instrument of power and terror for the Social Democrats and of downplaying the problems. In view of the protest rallies against incrased meat prices, for example, the *Alldeutsches Tagblatt* advised the "workers' circles" to eat legumes and dessert, inasmuch as meat was unhealthy anyway.[20]

Neither, of course, did the Christian-Socials, whose minister of trade was mainly responsible for the failed customs policy, make any preparations for meeting Social Democratic demands. Mayor Lueger disdainfully rejected requests for subsidies for the unemployed and homeless. These, he said, were "people who know how to exploit the population's charitableness all too well, so that they are able to lead a good life without working."[21]

The satirical magazine *Kikeriki* (Cock-a-doodle-doo) commented on the profound misery: "Public parks are the most popular restaurants these days. No less than hundreds of people sit there on benches at lunchtime, letting the sun shine into their stomachs. Sunshine, incidentally, will soon be one of Austria's most favorite of all popular meals."[22]

The protests against inflation lasted until the outbreak of the war in 1914 and had their climax in the fall of 1911 in mass riots, which the military suppressed violently.

Housing Shortages

In addition to climbing prices for food supplies, land and development speculation increased rents and exacerbated the housing shortage. Scores of old tenement buildings were demolished, making room for new, expensive luxury buildings. The prices for land climbed fast, particularly in the outer districts. In the most expensive place in Vienna, Stephansplatz, the price increased from about 100 kronen per square foot to over two hundred kronen between 1880 and 1910, while the suburbs had price increases of 2,650 percent, as the Arbeiterzeitung (Worker's newspaper) calculated.[23] Land in the outer districts was so sought after because tenement buildings with several stories and tiny apartments were built on the smallest space possible and as cheaply as possible, yielding exorbitant profits. In the three years between 1910 and 1913 alone, the rent index in Vienna climbed from 87.5 points to 101.8 points.[24]

As capitalists, Vienna's landlords became the poor's enemy per se. Tenants had no legal protection. At any given time, and without apparent reason, the landlord could give notice to a tenant, who then had fourteen days to move out. There were outrageous cases, widely reported by the newspapers, where apartments were vacated by force and the tenants stood in the streets with their belongings, infants, and sick family members, and no idea where to go. Kubizek, too, was disgusted about the extent to which the "professional landlords . . . are making a profit on the masses' horrible housing situation! The poor tenant usually doesn't even know them, for they don't live in their rental boxes, heaven forbid!, but out there, in Hietzing somewhere, or by the vineyards in Grinzing, in elegant villas where they have in complete abundance what they begrudge others."[25]

Yet taking action against the building owners was impossible. As early supporters of Lueger they constituted a powerful political group who enjoyed the mayor's special protection. What is more, he could rely on their votes in the old election system, which favored the rich and put the poor at a disadvantage. Municipal apartments were reserved for Christian-

Social party members. There was no public housing for working-class families.

During his first year in Vienna Hitler could still study the homeless problem with detachment and, as a future architect, think about the "solution to the miserable housing situation." Once he took Kubizek along to the working class suburb Meidling to get to know "the housing and living conditions of working class families through direct observation." However, according to Kubizek he was not interested "in individual lots," but "tried to establish an impersonal average."[26]

At night, Kubizek reports, "pacing back and forth between door and piano," Hitler gave him lectures "against land speculation and the exploitation by the landlords"[27] and, with the aid of a large city map, rebuilt Vienna from scratch: "On the drawing board of a nineteen-year-old youth, who was living in the gloomy back premises of a house in the suburb of Mariahilf, the old imperial city turned into a city extending into the open landscape, flooded by light, full of life, and consisting of four-, eight-, and sixteen-family houses."[28]

The horrible housing situation and the rent increases, exacerbated each year by never-ending floods of immigrants, finally also became a problem for those making more money. Households with many children had to accept subletters, even in the tiny apartments in the huge tenement buildings, in order to come up with their rent. In the workers' district Favoriten there were ten tenants per rental unit, which consisted of one room with kitchen, without running water in the apartment. Almost all cellars were utilized as spaces for living and all kinds of home-based work. Beds that were not used during the day were rented to so-called *Bettgeher* or *Schlafgeher* (literally, bed- or sleepgoers). These were allowed to use a bed for approximately eight hours at certain times of day or night, but were not allowed to stay in the apartment the rest of the time. In 1910 there were more than eighty thousand *Bettgeher* in Vienna,[29] among them four times as many Czechs as Germans.

Particularly during the ice-cold Viennese winters, tens of thousands of people who could stay in the overcrowded apartments only during the night looked for a place to go during the day. Those who still had some money went into taverns or the movie theaters, which were open from 10:00 A.M. until 8:00 P.M. and were very cheap.

The political parties tried to attract interested young men. They offered them warm rooms to stay in and reading rooms with newspapers and books, organized nightly discussions and lectures in very intimate circles, and offered all kinds of classes—with the aim of acquiring new and educating old party members in the spirit of their party, whether it was National, Catholic, or Social Democratic. All offered general and legal advice and tried to improve the individual's quality of life, to promote culture, to fight alcoholism, and to convey knowledge in history, geography, art, and music. Thus everyone could make up for his lack of formal education and educate himself politically.

The club members usually met in the back rooms of taverns, where there were only a few tables and benches. Above all, the "instructors of the people," committed students or teachers, got people to read, recommended certain books to them, and gave them brochures. In his memoirs, Social Democrat Julius Deutsch, five years Hitler's senior, describes the way he worked his way up the ladder from handiman to college graduate via workers' education associations. These groups didn't aim for "cramming a lot of knowledge into people's brains, but rather to form a weltanschauung." This path went "from popular brochures which one read by the dozen, to more serious books." The labor movement "had set as its task the reformation of the entire society, and as a starting point it reshaped the individual. The Socialists made up a self-confident community which almost had the character of a religious sect."[30]

The other parties shaped their apprentices after the same pattern. All parties' taverns were similarly decorated. The difference was mainly in the words on the posters and signs, which served as decoration. If, for example, the Social Democrats' room said, "Education liberates," in the Schönerians' room it said, "Through purity to unity," and in the Christian-Socials' room, who offered little in terms of education, was a saying by the pope. It is likely that young Hitler, too, attended a number of various party group meetings, without, however, actually joining one.

The cafes in Vienna also fulfilled an important social function. For the cost of a small coffee with cream or a mug of café au lait, which in the cheap popular cafes was only six heller, and subsequently as many free glasses of water as one wanted, one could sit there for hours, meeting friends, playing chess, or reading the paper. There were all kinds of cafes, those that catered to businessmen, to fraternity members, middle-class ladies' circles, and chess or pool teams. Aristocrats met at the cafe at the Hotel Imperial or the Hotel Sacher. The literati of Viennese modern met at the Café Central. Each cafe offered certain newspapers, according to the political and national taste of its regulars. There were German-National and Social Demoratic, Czech, Italian, and Polish cafes, those for art students where expensive art magazines were available, those with international newspapers, and so forth.

Young Hitler did not belong to any of these social circles. What was left for him were the cheap popular cafes in Mariahilf where the salesgirls went as well, and later on, the cafes in Leopoldstadt: *I believe that in 1909–1910 all girls in Vienna had lunch at the cafes, one cup of coffee and two rolls! In the small cafes the coffee was just as good as in the famous ones.*[31]

Even when he was Reich chancellor Hitler still liked to talk about Vienna's cafes, which he praised as *a source of quietude, meditation, and education.*[32] Accordingly, after Hitler's death Hermann Göring stated disdainfully that Hitler had been a bum from Vienna's cafes.[33]

The Construction Worker Legend

In late summer 1909 twenty-year-old Hitler's financial situation must have become desperate: while on August 22 he did move into an apartment as a "writer" in the distant Fourteenth District, 58 Sechshauser Strasse, first floor, door number 21, with Mrs. Antonia Oberlechner,[34] three weeks later at most he already moved out. The registration slip, issued on September 16, 1909, was filled out by someone else with the note: moved, "no forwarding address"—which strongly suggests that the twenty-year-old did not pay rent and disappeared. About the following three months we know nothing whatsoever, which suggests homelessness.

What is unique and certainly worthy of note is that after 1938 the Viennese newspapers made a point of presenting an apartment where young Hitler allegedly lived in 1909, at 11 Simon-Denk-Gasse in the rather bourgeois Ninth District. A wreath was put on the entrance to the building and decorated with a large picture of Hitler, with Hitler Youth standing by the entrance as guards of honor. The picture made the title pages of the magazines.[35] The official, illustrated volume *Wie die Ostmark ihre Befreiung erlebte* (How the Ostmark experienced its liberation) of 1940 even published a photograph of the interior: "The Führer's small and shabby apartment during his time in Vienna."[36] This leaves the impression that young Hitler had lived only there and nowhere else in Vienna. Other apartments were not mentioned.

But this address, which is far from any of Hitler's real addresses,[37] is nowhere documented. The fact that in 1938 the NSDAP party archive confiscated from the registration archive the registration slips of Hitler's apartments in Vienna very much looks like a deliberate deception with the aim to thwart any research on Hitler's whereabouts in Vienna. However, historians are not missing anything, for the originals remained in the party archive, and the registration office in Vienna furthermore prudently made copies. Yet there is no registration slip containing Hitler's room at the Simon-Denk-Gasse at either location.

In the fall of 1909 at the latest, twenty-year-old Hitler must have been forced to look for work in order to survive. *I looked for work only in order to avoid starvation, only to obtain an opportunity of continuing my education, though ever so slowly.*[38] His job hunt could not have been very successful: *I soon learned that there was always some kind of work to be had, but equally soon I found out how easy it was to lose it. The uncertainty of earning my daily bread soon seemed to me one of the darkest sides of my new life.*[39]

Mein Kampf does not provide any real information, except: *not yet eighteen years old*—in fact, he was already twenty—he worked *as a helper at a construction site and in the course of two years basically went through all sorts of occupations of the ordinary day laborer.*[40] In many of his future political speeches Hitler would amplify on his martyrdom as a construction worker in Vienna, for example, on May 10, 1933, at the German Workers' Front convention in Berlin, he declared that *due to the unique course of my life I am perhaps more than anybody else in a position to understand all social classes, because I was right in the center of life, because in a whim or perhaps by virtue of its providence fate simply threw me into the large mass of people. Because I myself worked for years as a construction worker and had to earn my living.*[41]

The work of a construction helper was extremely demanding. The *Arbeiterzeitung*'s social concerns reporter assessed the constant physical strain that was put on a stone carrier, for example. Each day he had to pile up three to four thousand paving stones, carrying 130,000 to 220,000 pounds—depending on the kind of stone used—on a daily basis. Working hours were from 6:00 A.M. to 6:00 P.M. with three one-hour breaks. Remuneration was six kronen a day. Construction helpers, whose work was hardly any less strenuous, made four kronen a day.[42]

Why should a foreman have selected twenty-year-old Hitler, of all people, out of the scores of men offering their services every day? Until that point, he had never performed any physical work. He was clumsy and lacked strength, possessed neither craftsmanship nor any technical or business or other practical skills worth mentioning. He was a homebody who had never gone in for sports and found dealing with people difficult. According to his relatives in Waldviertel, when he was young he did not even help with farm work in the summer but was content to take a few walks in the forest, otherwise keeping to himself.[43] He certainly did not possess those qualities he later on would love so much in young men: *swift as greyhounds, tough as leather, and hard as Krupp steel.*[44]

What a story of woe could Hitler have told if indeed he had worked as a construction worker! Yet it is conspicuous that in *Mein Kampf* he entirely failed to elaborate on the kind of work he did, simply saying, *I drank my bottle of milk and ate my piece of bread somewhere off to one side, and cautiously studied my new associates or reflected on my miserable lot.* He claimed that since he refused to join a union he had got into an argument with the Social Democratic construction workers: *A few of the spokesmen on the opposing side forced me either to leave the building at once or be thrown off the scaffolding.*[45]

In *Mein Kampf* this alleged political argument with union members served Hitler as a cue for starting in on a diatribe against the unions and Social Democrats he hated so much, what with their lack of national pride: *I wrestled with my innermost soul: are these people human, worthy to belong to a great nation?*[46]

Apart from the fact that there was hardly an employer who would have appreciated a new helper, rather than working, keeping the workers from doing their job by giving political speeches and preaching about the greatness of the German people, one thing is peculiar: in the Vienna of that time the claim that unions fought against all nonorganized workers on construction sites was a popular means of scaring people with the "Social Democratic terror."

The Christian-Social *Brigittenauer Bezirks-Nachrichten* (Brigittenau district news), for example, published an article under the headline: "Workers, Free Yourselves of the Pressure the Social Democrat Leaders Exert on You!" The "red leaders," the article reported, were trying "to force any National or Christian and even any nonorganized worker off his workplace and to deliver him to hunger and misery. And they have the gall to claim that in doing such a lovely thing they are representing the interest of all the workers!"[47] Or: Social Democracy "was ready at all times to persecute to death those workers who won't let themselves be pressured into the red organization, and to deliver them to hunger and misery."[48]

What is more, Hitler's description suspiciously resembles the statements made by Paul Kunschak, who in 1913 shot and killed the Social Democratic labor leader Franz Schuhmeier. This murder case made headlines because the perpetrator, an unemployed lathe hand, was the brother of Christian-Social labor leader Leopold Kunschak. In May 1913, during the trial, he stated that he had wanted to shoot a Social Democratic labor leader in order to punish him: years ago they had tried to force him to join the Social Democratic union in some company. When he had refused, he was fired. "After that he had much to suffer from the Social

Democratic workers." Kunschak said he had murdered a labor leader rather than a union member because it was the labor leaders who were to blame for "inciting the workers."[49]

The degree to which these statements coincide with Hitler's construction worker myth proves once more how much of a political propaganda piece *Mein Kampf* is and how little it resembles an "autobiography." As elsewhere, in *Mein Kampf* Hitler by no means reveals personal experiences but relates political stories à clef that he took from the rich source of Vienna's anti-Social Democratic propaganda.

There is no other source for Hitler's working as a construction worker in Vienna than he himself. At no time did a former colleague turn up, not even during those days when people were ferociously competing with stories about having known the "Führer" in his youth.

Here is another story: After 1938, while viewing a collection of antiques in the Art Historic Museum, Reich chancellor Hitler surprised his guide by asking him about a certain gem, an "Aspasian gem." During Hitler's years in Vienna it had been part of the museum collection, but in 1921 had been handed over to Italy as part of the reparation payments. At the guide's astonished question as to why he knew about this gem to begin with, Hitler replied that during his youth he had once assisted in repair work in these rooms and remembered this gem. Oral tradition has it that he was referring to gilding work in the museum.[50] In 1940 this story made some newspapers, but immediately had to be corrected by the statement that at the time the restoration took place, in 1906–07, Hitler was only sixteen years old.[51] It is more likely that Hitler noticed the gem not as a laborer but as a museumgoer and in his story in 1938 once again astonished the experts with his remarkable memory, thus feeding the myth about his past as a construction worker.

Charity in Vienna

It is a fact that the by now twenty-year-old did not manage to earn enough money even to make a bare living. For a standing-room ticket at the Opera he would have had to perform the heaviest labor at a construction site for at least seven hours. Since September 17, 1910—before the onset of winter—he was not only unemployed but also homeless. What he had so far witnessed and "studied" as an uninvolved observer he now experienced personally. He joined the legion of the poor, forced to claim the services of charitable institutions.

In 1914 Hitler complained to the Austrian authorities effusively about his distress in the winter of 1909. It had been, he said, *an utterly bitter time for me. I was a young, inexperienced man, without financial assistance, and also too proud to accept any from anybody, let alone to ask for it. Without any support, I was entirely on my own, and the few kronen, and sometimes only heller, for my work were hardly enough to afford a place to sleep* However, Hitler is exaggerating when he claims, *for two years I had no girlfriend other than worry and need, no other company than constant, unappeasable hunger.* Even five years later—in 1914—he claimed, he still had *mementoes in the form of chilblains on fingers, hands, and feet.*[52]

Poor relief in Vienna was still largely through private charity. Alms were collected, a lottery for the poor regularly brought in money, and each unclaimed inheritance collected interest for the needy. As in the Middle Ages, churches and cloisters had soup kitchens and were beleaguered by the poor every day. Rich houses had their "house poor" who were regularly fed. Selected needy were allowed to pick up leftovers from taverns and hospitals. Whenever a baker gave away bread, crowds came running, and there were brawls.

There was a vast number of private charities: for laborers, the blind, civil servants, middle-class widows, men disabled on active service, students, cripples, and others, and money was also handed out for clothes, places in daycare centers for pupils, meals for students, beds in hospitals, and so forth. The mass-market periodical *Illustrierte Kronenzeitung* regularly ran a column announcing such foundations, and owing to the tremendous interest in it even published its own foundation book for twenty-five heller.[53]

The most generous foundations were typically established by Jewish philanthropists, such as Baron Rothschild, Baron Königswarter, and Baron Epstein. Prominent lawyer Moritz Singer chaired the Association of Soup and Tea Institutions in Vienna, where, as the papers reported, after 1900 "a liquid little known even to the poorer parts of the population, cocoa with milk" and vegetables were distributed at cost. Viennese Jews financed children's homes and orphanages, *Wärmestuben* (warming-up rooms), thousands of places that offered food, and stipends for needy students. Still, they were not spared anti-Semitic malice. Jewish charity was nothing but a form of business, a Christian-Social paper opined: "It is interesting to note that those financing homes for laborers are always brewery owners making the comrades dependent on alcohol in return for the money donated or loaned."[54]

Hitler must have been one of those taking advantage of some of these charitable institutions, among them doubtless the free soup kitchen in the Hospital of the Sisters of Mercy near his first apartment in Vienna at Stumpergasse. At any rate, one of his former landlady Maria Zakreys's relatives once discovered him "as he was . . . standing in the cloister's soup line; his clothes looked very shabby and I felt sorry for him, because he used to be so well dressed."[55]

The *Wärmestuben* offered some food too. At those places people in need, "regardless of their age, sex, or origin, and without first having to prove their indigence," find "protection from the cold, there they receive every day a free bowl of strengthening soup and a piece of nourishing bread, there they find a refuge protecting them from the hardships of a winter night," as one newspaper put it somewhat poetically.[56]

The *Wärmestuben* typically opened their doors in mid-November and closed the following spring. Initially they were only open during the day and thus also offered some protection to those who did have a bed to sleep in but could not spend their days there, such as the so-called *Bettgeher*, some subletters, and inmates of those shelters that were closed during the day. On cold days families who did have an apartment but no money for heat went there too. Vienna's mayor's office distributed only six hundred kindling wood assignments annually.[57]

From 1909 on, when the housing shortage became more and more desperate, the *Wärmestuben* were also kept open during the night. Entire families, pressed up against each other on wooden benches, sought protection from the cold. Social-affairs reporter Ernst Kläger described one such *Wärmestube* in the Brigittenau worker's district: "We now stumbled through a dark gate, entering a large and only dimly lit room where long benches, on which people were squeezed together, were put up in all directions. The sight of these people, sitting in long crammed lines so that there was no room to move even slightly, caused us physical pain, and we hardly felt it when the warden used his elbows to make enough room for us to force ourselves into the long line of pent-up people." Kläger continued, "We sat in this painful position for hours. . . . Yet around us there was dead silence. As if under a spell, people remained motionless within the quadrangle of the benches, looking like a ghostly gallery of the dead whom someone had put one next to the other as if for some horrible amusement."[58]

On holidays, particularly at Christmas, the *Wärmestuben* became a stage where gracious benefactors could enter, among them, for example, the emperor's daughter Archduchess Marie Valerie, who was the protector of Vienna's *Wärmestuben* Association. Speeches were held, cookies and fruit were handed out, and clothing was distributed. Apart from soup and bread, sausages and beer were offered as well, plus a "real" lunch for free.[59] The newspapers had their touching Christmas story. And they wrote with the same eagerness about the benefit balls and soirées for the poor that aristocrats gave in their mansions.

This beneficent manner of providing a few alms for the hungry, accompanied by a great deal of self-promotion and applause from the society papers, embittered many of the socially disenfranchised. They felt humiliated, even though they were hungry enough to accept the donations. Kläger wrote in their behalf that "welfare institutions are society's failed attempts to rid itself of its guilty conscience. They appeared to me like a bad dream image, those vast crowds of believers who wait out there in the barren darkness outside the bright gates of our rich life, utterly blinded by its external beauty. One must have seen them the way I saw them: suppliant, with greedy eyes, threatening and foaming with rage in their powerlessness, thousands and thousands of society's enemies, raised by our mercy."[60]

In *Mein Kampf* Hitler inveighs against *the snobbish, or at times tactless and obtrusive, condescension of certain women of fashion in skirts or in trousers, who "feel for the people."*[61] And, this time even in unison with the Social Democrats: *During my struggle for existence in Vienna, it had become clear to me that social activity must never and on no account be directed toward philanthropic flim-flam, but rather toward the elimination of the basic deficiencies in the organization of our economic and cultural life.*[62]

To be sure, around 1900 these private charities were urgently needed in Vienna, for neither the federal nor the municipal authorities, nor welfare laws, for that matter, were able to master the problems.

In Subterranean Vienna

Those who at least once in a while wanted to be warm at night had to rely on illegal private lodgings in the suburbs. Smart apartment owners rented out virtually every available square foot, thus making good business: one night, if only on the floor, was sixty heller—far more per month than Hitler had paid Mrs. Zakreys.

Social-affairs reporter Winter wrote about such a "proletarian quarter" in Brigittenau: "Those who want to see only need to enter one of the houses, almost at random, where they can walk from apartment to apartment—particularly in the back premises—and view equally horrible pictures everywhere." Winter listed as characteristic qualities "overcrowdedness, many children, and living and sleeping together, frequently in one bed, of people who don't know each other at all." One single, tiny room often served as a place "to cook, wash up, live, sleep, study, and

Night shelter in Leopoldstadt,
photographed by social affairs
reporter Emil Kläger

work for money." Winter continued: "I found a stable that had become too inadequate for animals, as an abode for ten people, among them three children, who lived in random fornication among entirely run-down lumpenproletarians."[63]

During checkups with police protection, health-department officials arrested the occasional landlord and closed down illegal quarters here and there—thus making more people homeless.

Reporter Kläger spent a few nights in illegal quarters for a large number of people in Leopoldstadt. He revealed that it took some people three or four entire days without sleep "to become immune to the horrible bug infestation and the unbearable conditions." Squeezed into the two- to three-bedroom apartments in old, dilapidated buildings were eighty or more people, men and women, sick and healthy, alcoholics and hookers, and also children: "Everything around me was a confused mass of people, rags, and dirt. The room looked like a humongous dirt ball." The next morning everybody fled the shelter so that "they could escape the dreadful circulation as quickly as possible after a night's sleep."[64]

In such conditions, rats and other vermin multiplied and were extremely dangerous at a time of large migrations, when cholera, aided by malnourishment, was spreading everywhere in Europe. Furthermore, tuberculosis, also called "Viennese disease" or "proletarian disease," was rampant in the mass shelters, but also in the craftsmen's shops, where the supervisors and their assistants worked and slept in dark, damp cellars. Infant mortality in working-class districts was three to four times higher than in "better" neighborhoods. In cramped quarters crime, alcoholism, very cheap prostitution—and syphilis—bloomed.

According to Kubizek, Hitler, who had been raised in a perfectly clean household, particularly found poor hygiene painful to bear, even in Mrs. Zakreys's apartment at Stumpergasse: "His inner protest against social ills was a result less of hunger than of the uncleanliness in which he was forced to live."[65] Kubizek described the relatively harmless conditions at Mrs. Zakreys's as follows: "one single faucet out in the hallway, where eight parties have to go with pails and buckets. A highly unhygienic bathroom shared by the whole floor, where you almost need to establish a regular arrangement if you want to use it. And on top of all that—the bedbugs."[66] He reported that night after night, Hitler would go on a "hunt for bedbugs" and the following morning showed him "the specimen, which he had carefully impaled on a needle."[67]

Apart from the health hazards, everyone who observed these conditions also mentioned the moral hazards for children. Many a criminal career started out during childhood. Because begging was hardly profitable—apart from being illegal—child prostitution was frequently the only means of making money. In *Mein Kampf* Hitler describes these children and adolescents with palpable disgust: *Morally poisoned, physically undernourished, his poor little head full of lice, the young "citizen" goes off to public school. . . . When at the age of fourteen the young man is discharged from school, it is hard to decide what is stronger in him: his incredible stupidity as far as any real knowledge and ability are concerned, or the corrosive insolence of his behavior, combined with an immorality, even at this age, which would make your hair stand on end.*[68]

The standard solution to the problem was for the health-department police to conduct raids and pick up the waifs and strays to commit them to orphanages. But these too were overcrowded and too old, for more and more mothers were forced to surrender their children to public care.

When in 1908 the opposition in the city council demanded that heatable cots be put up and streetcar arches be opened to protect more people from the winter cold, municipal government officials pointed out how much public assistance the city was already handing out to the poor, claiming, against their better judgment, that it was "inconceivable that anyone in Vienna could possibly be without shelter during this cold season without bearing the blame for this himself."[69] Thus the City of Vienna took the position that the "innocent" could not be homeless, and directed the police to commit the homeless into the municipal *Werkhaus*, unless they put them straight into prison for some delinquency or other.

In those *Werkhäuser*, crowded together under the most miserable conditions, they had to paste together paper bags and pouches, make paper decorations, count and pack hairpins, fill straw mattresses, mend shoes, do laundry, and clean up and repair the shelter. The number of people in the *Werkhaus* climbed from 13,300 in 1905 to 67,100 in 1908, with costs decreasing from 59.92 to 43.10 heller per diem, despite inflation. Of that amount, merely 11 heller was for board, which only covered water, soup, and bread.[70]

Lowest on the social ladder were those homeless who, despite regulations, were forced to spend their nights in the open, in factory halls, under the streetcar arches, in the widely extended, stinking sewage system, and in the warm compost heaps in the gardener's shops. When they were picked up by the police, they were committed to the *Werkhaus*, arrested, or deported.

Hitler writes in Mein Kampf: *After the turn of the century, Vienna was, socially speaking, one of the most backward cities in Europe. Dazzling riches and loathsome poverty alternated sharply. . . . Outside the palaces on the Ring loitered thousands of unemployed, and beneath this* Via Triumphalis *of old Austria dwelt the homeless in the gloom and mud of the canals.*[71] And during one of his monologues he said, *In Vienna more than eight thousand people lived in the canals before the World War. These are rats that creep out when a revolution approaches.*[72] Max Winter described the homeless by the furnaces of the brickworks: "Dressed in rags, some barefoot, others in torn shoes. Everyone without cover, at best their coat, wet from the rain, spread over their shoulders, two bricks with their hats on top of them as pillows, the floor strewn with pieces of brick and dung as a bed. One of them with his upper body stark naked so he can escape the lice, another one who has collared one of the wheelbarrows as a bedstead."[73]

Yet here and in the sewage system the "oldtimers" defended the warm spots against newcomers as if it were their property. In this *subterranean Vienna*—to use the title of Winter's collection of social reportage—might was right. Homeless women with children, old, sick, or shy people did not have the least chance to make it there.

Growing Hatred of Foreigners

The housing shortage, inflation, and pressing unemployment fanned the flames of xenophobia in Vienna and exacerbated ethnic conflicts as the flood of immigrants continued to rise, aided by modern means of transportation, railways in particular. The fast extension of industry attracted more and more laborers. Between 1880 and 1910, for example, the number of factories in Vienna's outer districts increased by 133 percent.[74] It was impossible to keep up with the development of new apartments or social institutions. Hospitals, foundling wards, schools, and universities were overcrowded. More and more people called for giving natives a special status in hospitals and orphanages and for excluding certain groups, such as Eastern Jews and Slavs.

On December 2, 1908, the day of Franz Josef's anniversary, German students grabbed fellow students at the cafeteria of Vienna University and threw them out. German-radical deputy Eduard von Stransky justified this in Parliament by saying that the Slavs, in cahoots with the Jews, had "prepared and instigated rallies against our university's German character—a humane institution that is financed by public funds." He said the German students were thinking, "We now have enough, we don't want to be together with those people, the cafeteria should be segregated, non-German students and Jews should put their money together and found a non-German cafeteria. The Germans want their own cafeteria."[75] The cafeteria remained a place of conflict until this goal was reached. A cafeteria for Germans only was followed by a cafeteria for Jews only, then by one for Italians only, and so on.

After this dubious success other social institutions became targets: thus the Academic Association for the Care of Sick Students decided to collect dues at four times the regular rate from foreigners, Jews, and Czechs. The Zionist *Neue National-Zeitung* commented angrily, "Surely one can't create a social association in order to serve national aspirations . . . particularly not if you exclude poor Jews after successfully trying to collect donations from rich Jews!"[76]

In 1907 the Pan-German writer Jörg Franz von Liebenfels published a brochure entitled "Race and Welfare, a Call for a Boycott of Random Charity," in which he attempted to prove "that at least one third of diseases are a result of one's own fault or one's race," including tuberculosis, for "particularly people with mixed parentage have a great tendency toward it, and often sexual excesses are the underlying reason." He continued, "All those disgusting skin diseases originate in the East and are really diseases of filth and race. Even those of a higher race will be infected, as modern life, which no longer knows any boundaries between races, forces them to associate with members of lower races."

"Bad race," Lanz argued, was also the reason why "insane asylums and loonybins" were overcrowded: "If the federal government pursued a racial economy and gently annihilated those families with hereditary impairments, it would be possible to save a considerable part of the nine million kronen per annum!" He continued by recommending to make charitable donations dependent on race and only to consider "people with gold-blond hair, blue (or blue-gray) eyes, a rosy complexion, elongated skulls and elongated faces, high and small straight noses, well-proportioned mouths, healthy white teeth, round chins, with a balanced, tall physique, narrow hands, and narrow feet."[77] Even though no sensible person in Vienna took someone like Lanz seriously, his outpourings still indicate the spirit of the time in a perverted extreme.

Fearing deportation, a fate threatening anyone in Vienna who was unable to get by in a normal way, tens of thousands of unemployed immigrants lived underground. The names of those threatened with deportation and those who already had received a warning were listed in a "Register of Poor People's Institutions" in all public offices. Furthermore, the monthly *Blätter für das Armenwesen der Stadt Wien* (Publications concerning the poor in the City of Vienna) published a regular column with new names to be added to the register "for the protection against the improper collection of relief." This was an attempt to target particularly those "individuals who have come to Vienna on a chance, without being able to take root here," among them "vagrants," that is to say, the homeless, those unable to work on account of age or health, and those immigrants who "are incapable of withstanding the economic battle, in spite of numerously repeated subsidies, and are thus responsible for a critical increase in the already large population of poor natives." What was necessary in those cases was "the humanely executed resettlement of people in jeopardy in their native surroundings." The City of Vienna, the publication claimed, was unable to "shoulder the task of providing for the poor of all provinces of the monarchy."[78]

Hitler at the Homeless Shelter in Meidling

Otherwise so talkative, Hitler kept quiet about the details of those humiliating weeks and months. It is certain, and by way of a notice in the police records of 1910, that in the fall of 1909 he was so poor that he had to spend the night in the homeless shelter in Meidling.

This huge shelter, which in consideration for the decent citizens was built behind the Meidlingen cemetery, far from the residents, was not opened until 1908. It offered for free protection from the cold, food, showers, and baths to some thousand people. Contrary to the old municipal shelter and the notorious *Werkhaus* it was quite sought after as a place to spend the night. In the winter, hundreds of homeless waited to be

Dining room for men at the homeless shelter in Meidling

admitted night after night in long lines—and all too frequently were rejected because the shelter was overcrowded. Each night, groups of guards were watching, ready immediately to intervene in case of a riot.

Many people spent the nights hungry and freezing on the pavement in front of the shelter to at least have a chance the following night. The newspapers never picked up these conditions unless once again a child froze or starved to death in front of the shelter's gates, someone had committed suicide in desperation, or someone critically ill had not received any medical attention and had died outside the gates.

This shelter, and a second one in the Third District, was run by the privately owned, very efficient Shelter Association for the Homeless and almost exclusively financed by private donations and membership dues. Court bookseller Künast held the post of association director, and many prominent donors assisted him, among them the operetta composer Karl Millöcker. The association handed out clothing and financial contributions and, supported by the Social Democrats, ran the by far most successful job-placement program.

In view of the pressing need the association was downright desperate to gain new members and donations when in 1909 the City of Vienna cut the promised subsidies from 50,000 to 30,000 kronen per annum.[79] The *Arbeiterzeitung* commented: "Thus month after month the beggar's bag is being waved, with the municipality of Vienna, whose real social obligation is to help, idly watching. The fact that in the month of March more than 3,000 children—100 per day—had to seek shelter, doesn't in the least concern the gentlemen. After all, it's not their own children, and the others may rot and perish."[80]

The article said it was "Vienna's disgrace that it has no money to spare for this important responsibility. There has always been money for ... receiving princes and the hunting exhibition, or for banquets and drinking sprees," and certainly for the parade anyway, "but for the aim of no one living in this city having to spend the night outdoors, for women and children not having to be turned away from the shelter's gates, for that Vienna has no money. It is time to put an end to this disgrace." The article urgently demanded that municipal shelters be built—but to no avail.[81]

The problem was also exacerbated by the hospitals being overcrowded and many sick people seeking shelter. In its own column entitled "Vienna's Hospital Disgrace," the Arbeiterzeitung kept pillorying new cases of mothers and their feverish children or accident victims being sent from hospital to hospital and rejected everywhere.

At the Meidlingen shelter regulations for hygiene and order were strict. Admittance procedures were like a ritual: the "father of the house" received the new arrival, who would remain anonymous, and gave him a ticket that admitted him to the disinfection room and the bathroom and hall. The sick received emergency treatment. While the shelter occupants were washing up, their clothes were cleaned and disinfected. Then free soup and bread were handed out at a counter. With the ringing of a bell the dormitories were opened, where wire cots stood one next to the other. The next morning the shelter had to be vacated by 9:00 at the latest.

This institution served an important social function besides being a shelter and furnishing preliminary provisions: the occupants supported each other. Those with experience frequently gave the newcomers crucial advice regarding money or services, such as what shelter or Wärmestube could be recommended, where work was to be found, where begging was worthwhile, and what scheme would work. Each night, the large dormitories turned into bazaars. For a little money or a cigarette, tailors and cobblers would repair what was in most desperate need of fixing. Trade with tobacco, schnapps, and all kinds of things flourished. The most sought-after items were shelter tickets for additional nights; the shelter offered free lodging for one week only. Experts, however, had a special method: they stood in line for tickets but stayed elsewhere and sold the night places on the black market.

Hitler too found the help of an experienced colleague in the shelter: Reinhold Hanisch, who occupied the cot next to him. He lived under the assumed name Fritz Walter, was a dubious figure and something of a bum. He constantly moved from quarter to quarter and on his registration slips kept stating different facts: as his year of birth, 1884, 1886, 1889, and 1893; as his profession, salesman, stagehand, helper, servant, or draftsman; and as his place of birth, various towns in Bohemia, usually Grünwald near Gablenz.[82]

Hanisch passed on his impression of twenty-year-old Hitler: "The Asylum meant to him an entirely new world where he could not find his way." Hanisch said that the young man had seemed sad and was dead-tired and starved, with sore feet. Rain and disinfection had turned his blue-checked suit lilac. In his dire straits he must have long since sold the belongings he brought with him from Linz. For in the shelter, all he owned were the shabby clothes he was wearing.

According to Hanisch, Hitler said that his last landlady had evicted him. He then had spent a few evenings in a cheap cafe at Kaiserstrasse in the Sixth District, until he ran out of money. And so he had spent several nights on park benches, but the police had chased him away. One night in his need he had approached a drunk gentleman, begging him for some money, but the man, brandishing his cane, had insulted him. He hadn't eaten anything for days.

Their fellow occupants gave him a little bread. An old beggar advised him as to where he could get free soup and medical attention. Hanisch was popular because he told stories: "I spoke the Berlin dialect and all of them took me for a Prussian." In reality he had spent three months in jail in 1907 in Berlin for theft and six months in 1908 for forgery.[83] According to Hanisch, Hitler constantly wanted to hear stories about Germany, "because he was quite enthusiastic about the Reich."[84]

Because they were allowed to stay at the Meidlingen shelter only briefly, Hanisch reported, they both went to other shelters together, for example, to Jewish Baron Königswarter's private *Wärmestube* in Edberg, which was open at night as well, from there on to Favoriten, then back to Meidling—and so forth.

During the day they looked for work. After witnessing several futile attempts on the part of the young man, Hanisch came to the conclusion that young Hitler was much too weak and clumsy for hard work. Once, he wrote, a few men were needed for digging a ditch. Hanisch, however, had advised Hitler against it, for: "I knew Hitler couldn't have done such work for an hour." Hanisch also said, "I never have seen him do any hard work, nor did I hear from him the story that he did a worker's job in the building industry. Builders employ only strong and husky men."

According to Hanisch, Hitler sometimes went to Western Railway Station to carry passengers' bags. When winter set in, the unemployed stood in line to shovel snow. But, Hanisch said, Hitler didn't own a winter coat, was freezing miserably and coughing, and did that no more than a few times either. In short, the helpless and frail young man could hardly make any money and therefore was very poor, even compared to the other homeless. When Hanisch asked him what he expected from the future, Hitler answered: "I don't know myself." Hanisch commented: "I have never seen such helpless letting-down in distress."

Hanisch asked his young colleague a lot of questions. Hitler told him he had attended the Art Academy. Continuously looking for ways to make money, Hanisch now made a suggestion: If Hitler was an artist, why didn't he paint postcards? They could be sold in taverns. But Hitler did not dare walk into taverns as a salesman: he was too poorly dressed, plus he was afraid the police would make trouble, because he had no license. And so Hanisch offered to sell them for him. They agreed to split the profits.

However, Hitler had no money to buy paints and paper. Didn't he have any relatives, Hanisch asked, whom he could ask for money? The young man hesitated for a long time, but was finally willing to write a letter, yet he had no stationery. In the end, Hanisch reported, he and another fellow occupant took him to the Café Arthaber opposite the Southern Railway Station, so he could write a letter to "his sister" there, asking for money. This could have been neither Hitler's half-sister Angela Raubal nor his thirteen-year-old sister Paula. Only "Haniaunt" could have been the addressee, who by now lived in Waldviertel as a maid with her sister Theresia Schmidt. She helped out again.

Shortly before Christmas 1909 Hitler, standing in line before the Meidlingen shelter, pulled a fifty-kronen note out of his pocket. Hanisch wrote: "I told him not to show it so, because if anyone saw it he might be robbed or someone might ask for a loan." Now they acquired the supplies he needed to paint watercolors, plus a winter coat. Since, according to Hanisch, Hitler was afraid the secondhand clothes dealer in the Jewish quarter was going to cheat him, he purchased a coat in the Federal pawnshop, the Dorotheum, for twelve kronen.

Now Hitler began to paint postcards. Because the Wärmestuben were overcrowded, the only places where he could work were cheap cafes. Hanisch, who hoped to make some money himself through his friend, urged him to work, and proved to be an accomplished salesman. Thus they succeeded: the two of them were now making enough money to spare themselves both the humiliating search for strenuous odd jobs and standing in line for hours every day in front of some filthy place to stay for a night or a homeless shelter.

Hitler's darkest period in Vienna was over. According to the police registration records, on February 9, 1910, he moved into the Municipality of Vienna's men's hostel in the workers' district Brigittenau, where he stayed until May 1913, when he left for Munich.

From his safe, warm abode in the men's hostel he could follow the bad news from the Meidlingen shelter. A riot erupted there on April 3, 1910: some two hundred people seeking shelter were turned down and tried to take the overcrowded place by storm, but police used force to prevent them from doing so. The *Arbeiterzeitung* commented, full of anger and disgust, "Thus Vienna's disgrace has been made permanent, the disgrace of rich Vienna, where night after night hundreds of people are forced to crawl into miserable caves and we can't offer them shelter but only police sabers instead."[85]

In the fall of 1910 there was a small rally: as usual, the shelter refused to let forty-six families stay after one week, and in their helplessness the 108 people concerned went right through town to city hall to seek help there. The spectacle they created did not do them any good. The municipal administration did what it always did: it submitted those homeless with Vienna as their legal residence to the *Werkhaus*, and deported the others to their native towns.

If Hitler had been apprehended homeless and unemployed, the police would have forced him too after a warning to return to his sisters and his guardian in his native Linz. For Vienna was not his legal residence, and he could not claim welfare there.

6

As a Painter in the Men's Hostel

The Model Institution

The six-story men's hostel in Vienna-Brigittenau, 27 Meldemannstrasse, was among the most modern in Europe. Opened in 1905, it was funded by the private Emperor Franz Josef I Anniversary Foundation for Public Housing and Charitable Institutions, which was financed through donations, receiving significant contributions from Jewish families, particularly from Baron Nathaniel Rothschild and the Gutmann family. The hostel was administrated by the City of Vienna. The first blueprints caused a stir during an exhibition in the Künstlerhaus (artists' house). The hostel was not to have common sleeping areas but individual compartments for each of its up to 544 guests, excellent hygienic conditions, and many social events to enhance "education and sociability."

Brigittenau, at the outskirts of the city, had many new industrial plants, a great need for laborers, and the most rapid population growth in all of Vienna's districts. Its population increased from 37,000 in 1890 to 101,000 in 1910.[1] Most new residents were young single men who worked in the new factories and, because there were no cheap apartments, found places to spend the night as lodgers in overcrowded workers' apartments.

This new men's hostel was supposed to decrease the number of lodg-ers and thus protect the compromised morals of their host families. The foundation's principal trustee, Prince Carl Auersperg, pointed this out on the occasion of Emperor Franz Josef's visit in 1905: "In particular, this men's hostel seeks to give an actual example of the . . . chance to effec-tively fight the pernicious phenomenon of lodging, to offer single laborers a home instead of the dull and overcrowded emergency quarters, provid-ing not only an affordable place to stay but also providing the opportunity to nourish body and mind."[2]

Rent for one sleeping place was only 2.5 kronen per week, an amount a single handiman or craftsman with an annual income of 1,000 kronen could afford. In Vienna the hostel was thus praised as "a miracle of a divine lodging place on earth" and "a marvel of elegance and afforda-bility."

Viennese journalist Ernst Kläger, disguised as someone seeking shel-ter, spent a night at the hostel and wrote an article about it. The area between downtown Vienna and Brigittenau, beyond the Danube Canal, was desolate. Kläger passed through Wallensteinstrasse, "the main street of the poor people's district. It was around six o'clock, the time of day when the residents of Brigittenau take a walk of sorts. Laborers back home from work amble up and down the street with their wives and kids, past poorly lit shop windows with teasing arrangements of cheap goods with tags attached to them. Young fellows shunning the light lean on motley streetcorners. They are usually accompanied by hookers." Kläger walked on through narrow side streets and "uncanny gloom. The pavement is rather shot, and there are such few streetlights that you can't rid yourself of a sense of danger."

The Brigittenau district was not yet fully electrified. In the First District there were 231,396 incandescent lamps, and in the Sixth District, where Hitler initially lived, 77,076. Brigittenau had only 7,523 lamps. Even more telling is the number of incandescent lamps in taverns and cafes: in the First District, 11,015; in the Sixth District, 3,291; but in the large Twentieth District, there were only seventeen incandescent lamps in taverns and cafes, which indicates the small number of eating estab-lishments and the antiquated conditions in those that did exist; they still used kerosene.[3]

Finally Kläger found the new hostel: "A large electric arc lamp over the gate guides those who are stumbling up the hill of dug-up soil. Com-pared to the other, smaller houses around and the bare factory buildings in the back, the shelter looks proud. I open the door and to my surprise find myself in a vestibule which no good hotel would put to shame. I am embraced by comfortably warm air." The men's hostel had both electric and gas lights and was heated by a modern, central low-pressure steam heater. At the counter the reporter had no difficulty obtaining a ticket for one night for thirty kreuzer (sixty heller). Kläger described the dining room in the upper mezzanine: "Again I am pleasantly surprised by the elegance of the room, which is lighted by two arc lamps and whose walls are covered halfway up with pale-green tiles."

Then he tried the dirt-cheap food and found the meals "all very good." The occupants spent only an average of half a krone per day for food in the hostel—for breakfast, dinner, and snacks—in other words, only approximately fifteen kronen per month.

Kläger watched the lodgers: "The door opens constantly, and someone in a bad suit, usually a bag under his arm, enters. One could tell that most occupants were incredibly tired." Because most of them worked during the day, it was quiet in the afternoon. Yet in the evening "it was lively, gregarious, but by no means boisterous, until around ten-thirty."[4]

There were kitchenettes with gas rings and kitchen utensils for those who wanted to prepare their own food. Cooking teams were formed: one of the unemployed would remain in the hostel, go shopping, and cook for some of the laborers, and in return could eat for free. Initially Hitler tried to cook, but with little success, for according to Reinhold Hanisch, the Upper Austrian milk soup he proudly offered had curdled and turned out more like cheese.

Kläger made his rounds through the shelter and reported: "Right next to the dining room is a large, very nicely furnished reading room with two sections, one for smokers and one for nonsmokers. It has dailies and a nice library which is available to the lodgers. Most books are easy-to-digest novels and writings on popular science.[5] There are also desks with the necessary utensils for doing one's correspondence." On Sunday afternoons there was entertainment plus the opportunity for continuing education through concerts and lectures. On the lower mezzanine there were laundry and shoe-shining rooms, luggage and bicycle racks, and a cobbler and tailor room.[6]

Hygienic conditions were exemplary: a house doctor practiced for free, offering outpatient services in a "sick room" for minor illnesses. As in all shelters, there was a disinfection room for delousing the newcomers. Apart from lavatories, there were also a shaving room and a shower room with sixteen showers, twenty-five footbaths, and four bathtubs. One bath was twenty-five heller, about a third of the price in a public bath. All this bore fruit in the cholera year of 1910; the dreaded disease spared the fully occupied men's hostel.

The sleeping wing, comprising the four top floors, was opened at 8:00 P.M. and had to be vacated by 9:00 A.M. It consisted of long rows of tiny, separate sleeping compartments, each measuring 4.6 × 6.9 feet. There was enough room for a bed, a small table, a clothes rack, and a mirror. Permanent guests had their sheets changed every seven days, and one-night guests every day, as in hotels. As an extra convenience, each compartment had a door with a lock and a lightbulb. It was probably the first time Hitler had had electric light in his room.

There were constantly new occupants in the men's hostel, but altogether their age and social background remained constant: some 70 percent of the men—with a minimum age of fourteen—were under thirty-five years old. At 70 percent, laborers and handimen represented the largest group, and among them, those in the iron industry were in the majority: keysmiths, smiths, turners, and furnace men.[7] Yet other occupations were represented as well: coachmen, store clerks, waiters, apprentices, gardeners, many casual laborers and unemployed workers, but also some run-down aristocrats, unsuccessful artists, and divorced and bankrupt men. Some 80 percent of the hostel's occupants had an annual income of less than 1,200 kronen, which was below the lowest taxable income bracket.

The occupants' backgrounds were indicative of the multiethnic empire: 43.5 percent were from Lower Austria and Vienna, 23 percent from Bohemia and Moravia, 11.6 percent from Hungary, between 2 and 3 percent each from Styria, Upper Austria, Galicia, and Silesia; others came from Croatia-Slavonia, Tyrol, Bukovina, the coastal area, Salzburg, Dalmatia, and Bosnia. As for the foreigners, 4.5 percent were from the German Reich, 1.3 percent from Italy, and .9 percent from Russia.[8]

One example, discovered by accident, may serve to illustrate how disparate and complex here as everywhere the fronts in the Dual Monarchy were: In August 1909 a shelter occupant named Wilhelm Mandl was arrested after he threw a stone into a guardroom during German-national riots against the Czechs in Vienna.[9] Mandl was a photographer from Hungary with a prior conviction, three years Hitler's senior, who for decades lived in men's hostels and emergency shelters. That he was of Jewish faith[10] but an aggressive German nationalist provides insight into the complexity of the Dual Monarchy's "people's Babylon." Life in this multiethnic men's community must have been accordingly turbulent.

The shelter's administrator was strict and feared as an authoritarian. He lived in the shelter and demanded discipline, cleanliness, and quiet. Women were strictly forbidden to visit, even in the community rooms. Any violation of the house rules was punished by eviction.

Even though a similar shelter was opened in the workers' district Hernals at 89 Wurlitzergasse in the summer of 1910—where, contrary to some claims, Hitler never lived—the two shelters with 1,434 beds altogether did not nearly meet the demand. Furthermore, in 1911 by far most of the shelter occupants at Meldemannstrasse had been in the shelter for more than a year, [11] which left hardly any room for newcomers. Without being forced to, no one would relinquish his place.

Producing Paintings

In the safe, meticulously clean atmosphere of the men's hostel, Hitler sat in the nonsmoking section of the reading room and painted his pictures. The work went well. For the first time in his life Hitler was able to make a living by painting. Supposedly he had no artistic ambition. Art that aims at bread, he would say later on—albeit not in reference to his own work—is *for wage workers, commissioned by the consumer, nothing but a confectioner's artful tart or the rolls the baker sends along with the morning coffee.*[12]

Hitler soon no longer confined himself to offering painted postcards in taverns, but made pointed inquiries of craftsmen—for example, frame manufacturers who needed small watercolors to highlight their frames in the shop windows. In April 1910 upholsterer Karl Pichler in the working-class district Hernals, 30 Hernalser Hauptstrasse, ordered a spring and a fall landscape from him.[13] Later on Hitler also got commissions from the glazier Samuel Morgenstern.

Hitler painted what tourists wanted to see, above all, views of Vienna: Saint Stephen's Cathedral, Minorite and Scottish Church, Karl'skirche, City Hall, and Parliament. (Social romanticism could be found in Ratzenstadl, a run-down quarter in the Sixth District.) He copied nearly all his paintings from originals. But occasionally he had to draw from nature. Early one morning Hitler and Hanisch went near Gumpendorf church, a view of which had been commissioned but for which there was no model, to make sketches. But Hitler, Hanisch says, had nothing but excuses: it was too cold, his fingers were too stiff. At any rate, he produced nothing.

The daughter of frame manufacturer Jakob Altenberg complained about the poor quality of Hitler's paintings: "These were the cheapest items we ever sold. The only ones who showed any interest in them were tourists who were looking for inexpensive souvenirs."[14]

Between 1933 and 1945, however, Hitler's paintings were praised as great works of art. The cult around the Führer's artistic past and the steep

The Michaelerplatz in an eighteenth-century view, copied by "A. Hitler"; at the left, the Loos House during Hitler's time

price increases for his paintings went so far that Hitler felt forced to step in lest he be embarrassed in front of experts. In 1944, when the price for a "genuine Hitler" was up to ten thousand marks, he said to his friend, the photographer Heinrich Hoffmann, *Even today these things shouldn't cost more than 150 or 200 reichsmark. It is insane to spend more than that on them. After all, I didn't want to become an artist, I painted that stuff only to make a living and afford going to school.*[15] On March 28, 1938, he prohibited any publication of his works.[16]

At the time, however, he made only three to five kronen per painting, out of which amount Hitler had to buy paints and supplies. In order to make a living for himself and Hanisch, he thus would have to paint at least one picture per day—which he could not. To be sure, the two men now could afford room and board at the hostel, but hardly anything beyond that, above all, no new clothing and shoes. Hanisch urged the reluctant Hitler to work faster, with the result that their friendship cooled down drastically. Under Hanisch's angry eyes, Hitler increasingly attached himself to another hostel occupant: Josef Neumann. According to Vienna's Registration Office, Neumann was eleven years Hitler's senior, born in Vöslau in Lower Austria in 1878, single, Jewish, and a copper cleaner by profession. He was registered at the shelter at Meldemannstrasse from January 29 until July 12, 1910.[17] According to Hanisch, Neumann traded with all kinds of goods and works with another Jew who peddled secondhand clothes. Hanisch was particularly peeved that the two of them also sold paintings for Hitler.

Discussions in the Reading Room

Later Hanisch would criticize Hitler vociferously for having been lazy and refusing to paint from morning till night. Other interests, he reports, were more important to him: "In the morning he wouldn't begin work until he'd read several newspapers, and if anyone should come in with another newspaper he'd read that too."

Hanisch writes that Hitler's speeches and participation in political discussions took up most of his working hours: "It was impossible to make Hitler work. In the morning he sat in the hall of the Home, and was supposed to be making drawings while I was busy canvassing the frame manufacturers and upholsterers. But then political discussion would start and generally Hitler would become the ringleader. When I came back in the evening I often had to take the T-square out of his hands, because he would be swinging it over his head, making a speech."

According to Hanisch, Hitler revered Gottfried Semper and Karl May, got all excited about the Catholics and the Jesuits, went into the history of the revolution of 1848, and liked to lecture on Arthur Schopenhauer, the German nationalists' favorite philosopher. Hanisch reports that an older colleague in the shelter, called "the professor," had asked him whether he had ever read Schopenhauer. Hanisch writes, "Hitler turned crimson and said he had read some. The old gentleman said that he should speak about things that he understood." After that Hitler was more careful.

In the men's hostel, Hitler praised certain politicians. Hanisch says, "He was a great admirer of Schönerer. Karl Hermann Wolf too was his man." Schönerer, the leader of the Pan-Germans, and Wolf, the leader of the German Radicals, represented the most extreme German-national parties of the Hapsburg monarchy.

Hitler's admiration for Vienna's most popular politician, Karl Lueger, was also obvious. According to Hanisch, around Easter 1910—the time of Lueger's death—Hitler, "as if intoxicated," talked about a movie about a people's tribune who as an orator swayed the masses: "Hitler was aflame with the idea that this was the way to found a new party. I laughed at him and didn't take him seriously." Hanisch continues, "One day I told him to stop talking, he really didn't look the promoter of a political party, and he must do some serious work."[18]

As everywhere in the Dual Monarchy, the question of nationalities was discussed at the men's hostel as well. According to Hanisch, Hitler took a strictly centralistic position, just like the Schönerians. Hanisch claims that he defended Berlin's policies against the Polish minority in the German Reich and allegedly even expressed sympathy for the German minority's forcible denationalization in Hungary. "Hitler said this was unavoidable; a state must try to create a uniform nationality within its borders." Hanisch's comment: "I was very angry that Hitler always took the government's part. Whether the ruthless policy of Magyarization was discussed, or the policy in Posen, or Upper Silesia, Hitler invariably approved of all such violent methods as necessary for the state's sake." Hanisch had always opposed Hitler's view in such debates, "but opposition was useless because of his shouting." As a politician Hitler also would invariably criticize the Hapsburgs' federal principle toward the vastly different crown provinces. Thus he said in a speech in Munich in 1923: *Austria is lacking the spirit that is necessary to preserve a state. . . . Why did Austria not Germanize Trieste? To accomplish that you need an iron fist, an iron will, and that was lacking. Why? Because the press preached kindness and democracy. Yet countries have never been colonialized with kindness and democracy.*[19]

According to Hanisch, in 1910 there was also a discussion on Empress Elizabeth, who had erected a monument to the German poet Heinrich Heine on the Greek isle of Corfu. At first, this statement is somewhat confusing, inasmuch as Elizabeth, Emperor Franz Josef's wife, had been murdered twelve years earlier, in 1898. Still, Hanisch makes sense: in 1910 there were indeed renewed eager debates about Elizabeth, because

Emperor William II bought her castle Achilleion on Corfu from her estate and now, as a raging opponent of Heine, made it his first business to have the monument removed. Even during her lifetime, the Austrian empress had fallen under serious attack for her enthusiasm for Heine and had been counted among the "Jew lackeys."[20] Again a wave of Heine abuse swept the anti-Semitic press. If Hanisch is to be believed, Hitler defended Heine. He allegedly said that it was sad for Germany not to honor Heine's accomplishment with a monument and that although he did not agree with Heine's opinions, his poetry demanded respect.

Hitler diligently studied anti-Semitism. He was also strongly influenced by Jewish friends in the men's hostel, and he read pro-Semitic literature. Thus, Hanisch says, Hitler had quoted the parable of the ring from Lessing's *Nathan the Wise*, a parable of religious tolerance. Lessing had portrayed the Jews as the first civilized nation because they had been the first to abandon polytheism for the belief in one God. According to Hanisch, Hitler even had denied that Jewish capitalists were usurers and emphasized that the major share of capital was in the hands of Christians. It was the nobility, Hitler supposedly said, that practiced usury by using Jewish agents. Hitler praised the Jews' charitableness, mentioning great examples from history, such as Joseph von Sonnenfels, who during Maria Theresia's reign abolished torture. Hanisch also reports that when someone argued that Jews could not be artists, Hitler mentioned Felix Mendelssohn-Bartholdy and Jacques Offenbach as examples to the contrary.

What Hitler supposedly admired most about the Jews is the way they survived despite all persecutions. He praised Rothschild for refusing to convert simply in order to be permitted to practice in court. During nightly walks, Hanisch says, they discussed Moses and the Ten Commandments, which Hitler admired as the basis of all civilization.

Hitler congenially discussed Zionism with Neumann. Hanisch writes: "Neumann said that if the Jews should leave Austria it would be a great misfortune for the country, for they would carry with them all the Austrian capital. Hitler said no, that the money would obviously be confiscated, as it was not Jewish but Austrian. Then Neumann always made a joke; it would nevertheless be a misfortune for Austria, because when the Jews crossed the Red Sea all the coffeehouses in Leopoldstadt were deserted." The question as to what should happen with Jewish property in case of an "exodus" from Europe to Palestine was the subject of intense public debate at the time.

According to Hanisch, another current subject of debate, the charge of ritual murder, was also discussed. This was doubtless the consequence of the wildly controversial effort by some Liberals, among them Tomás G. Masaryk and pacifist Bertha von Suttner, to reopen the ritual murder trial of 1899 against Leopold Hilsner, a Jewish cobbler's apprentice from Galicia, in order to prove his innocence—and the absurdity of ritual murder charges in general. The liberal newspapers and, above all, the "Defense League against Anti-Semitism," supported the effort. The anti-Semites of all nationalities, however, from the Pan-Germans to the Czech National Socialists, upheld that the judgment had been fair. In this debate too, Hanisch maintains, young Hitler did not side with the anti-Semites but dismissed the ritual murder charge and remarked "that it was absolute nonsense, a groundless slander."

Hanisch, who was clearly jealous, leaves the impression that then twenty-one-year-old Hitler was entirely under the influence of his close Jewish friend Neumann. Yet young Hitler's stand was not unambiguous. When a foreman from Bavaria wondered why the Jews always remained strangers in nations, Hitler replied, according to Hanisch, "because they were a different race. Also, he said that the Jews had a different smell." Hanisch also says that "Hitler himself often remarked that descendants of Jews are very radical and have terroristic inclinations. He said that for a Jew to take advantage, to a certain extent, of a non-Jew, was not punishable according to the Talmud"—which is also an opinion that can be found in virtually any anti-Semitic newspaper of the time. According to Hanisch, Hitler liked to quote the saying that the end justifies the means and simply incorporated anti-Semitism as a powerful slogan in his "party program," which was apparently much discussed.

These statements offer a confusing picture—which in part may be due to the way Hanisch, who was not interested in politics, renders them. Whatever we may think of these statements, one thing is for certain: young Hitler must have thoroughly dealt with Judaism and anti-Semitism at that time, garnering his information certainly not from anti-Semitic sources alone.

Hanisch wrote his account in the thirties, with a clear anti-Semitic undertone and the obvious aim of discrediting the by now most famous anti-Semite, Hitler. At the time, Hanisch says, Hitler used to wear a long jacket that Neumann had not been able to hawk in the Jewish quarter and had given to him. The garment was apparently kaftanlike, although other witnesses described it as rather more like an old frock coat. At any rate, in the back the jacket had long frock tails, for—as Hanisch reports— the fellow occupants used this unusual piece of clothing to play a practical joke on Hitler: one colleague tied Hitler's long tails to the bench while someone else talked politics with him. "All of them then used to contradict him, a thing he could never stand. He'd leap to his feet, drag the bench after him with a great rumble. . . . When he got excited Hitler couldn't restrain himself. He screamed, and fidgeted with his hands." Hanisch comments mockingly that for some of their colleagues Hitler's ferocious political speeches were "a sort of amusement. . . . There was continual debating; often the Home looked as if an election campaign were in progress. . . . But when he was quiet it was quite different; he seemed then to have a fair amount of self-control and acted in quite a dignified manner. When speaking he was rigid."

Hanisch puts it on even thicker when he writes that Hitler "wore an incredibly greasy derby on the back of his head. His hair was long and tangled and he grew a beard on his chin such as we Christians seldom have, though one is not uncommon in Leopoldstadt or the Jewish ghetto." Somewhere else Hanisch employs more than patently anti-Semitic language when he maintains that at the time Hitler looked very Jewish: "Also he had big feet, as a desert wanderer must have."

Hanisch claims that all of Hitler's new friends at the men's hostel were Jews. Because Hanisch names names, it is easy to verify his statement by way of Vienna's Registration Office: "Robinsohn," the one-eyed locksmith he mentions, who allegedly received disability insurance and frequently helped Hitler out, was Simon Robinson, born in 1864 in Lisko, Galicia, a locksmith's assistant who from January 19, 1912, to November 27, 1913, lived off and on at the men's shelter at Meldemannstrasse.

Neumann's friend, who, as Hanisch reports, helped with the selling of Hitler's paintings, also can be found in the files of Vienna's Registration Office. He was Siegfried Löffner, born in Windig Jeniklau near Iglau in Moravia in 1872, a sales representative. He had a wife and two children in Teplitz in Bohemia but since 1914 was considered divorced. Thirty extant registration slips between 1914 and 1936 document a life in Vienna between men's and singles' hostels. For unknown reasons, however, there are no entries for him for the years before 1914.

Joint Enterprises

Hitler usually stayed away from social events. He did not participate in the popular nightly drinking, apparently already a teetotaler, as Kubizek corroborates. Lack of money also forced him to quit smoking: *I threw my cigarettes into the Danube and never took them up again.* His proud conclusion at the Wolfsschanze in 1942: *I am convinced that if I were a smoker,*

I would not have been able to withstand the troubles that have burdened me for such a long time. The German people perhaps owes its salvation to this![21]

Because the young man could not keep up in conversations about women either, he was regarded as strange. At eight at night, when the sleeping compartments were opened, he retired to his room with its light bulb (which was considered a luxury) and began his second life, into which the others did not get a glimpse, the time of his nightly "studies," a habit Hitler would keep all his life.[22] We have to believe what Hitler writes in *Mein Kampf* about this period: *I painted to make a living and studied for pleasure.*[23]

Hitler rarely participated in joint enterprises. Once, Hanisch relates, they went to the Prater together to see the American "scenic railway," a sort of grotto railway with opera scenes and gramophone music, among them a scene from *Tannhäuser*. Hanisch reports that on the way home Hitler explained the opera to his friends and sang some passages. Hanisch comments: "For Wagner he had great enthusiasm, and said sometimes that opera is really the best divine service." Mozart's *Magic Flute* was also played in the scenic railway. But, Hitler said, Mozart fit more in the old sentimental times and had been outlived. Wagner, on the other hand, had been a fighter. This attraction in the Prater must have served as a poor substitute for the opera performances Hitler was missing.

The Prater was the meeting and amusement place of the little people. Bohemian maids also spent their little leisure time there—according to the servants' statutes, they had seven hours off every other week—and met their admirers at dances. The writer Felix Salten remarked about this: "An entire young mankind, having no home in the vast city, being lost in the maelstrom of this buzzing life and lonely, finds a piece of home here, in the smoky-thirsty hall. . . . The simple, human drives reveal themselves simply here, as nowhere else. Woman's lust for man. Man's lust for woman. . . . The entire hall is steaming with youth, desire, intoxication, and giddiness."[24] Kubizek reports that Hitler was indignant about the Prater's silly wine-induced merriment.

Kubizek also tells the story of a joint visit to the Prater. However, Hitler did not like it: "He didn't understand people who wasted their valuable time with such silly stuff. When roaring laughter broke out in front of some attraction in a show booth, he would just indignantly shake his head at so much stupidity and ask me angrily whether I could understand why these people were laughing." Kubizek continues, "Furthermore, the motley crew of Viennese, Czechs, Magyars, Slovaks, Romanians, Croats, Italians, and God knows what else, who were pushing through the Prater, thoroughly disgusted him. . . . He found the motley crew that was milling through the Prater even physically unbearable. As much as he sympathized with the little people, he couldn't keep them far enough away from himself."[25]

Disagreement with Hanisch

Hanisch writes that at Easter 1910 he received forty kronen for a large order, which he shared with Hitler. Thereupon Hitler disappeared from the hostel with Neumann, failing to return for a week. The registration slip in Vienna corroborates this statement, although it puts the event at Whitsuntide: on June 21, 1910, Hitler gave notice at the men's hostel, and on June 26 he reregisterd.

We do not know how or where the two men spent these days. When Hanisch, irritated, asked upon Hitler's return where he had been, Hitler replied that he had gone sightseeing with Neumann and spent much time in the museum. Hanisch urged him to get to work, but Hitler declared he had to recuperate. The twenty kronen, Hanisch reports, were gone.

It is likely that Hitler, whose relationship with Hanisch had decidedly cooled, was not telling the truth. He may have gone to Waldviertel in those mysterious days in June, either with or without Neumann, to visit "Haniaunt." After all, a few months before, she had helped him out of the direst straits with the transfer of fifty kronen, and they surely still must have been in contact via letters. The aunt, who died of diabetes a few months later, was probably already sick in June. An indication of Hitler's visit to Waldviertel could be a watercolor view of Döllersheim that Hitler gave Joseph Goebbels years later. However, the watercolors *Hitler's Ancestral Home in Walterschlag* and *Cemetery at Spital with My Relatives' Graves*, dated 1910, are fakes.[26]

According to the registration slip, Neumann, whom Hanisch calls Hitler's true and closest friend, left Vienna on July 12, 1910. Hanisch reports that Neumann spoke of Germany with great enthusiasm and asked Hitler to come along. However, Hitler could not bring himself to comply. After that, there was no more news from Neumann.

After Neumann's departure, the relationship between Hanisch and Hitler headed toward a breakup. Hanisch says that Hitler produced fewer and fewer paintings, which might point to another money source, a transfer from his aunt. Hanisch reports that he himself now attempted to paint and make etchings so that he could fill orders that had been placed. In other words, Hanisch turned from colleague to competitor.

Hitler became suspicious and demanded that Hanisch give him a list of customers. Hanisch was well-advised to refuse, because—as he admits later on—he had secretly accepted a commission by Altenberg that was really meant for Hitler. What Hitler did not know is that the order was for cutting out silhouettes made of gilt glass, which was to become a constant source of income for Hanisch up until the thirties.[27]

In July 1910 the two had an argument. Hanisch writes: "I called him a hunger artist, and he called me a house servant, because I had once told him that I worked as a servant in Berlin. I replied that I was not ashamed of any kind of work; I had tried many different kinds and never shirked anything." After that Hanisch decided to work by himself and to leave the men's hostel.

Three weeks later Hanisch ran into an old acquaintance in the Fourth District (Wieden): "a postcard salesman named Loeffler, a Jew who also stayed in the Asylum and was one of Hitler's circle of acquaintances. I asked him what news there was from the Asylum, and he reproached me for having misappropriated a picture by Hitler." Loeffler referred to a view of Parliament that Hitler painted particularly carefully and that he expected to yield a larger than usual profit.[28] The two probably met in the store of framemaker Altenberg at Wiedener Hauptstrasse, which they now supplied as competitors. Loeffler—for there is no doubt that he was the friend of Neumann in question—was working as Hitler's salesman.

Hanisch continues in his report on his encounter with this man: "We had a violent argument. In the middle of it a policeman walked up and Loeffler told the policeman what the argument was about, so he had us come with him to the Commissariat of Police. Since I had no identification papers I was held." Loeffler—whose real name was Siegfried Löffner—at any rate was on Hitler's side, and charged Hanisch with misappropriation. It turns out that Hanisch lived in Vienna under an assumed name. According to Vienna's Registration Office, on July 13, 1910, Hanisch registered in the men's hostel at Wurlitzergasse under the name of Fritz Walter. Hanisch explains that the reason for taking on a false name was that he knew Hitler to be an irascible person and was afraid he would find him, and "if he lost his shelter in the Night Asylum because of his laziness I was afraid he would . . . be a burden to me."

Years later the police report, issued by the district police commissariat of Wieden on August 4, 1910, was transferred to the files of the NSDAP party archive: "Siegfried Löffner, agent, XXth District, 27 Meldemannstrasse, states: I learned from a painter at the men's hostel that the arrested man sold pictures for him and had misappropriated the money. I do not know the name of the painter, I only know him from the men's hostel, where he and the arrested man always used to sit next to each other."[29] Why Löffner claims not to have known Hitler's name is a mystery. He probably wanted to reinforce his statement, or Hitler had directed him to do so.

On August 5, 1910, Hitler is questioned at the Brigittenau commissariat. This record, too, is extant: "Adolf Hitler, artist, b. 4–20–1889 in Braunau, resident of Linz, Cath., single, XXth District, registered at 27 Meldemannstrasse, states: It is not true that I advised Hanisch to register as Walter Fritz, all I ever knew him as was Walter Fritz. Since he was indigent, I gave him the pictures I painted so he could sell them. I regularly gave him 50% of the profit. For the past approximately two weeks Hanisch has not returned to the hostel and misappropriated my painting *Parliament*, worth c. Kronen 50, and a watercolor worth Kronen 9. The only document of his that I saw was his workman's passbook issued to the name Fritz Walter. I know Hanisch from the hostel in Meidling, where I once met him. Adolf Hitler."[30]

Hanisch justified himself to the police by saying that Hitler had expected too much money for his pictures, that he, Hanisch, had received no more than twelve kronen for the *Parliament* picture and given Hitler half of it. Hitler denied this. Hanisch also had good reason not to mention the name of the buyer, framemaker Wenzel Rainer at Liechtensteinstrasse. At the time, he wrote in 1933, he had not refuted Hitler's statement "because I had gotten an order for several weeks by the private buyer of *Parliament*, which Hitler would have received if I had stated the place of the sale."[31]

On August 11, 1910, Hanisch was sentenced to seven days in jail. According to the Registration Office, after his release he moved under his real name into quarters in the Fifth District and as early as October 10, 1910, reappeared—as Friedrich Walter, this time a "stage hand" by profession—at Meldemannstrasse, where he stayed for one week. After that he kept returning sporadically, until in 1913 he stayed for three months. Thus Hitler was by no means rid of his deadly enemy, who surely made his life difficult as much he could.

It is very likely that Hanisch soon took his revenge for Hitler's denunciation via a friend from the men's hostel. The event can be retraced only by linking two independent sources together. A colleague from the men's hostel, Anonymous from Brünn, reports that in the spring of 1912 a painter—an art school graduate who owned an easel and made oil paintings—stayed at the men's hostel. He was Hitler's enemy. Anonymous stated, "When he accidentally, or sometimes intentionally, passed the place where Hitler was sitting, he never failed to glance at his work, and one could see in his face a malicious expression. Hitler instinctively distrusted him right away and told me K. probably wanted nothing but to ruin him, out of competitiveness and envy. It reached a point where Hitler covered his paintings or turned them around whenever he saw K. approaching."[32]

Anonymous continues to state that at the time—in 1912—Hitler was summoned to the Brigittenau police commissariat to make a statement. Someone had reported him as assuming a fake title, that of a painter with an art school graduate degree. His shabby shoes, however, allegedly kept him from complying with the summons. Thereupon a policeman came to the men's hostel. Hitler had to talk to the administrator and was admonished to stop using the fake title, lest he be punished. According to the statement, he suspected the painter of having incriminated him.

Independently of Anonymous, two decades later Hanisch also mentioned an art academy graduate who had known Hitler well. This painter, by the name of Karl Leidenroth, was still such a close friend of Hanisch in the thirties that on one hand he issued for Hanisch certificates of authentication of Hitler's paintings, but on the other hand he also claimed that he had personally witnessed young Hitler forging pictures in the men's hostel—clearly an attempt on the part of Hanisch and Leidenroth at blackmailing their now rich and famous former colleague. According to the documents in the Registration Office in Vienna, the person in question was the art school graduate, painter, and long-time hostel resident (November 1908 to April 1911) Karl Leidenroth, born in Oberölbingen in Saxony in 1882, who died in Vienna in 1944.

The two statements by Anonymous and Hanisch put together lead to the conclusion that Hanisch and Leidenroth were already in cahoots with one another back during their period in the men's hostel. Thus "K." was Karl Leidenroth, and his report to the police in 1912 was the revenge for Hitler's friend Löffner's reporting Hanisch in 1910.

After Neumann's departure and his argument with Hanisch, Hitler found other occupants to go selling for him, such as Löffner. But he now also overcame his resistance more and more often and sold paintings personally, if only to save the commission. He was able to use his established business connections, such as the one with Altenberg.

Jakob Altenberg, born in Grzymatow, Sk(r)alat, Galicia, in 1875, immigrated to Vienna as a young man and learned the craft of a gilder. He shed his Jewish faith, married a Viennese tavern owner's daughter, and fathered two children: Adele, born in 1896, and Jakob Jr., born in 1902. At almost thirty years of age he opened his first store as a frame merchant and gilder at Wiedner Hauptstrasse, and soon afterward a second one at Mariahilfer Strasse. Within a short period of time he advanced from small-time dealer to owner of a booming frame manufactory and four frame and art stores in Vienna. He also bought himself a house in the posh Fourth District.[33]

Around 1910 his ten-year-old daughter Adele occasionally helped out in the store and later remembered Hitler's "unkempt appearance," "but also his shyness and his manner of lowering his eyes and staring at the floor when talking with someone." Once he delivered a political monologue when he was with her father—we do not know on what subject. Altenberg, however, shut him down rigorously.[34] In 1911 or 1912, without an agent, Hitler established a business connection with glazier and frame merchant Morgenstern, a Jew from Hungary with whom he had a very good personal rapport.

On March 29, 1911, Hitler's aunt Johanna Pölzl died at forty-eight years of age in Spital near Weitra, where she was buried on March 31.[35] In any case, there was not enough time for Hitler to make it to Waldviertel. "Haniaunt's" estate must have contained indications that she had made cash payments as a gift to her nephew Adolf. At any rate, the Hitler family's book of household expenses proves that in 1908 Adolf received a loan from his aunt in the amount of 924 kronen.

Because Paula apparently got nothing, Angela Raubal finally had a reason to claim the entire orphan's allowance for her fifteen-year-old sister. Twenty-seven-year-old Angela Raubal had been a widow since 1910 and had to raise three small children plus Paula, who was attending high school in Linz, on her tiny civil servant's pension. Angela induced the guardian no longer to send Adolf's orphan's allowance to Vienna but to retain it. Then she involved the Austrian District Court in Linz. Twenty-two-year-old Hitler was questioned by the Austrian District Court Vienna-Leopoldstadt on May 4, 1911. He cannot but state "that he can support himself and agrees to give the full orphan's allowance to his sister."

The District Court in Linz noted that "furthermore it is claimed that during his education as a painter Adolf received significant amounts from his aunt Johanna Pölzl and thus was at an advantage with regard to his sister anyway; thus the Court, as the minors' Adolf and Paula Hitler's guardianship court, sees no reason to object to the orphan's allowance of Kronen 600 to be disbursed in its entirety for the education of the minor Paula Hitler." It authorized the guardian "to disburse Adolf Hitler's monthly premiums, which he has so far received, to his sister Paula Hitler."[36] Losing his orphan's allowance was bound to have been a serious blow to Hitler—after all, the twenty-five kronen covered his rent and modest food costs.

These court transcripts sufficiently prove that Hitler did not give up the money voluntarily at all, for sheer love of his sister, as many still claim. He did not respond to Paula's subsequent letter.[37] This court transcript is the only source for Hitler's biography for 1911.

The Election Campaign in Brigittenau in 1911

The lack of historical sources is all the more regrettable inasmuch as it was a politically momentous period: after endless riots, the Reichsrat was dissolved in 1911, which made new elections mandatory. A savage and ruthless campaign ensued.

In Vienna, the main competition in this election took place between the two largest parties, the deeply antagonistic Christian-Socials and the Social Democrats who, with the advantage of universal, equal suffrage, had a chance in the Reichsrat elections to prove their strength against the Christian-Socials, who constituted the ruling party in Vienna.

For months the Social Democrats had mounted political pressure against inflation and the housing shortage by way of mass demonstrations. Foreign observers—among them the German ambassador—noticed that "a large part of the bourgeoisie expressed its solidarity with the workers."[38] An unusually large number of women participated in the rallies ("We want cheaper bread for our children!"), and more and more civil servants in uniform: mailmen, post office employees, and streetcar conductors. For the longest time the lower middle class—the Christian-Socials' constituents—had experienced hardships as well.

The Viennese Christian-Socials' far-reaching corruption, which was uncovered after Lueger's death in 1910, finally turned the tide against the all-too-powerful party. The American chargé d'affaires in Vienna reported to Washington that people were bitter because the party leaders had shamelessly accumulated riches for themselves, at a time when their own traditional constituents were suffering.[39] The problem of increased meat prices was still unresolved and worked against the Christian-Socials as well, because the trade minister was one of their party members.

As a working-class district, Brigittenau was a bastion of Social Democracy—but only during national parliamentary elections. Brigittenau's labor leader, Wilhelm Ellenbogen, the district's deputy in the Reichsrat from 1901 to 1918, was once again slated to win by a landslide.

Ellenbogen, born in Lundenburg in Moravia in 1863, was as the son of a Jewish elementary teacher but had shed his faith. He was trained as

Wilhelm Ellenbogen, Ph.D., Social Democratic labor leader in Brigittenau

Dr. Viktor Adler, leader of Cisleithania's Social Democrats

a doctor and, like Viktor Adler, committed himself to the labor movement out of social concern. He was recognized as an expert on the economy, was a specialist on the railway system, and wrote numerous articles on basic political issues. Above all, however, as the party's man of letters and thoroughly knowledgeable in German Classicism, he was sought as a lecturer, whether on political or literary topics. His main concern was to get the laborers interested in the life and work of Richard Wagner.[40] It is certainly possible that young Hitler attended one or more of Ellenbogen's famous lectures in Brigittenau and thus was also educated by his political enemy.

Because Ellenbogen was Jewish, both the Christian-Socials and the Pan-Germans put their stake in anti-Semitic slogans during the campaign. A phrase by German-Radical Karl Hermann Wolf, who liked to call the labor leader a "red sewer rat," indicates how much some people hated the short, red-haired Ellenbogen.[41]

During the election campaign of 1911, two fronts were facing each other full of hatred: on one hand the anti-Semites in the coalition of Christian-Socials and German-Nationals, and on the other hand the "Jew parties," Social Democrats and German Libertines, called "Jewish liberals." One side conjured up the specter of "Jewish" rule over the City of Vienna, and the other the specter of a "rule of clerics."

As was predictable, Ellenbogen won in the first ballot: with 18,577 voters and 16,466 valid votes, he received 9,750 votes against 6,114 for the Christian-Social candidate. Of the smaller parties, the Czech candidate received 413 votes, and Georg Schönerer, who ran in all Viennese districts, an embarrassing 20 votes.[42]

On the night of election day the winner rode in a car with a red flag through Brigittenau and gave speeches to his followers. In front of one of the polls some eight thousand people had gathered to welcome him, waving red flags and cloths, and throwing flowers. The police were nervous. For reasons that are not clear the heated-up political atmosphere led to serious collisions between the police and the crowd. A large number of people were injured, receiving stab wounds, being hit by rocks, sticks, and beer mugs, and suffering saber cuts.[43] These riots must have had a strong impact in the men's hostel as well and heated up the political atmosphere there, which was inflamed to begin with.

Nationwide, the election strengthened the radical nationalist parties and weakened the moderate ones, including the Social Democrats. The Christian-Socials altogether lost twenty seats (seventy-six, down from ninety-six) and the Social Democrats five seats (eighty-one, down from eighty-six). Conversely, the Czech National Socialists, for example, improved to sixteen (up from nine), the German-Radicals to twenty-two (from twelve), the Pan-Germans to four (from three), and the new German Labor Party, which ran in the Sudeten provinces, for the first time gained three seats.

This result promised no moderation in the future Reichsrat. At the very first session of the new Parliament, on October 5, 1911, there were brawls between German and Czech deputies, and the minister of justice was shot at but was unharmed.

Rallies Against Inflation

Between the election and Parliament's convening in October, an extremely dry summer and a crop failure exacerbated economic hardships. During a huge rally on the morning of Sunday, September 17, 1911, Viennese workers marched in protest against meat price increases to Vienna's City Hall and thence through the city. The main organizer was sixty-two-year-old Anton David, a labor leader from Ottakring, an energetic and popular union man, who as a young man had worked at the Saint Marx slaughterhouse in Vienna, where he had accumulated his knowledge of a big city's food supply distribution problems.[44]

At this rally David, like Ellenbogen, was one of thirty party speakers party speakers who at strategical places propagandized against the government's failed customs policy. The speeches were drowned by fierce shouts and slogans such as "Long live the revolution!" and "General strike!" A large body of police and soldiers aggravated the demonstrators' nervousness. Apart from the police, three divisions of cavalry and seven batallions of infantry were posted against the demonstrators. The military also cordoned off all access roads to the Hofburg to protect the emperor.

It is very likely that Hitler witnessed this huge rally from the street. *I pondered,* he wrote in *Mein Kampf, with anxious concern on the masses of those no longer belonging to their people and saw them swelling to the proportions of a menacing army. . . . For nearly two hours I stood there watching with bated breath the gigantic human dragon slowly winding by.*[45]

The protest grew violent. Windowpanes in City Hall, in stores, cafes, streetcars, and cars were broken, and so were gaslights. The party leaders desperately tried to prevent transgressions, partly because they feared excesses would diminish the initial sympathies for the demonstrators. Yet even the labor leaders could not calm down the angry crowd. Someone tried to hit a policeman with a club. When David attempted to intercept, he was injured.

Then the military intervened, using Hungarian cavalry and Bosnian footsoldiers, the feared "Bosniaks." The *Illustrierte Kronen-Zeitung* wrote: "In every street through which the demonstrators passed, there were serious clashes, and the crowd's violent anger reached its climax when a squad of hussars approached on horseback. Shouts were heard: 'Now they're letting the Hungarians loose on the Viennese!' And then, when the Bosniaks advanced, there were piercing whistles, rocks were thrown, and people shouted, 'The Bosniaks have no business here!' " From that point on the rally threatened to turn into a revolution, comparable only to the one in 1848.[46]

The situation became most alarming in the working-class Ottakring district. The rioters erected barricades with benches and furniture that they acquired from the elementary school, and they threw rocks at policemen and soldiers. Angry housewives in the surrounding buildings took the demonstrators' side and threw irons and pots out of their windows at the policemen. The police responded with bayonets and sabers. Toward 1:00 in the afternoon the first shot was fired.

The "bloody Sunday" resulted in three workers dead and some one hundred injured: people stabbed by bayonets, cut by sabers, wounded by bullets, beaten up and stomped on. According to the *Deutsches Volksblatt,* when night descended Ottakring "resembled the picture of an army camp. Guards on horseback and cavalry patroled the streets, soldiers on foot stood ready at intersections or by their horses. Since the lights were demolished and the gas had been turned off, the whole area of the district was completely dark."[47]

The illustrated family magazine *Wiener Bilder* reported "with a feeling of utmost sadness": "Vienna, the patient, tolerant city, is up in arms." Certainly, the article argued, there were also members of the "lumpen proletariat" among the demonstrators, "who indeed have nothing left to lose. Yet in such tempestuous times, other people too, who don't know where they will spend the night with their families, don't heed the call for moderation. . . . Sunday's bloody events are a cautionary signal which no one in a position of responsibility in this country must ignore."[48]

Some forty thousand people attended the first victim's funeral at the Ottakring cemetery, monitored by a huge levy of military and police. In the meanwhile, Christian-Socials and German-Nationals exploited the disturbances for their party's political purposes and fanned the fear of the Social Democrats as revolutionaries and enemies of property owners and small business owners.

Clichés about Viennese Labor Leaders

Certainly during this election campaign and the rallies against inflation, if not before, Hitler must have thoroughly studied Social Democracy. *Depressed by the demonstration, he was driven by an inner voice to buy the Arbeiterzeitung and read it carefully. . . . More than any theoretical literature, my daily reading of the Social Democratic press enabled me* to recognize the essence of Social Democracy.[49]

Hitler also must have studied the Social Democratic leaders. In *Mein Kampf* he mentions four of them by name: Adler, Austerlitz, Ellenbogen, and David. To be sure, he mentions them in order to make a political point: the argument that Social Democracy was in Jewish hands, endeavoring to use their international slogans to alienate the German workers from their "folkishness": *I took all the Social Democratic pamphlets I could lay hands on and sought the names of their authors: Jews. I noted the names of the leaders; by far the greatest part were likewise members of the "chosen people," whether they were representatives in the Reichsrat or trade-union secretaries, the heads of organizations or street agitators. It was always the same gruesome picture. The names of the Austerlitzes, Davids, Adlers, Ellenbogens, etc., will remain forever graven in my memory.* He continues: *One thing had grown clear to me: the party with whose petty representatives I had been carrying on the most violent struggle for months was, as to leadership, almost exclusively in the hands of a foreign people; for, to my deep and joyful satisfaction, I had at last come to the conclusion that the Jew was no German.*[50] (It should be clarified that Hitler wrote these sentences ten years later, as a politician. What is documented from his period in Vienna is his constant reviling of the "Reds," but we don't know of any anti-Semitic statements about individual Social Democrats.)

These sentences about the labor leaders also contain Viennese clichés. Whenever they wanted to establish the "Jewish" character of Social Democracy, the anti-Semites in Vienna mentioned the names of Adler, Ellenbogen, and Austerlitz together. The Christian-Social *Brigittenauer Bezirks-Nachrichten* wrote in 1912: "If Adler, Austerlitz, Ellenbogen, and their comrades were ordered and paid for from abroad to do their infamous undermining, they couldn't act more efficiently to support Austria's enemies than they are doing now."[51] Usually Anton David was not included in those lists of names. That Hitler still mentions him ten years later must have something to do with David's leading role during the 1911 rallies against inflation.

None of the four politicians Hitler mentions was Jewish by faith. Party leader Dr. Viktor Adler, born in Prague in 1852, was from an upper middle-class family and was educated at the distinguished Catholic Schottengymnasium in Vienna. As a student of medicine he had been a founding member of the German fraternity Arminia in Vienna and of the German School Association. He was among the circle around Schönerer and a coauthor of the Social-Liberal Linz program of 1882, until the Aryan Clause that Schönerer later inserted drove him away. A doctor for the poor and a psychiatrist, he was confronted with the disastrous health and social conditions and the lack of legislation for the protection of workers, and turned toward Social Democracy out of a sense of social commitment. Steadfast in his attempt to merge a sense of nationalism and international solidarity in Cisleithania's workers, he unified the party in 1888 and became its leader. He turned Austria's Social Democratic Party into a united, nationally federative organization, but was powerless against the nationalism that around 1910 was surging in his own party as well.

Both Adler and Ellenbogen were part of Vienna's circle of modernists and friends with many artists and scientists. Their political opponents would always describe their upper-middle-class lifestyle as if they had taken the money from poor workers. The *Brigittenauer Bezirks-Nachrichten* wrote in 1912 that the Social Democratic Party imposed "party taxes which are very hard on the workers, but which allow the leaders to live well. It wants to keep the masses stuck in the proletariat, but the leaders build villas, acquire property, and play the fine gentlemen."[52] And: "It was by no means proletarians and wage workers who stood at the cradle

Friedrich Austerlitz, editor-in-chief
of the *Arbeiterzeitung*

Ottakring labor leader Anton David

of Social Democracy, but the well-to-do offspring of capitalists, none of
whom knew 'Mother Worry.'" Marx, Engels, and Lassalle, the article
read, had not been proletarians, any more than Adler or Ellenbogen.[53]

The fourth "Jewish" labor leader Hitler mentions in *Mein Kampf* was
Friedrich Austerlitz, a pugnacious man with a sharp tongue, editor of the
Arbeiterzeitung, which Hitler hated ferociously but read nonetheless. Every
day Pan-German as well as Christian-Social papers got all flustered about
the "Jewish workers' newspaper clique": "If any press is working with
sewage and mud, it is the Jewish press, plus the Social Democratic press,
which is edited almost exclusively by Jewish greaseballs, for these reptiles
stop at nothing, not even at the total destruction of lives, and we can
only be sorry about part of the Christian population still buying and
reading this printed pest."[54]

Hitler the politician liked to repeat the Viennese anti-Semites' slogans in the attempt to incite the workers against the Social-Democratic
party leaders. In 1920 he wrote in an article entitled *Some Questions for
the German Worker: How come our German labor leaders belong almost exclusively to a nation one never sees working? What's the percentage of Jews
among the total population, what's the percentage of Jews among the manual
laborers, locksmiths, smiths, miners, sanitation coachmen, scavengers, cobblers, etc., etc., but what's the percentage of Jews among the labor leaders?*[55]

Hitler conveniently ignored the Jews he knew who were among the
poor people—Robinson, the locksmith, Neumann, the copper cleaner,

Löffner, the sales representative. Neither did glazier Morgenstern or frame manufacturer Altenberg at all fit the cliché of the Jew who by nature refuses to work.

Hitler's Opinion of the Workers

During this period of more than three years at the men's hostel, daily contact acquainted young Hitler with a social class that up to that point was foreign to him: a purely male society of outsiders, workers in the nearby factories, but also men who had failed and were nowhere at home, as well as casual laborers. Hitler's image of "the worker" was clearly molded by these colleagues in the men's hostel, who included some dubious individuals. He had hardly met any workers as colleagues and at work, and most certainly had not met a community of workers with whom he could have felt some kind of solidarity. He learns about working-class families' problems through newspapers at best, not through personal experience.

Hanisch writes: "He repeatedly said of the workers that they were an indolent mass that cared about nothing but eating, drinking and women. He thought a revolution could only be the work of a student class, as in 1848." This statement coincides with a later one during a private conversation in the thirties: *the vast majority of workers want nothing but bread and games, they have no sense of ideal at all.*[56] And about construction workers: *I do not know what horrified me most at that time: the economic misery of my companions, their moral and ethical coarseness, or the low level of their intellectual development.*[57]

Hanisch describes an early conflict with Social Democratic colleagues in the men's hostel on May 1, 1910. A factory worker came into the reading room with a red carnation in his buttonhole, talking about the May Day parade in the Prater. Hanisch reports that Hitler "leaped to his feet, waving his hands wildly, and screaming: 'You should be thrown out; you should get a lesson!'" Hanisch adds: "Eveyone laughed at his excitement."

In his rejection of May Day parades Hitler was in agreement with the Pan-Germans, the German-Radicals, and the Christian-Socials. Mayor Lueger's phrase about "the people who on May 1 amble to the Prater," was quoted again and again: "These, sir, are nothing but rascals."

According to Hanisch, Hitler was against any form of terror or strikes. In the terminology of the Christian-Socials as well as the Pan-Germans, these two words clearly point to Social Democracy and its most effective means of political pressure—mass demonstrations.

In *Mein Kampf* too Hitler implies that he often had arguments with Social Democrats: *At that time I was still childish enough to try to make the madness of their doctrine clear to them; in my little circle I talked my tongue sore and my throat hoarse, thinking I would inevitably succeed in convincing them how ruinous their Marxist madness was; but what I accomplished was often the opposite.*[58] Yet these arguments do not take place on scaffoldings but in the men's hostel's warm reading room.

Hitler's later remarks on Vienna's workers were derogatory, conde-scending, uttered from the position of someone supposedly on a higher social plane, for example, in *Mein Kampf: Only in the smallest groups did I speak of the things which inwardly moved or attracted me. This speaking in the narrowest circles had many good points: I learned to orate less, but to know people with their opinions and objections that were often so boundlessly primi-tive. And I trained myself, without losing the time and occasion for the contin-uance of my own education. It is certain that nowhere else in Germany was the opportunity for this so favorable as in Vienna.*[59]

Apparently Hitler counted himself among the "educated," not at all among the workers. He called himself an "art academy graduate" and showed no signs of solidarity with the needy. Even his friend Kubizek had wondered about this during the hunger rally in 1908: "If he measured the situation against his own living conditions, his own economic situation, his own social environment, then there was no doubt that he was one of those people who were marching behind the hunger posters. His abode was the wretched back premises of a house full of roaches, and for lunch he often didn't eat more than a piece of dry bread on a bench in Schön-brunn. Many of the demonstrators were perhaps not even as bad off as he was. Why then didn't he march with these people? What kept him from doing so?"

Kubizek believes that the explanation lies in Hitler's awareness "that he belonged to a different social sphere by virtue of his background. He was the son of an Austrian civil servant. When he thought of his father, he saw him as the respected, esteemed higher customs official before whom people took their hats off when they saw him and to whom the burghers listened. In reputation and attitude, his father had nothing what-soever to do with this person in the street. As much as he was afraid of being infected by the general moral and political decay of the ruling classes, he was much more afraid of becoming a proletarian. To be sure, he was living as one, but he didn't want to be one under any circumstanc-es."[60] Kubizek also writes that this was the reason Hitler did not even consider getting into personal contact with his fellow sufferers: "contact with people simply was disgusting to him, even physically."[61] Kubizek sees in the "incredible amount of energy (Hitler) put into his autonomous studies . . . the instinctive intention to protect himself from the fall into the misery of the masses by way of educating himself as much and as thoroughly as possible."[62]

Hanisch, on the other hand, claims that in response to Hitler's statements he had said his friend did not know any real workers but merely the bachelors who lived in the men's hostel. "Only loafers, drunkards and the like stay for a long time in such a home." He claims to have argued that a real workingman soon "looks for board in a private house to enjoy family life." According to Hanisch, real workers hardly participated in the debates in the reading room either—and if they did, they barely took any notice of Hitler, "because they found his debates quite foolish."

Hitler the politician kept silent about his experiences at the men's hostel in Vienna, for good reasons. He became intoxicated with his own words when he said about the working people, *I stood with them at the construction site, I was hungry with them when we were unemployed, I lay in the trenches with them, I know them, that magnificent people!*[63] And when he cried out during an NSDAP meeting in 1920, *I am a working man, made of workers' flesh and blood,*[64] this was nothing but political propaganda.

The Sources on the Period in the Men's Hostel

There are five reports by hostel occupants concerning Hitler's stay at the men's hostel, which lasted more than three years, from February 1910 until May 1913. All are from different periods. Reinhold Hanisch documents the period in the homeless shelter in Meidling from the fall of 1909 until August 1910. After that, we have no eyewitnesses at all until early 1912. A shelter occupant referred to as "Anonymous from Brünn" covers the months from February to April 1912, and Karl Honisch writes about Hitler's last months before his departure for Munich in May 1913. Rudolf Häusler's verbal accounts, quoted here for the first time, cover February through May 1913. Furthermore, in this context the book by Josef Greiner requires a critical analysis. He moved his "friendship" with Hitler in the men's hostel to the years 1907 and 1908, which, however, is clearly false.

These five statements indicate the thin ground on which the historian writing Hitler's early biography moves. On one hand they cover only a very short time span among Hitler's years in Vienna; on the other hand, their value as sources is questionable throughout.

In 1939 the American magazine *The New Republic* posthumously published the three-part series "Reinhold Hanisch: I Was Hitler's Buddy."

The manuscript was most likely from the personal estate of Hitler researcher Konrad Heiden. We do not know if and how the latter edited the original, because the original manuscript was lost.[65] At any rate, the statements in this series coincide with those quoted by Heiden in his book,[66], which was published prior to the articles, as well as with the two-page (and hence much shorter) text that Hanisch wrote in May 1933 and that survived in the NSDAP's archive.[67]

Hanisch presents an abundance of facts and an altogether very lively and ultimately credible picture of young Hitler. For example, almost all the names Hanisch mentions can be found in the files of Vienna's Registration Office for the period he specified. Even the statement often considered not credible—that young Hitler preferred being around Jews—is corroborated by the registration files. Furthermore, the statements by Hitler that Hanisch quotes are all in agreement with August Kubizek's memoirs, with which Hanisch after all was not familiar. The events of 1910 that he mentions are correct as well, even though they seem to be false at first sight, such as the mention of Empress Elizabeth. The police records support Hanisch's credibility in regard to the fraud charge.

Hanisch clearly does not tell the truth mostly when dealing with the pictures Hitler painted at the men's hostel. In this area Hanisch pursues definite financial interests, for in the early thirties he mainly lived on the sale of "Hitler originals" he had forged, of whose high market value he took advantage as the absolute expert in the matter. Initially he was still careful and signed his own paintings with his initials, "R. H.," but in a way that made them indistinguishable from "A. H." so they could be sold "erroneously" as Hitler paintings. Hitler usually signed with "A. Hitler."

Hanisch used his interviews with journalists and his article for Heiden in order to validate his own forgeries, thus "incidentally" issuing himself certificates of authenticity. In that respect his statements are a web of lies that is virtually impossible to disentangle. Hanisch even went so far as to accuse Hitler of forgery in order better to sell these pictures, which were not forged by Hitler but by himself. False experts' certificates by the former men's hostel occupant Karl Leidenroth further sustained the fraud.

The fakes originating in Vienna in the early thirties also must have been embarrassing to Hitler because their quality was far below Hitler's artistic level, which was modest to begin with. As Reich chancellor he did everything he could to destroy the forgery center in Vienna. It was probably he who in 1933 put Franz Feiler, a nineteen-year-old streetcar conductor in Innsbruck,[68] on Hanisch's track via middlemen. Feiler was an enthusiastic, illegal National Socialist who knew Hanisch as a temporary neighbor in Vienna. He initially gained Hanisch's trust by promising Hanisch, who was in dire straits, to get him a commission for a painting from the NSDAP. In May 1933 Hanisch worked out a written plan for a painting that the party was to buy for 150 to 170 shillings to give to the Führer as a thoughtful present. The picture was supposed to touch on Hitler's predilections: Semper, Liszt, and Ludwig II of Bavaria, the Hofburg in Vienna as well as the court museums, and scenes from operas by Wagner.[69] The plan never materialized.

Feiler then came to the point and asked Hanisch to help him buy paintings by Hitler. At first Hanisch offered him a genuine painting from the remainders of frame salesman Jakob Altenberg for 950 shillings, plus two unsigned ladies' silhouettes made of gilt glass, remarking that their present owner had once bought them as works by Rudolf von Alt. A musical scene with Franz Schubert, also made of gilt glass, bore the signature of "Wiesinger-F." This referred to the painter Olga Wisinger-Florian, whose style Hanisch also imitated in flower paintings he sold as Hitler originals.[70]

Hanisch claimed that these three gilt glass paintings were forgeries by Hitler, and that three witnesses plus he himself could testify to that. Hanisch named "Prof. Leidenroth," a former fellow occupant at the men's hostel, as a witness "who from time to time watched Hitler working." "These 3 items are repurchasable at 300 shillings and I'm charging 500 shillings as immediate commission for my troubles. I am requesting an immediate response to this offer, as I am having others look for buyers who are also giving me their necessary trust. Don't look at me as a forger of these things in view of the witnesses."

Hanisch continued, "Should Hitler deny he made this paintings, the witnesses would amply refute him. In particular, Prof. Leidenroth, who was a real art school graduate, a student of Stuck in Munich, is a high-ranking public official and major in the Prussian army, and knows Hitler as well as I do. Because of us witnesses these three works actually do have historic value as forgeries by Hitler, even though Hitler will no longer play the role he did back then."[71]

The accusation that Hitler had produced forged gilt silhouettes was false. After all, it was Hanisch who in 1910 had collared this order for Hitler from Altenberg's firm, and who, as Altenberg's daughter confirmed,[72] had specialized in these works for decades.

At any rate, Reich chancellor Hitler must have felt extremely uncomfortable about the whole matter. The name Leidenroth, too, was bound to stir up unpleasant memories, because in the men's hostel he

had once denounced Hitler to the police for illegally assuming an academic title. The mention of this name made clear to Hitler that his two
enemies in the men's hostel, Leidenroth and Hanisch, were in cahoots
with one another, corroborating each other in their statements and accusations against him.

In a threatening tone Hanisch announced to Feiler further revela-
tions: "In a booklet about Hitler and his actual former political views as
well as his behavior in Vienna, which is about to be published, this fakes
is mentioned [sic] and Hitler will have ample opportunity for denial."
This may have been a reference to the pamphlet *Hitler wie er wirklich ist*
(Hitler the way he really is), which was allegedly published by Novina
Publishers in Pressburg and of which no copies have turned up to date.[73]
Hanisch reinforced this blatant blackmail by adding that he had done
research on Hitler's alleged studies in Vienna's Academy of Visual Arts:
"Found much additional material plus witnesses."[74]

Feiler purchased a view of the Michaelerhaus from Hanisch. The
picture was signed "A. H. 1910" and cost two hundred shillings. Feiler
gave Hanisch fifty shillings as a down payment, and on Easter Monday
1933 took the painting to Hitler in Berchtesgaden.[75] Hitler recognized
the watercolor painting as a fake and made Feiler go to the Vienna police
to charge Hanisch with fraud. In July 1933 Hanisch was in court once
again, was confronted with Feiler's statement, sentenced, and sent to jail
for a few days.

Several newspapers reported on the trial.[76] This made Hanisch an
important witness for Hitler's opponents in Austria. On August 21, 1933,
the liberal *Wiener Sonn- und Montagszeitung* published a long interview
with Hanisch under the sensationalistic title "Hitler as a Beggar in Vienna."

The article contains a number of mistakes for which the editor appears to be responsible. On the whole, however, the statements are in
agreement with those Hanisch made to Heiden as well: how he met young
Hitler in the homeless shelter, how he helped Hitler in all kinds of ways,
how the young man spent his money on newspapers and pastry with
whipped cream, his favorite dessert, how Hitler had not at all been anti-
Semitic, talked a lot about politics, and so forth. Hanisch then relates
the story about Hitler's 1910 report to the police charging fraud, defends
himself effusively, and enlarges upon the inferior artistic quality of Hitler's
paintings.

Here, too, Hanisch accuses Hitler of forgery: he claims Hitler told
him in the men's hostel "that even when he was still living in Linz he

painted small landscapes in oil, then roasted them in the oven until they turned all brown, and sometimes he actually did succeed in selling these pictures to second-hand dealers as old, valuable pieces." Thus the roasting of pictures is supposed to have taken place in Klara Hitler's small household. According to Hanisch, the procedure could not have been done at the men's shelter without being noticed.

As Hitler's only known colleague in Vienna and his open personal enemy, Hanisch, a veritable celebrity, was frequently interviewed and apparently made money on it, too. It was he who revealed that Hitler had lived in the men's hostel for years. He also told the writer Rudolf Olden a few things, and Olden quoted him liberally in his biograpy of Hitler, which was published in Amsterdam in 1935.[77]

There was a special connection between Hanisch and the writer Konrad Heiden. The latter, born in Munich in 1901, a staunch early opponent of the Nazis and the *Frankfurter Zeitung*'s correspondent in Munich until his emigration in 1933, had studied the Hitler movement since the early twenties. In 1932 his book *Geschichte des Nationalsozialismus* (History of National Socialism) was published in Berlin. He planned to write a biograpy of Hitler next. While gathering material, he also encountered Hanisch in Vienna. He interviewed him about his experiences at the men's hostel and subsequently hired him to look for additional material in Vienna. Thus in the Academy of Visual Arts' archive Hanisch found proof that Hitler had never formally studied art but had failed the entrance exam twice.[78]

Endangered as a known opponent of Hitler, in 1933 Heiden first emigrated to the Saarland in Germany, and from there to Paris. In 1936 the first volume of his book *Adolf Hitler: Eine Biographie* was published in Zurich. The subtitle was: *Das Zeitalter der Verantwortungslosigkeit* (The age of irresponsibility). The same year an American edition appeared in New York. In this book Hanisch is quoted as a source as well. Heiden's sensational revelations must have exacerbated Hitler's old anger against his archenemy from his years in the men's hostel.

After he was released from prison, Hanisch became even busier as a forger of Hitler paintings, their quality ever declining. A dealer by the name of Jacques Weiss sold the pictures all over Europe.[79] On November 16, 1936, Hanisch was again arrested. The search of his rental apartment brought to light not only manuscripts on Hitler but also concrete proof in the shape of additional forgeries. The burden of proof was overwhelming. On December 2, 1936, Hanisch was jailed in the Vienna County Court,[80] where according to the medical examiner he died on

Feburary 4, 1937, apparently of heart failure. According to the coroner's report, he was buried without charge, inasmuch as he had no assets.[81]

Berlin did not learn immediately about Hanisch's death. Feiler informed his friend at the NSDAP Main Archive only after the Anschluss on May 11, 1938, saying that Hanisch had died "one and one-half years earlier . . . of pneumonia, while in custody in the court hospital."[82] Feiler blamed the Schuschnigg government's Austrian police for Hanisch's death: "I know how they sometimes deal with a poor devil—particularly if he wears shabby clothes—at the police station and in court. When such a person turns out to be mentally far superior to those in whose hands he is, I start having my own thoughts about his totally unexpected death."

According to Feiler, Hanisch had "had his faults . . . but despite his poverty and need he was a noble character, and his death saddens me very much. He once was our Führer's friend, and I too am not ashamed of my friendship with Reinhold Hanisch." As for Hanisch's interviews, Feiler believed reporters had tricked him. Feiler offered to do further research on Hitler paintings in Vienna. However, he said that this would entail difficulties, for: "After all, I can't search homes. Perhaps with the support of the authorities something might turn up. I could then help by providing information."[83]

The forged paintings kept Hitler's associates busy for several more years. As late as October 21, 1942, Heinrich Himmler ordered at Hitler's instruction that three Hitler paintings forged by Hanischst be destroyed, along with the pertinent affidavits by Hanisch and Leidenroth from 1935.[84]

Contrary to Hanisch's, the next eyewitness report, covering the period from February through April 1912, is short, presenting only one problem: its author, called "Anonymous from Brünn," is careful enough to remain incognito, understandably so. His report appeared in Czech in Brünn's magazine *Moravsky ilustrovany zpravodaj* (Moravian illustrated observer) in 1935[85] and portrays Hitler critically and credibly. The usual criticism of this source is based on a lack of knowledge of the complete text and supported by individual, often incorrect, quotes that others have copied without checking them.

To be sure, Anonymous makes mistakes. Yet these concern mainly details about Hitler's family history, in other words, facts Hitler himself told Anonymous, who either must have mixed them up over the years between 1912 and 1935 or misunderstood them to begin with.

However, whenever Anonymous relates his own observations and experiences with Hitler, he is credible. The names and dates he quotes hold up under inspection. The political statements of Hitler's that mentions are in agreement with other sources as well—for example, Kubizek. It is also interesting to note an aside that states that Hitler's family came "from the Germanic part of Bohemia"—a sign of how seriously the Czechs considered Waldviertel as a national area under dispute.

A further, rather short report that does not yield very much about the first months of 1913 is by Karl Honisch. He was the only occupant of the men's hostel whom the NSDAP's party archive ferreted out after 1938 and interviewed about his experiences with Hitler.[86] Honisch was two years Hitler's junior, born in Moravia in 1891, single, and a "clerk" by profession. He went from Brünn to Vienna, where he was formally registered only in 1913, most of the time at the men's hostel at Meldemannstrasse, where he checked out shortly before Christmas 1913, destination unknown.[87]

The report Honisch wrote for the NSDAP in 1939 is objective only to a limited degree. Understandably, he was careful not to reveal anything negative about the man who was now "the Führer." Young Hitler is portrayed in an extremely favorable light; for example, Honisch writes that "Hitler was not an average person like us and despite his 24 years mentally superior to all of us." The hostel's personnel also "liked him a lot," and "—if I remember correctly, the administrator rather often wanted to talk to him. And that was an honor rarely bestowed on one of the occupants." Honisch's statement is a veritable walk on the wire in its attempt to sound credible on the one hand but, on the other, not to get himself into trouble.

Honisch also mentions Hitler's political concerns and his love of orating. He comments tortuously, "We didn't always understand his views." "Only now," in 1939, did Honisch "understand the essence of some of the things he said. There is no doubt that Hitler carried within him the germs of much of what he would later realize, that these were working and fermenting in him. That's probably where his mood changes came from." To be sure, at times he was "rather hot-tempered." However, Honisch confesses to the party archive, "We were familiar with these moods and respected them."

Honisch deftly avoids mentioning concrete details about former colleagues that the NSDAP would be able to check out. He is content to state that Hitler liked to talk to experts in various fields: "Thus I remember a thirty-year-old man by the name of Schön. He was an unemployed estate manager who apparently had a degree from a technical university.

Hitler and he would frequently discuss agrarian issues, and Hitler took this so seriously that he would often pick up pencil and paper to take notes. Then there was also a certain Mr. Redlich, who had a graduate degree. . . . And there were several others whose names I don't recall, among them also workers and craftsmen from whom Hitler was eager to learn about their professional fields."

The name Schön cannot be identified in the registration files because it occurs so very frequently, but Redlich can: it is a certain Rudolf Redlich, born in Cejkowitz in Moravia in 1882, single, a civil servant, and a Jew. The police register reveals that he was at the men's hostel at Meldemannstrasse from December 30, 1911, to June 28, 1914, at the same time as Hitler and Honisch.[88] Thus Honisch confirms that yet another Jew belonged to Hitler's close associates at the men's shelter.

Aside from that, Honisch fills many pages with detailed descriptions of the men's shelter, which he simply copies from an official pamphlet, the *Tenth Annual Report of the Emperor Franz Josef Anniversary Fund for 1905*, published in Vienna in 1906.

Honisch is the only source stating that Hitler did not go to Munich by himself. According to him he was "accompanied by a friend who also emigrated to Germany; I don't recall his name." This companion was Rudolf Häusler, born in Aspang in Lower Austria in 1893, who spent his childhood in Vienna, which was still his legal residence. A Catholic, Häusler was registered at the men's shelter at Meldemannstrasse from February 4 to May 25, 1913, during which period he was a pharmacist's apprentice.[89] Hitler and Häusler, who was four years younger than he, were so close that they shared a tiny room, a sublet with tailor Popp in Munich, from May 25 1913, until February 15, 1914—a longer period than Hitler and Kubizek had spent together in Vienna.[90] They kept in close contact until the outbreak of the war in August 1914 (see Chapter 12). Then contact broke off.

Häusler married in Vienna in 1917, and in 1918 his only child, Marianne, was born. In 1929 Häusler became a widower, raised the child himself, and never remarried. He worked as a merchant in various fields and ran a hotel in Czechoslovakia with his daughter's help. It was not until very late that he realized that his friend Adolf was identical with Germany's party chairman. In 1929 he became an illegal National Socialist. He mentioned his connection with Hitler only in internal party files in 1939.

He told his daughter that he had tried to contact Hitler personally during a six-week trip to Berlin in 1933. However, he said, he had not been admitted; the people in charge had not believed that he was Hitler's friend and did not want anything from the chancellor except to see him again. We cannot prove that Häusler kept something from his daughter—but there are indications of a pact of silence between the two friends. Until 1945, Häusler didn't breathe a word about his connection with Hitler. And strangely enough, the Popp family in Munich did not say anything about their second subletter either, which must have been in accordance with Hitler's express request.

From 1938 on Häusler advanced rather impressively, if not outstandingly, within the party: according to the Berlin Document Center's party files he was first department manager with the Deutscher Arbeitsfront (German Work Front) and in that function was responsible for allocating apartments. In addition, from 1940 to 1945 he was the NSDAP's central office manager in Vienna.[91] To be sure, in Vienna's district party files this career reads differently. In 1955 Austria's Ministry of the Interior stated that Häusler had been a candidate for party membership from 1938 until 1944 but had not been a party member, and that he therefore had a clean record.[92]

Häusler died in Vienna in 1973 at the age of seventy-nine, without leaving any record of his relationship with Hitler. Neither were letters or writings by Hitler among his personal effects. However, in the scrapbook of Häusler's younger sister Milli there still was a colored postcard by Hitler (see p. 364). There also were tracks in Häusler's mother Ida's estate in the form of two letters Hitler wrote in longhand from Munich in 1913. Of these letters, at least a fragment of a photograph has survived (see p. 400). The content of these few lines confirms what Häusler's daughter Marianne reports: that Hitler was a kind of mentor for Häusler, who was four years his junior, and enjoyed his mother's full confidence.

Because no historian ever even tried to contact Häusler, whose name was listed in Vienna's telephone directory until 1973, we still have no more than those scant statements about Hitler that Häusler made to Marianne, who readily shared them with me.

Thus the credibility of this witness, who was extremely close to her father, needs to be examined. Marianne, now Mrs. Koppler, energetic, intelligent, and not uncritical of her father, does not try for one moment to create a myth. In what she relates, she instead confines herself to the few things she knows and still remembers about her father and her grandmother. Her father, she says, was very reserved even toward his own family members, but at the same time was so domineering that neither daughter nor grandson liked to ask him about things he did not want to tell without being prompted. We have to consider it particularly fortunate that, according to her own statement, she was never interested in Hitler, because he had treated her father badly when they separated in 1914 and after 1933. Furthermore, we can believe her when she says she has never read a book about Hitler—which certainly increases the value of her statements.

Obviously, such a secondhand statement is not as valuable as if pointed questions had been put to Häusler directly. Yet Marianne Koppler's statements do contribute some important details on young Hitler (see Chapter 12).

The book by Josef Greiner, *Das Ende des Hitler-Mythos* (The end of the Hitler myth), published in 1947, is in stark contrast to the four statements just mentioned. As the first German-language report for the public by someone "in the know," the book was a guaranteed success.

Greiner claims to have known Hitler in 1907 and 1908 at the men's hostel at Meldemannstrasse—in other words, at a time when we know for a fact Hitler still lived in Linz and later on with Kubizek at Mrs. Zakreys's. Greiner even claims he received a thank-you letter, later lost, for his alleged help from Klara Hitler, written "with a trembling hand."[93]

The book was written in order to create a sensation. Greiner draws a horrifying picture of young Hitler, with all kinds of tasteless details— just what people wanted to hear after 1945. For example, Greiner claims that Hitler worked with an Eastern Jewish junk dealer to teach her to read and write, but at the same time earned money collecting bedbugs. One day he allegedly put these bedbugs into his employer's bed and was fired.[94] He then had given "Aryan" children some chocolate so they would call Jewish playmates "Jew pigs."[95] According to another anecdote Hitler demonstrated his anti-Semitism at the posh Café Fenstergucker next to the opera by putting a fish bladder full of red ink under the behind of a "Jewess" in festive attire,[96] and so forth.

Greiner's sexual fantasies culminate in the drawn-out story of young Hitler supposedly trying to rape and beat one of the models posing for him.[97] Furthermore, a prostitute in Leopoldstadt had given him syphilis.[98] The negative result of the Wassermann test in 1940 proves unambiguously that Hitler never had such an infection.[99] Greiner also suggests that Hitler did not commit suicide but escaped from Berlin on April 30, 1945, via helicopter: "deception tactics that resemble an ancient heroic epic."[100]

As a fringe benefit, Greiner creates with his book a politically opportune legend of himself as an allegedly active resistance fighter who even tried to assassinate Hitler. He claims to have pointed out to his former colleague in the men's hostel how reprehensible the treatment of

Jews as well as that of people from southern Tyrol was, and that he even declined an offer by Hitler to become a part of his administration as minister of economy. He reprints three long letters, allegedly written by Hitler in 1938, as "proof."[101] Yet they were clearly written after 1945, specifically for the book, and then predated.

Greiner sent his anti-Hitler book to politicians, for example, to "His Excellency Commander-in-Chief Stalin," along with a six-page letter dated May 14, 1947. In his letter he introduced himself as president of an "Austrian Pan-European League," an association founded by him but not even established yet, and as a member of the "Society for the Cultivation of Cultural and Economic Relations with the Soviet Union," and offered one of his inventions as payment for Austria's entire reparations to Russia—and furthermore to help save Austria and safeguard peace.[102]

As early as 1956 Franz Jetzinger proved by way of a detailed examination that Greiner's book is a "palpable web of lies."[103] Jetzinger says that Greiner gleaned the little real information his book contains from *Mein Kampf*, Heiden's book—and thus, via detour, from Hanisch—and conversations with Jetzinger. On account of the numerous, extremely strange mistakes in Greiner's book, Jetzinger considers it impossible that Greiner knew Hitler. Everyone studying the book and its subject matter is bound to come to the same conclusion.

On the other hand, however, there is Hanisch's article in *The New Republic*, which mentions a man in the men's hostel to whom Hitler got close in 1910, a signboard painter by the name of Greiner, who used to be a lamplighter at the Cabaret Hölle (hell). According to Hanisch, Greiner and Hitler had hatched odd schemes. For example, they planned to fill old tin cans with paste and sell them as an antifreeze for windows—but only in the summer, so that no one would be able to try out the merchandise. Hanisch says that when he voiced his doubts, Hitler had replied that "one must possess a talent for oratory." The two had also had the idea of protecting banknotes from being worn out by keeping them in a case of celluloid, for which purpose the banknotes would have to be made smaller—and so forth. Hanisch commented that Greiner "was a great talker" and "a bad influence on Hitler."

In his critique, Jetzinger suggests that Hanisch lied and simply made up this man called Greiner, and that Greiner for his part had exploited Hanisch's ravings about the men's hostel occupant, who was coincidentally a namesake, and built his web of lies on it.

However, it is not quite that simple. Once again, Vienna's Registration Office confirms Hanisch: there really was a Josef Greiner, born in

Styria in 1886, residing in various homes in Vienna between 1907 and 1911, among them, the men's hostel at Meldemannstrasse from January 15 until April 17, 1910, and later again four times for short periods. This Greiner is identical with the author of years later. Hanisch must have known him.

Why Greiner still does not know anything about Hitler and simply tells tall tales is puzzling. One explanation might be that Greiner was a mutual men's hostel colleague of Hitler and Hanisch, at least from February 9 (when Hitler moved into the hostel) until April 17, 1910, but did not really know him well. In that case Hanisch may have wanted to compromise Hitler by claiming he was a friend of this dreamer and swindler. Because Greiner was mentioned in Heiden's 1936 book as Hitler's alleged colleague in the men's hostel and their friendship was thus confirmed, he could capitalize on it. Heiden's book served him as a legitimization, and so he does mention it in the first sentence of his preface.

The 1947 book was already Greiner's second attempt at cashing in on his "friendship" with Hitler. In March 1938 he had self-published the hurrah pamphlet *His Battle and Victory: A Memoir of Adolf Hitler*. In that publication, however, which is only thirty-nine pages long and richly illustrated with pictures of the Führer, Greiner claims to have known Hitler in the men's hostel for one year, in 1912. There is, in short, no word about 1907, about Klara Hitler's death, or anything else Greiner relates in 1947. This booklet has not been known so far but is important for an assessment of Greiner as a source, so I will quote from it extensively.[104]

In this first publication Greiner does not mention any personal experience with Hitler, only the threadbare fairy tale that young Hitler had given a beggar child his dinner, "a roll with a piece of sausage, even though he had no money to buy himself another roll with sausage."[105] Greiner clearly follows *Mein Kampf* and Heiden's book and defends Hitler against his opponent Hanisch: "Because Hitler put in a good word for him, Hanisch was jailed for only one week. And now it is this very Hanisch who, in return for Hitler's magnanimity, can't tell eager antagonistic circles enough lies about Hitler's youth." In a glorifying tone Greiner praises Hitler as a "Messiah" and endows him "with a prophetic eye": "Adolf Hitler has started his work and within a short period of time reached a stage that outshines anything else created in the world so far."

Page after page, in a bombastic style, he heaps praise on the alleged genius, his former colleague from the men's hostel who meanwhile had become master of the "Ostmark," but he does not do so in a manner based on real knowledge: "During religious discussions he displayed profound knowledge, not only of Abraham, Moses, and Jesus, but also of Confucius, Rama, Krishna, Buddha, etc. The development of the Christian churches, their schisms into oriental and occidental directions, the attempts at reformation by Savonarola, Hus, Luther, Zwingli, and Calvin were his favorite subjects." And: "Hitler himself believed in God. Wherever he stood and walked, he admired Creation's infinity and wisdom, and the way its Works had developed."

Greiner continued: "It must have been the omnipotent God's will to let Adolf Hitler literally experience the hardship of the people in order to enable him to serve his people as a true Führer. Even young Adolf Hitler had a burning heart, a profound mind, and an iron will. The flame with which he kindled German souls is burning bright in all German regions. Hail to you, Adolf Hitler!" On Austria's Anschluss he commented, "And thus a miracle happened the like of which world history has never known. The entire people cried for Hitler. . . . The shout 'Heil Hitler' is now roaring over hallow German soil, from the North Sea to the Drau. The much-defiled German military turned out to be an instrument of peace. . . . Was not God Himself in Adolf Hitler's camp?"

Greiner sent his pamphlet with personal dedications to Hitler, Mussolini, Goebbels, and Göring. He presumed the NSDAP would publish it as a promotional booklet, thus making him rich.[106]

Hitler, however, had the sham pulped. A "cautionary note" was inserted in the party files that described Greiner as a "dangerous, notorious blackmailer" who was "not acceptable" to the party. Greiner's repeated applications from May 1938 on for NSDAP membership were denied, the reason invariably being that he was "someone who turns his nose to the wind and an unscrupulous wheeler and dealer. Furthermore, there is suspicion that he has a criminal record."[107] Greiner used this rejection after 1945 to fabricate the legend of himself as a resistance fighter.

In short, Greiner always did what promised success and political advantage—before 1945, the myth about "Messiah" Hitler, and after 1945, the myth about Hitler the syphilitic and fraud. In any case, his books do not constitute a quotable source.

This also means that those alleged facts about Hitler that originated in Greiner are false. For fifty years they have been readily accepted and repeated in the literature on Hitler, usually without reference to Greiner. Future biographers of Hitler will first painstakingly and carefully have to "cleanse" the extant literature of Greiner to get to a more realistic and genuine picture. This fact also invalidates all those theories that build on

Greiner's book, including the most famous one about Hitler's alleged infection with syphilis from a Jewish prostitute.

HITLER MYTHS

Reich chancellor Hitler controlled everything the press mentioned about his former life, insisting that *Mein Kampf* be the only biographical source to consult. Thus in 1940 the press was forbidden "to deal with alleged personal experiences and memoirs from the life of the Führer. . . . The Führer's work offers so much material that . . . going back to alleged events in his childhood, youth, and military service is not necessary."[108] Indeed, numerous myths about Hitler's youth are based on the only source known before 1945: Hitler's *Mein Kampf*. Hitler himself contributed tremendously to the creation of these myths, for as he grew older, he embellished his sufferings in Vienna more and more in many speeches and nighttime monologues.

We cannot check whether the following story, which Hitler told photographer Heinrich Hoffmann, is true and was rendered correctly. Once, Hitler said, he was recommended to a Viennese lady who led an affluent lifestyle and whose husband had just died: "A charming old Viennese lady!" She wanted a watercolor of the interior of the Capuchin Church, where she had been married. Even though he typically received no more than "fifteen to twenty kronen" per picture, this time Hitler was going to ask for two hundred kronen, but in the end was too nervous and responded to her question merely by saying, "I'll leave that up to you, ma'am!" The lady disappeared in an adjoining room "with a benevolent smile" and then gave him a sealed envelope. When he quickly tore it open in the stairway, he found, "paralyzed with astonishment," five one-hundred-kronen notes.[109] Should this be true, Hitler could have lived for half a year on the sale.

Another story originated with romantically inclined Henriette von Schirach, Reich governor Baldur von Schirach's wife. She said that during his last visit to Vienna in 1941 Hitler had taken a ride along a route where they passed his erstwhile "favorite motifs": "We were riding through the old center of town at walking speed, and Hitler talked about his youth as an artist. He had the car stop in front of Parliament and got out. Without a coat or hat on, he showed us the spot where he had stood painting the building." In other words, there was no mention of always copying from originals. "Then we slowly moved on to the Opera, to Schwarzenberg-Platz, to the upper Belvedere, to the Helden-Platz. . . .

The streets were empty, it was a bright moonlit night. We rode on to Saint Stephen's Cathedral, and from there to Karlskirche. How often, he said, had he painted the facade and the tall pillars. We rode through the quiet city for more than an hour—to Minorite Church, and to one of his favorite motifs, 'Maria am Gestade' (Mary on the riverbank)."[110]

I can quote only a few examples from the many myths about Hitler's in Vienna period. For instance, nowhere do the sources indicate that Hitler worked as a draftsman in the architectural firm Max Fabiani, and certainly not in 1912, as has been suggested.[111] This myth can be traced back to a 1966 Florence newspaper's interview with Fabiani, spectacularly entitled "L'uomo che licenziò Hitler" (The man who fired Hitler). There Fabiani, the architect of Vienna's Urania, stated about his alleged former employee, "I found him so determined. You realized immediately that he was a man who would achieve something in his life." Still, he claimed, he had fired Hitler after three months, for obstinacy, discrepancies of opinion, low efficiency, and "because he was too weary."[112]

Hitler's British sister-in-law Bridget Hitler made up an even more spectacular story: she claimed that Hitler, "a shabby young man," had been in Liverpool between November 1912 and April 1913, and had lived off her, her husband Alois, and their son Patrick, who was born in 1911. However, the painstakingly kept registration records in Vienna alone prove that this trip never took place.[113]

In her memoirs, Hofburg actress Rosa Albach-Retty—Romy Schneider's grandmother—mentions that the former manager of the Theater an der Wien had told her that one day a "delicate young man" in a "threadbare, much-mended suit" had auditioned for him as a choir singer, singing Danilo's entrance song, "Da geh ich ins Maxim"—of all pieces!—from Franz Lehár's *Merry Widow*, which was well enough known to be Hitler's favorite operetta. He had done very well. However, the young man could not be hired because he did not own a tailcoat. At the time, actors and singers had to provide their own wardrobe.

Neither is the anecdote that Rosa Albach-Retty claims to have heard at tea in a friend's house in "the early summer of 1910 or 1911" more credible. She was having workmen in her house and said that "one of the workers, a pale young man," had approached her and politely asked if he could borrow two volumes of Friedrich Nietzsche's works from her. "I promise you, ma'am, that I will cherish the books like life itself!" he said, "almost solemnly," promising to return them in three days at the latest. The friend added, "A strange man. He drinks only milk and is interested in *Zarathustra*." She had found a handwritten business card in the book, which was promptly returned. "A mason handing out cards! Have you ever seen the like of it?" "What's his name?" Rosa wanted to know. "Wait, it'll come to me in a second. Adolf . . . yes, Adolf Hitler!"

In March 1938 the two were standing on the balcony of the Court Theater, witnessing the Anschluss. "Who," Rosa comments, "was riding by, standing in an open car, passing us to frantic cheers? My friend Vally's mason! Now, however, our Führer, Adolf Hitler."[114]

Anecdotes of this sort express mainly one thing: how successful Hitler was with his touching story about the poor but clean Viennese construction worker who was thirsty for knowledge.

Theoreticians of Race and Explainers of the World

Private Studies

During his years in Vienna, he *studied as never before*, Hitler wrote in *Mein Kampf. At that time I read enormously and thoroughly. All the free time my work left me was employed in my studies. In this way I forged in a few years' time the foundations of a knowledge from which I still draw nourishment today.*[1]

Indeed, Hitler must have accumulated most of his knowledge of certain facts and details, which would so amaze people later on, during his years in Vienna, particularly as it pertained to architecture, German history, stagecraft, Richard Wagner's operas, and politics. "He never read books for enjoyment or distraction. Reading books was dead-serious work to him," August Kubizek reports: "Once he had appropriated something in this manner, it occupied its firm and proper place in his memory. He knew where to recall it—and always had it handy, as fresh as if he had just read it. . . . It almost seemed as if his memory kept improving, the more material it absorbed."[2]

Hitler studied haphazardly, without direction, utterly contemptuous of schools and universities, without belonging to a fraternity, a workers' association, or anything of that sort. He got his information from books at the public library and booklets published by political parties and associations. Above all, he studied newspapers, which he read voraciously and would later praise as *a sort of school for grown-ups: By far the greatest share in the political "education," which in this case is most aptly designated by the word "propaganda," falls to the account of the press.*[3]

Otto Wagener, Hitler's confidant at the time, conveys a similar picture of the period around 1930 as Kubizek and Reinhold Hanisch did for the years in Vienna. "He didn't care who had written [an article], or what newspaper had published it, he simply took in whatever interested him and assigned it to the place in his brain where it fit in, where it either confirmed his own ideas or opinion or perhaps even gave it a foundation. Whatever ran contrary to his own ideas, he rejected and didn't even take in to begin with."[4]

Hitler developed this method of appropriating knowledge and what he called *weltanschauung* by memorizing other sources word for word and internalizing them as his own opinion when he was still young, during his period in Vienna. Reading supplied him with *tools and building materials*, as he said in *Mein Kampf*. *Like a stone of a mosaic*, this material *should fit into the general world picture in its proper place.*[5]

He would memorize what he had read by extensively talking about it over and over again. Kubizek, who at Stumpergasse in 1908 had to endure hour-long monologues at night, reports: "as soon as a book took hold of him, he started talking about it. Then I had to listen patiently, whether the topic interested me or not."[6] Rudolf Häusler made similar statements regarding the years 1913 and 1914. Clearly Hitler used his audience for his purposes, allowing neither objections nor discussion about what he said.

His secretary Christa Schroeder also reported about Hitler's "mental calisthenics," his habit of "talking several times about a topic which he remembered from his reading in order to imprint it ever more firmly in his memory" during the nightly tea by the open fireplace. As messy as Hitler was otherwise, Schroeder said, "his memory certainly was in perfect order, a bona fide mental chest of drawers from which he knew how to profit optimally."[7]

According to Schroeder, he never quoted the sources of his knowledge but always gave the impression "that everything he said was the result of his own ruminations, his own critical thinking. He could cite whole book pages, leaving the impression that what he said was the result of his own understanding." That was the reason why many people were convinced that Hitler had an "exquisitely astute and analytical mind."

The secretary reports that she once recognized much to her astonishment a "downright philosophical treatise" by Hitler as a "rendition of a page of Schopenhauer."[8]

That is probably exaggerated, but on a smaller scale, one cannot ignore that statements by Hitler from a later period were exactly identical with other sources—some of them from Vienna. What is quite clear are the traces of radical National Viennese papers, in particular the *Alldeutsches Tagblatt*, Franz Stein's *Hammer*, or the Christian-Social *Brigittenauer Bezirks-Nachrichten*—and of many booklets whose contents resembled these publications. Even as Reich chancellor Hitler was still clearly influenced by the German-National zeitgeist of Vienna's fin-de-siècle.

In the early nineteenth century, Romanticism and the liberation wars against Napoleon had awakened nationalism throughout Europe. Everyone was now interested in his own origins: the Czechs, Hungarians, Poles, Serbs—as well as the Germans, who were now rediscovering Germanic culture. The simultaneous search of various peoples for their own identity was particularly explosive in the Dual Monarchy's huge melting pot. The more a people nourished its own image as a people, the stranger the other peoples appeared to be.

In the second half of the nineteenth century, this shift of focus on one's national origins combined with Darwinism, whose theories on plants and animals were applied to individual people and entire peoples. The thesis of man's origin, which was greatly popularized, and his natural development from the ape in ancient, barbaric times to a more sublime "noble man of the future" consequently led to comparisons. The argument was that supposedly there were "strong" and "weak" peoples, peoples on the rise and peoples on the decline, developed and undeveloped peoples. Theories of race indicated ways to accelerate the "refining" of one people as compared to others. Everyone wanted to belong to the "strong," "more highly developed" one. "Purity of blood" and a clean pedigree were looked upon as strengths, a mixed background, as a weakness. It was considered to be in the vital interest of one's own people to nourish its "folkish" individuality and to avoid anything foreign as much as possible.

This "folkish defense battle" was fought on two fronts: on one, against the other nationalities within the Hapsburg empire, and on the other, as an internal fight for "racial hygiene," a policy of "keeping one's own folkdom clean," of "segregating" from the members of an "alien race." "Breeding rules" became popular, which everyone who valued "his people" was supposed to follow—including the suggestion to be careful in choosing a "racially valuable" spouse or in conceiving racially pure children, who were supposed to be strong and healthy too. There were regulations on hygiene meant to keep one's race healthy, and sports and gymnastics associations to develop physical strength for the imminent battle against the "foreign peoples." For after all, according to Charles Darwin, the "strong" were bound to be victorious, and the "weak" to perish.

All of a sudden, the mixing of nationalities, which for centuries had been an ordinary occurrence in the Dual Monarchy, was looked upon as a menace to one's "own folkdom." More and more people feared their national identity was going to get lost in this "people's mix." Around 1900 the new race theories were ubiquitous, like a religious doctrine. Writers and philosophers dealt with the subject, particularly in the wake of Gobineau, the classic race theorist, whose *Essay on the Inequality of the Human Races* was published in a German edition in 1900 and assigned to the "white race" superiority in beauty, intelligence, and strength, proclaiming it was destined to bring order into the world. These theories were used as explosive ammunition in the daily battle between the Austro-Hungarian nationalities, where they were far more extreme than they were in the neighboring nation states, including the German Reich.

Houston Stewart Chamberlain, who had been born in England and was raised in France, wrote his book *The Foundations of the Nineteenth Century* in Vienna. He, too, called for "selective breeding" according to Darwinist priniciples: "Once you have recognized the miracles selection can achieve, how a race horse or a dachshund or an 'exuberant' chrysanthemum is gradually bred by carefully eliminating all inferior elements, then you will also recognize the efficiency of the same phenomenon in the human race." Chamberlain also referred to "the marooning of frail children" with the aim of strengthening the race as "one of the most beneficial laws of the Greeks, Romans, and Germans." "Tough times" too, "in which only the robust man and the tough woman survive, have a similar effect."[9] Chamberlain considered the Jewish and the Aryan principles incompatible. Neither assimilation nor conversion, he argued, would turn a Jew into a non-Jew. This view made him an important proponent of racial anti-Semitism.

In the 1890s Chamberlain was integrated in Vienna's intellectual life. He was part of the reputable Society for Philosophy and an honorary member of the Richard Wagner Association, which had been cofounded by Schönerer, putting Chamberlain in close proximity to the Pan-

Germans. As Wagner's daughter Eva's husband, Chamberlain lived mostly in Bayreuth while Hitler was in Vienna, but the city's Pan-German press quoted him frequently.

In their popularized form, race theories could be found in all of Vienna's national newspapers. For example, the *Wiener Deutsches Tagblatt* called for "anthropological politics": "It is silly to claim that the state has no right to limit personal liberty by way of moderate legal natural selection. . . . We have to walk all the way to the top, toward the creation of the healthy new man, lest we want to suffocate in a growing heap of misery."[10]

"Folkish" circles practiced a great deal of genealogical research and called for the legal recognition of marriages according to "biological-social" aspects. See, for example, Schönerer's *Unadulterated German Words* in 1908: "We have forgotten to appreciate the value of breeding, in other words, of knowing that all noble species can be but the result of well-planned breeding with a strict selection of mates. The phrase about the equality of all men has clouded our brains. The much-praised freedom of traffic has facilitated the mixing of peoples that are foreign to each other."[11]

The zeitgeist was saturated with terms like "master race" and "inferior race." In order to corroborate race theories scientifically, many "researchers" went haywire, measuring and comparing skulls and extremities, establishing alleged racial differences in the blood, in the electric resistance, and in the breath, which was supposed to express some kind of primal personal power. Racial hierarchies were constructed. Everything, even differences in the evolutionary levels of Austro-Hungary's various nationalities, was explained by way of "race." German-Austrians liked to interpret higher education and a larger share of the tax burden as proof that there was a "master" or "noble race." Poor social conditions, a backward economy, and poor education, on the other hand, were considered indications for the presence of a "slave" or "inferior race." All race theoreticians rejected the fundamental principles of legal equality and democracy: the "slave peoples" were not considered worthy of the same rights as the "master peoples."

These theories were propagated by a large number of pamphlets penned by various authors. It is difficult to assess which one of the many writers—all of whom are virtually unknown today—influenced young Hitler, inasmuch as they all very much resembled one another both in their terminology and in their lines of argument.

Viktor Lischka, editor of the *Alldeutsches Tagblatt*, published a number of pamphlets during Hitler's Vienna years, for example, one in 1908:

"Der Kampf gegen das Deutschtum in der Ostmark" (The fight against Germandom in the Ostmark). It suggested that the House of Hapsburg had given "the still uneducated and uncivilized peoples" equal rights, making these "raw fellows" masters "before they had their apprenticeship or journeymen years." Universal, equal suffrage, the pamphlet claimed, had tried to sentence Germandom in Austria to perdition. However, "if one part should have to perish entirely in the process, it should be the state rather than our people! . . . By not wanting to let us live in the state, they force us to destroy it in self-defense. We are fighting for our very existence as a people!" The article said that a "decisive war" was being waged "about whether our people is destined to be or not to be." "We have no intention of playing yeast in the otherwise culturally almost worthless and useless mash of peoples!"[12]

Another example comes from a Pan-German flier: "The battle among the peoples is an issue not of right but of might. From the Germans' point of view, only German concerns are valid, and not those of other peoples; for no one can serve two masters who have been enemies for centuries and must needs be natural enemies. Fate hasn't meant for us Germans in Austria to form a peace league. We are enmeshed in a battle."[13]

As far as the issue of race was concerned, the Austrian Pan-Germans regarded themselves as pioneers. Pan-German writer Jörg Lanz von Liebenfels wrote in 1908: "Thanks to Schönerer's work the loyal German-Austrians are fifty years ahead of the German Reich on the issue of race policies! . . . The tough fight we, who are excluded from the Reich association, have to fight . . . has . . . trained us in regard to race policies and strengthened us racially. . . . We know from everyday experience what an inferior race means as regards moral stance and politics." The German Reich, on the other hand, whose only problem was Polish immigrants, as far as Lanz von Liebenfels was concerned, had only now arrived at the point marked by Gobineau's writings: the "racial recuperation of the entire German people" had to start "with the racially trained Austrians" as the "renewers of Germanic racedom."[14]

In 1906 Pan-German author Harald Arjuna Grävell van Jostenoode came up with practical suggestions for reaching the great goal of "establishing Germanic world rule." For example, he proposed a "Germanic education law" with "Germanic education fortresses": "Some large model schools in a beautiful environment should be available at no charge to the offspring of a pure race. These would be breeding grounds of the new spirit"—a plan that resembles Hitler's Napola schools. The author called for a caste system just as the one of the "Aryan Indians," "to counteract democratic consciousness. Everybody should be listed with his precise ancestry so one could verify where he belongs and establish how much pure blood there is within an ethnic group."[15]

Guido von List

Guido List, born in Vienna in 1848, who adopted the noble "von" as an expression of his belonging to the "Aryan master race," was the venerated head of a sworn community of "initiates" who around 1900 gathered in secret circles and groups. As a writer and "private scholar," he put his main emphasis on studying and explaining Germanic history, culture, myths, fairy tales, and legends.

A prolific writer, List's first success was *Carnuntum*, a novel in two volumes published in 1888. The book portrays the Germans, ever brave, forceful, and morally pure, as they reconquered the Roman garrison Carnuntum—which was allegedly rundown and immoral—in the fourth century and subsequently established a new Germanic empire. In his book *Deutsch-Mythologische Landschaftsbilder* (German-mythological landscape portraits), published in 1891, he started out with a description of landscapes and their names to develop an Old German cultural history, which he suggested had to be revived. In addition, he wrote epics, such as *Walküren-Weihe* (Valkyrie's consecration) in 1895 and *Ostaras Einzug* (Ostara's entry) in 1896, in both of which Wodan, the father of the gods, is implored to call on his Germans to rise from supression and reclaim power after a thousand-year twilight. At that point Ostara, the Germanic goddess of spring, will enter into the land dedicated to her: "Ostar land" = Austria.

In 1902 List became temporarily blind and had visions which he believed revealed to him the secrets of the Eddas and the Old Germanic runes and symbols. These visions gushed forth on paper in a sheer flood of words. The first manuscript, which he proudly submitted to the Imperial Academy of Sciences in 1903, was immediately returned without comment.[16] When no one else wanted to publish it either, the disciples of the seriously hurt man founded the Viennese Guido von List Association in 1907 so they could collect the money needed to print their master's writings.

All Pan-German publications promoted List and urged people to join the association, which was located near Hitler's first apartment in Vienna, at 25 Webgasse in the Sixth District.

During Hitler's years in Vienna, List's main works appeared in quick succession. The Pan-German publications dealt with and quoted them so

Guido von List

extensively that any of their readers could thoroughly familiarize them-selves with them. For example, *Die Rita der Ariogermanen* (The Rite of Aryo-Germans, 1909) offered an introduction into Germanic tribal and men's law, and called for a revival of Old Germanic laws such as the donkey ride for unfaithful women and "the wearing of shameful insignia in public. The fact that Jews had to wear a pointed hat, the so-called . . . 'Jewish hat,' was a 'telltale reference' which would serve its purpose as a sign of greed even today."[17]

List divided mankind into two groups: the Aryan "masters"—also called Chosen Ones or Initiates—and the "herd people," also called slaves, servants, or "chandals," after an Old Indian term for people with mixed ancestry. According to List, the Aryans were from a continent near the north pole, from where the Ice Age had driven them away; they had moved southward and brought culture to all of mankind. By mixing with the southern races they had decreased the degree of their own ethnic purity but raised the quality of the inferior southern races and making them capable of culture. According to List, the Aryan race lived on in a pure state only in the north.

List argued that this pure Aryan master race should be regained by "demixing" and strict segregation from the mixed peoples. Mixed marriages should be prohibited. The noble Aryo-Germans, destined by God to rule the world, should be privileged everywhere, and the "mixed peo-ple" should be assigned the position of servants: "Only members of the Aryo-German master race enjoy civil liberties and civil German law.

Members of the inferior mixed races are ruled by the law for foreigners and cannot attain any civil master privileges."[18] And: "Members of inferior races are ineligible for land ownership and leading positions, and prohibited from establishing their own enterprises and receiving any higher education."[19]

List wrote: "Yes, the immense pressure weighing on the racially pure German who is conscious of his nature seems to have had some unexpected consequences. A complete awakening of the Aryo-German mind is about to take place, if for the time being only in a minority of people." This minority, List argued, had to actively work toward the promulgation of old ideals, toward "racial awareness, the command to keep one's blood pure—in short, the most sacrosanct element of Germanic marriage, the breeding of the noble Aryan." This would—just in time, before the fall into the abyss—open up the path "toward the ancient heights of pure-blooded German heroism, toward the Holy Grail, toward Aryo-Germandom." Yet his goal could be achieved only in combat and "after a new period of heroism": "no one should spare one's body." Rebirth was certain.[20]

According to List, the master race's worst enemies were the "internationals": the Catholic church, Jews, and Freemasons, who were waging a war of extermination against the Aryan race. "Through lies and acts of violence," List said, "the clerics in Rome and the aristocracy they rule have suppressed and destroyed German customs, the German way of thinking, and German law." List predicted an "Aryo-German world war in the future," which had to be waged "in order to establish order and to regain the master privileges which were cunningly taken away from the *herrenmensch*, and also so that the herdman will again live in an orderly situation where he will find his happiness too."[21] At issue was nothing less than world dominance and—as a first step—a "pan-Germanic Germany," consisting "of Germans, the British, Dutch, Netherlanders, Danes, Swedes, and Norwegians."[22] List wanted a "Germanic agriculture," new settlements in border areas by organized, cooperative German farmers' families, as the basis for the renewal. The Aryans were supposed to regain their health by working the soil, but should always be on the lookout for enemy nomads—the Jews. According to List, the Jews were so dangerous because they were spoiling the Aryan "noble race" by way of mixed marriages. Therefore they had to be fought: "If a people lets the parasitic nomad live with them and if it makes him even a judge, a teacher, or the leader of an army, then he will turn his host's cultivated land into a desert. Therefore, let's get rid of nomadism!" And: "To be sure, they don't tell you they are nomads, they disguise themselves by wearing clothes of your own kind in order to deceive you, but they try to steal your property from you. Therefore send the nomad away." The nomad was a pest and enemy who turned "the land you have cultivated into a desert and you personally into an unsettled, itinerant have-not."[23]

The Swastika

In List's work, "serving the people" and fighting against all those not belonging to that people take on a virtually religious dimension. List founded secret societies modeled on the Freemasons he hated so much, in order to prepare for the upcoming battle between the races. Thus in 1907 the mystical association "Armanenschaft" (Armanship) was founded, whose members were personally selected by List. According to him, the Armans were the pre-Christian "noble race of the people," the "truly noble ones" as a result of years of careful breeding.[24] To be sure, the Order's brethren were actually not overly noble, as List preferred well-to-do men who generously supported his work. In such cases it was not difficult to ignore the fact that someone's ancestry was not entirely "pure." In 1911 the organization HAO was founded—"Hohe Armanen Offenbarung" (High Armans' Revelation).

These secret societies were inextricably intertwined with others in various ways, particularly after List's death in 1919. There were connections with the secret order surrounding List's disciple Jörg Lanz von Liebenfels, with the Artamans, who entirely focused on folkish agriculture, with the Bayreuth circle, the Sollnian circle, the "Thule Society," and several others.

The swastika gradually became these Arman fraternities' secret sign of recognition, and by and by it was also used in other German-folkish circles. The swastika can be traced back to ancient times, but before 1900 it was not generally known. *Meyers Konversations-Lexikon* of 1888, the standard encyclopedia of the time, explains the term in only one sentence: "The swastika can be found on prehistoric vessels and tools and is also a religious symbol of the Buddhists in India."

Early books by List contain the swastika as a sign of the "invincible," the "strong one from above," that is to say, of the Germans' savior. Other folkish circles adopted the symbol from List, for example, the New Templers around Lanz von Liebenfels. In 1907 Lanz hoisted a swastika flag for the first time on the tower of his order's castle, Werfenstein in Wachau, "as a sign of battle and victory of the Aryan ethnic spirit"—its colors, however, were blue and silver.

Even as an adolescent in Linz's high school, Hitler, like many of his

Guido von List
Das Geheimnis
der Runen

The secret of the runes

friends, became excited about the Germanic heroes and knew from his history lessons with Professor Poetsch a great deal about Old Germanic history. August Kubizek reports that in 1908 in Vienna he carried around two books for a few weeks, apparently from the public library, one containing Nordic myths, and the other, "illustrations of excavations and discoveries which permitted inferences on the Germanic tribes' level of cultural development. Adolf often talked to me about the two books and showed me illustrations." The friend remembers two illustrations: one, a ram with a sign of the sun, and the other, "the swastika, really." Adolf then told me that the German people needed a symbol, a sort of military badge representing the international concept of 'the German.' "[25] The tome was probably List's book *Das Geheimnis der Runen* (The secret of the runes), which was published in 1908.

When Hitler explained the swastika in 1920 in Munich's Hofbräuhaus, he was repeating List's teachings: that the Aryans had brought the "sign of the sun" from their home, the ice-cold North. *They build all their cults around light and they find the sign, the tool for lighting a fire, the whisk, the cross. . . . It is the swastika of the communities once founded by Aryan culture.*[26]

In *Mein Kampf* Hitler indirectly confessed his adherence to List's "Aryan mission" when he explained the political meaning of the swastika: *As National Socialists, we see our program in our flag. In* red *we see the social idea of the movement, in* white *the nationalistic idea, in the swastika the mission of the struggle for the victory of the Aryan man.*[27]

Hitler and Guido von List

Hitler's personal library, fragments of which have survived, contains a book on nationalism by Tagore, with the dedication in longhand for his birthday in 1921: "To Mr. Adolf Hitler, my dear Arman brother, B. Steininger."[28] Babette Steininger was an early party member in Munich.[29] This might be an indication that Hitler was in contact with one of the secret associations around List, but probably not until he was in Munich. However, the word "Arman" might also have had a more general meaning, underscoring Hitler's high rank within the "Germanic" hierarchy.

Other statements should be treated even more carefully, if only because they are merely secondhand information. For example, as Hitler later told a List disciple in Munich, he supposedly had a recommendation letter to big businessman Oskar Wannieck, the Munich industrialist, honorary chairman and most important patron of the List Society.[30] However, Wannieck died as early as July 6, 1912, and had long been buried in his cairn at Munich's Waldfriedhof when young Hitler arrived in Munich in 1913.[31] We have to be similarly skeptical with regard to Hitler's alleged statement that upon the recommendation of the "Vienna organization"—apparently the List Association—he had before 1914 worked as a servant at the Solln circle's club in Munich for a short while. According to the rumor, he "soon gave up this inferior position, since he didn't feel comfortable in this circle of college graduates, officers, and businessmen."[32] Rudolf Häusler, at any rate, who was extremely close to Hitler during his first years in Munich, did not indicate anything even remotely pointing in that direction.

Yet there can be no doubt that young Hitler was familiar with List's theories while he was in Vienna. Thus in a speech in Munich in 1920 he talked at length about the Aryans from the north as the originators of all human culture: In the *incomparable ice deserts* of the north, he said, *a race of giants in strength and health had grown in ethnic purity. . . . Now that race, which we call the Aryans, was in fact the originator of all major cultures of the future. . . . We know that Egypt reached its high cultural level on account of Aryan immigrants, as did Persia and Greece; the immigrants were blond, blue-eyed Aryans, and we know for a fact that no cultural nation has been founded on earth except for those countries. To be sure, there were mixed races in between the black, dark-eyed and dark-skinned southern race and the immigrants of the northern race, but there were no great independent, creative cultural nations.*[33]

That is exactly what List wrote in his book *The Names of Germania's Tribes*, where he listed all the cultures who allegedly owed their existence to Aryan immigrants, from the Chinese to the Persians and Indians, adding "that the Old Egyptian culture too originated under their influence. Buddha, Osiris, and many others, were verifiably Aryans."[34]

Statements by Hitler such as the following also clearly carry the mark of List: *Human culture and civilization on this continent are inseparably bound up with the presence of the Aryan. If he dies out or declines, the dark veils of an age without culture will again descend on this globe.*[35]

Time and time again, one can detect in the Führer's utterances List's ideology of a "cleansing" of the Aryan race so it can once again become a heroic people, for example, in 1935 when he exclaimed in front of 54,000 Hitler Youth: *We have to raise a new man lest our people perish of the symptoms of degeneration of our time.*[36] Or in 1929, in a speech in Munich: *Maintaining the purity of one's blood is the first and foremost task. When a people loses its blood value, it perishes. . . . my weltanschauung tells me that I must keep the body of our people free of foreign blood. And: before us there are only Germans, and we know only one border: we won't lift a finger for those who don't belong to our people, let them take care of themselves, may the community of their people use them for its purposes, they have nothing to expect from us.*[37]

And after suggesting that the German people was *a people in decay*, he offered the following solution: *We know only one people for which we fight, and that is our own. Perhaps we are inhuman! Yet if we save Germany, we have accomplished the greatest deed in the world. Perhaps we are unjust! Yet if we save Germany, we have removed the greatest injustice. Perhaps we are immoral! Yet if our people is saved, we have once again paved the way for morality.*[38] And: *In the fight for one's race there is no such thing as making contracts! We cannot accept a lowering of our racial level through bastardization. There is only one question: Who's in charge? There is no room for protest in these matters, there's only revenge and action! If you are finally determined to defend yourself, my German people, then do so ruthlessly!*[39]

Even the NSDAP's party platform of 1920 met the demands of Guido von List and the Schönerians, who were closely connected to him; see in particular clause number four: deprivation of the Jews' civil rights; number five: subjugating them to laws for foreigners; and number six: stripping them of the right to hold public office.

Hitler's solid knowledge of List's writings was also confirmed by his Munich bookseller, List disciple and genealogist Elsa Schmidt-Falk. She testified that Hitler owned a copy of List's *Deutsch-Mythologische Landschaftsbilder* (Images of German mythological landscapes) and was familiar with his main works. Once he told her in jest that when Austria belonged to

Germany, he would have the swastika excavated that in a maudlin midsummer night List and his friends had assembled near Carnuntum by Vienna from empty wine bottles and buried under a brick.[40] At any rate, Hitler had enjoyed talking to her about List and "our mutual homeland, Austria."[41]

With all the necessary reservations against a second-hand source,[42] we can probably believe Elsa Schmidt-Falk's statement that Hitler appreciated List's book *Der Unbesiegbare* (The invincible) and believed that List's prophecy about the "strong man from above" referred to himself. "The invincible" one was that heroic Germanic prince whose appearance had allegedly been predicted early on, in the *Edda*. List regarded it as his life's work to make the preparations for the age of this "strong man from above" and for Germanic world rule.

List's book *The Invincible: Basics of a Germanic Weltanschauung* appeared in Vienna in 1898 in the format of the little catechism, with ten "divine laws," number ten being: "Be loyal to your people and fatherland until you die."[43] The book set out to describe "a weltanschauung in a Germanic sense, in brief, comprehensible sentences," and to show "how a noble German people could be raised, both mentally and physically healthy and able to withstand the tempests of the future and to meet all demands, even the highest ones, of all times to come."[44]

List said in his preface: "For centuries those in power, who were in charge of mankind's education, tried to hone down and ultimately erase the individual peoples' basic national characteristics so they could keep chasing after the total illusion of the leveling of all tribal differences; they were led by the horrible intention of starting to raise a uniform mankind. . . . Blinded by a misunderstood love of mankind, they propagated among the peoples the absurd misconception of general cosmopolitanism with its pernicious fallacy regarding the one herd and the one shepherd."[45]

However, now that the "people's spirit" had awakened, the Aryo-Germans had to aspire to "the goal of the highest possible refinement of their people." In order to achieve this, a "national people's education" with a "people's moral teaching (national ethics)" was necessary; instead of traditional religious instruction in schools, "secular, national teachers" should educate the children toward "a religiousness budding from a national sensation . . . as the best defense against the decline of the nation."[46]

These efforts, List promised, would be rewarded, for "God loves and protects diligent, courageous, loyal, and just peoples and rewards them with prosperity and liberty. In return he sends them great men who lead them to power, greatness, and wealth."[47]

Dieſe Geheimlehre ruht nun in der Urſprache als der Myſteriumſprache unſeres Ariogermanentums und mit vorliegendem Buche biete ich dazu den Schlüſſel. Wer dieſen zu gebrauchen befähigt iſt, dem ſteht der Hehre Tempel ⌐┘ Arehiſoſur ┗┑ der Geheimlehre offen und er trete ein als deren Hierophant!

Ich biete mit dieſem Werke das Höchſte, Heiligſte, was ſeit langen Jahrhunderten ge-boten wurde, die Verkündigung der ario-ger-maniſchen Götter-Morgen-Dämmerung; — der Starke von Oben, er iſt im Heraufſtieg!

!!!   ⌐┘ **Arehiſoſur** ┗┑   !!!

"The strong one from above, he is ascending!" From the preface of List's *Original Language of the Ayro-Germans*

According to List, the longed-for popular Germanic leader, the "strong one from above," would reign as a god-man, without being subject to any law. The heroic prince could be recognized by leaving each battle as the victor. The "strong man from above" was always right, for he was in harmony with natural forces and appeared even in old legends as the Germans' savior. He could never be wrong. He was sure to attain the "final victory."

Those familiar with List's theory about the "strong man from above" being recognizable in his victories, understands Hitler's seemingly absurd sentence: *If Genghis Khan really was the great man as whom history portrays him, then he was an Aryan and not a Mongol!*[48] This remark alone proves that Hitler was very well informed about List's theory regarding an infal-lible and invincible "Aryan" savior.

Hitler's well-known, obstinate refusal ever to admit a mistake, his con-viction to be infallible, might well be traced back to this belief. In *Mein Kampf* Hitler wrote that a leader who recognizes his weltanschauung to be false should *renounce the public exercise of any further political activity. For since in matters of basic knowledge he has once succumbed to an error, there is a possibility that this will happen a second time.*[49] According to List, such an error would be proof that he is not the "strong man from above," after all.

Thus List's theory concerning an Aryo-Germanic leader, the "invin-cible one" prophesied in the days of old, was probably at least an early step toward Hitler's later Führer cult. In *Mein Kampf* he construed the necessary prehistory, a clear, organically grown and never contradictory "weltanschauung" early on—that of a "strong one from above." Trying to maintain this claim was part of the reason why he had to extinguish his traces in Vienna. His friendly relations with Jews in the men's hostel, for example, would have contradicted his assertion that his development had been straightforward, which would have weakened his claim to be the "strong one from above."

After 1933 and his government's numerous initial successes, which had been considered inconceivable before, Hitler's belief in his being chosen must have been strengthened until he virtually identified himself with this "strong man from above." In 1936 he said, *I am walking with the confidence of a sleepwalker the path Providence tells me to walk.*[50] In 1937: *If this omnipotent power has blessed a work the way it has blessed ours, then human beings can no longer destroy it.*[51] And: *If I look back at the past five years, I believe I can say: That was no mere human accomplishment. If Providence hadn't guided us, I often wouldn't have found those dizzying paths.*[52]

The self-assurance with which Hitler conducted his daring political adventures in the thirties might be linked to this belief—as well as to his being removed from reality. His Reich press spokesman Otto Dietrich later wrote about the years leading up to the war: "He was like a gambler winning in roulette who can't stop because he believes he possesses a system which allows him to make back everything he has lost and to break the bank."[53] Apparently his conviction to be invincible also fed into his certainty in April 1945 to be saved at the last minute—similar to Frederick the Great's conviction in the Seven Years' War.

List may have given additional support to Hitler's belief in being chosen. He suggested that remnants of the pure Aryo-Germanic race had been preserved in faraway areas, "in Old Saxony, in the Elbe lowlands, in Lower Austria, in the valleys of the Krems, the Kamp, and the Isper."[54] The Kamp flows through Waldviertel, where all of Hitler's ancestors were from.

Yet this illusion or this autosuggestion to be the national savior and unifier such as had been prophesied was partly also political calculation. The teachings of Gustave Le Bon, whose book *The Psychology of the Masses* Hitler had perused during his years in Vienna, might also have played a role. Le Bon wrote about the "great leaders" of the masses: "Creating belief, that is the special task of the great leaders. They don't create until they themselves have become fascinated with a belief. The strength of their belief lends their words great suggestive power."[55] According to this, such a charismatic leader would first have to get worked up about his own belief before he could dare move the "masses" to believe in him.

Hitler wanted to force the German people to its happiness: *We see in these historical materializations of Germandom fate's invisible order to unite this obstinate German people by force if necessary.*[56]

Lanz von Liebenfels

Guido von List's closest disciple was the writer Joseph Adolf Lanz, born in Vienna in 1874 as the son of the teacher Johann Lanz and Katharina, née Hoffenreich. At nineteen he joined the order of the Cistercians of the Chapter of the Holy Cross in the Vienna Woods as the novice Brother George. There he studied the history of the order and local history and became preoccupied with astrology and Bible studies. Like List, he had a "dream vision," which was triggered by an old gravestone depicting a knight pinning a monkey to the ground with his foot. Lanz interpreted this as a reference to the need for aristocratic "masterman" to subjugate "monkeyman" and from then on placed himself in the service of this idea, which had come to him in a dream.

In 1900, one year after he had been ordained into the priesthood at the age of twenty-five, Lanz left the order on account of "growing nervousness"[57] and founded the Order of the New Templars, whose cornerstones were the myth of the Grail, men's rights, and the ideal of racial purity. As a Knight Templar he gathered honorable, rich, and "racially pure" men around himself and with their money bought a castle just for his order, the dilapidated Werferstein in the Nibelung District in Wachau.

In 1902 Lanz gave himself a new identity. He changed his date and place of birth, claiming he was born in Messina, Sicily, in 1872. He assumed a fake doctorate and in all documents changed the names of his parents, who were still alive. The teacher Johann Lanz became "Baron Johann Lancz de Liebenfels" of allegedly old Swabian nobility. Lanz entirely obscured the identity of his mother Katharina, who lived until 1923, by giving her the name Katharina Skala. List backed his disciple by publishing his fabricated family tree with a detailed description of "Lanz von Liebenfels's" allegedly "genuine heraldic figures of the Armans and Femans."[58]

Later on Lanz would explain these manipulations by saying he wanted to avoid astrological checkups of himself. However, the real reason was the Hoffenreich family's Jewish ancestry,[59] which made Lanz fail to meet his own racial criteria in the Order of the New Templars. He did succeed in sneaking these false facts into the City of Vienna's official registration files.[60] Thus Adolf Lanz became the "Aryan" Baron Adolf Georg (Jörg) Lanz von Liebenfels, Ph.D.

Lanz made his living by writing numerous articles for Pan-German newspapers in the service of notoriously generous Georg Schönerer. He knew no bounds in praising his sponsor, placing him even above the Pan-Germans' superidol, Otto von Bismarck. To be sure—he argued—Bismarck had put the German people "in the saddle" by awakening its "folkish consciousness." Schönerer, however, was teaching it how to ride, with the help of his "young race operation."[61]

The former monk became an ardent opponent of the Catholic Church, especially the Jesuits,[62] and an eager proponent of Schönerer's "Away from Rome" movement, which he propagated as an "Aryan race movement": "Before our eyes a new chapter in world history is beginning. It is becoming increasingly clear that the religious controversies of former times and the national wars of the most recent times are but the forerunners of a tremendous struggle among the races for global predominance. Already we see everywhere the signs of this most enormous of all battles appear. . . . The Mediterranean countries, Mongols, and Negroes are getting ready for their joint fight against the Germanic race." It was in Rome, Lanz said, "the Germans' most embittered enemy," that they found their general.[63] However, the Germans' goal was a "unified, undivided Germanic people's church without Rome."[64] Lanz was not true to his own principles and never converted to Protestantism.

Lanz's "dream vision" turned out not to be original at all, for it was a potpourri of contemporary theories, most importantly List's race theories. "Just like every Aryan feels overwhelming repulsion at the sight of a Mongol's distorted mug or a Negro's grotesque visage . . . so the eyes of any member of an inferior race flare up in age-old vicious hatred at the sight of a paleface. One feels his own superiority and recognizes his divine origins, and the other still has the feelings of the untamed, savage ape which at such a moment awaken as the inheritance from the ancient past. . . . If our ancestors had not courageously taken up this fight, the earth would be populated by gorillas or orangutans today."[65]

Lanz was a crucial voice in the List Society, was accepted into List's mystical "Armanship," and for his part accepted List as a member into his Order of New Templars. The swastika, which List promoted, was incorporated into Lanz's new coat of arms and the New Templars' flag.

In 1906 Lanz's most important work was published, *Theozoologie oder die Kunde von den Sodoms-Äfflingen und dem Götter-Elektron* (Theozoology, or the news about the little Sodom monkeys and the gods' electron). A member of his generation, which experienced electricity as an overwhelming phenomenon, Lanz ascribed to the Aryan gods electric powers and borrowed ideas from Carl von Reichenbach's theories on magnetism

Flag of the New Templars with swastika

and the breath of life: the human brain, for example, was described as a "breath accumulator."[66] He corroborated his obscure ideas with "Biblical sources" and arrived at conclusions such as: "Christ proven to have been an electric human being during the Tertiary."[67]

Lanz's formula for the entire area of what was "moral" sounded like List's: "Everything that is good for the superior race is moral, and everything that is harmful, immoral." "The divine remains in superior human beings only when they remain among themselves. Then they will more and more become like God by way of progress and improvement. However, if they don't do that, if they mingle with inferior races, then the divine in them will gradually disappear as well."[68] "The possibility," he also wrote, "to refine and improve one's race through purebreeding [is] the only genuine and effective kind of 'repentance' for the sin of intermingling."

As the ideal way of keeping the blond race pure Lanz promoted "purebreeding colonies" in remote rural areas with strict segregation of the "brood mothers": "We have protected our cattle against racial degeneration and contamination by way of cattle breeding tariffs, but we still render unprotected human beings to contamination and blood adulteration through lecherous bastards from the East and the South."[69] In addition, he called for the legalization of polygamy for heroic soldiers.[70]

From 1906 on Lanz published the magazine *Ostara*, "the first and only periodical dedicated to the research and cultivation of heroic racedom and men's rights," with detailed reviews of the latest publications on the "race business." At first the series was a forum for Pan-German authors. Thus the first two issues made a case against universal suffrage and against Hungary. From 1908 on Lanz wrote most *Ostara* issues himself: "Race and Woman and Her Predilection for the Man of a Lower Nature," "Introduction to Racial Science," "The Dangers of Women's Suffrage and the Necessity of Master Ethics Based on Men's Rights" (1909), "Judging Character by the Shape of the Skull" (1910), "The Love and Sex Life of Blond and Dark People," "Introduction to Sexual Physics," "Moses as a Darwinist," "Callipedics or The Art of Deliberate Conception," a primer in eugenics for fathers and mothers, and many more.

Discovering the "race business" had turned out to be lucrative for Lanz, who thoroughly took advantage of it. For a fee he issued certificates of "race beauty prizes" according to a "racial value index" he had developed. For a while he inserted collectible "coupons for the racial beauty prize" in issues of *Ostara*. Readers had to send in a certain number of coupons to receive a "racial certificate"—without any actual "racial" checking.

Lanz used strong and violent language to express his extreme misogyny and to fight for men's rights. "The German woman," he wrote, preferred men of inferior races or "half-monkeys" as sexual partners owing to their greater "virility." In order to illustrate his points, Lanz liked to use stories about bitches that did not become pregnant by pedigree dogs, only by bastards. Yet, he claimed, because a woman's first lover "impregnated" her with his semen, thus appropriating her, the children from future partners would have characteristics of this first lover. Therefore the "race" was spoiled. Virginity didn't "merely have amusement value but the greatest value as regards eugenics."[71]

Lanz strongly suggested that a man have a doctor check his bride's virginity and to guard her extremely carefully after the wedding, for: "This is the tragedy of heroic man's erotic life: that both the women of his own race and even more so the women of inferior races find him not enough primitive-sensual. . . . Primitive-sensual dark men of inferior races who live among us have thoroughly spoiled our women's erotic taste both psychologically and physically."[72] Women, he argued, had been given to men as their "possession," "indeed, Nature herself has destined them to be our slaves. . . . They are our property, like a tree that bears fruit is the property of the gardener."

Yet prior to 1914, anti-Semitism was not yet at the center of Lanz's theories. His main enemies clearly were, above all, "German women," but also the "Mongols," the "Negroes," and the "Mediterraneans," which in his terminology included the Jews. Because he considered miscegenation the basic evil, he was not particularly interested in those groups of people who themselves placed great importance on being homogenous, such as the religious Jews, particularly the Zionists. Lanz wrote: "We walk on the right side, the Jews on the left; we want nothing but strict segregation, which will occur all the more quickly and easily the sooner the Jews start with their national pure-breeding." He figured the problem to be people of a mixed racial background, especially the assimilated Jews. To quote Lanz: "What shall we do with the many millions of uncircumcised and baptized people of mixed parentage who are 'partly German' and even 'Germanic,' who populate our fields of industry and big cities and have made Germandom the target of scorn around the world?"[73]

On the other hand, Lanz did not conceal his fervent admiration for one such "mixed" man, the baptized Jew Karl Kraus, mainly on account of the latter's ongoing battle against Vienna's liberal press. Lanz did not tire of trying to turn his idol into an "Aryan": "Anyone who has ever seen Kraus will instantly admit that he doesn't display the signs of either the Mongolian or the Mediterranean type. . . . He has dark blond hair that must have been light blond when he was young, a well-formed angular-round forehead and an otherwise heroic, well-sculpted face, particularly the upper part. His eyes are blue-gray. I have never personally associated with Karl Kraus. I do not know the exact measurements of his skull. . . . Heroic man is also the ingenious man. Karl Kraus is a genius, a genuine genius, for his work is that of a pioneer and creator. That alone says something about his true race."[74]

Kraus, noticeably disgusted by the debate, responded with a long, biting article entitled "He's a Jew After All!" He ranted: "I don't know from race. What the stupidity of German-folkish scribblers and politicians is thinking when it addresses me as one of theirs, and how that kosher intellect arranges things when it claims me as one of ours, and vice versa—I don't know that, that doesn't bother me, that goes in one ear and out the throat."[75]

From the twenties on, Lanz sought to be recognized as one of those having blazed the trail for Hitler. In 1926 Lanz's publisher sent his new book, *The Book of Psalms in German: The Aryosophes', Racial Mystics', and Anti-Semites' Prayer Book*, to Hitler with a dedication.[76] Friends of Lanz thought "basically the swastika and Fascist movements are merely side effects of the ideas expressed in *Ostara*."[77] On the occasion of his alleged sixtieth birthday in 1932 Lanz had people celebrate him with the words, "The pioneer of National Socialism is the modest, simple monk Jörg Lanz von Liebenfels."[78]

After 1945 Lanz lived mainly in Vienna and liked to tell reporters about his alleged connections with Hitler, which acutely embarrassed his family. His brothers Heinrich and Fritz Lanz commented, "Why don't you finally leave the old fool in peace!" The Hoffenreich side of the family considered Lanz "mad." His nephew Luigi Hoffenreich said, "At home we only called him Cuckoo."[79]

In 1951 seventy-seven-year-old Lanz also told depth psychologist Dr. Wilfried Daim that in 1909 he had personally met twenty-year-old Hitler in Vienna. He claimed Hitler had called on him in Rodaun to ask him for a few *Ostara* issues he was missing. Lanz said he had complied with Hitler's request and even given the young man, who looked "quite poor," two kronen for transportation.[80]

It is virtually impossible to verify Lanz's statement. Eyewitness Elsa Schmidt-Falk knew nothing about any personal connection between Lanz and Hitler. She says Hitler didn't even talk to her about Lanz and only once briefly mentioned "Lanz and his homosexual clique."[81] The List follower called Lanz "a dreadful person," "pseudo aristocrat," and "a monk having jumped out of his frock."[82]

Whether or not Lanz and young Hitler briefly did meet in Vienna is rather inconsequential. However, what is certain is that Hitler was familiar with the *Ostara* series and with Lanz as a prolific writer publishing in the Pan-German newspapers. Old Lanz's statement three years before his death mainly proves that even after all the catastrophes triggered by Hitler he was still keen on stressing his historic significance as the alleged "man who gave Hitler his ideas"[83]—and simultaneously, by the way, on his alleged influence on Lenin.

To be sure, among the Pan-German writers Lanz was the most outrageous. Yet the parallels with Hitler's weltanschauung are not as convincing as in List's works, for example. Furthermore, around 1900 the theories about eugenics and "maintaining pure blood" of genuine Aryans and inferior mixed-breed races were so widespread that no one author can be determined as Hitler's source. What reminds us most of Lanz is Hitler's language, for instance, when he writes in *Mein Kampf: With satanic joy in his face, the black-haired Jewish youth lurks in wait for the unsuspecting girl whom he defiles with his blood, thus stealing her from her people. With every means he tries to destroy the racial foundations of the people he has set out to subjugate.*[84]

The fact that Hitler the politican frequently mentioned "Negroes" and Jews as joint spoiler of "the German woman" and thus the "German race," is reminiscent of Lanz. For instance, in connection with the French occupation of the Rhineland in 1921 he said: *The Jew wants to violate, to completely ruin our German race; that's why he throws German women in the Rhineland to the Negroes as well.*[85]

Part of the reason why Hitler did not simply adopt the radical theories of a Lanz was certainly political tactics, particularly as far as the latter's misogyny was concerned. The folkish sectarians threatened to turn into a liability for the Reich chancellor, so he shook free of them. In *Mein Kampf* he raved with pronounced animosity about those *antiquated folkish theoreticians*, deutschvölkisch *wandering scholars*, and *folkish Methusalah*[s] who were all at variance with each other: *For the same people who brandish scholarly imitations of German tin swords, and wear a dressed bearskin with bull's horns over their bearded heads . . . run away as fast as they can from every Communist blackjack.* No one, Hitler maintains, was taking them seriously: the Left *lets them talk and laughs at them.* And: *They are not only cowards, but they are also always incompetents and do-nothings.*[86] In March 1936 Lanz was critically mentioned in an official article on "The Falsification of Racial Thoughts through Esoteric Doctrines."[87]

An eyewitness from the thirties reported that Hitler had little patience for "national sectarianism" and preferred script to Gothic writing. Once, the eyewitness said, when some overly eager man gave him a new "Aryan" libretto for *The Magic Flute* to replace "Schikaneder's text, which allegedly was a product of the Jewish mindset," Hitler rejected it, commenting that "he had no intention to make himself look ridiculous in the eyes of the world." In a small circle, the eyewitness said, he had also openly made fun of "Himmler's Germanic home-made platitudes."[88]

Hans Goldzier

Hitler later told Otto Wagener, who as a top-ranking party functionary was among those closest to him between 1929 and 1933, that during his Vienna years he had also perused the writings of Vienna engineer Hans Goldzier: *Judging by his name, he could have been a Jew, which may be the reason why he also used the pen name Th. Newert initially. Goldzier's ideas impressed me very much, but I never again heard about him or his theories later on. I only know that he was employed as an engineer during the construction of the Simplon tunnel.*[89] The name "Th. Newer" must be a mistake made during copying, for Goldzier wrote under the pseudonym Th. Newest.

From 1905 on Goldzier published a number of pamphlets in Vienna on the general topic of "Some Problems of the World." He posited a number of theories that explained virtually all the world's problems at once and supposedly disproved science, Goldzier's great enemy: "Good Lord! What did science not count, weigh, and prove! And yet, all that rubbish which was so carefully figured out fell apart when someone capable of judgment looked at the whole thing from the right angle or when a new discovery revealed the real facts."[90]

Goldzier particularly targeted Newton's law of gravity: "The Theory of Gravitation—False!" He polemicized "Against the Chimera of the Hot Center of the Earth," supposedly solved conundrums of astronomy— "From the Illusion of Comets to the Reality of the Last Things"—and unraveled all laws regarding origin, life, and death of the universe, from the Milky Way to the deluge, ice ages, prehistory, and the future. He elaborated on the location of paradise, which like Guido von List he believed to be near the North Pole. In his opinion the moon was made of iron, and the lunar craters were iron bubbles, like the air bubbles in bread dough.

And so forth: electricity was the primary force and the motor of all life; it governed people, who were "basically marionettes . . . which are wriggling on invisible threads, exactly like . . . electric fish, which pursue or abandon their goals according to the direction of electric currents."[91] He also argued that it was electricity that "decides on the individual's happiness or misfortune."

Goldzier offered some guidelines for effectively dealing with this crucial force. For example, he exhorted parents "not to tempestuously kiss their children, because repeating such caresses will frequently withdraw life current from the child.[92] Here is what Hitler told Wagener for comparison: *That's why a child screams and rejects a grandmother who doesn't stop trying to hug him; he doesn't want to waste his strength on someone who is dying. And Grandmother takes the child into her arms only because she wants to seize his surplus powers—subconsciously, of course.*[93]

Goldzier also applied this theory to entire peoples and "races," always using the Darwinist principle of "the strong ones" triumphing over "the weak ones." He argued that those short of life breath and "overly cultivated" were declining, approaching distinction, and were therefore eager to rob the healthy of their life current, thus destroying them. In short, Goldzier suggested, the weak, who were not able to live independently, represented a parasitic life form. His conclusion was: "Every people has the right vigorously to fight the willful and deliberate deterioration of its race." And: "If the individual's or society's way of life preserves and improves the species, it is good. Everything that doesn't, is bad."[94]

Little can be uncovered about Goldzier's life. Vienna's registration office has an entry on a "book printing shop owner" by the name of Hans Goldzier who is probably identical with the writer. Born in Vienna on

February 23, 1861, he had many different addresses and in 1908 moved to Baden near Vienna. His date of death is not known.[95] Goldzier's pamphlets were apparently published in his printing shop. Priced at 2.40 kronen, they were rather expensive. Yet the author emphasized that he was willing to give them at no charge to those in need, asking them to contact him.

In his conversations with Wagener, Hitler transposed Goldzier's theory of races that were strong and vigorous on the one hand and weak and parasitic on the other into politics: after longwinded explanations regarding hoarding animals, worker bees, drones, and factory owners, he reached the following conclusion: *Thus the elimination of the life that is not worth living is a consequence dictated by nature, which can be deduced from the purpose of human existence and the existence of all organisms in general.* He then referred to Moses, Confucius, Christ, and Mohammed, coming to the realization that it was only logical that the masses revolted against their exploiters, perhaps *because they instinctively recognized the true cosmic interconnections.* Ultimately Hitler again ended up with the Jewish *race of parasites.*[96] Hitler followed Goldzier in explaining in detail the effect of electricity, suggesting that it emanated from the center of the earth into the universe as "latent warmth," and looking for "ideal conductors": *this is how plants, organisms, and ultimately human beings come into existence.*

Goldzier, the Viennese explainer of the world whom science was well advised to ignore, achieved unexpected eminence only posthumously, by way of German Reich chancellor Hitler, who did admit to Wagener *that Goldzier wrote totally unscientifically. And since he attacked the dogmatic doctrines of academic scholars and posited unproven and perhaps unprovable theories, his views had no chance of ever attaining a fate better than that of Galilei and others.* Here Hitler was adopting Goldzier, who often liked to compare himself to Galileo Galilei. The chancellor continued: *So the question of in what respect these theories are correct or incorrect is none of my concern, and was none of my concern even back then.*

We know that Hitler studied Goldzier only from Wagener's memoirs. This example illustrates how longwinded and odd Hitler's monologues could be and explains why so few of his listeners bothered to write down all he said, page after page. They typically confined their minutes, which they took from memory, to politically or otherwise significant remarks and skipped long reports on little-known authors such as Goldzier. There must have been other similar sectarians in Hitler's life. Perhaps he even talked about them in detail at some point, but there were no stenographers as eager as Wagener around.

Hanns Hörbiger and the World Ice Theory

Contrary to his studies of List, Lanz, and Goldzier, Hitler probably didn't read three Viennese theoreticians—Hörbiger, Weininger, and Trebitsch—until he lived in Munich. However, they are intricately intertwined with the former three and apt to round off the image of what contributed to Hitler's early weltanschauung.

Hanns Hörbiger, Viennese engineer and technician, born in 1860, was a respected designer of steam engines whose invention of the "Hörbiger valve" made him a prosperous man. He arrived at his "world ice theory" not by way of scientific research; rather, he "received" it intuitively, as a "vision": "My glacial cosmogony is not an intellectual construction, it is a sublime gift. Two decades ago, in utter desperation of the soul, a vision was received whose cosmic, abysmal profundity made the body tremble in sickly shudders." Thus he was "the almost incidental finder of the key which deciphers the lunar hieroglyph and reveals the secrets of the Milky Way, the earthly atmosphere, and the coal seam."[97]

The similarities with Guido von List are obvious, particularly because Hörbiger, too, used not only astrology but especially Old Germanic legends as a source for his findings. Even an early text such as the *Edda*, he argued, had described the creation of the world from ice, it was just that no one had interpreted the text correctly so far.[98] Just as List's work, so does Hörbiger's have a mythical "Atlantis" in the ice-cold north as the Germans' homeland.

The world ice theory explained virtually all phenomena in the universe and also established links to other scientific theories. According to Hörbiger, at the beginning of the world was a catastrophe: huge blocks of raw ice fell into the sun, triggering an explosion and, through a splintering of the sun, creating the universe. The Milky Way was made of ice. The great revolutions in world history were likewise marked by catastrophes in certain long time intervals.

Even though Hörbiger was already working on his theory around 1900, it did not become known until its publication in 1913 and not really famous until the twenties. It is possible, but rather unlikely, that young Hitler ran into this theory via lectures or newspaper articles while he was still in Vienna. However, he must have extensively dealt with it in Munich. At any rate, he was an acknowledged follower of Hörbiger and loved indulging in monologues on the world ice theory in evening discussion circles.[99]

In the twenties and thirties Hörbiger had many followers, among them the Viennese man of letters Egon Friedell, who in his *Cultural History of the Modern Age* explained the world ice theory by arguing "that in the field of biology, evolution had to take place in the form of explosive beginnings and ends of the world. . . . According to the age-old, wise teachings of the astrologers . . . the course of world history always runs in 2,100-year-long ages, which are always determined by the sun's spring equinox and the position of the zodiacs."

According to Friedell, the Age of Aries comprised antiquity between 2250 and 150 B.C. The Age of Pisces, the era of the Occident, was coming to an end around 1950. Astrology predicted a new Hyksos rule, just as it had once conquered Egypt, for the period of transition into the Age of Aquarius. Friedell interpreted this exactly the way Hitler and many of his contemporaries did: "This can only refer to Bolshevism."[100]

Hörbiger's followers were outraged at the lack of applause his theory received from the scientific field, which also reinforced Hitler's desire to defend him. He believed that many questions could only be solved *if one day someone intuitively recognizes the connections between phenomena, thus giving precise science a direction. Otherwise we will never be able to look behind the veil which that catastrophe* [of the blocks of ice falling into the sun] *threw between the prehistoric world and our own life.*[101] He planned on practicing a *kind of artistic and scientific patronage* in the exemplary case of Hörbiger, as *the most beautiful thing there is in this world. If I can find a researcher who is looking for a new way,* he would help him in his opposition to *precise science,* which rejected everything new anyway.[102]

The world ice theory was supposed to be the pinnacle of the planetarium Hitler had planned to build on Linz's Mount Pöstling: according to the plan, the ground floor was going to have a representation of Ptolemy's universe, the middle floor, of that of Copernicus, and the top floor, of Hörbiger's theory. Hitler raved in 1942: *I see the building before my eyes, it is classic, as beautiful as anything. . . . I'm going to remove the temple of the idol that's there* [meaning the Baroque Wallfahrtskirche (pilgrimage church)] *and put this one up instead. In the future, tens of thousands of people will pass through there every Sunday, and they will all be filled with wonder at the size of our universe.* He said it was the purpose of the planetarium *to give people visiting such planetariums an even more sublime* ersatz *than the church, and to demonstrate to them the way omnipotent God works.* It was supposed to bear the inscription: "The heavens sing eternal God's praise."

District Leader August Eigruber, who recorded these statements, added: "The Führer explicitly remarked that his experiences in the East confirmed to him Hörbiger's views, even though the 'projects' didn't share this opinion."[103] The experiences in the East were a reference to the first war winter in Russia, and the "projests," the professors who sneered at the world ice theory. Hermann Giesler, the architect working on the Linz project, remembered Hitler's words: *Think of the immediate past, when a quarter of a million people froze—perhaps I'm biased—we'll see. But the sentence alone, 'Ice is not frozen water, water is melted ice,' deserves at least to be considered.*[104]

Hitler's tendency to view history in terms of eons, not to measure it on a human scale but according to cosmic laws governing human history, and finally, the illusion of building a "Thousand-Year Reich" with solid buildings meant to survive all catastrophes on earth—all this reveals that he was an eager disciple of Hörbiger and List: *Believe you me, all of National Socialism wouldn't be worth a thing if it were limited to Germany and didn't finalize the rule of the superior race over the whole world for at least 1,000 to 2,000 years.*[105]

Incidentally, Hörbiger was an opportune "Germanic" counterpart to the "Jewish" Albert Einstein and his theory of relativity, which was developed around the same time and was much harder to grasp than the world ice theory. But let us not forget: Hörbiger died in 1931 and never met his fervent follower Hitler personally.[106]

Otto Weininger

Among the six Viennese theoreticians discussed here, the philosopher Otto Weininger surpasses the others by far in intellectual depth and posthumous significance, and constitutes a special case.

Born in 1880, Weininger, a Jew who converted to Protestantism, was a profoundly unhappy man of great integrity who perished of his own philosophy, taking his own life at the age of twenty-three. What made him famous was his dissertation, which was repeatedly reissued as a book entitled *Geschlecht und Charakter* (Gender and character).

Weininger's book is a sort of typology: the male principle ("M"), representing the intellect and the creative force, is juxtaposed to the female principle ("W" for "weiblich"), which stands for being governed by instincts and the noncreative, "degenerating," feminine-Jewish principle. Weininger wrote: "for the genuine, real Jew, like woman, has no self and thus no value in himself."[107] The book is a testimony to man's fear of woman, who is supposedly menacing, devouring him and making him sick, thus representing the flip side of the sexual permissiveness glorified by Viennese modernism. At the same time it is the expression of a profound Jewish identity crisis in the grueling battle between assimilation and Zionism.

Weininger, the Jew desperately wrestling with himself and his background, was expressing his fear of the alleged agnostic, destructive power of being Jewish. Among Weininger's oft-quoted phrases were: "The spirit of modernity is Jewish, no matter how one looks at it. . . . Women and Jews are pimps, it is their goal to make man guilty. Our era is not only the most Jewish, it is also the most feminine of all eras," "the age that . . . no longer has a single great artist, a single great philosopher, the age of the least originality and the biggest hunt for originality."[108] Weininger critiziced modern art, this "whole modern intercourse culture," as an alleged "Jewish art," since it was not rooted in a homeland.[109] In all of this, he appropriated those very accusations which his great idol Richard Wagner had leveled against the supposedly uncreative Jews in his essay "The Jews and Music."

Weininger also argued that modern science, in particular medicine, "to which Jews turn in droves," should be rejected: "The Jew has no awe when it comes to secrets, because he never senses any." And: "The shameless tackling of those things which the Aryan at the bottom of his soul always experiences as fate entered science only via the Jews."[110] Clearly, Weininger protested against Viennese modernism's "pansexualism," and against Sigmund Freud and psychoanalysis in particular.[111]

The young man, who could not come to terms with his sexuality any more than he could with his Jewish background, called for sexual abstinence, inasmuch as sexuality belonged to the "realm of pigs": "There is only one love: it is the love for Beatrice, the adoration of Madonna. After all, for intercourse, we have the Babylonian whore." And: "The fact that a couple who really found one another forever and ever—Tristan and Isolde—walk into death rather than into the bridal bed, is also absolute proof of someone higher up above."[112]

Woman, he said, was "universal sexuality," blind instinct, vice, and immorality. Her only goal was use the sexual act to rob creative man—who was equipped with reason—of his creative power and to ruin him. Weininger was even so radical as to reject marriage and family, accepting the fact that humankind would die out, only so that "pure man," "God's image," could be saved. "The fear of woman, it is the fear of meaninglessness: it is the fear of the enticing abyss of nothingness."[113]

W(oman) and M(an), he wrote, had to meet the tasks dictated by nature: "Thus, while W is entirely satisfied and taken in with sexuality, M still knows of a dozen other things: fight and play, conviviality and feast, discussion and science, business and politics, religion and art."[114]

Weininger compared the Jews—and Lanz von Liebenfels adapted this—with Mongols and "Negroes": "anthropologically, the Jews seem to be somehow related to both races mentioned above, to the Negroes as well as the Mongols. The curly hair points to the Negro, and the completely Chinese or Malaysian shapes of their skulls, which one so often encounters among the Jews—who then also invariably have a yellowish complexion—point to partly Mongolian blood."[115]

Negroes, like Jews and women, Weininger argued, should not be "emancipated": "The thing about the emancipation of women is just like the emancipation of the Jews and the Negroes." To be sure, no one should be suppressed, "even though he may feel comfortable only in the state of suppression. . . . Women and men have equal rights." However, this did not mean that women or Jews should share in political power. "Just as one is well advised to not give children, the mentally retarded, or criminals any influence in the government of the community, even if all of a sudden they were to be equal in number or even gained the majority, so women may be kept from something for the time being if we have reason to fear that the issue at stake would be harmed through the impact of women."[116]

Yet as clear as Weininger's opposites of man-woman and Aryan-Jew seem to be at first sight, and as primitive as they sound in the mouths of some of his followers, they express complex thoughts and feelings. For Weininger borrowed from Freud the principle of bisexuality, according to which every human being had both masculine and feminine traits. Man's fight against immoral woman thus turned into man's fight against the feminine within himself—plus, in Weininger the Jew, into the fight against his own Jewishness. Sexuality remained enticing, even if "woman" was despised. One could not shed one's Jewishness through conversion.

The twenty-three-year-old did not see a way out of this dilemma and ended his own life in 1903 in a carefully staged suicide in the house in which Beethoven had died. His suicide has been interpreted as the desperate act in a Jewish identity crisis, or, as his friend Arthur Trebitsch wrote: "morbus iudaicus," the Jewish disease, had "killed off all joi de vivre" in Weininger, and "confused and darkened his mind in its ever-present turmoil. . . . Thus he put an end to his unbearable life, killing in a manner of speaking with his own self and his death the 'eternal Jew' in the world."[117]

His death even intensified the Weininger myth. The unfortunate man's funeral was attended by Karl Kraus, Stefan Zweig, and fourteen-year-old Ludwig Wittgenstein. The fervent admirer of Weininger and misogynist August Strindberg penned an obituary on a "courageous manly thinker."[118] An expression of the zeitgeist around 1900, *Geschlecht und Charakter* became a cult book. It influenced very different thinkers, Kraus as well as Strindberg, Wittgenstein, Robert Musil, Georg Trakl, Arnold Schönberg, Franz Kafka, Elias Canetti, Thomas Bernhard, and others, including of course those who followed contemporary trends, like Lanz von Liebenfels.

On the other hand, Weininger's desperate words about Judaism were highly welcome to anti-Semites, who quoted them a great deal and often misused them. Among Weininger's admirers was Benito Mussolini as well as Hitler. In 1941 the latter approvingly repeated the opinion of his friend Dietrich Eckart, that *he had met only one decent Jew, Otto Weininger, who killed himself when he realized that the Jew lives on the corruption of others' folkdom.*[119]

Hitler's personal lawyer, Hans Frank, also reported how opportune this Jewish anti-Semitism was for Hitler, and how "particularly happy" he was about it: "The pertinent remarks in the writings of Viennese Jewish philosopher Otto Weininger were important to him as proofs of his own lines of argument. He often talked about these and similar fruits of his nightly reading." Frank revealed that in 1937 Hitler had said: *I am an innocent lamb compared to the revelations by Jews about Jews. But they are important, these disclosures of the Jews' most secret, always totally hidden qualities, instincts, and character traits. It isn't I who say this, it is the Jews themselves who say it about themselves, about their greed for money, their fraudulent ways, their immorality, and their sexual perversions.*[120]

An allusion during a 1920 speech in Munich reveals at what length Hitler must have studied Weininger: in view of the *Jewish danger,* he said, it was crucial for every individual *to start removing the Jew in himself, and I am very much afraid that this whole line of argument was developed by none other than a Jew himself.* The audience's response in the Hofbräuhaus was one of "amusement."[121] Hardly anybody would have understood that Hitler had alluded to Weininger.

Arthur Trebitsch and Others

Before 1914 Viennese writer Arthur Trebitsch, like his friend and schoolmate Otto Weininger born into a rich Jewish family in 1880, was known only to a small circle of followers in Vienna. As a young man he was, like Weininger, part of the circle around Houston Stewart Chamberlain and dabbled as a writer, always in competition with his successful, older half-brother, Siegfried Trebitsch.

Trebitsch lived in a great style, but was hurt by the fact that his guests appreciated him mainly as a rich man and less as a writer and thinker. To his embarrassment, in March 1910 a lecture of his bombed in the Philosophical Society. This experience increased his hatred of philosophers and professors and fed his paranoia about being persecuted and systematically destroyed by them.

Two of his books, published in 1909 and 1910, were unsuccessful as well. When he could not find a publisher, he founded his own publishing house, naming it Antaios (Antaeus) after the Greek giant, the son of Poseidon and Earth Mother Gaea, who was invincible as long as he remained in touch with Mother Earth, who protected him. Antaeus is also mentioned in Richard Wagner's essay "The Work of Art of the Future," an exhortation to produce art that is close to the artist's soil and people.[122] When he was Reich chancellor, Hitler once mentioned the ancient giant Antaeus in passing, *who becomes stronger every time he falls to the ground,*[123] thus displaying before his astonished audience his knowledge of Greek myths.

In January 1909 Trebitsch officially left the Jewish religious community in Vienna, as a "List of Former Members," published in the Zionist *Neue National-Zeitung*, reveals.[124] From now on he denied ever having been Jewish: "I am not a Jew, I never was one, and I will never be one." To be sure, his great-grandfather had been a member of the "slave race of racelessness"—"I, on the other hand, free-born, highborn, and to the manner born, after three generations of being firmly rooted in my well-earned home soil, have nothing whatsoever to do with that racelessness and am as genuine and real a German-Austrian as anyone."[125]

Trebitsch's name came up in the Viennese newspapers before 1914 on account of a number of duels and slander suits he filed against all those who called him a Jew. In 1912–13 he heaped public scorn on himself by suing his half-brother Siegfried and the critic Ferdinand Gregori at the District Court: Gregori, Trebitsch charged, had called a novella of his "rubbage and garbage." Siegfried had agreed, saying he had only once read something of his brother's, which had been "amateurish." Arthur, he had suggested, was suffering from "megalomania and paranoia."[126]

During World War I Trebitsch become a "politician out of desperation," putting himself entirely in the service of "Germandom," which he idolized and believed to be threatened by the Jewish powers that be. In 1916 his polemic pamphlet "Frederick the Great, an Open Letter to Thomas Mann" appeared, in which he, the Austrian, accused the Northern German to have travestied the Prussian king, this "truly heroic and great man."[127]

Trebitsch's 1919 "confession" *Geist und Judentum* (The Jews and the mind) contained longwinded variations on Weininger's arguments but hardly anything new. The author claimed that the Aryans possess the "primary" intellect, all that which is rooted in the soil, work, the artistic, and the "creative," whereas Jews have only a "secondary" intellect and possess the qualities of "hoarding," making a profit on the works produced by the Aryans. To him, Sigmund Freud's psychoanalysis was an expression of typically Jewish "erotomania": "for they so like to work everything intellectual off sexually, where a sounder and more self-assured Nordic German knows how to sublimate all his sensuality by working and being active."[128]

He claimed that "morbus iudaicus," the Jewish disease, was poisoning "the whole world of host peoples," and that the world was "wasting away because of the disastrous consequences of the horrible infection!"[129]

After 1918 Trebitsch went from town to town as a lecturer, warning people of the "Jewish danger" in papers entitled "Germany or Zion" or "Germans and Their Rescue." Jewish philosopher Theodor Lessing observed that Trebitsch looked at each of his lectures "as a manifesto to the German people. And while speaking to a few hundred people who are not prejudiced, he feels that what he does is on the same level as Luther's deed when he burned the Pope's bull of excommunication." Trebitsch, Lessing said, was considered a "maverick weirdo": "No group takes him quite seriously."[130]

In 1919, during a lecture in Berlin, Trebitsch's paranoia became so acute that he barely escaped being submitted to an institution. His next book published with Antaios Publishers turned out all the more aggressive: *Deutscher Geist oder Judentum* (The German mind or Judaism), which was full of warnings of being "poisoned" by the Jews and of an alleged impending Jewish world rule. According to Trebitsch, the Jews were fighting along with the Socialists, the Catholics, the Jesuits, and the Freemasons to ruin the Aryans and seize power. Thus the German people was in danger of perishing if it did not defend itself. It also needed a leader who was "born and sent by God. Yet to serve the will of such a Führer means submitting oneself to the total will of the entire German people and serving that will, which has remained mute so far and become loud and clear only through this leader."[131]

The author believed he was persecuted by Jews who were supposedly trying to poison him with electric rays. In 1923 he listed all these disgraceful acts in the book *Die Geschichte meines "Verfolgungswahns"* (The story of my "paranoia"), which contained the dedication: "You will not catch me with your tricks, you Jew, / You cunning mob! For I'm a match for you."

His German identity so took over that—blond and tall as he was— he stylized himself into a sort of Aryan messiah and Germanic hero. Like

Weininger, he conjured up Christ as someone who had completely overcome his own Jewishness. For a while Trebitsch even made a claim to
leadership in German-National circles, but did not prevail.

In the early twenties Trebitsch came in contact with Hitler and his
mentor Dietrich Eckart in Munich and became one of the first patrons
of the new National Socialist party under Hitler.[132] Eckart mentioned
Trebitsch in his booklet "Dialog between Hitler and Me": "You do know
what a certain Trebitsch has said," Eckart says to Hitler: "Germany Bol-
shevist, and the Jews will easily overcome Rome. As a Jew he must know."
To which Eckart added the snide comment: "Arthur Trebitsch, Jewish
writer writing against the Jews, or at least thinks he does. His every other
word is, 'We Aryans.' "[133]

In March 1935 Hitler advised an acquaintance of his to study Trebitsch's writings: *Read every sentence he has written. He unmasked the Jews
as no one else did.* However, Hitler added, Trebitsch had believed he,
Hitler, had *a blind spot in his eye. A blind spot for the smart-alecky Zionist
snakes in the party's cadre. . . . Born Jews and Judases, he believed, were
controlling the movement, and the party would be at their mercy.* Hitler added:
*He didn't like Streicher, or Strasser, or Ley, Frank, Rosenberg, and others—
he had a whole register of names.* Hitler said he had revered Trebitsch so
much that he had even considered giving him Alfred Rosenberg's office
of *supervision of ideological training.* He had been sorry when Trebitsch left:
I know nothing about him. But I haven't forgotten what he wrote and said.[134]
In 1935 Hitler still had not learned that Trebitsch had died in 1927.

It is impossible to uncover completely all the sources of Hitler's weltanschauung, for he hid them very carefully. The most we can hope to
achieve is to get closer to this mosaic, the product of the books he read.
Furthermore, I need to stress that young Hitler did not usually gain his
knowledge directly from such philosophers and theoreticians as Darwin,
Chamberlain, Dühring, Le Bon, Nietzsche, Schopenhauer, or Schiller,
but instead from reports in newspapers, pamphlets, and popular periodi-
cals, which regurgitated the main theses of the writers who happened to
be in vogue. Trying to trace these dark sources individually is almost
hopeless unless Hitler himself gives us a clue. However, at least some
basic features are emerging. Almost all of the theories Hitler preferred
have in common that they were not in agreement with academic science
but were the products of the idiosyncratic thought processes of private
scholars who were full of contempt for established scientists, who hardly
ever accepted them either, and for good reason.

All this was in line with the zeitgeist, which in certain circles virtually worshipped dilettantism. Chamberlain, for example, proudly stressed in the very first sentence of his two-volume work that he was an "unlearned man." He then went on to make a case for dilettantism's "important task" as a "reaction to science's authoritarian rule": "Only the mediocre ones among them can bear to permanently breathe prison air." And: "Isn't it possible for some comprehensive unlearnedness to do more justice to a large complex of phenomena than the kind of learnedness which has predetermined the course of one's thoughts through strict and lifelong specialization?"[135]

To stick with this example: Hitler in fact dropped many similar remarks. However, he did not necessarily read this in Chamberlain directly but may have repeated the opinion from one or more of the numerous popular copiers and admirers of Chamberlain within Vienna's German-National circles. Furthermore, such remarks were part of the current trend against enlightenment and the exact sciences, and toward a new mysticism, toward revelations and the precedence of intuition and feeling. Politicians such as Dr. Karl Lueger, whom Hitler so revered, had tremendous success with the "people" when they dropped snide remarks about the "professors."

Hitler construed a clear and organized weltanschauung that gave preference to bipolar theories: the theory about masters and slaves, about strong and weak, blond and dark people, accompanied by a clear distinction between good and evil, as in Karl May's *Ardistan and Djinnistan* (see pp. 382 ff.), for example, between valley and mountain in Eugen d'Albert's opera, and—on a much higher level and in reality not at all as simplistically as Hitler understood it—Weininger's masculine and feminine principles as corresponding to the contrast between Christian and Jewish elements. All these theories have a distinct pattern of friends versus enemies.

Apparently such a bipolar view of the world was in agreement with Hitler's way of thinking. Albert Speer reports that as Reich chancellor Hitler's pet phrase was, "We have two possibilities here," which he used so often that his closest surroundings, including the secretaries, made it a running joke.[136]

On the other hand, this tendency to see things black-and-white was also political calculation on the part of Hitler—as it is for any politician who sees himself as a "people's tribune" and wants to manipulate the masses. Hitler did not at all hide the fact that he used this method. In *Mein Kampf*, he wrote: *The broad masses of people consist neither of professors nor of diplomats. The scantiness of the abstract knowledge they possess directs their sentiments more to the world of feeling. That is where their positive and negative attitude lies. It is receptive only to an expression of force in one of these two directions and never to a half-measure hovering between the two.*[137]

And to quote one more example from the many: *The people in their overwhelming majority are so feminine by nature and attitude that sober reasoning determines their thoughts and actions far less than emotion and feeling. And this sentiment is not complicated, but very simple and all of a piece. It does not have multiple shadings; it has a positive and a negative; love or hate, right or wrong, truth or lie, never half this way and half that way, never partially, or that kind of thing.*[138]

For Hitler, not the human being is in the center, but one's people and race, whose history unfolds in harmony with cosmic cycles, such as the ice ages. Within these cycles, the individual has no value other than being part of a people and a race and to help secure their survival in the battle against other peoples and races. Guido von List argued that in order to attain global predominance one day, the "Aryan race" had to be "pure," free of all influences "foreign to its race." In these theories, the system of rigorous "eugenics"—the German term literally meaning "racial hygiene"—with its strict marriage laws, "selective breeding," and the "meting out" of the sick and weak, which was usually explained by using the example of plant growing, appeared as a quasi-cosmic law, which in the circle of Schönerians and their sympathizers was postulated more fervently and radically than anywhere else.

What these theories make very clear is the basic Darwinist idea (which is typical of the zeitgeist around 1900 as well) that the weak will perish just as inevitably as the strong will prevail. Hitler said in 1923: *All of nature is a permanent battle between strength and weakness, a permanent victory of the strong over the weak.*[139] It is in this context that we also have to read remarks such as those Hitler made to Goebbels in the winter of Stalingrad, in February 1943: *If, however, the German people were to become weak one day, it wouldn't deserve anything but to be eradicated by a stronger people; in that case, Hitler said, one wouldn't be able to pity it either.*[140]

8
𝕻olitical 𝕽ole 𝕸odels

Georg Schönerer—The Leader

When I came to Vienna, my sympathies were fully and wholly on the side of the Pan-German tendency, Hitler wrote in *Mein Kampf*,[1] and there is no reason to doubt the validity of this statement. Even while he was still in Linz, Hitler had developed a marked preference for this political camp, of which his colleagues in the men's hostel were aware as well.

It is unlikely that Hitler ever met his political role model, Georg Schönerer, the leader of the Pan-Germans. After Schönerer lost his seat in Parliament in 1907, he hardly ever returned to Vienna. When he made his last appearance in the capital during the centenary celebrations of the Battle of the Nations* near Leipzig in October 1913, Hitler had already moved to Munich.

There is no doubt, however, that Hitler witnessed the cult the Pan-Germans created around their idol, particularly in party newspapers such as the *Alldeutsches Tagblatt*. The Pan-Germans pledged to their Führer loyal allegiance, sang Schönerer songs, and wrote poems in his praise. Entire pages of congratulations appeared in the *Alldeutsches Tagblatt* under

---

*A major victory for the German coalition armies against Napoleon. (*Translator's note*)

the title "Heil to the Führer!" and such arch tributes as "We love, we revere, we admire you and laud you as the best man our people has had since Bismarck."

Schönerer thanked his followers with a Bismarck quote: "That which is German, will sooner or later return to Germany," reminding them: "So we should continue our fight against the black and red enemies in Bismarck's spirit, and the Germanic way of viewing the world and life shall once again blaze the trail. Therefore: *Away from Judea!* And: *Away from Rome!*"[2]

Hitler witnessed the three Pan-German deputies' aggressive behavior in parliament, for example, Karl Iro's speech against the Gypsies. In the streets of Vienna he could observe the Pan-Germans' terror against Jews and Czechs. However, he gained by far the largest part of his no doubt profound knowledge of Schönerer from reading the Pan-German newspapers, the *Alldeutsches Tagblatt*, the *Unverfälschte Deutsche Worte* (Unadulterated German words), Franz Stein's *Der Hammer*, and Schönerer's speeches, which were sold as pamphlets with large print runs.

He also must have been familiar with the extensive Schönerer biography, which was penned by Schönerer's disciple Eduard Pichl and whose first volume appeared in 1912 on the occasion of Schönerer's seventieth birthday. This tome was a bona fide bible to Pan-Germans. Its epigraph read, "Through purity to unity!" and its dedication, "To the German men in the *Ostmark*." It is from this book, which young Hitler is certain to have perused, that he became familiar with Schönerer's political work in historical retrospect. Later on he would again and again refer to the Schönerer of the early days and of the nineties, which he had of course not witnessed in Vienna firsthand.

Georg Ritter (knight) von Schönerer was born in Vienna in 1842, the son of a rich railway businessman; after attending agricultural schools he became administrator of his father's large estate of Rosenau near Zwettl in Waldviertel in 1869. He proved to be extremely diligent, liberally modernized the estate, and kept an eye on profitability, but at the same time was like a benevolent father to his employees, those dirt-poor farmworkers who typically were suppressed and exploited by the landowners. He dealt with their concerns, founded a society for agriculture and forestry in Zwettl with some two thousand members in 130 local groups, and conducted seminars on modern agriculture.

Schönerer's financial generosity has been proverbial in Waldviertel to this day. He financed the establishment of two hundred fire departments and twenty-five public libraries, donated gymnastics equipment for the physical education of the rural youth, and gave money to the sick

Georg Schönerer around 1910

and poor. He tried to advance the farmers' social status and old peasant culture, costumes, and customs. In short, he became a venerated "peasant leader" in Waldviertel.

As a twenty-four-year-old, Schönerer witnessed the Hapsburg Empire's defeat by Bismarck's Prussia in the battle of Königsgrätz in 1866. Like many German-Austrians of his generation, he felt Austria's exclusion from the German Confederation* was a disgrace but not a definitive fact. In other words, he was among those who believed that the timely "perfecting" of the German Reich by an Anschluss of Austria's German parts was in the natural course of events. Schönerer wrote letters of tribute to his idol in Berlin and did not even budge when he received an unmistakably reserved response in which Bismarck let him know that he found any tempestuous Austrian-German nationalism politically inopportune. The statesman Bismarck was not interested in utopian nationalist dreams. He did not dream of letting the Schönerians jeopardize his Double Alliance policy.**

*The German Confederation was formed in 1815, after the Liberation Wars against Napoleon and the collapse of the Holy Roman Empire of the German Nation. Parts of Prussia and Austria were among the Confederation's thirty-nine members. (*Translator's note*)
**The Double Alliance was formed between Prussia and Austria at the Berlin Congress in 1879. (*Translator's note*)

Yet Schönerer continued to indulge in his hero cult, filling Wald-viertel with devotional Bismarck articles. He had a Bismarck tower made of granite blocks built in the park of Rosenau, on whose top a summer-solstice fire was lit every year; he had "Heil Bismarck" chiseled in large runes into some of the erratic granite blocks from the Ice Age that are characteristic of Waldviertel. He donated embellished signs to village taverns, bearing names such as "Iron Cross," "Prince Bismarck," and "The German Guard at the Kamp." He planted Bismarck oak trees and pleased the young people in Zwettl by distributing hundreds of spiked Prussian paper helmets.[3]

In 1873, at the time of the stock exchange crash and the ensuing economic crisis, thirty-one-year-old Schönerer was voted into the Reichs-rat as a representative of the German Progressive Party—that is to say, the Liberals. He made a name for himself as a bullheaded speaker with a temper and soon had a fight with his own party, which he left in 1876. From then on he fought Liberalism, capitalism, and "the Jews," became increasingly German-national, and earned a reputation as a fighter against corruption.

As a German-national, Schönerer was one of the main speakers against Austria's superpower policy during the occupation of Bosnia and Herzegovina in 1878, which in his opinion undermined German concerns and placed an excessive financial burden on the German-Austrians. "More and more, and ever more loudly, one can hear the German crown provinces exclaim: If only we already belonged to the German Reich and were finally rid of Bosnia and its entourage!"[4]

Schönerer used the slogan "people's law supersedes federal law" to declare the Hapsburg dynasty expendable in the "German people's" in-terest. The Hohenzollerns, he said, were the real ruling dynasty of all Germans. This made Schönerer a public enemy who from then on was under police observation.

In 1879 a government informer submitted a report about an over-crowded assembly in the town of Ottenschlag in Waldviertel, where Schönerer berated the Dual Monarchy's policy of dealing with the various nationalities, in particular, the occupation of Bosnia: "He said 10 million had been spent on Bosnian refugees, with the money taken from the Austrian people."[5] The observer continued: "People are extremely agi-tated, Schönerer's opponents constitute only a tiny minority, and every-one supports Schönerer as the real representative of the people—he is crude and unpretentious, as if made for the people."[6] From Gmünd he reported: "The atmosphere in Gmünd is malicious, antipatriotic, even downright Prussophile, Schönerer himself is idolized there."[7]

When Schönerer was on the attack, he always referred to the "will of the German people," which felt its interests were not properly represented, either in the Dual Monarchy, in the Reichsrat, or in the press, and which had made him its spokesman. In gatherings that grew larger and larger, he proved to be a people's tribune with great charisma and remarkable rhetorical abilities, which even his opponents had to acknowledge: "Physically Schönerer is short and stocky, and his fat, red beer face with its fat eyes does not leave a pleasant impression at first sight. Yet when the man speaks, he looks different. Then those otherwise weary eyes begin to glow, his hands start moving, and his features become very lively, while the words reverberate from his lips throughout the room. He accentuates carefully what he wants to come across to his audience."[8]

The German fraternities,* which upheld the national ideals of 1848 and also dreamed of a "Greater German" Reich, joined the new leader. During those years Schönerer's attraction was so strong that able young reform-minded and socially conscious politicians gathered around him. In the 1880s this circle produced an abundance of ideas and political actions, for instance, the founding of the "German School Association" in 1880 for the financing of German schools and preschools in mixed-language areas. Schönerer's most important colleagues were the young German-national intellectuals Dr. Viktor Adler, Engelbert Pernerstorfer, the historian and journalist Dr. Heinrich Friedjung, and Dr. Karl Lueger, who did not go his separate political way until a few years later.

It was this small circle that in 1882 created the "Linz Program" with Schönerer's motto "Not liberal, not clerical, but national." This basic document of the German-nationals called for social reform, including pension and disability insurance, limiting women's and child labor, democratization, and freedom of the press and of assembly. It proposed a complete restructuring of the multiethnic empire in order to make sure the Germans would be in the lead position. Hungary was supposed to become virtually independent and remain connected with Cisleithania only through personal union. The crown provinces with the largest share of non-Germans and simultaneously the greatest need of financial assistance—Galicia and Bukovina—were to be separated from the empire. (Roughly one million Jews lived in Galicia and the Bukovina.) Dalmatia, Bosnia, and Herzegovina were to be handed over to Hungary, where, along with Croatia, they were meant to form the nucleus of a South Slavic empire.

---

*The German fraternities, important carriers of the ideal of national unity, were instrumental in the (ultimately unsuccessful) revolution of 1848. (*Translator's note*)

Austria's remaining patrimonial lands and Bohemia were supposed to be linked together more closely, with German as their national language, and to aim for a tariff union with the German Reich. The authors of the Linz Program supported universal, equal suffrage only on the basis of a guaranty for a German majority and for German as the national language.

Virtually all German parties considered the Linz proposal for restructuring to be at least debatable, and so did the Hungarians—who were thirsting for freedom anyway—and most Poles, who endorsed increased independence as a start for reaching their ultimate goal, a sovereign Polish state. However, the emperor would have never voluntarily agreed to further splintering, and the Czechs would not have agreed to German as the national language.

Ethnic Anti-Semitism

In the 1880s Schönerer's struggle "for the German people" turned into a bitter fight against "the Jews," initially mainly the Russian Jews, who had been fleeing the pogroms in the Czarist empire since 1881. Again, Schönerer made himself spokesman of the "people" and on May 11, 1882, protested in the Reichsrat against the "mass influx of an unproductive and foreign element," whose number had doubled in Austria in the last twenty years, "and in Vienna, even tripled." He requested that further immigration be limited, following the pattern of the United States' anti-Chinese bill, but he did not prevail.[9]

In 1883 Schönerer appropriated Richard Wagner, who had just died, for his nationalistic purposes, turning a memorial drinking and mourning ceremony of the fraternities into a powerful political rally.[10] The New Richard Wagner Association in Vienna, which was founded a few years later, became a nursery for the cult of Germans and of anti-Semitism; its self-proclaimed aim was "to free German culture of all its fake and Jewish elements."[11] German-national celebrations were always accompanied by Wagner's music, for instance, the great School Association celebration in Vienna on December 8, 1909, which started with the *Rienzi* overture and ended with music from the *Meistersinger*.[12]

Schönerer became the most vociferous and popular promoter of ethnic anti-Semitism. In his ideology he referred to Berlin philosopher Eugen Dühring and his book *The Jewish Question as a Racial, Moral, and Cultural Issue*.[13] During Hitler's Vienna years all pan-German collections of quotes contained Dühring, for example, his remark: "It is the duty of the Nordic man, who has ripened under a colder sky, to eliminate the parasitic races, just as one simply has to eliminate dangerous poisonous snakes and wild beasts of prey."[14]

Schönerer used the slogan "Jewish or Christian, it's only race, and nothing else, that's the disgrace" to request special laws for Jews in Austria, even when they were baptized, and to repeal emancipation. He said: "We German-nationals view anti-Semitism as a keystone of the national idea, as a main support of a true folkish mentality, and thus as the greatest achievement of this century."[15] He demanded that his followers and "the German people" strictly segregate and reject everything "Jewish," according to the slogan "Through purity to unity." On February 18, 1884, at a mass gathering of Schönerians, for the first time displayed a poster reading "No Entry for Jews!"[16]

In 1884 Schönerer proceeded against the monarchy's most powerful Jew, Baron Rothschild, the main shareholder of the Emperor Ferdinand Northern Railway. In the Reichsrat Schönerer called for an annulment of that contract and the nationalization of the highly profitable railway. He submitted a list of almost forty thousand signatures in support of his motion—as a "scream of the people" against the Jewish threat. In addition, he was supported from Parliament's visitors' gallery by cheering and hecklers yelling anti-Semitic insults against the "Northern Railway Jews." This spectacular action did have the effect of Rothschild paying the City of Vienna a much higher price for extending the contract than had been planned. Thus Schönerer, the "dragon slayer" against "Jewish corruption," gained additional supporters.

In 1885 Schönerer arbitrarily, and belatedly, added the Aryan Clause to the Linz Program. His reasoning was: "In order to carry out the reforms that we seek, it is imperative that Jewish influence in all areas of public life be eliminated." This meant that he had to separate from his proven German-national colleagues Viktor Adler and Heinrich Friedjung, who were both baptized but had Jewish parents. Schönerer's slogan "Germany to the Germans" was thus directed not only against the monarchy's non-German groups, but also against those Jews who during each census indicated German as their native language, and who felt German and were politically active as German-nationals. From now on Jews were no longer supposed to be Germans.

The Aryan Clause soon found imitators: the German fraternities expelled their (thoroughly German-national) "Jews," among them Theodor Herzl, Viktor Adler, and Arthur Schnitzler. The Waidhofen Resolution declared Jews unqualified to give satisfaction in a duel. Schnitzler quoted the pertinent passage in his memoirs with great bitterness: "Every son of a Jewish mother, everyone in whose veins flows Jewish blood, is without honor by birth, devoid of any sublime emotion. He cannot differentiate between what is filthy and what is poor. He is a morally unworthy person. Therefore associating with a Jew is dishonorable; one must avoid the company of Jews. One cannot insult a Jew, therefore a Jew cannot demand satisfaction for insults suffered."[17]

Other German associations, from the Alpine Association to gymnastics, language, reading and singing clubs followed suit and typically expelled Slavs along with the Jews. On April 11, 1908—during Hitler's Vienna years—the Lower Austrian Gymnastics District celebrated the twentieth anniversary of its "de-Jewification" with "exhibition performances."[18]

Schönerer resolutely silenced doubts by dropping remarks such as, "And if certain gentlemen assure me: There are 'exception Jews'!, I reply: As long as they can't show me an 'exception bark beetle,' I won't trust these assurances."[19] Again and again he drilled into his followers' heads: "Concerning the Jews, our standpoint remains irreversible: A Jew remains a Jew, whether he is baptized or not!"[20]

The social pressure on "Aryans" with Jewish friends was increasing: those who were not willing to go along with anti-Semitism were decried as "traitors of the German people" and "Jew servants," according to Schönerer's principle: "We consider anyone a renegade of his people who knowingly supports the Jews and their agents and comrades." Schönerer appealed to his followers to prepare for a big battle: "If we don't expel the Jews, we Germans will be expelled!"[21]

The "Movement" and the Community of Faith

Schönerer turned "Germandom" into a matter of faith and a kind of religion. As early as 1883 his publication "Unadulterated German Words" published articles on "The Aspect of Faith of the New Religion of Germandom": "The folkdom of those who are German from the bottom of their beings," it read, was "a perfect substitute for religion, if not in the sense of a great number of dogmas in whose belief man's eternal bliss depends. . . . A stronghold of morality, that is what the German view of life is meant to be."[22]

The Schönerians had their own symbols and signs of recognition: the cornflower, runes, the "Heil" greeting, and German battle songs. They celebrated summer and winter solstices and observed the Ostara holiday. In historical get-togethers, the German past was conjured up. German songs were sung by the camp fire. Art was "folkish," and Viennese modernism was rejected as "international" and "Jewish."

The movement exerted its influence on family life: spouses, friends, and colleagues could only be Germans, not Jews or Slavs. Before getting married, the future spouse's Aryan descent and "biological health" had to be checked. Children received Germanic names and were raised according to "old German custom," girls being protected from the dangers of modern emancipation so they could be turned into "good German mothers." Women didn't wear makeup, had simple hairdos, and wore modest clothes. Young people were supposed to learn practicing self-deprivation and abstinence in order to stay healthy for the good of "the German nation." The Schönerians were mostly vegetarians. They strengthened their bodies through gymnastics and calisthenics, if possible in the open air.

All these rules on how to live were practiced in small groups and clubs. Vienna University had the German Students' Association for Folkish Efficiency, whose members were required to "educate" themselves "conscientiously in our way of life in order to refine and deepen our nationalism." This included abstinence, "in the awareness of the damage which the consumption of alcohol and drinking customs cause through their paralyzing effect on the individual as well as the entire people": "He who endeavors to make the best of himself in strict self-discipline and the rigorous perfomance of his duty so he can place this better person in the service of his people, performs a German deed."[23]

"Through purity to unity" also meant strictly Germanizing foreign words and phrases. The Viennese expressions "Servus" and "Prost"—"hi" and "cheers"—were replaced by the Old Germanic "Heil!" Dictionaries of Germanized expressions were put on the market.

According to an old Germanic custom, Schönerer had people pay tribute to him as the sole and absolute "Führer." To his followers, whatever he said was the law. There were no discussions on basic political principles. Those who expressed a differing opinion even on a single issue were ousted from the movement, the reason being: "Without agreement with Schönerer, the leader and creator of our program, no Pan-German . . . is entitled to publicly pronounce deviations from Schönerer's program or from the principles he represents. No one but Schönerer is entitled to change . . . Schönerer's program or the principles he represents, and there is no one among us who has either the necessary or the acknowledged authority to endorse programmatic reforms within the ranks of the Pan-Germans against our leader Schönerer's will."[24] Only a select few assisted their leader.

Schönerer's Germanic cult finally turned sectarian after 1887, when he celebrated the "two-thousand-year anniversary of Germanic history," in memory of the Battle of Noreia in 113 B.C., in which the Germanic tribes of the Cimbri and the Teutons defeated the Romans for the first time. A public plea of 1888 said: "Against the backdrop of the coarse battle cries of the Cimbri and Teutons with their primal force, the strong foundation of the Roman Empire trembled as a first warning of their destiny: 'Make room for the Germans!' " The anniversary was celebrated with a "Germanic festival" on June 24, 1888, the summer solstice, in Wachau, "according to the old German custom at the place of the oldest settlements in our mark with bonfires on the summits of those mountains at whose feet the River Danube flows as an eternal symbol of the never-resting, powerful German spirit."[25]

On the occasion of this celebration, Schönerer abolished the Christian calendar and introduced a new calendar. From now on the Schönerians no longer counted years after the birth of Christ but "after Noreia" ("n.N." for "nach Noreia"), which turned A.D. 1888 into the year 2001 n.N. Furthermore, the Roman names of the months were changed to Old Germanic names. Thus Schönerer's birthday, for instance, changed from July 17, 1842, to "17 Heuerts 1955 n.N." However, after a few years the complicated calculations became too bothersome even for staunch Schönerians. To make it easier for themselves, many started using both calendars simultaneously.

Every day the Schönerians evoked the dogma about the "German people's" alleged natural superiority to all other peoples. The Schönerians surrounded themselves with anti-Semitic riffraff. There were canes with Eastern Jews' heads as knobs, "Jew biters cigarette tips" with pictures of Schönerer for 20 kreuzer, which, however, cost "25 kreuzer for Jews, Jew lackeys, and dirty swine."[26] Particularly efficient were cheap stickers with anti-Semitic sayings. Once Schönerer bought forty thousand such coupons all at once and had them distributed in the city,[27] on mailboxes, the doors of Jewish shops, billboard posts—and sometimes even the latest newspapers in the cafes. However, the police removed the coupons, because posting them was illegal.

The *Alldeutsches Tagblatt* printed the club news, for example, those of the Pan German Club for the Ostmark, the Association for the Preservation of Germandom, and of many others, and anounced pan-German events. There were gymnastics and song festivals, beer, and lecture evenings. The Germanic League had a "German-folkish Job Placement Agency." The German Singing Society was looking for "fellow Germans who can sing." Summer rentals were offered "only for German Aryans." There were pan-German savings associations that gave out loans, and pan-German bookstores.

Particularly in the First District, where Hitler lived, in Mariahilf, there were a great number of these associations all around the *Alldeutsches Tagblatt*'s editorial offices. The chairman of the Pan-German association German Oak, Karl Geiger, lived at Stumpergasse 1. The club members met Mondays, Fridays, and Sundays in the nearby Oetzelt Tavern at 15 Bürgerspitalgasse. The tavern Zur schönen Schäferin (The beautiful shepherdess) at 101 Gumpendorfer Strasse was the regular meeting place of the local branch of the Pan-German Club for the Ostmark. Also nearby was the headquarters of the club Südmark, at 6 Magdalenenstrasse.

All these groups welcomed sympathizers. Thus a whole web of pan-German institutions was available to young Hitler, who certainly took advantage of them, if only to read the various publications or attend the lectures being offered. And even if he were to carefully hide these sources of his political education later on, they still reveal themselves, against his will, through the way he expressed himself, which clearly had Viennese pan-German sources.

Activities Against the "Jewish Press"

Schönerer had his most spectacular successes in the 1880s with his campaigns against the liberal Viennese newspapers. Initially these had attacked and ridiculed him, but subsequently they completely ignored him. Schönerer accused them of being in the service of "Jewish big business," of insulting, exploiting, and deceiving the "German people" and always merely representing the concerns of "the Jews." At mass rallies he thundered against "these obscenely sensationalistic Jewish animals from the press," "this Semitic lindworm." "Like vampires," he said, the Jews wanted "to suck their vital force from the strength of the Aryan peoples." And: "Every German has the duty to help eliminate the Jews as much as he can."[28] Schönerer's appeal to the emperor became proverbial: "Your Majesty, deliver the people from the yoke of the Jewish press!"

The battle against the "Jewish press" had its climax in March 1888, when Schönerer and some of his friends forced their way into the editorial offices of the *Neues Wiener Tagblatt* and physically attacked the editors with clubs. The reason for this was that they had announced ninety-one-year-old Emperor William I's death a few hours too soon.

This time Schönerer was put before a court, with the active help of Crown Prince Rudolf, and sentenced to four months in high-security prison for committing a public act of violence. He also lost his noble title and his political rights for five years, and thus his seat in Parliament.

In the eyes of his followers, this tough sentence turned Schönerer into a victim of the legal system and a martyr. In the evening people made demonstrations of their respect for him before his apartment in Vienna. All of a sudden, "Die Wacht am Rhein" could be heard everywhere in Vienna as a threat against the House of Hapsburg, which in the person of Crown Prince Rudolf had clearly taken the side of the "Jewish press." Overnight, stickers with the phrases "Hail to Schönerer!" and "Down with the Jews!" covered the whole city.

When Schönerer started serving his term, he rode from the train station to prison through a lane of followers shouting "Heil!" Even Christian-Social Prelate Dr. Josef Streicher was among the "Heil Schönerians": "After all, he had been the Siegfried* who had first set out to fight the dragon of the Jewish press."[29]

. None other than the crown prince ran coincidentally into such a mass demonstration in his car. Wedged in and unable to move on, he was faced with the anger of the National Socialist and anti-Semitic crowd. That evening his pessimism regarding the future of the multiethnic empire increased critically, becoming one of the many reasons for Rudolf's suicide a few weeks later, in January 1889 in Mayerling.[30]

Yet at the same time Schönerer's triumph was the turning point toward his political and personal decline. His incarceration, and even more so his forced political absence for years and his excessive alcohol consumption, weakened him and cleared the way for other parties. In 1888–89 two mass parties formed, the Christian Socials under Lueger and the Social Democrats under Adler, both of them former colleagues of Schönerer. Lueger tried to win voters by using the very slogans that had proven so successful for Schönerer, in particular the anti-Semitic platform, the call for the nationalization of large companies now in "Jewish hands," and the battle against "capitalism," the "Jewish press," and Viennese modernism.

When Schönerer returned to the Reichsrat in 1897, the German-Czech battles during the Badeni crisis** were heading toward their climax. Fifty-five-year-old Schönerer once again distinguished himself by shouting insults against the Czechs and brawling in Parliament. As a newspaper reported, "In view of the German representatives' predicament, Representative Schönerer grabbed a ministerial armchair and brandished it against the Czechs, who were ever more fiercely on the attack.

---

*Allusion to *The Song of the Nibelungs*, the great Middle High German epic, in which heroic Siegfried slays a blindworm. (*Translator's note*)
**Prime Minister Count Badeni's language statutes for Bohemia and Moravia. (*Translator's note*)

They tore the heavy chair out of his hands twice, but Schönerer got hold of it a third time. Thereupon German-Clerical representative Hagenhofer grabbed him by the throat so that Schönerer staggered backwards; but he quickly struggled back to his feet and started beating on Hagenhofer with his fist. Count Vetter, who was standing by the president's seat, grabbed a glass of water and poured it into the crowd."[31] And so forth.

Away from Rome

Around 1900 Schönerer's attraction was fading. Consequently his obsessions became all the more extreme, and he now made the Catholic church the object of his hate. A genuine German, he said, should serve neither the House of Hapsburg nor the Catholic church, the "Romelings." Rather, he had to return to the "German" religion, Lutheranism: "So, away with those fetters that bind us to a Church inimical to Germany. Not a Jesuit but a Germanic spirit shall rule and govern in German lands!"[32]

Employing the slogan "Away from Rome," he called on people to convert to Protestantism, which he himself did in 1900. Schönerer's disciple Franz Stein revealed the "Away from Rome" movement's underlying political agenda: "It was founded with with the express purpose of facilitating the Anschluss to the German Reich in another decade."[33]

Intolerant and malicious, Schönerer launched one attack after the other, first against the Jesuits, then against confession: he argued it corrupted one's chastity and dignity, inasmuch as immoral questions upset and even ruined girls and women.[34] The "Unadulterated German Words" contained reports on sexual offenses by priests and monks in a downright pornographic style. This did not fit in with the Viennese-Catholic mindset and repelled potential sympathizers, particularly since the "Unadulterated German Words" brazenly asserted "that the Jewish bible is not a German moral-religious book, and that the founder of Christianity, as the son of a racial Jewess and a descendant of David, is not an Aryan, is a fact that simply can't be reversed."[35]

Statements like this appalled all those who had converted to Protestantism out of religious conviction. Soon Protestant pastors complained about the offensive movement.[36] When Schönerer made conversion to Protestantism a requirement for being accepted into the Pan-German Party, its fate was sealed.

Even the highly successful and efficient German School Association now went into opposition. It refused not only to support the "Away from Rome" movement but also to introduce the Aryan Clause. The association continued to accept Jews, Catholics, and Protestants as teachers and pupils. Schönerer, who had since gone mad, severed his ties to the School Association and founded the School Association for Germans, which was allowed to accept only Protestants—to pathetically little success.

In response to this, Franz Ferdinand, the successor to the throne, became patron of the Catholic School Association in 1901, subscribing to the slogan, "Away from Rome means away from Austria!" The association accepted only Catholics as pupils and teachers and was under the special protection of Vienna's mayor Lueger. To the great applause of the Viennese, the latter deftly distanced himself from his former political friend: "These are not Germans but political buffoons." Schönerer returned the insult, calling Lueger "this leader of political tricksters and careerists" with his "priestly rule."[37] But at that point hardly anyone took him seriously anymore.

Schönerer increasingly became a comic figure. His slogan "Without Judea, without Rome, we'll build Germany's church and dome!" now triggered derisive laughter—as did his annual pilgimages to Bismarck's grave in Friedrichsruh near Hamburg.

Hitler the politician would stress in later years that the "Away from Rome" movement had been a serious political mistake on the part of Schönerer. The struggle against the church, he said, made the Pan-Germans *impossible in numerous small and middle circles*. This mistake had happened because of the Pan-Germans' *insufficient understanding of the psyche of the broad masses.*[38] *Its struggle against a definite denomination, however, was actually and tactically false.*[39]

Yet while he was still in Vienna, young Hitler must have sympathized much more with the anticlerical movement than he later admitted. Almost all eyewitnesses from his Vienna period mention his hatred for the Catholic church. According to August Kubizek, he said in 1908: *These world Churches are in any case foreign to the soul of the people, and the Church's cult is essentially foreign to them, they don't even understand the Church language, everything is filled with a strange mysticism. Only those princes prevailed who served the Church, which is why we have the term "by the grace of God," which really means, "by the grace of the Church." And: It is one of the cultural tasks of the future to liberate the German people from this yoke.*[40] This is exactly Schönerer's language.

For the years 1909 and 1910, Reinhold Hanisch reports that in the men's hostel Hitler criticized the Catholic church's "Germanophobia," arguing that the Germans would be a united nation and would have reached a higher standard of civilization if they had remained faithful to their old mythology. The Catholic church, he said, had spilled more blood than any other religion.

Anonymous from Brünn reports about 1912; "Hitler said the biggest evil for the German people was accepting Christian humility," for it was not Christian but had "its origin in Oriental idleness." Anonymous says that Hitler had not appreciated Charlemagne at all, for this fighter for Christianity had really been *the Germans' executioner*, halting the course of German history for at least five hundred years. *Without Charlemagne interfering, both the Franks and the Langobards would have learned the German language.* These too were typical arguments of the Pan-Germans prior to 1914.

According to Anonymous, Hitler revered Luther: "He said Martin Luther did a great service to the German people, not only because he gave it a new language, but mainly because he led away from Rome, back to a genuine Germandom." Hanisch claims that Hitler had said in the men's hostel Protestantism was the true German religion, and that he had admired Luther as the greatest German genius. Karl Honisch reports for 1913 that in the men's hostel, Hitler had mainly complained about "the Reds and the Jesuits."

All of this indicates Hitler's sympathies for Schönerer's "Away from Rome" movement. Yet officially he never left the Catholic church. Thus he never had to deal with that liability when he was a politician. He would counter pertinent accusations by saying that he had never been part of the "Away from Rome" movement.[41]

In 1902, shortly after the Schönerians had finally given their party a name—from 1901 on they called themselves Alldeutsche Vereinigung (Pan-German Association)—the "Away from Rome" movement caused the party's first internal irritation with its "leader," who was becoming increasingly erratic. Schönerer's most able and popular party friend, Karl Hermann Wolf, did convert to Protestantism but refused to make such a private affair a requirement for party membership. This led the opposition within the party to gather around him.

The controversy revived many old conflicts and basic differences of opinion. Instead of hanging on to unrealistic greater German dreams of an ideal future, as Schönerer did, Wolf saw greater opportunity in pressing for German rights in Cisleithania. In 1902 he separated from Schönerer and founded the "Free-Pan-German" or "German-Radical" party. Four of the twenty-one Pan-German deputies in the Reichstag defected to him. The Pan-German associations, down to the tiniest gymnastics and fencing clubs, cycling teams, and dancing circles, split into Schönerians and Wolfians.

Because the successful *Ostdeutsche Rundschau*, which was edited by Wolf but largely financed by Schönerer, joined the German-Radical camp, Schönerer had to found a new daily in 1903: the *Alldeutsches Tagblatt* at Stumpergasse. This paper never became as influential as the *Ostdeutsche Rundschau* and could barely stay alive. Only the fact that young Hitler habitually perused this obscure little paper while he was living in Vienna imbued it with some unexpected significance after the fact.

Politically, Schönerer, who was now considerably weaker, concentrated on his battle against the introduction of universal, equal suffrage, and thus, against the Social Democrats. Yet his painfully longwinded speeches and vicious tirades revealed his mental decline. He no longer had anything important to say. After the introduction of the new electoral law, Schönerer was no longer voted into Parliament. His party shrank from twenty-two to three seats, which did not give it even the slightest chance of effecting anything in a parliament of 516 representatives. Hitler argued in *Mein Kampf* that the fact that the Pan-Germans still shifted the weight of their activities to parliament instead of the people by way of an external opposition was *one of the main causes of the collapse of the movement.* He maintained that *even in Vienna* he had *pondered this very question with the greatest care.*[42]

Schönerer died a lonely man in Waldviertel in 1921. According to his request, he was buried in Friedrichsruh near Bismarck's grave.

Posthumous Honors

Posthumously, Schönerer won high honors through his admirer Hitler, whom he had not known. All his life, Hitler would praise this politician of his youth, dedicating several pages in *Mein Kampf* to him, lauding above all Schönerer's persistency, faithful adherence to his principles, and immutable love for the "German people."

Indeed, one cannot overlook the fact that Hitler not only adopted Schönerer's political principles but also virtually copied them. His views on ethnic anti-Semitism, the "Jewish press," Hapsburg's multiethnic empire, the precedence of the "noble German people" over all other peoples, and the Germanic cult of the leader were as much in line with Schönerer's doctrines as was his hatred of "Jewish-undermined Social Democracy," of universal and equal suffrage, democracy and parliamentarism, the Jesuits, the House of Hapsburg, and many other objects of his contempt. No doubt Hitler's early conviction that the Dual Monarchy had to be demolished in order to make possible the "unity of the German people" also goes back to Schönerer. Hitler the politician would turn Schönerer's motto "popular law supersedes state law" into the slogan *human right supersedes the state's rights*, by which he meant precisely what Schönerer had always said: that everyone's main obligations were to one's people, and not to the state to which one belonged; and, that a people was not bound by national borders but had to overcome them in order to achieve unity. This, however, was a principle which had followers among all nationalities in the multiethnic empire.

Hitler portrayed the Pan-Germans as *men of national and patriotic mind* who rebelled against the *Slavization policy* and the disenfranchisement of the Germans: *If, by the instrument of governmental power, a nationality is led toward its destruction, then rebellion is not only the right of every member of such a people—it is his duty.*[43]

He argued that Schönerer had showed the German people, which was allegedly threatened by extinction, the only possible way to go: a "Pan-Germany," that is to say, the German-Austrians' Anschluss to the German Reich. *That they mustered the courage to cry "Hoch Hohenzollern" impressed me as much as it pleased me; that they still regarded themselves as an only temporarily severed part of the German Reich, and never let a moment pass without openly attesting this fact, inspired me with joyful confidence; that in all questions regarding Germanism they showed their colors without reserve, and never descended to compromises, seemed to me the only still passable road to the salvation of our people.*[44]

Like his Viennese model, Hitler adopted the title "Führer" and introduced the "German greeting": "Heil!" Like Schönerer, he did not tolerate majority decisions in his "movement," but only *the truly Germanic democracy characterized by the free election of a leader and his obligation fully to assume all responsibility for his actions and omissions. In it there is no majority vote on individual questions, but only the decision of an individual who must answer with his fortune and his life for his choice.*[45] Only a small group was supposed to aid the leader: *What is crucial is not the quantity but the will. A minority's will that is led forcefully is always larger than a white-livered one.*[46]

Yet Hitler did not simply copy Schönerer, but also examined his political mistakes—and avoided them. For example, he wrote that the Pan-Germans had not realized that *one should, on purely psychological grounds, never show the masses two or more opponents, since this leads to a total disintegration of their fighting power.*[47] This realization led Hitler the politician not to fight, like Schönerer, against the Freemasons, Jesuits, capitalists, Catholics, parliamentarians, and many other enemies, but to focus on one single enemy: the Jews, whom he made responsible for virtually everything that was wrong.

In 1938, as "Führer of the Greater German Empire," Hitler paid homage to the idol of his youth by supporting the final two volumes of Eduard Pichl's Schönerer biography, which still had not been published yet, purchasing half the edition of one thousand copies.[48] In 1939 Munich's Hapsburg Square was renamed Von Schönerer Square as a tribute to the Hapsburgs' greatest opponent prior to 1918.

On April 27, 1941, Hitler had a Schönerer memorial plaque affixed on the house of the former Austrian Reichsrat, which now served as the NSDAP's Viennese District Building.[49] The aggressive opponent of democratic suffrage, Franz Stein, Schönerer's last disciple, delivered the ceremonial speech.

Schönerer's hundredth birthday observance in 1942 was celebrated with a large exhibition in Vienna's Messepalast. Called "Georg Ritter von Schönerer, Herald and Pioneer of the Greater German Reich," it was organized by the old Schönerians Pichl and Stein. The high point of the exhibit was a quote from Schönerer, prominently displayed: "Pan-Germany is and has been my dream, and I am concluding with a *Heil* to the Bismarck of the future, the savior of the Germans and the shaper of Pan-Germany!"

The Special District Office "Inner Front' " press office also dug out the following quote from the large treasure of Schönerer quotes, which was fitting to the war: "I am the first one to confess not only preaching love but also hate, and I am the first one to stand up for the fact that everyone who loves his people must also be capable of hatred. And as soon as my son has grown up, I will ask him: Can you love? And if he says yes, I will reply to him: Well then, love everything that is good and beautiful in the German nation! And then I will ask him: Can you feel hate too? And if he says yes, I will say to him: Well then, hate everything that is bad and everything that is harmful to the German people."[50]

In an advertising brochure for the Schönerer exhibit in 1942, Stein even troubled John the Baptist to provide a quote to the effect that Schönerer was "the voice, forerunner, and seer . . . who could not live to see fulfillment so that someone mightier could come after him to complete what he started."[51]

Franz Stein and the Pan-German Labor Movement

During Hitler's Vienna years, when Schönerer was still his followers' cult figure but no longer personally present, Franz Stein embodied the Pan-

German policies in the form of an aggressive, antiparliamentary opposition, as the head of the Pan-German labor movement and editor of the Viennese newspaper *Der Hammer*.

Because Schönerer no longer gave speeches in Vienna, Stein took over his role, even during the annual Bismarck celebrations. These always took place on the eve of Bismarck's birthday, at the restaurant Englischer Hof at 81 Mariahilfer Strasse, very close to Stumpergasse. On March 31, 1908, ten years after Bismarck's death, it was again Stein who delivered the ceremonial speech. At a ticket price of forty heller, the evening offered plenty of music by Richard Wagner—the *Rienzi* overture, the Entry March from *Tannhäuser*, and arias from *Lohengrin*—and, as always, concluded with the "Wacht am Rhein." It cannot be proven, but is likely, that in his first year in Vienna young Hitler would not have wanted to miss such a large Pan-German event close to his home and on that occasion for the first time heard Stein as a speaker.

He must have been familiar with Stein as a diligent and prominent writer for the *Alldeutsches Tagblatt*, for instance, from the Bismarck anniversary issue of 1 "Ostermond" ("Easter Moon" = April) 1908, where Stein concluded his homage with the words: "Perhaps the German people will be fortunate enough to receive a man of deed, born in the twentieth century, as tall and strong, glorious and magnificent as Otto von Bismarck, to bring the unfinished task to its conclusion."[52]

It is not known whether there was any personal contact between Stein and young Hitler.[53] This would have been most likely to happen in one of the small labor groups Stein organized in Vienna, where he frequently appeared and participated in discussions. Stein's fraternity Germania administered two somewhat large clubs with libraries and frequent evening lectures, the larger one in the Eighth District at 2 Bennoplatz. The monthly membership fee was only forty heller.[54]

Franz Stein, born in Vienna in 1869, the son of a factory worker, was trained as a mechanic. In 1888, as a nineteen-year-old associate, he had his crucial political experience: he was among the approximately five thousand people in the audience in Vienna's Sofie Hall listening to Schönerer's famous speech against the "press Jews." Schönerer's attack on the editors of the *Neues Wiener Tagblatt* shortly afterward, the trial, but above all, Schönerer's sentencing and incarceration entirely won Stein over to the camp of this "victim of the law."

Later Stein liked to describe Schönerer's triumphal procession, right after he had been sentenced, from the District Court to the house near Bellaria where he lived. His followers unharnessed the horses and pulled the carriage of the judiciary's victim. Stein talked about the shouts of

"Heil!" for Schönerer and "Boo!" for the government, and about the singing of German-national songs. Nineteen-year-old Stein was allowed to accompany Schönerer in his car to attend the tribute for him at night and to hold the famous bunch of cornflowers that Lueger handed to Mrs. von Schönerer. Hundreds of cards pledging allegiance to Schönerer were tied into the bunch.

When Schönerer started serving his term in August 1888, Stein was among those who cheered him from the edge of the street. He reported on the court's fear of these rallies and on how the gates of the castle were closed to protect the emperor, and how nervous policemen arrested honorable men for "ostentatiously waving their hats."[55]

After his release from prison Schönerer invited the young admirer to Rosenau Castle in Waldviertel. Thus began Stein's political career. Schönerer directed Stein to build a Pan-German labor movement and to win over German voters from the despised "international," "Jewish" Social Democrats. At first he sent the young man as an itinerant speaker through the area that was particularly open to German-national slogans because of the continuous influx of cheap Czech labor: highly industrialized German-speaking Bohemia, the "Sudetenland."

Stein was extremely active. In 1893 he founded the "German-National Workers Association." He also wrote for Schönerer's publications and in 1893 published his first own pamphlet, Schönerer and the Issue of the Workers. In 1895 Schönerer made him the editor of a German labor newspaper, Der Hammer. The title was an allusion to Bismarck as the "smith of the German Reich," who was often portrayed standing by an anvil, forging Germania's sword with a hammer. The new publication's subtitle was "Periodical for Social Reform and Pan-German Policy" and as a program had in its heading Bismarck's phrase: "Give the worker the right to work as long as he is healthy, make sure he gets care when he is ill and support when he is old." Stein called for social reforms modeled on Bismarck's policies, in particular—as a precondition for any social reform—the national unification of workers in their struggle against Czech competition on one hand, and Social Democracy on the other hand. Otherwise, the paper supported Schönerer's ideology, from ethnic anti-Semitism to the "Away from Rome" movement.

Stein's Hammer had nothing in common with the Leipzig periodical Der Hammer: Blätter für deutschen Sinn (Publications for the German spirit), which was founded by Theodor Fritsch in 1902, except that both shared a Pan-German political alignment and occasionally some writers. In the Reich there was clearly less interest in the German-Austrians' national longings than in Reich-German dreams of being a superpower, for instance, regarding the colonies in Africa and China and the program to build a world-class navy. Schönerer had complained about that, and Hitler reiterated these complaints when he praised *the greatness of the Germans in the Reich's old Ostmark* in *Mein Kampf*, *who, with no one but themselves to depend on, for centuries protected the Reich against incursions from the East, and finally carried on an exhaustive guerilla warfare to maintain the German language frontier, at a time when the Reich was highly interested in colonies, but not in its own flesh and blood at its very doorstep.*[56]

In 1897 Schönerer took Stein along to his new district of Eger in Northern Bohemia and in addition made him the editor of the *Egerer Neueste Nachrichten*. There Stein also published cheap pamphlets with titles such as *Social Democratic Bestialities, Unheard-of Red Terror*, and *Emergency Call of a Workman Ruined by Social Democratic Terror*.

In 1899 Schönerer, Karl Hermann Wolf, Stein, and youngish workers such as Ferdinand Burschofsky and the weaver Hans Knirsch organized the first "German-folkish Labor Day," in response to the Czech Labor Party, which had been founded shortly before under the name Czech National Socialists or Czech Radical Party and in their struggle against the German-Bohemians combined socialist and nationalist goals.

In the "Oath of Eger," deputies from ninety Bohemian towns promised to put aside all social and economic differences in order to serve the national cause. The working class, they pledged, was uniting "with the other estates of the German people who do honest work, with the farmers, tradespeople, and merchants, and the brainworkers for the joint struggle for political and national rights as well as an improvement of their social position."[57] The program had a "racial-folkish basis," excluded Slavs and Jews, and called for the introduction of protection for the workers, unemployment compensation, and health insurance for workers for their "folkish fellows."[58] Differences between social classes were to be eliminated among Germans.

On the basis of the Eger Program, Stein founded the Reich Association of German Workers Germania in the Bohemian provinces and subsequently also in other crown provinces and in Vienna, plus a number of German-folkish associations in the service industry—for example, the German Workers' Office in Eger in 1901, which offered a job placement service and legal counseling.

As a representative in the Reichsrat from 1901–06 Stein distinguished himself as probably the most vociferous speaker against the introduction of universal, equal suffrage: "Now they want to give the same illiterate man who can write neither his own name nor that of the candidate the right to cast a secret vote in an election. . . . The ballots will

Franz Stein

be cast by corrupted officials, in the clergymen's offices, and in the Social Democrats' agitprop centers—that's where the constituents will be driven to the polls by the masses."[59]

Stein distinguished himself by insulting the Hapsburgs. For instance, he said, "Austria is really only an ill-conceived geographic formation. If you look at the map, you'll have to admit that Galicia, Bokovina, and Dalmatia don't actually fit in, and Tyrol and Vorarlberg should also finally be annexed by a neighboring German state. So dividing up the Empire would not pose any great geographic difficulties." And: "The state is dying, and like all philanthropists wishing someone who is terminally ill a quick end, so I and my political friends wish this state a quick and painless end."[60]

In Parliament Stein said that the Pan-Germans could "not be got to do anything for this state of Austria, but what we do we do, only for the German people in this state. We could not care less about the dynasty and the Austrian state; on the contrary, we hope and wish finally to be delivered from this state, that what is bound to happen by nature will finally happen: the disintegration of this state so that in the future the German people in Austria can live happily outside of this state under the glorious protection of the Hohenzollern."[61]

Stein viewed the "international" and "Jewish" Social Democrats as the German workers' main enemy. In a speech that was reissued many times and was still sold during Hitler's Vienna period, Stein explained "the Differences between the Views of the German-folkish and the Social Democratic Workers." In this speech he called on the German workers to fight more actively against the monarchy's "inferior peoples" and finally to establish German predominance. He justified this by tradition, the Austrian-Germans' allegedly higher cultural level, and their superior economic power: surely, he said, one could not put "the culture of the lattice binders, the Slovaks," on the same level as that of the Germans: "Each railway car, each steamship, even the lighting in this room is a cultural product of the German mind. For centuries we Germans . . . performed the duty, not only in Austria . . . of raising culturally backward peoples to a higher level." The Slavs, he said, owed it to the Germans "having learned how to read, write, and add and subtract."

As for taxes, Stein figured out "that the German peoples pay three times as much as the Poles and seven gulden per person more than the loudmouthed Czechs, and therefore we demand that on the basis of our high tax contribution we Germans not be controlled and ruled by the other, inferior peoples." And: "When our farmers are unable to pay their taxes, the tax collector comes and takes away their last piece of cattle in the stable to turn it into money. And these taxes go to the promised land of Galicia, which gives us Polish schnapps, Polish Jews, and Polish ministers in return. We are fed up with constantly serving as a gold mine and finally have to aim toward gaining something for our people." The "inferior peoples," he said, expressed their "thanks" by "wanting to be the masters in this state, which was founded by Germans . . . and by wanting to push us down to the level where they are. We cannot allow this to happen, we Germans will never give up the privilege we deserve." In addition, Stein—like the Social Democracts—called for a reform of the tax system, for abolishing all indirect taxes and the introduction of a luxury and stock exchange tax instead.

Stein then pleaded with employers and workers alike to overcome class differences: "At a time when we are under such serious pressure from all sides—Czechs, Poles, Slovenians, Italians, etc.—every single person [had to] do his duty in the service of his people, no matter whether he is a factory owner or a worker, a scholar or a farmer, a merchant or a tradesman." And: "With German strength and German courage we will over time succeed in demolishing the international Social Democratic Party under its Jewish leadership."[62]

As for Stein's choice of words and the large degree of his anti–Social Democratic animosity, he was hardly surpassed by any other politician—and if he was, it was by the politician Hitler later on.

When young Hitler became familiar with Stein in Vienna, the latter had lost his seat in Parliament, was more radical than ever, and was the main

agitator of the Pan-Germans' extraparliamentarian opposition to democracy, Social Democracy, the multiethnic empire, Czechs, and Jews. He
was usually mentioned in the newspapers in connection with violent acts,
particularly constant brawls with Social Democratic, Czech-National, or
Christian Social workers. When his immunity expired, he was presented
with old bills: for example, in order to avoid being sued, he had to formally
apologize in March 1908 to Czech deputies because he had once thrown
inkwells at them. The *Arbeiterzeitung*, of course, could not possibly pass
up on this humiliating event.[63]

In 1907 Stein made the *Hammer's* political leanings more radical,
turning it into an outspoken polemic pamphlet with a Bismarck quote in
its logo: "Let's make no mistake about it, we are not calmly discussing
things with Social Democracy as with a party of brethren; it is at war
with us and will start attacking as soon as it believes it is strong enough
to do so."

The *Hammer* condemned the German Social Democrats' "father-
landlessness," "the worst kind of class rule, the tyranny of the masses,
which caused the magnificent old cultural world's ruin. . . . They speak
about liberty; yet they exercise the most incredible terrorism against all
workers who refuse to submit to them." Social Democrats, he said, were
anarchists who "so far have glorified any propaganda of deed, all assassi-
nations, and have praised the criminals among them who were executed
as martyrs."[64] An article on Spanish anarchists was entitled "Eliminate
the Bloodhounds!" Compassion was uncalled-for, the article argued, for
"sensations of humaneness are in contradiction to proud, purposeful ethnic conscience."[65]

Stein tried every available means to incite the Social Democratic
workers with anti-Semitic slogans against the "Jewish" party headquarters
in Vienna, tactics other anti-Semitic parties, such as the Christian Socials, also greatly favored. Hitler too liked to apply them later on. In 1942,
for example, he praised Julius Streicher's accomplishments: "He said that
by incessantly and obstinately lambasting against the Jews, he had succeeded in separating the workers from their Jewish leaders."[66]

Stein's aggressiveness could not stop the decline of the Pan-German
labor movement, which had started with the party's schism in 1902. At
the time, of the 4,320 members of his Germania, only 2,840 remained.
Most others switched over to Wolf,[67] Stein's great competitor, who also
enticed members by promising them to give them more independence
than they could ever hope to achieve under the imperious Schönerer and
his vassal Stein.

Labor leaders such as Knirsch and Burschofsky, who had switched over from Stein to Wolf, and the large Union of German Railway Workers formed the German Workers' Party (Deutsche Arbeiterpartei, DAP) in 1903, which also mainly fought against Social Democrats and Czechs. The various German-national labor groups exhausted themselves in endless venemous arguments that confused their followers. Even party historiographer Alois Ciller wrote: "Only rarely in the tumultuous history of German parties has such a vivacious movement, which could instantly excite poor and rich, young and old, farmers, the middle class, and workers, come to a more inglorious end."[68]

In 1909 Wolf released the DAP into independence, but continued to support it. The young generation became very much involved: in 1910 Dr. Walter Riel switched over from the Social Democrats to the DAP and tried to tighten the party line in the struggle against the Czechs in Bohemia. The DAP, running by itself for the first time in 1911, obtained three seats in Northern Bohemia; Knirsch and Riehl were among them. In other words, these were those people from Hitler's generation who became politically active in the national struggle in Northen Bohemia, who formed the first NSDAP in what was to become Czechoslovakia, and who later on formed the personal connection to Hitler's party in Munich.[69] However, there is no indication that young Hitler knew these young DAP functionaries in the Sudetenland while he lived in Vienna.

As leader of his party, Hitler avoided repeating the Pan-Germans' mistakes and made a point of integrating all the former Dual Monarchy's German-national labor groups equally in his NSDAP and to quench old rivalries. He paid homage after the fact to Schönerer as well as Wolf, Stein, and Lueger, and also accepted the new generation in the successor states, particularly in Northern Bohemia—which was now part of Czechoslovakia—with all honors as members of his party. Knirsch as well as Riehl would later proudly emphasize their claim to have been predecessors of Hitler's NSDAP in the Sudetenland. When Hitler took power in 1933, Riehl gave him a book on the early days of the DAP, in which he inscribed the dedication: "To the savior of the swastika, Reich Chancellor A. Hitler, dedicated at the end of July 1933 by his faithful 'Johannes.' "[70]

Stein paid allegiance to his leader Schönerer beyond the latter's death, through his club "The Last Schönerians," which shrank down to thirty-five members by 1938.[71] In the corporative state of Austria Stein was put in prison for his anticlerical and anti-Austrian stand, and afterward was unemployed and impoverished.

He was saved by a new Führer, who confessed to be an admirer of Schönerer: Adolf Hitler. Now Stein received great honors. As early as

1937 Hitler granted the old Schönerian financial support.[72] Before the referendum in April 1938 Stein made a reappearance as party speaker, and his name was on the ballot for the Greater German Reichstag. In 1938 Hitler invited Stein to a four-week vacation to Germany. On his seventieth birthday in 1939 he sent him a "Führer portrait" in a silver frame, with a cordial dedication. From June 1, 1939, on Stein received a lifelong, tax-free honorarium in the considerable amount of three hundred marks.[73] During the festivities for Schönerer's hundredth birthday in 1942 Stein appeared as a ceremonial speaker and also organized the Schönerer exhibit in Vienna.

Stein's funeral—he was interred in an honorary grave in Vienna in 1943—turned into a momentous party event. The NSDAP's top brass appeared, led by Reich Director Baldur von Schirach. The coffin was covered by a swastika flag; Hitler's wreath consisted of "oak leaves, fir sprigs, and gladioles." The police band played Beethoven.[74] "On towering pylons the sacrificial bowls were burning," the newspapers wrote.

Karl Hermann Wolf: The German-Radical

Karl Hermann Wolf, the leader of the German-Radical Party, was probably the only one of Hitler's political models in Vienna to whom he could personally convey his appreciation when he had become a politician himself. The meeting took place at the 1937 party convention in Nuremberg. After returning from a spa in Bavaria at the NSDAP's expense, seventy-five-year-old Wolf, who was very ill, almost deaf, and walked on two crutches, was invited as Hitler's guest of honor. The newspapers reported that at the end of the party convention, Hitler, as usual, received a few important people, "some of them from the circle of Germans living abroad and ethnic Germans." "Among them was a somewhat frail old gentleman dressed in a rather old-fashioned way. When district leader Hans Krebs introduced him to the Führer, Adolf Hitler stepped right up to him, took both his hands, and shook them for a long time. Then he immediately began to talk very animatedly about how during his Vienna years he used to attend meetings with Karl Hermann Wolf—for that's who the old man was—at the Wimberger tavern and other halls in Vienna, commended Wolf on his accomplishments, and promised to take special care of him."[75] That young Hitler did indeed revere this politician was no secret in the men's hostel. Reinhold Hanisch stated that apart from Georg Schönerer, "Karl Hermann Wolf too was his [Hitler's] man."[76]

After the Anschluss Wolf's name, like that of his old enemy Franz Stein, was on the Führer's list for the referendum and the election to the

Greater German Reichstag on April 10, 1938. From June 1938 on, indigent Wolf too received an "honorarium from the Führer." Until then, his second wife had supported him with great difficulty by running a tobacco store.

After his death in 1941, Wolf was also honored by the NSDAP by receiving an honorary grave in Vienna's Central Cemetery and a solemn party funeral. Baldur von Schirach paid homage to the deceased in Parliament as a "standard-bearer of Germandom," describing his "impassioned defensive struggle" against the Czechs. The Führer, von Schirach said, had enthusiastically listened to Wolf during his Vienna years. It had been Wolf who had made him "conscious, for the first time, of the might of the spoken word and its power of conviction."[77]

Aside from many prominent party members, storm troopers of honor of the SA, a formation of political directors, and guards of honor of the Hitler Youth paid the old warrior their last respects. The State Opera choir sang Franz Schubert's "Litany," and a trumpet ensemble played while the coffin was being lowered. Then the mourners threw cornflowers into the open grave. Hitler's wreath of oak leaves and lilies bore the dedication "To the pioneer of the idea of the Greater Germany."[78]

When Hitler arrived in Vienna in 1908, Wolf was forty-six years old and at the pinnacle of his political career. He was founder and chairman of the German-Radical Party and a well-known representative in the Reichsrat. To be sure, the center of his activities was in the Sudetenland; but on account of the Reichsrat alone, he was often in Vienna, where he appeared at many national gatherings, for example, at the tavern Wimberger in Mariahilf, where young Hitler heard him.

Wolf was considered the most vigorous fighter for "German folkdom" in Austria. He was the German students' idol and generally extremely popular, mainly because he was quick at repartee and witty. He was short and, although he limped, very agile. He liked to garnish his speeches with classical quotes, was as comfortable among students as he was among workers, and was very self-confident. He was in every respect the opposite of Stein, who was huge, had a resounding voice, was awkward, had no sense of humor, was vulgar and aggressive, and in general repeated what his leader Schönerer said as well, only in much coarser words.

Wolf lived mainly in the Dual Monarchy's mixed-language areas or in German-speaking enclaves. He was born the son of a high school teacher in Eger in Northern Bohemia in 1862 and went to college in

Prague, where he majored in philosophy and became very active within his German fraternity. In 1884 he was sued for lese majesty, fled from the impending trial to Leipzig, and dropped out of school. In 1886 he became an editor at the *Deutsche Wacht* in Cilli, which at the time was a German-speaking city in Slovenian surroundings in Lower Styria, and then at the *Deutsche Volks-Zeitung* in Reichenberg in Northern Bohemia.

Confronted with the language battle early on, he believed the German people was threatened from all sides: "In the North, where German strength is protecting its rights against Czech arrogance, in the imperial capital, where the national idea frequently still knocks on the doors of the Phaeacians who, nationally indifferent and politically insignificant, aren't listening, in the valleys of the Alps, where the clergy's lust for power tries to keep the people in the fetters of ignorance, and even here at home, where we are building the German guard against Slovenians and fanatical darklings in the South of Styria."[79] Wolf saw the escape from the "German predicament" in vigorous national self-help on the part of the Germans.

In 1889 Wolf went to Vienna as a newspaper editor. He found a patron in Schönerer, who in those years had to keep away from politics. Schönerer also financed Wolf's new newspaper, the *Ostdeutsche Rundschau*. The title alone was provocative. For *ostdeutsch* (Eastern German) referred to the "Ostmark," and instead of the double eagle, the newspaper's logo contained the one-headed eagle, which was interpreted as a German eagle. The snake it held in its claws was interpreted as a symbol of the Jews.[80]

In the 1890s Wolf quickly also made a name for himself in Vienna as an orator. An otherwise critical contemporary commented on the little-respected Schönerians of the time: "Only one of them, Karl Herman Wolf, distinguished himself from the others, in some respects certainly to his advantage. Exquisitely talented and an excellent speaker with a deep, mellifluous voice, he sometimes found words which left the impression of genuine conviction, even true warmth of feeling, and directly spoke to the heart. . . . All the while this little, homely man with the limp food was quite an audiacious brawler."[81]

The Badeni riots in 1897 made Wolf a hero of the German-nationals. This most dangerous national crisis since the revolution of 1848 was triggered by the language laws of prime minister Kasimir Count Badeni from Poland. According to the new statutes, all federal civil servants in Bohemia had to prove their bilingualism within four years—and in purely

German areas as well. This would have meant the replacement of most German civil servants, for few of them spoke Czech, whereas the Czechs tended to be bilingual.

For months the western part of the empire did not come to rest. The mood became more and more extreme, even within otherwise moderate parties such as the Christian Socials and the German Social Democrats. The government was unable to quench the unrest, which first broke out in Northern Bohemia and then spread to Prague and Vienna, growing into a veritable German-national revolution against the multiethnic empire, the "Polish" government, and the imperial family. Eventually a state of emergency had to be declared in Bohemia.

From the start, the Schönerians' main political area was in the Sudetenland, where Schönerer's, Wolf's, and Stein's electoral districts were. They believed their time had now come. From the street they pressured the government by using the slogan "Only German public servants in German-speaking areas," to wide popular acclaim. In radical popular speeches, it was particularly Wolf who turned the struggle between nationalities into the Germans' liberation battle and was several times reported to the police for high treason and lese majesty.[82]

The situation started to threaten the security of the state when the Germans began to paralyze Parliament through filibusters, with the clear aim of toppling the Badeni government. Again Wolf distinguished himself through a veritable terror of the minority against the majority, and with language as aggressive as had hitherto been unheard-of in Parliament: "Now they want to use the Polish scourge to whip the German people in Austria out of its own and into the Slavic skin. Yet there are still fellows around who know what's right and what's wrong. We won't be cheated out of the most sacrosanct thing we have, our folkdom. All violence they use against us will only incite the people's wrath even more. There is a closed phalanx which is ready to set everything aside for the honor of the German people."[83]

In this revolutionary atmosphere, other non-German nationalities joined the troubled Czechs, in particular the Poles. Orgies of invectives, brawls, and fistfights took place almost daily in Parliament. The members of the German fraternities made rallies in front of the Reichsrat, celebrating their heroes.

According to a witness report, Wolf targeted Badeni personally: "Limping back and forth before the minister's bench, he fixated him in the most insulting manner, hissed provocative words at him, and sneered right in his face."[84] Count Badeni let himself be caught in the trap: he challenged Wolf to a duel. The latter accepted immediately, thus getting

Badeni precisely into the serious predicament he had intended. For although duels were part of the code of honor and almost never punished, legally they still were considered crimes. A prime minister who was guilty of a crime by taking part in a duel was politically hardly tolerable. Badeni offered the emperor his resignation. Franz Josef refused to accept it. The duel between the prime minister and Parliament's most extreme radical took place with pistols and an exchange of three bullets. Wolf, experienced in duels, won, injuring Badeni's arm. The news about this was an international sensation, and the monarchy's reputation was seriously damaged. Wolf was now a famous man.

The riots against the language laws continued. In November 1897 the police forced Schönerer, Wolf, and a few German Social Democrats to leave Parliament, and demonstrators received them in front of the building with ovations. Wolf was taken into custody for committing violent acts in public and submitted to the district court—which in turn triggered demonstrations before the courthouse as well, with the obligatory singing of the "Wacht am Rhein." In the streets, students and workers joined together against the Polish prime minister, who now, when Mayor Dr. Karl Lueger turned against him as well, resigned. A few hours later Wolf was released and celebrated as a hero. Someone composed a "Karl Hermann Wolf March." Karl Hermann became a popular Christian name for German boys. In the following elections in 1901, the Schönerians increased their number of seats from eight to twenty-one, mainly on account of Wolf.

The statutes under discussion were rescinded. Still, the situation did not calm down. For now the Czechs, rather than the Germans, went into opposition. They paralyzed the Bohemian Parliament and the Reichsrat in Vienna through filibusters. The hatred between Czechs and Germans in Bohemia became utterly divisive. The few who kept a cool head amidst all this chaos had every reason to worry about the Dual Monarchy's governability and future.

Wolf's triumphs placed a burden on his relationship with Schönerer. In 1902 Wolf separated from the "Führer" and founded the "Free-Pan-German" or "German-Radical" party, explicitly not a small elitist party but one for the masses. He declared his loyalty to the House of Hapsburg and the Dual Monarchy, was willing to cooperate with the Government, and actively worked with it on specific issues. In the center of his activities was his support of the German minorities, wherever they were—particularly in Bohemia, but also in Galicia, Slovenia, and elsewhere. All German fraternities joined his camp.

Ein Wahrzeichen.

"A symbol." "Pan-German Eagle for Pan-German Clubhouses": a jibe
at the battle between Schönerer (left) and Wolf

As for his party program, Wolf essentially adhered to the Linz Program of 1882—in other words, separation of church and state and a liberal
reform of domestic relations law and education. He did, of course, also
call for making German the national language in Cisleithania, as well as
for naming the western half of the empire Austria.

The Wolfians supported universal, equal suffrage, and during the annexation crisis of 1908 also voted in line with the Government. Thus they put their loyalty to the Hapsburgs above that to Germandom, which angered not only the Pan-Germans but also even the Social Democrats. Friedrich Austerlitz wrote in the *Arbeiterzeitung*: "They call themselves German-Radicals, but black-yellow veterans, obsequious court lackeys, that's what they are!"[85] Self-confident Social Democrat Engelbert Pernerstorfer mourned Wolf as the German-nationals' evaporated hope: "If he had had self-control and been serious, he could have become a leader."[86]

After Lueger's death in 1910 the Wolfians adopted his slogan about "Greater Austria," giving it their own twist: "By this term we mean a uniform, centralistically governed and administrated state comprising the entire Hapsburg Monarchy, in which there is no room for an independent kingdom," which was a reference to Hungary. "Such a Greater Austria could not even exist other than with German predominance," for after all, the German people was "the largest and most powerful uniform people," whereas the Slavs belonged to various different peoples.

Wolf was against pursuing the Anschluss to the German Reich because it could not be accomplished without leading to a catastrophe: "Yes, we certainly do need a German policy, but one that is also reasonable and has attainable goals." "The power of the crown," he continued, was still "great enough, and the German people is still strong enough to dare a thorough change of direction of the entire interior statecraft."[87]

Wolf was successful with his moderate course: in the 1907 elections his "German-Radicals" gained twelve seats, and the Schönerians, only three. In 1911 twenty-two seats went to Wolf, and four to Schönerer.

During that time, when Wolf pursued policies within the framework of the Dual Monarchy yet pushed toward a centralized state, young Hitler heard him speak, probably as a famous orator in Parliament, but also during many large appearances in Vienna, such as the tavern Wimberger mentioned above, a traditional German-national gathering place in Vienna. In 1913, only a few days before Hitler emigrated to Munich, Wolf gave a major speech at an event organized by the German School Association in Vienna's City Hall. In the name of the Sudeten Germans he expressed his disappointment at the Germans in Austria having to defend their linguistic boundary while "just being able to scrape together enough alms and subsidies" and about the state's "animosity" toward them: "When we saved five children from Slavization at one place, we were sent ten Czech civil servants in return."[88]

*　　*　　*

Wolf had to pay a high personal price for switching parties: Schönerer's revenge consisted of a defamation campaign that almost drove Wolf, who was equipped with an exaggerated sense of pride, to suicide. There were rumors about bribery, forged IOUs and corruption, and the rape of two young women. A series of suits followed, among them a particularly troublesome one for adultery. Wolf's personal life was dragged into the open to prove his "moral decay."

In his hatred Schönerer went so far as to winning Wolf's wife over to his side by paying her money. She left Wolf with their two little children and divorced him in 1903. Schönerer even paid for her divorce lawyer and her flight with her children to England. Wolf, to whom the court had granted custody of the children, was powerless, because he did not have the money for a legal battle. He never saw them again.

Accusations that the sugar cartel had bribed his troubled *Ostdeutsche Rundschau* to prevent criticism of manufacturers' exploitation of turnip farmers made Wolf seethe with rage. From now on, whoever wanted to infuriate Wolf would allude to the sugar cartel. The *Arbeiterzeitung* wrote: Amidst all the noise, "Czech representative Karta grabs three sugar cubes and throws them at Wolf. Wolf jumps out of his chair in extreme agitation, rushes toward Karta, hits him on his hand and is about to slap him in the face." His fellow party members prevented the furious man from doing so.[89]

Wolf considered the Czechs to be the Germans' main enemy. In comparison, his anti-Semitism vanished in the background. After all, the main emphasis of Wolf's work was not in Vienna but in mixed-language Bohemia, where an overly rigorous anti-Semitic attitude would have been politically rather unwise. For at that time, the majority of the Bohemian Jews, who embodied the middle class, tended to favor Germandom and sent their children to German schools. They made generous donations to German purposes and voted for German-national parties, even the Wolfians. Wolf could not and would not do without them as Germans in Bohemia, according to his principle that all Germans had to stick together in a "threatened land," be they Jewish or Christian.

The German-Radical newspapers rigorously followed that line. The *Deutsches Nordmährenblatt*, for example, wrote: "If Jewish influence helps to keep a town, a city, or a chamber of commerce German, it would be more than folly to fight that 'influence.'"[90]

Again and again Wolf warned his fellow party members against the danger of forgetting "the forceful defense against Czechdom" over the battle against the Jews.[91] Anti-Semitism, he argued, must not be made the "main and cardinal issue" of the national program. He also resolutely supported the successful German School Association with its almost 200,000 members and more than 2,000 local chapters, which still refused to introduce the Aryan Clause. Not only Schönerians but also Christian Socials accused the association "of instructing the Jews as Germans and then sending them over to us so they can lead our people into economic servitude."[92] Here, too, Wolf's stance was unambiguous: the main issue, he said, was the protection and spread of German language and culture, which was an issue where they could not do without the German-conscious Jews.

Wolf was similarly pragmatic in the matter of the League of Christian Germans in Galicia, founded in 1907, which was supposed to support the approximately 100,000 members of the non-Jewish German minority. At Wolf's direction, the *Deutsches Volksblatt für Galizien*, published by the League, appealed to the Christian German Galicians: "Neither should we spurn support from the Jews on this issue. As little as we can possibly be interested in a mixing of Germans and Jews, we still do have good reason to try to strengthen our position by establishing links with the German-ophile Jews." All Germans, whether Jewish or Christian, should co-operate: "Now show them, Fritz, what you can do! Work—constant work!—sacrifice, devotion to the German people! That must be your motto now. Otherwise, the others will pass you by, and you will stay behind."[93]

Stein, however, took the opposite stand in the Reichstag in 1905: the question was what should happen to the German minority in Galicia after its separation from Bukovina, which the Pan-Germans called for. Stein said, "The overwhelming majority of the population in Bukovina, who is now pledging allegiance to Germandom, consists of Jews." The Pan-Germans, he argued, would "never ever take those who are not of our blood under the wings of the great Pan-German idea."[94]

Even though Wolf was not exactly coy about voicing anti-Semitic statements during his appearances in Vienna, the Schönerians as well as the Christian Socials berated him as a bad anti-Semite. Christian Social representative Hermann Bielohlawek shouted in Parliament: "You can take your hats off to any Jew, but not to Wolf! Jew slave! For ten years we fought agains the Jews so that Wolf can now help the Jews to regain power! How much are they paying you for this, Herr Wolf?"[95]

Wolf was the German fraternities' unchallenged leader. Again and again he spurred the students on to devote themselves to the "service of the German people" and the "defense against the Slavs." He believed that education had to play an important part in this so that everyone would be mentally alert enough to withstand the Slavic "assault." Early on he personally became involved in organizing national reading and education clubs, traveled around as a political itinerant preacher for national enlightenment, and created a tight web of German-national table societies as "focal points of a large and united people's community."

These smallest groups of Pan-German—or, since 1902, German-Radical—propaganda met once a week in private homes to read German-national pamphlets and newspapers together, to discuss issues, practical mutual help, and for "political and national self-education." They sang national songs and listened to lectures: "This strengthens the sense of national solidarity, widens the horizon, and instills an understanding; everyone feels like part of the whole, like a wheel in the great clockwork of the nation."[96] The students played an important role in this as organizers.

To quote an example: In 1908 Wolf's *Ostdeutsche Rundschau* promoted a German-Radical political oratory school in Vienna. Subjects offered were the history of German and Austrian Social Democracy and "Socialism and Nationalism." The school also offered for discussion Social Democrat Otto Bauer's new publication, "The Issue of Nationalities and Social Democracy," which stressed the precedence of class consciousness over national consciousness, and Karl Renner's pamphlet on "National or International Trade Union." Any member of any German-national club could join.[97]

During Hitler's Vienna years the club "German History," of whose executive committee Wolf was a member, was located in the Sixth District, at 21 Sandwirtgasse. The club's aim was to create a sense of pan-German nationalism, which it tried to convey through popular lectures and cheap pamphlets: "In pamphlets on the works and deeds of our people's great men, from Arminius to Bismarck, on great eras of our history, from the demolition of the rotten Roman Empire through Germanic might, the glorious time of the Hohenstaufens, the liberation act of the Reformation to most recent times, in which the united people created its new Reich, we shall convey the conviction to the new generation . . . that the German people stands high above all the other ethnic tribes of the multilingual state in strength and culture."[98]

On the other hand, Wolf was responsible for the radicalization of the battle between nationalities at the universities. He, who was considered the monarchy's most savage political brawler, encouraged his fraternity members in their daily battle against non-Germans. Even newspapers that looked unfavorably on him reported in detail how on December 1,

1908, shortly before martial law was declared in Prague, he was surrounded by hundreds of brawling and jeering Czechs, but went from the German casino to the university cafeteria unperturbed, while the police were unsuccessfully trying to protect him. The *Neues Wiener Journal* described the event: "The situation became more and more threatening, since the crowd kept yelling: 'Hang him!', 'Slay him!', 'Throw him into the canal!', 'Sugar! Sugar!' A rock which was thrown at Wolf hit one of the German students accompanying him."[99]

Wolf was also the terror of the Bohemian Assembly, which became nonfunctional largely through his German-Radicals' filibusters. He stirred hatred between Germans and Czechs and, along with his fellow party members, took the conflicts from Bohemia's Assembly straightaway to the Reichsrat in Vienna, where he continued to brawl. In mass gatherings he again and again fanned national hysteria, which had been rampant to begin with.

In the Reichsrat Wolf kept submitting urgent motions against the Czechs, for instance, on January 22, 1909, "against the permanent threats against the German students as well as the German minority by the mob in Prague." After he had berated a Czech deputy, a priest, as a "black parson" and "impertinent fellow," he complained about the "gall" of the Prague Czechs, a "mob . . . you couldn't find any more depraved and debased in any big city." "Our German students have an unquestionable right, acquired over centuries, to wear their colors on the grounds of the oldest German university, to actively affirm their Germandom." This speech was immediately followed by a Czech National Socialist's filibuster in Czech, which lasted for hours. Once again parliamentary work was blocked.[100]

In Vienna Wolf concentrated on motivating the German students for the battle against their non-German fellow students: "We simply owe it to our historical position to protect at all events the birthright of the German language and the German spirit on this soil, which were established through German diligence and defended by the strength of German arms."[101]

When in November 1908 two hundred Italian students rallied for the establishment of an Italian law school in Vienna, some thousand fraternity members gathered in the university's assembly hall. Italian national songs were drowned by the "Wacht am Rhein," and eventually students went at each other with clubs. The brawl escalated to shouts of "Boo!" and "Throw the Italians out!" and whistles, and on the Italian side to shouts of "evviva" and "corraggio." Then eighteen shots were fired, clearly from the Italians' pistols. A panic ensued. Several students re-

Riots between German and Italian students at Vienna University in 1908

mained behind, seriously injured. The police confiscated two revolvers, a dagger, knives, blackjacks, brass knuckles, rubber-covered lead clubs, and a vast number of broken clubs. The university was closed for a few days.[102]

As a consequence of many such clashes, all students became more and more radical. Now the Jewish students too, expelled from the German fraternities, started to organize in their own fraternities. The first and most important one was the Zionist Kadimah (Onward), founded in 1882 by Galician students in Vienna, but dominated by Western Jews around 1900. The Kadimah nurtured the ideal of the manly, brave, steely, and athletic Jew who no longer wanted to be passive but to fight.

Now that the Jews no longer fought as "Germans" but as Jews, there were national riots on that front too. At the end of February 1908, when Hitler had just arrived in Vienna from Linz, students used not only clubs but also cowhides as weapons during such a fight, and both sides drew blood. Such clashes happened several times that year, for example, on November 10. First a member of the fraternity Alemannia insulted Jewish students. Thereupon a Kadimah student challenged him to a duel. When the fraternity member declined by giving the usual reason of not dueling with a "non-Aryan," a free-for-all ensued. The Alemannians occupied the entrance of the university to deny admission to the Kadimah and shouted "Down with the Jews" and "Off with them to Zion!" The brawl ended with the collapse of a large stone ramp by the university entrance, which left sixty people injured. Similar occurrences took place at all other universities in Cisleithania, wherever non-German groups tried to claim their rights. In addition, the Cisleithanian universities witnessed riots that erupted for ideological and political reasons, for instance, between Clericals and Liberals, Pan-Germans and Hapsburg-Germans, and, of course, ethnic fights between Italians and Slovenians, Poles and Ruthenians, and many more.

Stefan Zweig remarked with the experience of the years afterward: "What the SA members do for National Socialism, the corps students did for the German-nationals, who under the protection of academic immunity established an unparalleled terror of physical violence, marching up for every political action in military order, shouting and whistling. Grouped into so-called 'fraternities,' with dueling scars on their faces, drunken and brutal, they held sway over the university's assembly hall . . . armed with hard, heavy clubs. . . . Incessantly provoking people, they now hit the Slavic, now the Jewish, now the Catholic, and then the Italian students, driving the defenseless men out of the university. At every 'stroll' . . . blood flowed. The police . . . could only confine themselves to carrying away the injured who, bleeding, were thrown down the stairs into the street by the national hooligans."[103]

Dr. Karl Lueger: The People's Tribune

As a convinced Schönerian, it took young Hitler a while to appreciate Schönerer's archenemy, Vienna mayor Dr. Karl Lueger, and his Christian Social Party: *When I arrived in Vienna, I was hostile to both of them. The man and the movement seemed "reactionary" in my eyes.*[104] Lueger was the "Lord of Vienna," his party omnipotent in the city. Georg Schönerer, on the other hand, to whom Lueger had once paid tribute by handing him a bunch of cornflowers, was politically as good as dead after 1907.

The followers of the two continued to feud with one another. The party newspapers raged against each other every single day. Yet Lueger always emerged as the stronger of the two. He prohibited Schönerians as well as Social Democrats from obtaining municipal positions, refused to hire them as municipal suppliers, and—as a special disgrace—forbade them to use the municipal school gyms. The reason he gave was: "I don't need any revolutionaries or admirers of the Hohenzollern in Austria, I need good, loyal, dynastic men in Austria!"[105]

The fact that young Hitler, a declared Schönerer sympathizer, allowed himself to be impressed by Lueger indicates a degree of political independence. However, he did not join the Christian Social Party. It was not Lueger's party but his outstanding personality that thrilled and stimulated Hitler. If one is to believe *Mein Kampf*, it was anti-Semitism and a newspaper that showed young Hitler the way to Lueger. In connection with the liberal "Jew press" and its alleged Germanophobia he wrote: *I was forced to recognize that one of the anti-Semitic papers, the* Deutsches Volksblatt, *behaved more decently. . . . I sometimes picked up the* Volksblatt, *which, to be sure, seemed to me much smaller, but in these matters somewhat more appetizing. I was not in agreement with the sharp anti-Semitic tone, but from time to time I read arguments which gave me some food for thought.*[106]

The *Deutsches Volksblatt*, which had a large circulation and once had switched over from Schönerer to Lueger, represented the German-national wing of the Christian Socials and distinguished itself through its aggressive anti-Semitism. *At all events, these occasions slowly made me acquainted with the man and the movement, which in those days guided Vienna's destinies: Dr. Karl Lueger and the Christian Social Party.*[107]

As he recalled later, he first heard Lueger speak in 1908, in the city hall's Volkshalle: *I had to wrestle with myself inside, I wanted to hate him, but I couldn't help myself, I felt compelled to admire him; he had absolutely outstanding talent as an orator.*[108] In the Volkshalle large events took place, for example, the swearing-ins of the City of Vienna's new residents. They had to solemnly pledge their "citizen's allegiance to Vienna" before the mayor and promise to uphold the "German character of the City of Vienna." Non-German settlers had to forswear their national backgrounds. On July 2, 1908, at a time of great national tension between Germans and Czechs, Hitler might have witnessed such a swearing-in. As usual on such occasions, Lueger used the opportunity to formulate a few principles on the national question in Vienna. The *Deutsches Volksblatt* reported: The mayor "refused to despise the Czechs, but he stressed with great determination that it is the Germans who will continue to have the controlling voice in the imperial residence, that everyone else has to do what we say, in short, that the Czechs coming to Vienna have to adapt to their environment and Germanize." Everyone had to realize "that the

Dr. Karl Lueger, mayor of
Vienna 1897–1910

soil on which the old imperial city stands is German soil and will remain
German soil, that Vienna is not in a position to make any concessions
to the Slavic elements who are pouring into the center of the Empire,
but on the contrary, that it is up to the Czechs, etc., who accept Vienna's
hospitality, to forswear any conspicuous display of their tribal affiliation
and to get accustomed to the German environment."[109] Lueger's oft-
repeated slogan was, "Vienna is German and must remain German!"—
with German, as usual, designating the language and having nothing to
do with an Anschluss.

In 1908, when Hitler settled in Vienna, Lueger was sixty-four years
old, had been mayor for eleven years, and was more revered than any of
his predecessors or successors. Although he was already weakened by a
serious kidney disease and almost blind, every one of his by now rare
appearances was a municipal event. In a commentary on his popularity
in the *Arbeiterzeitung*, even his political opponent Friedrich Austerlitz
admitted that the mayor was "a sort of uncrowned king, and City Hall,
no less than a *Hofburg*. . . . He was more popular than any actor, and more
famous than any scholar; he was a presence and an influence in politics
as no big city can flaunt and as could develop only in Lueger. . . . Could
this constant Lueger brouhaha have prevailed anywhere else in the
world?"[110]

Hitler's enthusiastic verdict was in agreement with the general opinion than Lueger was *in community politics, the most ingenious mayor who has ever lived among us.*[111] And: *Under the rule of a truly gifted mayor, the venerable residence of the Emperors of the old régime awoke once more to a miraculous youth.* Lueger, Hitler wrote, was *the last great German to be born in the ranks of the people who had colonized the Ostmark.*[112] And: *If Dr. Karl Lueger had lived in Germany, he would have been ranked among the great minds of our people; that he lived and worked in this impossible state was the misfortune of his work and of himself.*[113] And: *Whenever Lueger gave a party at city hall, it was absolutely magnificent; he was a sovereign king. I have never seen him ride by in Vienna without everybody in the street stopping to greet him.*[114] Hitler is said to have revered Vienna's mayor so much that even "during the time of the *Kampf*" he had carried a small Lueger medal in his wallet as a good-luck charm.[115]

Lueger loved to appear in public as "handsome Karl" with his golden mayor's chain, surrounded by a throng of public-sector workers and municipal civil servants, particularly by priests in their vestments and altar boys, who during all inauguration ceremonies waved holy-water containers, whether it was the opening of a utilities factory or Vienna's Public School 85. Those closest to him wore a special "court uniform," consisting of a green tailcoat with black velvet cuffs and yellow coat-of-arms buttons.[116] Military bands played the *Lueger March*.

He had words of praise engraved for posterity in hundreds of stone plaques, which still exist in Vienna, reading "Constructed under Mayor Dr. Karl Lueger." Hitler was well familiar with this custom, which he mentioned as late as 1929 at an NSDAP gathering in Munich: *These show us how in Austria Mayor Dr. Lueger came to power in Vienna and how he then tried to solidify and immortalize the power of his movement through magnificent buildings, according to the idea that if words no longer speak, then the stones must speak. They chiseled in everywhere: Built under Dr. Karl Lueger.*[117]

Vienna tended to smile benevolently on Lueger's vanity. Thus a comic paper published the photograph of an elephant baby from Schönbrunn Zoo with the caption: "Born under Mayor Dr. Karl Lueger."[118] Even Lueger's fellow party member Prelate Josef Scheicher attested to Lueger's "touch of Caesarean madness and cynicism."[119] He said that Lueger had felt "an almost childlike joy when the potentates of this world hanged as many of those toy bands and ribbons as possible on him."[120] There had been many people "who lay before him on their bellies and, wielding the holy-water barrels on their knees, murmured: You are great, magnificent Fo!"[121]

Lueger's opponent Austerlitz wrote, "Perhaps the popularity Lueger enjoys is not at all something Vienna should be proud of. For Lueger's life was consumed by one single idea: the quest for power." "State, people, and party," he continued, had had "their focal point only in his own ego," and it had been the "pathological power of suggestion . . . which let a great city degenerate into the pedestal of one person's ambition."[122]

Lueger had earned his popularity by way of indubitably great achievements. His tenure, which lasted from 1897 to 1910, forms a singularly clear and defined picture amid the confusion of Austro-Hungarian policies. No doubt he was a strong leader. He possessed political charisma and was a politician who listened to constituents, passionately and energetically fought for his "people of Vienna," and vigorously worked toward the city's welfare. In the face of his accomplishments, the reverence for the "Lord God of Vienna," the "citizen mayor," which has lasted to this day, is certainly understandable.

Part of the reason why Lueger's light shone so brightly was that his political surroundings looked so gloomy: an old, depressed emperor who, equipped with little political talent to begin with, entirely depended on the advice of mediocre ministers and court dignitaries, and who practiced the proverbial policy of "blundering along," without any concept or political leadership. Governments changed all the time. Parliament was paralyzed by the battle between the different nationalities. The country was beset by social misery, unemployment, inflation, lack of social protection, controversies, and declining loyalty to the multiethnic empire.

The large, crumbling empire had only one bastion of clear, successful policies: the City of Vienna under Mayor Lueger. Hitler's opinion in *Mein Kampf* was that of the majority in Vienna: *Vienna was the heart of the monarchy; from this city the last flush of life flowed out into the sickly, old body of the crumbling empire.*[123]

Vienna, the Modern Metropolis

In 1908 Vienna had two million people, making it the sixth largest city in the world. The three next-largest cities in the Dual Monarchy, Trieste, Prague, and Lemberg, had only some two hundred thousand people each.[124] Between 1880 and 1910 Vienna's population almost doubled, in part because of vast floods of immigrants at a time of rapid industrialization, and in part because of the incorporation of the suburbs in 1890 and of the large area on the opposite side of the Danube—Floridsdorf—in 1904, the latter a natural area of extension toward the fulfilment of the dream of a city of four million people. Annual immigration was at least thirty thousand people.

The rapidly growing city needed new structures, from the traffic network, gas, electricity, and water supply to hospitals, baths, churches, and public schools. Under Lueger the city managed these tasks in a grand style and, in many areas, in an exemplary way; during his tenure, Vienna turned into a modern metropolis. The most important secret of Lueger's success was the municipalization of utility companies such as the gasworks and power stations and the transport services, which previously had been in the hands of mostly foreign stock corporations. Yet he also municipalized the waterworks, the slaughterhouse, and even the brewery, established municipal banks against the competition of "Jewish" banks and— as a measure against overpriced funerals in Vienna—a municipal mortuary service.

The former horse trams made way for an electric streetcar system that was some 120 miles long, the best-developed system in Europe. The metropolitan railroad, designed by Otto Wagner, has been a gem of city planning until today and was admired even by Hitler. The second aqueduct supplied water from the high-altitude area of Hochschwab, providing the city with its legendary good water. Lainz's "attention house," with clinics built in a pavilionlike style amid an urban landscape of parks and meadows, still in operation, was the most modern hospital and convalescent home in Europe.

Besides that, the mayor prevailed in establishing a beautification program. Because he did not want to turn Vienna into a "heap of rocks," he also had parks and smaller "green zones" built. A band of groves and meadows under a construction ban preserves the idyllic landscape of the Vienna Woods as a nearby spa area to this day. The seawater Gänsehäufel swimming pool with its rural surroundings offers the city's residents a welcome chance to relax.

Lueger came up with the money all this required by way of long-term domestic and foreign loans. (Some of the debts were taken care of during the time of inflation. However, the foreign loans that had to be paid back in gold turned into a problem for the small Republic of Austria after 1918.) The claim that Lueger had financed his huge construction projects exclusively by the large profits gained from "foreigners," was Christian Social propaganda. Thus Lueger's first biographer, fellow party member Reverend Franz Stauracz, wrote in his hurrah pamphlet on the occasion of the ten-year anniversary of Lueger's tenure in 1907: "His liberal predecessors also went into debt but didn't accomplish anything;

yet the interest on our present loans is paid from the profits on the enterprises and amortized, without costing people a cent. Previously, every year the income from the gasworks, the tramway, etc. went mainly into the pockets of English Jews, but today it is the general population that profits from them."[125] Hitler reiterated this propaganda as late as 1941: *Everything we have today in terms of municipal autonomy goes back to him [Lueger]. He turned those businesses that were private elsewhere into municipal enterprises, which is why he could make the city of Vienna more beautiful and larger without raising taxes even by one cent: he had at his disposal those sources of income which used to be private companies.*[126]

A glance at the news reports of 1908 renders Lueger a kindly, humorous city father who dealt with everything, even the tiniest problem, according to his motto: "We must help the little man." For example, he received enthusiastic applause when he said that he would like nothing more than to "provide every citizen who has caroused through the night with a cab."[127]

Before the assembled city council he put the blame for the increase of milk prices on the allegedly greedy merchants—everyone knew that he was referring to the Jews—warning them: "If nothing else prevails, I will take care of the selling of milk myself. (Demonstrative, long applause.) I already supply so much, I supply electricity, gas, beer, I supply all kinds of things, why shouldn't I also supply milk?"[128]

Garbage, too, occupied him, as he explained during a meeting with the press: "After that, household trash shall be burned and, through some special procedure, turned into the generation of energy. Street garbage, on the other hand, shall be used as fertilizer. This would create new revenues for the city, which shall cover part of the cost of garbage disposal."[129]

The Lower Austrian state elections in 1908, the first elections Hitler personally witnessed in Vienna, turned into a triumph for Lueger. In Mariahilf each of the three Christian Social candidates received more votes than all other candidates put together.[130] This success rested on the old electoral law. Lueger refused to introduce universal, equal suffrage in Lower Austria or Vienna, thus guaranteeing that his Christian Social Party would rule over the Social Democrats.

The rage of the liberal press—to which the mayor referred as "Jewish press"—against Lueger, the people's tribune, was futile. No matter how fiercely the press attacked him, Lueger's followers would not be swayed against their idol. In 1942 Hitler mentioned this phenomenon in connection with the British press during World War II: *Hitler said that it could even go so far as the press no longer reflecting popular opinion at all; proof of that was the Viennese press's stance during the era of Mayor Lueger. For even though the Viennese press was entirely Jewish and liberal, Mayor Lueger had always gained an overwhelming Christian Social majority during municipal elections, and thus popular opinion had no longer coincided with that of the press at all.*[131]

Concerning Lueger's Biography

Lueger was "Viennese through and through." Born in 1844, the son of a military invalid and school janitor, he was raised by his soon-widow mother, who worked hard so that the highly talented young man could go to law school. Lueger graduated from law school in 1866, joined a law firm, and quickly made a name for himself as an advocate of the "little people," whom he supported vigorously and selflessly in disputes with "the big shots." He received the impulse to go into politics and his crucial political influence from the Jewish doctor and local politician Dr. Ignaz Mandl. Like Mandl, Lueger went to taverns and beer parlors and from one popular assembly to the next to deliver his political speeches. He listened to people's complaints and acquired a reputation as an advocate of the disadvantaged.

During the time of economic hardships, after the crash of 1873, popular wrath turned against ruling Liberalism, against the "capitalists" and "the Jews." Lueger deftly took up these trends and focused his work on two basic enemies: on one hand, big business, factories, and department stores, which endangered the small merchants—and on the other hand, the "proletariat," rising Social Democracy, which was perceived as revolutionary and, according to propaganda, tried to wrest whatever little property the good citizens had away from them. To these enemies were added the "foreigners," the immigrants.

Lueger, downright possessed with politics, worked extremely diligently and did not even shy away from brawls with political opponents. Lower Austrian governor Erich Count Kielmansegg wrote about his political opponent: "A strong will and an innate instinct to exactly assess the popular mood at any given time and to find the right slogan, made him reach his goal brilliantly."[132]

In 1875 this large lower middle class, which until then had hardly been noticed by politicians, elected Lueger as well as Mandl into the city council, initially as Liberals. There the two friends switched over to the Democrats and with their aggressive opposition toppled the Liberal mayor. Lueger supported Schönerer's German-national reform movement, and on the Northern Railway issue in 1884 fought at Schönerer's side against the Rothschild family and for nationalization. He then switched parties. His sole great goal was to become mayor of Vienna. To achieve this, he secured the support of important local and professional organizations, most notably of the butchers, bakers, and teamsters, but also of Viennese homeowners. Hitler commented on this issue: *By aiming essentially at winning the small and lower middle classes and artisans*, Lueger's party *obtained a following as enduring as it was self-sacrificing.*[133]

The extension of suffrage in 1885 led to Lueger's predictable rise: now the "five-gulden men" were allowed to vote, those men who were legal residents and paid taxes. This drew Lueger's followers to the polls. The "people of Vienna" loved him and voted for him personally, no matter what party he happened to represent. He soon distinguished himself in the Reichsrat as a spirited warrior against the "Jewish liberals," against corruption, foreign stock companies, and—in as yet peaceful competition with Schönerer—against the "Jewish press."

In 1887 Lueger turned to the small, antiliberal, Catholic reform Christian Social Association, which was about to develop a modern social platform. In addition, the association strove toward a "re-Catholicization" in its fight against "the Jews," and was pointedly anti-Semitic. His joining the association marked a turning point in Lueger's politics: from now on he appeared as an anti-Semite in public. This also entailed his separation from his friend and sponsor Ignaz Mandl.

Lueger soon became the group's leader and within a few years turned it into a modern mass party into which he integrated all of his former followers, from the landlords to the butchers, and from the democrats to the German-nationals. Anti-Semitism provided these entirely different groups with a common symbolic enemy. Adopting the modern term, which had been coined only recently, the association referred to itself as "The Anti-Semites." Only in 1893 did it choose the official name Christian Social Party, still keeping the designation "The Anti-Semites."

Lueger owed his meteoric rise not least to Schönerer's leaving politics in 1888. He very skillfully managed to pay tribute to the martyr Schönerer in public and at the same time to win over his followers to his own side. Not without justification, Franz Stein reproached Lueger for taking "advantage of ethnic anti-Semitism as developed by Schönerer . . . in order to promote himself" so he could quickly become mayor, and for "grabbing voters" among the Schönerians.[134]

In the Reichsrat, too, Lueger entirely focused on Vienna's problems and his enemy, the Jews, with the rousing slogan, "Greater Vienna must not turn into Greater Jerusalem." In 1890 he gave a famous speech against the Jews that was to be quoted for decades: "Yes, in Vienna the Jews are as numerous as grains of sand on the shore, wherever you go, nothing but Jews; if you go to the theater, nothing but Jews, if you walk on the Ring Boulevard, nothing but Jews, if you go to the concert, nothing but Jews, if you attend a ball, nothing but Jews, if you go on campus, again, nothing but Jews." And: "Gentlemen, don't blame me for the fact that almost all journalists are Jews and that they keep a token Christian editor here and there in their editorial offices, whom they can show off just in case someone might stop by and get frightened." On account of the Jewish press, he argued, "the movement against journalism naturally was forced to take on an anti-Semitic character."[135]

In any case, Lueger was far more successful with his anti-Semitic stand than Schönerer was. A leading Pan-German remarked with resignation that Lueger had known "how to make himself personally appear to be the embodiment of anti-Semitism in the mind of the public, to such a degree that everyone with a less than an independent mind equates opposition to Dr. Lueger with a rejection of anti-Semitism."[136]

In the face of Christian Social successes, Lueger's enemies, the Liberals, as well as the conservatives at court and the high-ranking clergy, joined forces in a spectacular concerted action: Cardinal Count Schönborn went to Rome to see the Pope. In the name of the Austrian bishops he pressed formal charges against the Christian Socials: according to the complaint, the party was "not Catholic but revolutionary and seditious," and its language respected no boundaries, poked "popular passions," incited "base desires," and identified with anti-Semitism. Pope Leo XIII, however, let himself be convinced by the Christian Socials' defense plea, in particular by its program of social reform, and sent Lueger his blessings.[137]

This sealed Lueger's success. In the following local elections, in 1895, the Christian Socials gained the majority of seats. Lueger had reached his goal—or so it seemed at least—and was elected mayor of Vienna.

There was a storm of protest against this election on the part of the Liberals. The Neue Freie Presse warned that under Mayor Lueger, Vienna would be "the only large city in the world carrying the stigma of an anti-Semitic administration." This, it argued, was "degrading to the old imperial city," and with Lueger, "the dregs [was rising] to the surface."[138]

To everyone's surprise, Emperor Franz Josef withheld his required endorsement of the election. He did this at the advice of his prime minister Badeni, as well as of high-ranking aristocrats and his female companion Katharina Schratt, but also because he believed that the legal

principle of his empire—that of all citizens being equal before the law—
was now in jeopardy.

The election was held a second time. The emperor again refused to
accept it. He did so altogether four times, for two years. With each imperial refusal and each new election this necessarily entailed, Lueger
gained more votes. He became a martyr and popular hero in an unparalleled victory march. What no one thought possible, happened: the emperor's authority suffered severe damage in this tug-of-war.

On Corpus Christi Day 1896, this became apparent to everyone. As
usual, the emperor was the first person to walk as a humble Christian
right behind "heaven" with the Most Holy Sacrament. In front of the
baldachin were various dignitaries, among them, Lueger. Eyewitness Felix
Salten reports: "The bells are ringing, the Church's flags are waving, and
the roaring shouts of the crowd welcome the beloved man, who thanks,
waves, and smiles to everybody. He is glad. For the Emperor, who is
following the baldachin, is bound to hear the thunder of the thousands
of voices. These shouts of joy resound all the way, right before the Emperor, this exultant yelling, which is meant for someone else. . . . The
Emperor walks in the procession as if in the wake of that man. Before
him, the roaring of the ovations, and around him, silence. It was Lueger's
triumphant march."[139]

It was not until the elections of 1897, which were overshadowed by
the Badeni riots and the intense fear of revolution, that things turned
around. Compared to the Social Democratic "revolutionaries," the Catholic Christian Socials now appeared as the lesser evil. Lueger's friends
prevailed in court, above all, Archduchess Marie Valerie, who was entirely under the influence of her confessor, Father Heinrich Abel.

Thus in 1897 Lueger finally became mayor of Vienna, which he
celebrated enthusiastically. At this very moment of triumph his political
abilities became apparent. Unlike Schönerer, he did not go into opposition to the imperial family, but assured the emperor of his loyalty. In the
eyes of his followers, the "martyr" magnanimously forgave his emperor,
which only further enhanced his popularity. The two most popular men
in Vienna—Emperor Franz Josef and the "people's emperor," Lueger—
were now reconciled. Salten sarcastically commented: "Having reached
his goal, he took the black-yellow mentality under the city's wings, made
loyalty to the Emperor part of the municipal administration, and made
Vienna the conductor of the people's anthem."[140]

Lueger, the People's Tribune

To the same degree that the electoral vote was extended, new social classes gained in political importance to which until then politicians had paid hardly any attention: the "little people." On account of their large number they now increasingly determined election results. Therefore new ways of approaching these voters, who escaped traditional means of propaganda, had to be found.

On all political levels a new type of politician appeared: the "people's tribune." He was thoroughly distinct from the type of the liberal politician, who attached great importance to being educated and having a distinguished demeanor, liked to talk down to people, considered himself to be an educator of the people, and was personally unapproachable. The new politicians, who, like Schönerer and Lueger, early on saw the writing on the wall, sought contact with the people: in taverns, beer parlors, in marketplaces, and in factories.

People's tribune Lueger liked to deliver his speeches in the native dialect, adjusted to the intellectual level of his audience, simplified everything that was complex, and spiced up his speeches with jokes. And he did what yielded the most votes: he attacked his voters' enemies and exacerbated their antipathies, not only against politicians but also against national and religious minorities, "the rich up there," "the mob down there," the "nonbelievers" and the "foreigners, who take away our women, apartments, work, etc." He deliberately appealed to emotions and instincts rather than the intellect and critical faculties. Hugo von Hofmannsthal said at the time: "Politics is magic. The masses will obey he who knows how to appeal to them."[141]

Thus the effect of Lueger's speeches on his audiences was that of mass suggestion. His lover Marianne Beskiba reports that Lueger "was able to transfer his will onto others in an almost supernatural way": "With flashing eyes and raised arms—all gesticulation—he let his voice thunder. . . . In drastic words he described the damage done by the previous liberal regime, developed his ideas for the common welfare of the people, and declared war 'to the knife' on his enemies.—Thundering applause accompanied each sentence, and he was often prevented from going on by enthusiastic cheers that didn't seem to end. Bathed in sweat, he finally returned to his table."[142]

Lueger gave the "people of Vienna" self-confidence. Salten writes: "He alone takes even the Viennese people's fear away. Until then, they were berated. He commends them. They demanded respect of them. He delivers them from all respect. They told them that only the educated should govern. He shows them how poorly the educated know how to govern. He, an educated man, a doctor, an advocate, rips into the doctors, tears the advocates apart, berates the professors, jeers at science; he surrenders everything that intimidates and confines masses, he throws it down, stomps on it, laughing, and the cobblers, the tailors, the coachmen, the greengrocers and shopkeepers rejoice, they roar with enthusiasm and believe the new age has begun, which was foretold in the words: Blessed are the weak in spirit. He validates Vienna's lower class in all its qualities, in its lack of intellectual wants, in its distrust of education, in its tipsy silliness, in its love of street songs, in its adherence to the old-fashioned, in its boisterous smugness; and they rave, they rave blissfully when he talks to them."[143]

To be sure, this way of talking to people lost its magic effect with an educated audience. An eyewitness reports: "How comfortably he moved in the morass of popular commonplaces and trivial jokes! As if he had always talked just to his suburban voters! He congratulated the directors of an architecture congress on their choice of a conference place because—Viennese women were 'well built.' In front of the scholars at a music history conference he wasn't able to describe music as a global language any better than by saying all Viennese waltzes got into everyone's feet and people danced the Czech polka in Vienna too." This critic attributed the fact that Lueger was successful even with speeches of that kind to the "pull of what was indigenous and had genuine roots as opposed to all that stuffy international fuss."[144]

Not without admiration, Salten observed about Lüger's speeches: "If a thinking person read them, he couldn't help smiling. . . . Yet if a thinking person listened when Lueger was talking, then being a thinking person was of no avail at all, then one's own thoughts disappeared, then one was grabbed by an elementary force, and carried along defenselessly."[145]

The attraction Lueger had for Hitler was clearly in his spectacular effect on a mass audience. Later on, when he studied problems of mass suggestion or mass fanaticizing, or when he remarked on the value of political propaganda, Hitler would come back to Lueger again and again. Using Lueger as an example, he discussed the political value of the *power of the spoken word* in *Mein Kampf* and talked about the *firebrand of the word hurled among the masses.*[146]

In contrast to Schönerer, Hitler wrote, Lueger *had a rare knowledge of men and in particular took good care not to consider people better than they are.*[147] All propaganda had to adjust *its intellectual level . . . to the most limited intelligence among those it is addressed to. . . . The more modest its intellectual ballast, the more exclusively it takes into consideration the emotions of the masses, the more effective it will be.* The point was not trying to achieve *success in pleasing a few scholars or young aesthetes.*[148]

Lueger's Anti-Semitism

Lueger knew how to focus all his voters' negative images in one powerful movement: anti-Semitism. He reduced everything that was contrary to the simple formula: The Jew is to blame. "We fight against the suppression of Christians and against the replacement of the old Christian Empire of Austria by a new Palestine."[149]

Lueger picked up Catholicism's ancient anti-Semitism, which was directed against the "Christ killer people" with its centuries-old roots, with antiliberalism and anticapitalism, the hatred of "money and stock exchange Jews," "press Jews," the intellectuals ("ink Jews"), Social Democracy ("Jew protection corps"), the Eastern Jews as ("beggar Jews"), allegedly "Jewish" modern art, and women's liberation. According to Kielmansegg, Lueger's invective against the Hungarians alone—"Judeo-Magyars"—won him "thousands of followers at the time."[150]

The Christian Socials considered it their most important political task to reduce the "power of the Jews," which had grown rapidly, and "to bring about some agreement between all Aryan-Christian nations in order to establish a majority in the Reichsrat which will allow to pass laws on the elimination of equal rights for Jews, on the confiscation of Jewish property, and the expulsion of the Jews."[151]

Lueger made himself the spokesman of his constituents: "In Vienna, the poor craftsman has to go begging on Saturday afternoon in order to get something in exchange for the product of his handiwork, he has to beg from the Jewish furniture store owner. Here at home, all the influence on the masses is in the hands of the Jews, the major part of the press is in their hands, by far the largest part of capital and, in particular, of big business is in Jewish hands, and the Jews are practicing a kind of terrorism here which couldn't conceivably be worse." "In Austria, the point was above all to liberate the Christian people from Jewish predominance. (Loud applause.)" And: "It is our task to conquer liberty for our Christian people and to hold on to it. . . . And if they all lose their courage, Dr. Lueger and his party will march on courageously. (Thundering applause, Bravo Lueger!)"[152]

The mayor was not squeamish: when a liberal Jewish deputy protested in the Reichsrat against the incitement of people to anti-Semitism, Lueger replied that anti-Semitism would "perish, but not until the last Jew has perished." When his opponent recalled Lueger saying, during a mass rally, that he did "not care whether the Jews are hanged or shot," Lueger, unfazed, interrupted him to correct him: "Beheaded! I said."[153]

Felix Salten explained Lueger's unparalleled success by the lack of orientation of the "petty bourgeois," who couldn't find a political home, be it with the upper-class Liberals or the "proletarian" Social Democrats: "The broad masses of the petty bourgeois, however, go without direction and leader, from assembly room to assembly room, bleating like an orphaned herd. And they all are weighed down by Austrian self-criticism, by skepticism, by Austrian self-irony, to the point of despondency. And there comes that man and slaughters—for he fails in all other arts—a Jew before the howling crowd. He slaughters him on the rostrum with words, he stabs him to death with words, tears him to shreds, and throws him at the people as a sacrificial offering. This is his first monarchic-clerical deed: directing general discontent toward Jew Lane; may they work off their anger there."[154]

Aggressions were stirred in the service of party politics, by Lueger's fellow party members even more so than by him. Thus, during a debate in the Reichsrat on wheat inflation, Josef Gregorig said that the high price of bread, just like the expensive artificial fertilizer, could be attributed to "Jewish fraud," and: "I would very much like to see all Jews ground to artificial fertilizer . . . (His fellow party members express their amusement) I would like that very much." And he suggested tongue-in-cheek as an additional means to reducing prices, "If you go and hang 3,000 stock exchange Jews today, wheat will be cheaper tomorrow. Do that, it's the only solution to the bread issue. (Applause from his fellow party members.—Merriment.)"[155]

Ernest Schneider made the much-quoted comment that "someone should give him a ship on which all Jews could be packed together; he would steer it into the open sea, sink it, and as long as it was sure that the last Jew was drowning, go down with them himself in order to do the world the greatest service imaginable."[156]

Around 1900, accusations of ritual murder, which had originated in the Middle Ages, were also revived in order to justify anti-Semitism. Whenever a child disappeared somewhere, particularly in the rural areas of Hungary or Galicia, there were rumors about a Jewish ritual murder, which in turn offered a welcome reason for terror against Jewish families.[157] Mostly responsible for spreading many horror stories were Catholic clergymen, who also contributed the accompanying literature, for example, Father August Rohling's popular pamphlet *The Talmudic Jew* or Reverend Joseph Deckert's 1893 *A Ritual Murder: Documents Prove It*.

Lueger's contribution to this wildly controversial parliamentary topic is an impressive example for his political maneuverings between the fronts: "It has happened that Jews used blood in violation of their own command, or that they got soiled with blood. What used to happen in the old days, can't it happen again now?" He then put forward long quotes from the prophets Isaiah and Jeremiah, whom he used as witnesses against the Jews: "For your hands are defiled with blood, and your fingers with iniquity; your lips have spoken lies, your tongue hath muttered perverseness!" And: "They hatch cockatrice's eggs, and weave the spider's web: he that eateth of their eggs dieth, and that which is crushed breaketh out into a viper." Lueger commented: "Well, I believe that the Jews are not the martyrs of the Germans, but the Germans, the martyrs of the Jews." "Wolves, lions, panthers, leopards, and tigers are human next to these beasts of prey in human form."[158]

Lueger said he was convinced that during the next revolution "poor monks" would no longer be "shot but that other people would be uncomfortable if such a revolution broke out." The Catholic church, he said, had to serve as "protection and shield against Jewish suppression" and to deliver the Christian people "from the shameful fetters of Jewish servitude."[159]

In their choice of words and frequent animal metaphors, prominent priests too, such as prelate and Christian Social parliamentarian Josef Scheicher, placed "the Jews" outside of human society. He called them a "swarm of migratory locusts" and used the phrase about the Jews who "web in and suck the Aryan people like a spider does the fly it has caught in its web,"[160] and: "The eternally Jewish is the mortal enemy of the Aryan, but always finds room there too, like the woodworm in the trunk until, full-grown and fat, it goes into a cocoon in order to take a higher-standing place in society as a new baron! Always taking pains to make sure that new young woodworms will never be denied admission to the Christian wood."[161]

Because pastors also preached anti-Semitism from the pulpit, Lueger's followers considered it less and less an injustice when they harassed the "godless ones." Felix Braun, a writer born Jewish, four years Hitler's senior, remembered his bitter childhood when "the political movement in Vienna became more agitated and degenerated into savage violence during gatherings and even in the streets. Even children had adopted the slogans of the new party, and they scornfully reproached me in the playgrounds in the gardens and even in school for being a member of my faith. During elections many Jewish children didn't dare leave the house." At home the young gardener's helper had also insulted him as a Jew and beaten him.[162]

In the wake of their Catholization campaign, the Christian Socials also took their anti-Semitism into crown provinces that were "rich in Jews," particularly Galicia and Bukovina, and financed a number of new "popular papers" for that purpose. For example, in July 1908 the *Bukowinaer Volksblatt* suggested strategies in the battle against the Jews. First, it said, Christians should study the enemy carefully: "If the enemy threatening you is a wolf, you'll grab a gun, invite a few friends, and in a nice, fun chase you hunt down as many of the harmful animals as you can." From bears, foxes, and snakes the article arrived at smaller vermin: "One best attacks bedbugs with hot water, insect powder, and various lotions." However: "The enemy who is more dangerous to Christians than any of those mentioned above, is the Jew—more dangerous, because we are still not quite equipped to fight him properly and the fight tends to be one with insufficient means, for bedbug lotions against bedbugs and drawn guns against beasts of prey have all been used for a long time, while we first have to invent a Zacherlin shot against the Jews." (Zacherlin was the most popular insecticide of the time.)

Again "the Jews" were compared to locusts and a raging fire. "That this comparison is again much too weak for these leeches becomes clear if we consider that both locust and fire only take away the fruits of your labor, whereas the Jews even take away the piece of soil you have held on to, thus leaving you not even the slightest hope for a better future. That is the intention of those leeches, that's what these lovelocked locusts are aiming for. So you see, my Christian people, that locust, raging fire, and the plague are no worse danger for you, for they leave you the hope for a better future, and if not that, at least the hope for a better Beyond, whereas the Jew with his sucking nipples gnaws like a slowly killing poison at your possessions and even at your body and soul."

In an interpolation to the prime minister, Benno Straucher, a Zionist deputy from Bukovina, submitted the pertinent newspaper issue to Parliament in July 1908, protesting against this "unconscionable political agitation," and pointing out "that these brutalities openly promote a ruthless internecine war against the Jews, and that silently tolerating this pernicious smear campaign . . . creates the impression of the Jews being downright outlawed in this state."[163]

To this day some Viennese protest that Lueger acted like an anti-Semite but was not serious about it. For he had even had Jewish friends, and after all, nothing ever really "happened" to any Jew. Indeed, despite his public display of anti-Semitism, Lueger did associate with Jews, and even sought the Jewish religious community's close cooperation. He took the liberty of making exceptions by way of the much-quoted saying, "*I* determine who's a Jew." He tolerated all those who supported him politically. Because in contrast to the Schönerians he did not define Jewishness by race but by religion, he could accept baptized Jews into his innermost circle, to the dismay of many of his fellow party members.

Whenever it was to his advantage, Lueger liked to tone down his anti-Semitism by arguing that he was only employing it as an effective political means. Anti-Semitism, he suggested, was "only a slogan used to bait the masses, and that he personally respected and appreciated many Jews and would never deliberately do an injustice to any of them."[164] He jovially told the merchant Sigmund Mayer, who was an important member of the Jewish religious community and politically important to him, "I like the Hungarian Jews even less than the Hungarians, but I'm not an enemy of the Viennese Jews; they're not in the least all that bad, and we couldn't even do without them. My Viennese constantly feel like taking a rest, and the Jews are the only ones who always feel like working."[165]

Empty talk like this, however, hardly convinced the oft-insulted members of the religious community. And what Mayer found particularly despicable was that Lueger employed anti-Semitism as a political means that ran counter to his convictions: "The man is lacking the most basic element that is what gives a human being his own character: honesty." Mayer said to Lueger, "I am not blaming you for being anti-Semitic, I'm blaming you for *not* being anti-Semitic."[166]

To be sure, if Lueger did use anti-Semitism, against his better judgment, as a means to an end and as a device of political enticement and propaganda, he would have been far more deceitful than his followers. They, at any rate, were convinced that what they did and said was the right thing to do. Arthur Schnitzler was among those who were not ready to accept all of those excuses that were put forward for Lueger. On the contrary, he said, "I always considered this the best proof of his morally dubious character."[167]

Politically it is a moot point to ask if and how many Jews may have been among Lueger's personal friends. What is important is only the effect his inflammatory speeches had, and it was devastating. A mesmerizing orator, Lueger infected for decades the masses who revered him with anti-Semitism, and the vulgar gaffes of his fellow party members and friends among the clergy, whom he did not contradict, poisoned the atmosphere. Even if no Jew was killed, people's old prejudices were confirmed by their idol, which brutalized them.

It was precisely anti-Semitism's political opportuneness that Hitler stressed in one of his monologues, full of respect for its stunning success. Lueger, he said, became a Christian Social *because he viewed anti-Semitism as the way toward the salvation of the state and because in Vienna anti-Semitism could be established only on a religious basis.* Thus Lueger had succeeded: *there were 136 anti-Semites among the 148 city councilmen.*[168]

But Hitler the politician criticized Lueger's Catholic anti-Semitism as not radical enough: *If the worst came to the worst, a splash of baptismal water could always save the business and the Jew at the same time.* Lueger, Hitler wrote, had made anti-Semitism *an attempt at a new conversion of the Jews.* And: *Lacking was the conviction that this was a vital question for all humanity, with the fate of all non-Jewish peoples depending on its solution.* Schönerer's disciple Hitler condemned this *half-heartedness* and sham *anti-Semitism, for it lulled people into security; they thought they had the foe by the ears, while in reality they themselves were being led by the nose.*[169]

The Church as Electoral Assistant

Lueger used the slogan "Catholic, Austrian, and German" to link his political concerns and that of the Catholic church. This earned him the support first of the low-ranking clergy and then the entire church. Preachers fought for Christian Socialism by exerting their influence on the pulpit in support of Lueger's party and against "Jewish liberals." Lueger, in turn, called for increased church attendance and during his public appearances liked to surround himself with clergymen and nuns.

Back on New Year's Day 1889, Lueger had received enthusiastic applause when he exclaimed, one hundred years after the French Revolution: "The year 1889 will be a sort of touchstone for our party. . . . We must not content ourselves with reestablishing the Christian world order. In 1789 there was the Revolution, in 1889 we have to revise the Revolution, Catholic priests must lead again, they must make it clear that they are the leaders of the people, and that the entire people stands behind the Catholic movement."[170]

In return for helping the church, Lueger was in the extremely fortunate position of being able to use all of the church's organizations, its entire sinecures, its mothers' associations, its church choirs, cloisters, and schools. Hitler acknowledged the importance of this tactic. In *Mein Kampf*, for example, he stressed that Lueger had been deft at correctly gauging the value of *existing institutions*, which enabled him *to make use of these institutions as instruments for the achievement of his purposes.*[171] The Christian Social Party *avoided any struggle against a religious institution and thus secured the support of that mighty organization which the Church repre-*

sents. . . . It recognized the value of large-scale propaganda and was a virtuoso in influencing the psychological instincts of the broad masses of its adherents.[172]

The Christian Women's Association in Vienna, called "Lueger's Amazon Corps" or "My Harem," was politically also very important for Lueger. Enthusiastically serving their idol, its members performed efficient political work and contributed essentially to Lueger's successes. Count Kielmansegg commented on the women's associations: "Their purpose was utterly political, to wit: to support Lueger's party by making propaganda for him at home and to endorse and support the party at home and in public."[173]

Lueger was adept at using his considerable charm to flatter women and motivate them to work for him. In the example of "handsome Karl," young Hitler could study how a charismatic politician turned women into willing and enthusiastic work forces, ready to make sacrifices. After all, after many years of service in the clergymen's offices they were frequently already used to zealously obeying authority.

Lueger's most efficient assistant was Jesuit priest Heinrich Abel, who indulged in tirades against the Jews, Liberalism, Social Democracy, and, above all, against the pernicious influence of Freemasonry, a "pack poisoned by Satan," which he made responsible for all democratic and national movements and numerous alleged political murders. Using clichés such as "Freemasonry's world conspiracy," "demagogues," "clandestine powers," and an alleged "secret world government," he declared from the pulpit that all evil was "Jewish-Freemasonic," and called on his men to fight an unrelenting battle against these "godless enemies" and for the church and the Christian Social Party.[174]

Neither did Abel make any bones about his anti-Semitism in his personal life. Thus he boasted to own a cane which his father had once used to thrash a Jew—and gave that cane to a political friend as a sign of his friendship.[175]

Every year Abel organized men's pilgrimages to Mariazell and Klosterneuburg. Mayor Lueger usually was among the participants. In his ceremonial addresses Abel berated "the horrible terrorism which Social Democracy practices against the little people" and "the absolutism of liberal bureaucracy," particularly of the "Jewish press." In Mariazell in 1906, his colleague, Jesuit priest Viktor Kolb, also became active in the election campaign: "The parliamentary election is not only a political election—it is, above all, a religious act; it is a pledge to or against God, to or against faith."[176]

This brand of politically active Catholicism, which on account of the Hapsburgs alone had a centuries-old tradition in Austria, further wid-

Inauguration of Vienna's municipal gasworks. The mayor is behind the archbishop.

ened the gap between "Clerical liberals" and "Jewish liberals." Around 1900, the Church was an uncontrollable political power factor, at least in Vienna, with the Christian Social Party as an extension of its arms.

The laws of 1867, which had established not only the emancipation of the Jews but also a liberal education policy, played a central role in the battle against the Liberals. Referring to the "Catholic people of Austria," the Church as well as the Christian Social Party called for "re-Catholicization" and a more "Christian spirit." This implied calling for the removal of the Jews from all public sectors, particularly their dismissal as teachers and university professors.

Orphanages, for example, were organized as strictly Catholic and German institutions in order to secure new members for the Church and for "Germandom" in Vienna. Talented sons of Christian Socials were accepted into the City of Vienna's famous Knabenhorte (boys' hostels), to which the mayor gave his generous financial support. These institutions subjected the children, the Catholic leaders of the future, to a strictly military, Catholic, and German education.[177]

Vienna's Popular Education Association steadfastly refused to comply with the mayor's wish to exclude "Jews, people of Jewish ancestry, and Jew lackeys."[178] Permissions to use lecture halls were withdrawn, moneys frozen, and honorable members branded as "Jewish-freemasonic" demagogues. Not even the fact that the prominent historian—and

"Aryan" Catholic—Alfred von Arneth, president of the Imperial Academy of Sciences, was also president of the Popular Education Association, made any difference. Under Lueger, "professor" was an insult anyway.

Anti-Semitic pamphlets were sold in Catholic clubs and clergymen's offices. Among them was the little book *From the Year 1920* by Lueger's fellow party member Scheicher. In this pamphlet the prelate related his "dream" of what the provinces of the Dual Monarchy would look like in 1920, which by then would have fallen apart: after rigorously exchanging minorities, the lands of the "Eastern states" would now be nationally organized and independent. Austria's old provinces, including Vienna, would now be called "Ostmark," Corinthia and Krain, "Südmark" and Sudeten "Nordmark." There would be a Czech Bohemia, a Polish Poland, a Ruthenian Ruthenia, and so forth. In Scheicher's vision, Lueger was by now retired as a "state elder of the *Ostmark*." Vienna had been renamed Luegerville in his honor. For the city was now "Jew-free," because the Christians had driven the "flatfeet," "crooked-noses," and "Yiddish gabbers" to Budapest by way of a total economic embargo.

Jewry had "raged worse than the plague in the lands of the former Austria," Scheicher wrote. "It drove young and old toward vulgar fornication, and systematically undermined the sense of purity and morals. Syphilis and scrofula were the results."[179] "The universities, the schools, the hospitals, the squares and streets, everything, everything built with Christian money! Still, the arrivals from the East, the barely civilized Semites from Galicia and Hungary, were generously allowed their share in all Christian foundations!"[180] Now, finally, the Jews were gone, and Vienna was clean. All that remained were the "crypto-Jews," that is to say, the baptized, "clandestine" Jews, an issue for which the prelate recommended the practices of the Inquisition.[181]

With the exodus of the Jews, Scheicher wrote, parliamentarianism's "Witches' Sabbath" was over as well. Brotherly love now reigned among Christians. Lueger had those few who had protested the abolition of democracy in Parliament picked up and committed to mental hospitals. Now a chamber system, organized by social estates, was in place. Referendums were held where black and white balls could be handed in as yea or nay votes on certain issues: "It was a salvation from the unbearable rule of demagogy and nonculture"—meaning Parliament.[182]

All big businesses were now nationalized. There were no longer any millionaires. All diligent people were living in peace. Demonstrations, as they once had been organized by the "Jew commies" in Vienna, were illegal. "We have cleaned things up. He who offends against the state will be mercilessly hanged. We once hanged three hundred Jews and twenty Aryans in Vienna in one day." And: "We have had to hang thousands in the state of Poland and the state of Ruthenia, until all sinners came to realize that we were serious." Pimps would also be hanged.[183]

Prelate Scheicher was hardly the only one yearning for a violent solution to the multiethnic monarchy's problems. However, he was the only one who recorded his political dreams. Dreams about a "priestly rule" in an allegedly morally pure, totalitarian state without Jews was part of Vienna's zeitgeist prior to 1914.

The Right Party Membership Card

One of the secrets of Lueger's success was the special and exclusive care he took of his constituents, whom he made dependent on himself and his party by offering many different kinds of relief. Lueger did not leave the slightest doubt about his feeling obliged to extend charities only to them and by no means to all Viennese. For instance, in 1905 he proudly pointed out in the Reichsrat again and again: "I am responsible only to my constituents, responsible only to those city councilmen who have voted for me."[184]

In Vienna there certainly was a great deal to hand out around 1900, as the city was one huge construction site for decades, with great demand for labor and a large volume of commissions for artisans and all kinds of businesses. The municipality of Vienna paid better wages than the federal government. Yet in order to obtain such a sought-after position with the city—or a city-owned apartment, a fellowship, or anything else for that matter—one had to be a member of the Christian Social Party, in other words, carry "the right card," a custom that was to play an infamous role in Austria. In addition, every city employee, most notably every teacher, had to swear an oath at the beginning of his tenure that he neither was nor would become either a Social Democrat or a Schönerian. Thus Lueger's followers, who always enjoyed privileges, could consider themselves to be among the chosen.

There was a great deal of corruption in the city government, which was hardly possible without Lueger being aware of it. Yet even his worst enemies admitted that the mayor was not personally corrupt or tried to enrich himself. The *Wiener Sonn- und Montagszeitung*, which was not favorably inclined toward the Christian Socials, acknowledged: "Around him, everything relishes in gold and medals, in titles and rich sinecures, but he only wants to remain the popular man holding all the strings, he, the maker of kings, who keeps reminding the majesties by his grace that it was he who created them."[185] In *Mein Kampf* Hitler too stressed in connection with both Schönerer and Lueger: *Amid the morass of general political corruption their whole life remained pure and unassailable.*[186]

Lueger remained adamant in his hatred of his political opposition, the "Jew commies," whom he never ceased to mock. The Social Democrats, he said, shied away from work: "They don't much care whether or not they're in jail for a few days. They don't work while in or out of custody, they don't work, at most they sing the 'Song of Work': 'Let's praise work!', except with the addendum: 'As long as someone else does it.' (Loud amusement.)"[187]

After the city council had authorized the mayor in 1909 to make all financial decisions alone, Lueger said sarcastically that according to standing orders, it was now Social Democratic city councilor Jakob Reumann's turn to speak: "Well, Reumann is proud now, he's allowed to speak until December 31, 1909. For that time period the city council has given me the authority to do business even without a budget, but after that his head will fall. He's going to be beheaded. The whole world is laughing at this comedy. I will hardly let anyone take the helm out of my hands. I'm remaining the boss here, and the more obstinate they are, the stronger I get."[188]

The antagonism between Christian Socials and Social Democrats led to the formation of two very similar social groups with similar political goals—such as anticapitalism—but opposing one another: craftsmen, farmers, and small tradesmen were building a front against industrial workers, and vice versa. Again and again there was controversy between these two groups, particularly when the craftsmen, under Lueger's protection, demanded excessive prices—to the protest of the workers.

For example, the Viennese butchers' privileges, which were a consequence of their party membership, led to meat prices that were inflated for years. The teamsters and, above all, the homeowners managed to achieve the same thing. In the interest of tourism, the governor of Lower Austria tried to abolish abuses in this area, but to no avail. Political corruption prevented reforms, "which is why within a few years Vienna earned a reputation as one of the most expensive cities in Europe and tourists therefore began to avoid the capital."[189]

In order to fight the Viennese bakers' dictating prices, the Social Democrats resorted to self-help and founded the Hammer bread factory which, according to its advertising slogan, was "a Viennese workers' plant" and "the Monarchy's most modern bread factory."[190] It distributed its goods through Social Democratic party organizations and left no doubt that it would not try to avoid confrontations.

To support the interests of the bakers, the Christian Socials assaulted the "red" bread factories. The topic was addressed at nearly every election rally, for example, at the Christian Social election meeting in a gymnasium in Brigittenau in 1911.[191] The *Brigittenauer Bezirks-Nachrichten* fumed that the "Jewish big business company" of the Hammer bread factory was trying to kill the entire baker's trade and establish the "rule of Jewish big-time operators and Jewish Socialist leaders."[192]

Hanisch indicates that the Hammer breadworks was a topic at the men's hostel as well. He says that young Hitler, anyway, had mentioned how good the bread from the two factories Anker and Hammer was— which, in view of Hitler's constantly berating the Social Democrats, was noted as being peculiar.

The Germanization of Vienna

All the Dual Monarchy's national problems came into focus in Vienna, which all the peoples in the Hapsburg Empire rightly considered "their" capital and imperial residence. Accordingly, Vienna should have been a multinational city—and it was, too, as far as immigration statistics were concerned: more than half of all Viennese residents were born outside of Vienna. The ratio between natives and immigrants was particularly extreme in Brigittenau, where Hitler lived: in 1908, only 17,200 out of 71,500 people could claim Vienna as their legal residence.[193] Hitler said in 1941: *What makes Vienna difficult is the difference in blood within its city walls. The offspring of all those races which comprised the former Austria live there, and so everybody listens with a different receiver, and everybody has a different sender!*[194]

This enormous migration of peoples changed the ratio of nations within a short time period: the German population's share decreased in the German-speaking parts of the country, especially in Vienna. The specter of alienation haunted the city. The natives felt threatened by the masses of poor, foreign-speaking immigrants, felt they had lost their power in their "own" country and did not get enough protection from the state—all the more so, the more unemployment and inflation increased. Thus they became receptive to radical national slogans.

All these shifts changed the zeitgeist within one generation. Whereas the fathers had still been liberal and cosmopolitan and proud of their monarchy, the sons were national. Hitler's contemporary Oskar Kokoschka, who was three years his senior, describes this rupture in his book: "Families from almost forty different peoples had known one another and married among each other. They had traded among each other. It looked as if in its almost one-thousand-year rule this old Hapsburg Monarchy had learned the art of teaching its peoples to live at peace with one another," which could serve as "a model of social ethics." However, "This empire all of a sudden seemed to have become so small that one threatened to step on the other's toes." And: "At that time the intellectual elite of different nations started to smash windows; internationally minded workers used paving stones to build barricades. National politicians demanded that their countries alone be allowed to exploit their mineral resources, at the expense of the general population. The Roman statesman's allegory of the limbs that have been severed from the body not being able to live an independent life, was forgotten."[195]

From the start, Mayor Lueger vigorously tackled the capital's most pressing problem, that of unstoppable immigration. According to his motto, "Vienna is German and must remain German," which he constantly reiterated, he adamantly enforced Vienna's German character against the efforts of the monarchy's non-German nationalities.

In this respect he was following the example of the empire's second capital, Budapest, which was strictly Hungarian, and vigorously magyarized the other nationalities. Yet he was also following the capital of other crown provinces, which remembered their national roots and relentlessly nationalized their people as well: during those decades, Prague became a Czech, Lemberg a Polish, Trieste an Italian, Laibach a Slovenian city. And everywhere there were national battles between the majorities and the minorities.

Lueger started the rigorous Germanization of Vienna precisely at the multiethnic empire's definition of nationalities—the everyday language people used—and demanded that each immigrant speak German. He then began to formulate Vienna's immigration law of 1890, which established that those could become legal residents in Vienna who had continuously lived in the city for ten years and paid taxes for just as long, who were economically independent and promised the mayor by oath that they would "conscientiously carry out their duty according to the regulations set forth in the municipal statutes, and who contribute to the well-being of the community to the best of their ability." Lueger then added the requirement for each applicant to swear to preserve "the city's German character to the best of his ability."[196] In addition, he always took the occasion of the nationalization oath ceremony to solemnly confirm his maxim of Vienna being a German city.

The oath strictly compelled immigrants to assimilate and Germanicize; furthermore, it was a political instrument in order to proceed against non-German clubs and schools. For the new legal residents, who had sworn to be German, now risked being sued for perjury if they got caught speaking Czech or Polish or being active in a non-German national club. To be sure, all this was legal according to federal law, but it contradicted the naturalization oath. This opened the doors wide to informers.

The mayor did not beat about the bush when it came to the Czechs—for instance, when he shouted at a residents' gathering in the fall of 1909: "Whose bread you eat, his song you sing, and his language you speak. I know that there are Czechs who don't want to yield under any condition; those who don't bend simply have to be broken. . . . The German language is valid, and it rules here in Vienna and in Lower Austria."[197]

However (and this proves Lueger's political sensibility): as long as the Czechs assimilated and were decent "German" citizens, the mayor offered them his protection and help, saying, according to the famous motto, "Leave my Bohemians alone." In a deft move he put Viennized Czechs into high positions, creating devoted personal guards who obeyed him unconditionally. Many small tradesmen and craftsmen who were originally Czech turned into fervent Lueger fans—to the annoyance of the national Czechs in Prague, who commented that it was an "extremely sad sign . . . for the Viennese Czech middle class, of all social groups, to provide the best servants to Lueger's Clericalism."[198]

It was not least Vienna's strict Germanization under Lueger that established his fame and also triggered young Hitler's *unconcealed admiration* for *the greatest German mayor of all times*.[199]

When in 1908 the question became pressing of whether an Italian law school—and perhaps even a Slovenian university—should be established in Vienna, the basic principle of whether Vienna was or was not a multinational city was also on the agenda. Minister of Finance Leon von Bilinski, who hailed from Galicia, meekly gave the German ambassador the following reply: "He said it would be absurd to artificially plant an Italian and subsequently perhaps even a Slovenian university here." The reason was: "In a national sense, he said, Vienna was no longer Austria's capital; it was a German city, and nothing could be done about that any longer."[200]

Lueger's Death

The mayor's slow death in the spring of 1910 moved people in Vienna. There was only one topic in the entire city: the virtues and flaws of "the Lord God of Vienna." Hanisch reports that in those days there were spirited discussions in the reading room of the men's hostel at Melde-

mannstrasse. The Social Democrats were hoping to achieve some successes now that the Christian Socials had no leader, and they did not
hold back their criticism. This in turn angered Lueger's followers, among
them—Hitler. He told his colleagues in detail about Lueger's career,
which he had apparently studied thoroughly. There was more than
enough material available. The newspapers were full of stories about Lueger, and since 1907, there was also Lueger's first biography, by Franz Stauracz, which had a large print run and was available in all libraries and
schools in Vienna, and certainly also in the men's hostel.[201]

Lueger died on March 10, 1910. His funeral made history as "the
most beautiful corpse" among Vienna's obsequies. The German ambassador reported to Berlin: "No sovereign could be buried with higher
honors."[202]

The mourners went from City Hall to Saint Stephen's Cathedral via
the Ring, where the consecration took place in the company of the emperor, many archdukes, ministers, and other top-ranking dignitaries. Then
the procession went on through Rotenturmstrasse via the quai. At As-
pernplatz more than a thousand cars waited to drive the mourners all the
way to the central cemetery. At the cemetery the public was excluded,
and all streetcar service in that direction was suspended. Initially Lueger
was interred in the grave of his parents, because the crypt of the newly
erected "Dr. Karl Lueger Memorial Church" was not yet completed.

Most stores were closed, and flags of mourning were hanging from
windows. As always during such huge events in Vienna, sausage stands
had been put up. A lane of some forty thousand men in uniform framed
the procession: Vienna's garrison, veterans, the uniformed municipal associations, marksmen's associations, the local chapters of the Christian
Women's Association with their many-colored flags. In short: Vienna had
a great party. *When the mighty funeral procession bore the dead mayor from
the city hall toward the Ring, I was among the many hundred thousands looking
on at the tragic spectacle.*[203]

We may assume that young Hitler also read many of the newspaper
obituaries, probably being most interested in the one by Lueger's greatest
political opponent, Friedrich Austerlitz, in the *Arbeiterzeitung*. Austerlitz
presented a brilliant analysis of the course of Lueger's political success,
which reads like a primer for an ambitious politician. Lueger's life, Austerlitz wrote, had been one of "tenacious strength and passionate will,"
"strength which achieves what the will has set as its goal." "He didn't
join a party, he created one within himself; he didn't rise according to
the law of seniority, but the leader was there before the party was. With
no other means than his fresh speech he conquered city and country,

shaping its representation according to his image. How did that become possible? Lueger was simply the first middle-class politician who took the masses into account, who moved the masses and dug the roots of his power deep into the soil." Lueger, Austerlitz continued, realized "that in this day and age political consequences can happen only from great powers and that the core of political activity is organization."

Yet according to Austerlitz, Lueger not only stirred up strength, "but also devastated ideas," replacing "the fruitful ideas of democracy by unscrupulous demagogy." "Like a virtuoso" he developed a "harshness of the tone that doesn't shy away from the most vicious slandering of one's opponent," and "a malicious terrorism that wanted to turn political antagonism into a war of total destruction." This, Austerlitz argued, was where "the ruthless abuse of the power of the authorities for partisan goals" was rooted. And: "The art of making blind promises, the art seemingly to unite opposites, to act agrarian today and industrial tomorrow, to work for the employers and to cajole the workers, to be loyal to the government and to appear to be in opposition, this too is Lueger's invention."[204]

Lueger's death triggered the Christian Socials' decline. Entangled in internal battles, competitions, and the disclosure of cases of corruption of gigantic proportions, the leaderless party shrank from ninety-five to seventy-six parliamentary seats in 1911. The Lueger cult flourished all the more.

The fact that with Lueger's death his party's great era was over as well was apparently also a topic of discussion in the men's hostel. Hanisch tells as that in connection with Lueger's death Hitler argued that a new party was necessary: it needed a name that sounded good and should adopt the best slogans from the other parties in order to win as many followers as possible. According to Hanisch, none of the parties in existence at the time was quite to young Hitler's liking.

Hitler remained the outsider, the "analytical" observer: *Since I saw my conviction realized in no other party, I could . . . not make up my mind to enter, let alone fight with, any of the existing organizations. Even then I regarded all political movements as unsuccessful and unable to carry out a national reawakening of the German people on a larger and not purely external scale.*[205]

However, in their virtues as well as their flaws the two Viennese politicians Schönerer and Lueger served Hitler as political models to whom he devoted many pages of his book: *It is infinitely instructive for our present day to study the causes for the failure of both parties. This is particularly useful for my friends, since in many points conditions today are similar to then and errors can thereby be avoided.*[206] And: *This whole process of the growth and passing of the Pan-German movement on the one hand, and the unprecedented rise of the Christian Social Party on the other, was to assume the deepest significance for me as a classical object of study.*[207] And: *Schönerer was more consistent, he had determined to smash the state. Lueger believed he could preserve the Austrian state for the Germans. Both of them were absolutely German men.*[208]

Yet despite the mortal enmity between the two parties, the fact that—as he wrote in *Mein Kampf*—Hitler turned from the Pan-Germans to the Christian Socials when he was in Vienna, does not at all signify a political about-face. For the Pan-Germans were just as German-national, antiliberal, anti-Semitic, and anti–Social Democrat as the Christian Socials. The aggressive language of the newspapers of both of them is identical.

What with all his admiration for Lueger, Hitler by no means became one of his "disciples," but again only adopted those parts of Lueger's policies that fit into his weltanschauung. Thus his sympathies definitely ended where Catholicism began. Even back when he was still in school he was not religious, and no eyewitness ever mentioned that he ever went to church. August Kubizek wrote: "For as long as I knew Adolf Hitler, I don't remember him ever attending a service."[209] He maintained that despite his great reverence for Lueger, he had not joined the Christian Social Party because "he was bothered by the ties to the clergy, which constantly interfered with politics."[210] Neither can Hitler's constant invectives against "the Jesuits" be brought into agreement with the spirit of the Christian Socials. Hanisch does find it worth mentioning that young Hitler once sided with the "Clericals": when there was a battle against the Social Democrats. At the time, Hanisch reports, the *Arbeiterzeitung* had mocked the Corpus Christi procession, and on that occasion young Hitler had "defended religion."

What Hitler mainly criticized in Lueger was that he was never really able to embrace the racial principle, both as far as Jews and Slavs were concerned, in which area he considered Schönerer to be more consistent. Yet he did admire Lueger, the "people's tribune" and "German man," as well as his tactical skill in not presenting to the "people" many different enemies like Schönerer, but to confine himself to one single enemy—the Jews: *In general the art of all truly great national leaders at all times consists among other things primarily in not dividing the attention of a people, but in concentrating it upon a single foe.*[211]

After the Anschluss the Lueger cult once again came to life. The NSDAP arranged a solemn funeral for Lueger's sister Hildegard in an honorary grave. The film *Vienna 1910*, in which a great number of stars appeared and which had its premiere in 1943, was a tribute to Lueger. The fact that, in a crude black-and-white way of presenting things, Schönerer served as Lueger's negative antipode, angered "the last Schönerians." In response to Stein's protests, Joseph Goebbels noted in his diary: "There is a radical political clique in Vienna which wants to make this film fail. I won't allow that to happen." However: "No doubt Lueger was somewhat heroized." Yet "apart from a very small circle of interested people," no one was familiar with all these events anyway.[212]

9
Czechs in Vienna

A Wave of Immigrants Around 1900

After 1867, the political distribution of power in the Dual Monarchy continuously diminished the significance of the empire's Germans, first on account of the split into Cisleithania and Transleithania, and then within the empire's Western half as a result of the basic laws of 1867, which guaranteed national rights to every citizen. The introduction of universal, equal suffrage in 1906 finally reduced the Germans' significance to the place they had by virtue of their share of the population. In Cisleithania, this was no more than 35.6 percent, and in all of Austro-Hungary, much less. In this new democratic system the Germans were forced to relinquish their former position of predominance, to share their rule with the empire's other nationalities, and ultimately to submit themselves to the non-German majority.

In Cisleithania, the Czechs were the most powerful nation after the Germans; they were highly educated and economically very productive, and they represented a fierce competition to the German-Bohemians, particularly because they were a source of cheaper labor. Under the fierce national pressure, many German-Bohemian workers emigrated to Saxony or Lower Austria. Czechs immigrated, and thus several German-speaking communities tended to become bilingual, all the more so because the Czech birth rate was much higher than the German.

To give an example: around 1850, the Southern Bohemian city of Budweis was almost exclusively German. In 1880, Germans and Czechs had an approximately equal share of the population. By 1910, the Germans' share was only 38.2 percent, with their number declining.[1] Also counting the suburbs, there still were 228,019 Czechs and 41,975 Germans around 1880—roughly 82 percent compared to 18 percent. In 1900, the ratio was 92.3 percent to 7.5 percent.[2] In 1910, there were no Germans on the city council.

In 1909 the German embassy transmitted a concerned report to Berlin: "The Germans in the Sudeten lands have long since been on the defensive against the Czechs." Formally they still had equal rights, "but in reality, they are being Slavicized or pushed back. . . . The Czechs' tactics aim toward not leaving any part of Bohemia exclusively German."[3]

While in 1905 there was a satisfactory national compromise in Moravia, the negotiations on a compromise with Bohemia was drawn out for years, led to several governments being toppled, and never came to a conclusion. The problem of the capital, Prague, turned out to be unsolvable. The Czechs insisted on Prague's being an exclusively Czech city. The German minority wanted a bilingual Prague. In return, the Czechs demanded a bilingual Vienna.

Between 1851 and 1910, the quota of Czechs in Vienna increased approximately tenfold.[4] By 1910, one out of five residents was of Czech origin, and immigration kept increasing. Thus a development toward a bilingual Lower Austria and a bilingual capital, Vienna, was certainly possible, but only if the immigrants remained Czech rather than assimilate. In *Mein Kampf* Hitler mentions this issue, which was a consistently hot topic during his youth in Vienna: *Purely German towns, indirectly through government officialdom, were slowly but steadily pushed into the mixed-language danger zones. Even in Lower Austria this process began to make increasingly rapid progress, and many Czechs considered Vienna their largest city.*[5]

Complaints about "Slavization" were by no means confined to the followers of the radical-national parties. All German parties emphasized their nationality—albeit in various degrees of intensity—even the German Social Democrats, the liberal parties, and the Christian Socials. The German self-image of being part of an elite faced strong, growing, national and economic self-confidence on the part of the Czechs.

German-national statistician Anton Schubert tried to establish alienation as a fact by performing "ethnic examinations" in every village and every ministry. He took as a basis not the everyday language people used, but where they came from, which he deduced by their names—a thoroughly questionable approach, considering the fact that the population had been mixed for centuries. According to this method, about one in four people in Vienna today would be a "Slav."

Because that was not enough to portray alienation as sharply as necessary, Schubert eliminated from the start a few social groups as "non-German," for example, the aristrocrats, even if they were German-speaking, and "nationally indifferent middle-class Germans," mainly the Liberals. One of the results of these calculations, for instance, was that only .8 percent of federal centers was in German hands: "Today the centers are entirely ruled by Czechs, Poles, Southern Slavs, and noblemen; yet the real German is dead and extinct there."[6] These statistics appeared in 1905–06 in three volumes and were constantly quoted, serving as welcome national-political ammunition.

The method of painting a horrific picture of "Slavization" with the help of highly questionable means was widespread. To give one example from the *Unadulterated German Words* of 1908 about the "Slavization attempts" of Czech railway workers: In the Lower Austrian town of Amstetten, it said, "fifty sons of Wenzel" were already employed in a workshop, one sixth of all employees. When those concerned demanded that this situation be corrected, the publication argued it could not get into the fact "that the corrector only counts six Czechs in the workshop by no longer counting Slovenians and those Czechs who had lived there for quite a while already, as Germans rather than Czechs."[7]

Hitler displayed his familiarity with these kinds of numbers when, as late as 1942, he remarked during a dinner with Heydrich: *The Czechs, he said, are masters of subversion, and that the example of Vienna proved this. Before the world war, there had only been some 120 Germans among the 1,800 Austro-Hungarian*[8] *court officials, everyone else, all the way to the top-ranking posts, was Czech.*[9] According to official numbers, if counted the traditional way—by everyday language spoken—of 6,293 ministry officials on January 1, 1914, 4,772 (75.8 percent) were German, and only 653 (10.8 percent) Czech.[10]

Yet there is no doubt that in Vienna, which on account of unemployment, the housing shortage, inflation, and unstable political conditions was in a difficult situation to begin with, the natives' fear of additional immigrants, in particular the Czechs, was very real. A Viennese proverb at the time exemplifies that: "There's only one imperial city, there's only one Vienna, the Viennese are outside, the Bohemians within!"

Nach der Volkszählung.

"After the Census." The overpowering Czechs and Jews versus the gnomelike German Gullible Fritz (1910): "I gotta be careful now, otherwise those two will become taller than me." (*Kikeriki*)

One cannot tell precisely how many Czechs lived in Vienna around 1910. All we know is that the number established in the census of 1910, approximately 100,000, is too low. If the Czechs in Vienna did not want to subject themselves to harsh discrimination, they were forced to indicate in the questionnaires German as their native language, and were therefore registered as Germans. The legal citizens of Vienna were considered German anyway.

If we count according Vienna's population's origins, we arrive at an entirely different picture. According to this method, slightly less than five hundred thousand of Vienna's two million people were from the Bohemian countries. If we include the parent generation, this number almost doubles, with the quota of Czechs being larger than that of the Germans.[11] Yet it would be a mistake to draw a conclusion from the immigration figures of Czechs to the Czech population quota. For assimilation often took place so quickly that the immigrants were already "Germanized" after just a few years.

The Czechs came to Vienna as industrial workers, as maids, cooks, nannies, cobblers, tailors, and musicians. Because many of them lived with their employers, they were dispersed over all the districts and did not live together in one concentrated area, such as the Viennese Jews did in Leopoldstadt. This furthered assimilation.

Professional touts also brought very young, often only ten-year-old boys, who were selected by Viennese craftsmen at the Franz Josef train station as if at a slave market.[12] By paying a premium and reimbursing travel costs they took the children, who usually did not speak a word of German. Around 1910 there were already more than twice as many Czech apprentices as Germans with the Viennese tailors, cobblers, and carpenters, who tended to be of Czech origin themselves.

Apart from the Czech residents of Vienna, there were many seasonal workers who worked only from spring until fall, at construction sites or in brickworks, and in the wintertime returned to their families in Bohemia. Furthermore, many young men came to Vienna for only a few years, made some money there, gained experience, and then returned to Bohemia. There they bought a store or a house, thereby furthering the economic boom in Bohemia. Thus there certainly were many Czechs in Vienna, but always different ones. Historian Monika Glettler compared this to a "hotel which is always occupied, but always by different people."[13]

The German-nationals vented all their anger at "Slavization," exacerbated by Czech acts of terrorism against the Germans in Prague and the paralyzation of Parliament by the Czech National Socialists in Vienna at the weakest link of the chain: the Viennese Czechs. Most of them were apolitical and wanted to live and work in peace. Yet they got caught against their will in the machinery of the national battles in Bohemia and were used by the Czech radicals as a means of propaganda in Vienna, particularly after the events of the anniversary year, when a state of emergency was declared in Prague. The German radicals, on the other hand, used the Viennese Czechs as pawns to hurt the overpowering Czechs in Bohemia.

In short, in Prague as in Vienna it was the weakest ones who were hurt and could no longer live in peace. If there was an act of terror in Prague against the German minority, the next day there was going to be an act of terror in Vienna against the Czech minority, and vice versa. If in Prague German stores were boycotted with the slogan "Don't buy from Germans," Czech stores were boycotted in Vienna with the slogan "Don't buy from Czechs"—and vice versa.

Every gathering of Czechs in Vienna was now threatened by riots. The German nationalists fanned the fear of the "rule of the Slavs" and maintained "that Austria's large cities, built by German strength and German diligence, were now threatened by Slavdom. Prague had already fallen, Brünn was engaged in a difficult fight with the opponent, and to the disgrace of Germans, Vienna was called the largest Slavic city on the continent today."[14]

The Czechs' growing economic self-confidence was noted with sus-

Ein Soldatenliebchen.

"A Soldier's Girl." The typical anti-Czech cliché: good old gullible Fritz has to pay, and the Czech eats everything all by himself. ("Cook Austria: Sir, the money for your board, please; but I sure have no use for you in the kitchen!") (*Kikeriki*)

picion. In 1912 there were already four large Czech banks in Vienna. The *Brigittenauer Bezirks-Nachrichten* complained about their obvious success and eagerness to do business: Czech banks were open from 8:00 A.M. until 7:00 P.M., but German banks only from 9:00 A.M. until 4:00 P.M. Furthermore, the Czechs enticed customers by offering them higher interest. According to the Christian Social newspaper, the numerous small Czech savings and loan institutions tried "to make first advances toward bilingualism with their Czech signs in the streets of Vienna."[15]

The Pan-Germans called on people to boycott Czech newspapers and threatened to publicize the names of those store owners who sold them. German companies that employed non-German workers were ostracized economically and socially. According to a newspaper report, an itinerant speaker from the Südmark said, "Throwing out 200 Bohemians is a better national deed than 300 protest rallies and 1,000 shouts of *Heil*."[16]

No reason was too small to trigger controversy. For example, when the Czech cashier of an Austro-Hungarian musicians' welfare association took off with eight thousand kronen, the *Alldeutsches Tagblatt* wrote that the man was "a dilettante as a musician, he is hardly good enough to turn the pages of the sheet music, and with his ears, which stick out, his earth-pale complexion, his low forehead, his awkward round head, and his malicious gaze he only too closely resembles those 'individuals' and 'thieves' whom you can watch in Präuscher's waxworks in the Prater for twenty heller."[17] This subliminally suggested the image of the "inferior" Czech, quite similarly to the way Vienna's cartoon newspaper *Kikeriki* practiced on a daily basis. The Pan-Germans believed that the "Czechization of the city" equaled cultural regression, and furthermore, that tourism would decrease "if the streets of Vienna are made unsafe by the Czech mob."[18]

Popular Budweiser beer was boycotted. The windowpanes of the Budweiser beer parlor were repeatedly smashed. Innkeepers who served Czech associations were forced to fire them. If they did not, they were terrorized: in one tavern, Czech newspapers were torn up and a bust that Czechs had put up there was covered with army treasury coupons.[19]

Even the foundlings and orphans were drawn into the national controversy. Because they were overcrowded, the foundling hospitals had for years passed many children on to foster families—to farmers in the area, but also to poor Czech families. The German-nationals started protesting against that: the children, they said, were being "Czechisized" and "alienated from Germandom."

Mayor Lueger appeased them by building a large municipal foundling hospital. The foster children were taken away from the Czech families and instead raised in the new institution, in the spirit of the Christian Socials: German and Catholic. Hermann Bielohlawek, a Christian Social of Czech origin, was among those proudly mentioning the new regulation: "Hundreds of German children who during the liberal era were Slavicized by Czech foster parents," would now be "preserved for their people" on account of the reform of foundling care.[20]

The German parties vehemently rejected Czech complaints in Parliament. Interrupted by many interjections, Pan-German Vinzenz Malik said sarcastically: "We don't mind if the Czechs and other nations live here in Vienna, but they have to be nice and modest. They are here as guests, and we will never allow them to be impertinent. If they are, we will always proceed against them and be ready to face the whole world."[21]

More and more Czechs were afraid to socialize with one another. Czech gymnastics or savings clubs, reading circles, and hiking and biking clubs became smaller. A plea to the Viennese Czechs to shop only in Czech stores was dismally unsuccessful: of thousands of Czech shop owners in Vienna, only a few had their names put on the Czech list—because they were afraid of terror, and worried to lose their German customers. Tired of the battle, they heeded the police's advice to resort to self-help, taking their Czech company signs off and putting up German signs instead.[22]

During those years many people in Vienna left their families' Bohemian past behind and Germanized their names to once and for all rid themselves of all difficulties. Others tried to make up for their Czech origin, which they felt to be a flaw, with an all the stronger pledge to

Germandom, as did, for instance, Christian Social Bielohlawek, who emphatically said in the Lower Austrian assembly: "Some who are Germans by license assault me for not being German enough and because my name vaguely indicates that fact. My accent tells them that I am no Czech. Yet among those who attack me at every opportunity, there is one who used to bear the name Vrputofatel and who now calls himself Emanuel Weidenhoffer."[23] He was a deputy of the German Nationals.

The Battle for the Nibelung District

In the summer of 1909 the German-national terror reached one of its peaks. It was triggered by an insignificant event: a Viennese Czech tourist club planned a Sunday boat trip on the Danube to Wachau, failing to consider the fact that many hundred years before, the Nibelungs had roamed through that very landscape, which was why the German-nationals claimed the area for themselves as "arch-Germanic." Here, in Wachau, was where the Schönerians had celebrated the two-thousand-year anniversary of the Battle of Noreia at the summer solstice in 1888 and introduced their Germanic calendar. Here was where the German-Templars around Jörg Lanz von Liebenfels had their order's castle, Werfenstein.

At any rate, the Pan-Germans were not willing to allow the "desecration" of the German Wachau by the "Slavs" and called on all pan-German clubs to travel to Melk and "receive" the Czechs there, for, as the *Alldeutsches Tagblatt* wrote, "a mass rally such as the state of Lower Austria has never seen, shall destroy the desire of these Slavic intruders, and of those Social Democratic gentlemen too, ever again to feel like going on such 'harmless' tourist outings," and, in the words of a spokesman of the "League of Germans in Lower Austria," "Melk will resemble an army camp this Sunday—already, four to five thousand guests are announced."[24]

Many members of the Czech tourist club were workers and members of the Social Democratic Party, which offered to help them in their troubled situation. Yet the club refused the offer, as it did not want to politicize the conflict unnecessarily.

The *Arbeiterzeitung*, at any rate, took a clear stand, in a scoffing editorial on the "Wachau Landsturm": "Six hundred tourists with their wives and children a danger to German Melk! And the ghosts of the Nibelungs are being conjured up! Our worst enemy couldn't have construed a more ridiculous situation for the German people in Austria." The editorial continued by saying that the tourists were workers "who have laid aside dime after dime for a long time to afford the modest and harmless pleasure of a ride on the Danube for themselves and their families. If for no other reason, the brutality alone would be disgusting with which the hard-earned, sorely deserved pleasure for people who surely have hardly any joy and recreation is being interfered with and spoiled, for the sake of a pathetic brawl." Such "absurd brawling" created "a situation which is intolerable in a metropolis."[25]

During a talk with Vienna's police president, the tourist club's president agreed to the suggestion not to dock the boat in Melk so as not to endanger "the women and children on board." Under German-national pressure, the Chapter of Melk kept its gate locked anyway, and Melk's innkeepers wanted to "refuse serving food and drink to the tourists." The club's president promised that the club would "preserve its character as an apolitical tourist and entertainment club at all cost" and also do without national flags and emblems.[26]

After this compromise was reached, the authorities permitted the trip. This meant total police protection during the entire ride. The military was kept ready. Mounted police oversaw the embarkation near the Reich Bridge on Saturday evening, and police also closed bridges over the Danube to prevent protesters from throwing stink bombs and fireworks on the boat. In any case, the federal authorities did everything they could to protect the citizens' rights.

The German-nationals protested against these police measures: "Since the Government didn't protect the Germans," they said, "the Germans would have to resort to self-help." To underscore that, rioteers roamed through the city, broke out into shouts of "Boo!" in front of Social Democrat deputy Franz Schuhmeier's house, and made much noise in front of taverns where Czechs met.[27]

The much-discussed Wachau trip turned out to be relatively harmless: toward six in the morning the boat *Franz Josef* passed Melk's dock in a considerable distance. Because the early train from Vienna still had not arrived, the number of demonstrators was limited. Waving black-red-gold flags, they rushed to the embankment. "They menacingly brandished their sticks, there was a deafening noise, and there were piercing whistles and roaring shouts of 'Boo!' in the air"—this is how the *Arbeiterzeitung* described the event. Several trains with demonstrators arrived in the morning. The mood heated up under the influence of the heat and alcohol.

When the boat returned around noon, the early-morning spectacle repeated itself. According to the *Alldeutsches Tagblatt*, approximately nine thousand demonstrators lined up against the Czechs at the dock, which

Die Wachaufahrt des tschechischen Touristenvereines.

The Czech tourist club's Wachau trip

was not used: "Thousands of Germans were posted in a long line. The black-red-gold flags fluttered in the wind, and indignant shouts rose powerfully across the river to the blinding white boat with its Czech cargo, which couldn't be set ashore. The 'Wacht am Rhein' concluded the magnificent defense rally of Melk." Afterward the demonstrators went into the taverns, where more speeches were held. To quote an example: "This defense has achieved everything it set out to achieve—keeping the Czech club from touching the German Wachau's soil with their Czech club motto. . . . Let us rejoice, Germans, at the success of our defense!"[28]

The Third Reich made a point of picking up the Wachau's German-national tradition. Thus at a significant date, the day of the referendum on the "Greater German Empire," on April 10, 1938, the NSDAP's *Völkischer Beobachter* published an enthusiastic two-page article, "The Wachau as a German Stronghold." Germans had settled there as far back as the Stone Age, it reported: "Proud Germans grew up on magnificent soil." "Heroic Germanic courage" had vanquished all enemies, even the Romans: "They slayed lions which were sicked on them in battle with oak sticks from the German forest." The article described the era of the Hapsburgs and the World War: "Degenerate people, aliens in the German nation, roamed through the Ostmark with a false name of God and their Heimat on their lips. German heroism and the German spirit were maimed and disfigured, and ridiculed. . . . The German character was considered strange in their own country."

The article concluded: "Then one day loud, unanimous shouts of joy rose to the sky: 'Adolf Hitler has liberated the Ostmark!' . . . Only now have the land of the Nibelungs and Wachau regained their true destination: to be a bulwark of the Greater German Empire."[29]

The Battle for the Komensky Schools

In their effort to make Vienna a bilingual city, the Czech-nationals leaned on clause nineteen of the national basic law of 1867: "The State acknowledges the equality of all traditional languages in schools, public offices, and public life." All nationalities had the right to raise their children in their mother tongue with the government's support.

Furthermore, the languages of all minorities who had a share of more than 25 percent of the population were legally recognized as "traditional languages," which gave these minorities a number of rights, for example, the right to form their own parties, to nominate their own city councilmen, and to keep their own schools.[30] Yet due to Lueger's Germanization campaign, at the 1910 census, officially the Czechs in Vienna had only 6.5 percent.

The sensitive topic of schools kindled harsh conflicts. Since 1883 the Czech school association Komensky had administered a Czech private school in Vienna's district of Favoriten, which greatly bothered the German-nationals. Komenksy teachers were constantly harassed by the Viennese authorities and were frequently checked and spied on. A retired teacher lost his Viennese civil rights because he taught in the Komsenky school. The reason given was that this was "not only infamous treason against his hometown, which fed him and bestowed a post and honors on him, but also a violation of the Viennese citizens' oath." Under the headline "Only German Teachers for Viennese Children," the Deutsches Volksblatt said that during the last census a district teacher, who was mentioned by name, had indicated "Czech" as his everyday language. He should be rigorously dismissed: "The people no longer abide the City of Vienna . . . hiring a Slav, who is always an enemy of the people. . . . We finally have to set an example!"[31]

During the riots about the trip on the Danube, violent acts were committed in protest against a garden party of the Komensky club in the Simmering labor district in August 1909. There was brawling. People threw beer mugs. The compartments of a streetcar were seized, Czech-speaking passengers were insulted. Traffic was stopped.

Mounted police had a very difficult time keeping the approximately two thousand Czech "defense fighters," who fled from the overpowering crowd in fear. For lack of the real victims, the demonstrators then attacked the police with canes, and threw rocks and beer mugs at the police horses. Finally they withdrew, "singing folkish songs," marched through the city in rows of eight, and sang, bareheaded, the "Wacht am Rhein" and the Bismarck song at Schwarzenberg Square, in front of the French embassy, of all places. The final speech culminated in the demand that the empire's capital, Vienna, be German and remain German.[32]

The tension was exacerbated by more and more hectic collections for the various national school associations. In 1909, the year of crisis, the Czech School Association's collection brought in 1.4 million kronen, which was more than the simultaneous collections by the Polish and the German school associations. Thus Lower Austria and Vienna had enough money for Czech schools.[33] Czechs as well as Germans quoted an official number of 22,513 Czech pupils in Vienna[34]—with the former pointing out the significant lack of schoolyards for Czech children and the latter painting the grisly picture of the "Slavization of Vienna" on the wall. The German-national parties and the Christian Socials thus tried harder than ever to push through the "lex Kolisko," a proposal for making German the only language in all the schools of Lower Austria and Vienna, independent of the size of their national minorities. This was in contradiction to clause nineteen, and the Social Democrats cautioned that this would be dangerous: "You are not serving . . . national peace but are throwing a burning torch into all states and state parliaments, whipping up the individual parties to fight for every school."[35]

The situation became worse for the German minorities in the Slavic regions. In Galicia, for instance, where the German minority demanded the same as the Czechs demanded in Vienna, Vienna's school policy served as an excuse to reject the demands. The Polish newspaper *Nowa Reforma* wrote in 1909: "In all of Galicia there are fewer Germans than Czechs in Vienna. If the Czechs in Vienna are not recognized as a people and their language not regarded as 'traditional,' then there is much more justification in adopting this view to the Germans in Galicia. . . . At any rate, by supporting the lex Kolisko the Germans have lost every right to make any demands in Galicia."[36]

In 1909 the Emperor tried to pour oil on the waters by making a compromise. He signed the "lex Kolisko," but only partially, granting German as the obligatory language of instruction only in schools for teachers and technical high schools in Lower Austria, but not in public and middle-class schools (which after all were the main issue). This exacerbated the indignation on both sides.

Lueger, on the other hand, received enthusiastic national applause when during the Vienna residents' oath he once again confirmed: "This oath now possesses heightened significance, because there are attempts to give our city a bilingual character. If Vienna becomes bilingual, then it loses the significance it has had until now. For Vienna can only be the Empire's capital and imperial residence if it is monolingual. For if one wanted to draw a conclusion from bilingualism, Vienna would not be bilingual but become mono- or multilingual—a situation which would be downright intolerable." Alluding to the Komensky schools, he added: "I will strictly see to it that there is only one German school here in my hometown of Vienna, and not any other."[37]

The state, which found itself obliged to protect the basic laws, including the rights of the minorities, was once again confronted with Lueger's policy of Germanization. The "people of Vienna" was clearly on Lueger's side, in opposition to the government and the emperor.

In 1911 the riots spread over to Vienna's second Czech school, which was being established in the Third District. The situation was confused because the authorities could not come to an agreement: The ministry of education allowed the school to be run until further notice, but the state education council ordered that the school be closed. The situation deteriorated all the more as the Czech National Socialists interfered vehemently, which turned the anger even of moderate people in Vienna against the Czechs.

The daily struggle for power was carried on on the backs of the pupils. The City of Vienna closed the new building because of alleged flaws in sanitary facilities—the flaws consisting of coat hooks that were too low. The federal authorities ordered the school to be reopened. New harassments followed, and it was closed again. Allegedly the building was too narrow for the alleyway, plus the barking of the dogs in the nearby School of Veterinary Medicine interfered with instruction, and so forth.[38] There was no end to the back-and-forth about the Komensky schools.

Toward the end of September 1911 the police sealed off the gates of the Czech schools, locking the students out. People were very bitter, particularly because these disturbances coincided with the unrest about inflation. The Czech National Socialists took up their Viennese compatriots' cause: on October 5, 1911, they took the Komensky pupils and their parents into Parliament, which led to brawls between German and Czech deputies in the parliament building's columned hall. On November 3, 1912, four thousand Viennese rallied, shouting the slogan: "Down with the Czech school!" The problem remained unresolved until 1918.

Attempts at Mediation

The Social Democrats were the ones most eager to reconcile the various nationalities. The party itself was supranational: of its eighty-seven Reichsrat deputies in 1908, fifty were German, twenty-four Czech, six Polish, five Italian, and two Ruthenian.[39] The party consistently supported the various minorities, for example the establishment of a Ruthenian university in Lemberg and a Czech university in Brünn.

In return for their commitment they were insulted as "Jew commies" and "friends of Slavs and Czechs" who supported "the Slavs' desire to expand." The Christian Social *Brigittenauer Bezirks-Nachrichten* wrote during the election campaign: "Every Social Democratic deputy equals one Czech deputy," and therefore every vote for the Social Democrats was one for the Czechs. And: Social Democracy posed "the greatest threat to the City of Vienna's German character." And: "Why would Dr. Adler and his comrades mind, they are Jews and therefore insensitive to our national feeling, which is why they couldn't care less whether Czechs or Germans rule the roost in Vienna."[40]

It was very difficult for Adler to contain the battles between his Czech and German fellow party members, and he finally found himself between all stools: the Czechs withdrew their allegiance from Vienna's central party office, feeling they were being patronized and "Germanicized," whereas the Germans accused it of being too Slavophile. According to historian Hans Mommsen, this nationalism, even within Social Democracy, was "a mass psychological phenomenon," "a collective hypnosis from which even the more sensible among the Czech party leaders could not disentangle themselves."[41]

At first things were fermenting among the unions. The German union members accused their Czech colleagues of keeping down wages and of being scabs, and the Czechs refused to send their contributions to

"The mayor drives the Czech offspring out, and the governor lets them back in through the back door." Caricature on the power struggle between the Christian Social city administration and Lower Austria's liberal governor, Erich Count Kielmansegg.

Vienna. Even when the Czechs achieved a change in the national union statutes and thus, to a large degree, independence, the conflicts did not let up.

As early as 1901 Adler complained in a letter to Karl Kautsky*: "In Vienna & all of Austria their understanding of 'national autonomy' is to

*Karl Kautsky (1854–1938), friend of Friedrich Engels, main founder of the modern Social Democratic Party in Germany. (*Translator's note*)

found local Czech chapters of all unions and, of course, their own political organizations as well, & to nationally divide virtually all companies. Since they are in a weaker position, it is difficult to attack them, & they turn their inferiority into their very strength. We are smarter and always give in! Then there's the financial aspect: we pay for the whole international shtick without a thank you, and even get the bad rep of being rich show-offs. I tell you, it's unbearable. Just making it look like it's more or less working, takes a lot of sweat and eating crow."[42]

In 1910 the majority of Czech Social Democrats left the party and founded the Czech Workers' Party (also called "Autonomists"). Only a minority remained loyal to Vienna's headquarters and formed the Czech Social Democratic Workers' Party ("Centralists"). When Kautsky, at a loss, inquired in Vienna why headquarters did not invest more energy in fighting the separatists, Adler's son Friedrich replied helplessly: "Our German comrades would be immediately ready to fight, on the contrary, we need to restrain them, for within no time at all, this battle, which would start out as a battle for internationalism, would be nothing else but a battle against the Czechs. In Vienna . . . this constitutes an imminent danger, and it is very likely that there will be very nasty conflicts, particularly among the metal workers, which will probably lead to Czech workers being literally whipped out of their factories. As horrible as we find this, there is absolutely nothing we can do."[43]

During the 1911 election campaign, when the Autonomists and Centralists competed in Bohemia for the first time, the separatists received 357,000 votes and twenty-six parliamentary seats, but the Centralists, only 19,000 votes and one seat.[44]

In the Dual Monarchy the ideal of socialist solidarity among the peoples turned out to be unfeasible, much to the other parties' glee. Franz Stein's *Hammer* jeered, saying that the idea of "pacifying" the Czechs had remained "an empty illusion": The Czechs, "heavy with loot, move into the house the Germans, good-natured and hanging on to false ideals, have put together, spit on their educators and benefactors, beat up their children and, whenever possible, cut off their livelihood. In the German *Ostmark* the Germans have sold their birthright for the bowl of lentils of universal, equal suffrage—now let them watch the Czechs establishing their army according to plan, from the bottom up!"[45]

Neither were the pacifists' attempts at mediation very successful. In 1909 some liberal intellectuals around the writer Hermann Bahr and Nobel Peace Prize winner Bertha von Suttner founded a Czech-German Cultural Committee, "which publicly opposes both peoples' excesses and shall publicly repeat at every opportunity that we belong together and don't fight, but that we want to get along with each other and view each oppression of the other nation as harm done our own."[46] Yet this attempt did not lead to anything either.

On the side of the Czechs, there were appeals to tolerance and co-operation, mainly and repeatedly from Tomás G. Masaryk. He tried to help the Viennese Czechs by voicing dispassionate arguments and asking the Viennese to understand the Czechs' situation. In Parliament he liked to quote German classicism's ideals of humanity: "I am Czech, you are German, he is Ruthenian; we have to make the policy of humaneness concrete and turn it into practical political work."[47] The empire's split, he argued, would have to make way for a wider distribution of power in favor of the non-Germans, in particular, that of the Bohemians, on the basis of the "simple idea of equal rights," the idea "that a people shall have the same value as another one, whether it is larger or smaller, whether it has more culture or less culture. You see how this idea is breaking through and has to break through."[48] Yet Masaryk's pleas to respect equal rights were hardly appreciated within or outside of Parliament. He was attacked by all parties, both Czech and German, as a prototype of the liberal, a "Jew lackey," as well as an intellectual.

Among the integrating forces was the Bohemian aristocracy, which followed a consistently supranational, pointedly "Bohemian" line and, of course, raised its children bilingually. Therefore the German-nationals accused them of forming "Czech colonies" in German Bohemia with their Czech servants, with civil servants, and the clergy.[49]

The main target was Bohemia's most powerful aristocrat, Prince Schwarzenberg. In 1910 he brusquely rejected the demand of "hiring only German civil servants in German areas," and curtly replied to his critics: "As far as filling my civil service positions, I cannot for a moment enter-tain the notion of taking their nationalities into consideration." Unper-turbed, he sold a piece of land for the construction of a Czech school, despite German protests: "Why should . . . Bohemian children . . . not be allowed to attend a Bohemian school!"[50] On the other hand, the Czech radicals criticized him for employing too many Germans on his estates.[51]

Even years later Hitler would complain that in the Dual Monarchy, the high nobility, just like the Social Democrats, had *agreed with the Czechs*.[52] When in addition to that the Schwarzenberg family turned out to be self-confident and after 1939, opposed him, he remarked *that the Schwarzenberg family had always been anti-German*. In 1941 Hitler had the Schwarzenbergs' property appropriated.[53] Other aristocratic families in Bohemia suffered a similar fate.

One enemy of the German-nationals, even during Hitler's school years in Linz, was the Catholic church. In *Mein Kampf* Hitler cites the example of the church's deliberately sending Czech clergymen to German communities in order to attain *a general Slavization of Austria. The process took approximately the following form: Czech pastors were appointed to German communities; slowly but surely they began to set the interests of the Czech people above the interests of the churches, becoming germ-cells of the de-Germanization process.* The German clergy, on the other hand, had turned out to be *completely useless* for the national struggle. *Indirectly, by the misuse of religion on the one hand, and owing to insufficient defense on the other, Germanism was slowly but steadily forced back.* And: *Thus the Church did not seem to feel with the German people, but to side unjustly with the enemy.*[54]

Indeed, around 1900, more clergymen of Slavic descent were appointed to German communities in Cisleithania than the other way around. Yet contrary to German-national propaganda, this had mainly a practical reason, in that the Slavs had a far greater pool of young priests than the Germans.[55] The church's general stance was supranational and conciliatory toward Catholics of all nationalities, with the major exception of its close ties with the Christian Socials.

In their attempts to make supranational contacts the universities too became the object of much animosity. When the University of Vienna, for example, innocently appointed a man named Dvořák as professor of art history in 1909, the Pan-Germans protested. A "Czech," they said, should not be allowed to teach "German" art history at a "German" university. They included in their attack those German professors who had personally nominated Dvořák, accused them of "betraying the people" and "mocking Germandom"—for instance, Professor of Law Dr. Josef Redlich from Moravia, who was also a German-Liberal deputy in the Reichsrat, and Jewish.[56]

Hitler on the Czechs

August Kubizek relates about young Hitler: "When we walked home through the districts of, say, Rudolfsheim, Fünfhaus, or Ottakring and workers passed us returning from work, it would happen that Adolf tightly grabbed my arm: 'Did you hear, Gustl?—Czech!' Another time we went all the way to the *Spinnerin am Kreuz* (spinner on the cross), because Adolf wanted to see this old Viennese landmark. We encountered brickworkers who loudly spoke Italian, wildly gesticulating. 'There you have your German Vienna!' he shouted indignantly."[57]

Apart from this remark, no other anti-Czech utterances are documented from Hitler's Vienna years. None of the eyewitnesses, for exam-

Undated note by Hitler for a speech: "The aim of the Czechs / what are the Czechs aiming for? / planned-out preliminary work / Czechization in the former Austria"

ple, mentions any bad experiences Hitler had with Czechs, but no friendships, either—contrary to Hitler's manifold relationships with Jews in Vienna. There is only one documentable personal relationship between young Hitler and a Czech: Maria Zakreys, his first landlady in Vienna, an immigrant from Moravia with a thick Czech accent and, as far as her writing abilities were concerned, a poor knowledge of German. Young Hitler got along exceptionally well with her. According to Kubizek, in 1908, Mrs. Zakreys, a Czech, was even "the only human being in this city of millions of people with whom we would associate."[58]

Hitler would hardly have been aware of a slight Czech-Viennese touch: when he called Eva Braun his "Tschapperl," this—coming from the Czech word "capek," awkward person—something like "awkward child" with the connotation of "silly little one."

Hitler's later remarks about "the Czechs" had hardly anything to do with personal experiences but were clearly only repetitions of old Viennese clichés, for instance, when he said in 1942: *Every Czech is a born nationalist who subjugates his interests to all other obligations. One must not let oneself be deceived, the more he bends, the more dangerous he becomes. . . . Of all the Slavs, the Czech is the most dangerous one, because he is diligent. He has discipline, is orderly, he is more Mongoloid than Slavic. He knows how to hide his plans behind a certain loyalty. . . . I don't despise them, it is a battle of destinies. An alien racial splinter has penetrated our folkdom, and one must yield, he or we. . . . That's one of the reasons why the Hapsburgs perished. They believed they could solve the problem through kindness.*[59]

Another catch phrase often employed in Vienna was that the Czechs were *"apple-polishers . . . who are subservient to their superiors but kick their inferiors.* Both Poles and Czechs, he said, knew from the experience of *a half thousand years . . . how best to act like vassals without arousing suspicion. How many Czechs, he said, were gadding about in Vienna when I was young, quickly learned the Viennese accent, and then deftly maneuvered themselves into important positions in Government, the economy, and so forth.*[60]

We can also detect the old Viennese condescension toward the "diligent" Czech who was fit to be a vassal, when in 1942 Hitler told his guest, Reich Leader SS Heinrich Himmler: *The Czechs were better than the Hungarians, the Romanians, and the Poles. A diligent petty bourgeoisie had formed which was keenly aware of its boundaries. Even today they will look up to us with both anger and boundless admiration: We Bohemians are not meant to rule!*[61]

Hitler considered Lueger's system of "Germanizing" the Czechs via the language not resolute enough. *Nationality or rather race does not happen to lie in language but in the blood.* Hitler said that *I remember how in my youth Germanization led to incredibly false conceptions. Even in Pan-German circles the opinion could then be heard that the Austrian-Germans, with the promotion and aid of the government, might well succeed in a Germanization of the Austrian Slavs; these circles never even began to realize that Germanization can only be applied to* soil *and never to* people. *For what was generally understood under this word was only the forced outward acceptance of the German language. Yet it was a scarcely conceivable fallacy of thought to believe that a Negro or a Chinese, let us say, will turn into a German because he learns German and is willing to speak the German language and perhaps even give his vote to a German political party. That was a de-Germanization and the beginning of a bastardization and a destruction of the Germanic element.*[62]

In any case, Hitler planned "to resettle all elements that are racially of no value from Bohemia to the East" after the war. "The individual Czech, he said, was diligent, and if they were spread over the occupied Eastern territories, they might be quite good as supervisors. The Führer stressed again and again that he personally knew the Czechs extremely well."[63] On the other hand, he found the resettling of the Czechs and the aimed-for "Germanization" of Bohemia and Moravia too slow, which is why later on he believed a Germanization was possible, but only if merciless strictness was exercised toward rebels.[64]

When in 1939 he moved his troops not only into the Sudetenland but also into the clearly non-German "rest of Czechoslovakia," this was hardly in line with his slogan "One people, one Reich, one Führer." He used flimsy excuses and referred to the Hapsburgs' tradition, for instance, in 1942: *Czechoslovakia, he said, just wasn't a structure that had internally grown into an independent state; rather it had remained a former Austrian nation state beyond its modeling itself after German culture.* Hitler said that even Czech president of state Dr. Emil Hacha had told him that the Czechs were *not a people of masters*. And Tomás G. Masaryk, with whom Hitler was well acquainted from his Vienna years, Czechoslovakia's first president of state and "father of the fatherland," who died in 1937, *had written somewhere that no one had been respected in his family who had spoken Czech*. In 1942 Hitler remarked that *with firm direction* it should be possible *to force the Czech language back to the significance of a dialect twenty years from now*.[65]

And not least, Czechs, like Jews, signified for Reich chancellor Hitler Viennese self-confidence, which refused to meet his demand for subjecting itself to the German unified state. In 1941 he said, *grumblings of [Vienna's] population was a consequence of the strong Jewish-Czech mix*.[66] And after the celebration of the "Jew-free Vienna festival," Hitler said in a monologue in a small circle on June 25, 1943: *I've managed to get the Jews out of Vienna, now I also want to get the Czechs out of there*.[67]

10
Jews in Vienna

Historical Background

Around 1150, when the dukes of Babenberg made Vienna their residence, they brought Jews into the city, who settled in the area of today's Juden-platz (Jew square), worked as money lenders and tradespeople, and enjoyed the sovereigns' special protection—paying considerable taxes in return. As early as 1200 Vienna had its first synagogue.

Over the course of the centuries, there were intermittent phases of expulsion, "Jewish auto-da-fés," and resettlements. The situation became particularly dangerous at the time of the Turkish Wars in the seventeenth century, when religious fanaticism was by no means directed only at the Turks but at the native Jews as well. In 1623 the 130 Jewish families in Vienna were banned from the inner city and forcefully resettled in a new ghetto between the forks of the Danube. At the instigation of his Spanish wife Margarita Teresa, Emperor Leopold I had all Jews expelled in 1670. They lost their property and all valuables, were only allowed to take with them what they could carry, and had to consider themselves lucky that they did not lose their lives. The Viennese set fire to the synagogue and in its place erected a church dedicated to the Emperor's saint. The ghetto turned into a new Catholic suburb, Leopoldstadt. Only a few years later the emperor, now a widower and in need of money, brought the Jews back to Vienna. They again settled in what was now Leopoldstadt, which was soon scornfully nicknamed "Matzohville." As late as 1900 approximately one third of all Viennese Jews lived there.

The Christian Socials compared the existential battle between the Christian Occident and the heathen Turks to the "defense battle" against the Jews. Thus during the mayoral campaign of 1895 Lueger shouted: "Today is the memorable day of Vienna's liberation from the Turks, and let's hope that we . . . can avert a danger from us that is greater than the Turkish threat: the Jewish threat." According to a newspaper report, the speech was followed by "thundering applause and endless shouts of 'Bravo!' "[1]

Modern anti-Semitism hit the Jews in Austro-Hungary in what was probably the happiest phase in their history. After centuries of oppression, the liberal national basic law of 1867 had brought them equal rights, completely and without qualification. Now they could finally enjoy all those large and small liberties that had been denied them for centuries. They were allowed to own property in the capital, could choose where they wanted to live, become governmental civil servants, attend universities without restrictions, and more.

An immediate consequence of emancipation was a wave of Jewish immigrants into the capital and imperial residence. Before the emancipation, in 1860, 6,200 Jews lived in Vienna, which represented a 2.2 percent share of the population; in 1870, there were 40,200 Jews, which was 6.6 percent; in 1880 the numbers were 72,600 and 10.1 percent, respectively. In 1890 Vienna had 118,500 Jews who, however, after the incorporation of the suburbs, only represented 8.7 percent. This percentage remained a constant in the rapidly growing city. In 1900, 147,000, and in 1910, 175,300 Jews lived in Vienna—religious Jews, to be sure. Following the criterion of ethnic anti-Semitism, which had become popular by then—that is to say, including assimilated and baptized Jews—the numbers were much larger.

Most of these 175,300 religious Jews, 122,930, were part of the German share of the population, including the Eastern Jews, whose Yiddish was regarded as German. According to their everyday language, the rest were Poles, Czechs, Romanians, and others. The 51,509 Jews in Vienna who were registered as "aliens" were mostly Hungarians. These statistics do not reveal how large the share of Russian Jews was, for most of the refugees had not settled yet and were not included in any statistic.[2]

Among the Dual Monarchy's cities, Vienna had by no means the largest share of Jews. In Cracaw they represented 50 percent, in Lemberg and Budapest, 25 percent, and in Prague, 10 percent. Compared to other large cities in Europe, however, Vienna's share was very high. The Jewish share in Berlin was between 4 and 5 percent, and in Hamburg 2 to 3 percent.[3]

The euphoria triggered by the freedom the immigrants had finally achieved, motivated many of them to great achievements. All doors seemed to be open to those who worked hard. Emancipation fanned their desire to become respected members of society by way of achievement and education.

In the Catholic-conservative atmosphere of Vienna, which was still largely characterized by bourgeois complacency and had a hard time dealing with the innovations of the modern age, the Jews who were education-conscious and eager for success encountered little competition. The writer Jakob Wassermann, for example, who had immigrated from Berlin, noted this with astonishment. The nobility, he observed, which had formerly been the leading social class, was "entirely indifferent": it "not only kept cautiously away from intellectual and artistic life, but was also afraid of it and despised it. The few patrician bourgeois families imitated the nobility; an autochtonous bourgeoisie no longer existed, and the gap was filled by civil servants, officers, and professors; below them was the closed bloc of the petit bourgeoisie." In short: "The court, the petit bourgeoisie, and the Jews gave the city its character. That the Jews as the most mobile group kept all the other groups constantly on the move, is no longer astonishing."[4]

The Jews' different driving power and value systems expressed themselves mainly in their eagerness to get an education. In 1912 one out of three high school students in Vienna was a religious Jew—three times more than their share of the population.* All types of secondary schools put together, the share of Jewish students was 47.4 percent in 1912— almost half.[5] Although if theology is excluded only 5.3 percent of altogether ten thousand Christians attended university between 1898 and 1902, the figure among Jews was 24.5 percent. Jewish students made up almost one third of all university students in Vienna.[6]

Jewish students' preferred majors were medicine—in 1913, they constituted more than 40 percent of all students of medicine in Vienna— and law: in 1913 more than one quarter of all law students were Jewish.[7] Jews preferred the independent professions of lawyer and doctor. Of al-

---

*In Austria, attending high school is not obligatory but one among several possible ways of receiving a "higher education." Pupils can attend elementary school up to the age of fourteen and then move on to professional schools. (*Translator's note*)

together 681 lawyers in Vienna in 1889, more than half—394—were Jewish. Twenty years before, there were only thirty-three.[8]

In Cisleithania, most Jews adopted the dominant nationality, at least culturally and economically: German. They loved German language and culture, were enthusiastic about Richard Wagner, whose most modern interpreter was Gustav Mahler, and felt themselves to be German-Austrians. Between 1867 and 1914 Vienna became a metropolis of modern art and science, especially in the fruitful symbiosis of Viennese and Jewish elements.

There were spectacular success stories in trade and economy, such as that of department store king Alfred Gerngross, which after his death in 1908 was told everywhere. Having emigrated from Frankfurt to Vienna with his brother in 1881, he opened up a fabric store, then bought one house after the other on Vienna's largest business street, Mariahilfer Strasse, and built a huge department store. He left his eight children a fortune of more than four million kronen.[9] Those craftsmen whom Hitler knew personally as buyers of his pictures were successful too: framemaker Jakob Altenberg from Galicia, glazier Samuel Morgenstern from Hungary.

"Jewish intelligence" became a standing expression in Vienna around 1900. The writer Hermann Bahr joked that every aristocrat "who is a little bit smart or has some kind of talent, is immediately considered a Jew; they have no other explanation for it."[10]

Although Gustav Mahler had been baptized long before, Alfred Roller believed he could detect in his friend a downright "Jewish" compulsion to work hard: "Mahler never hid his Jewish background. But it didn't give him joy. It motivated and urged him on to higher, purer achievements. 'Like when someone is born with one arm too short: then the other arm has to learn to accomplish even more and eventually perhaps accomplishes things that both healthy arms couldn't have achieved.' That's how he once explained to me the effect of his background on his work."[11]

The growing social reputation of Jews who had become rich found its expression in mansions on the Ring Boulevard, which were as if in competition with the palaces of the old nobility, in the medals and titles which the emperor bestowed on them in return for their accomplishments and generous donations, and in spectacular marriages of rich Jewish women with impoverished aristocrats.

The solution to the Jewish question, which was thousands of years old, finally seemed to be in sight in the form of total assimilation, including conversions and mixed marriages. In this respect, however, there were obstacles to overcome. Mixed marriages between religious Jews and religious Christians were prohibited. In order to get married, one of the partners either had to convert to the faith of the other or declare himself or herself unaffiliated with any church. Either step was usually taken by the Jewish partner. Between 1911 and 1914 such marriages occurred almost ten times as frequently as marriages between Catholics and Protestants.[12]

Politically the Jews tended to be in the liberal or Social Democratic camp, as Representative Benno Straucher emphasized in the Reichsrat in 1908: "We Jews were, are, and will remain democratic, we can only flourish in democratic air, for us, reactionary air is stuffy, we subscribe to a free, democratic weltanschauung, therefore we can only pursue truly liberal policies."[13]

This did not mean that they agreed on party politics. The Zionist *National-Zeitung* complained in 1908: "The fourteen Jews in Parliament are members of five different parties."[14] Only the four Zionists and one "Jewish Democrat" were openly Jewish, the others were Social Democrats or in the liberal camp. Of the six Jewish deputies from Galicia, for example, three were Zionists—that is to say, nationalist Jews—the other three were Social Democrats.

The success of Jewish immigrants aroused jealousy and hatred in those native residents who were left behind by the sudden competition and could not deal with the modern era's innovations: the craftsmen who lost their livelihood to the factories, the store owners who were put at a disadvantage by the department stores. Only six years after emancipation, during the crash of 1873, a new wave of anti-Semitism was vented against the "capitalists," the "liberals," and the "stock exchange Jews."

In 1876 a storm started brewing at the universities, which was triggered by the famous professor of medicine Theodor Billroth's criticism of what he considered the disproportionately large share of Jewish medical students from Hungary and Galicia. Billroth questioned the success of assimilation, arguing "that the Jews are a sharply defined nation, and that no Jew, just like no Iranian, Frenchman, or New Zealander, or an African can ever become a German; what they call Jewish-Germans are simply nothing but Jews who happen to speak German and happened to receive their education in Germany, even if they write literature and think in the German language more beautifully and better than many a genuine Germanic native." "Therefore [we should] neither expect nor want the Jews ever to become true Germans in the sense that during national battles they feel the way we Germans do."

Those Jews who had immigrated from the eastern countries, he ar-

Playmangel an der Wiener Universität —

aber nur für Arier.

Not enough room at Vienna University—but only for Aryans

gued, were lacking "our German sentiments," which were based on "medieval Romanticism." Billroth admitted that inside, "even though I have reflected about this a great deal and do like some of them individually," he still felt "the gap between purely German and purely Jewish blood to be just as wide as the gap a Teuton may have felt between himself and a Phoenician."[15]

Now the German fraternities felt authorized to expel their Jewish fellow students. The fraternity Teutonia introduced the "Aryan Clause" as early as 1877, and the other fraternities followed suit. The fraternities justified their actions with an appeal to the Berlin philosopher Eugen Dühring and his much-quoted remark: "The German students must regard it as their honor that the sciences are presented to them—or rather, bungled and contaminated in a Jewish way, and traded off—not by an alien and much inferior race which is entirely incapable of serious science."[16]

The Eastern Jews' Mass Migration

In 1881 Russian Czar Alexander II was assassinated. "Jewish revolutionaries" were blamed and pogroms were decreed, which led to actual massacres. Fearing for their lives, people fled across the border to Galicia, which was already overpopulated, had the largest percentage of Jews among its population, and was suffering from unemployment and starvation. Some 200,000 Jewish itinerant beggars roamed through the land and were called "air people," for nobody really knew what they lived off and where they belonged.[17]

The army of begging Jews was now multiplied by the Russian refugees. Many moved to the large European ports in order to emigrate overseas, and into the big cities: Vienna, Berlin, Prague, and Budapest. Before 1914, some altogether two million Eastern Jews set out on their journey. Along their way, they faced xenophobia and anti-Semitism to an extent they had never experienced before.

As early as 1882 the First International Anti-Jewish Congress convened in Dresden. In a manifesto the participants called for a battle against the foreign Jews and unsucessfully demanded that the European governments put a stop to Russian-Jewish immigration and militarily secure their borders. Anti-Semites of all different orientations and from almost all Western European countries were in agreement in their demand to rescind the emancipation of the Jews. They requested that the Jews—all of them, even those who had been in their new home country for a long time—be subjected to alien law, inasmuch as they allegedly could not be assimilated, representing a threat to Christians.

The Austrian Jews, however, knew that they were safely protected by the federal authorities. Those in danger received police protection. Anti-Semitic brochures were confiscated. This kind of legal protection was easier to put into effect in the cities than in the country—in, say, Galicia or in Hungary—where anti-Semitic riots repeatedly took place. Therefore even more Eastern Jews immigrated to the capital, even though since 1897 Vienna had been ruled by the anti-Semites under Lueger. Yet the Emperor was also in Vienna, and particularly the Eastern Jews expressed their loyalty to him. Vienna's chief rabbi Dr. Moriz Gründemann said in 1908: "Our Emperor has repeatedly said that all subjects of his large Empire are equally close to his paternal heart, regardless of their nation or faith. . . . After all, it is precisely the lack of distinction and equal rights for all which the Emperor has sanctioned and regards as sacrosanct, which obliges the Jews to feel the deepest gratitude to him."[18]

However, the flood of anti-Semitism sometimes put the emperor himself at a loss. He expressed this among his family; his daughter Marie Valerie recorded in her diary: "We talked about hatred and Pa said: Yes yes, of course we do everything we can to protect the Jews, but who really is not an anti-Semite?"[19]

Anti-Semitic politicians quickly rose to the top in Vienna. In the 1880s Schönerer collected the votes of farmers and students. In the 1890s Lueger experienced his triumph by being even more successful in winning the votes of the small businessmen and craftsmen.

The Christian Social *Brigittenauer Bezirks-Nachrichten* compared the "battle" against the Eastern Jews to the uniting of the nation in the liberation wars against Napoleon: This time, "not a mass of men on horseback, but a dark menacing, filthy cloud of powerful men from the East is banking up . . . threatening to completely suppress and stifle our liberty. Who wants to and who can deny that we are already do languish under Jewry's yoke and things are happening which must needs turn any German's face crimson with shame?"[20]

Statistics were put together in schools, theaters, factories, and in Parliament to prove the alleged "Judaicizing" of Vienna. For that purpose, religious and baptized Jews, people belonging to a Jewish "clan" or married to a Jew or with Jewish-sounding names, and even liberals, Social Democrats and other "Jew lackeys" were lumped together, regardless of their origin or denomination, in order to paint the desired horrific picture. A Berlin observer reported with astonishment on the extent of the anti-Semitic movement in Vienna: "Vienna's anti-Semitism differs enormously from that in the German Reich, for while it is only a national animosity in Germany, in Austro-Hungary it is clerical—German-national—strictly Czech-Catholic! In other words, a sea serpent of the various parties' special national-political interests, all of which believe they possess in anti-Semitism the ultimate means of making people happy."[21]

Around 1900 the itinerant peddlers and white slave traders served the anti-Semites to form a stereotypical image of the Eastern Jews as enemies. On his way westward, the "Handeleh" made ends meet by selling odds and ends, thus competing with the old-established merchants, who could now no longer dictate prices. The first rallies against the peddlers took place as early as the seventies. After a struggle that lasted for years, the Christian Social minister of trade prevailed in prohibiting peddling in Vienna in 1910, "for the protection of the honestly working trades-people residing in Vienna." In *Mein Kampf*, Hitler also used this cliché when he tied his alleged transformation into an anti-Semite to his encounter with a Viennese Handeleh.[22]

The slogan "Don't buy from Jews!" was applied to peddlers as well as department stores and was bandied about by anti-Semites of every political ilk. Under the title "German Women! Avoid Jewish Stores When You Shop!" the Pan-German *Yearbook for German Women and Girls* read in 1904: "For example, what disgrace it is for a German family when on and under the shining, arch-German Christmas tree there are presents for the dear ones that were bought in Jewish stores! Any German who buys his Christmas presents from Jews dishonors himself and be-

In Leopoldstadt

smirches his own nationality."[23] In order better to enforce the shopping embargo, a petition was made in the Lower Austrian state parliament even to segregate the stands of Jewish and Christian merchants in the marketplaces—which the Chamber of Commerce was able to strike down after protests from the Jewish community.[24]

The second inimical image of the Eastern Jew, the white slave trader, took up the old cliché of the Jewish seducer. On the other hand, around 1900 there were indeed a number of criminal cases in which Eastern Jews were implicated. Contrary to the anti-Semitic stereotype, however, these incidents were not about the seduction of "blonde" Christian girls, but the trade with poor Jewish women from the Eastern European shtetls, some of them from Galicia.

The white slave traders always employed the same methods: the well-dressed, obviously well-to-do trader appeared in the shtetl, approached a poor family with many children, acted like the future son-in-law, and married the girl, who was still a child, in a Jewish rite. To the joy of her parents he refused to accept a dowry and took "his wife" along with him, offering her a supposedly nicer life. This method could be used any number of times, because a ritual wedding was not legally binding. Another method was to take advantage of the desolate situation of those young women whose husbands were itinerant beggars and had been missing.

These women were indigent but were not allowed to remarry, inasmuch as they were not divorced. If they let themselves be seduced and were thus "disgraced," the white slave traders could easily take them along. In particularly poor families with many children there were even instances of child trading.[25] Typically the girls and women were illiterate, spoke only Yiddish, and were completely at the criminals' mercy, especially because they were emotionally bound in their marriage. Before they realized what was happening to them, they ended up in Hamburg brothels— usually via Serbia—which were called "girl export depots," or on a ship heading overseas. Prices in Odessa ranged from five hundred to two thousand rubles rubel per girl; in Hamburg the going rate was fifteen hundred marks.[26] In Buenos Aires, for example, the girls were typically sold to brothel owners right at the landing dock for prices between three thousand and six thousand francs. There the girls from Galicia, called "Austríacas," represented the third-largest group of prostitutes, after the natives and the Russians.[27] The traders—among them women—constantly changed their names and carried forged documents, often British or Turkish passports. A great deal of bribe money was paid to civil servants during these transactions.

The Jewish communities supported the fight against crime with all their might, for several reasons: to help the girls, to stop the criminals in their tracks, and also to stop providing fuel for anti-Semitism. Thus Vienna's Zionist *Neue National-Zeitung* reported in 1913 that of thirty-nine white slave traders in Galicia, thirty-eight were Jewish.[28] Another time they reported that 90 percent of the three thousand prostitutes in Argentina were Jewish.[29] They invariably combined their reports with urgent calls to do everything imaginable to put an end to these crimes. The international conferences on fighting the white slave trade were attended by rabbis as well. Such a conference took place in Vienna in October 1909—during Hitler's Vienna years—eliciting a large, controversial response in the press.

Itinerant teachers and woman social workers traveled to Galicia to educate and warn people, and to aid girls and their parents. One of these Jewish activists was a woman who played an important role in the history of psychoanalysis: Bertha Pappenheim, that "case of Anna O." that served Freud to conduct his *Studies on Hysteria* and to develop the concept of psychoanalysis. Affluent and single, she devoted herself to the welfare of women, established homes for endangered girls, studied social conditions on travels through Russia, Romania, and Galicia,[30] and also supported the establishment of a small industry for woman workers in Galicia—

for example, lacemakers and seamstresses—so they could earn "decent" wages after attending training courses.[31]

There was also support from the private foundation of Baron Moriz Hirsch, who enforced the building of schools in Galicia, for Jewish as well as Christian children, both boys and girls. After all, part of the reason why Eastern Jewish girls were so behind in education was that they were not accepted into the religious "Chedorim" schools.

But all of this took a great deal of time, and all the while anti-Semitism kept getting worse. In any case, particularly the standing expression "Jewish white slave traders" was a popular anti-Semitic term that Hitler too used in Mein Kampf: *The relationship of Jews to prostitution and, even more, to the white-slave traffic, could be studied in Vienna as perhaps in no other city of Western Europe, with the possible exception of the southern French ports.*[32]

Parliamentary Debates

The few Jewish delegates in Parliament fought for the realization of "the natural, inalienable right of every people to full, truly equal rights, and to absolute equality before the law" for the Jews. Yet considering what German Radical representative Eduard von Stransky shouted full of satisfaction in June 1908, they had hardly any chance: "Thank God, the majority of this House is anti-Semitic!"[33]

Zionist representative Dr. Benno Straucher from Bukovina, an advocate and director of the Jewish community in Czernowitz, complained: "Of all the parties in this House, which are all brimming with freedom, liberty, progress, equal rights, and justice—for themselves: none offers any protection for the Jews; when it comes to Jews, all witnesses become silent, the open and the clandestine anti-Semites have done their job well and planned their tactics carefully. No one supports us out of a sense of liberty and justice, no one wants to be called a Jew lackey, a mercenary of the Jews." Tired of the Christian Socials' constant interjections, he said: "With you, one doesn't need to prove anything, know anything, have learned anything; it is enough simply to say 'Jew,' that's proof enough for anything."[34]

In 1908, when young Hitler frequented Parliament, the Christian Socials proposed a law to limit the number of Jewish university and high school students. Only a number of Jewish students corresponding to the Jews' share of the population should be admitted.

In the course of the heated debate Straucher cautioned against such a step, which would ultimately be harmful to the German-Austrians. After all, German students had such a high percentage partly because "so far, a large part of Jewish students has made a pledge to Germandom and registered as Germans." For example, without the Jews, the Germans would not constitute 47.1 percent at Austria's technical universities, but only 31.05 percent, and at *Realschulen*, not 48.61 but only 37.07 percent—which would make them even weaker against the Slavs. Stransky interjected, "If we have to perish without the Jews, we'd rather perish than exist with the Jews!" Straucher replied, "Other Germans say that the German-speaking area should be increased, but you want to shrink the German-speaking area." He also reminded the representatives of the fact that the taxes the Jews paid were always counted as part of the Germans' taxes in order to derive claims against the Slavs. He said: "Only if we add the Jewish tax contribution do the Germans in Prague and Bohemia pay half of all taxes." "But did the Jews get anywhere a parliamentary seat from the Germans in return for that?" And: "I would particularly like to remind the German parties' anti-Semitic groups that we Jews have allied ourselves most faithfully with the German people for centuries; this earned us the other nations' hatred and animosity. . . . The Germans' enmity and their incessant attempts to disenfranchise us has disappointed us most painfully and bitterly. We certainly haven't deserved this in regard to Germandom."

Christian Social Julius Prochazka argued: "Christians are not accepted into schools because Jews have taken their seats!" And: "We don't want any preference for the Jews!" (In comparison, Hitler wrote in 1929: *Thousands, even tens of thousands of our people's sons who are blessed with talent, can no longer go to school. . . . You are raising an alien people at our universities, at the expense of numerous Christian fellow citizens!*[35])

Straucher: "In what respect are the Jews given preference? Do we keep anyone else from going to school? Enlighten your young people so that more of them attend school!"

Prochazka: "Build your own schools!"

Straucher: "Really? And what do we pay our taxes for and assume all the other obligations just like all other citizens?"

Again someone said, "Jew!" Straucher replied: "You and the term 'Jew'—I am proud to be a Jew, just as you are proud to be a Christian. For Jews and Christians possess the same religious truths."

Interjection by Polish provost Leo Pastor: "No, no, not that!" Another exclamation: "We pay the taxes and the Jews eat them up. Establish Jew schools!"[36]

The Christian Socials' proposal was voted down; but no less than

162 deputies voted for it—Christian Socials, German-Nationals, German-Radicals, Pan-Germans, and splinter groups.

The Zionist weekly *Neue National-Zeitung*'s response to this debate was a pointed editorial entitled "Away from Germandom!": "That's the thanks we get for the Jews in the Slavic countries having their heads beaten to pulp for Germandom. . . . That's what we get for clinging to German culture and standing up for it. This German culture forms the intellectual life of those men who want to take away from the Jews any chance to get an education and thus deny them any part in the intellectual achievements of our time. A sad culture." The result: "It was high time for a large part of our people to have disowned Germandom and its culture."[37]

Western and Eastern Jews

In the face of devastating anti-Semitism, which was spreading more and more and was clearly turning into ethnic anti-Semitism, the old-established, assimilated Viennese Jews felt insecure. They had done everything they could in order not to be conspicuously Jewish, to adapt and wholly belong. Many had long since been baptized and thought they could forget about their Jewish background. Now that they were suddenly put on the same level as their ragged brothers in faith from the East, they felt their entire hard-earned existence was threatened.

The Eastern Jews were conspicuous in the streets, for they had forelocks and wore traditional garb as signs of their Orthodox faith. They communicated in Yiddish, Russian, or Polish. They did not try to adapt to their environment, and their strange appearance made them look to some Viennese like a conspiratorial group.

The Jewish community tried very hard to assimilate the immigrants as quickly as possible. The "caftan Jews" were given inconspicuous clothes. Their children were supposed to learn German quickly in their own schools. The community provided for the immigrants as much as possible, not letting them become recipients of public welfare. The rich Jews donated more generously than ever to *Wärmestuben*, soup kitchens, and hospitals. There were conferences on the "evil" of "itinerary begging" to discuss strategies on advancing assimilation.[38] Yet the more generous the Viennese Jews were, the more people in need came. And the more Eastern Jews arrived, the more the fear of even worse anti-Semitism grew.

Furthermore, it turned out that many poor Eastern Jews didn't appreciate at all the charitable acts of their rich brothers in the West. They insisted on their old ways and customs, their traditional clothing and language. They were full of pride and self-confidence, and even displayed a sense of superiority toward the Western Jews: they were conscious of their "true Jewishness." They had faithfully preserved their old belief and rites, and adhered to their fathers' customs—thus turning into a personified reproach for the Western Jews whose faith had lost its firmness, and who were assimilated or even baptized.

Despite all attempts at conciliation, Eastern and Western Jews remained strangers to each other. The German-Jewish writer Wassermann wrote: "If I saw a Jew from Poland or Galicia, if I talked to him and tried to probe into him to comprehend his way of thinking and living, he could definitely touch or surprise me, or move me to compassion and sadness, but I certainly didn't feel a sense of brotherhood or even relatedness. In everything he said and breathed, he was a total stranger to me, and when there was no human-individual symbiosis, I even found him repulsive."

Wassermann—and he is only one example, for Elias Canetti made similar remarks—sensed a gap between "Jewish Jews" and "German Jews": "Aren't they two kinds of people, two races almost, or at least [representatives of] two different ways of living?" He, the German Jew "on an outpost," wanted "merely to bring to expression myself and my world, and turn it into a bridge." "Doesn't that ultimately make me more useful than someone who has been sworn into following a certain direction?"[39] Concerned, he lamented the assimilated Jews' "terribly uneasy situation": "German Jew; listen to these two words very carefully. Take them as the last stage in a long-drawn-out development. His double-love and his struggle on two fronts have pushed him close to the abyss of despair."[40]

The Eastern Jew Joseph Roth naturally analyzed the assimilated Jews' way of thinking more critically: "It is an oft-ignored fact that Jews can have anti-Semitic inclinations too. One doesn't want to be reminded of one's grandfather, who was from Posen or Kattowitz, by some stranger who has just arrived from Lodz. That is the ignoble, but understandable attitude of an endangered petit bourgeois who is just about to climb the rather steep ladder to the terrace of the haute bourgeoisie with its free air and magnificent view. Looking at a cousin from Lodz, one can easily lose one's balance, and fall." The Western Jew, he said, had become "haughty. He had lost the God of his fathers and won an idol, civilizationary patriotism."[41]

Ethnic anti-Semitism inextricably intertwined religious and orthodox Jews, no matter how different they might be. Max Nordau said: "No matter what we do, in the opinion of our enemies, the Jewry of the whole world is one. . . . Our enemies forge an iron clasp of solidarity around all of us, which we can't break." And: "It will always be the Jew of low standing who will determine the measure. . . . They cannot shake the caftan Jew off the coattails of their elegant tailcoats!" And: "While the itinerant anti-Semite who is spitting with impunity and without having to fear repercussions on the rags of our outlawed, unhappy brother in the East, he thinks of the Jewish baron, privy councillor, and professor at home."[42]

Not conversion, nor baptism, nor their German identity, no matter how fervently they adopted it, saved the assimilants from being inveighed against as "Jews." All of a sudden all their efforts at assimilation had come to naught, and the way out of the Jewish community of fate was blocked. Many were thus led into existential crises and to desparate, even suicidal self-hatred. How thoroughly and with how much pleasure the anti-Semites observed this is detectable in Hitler's writings—for example, when he discusses Otto Weininger and Arthur Trebitsch.

Wassermann, who witnessed the hopeless situation of many assimilated, German-conscious Jews in Vienna, wrote, "I know and knew many who pined away, full of yearning for the blond and blue-eyed man. They were lying at his feet, they waved incense barrels in front of him, they believed his every word, every time he blinked it was an heroic act, and when he spoke of his soil, when he beat on his breast as an Aryan, they became hysterical and started to howl triumphantly. They didn't want to be themselves; they wanted to be the other; if they have chosen him, they are chosen along with him, it seems to them, or at least they are forgotten as the flawed and veiled as the inferior men they are."[43]

Others, however, who had long since been assimilated, rediscovered their Jewishness. Arthur Schnitzler fought anti-Semitism in his novel *The Road into the Open* and the play *Professor Bernhardi*. His compassion for the Eastern Jews led the *Neue Freie Presse*'s literary critic, Theodor Herzl, a former member of a German fraternity and an enthusiastic assimilationist, back to his Jewish roots. In his novel *The Jewish State*, published in 1896, he suggested a vision as a way out of the misery: the Promised Land, Palestine. The novel argues that Palestine could offer the poor Eastern Jews a haven from oppression that could contain the flood of immigrants to Western Europe, and thus, one could dare hope, from anti-Semitism as well. The rich Western Jews were supposed to finance the acquisition of land and settlement in Palestine, which was then under Turkish rule.

Zionism, the Jewish national movement, originated as an act of self-defense. Roth wrote about the Zionists: "They replaced the lack of their own 'turf' in Europe with their search for a home in Palestine. They had always been people in exile. Now they became a nation in exile." Consequently, Roth maintained: "Modern Zionism developed in Austria, in Vienna. It was founded by an Austrian journalist. No one else could have founded it."[44]

Herzl's friend and combatant Max Nordau, also a former assimilationist, declared his commitment to the Eastern Jews: "Our brothers down there are suffering, yelling, 'Help!' We are rushing to their side. They are a chaotic mass. We organize them. They stammer their complaints in a gibberish incomprehensible to educated people. We lend them our civilized tongues. They are pushing impetuously, without direction. We show them the way they have to go. They have an undefined longing. We put it into words."[45]

Nordau was more aggressive than Herzl: "We don't have the ambition to disarm the anti-Semites through humility and obsequiousness." And: "Jewry cannot wait until anti-Semitism has dried up and a rich crop of altruism and justice starts sprouting in its dry bed." Zionism, he argued, was "the only way the Jews can be saved, without it they would perish."[46]

Having a new national identity, the Zionists also strove for legal recognition. Yet the criterion for establishing a nation, one's colloquial language, was an obstacle to these plans. For the Jews spoke different languages and therefore were of different nationalities. In 1909 the advocate Max Diamant from Czernowitz submitted a complaint in federal court, requesting that the Jews from Bukovina be recognized as a tribe proper, with Yiddish as its native tongue. The president of the federal court, eighty-one-year-old baptized Jew Josef Unger, a liberal, rejected the complaint, citing the usual reason: that the Jews were a religious community and not an ethnic people. One could only speak of a native language if all members of a people mastered it. Yiddish, he ruled, was only "a sort of [German] dialect" but not a language.[47]

During inscription in 1910, Zionist students listed "Jewish" as their native tongue, which was not on the list of the Dual Monarchy's languages. On an international level, however, the Zionists were already discussing the question of whether Hebrew wasn't preferable to Yiddish as their national language.

The language debate increased the rift between Western and Eastern Jews even more. Embittered, the assimilationists argued that with their goals, the Zionists precisely fulfilled the anti-Semites' wishes: by no longer regarding themselves as Germans, Czechs, or Hungarians of the Jewish faith, but as members of their own Jewish nation, and by striving toward emigration, they were setting themselves apart, trying to achieve exactly the same as the anti-Semites: a "Jew-free" Europe.

Nordau replied sharply that this attitude of the Western Jews expressed a "naive impertinent egotism": it ultimately implied "that a minority of approximately one fifth of smug Jews living in comfort is telling the majority of four fifths, consisting of desparate Jews who are ready to commit the most extreme acts of self-help, 'How dare you disturb our digestion with your savage appeal to Zion? Why don't you swallow your suffering? Why don't you starve quietly?' "[48]

Yet the Dual Monarchy's assimilated Jews did not consider themselves to be members of a foreign nation. Should they now learn their national language, Yiddish, that language that in "good houses" was rejected as a vulgar hodgepodge of antiquated German and Polish, and that did not allow one to climb the social ladder in Vienna? Should they renounce their German identity and existence, which they had worked so hard for, and move to Palestine as Jewish farmers? Should they now let themselves be robbed of their homeland not only by the anti-Semites but by the Zionists as well? Couldn't they decide for themselves what they wanted to be, Jewish or Protestant, or nondenominational—or Jewish, German, Polish, or Hungarian?

Karl Kraus made himself the spokesperson of Herzl's opponents, angrily declaring that he, a baptized Jew, wouldn't pay one "krone for Zion."[49] The rift between Eastern and Western Jews threatened to divide the Jewish community in Vienna.

In this conflict, even Nordau displayed sympathy and even compassion with the Western Jews. He wrote: "To the German Jew, Germania is the mother he worships. He knows that he is the Cinderella among her children, but still, he is her child too; he *is* part of the family. . . . They will be stabbed straight through their hearts and the secret wound will make them bleed to death." Even if they brought themselves to decide to go to Palestine, once there, they would "think of Germany, even their most distant grandchildren would, as if of a lost love of their youth."[50]

Hitler the politician, however, was not prepared to differentiate in this matter, dismissing even the controversies he personally witnessed as mock fights: *In a short time this apparent struggle between Zionistic and liberal Jews disgusted me.*[51] Whether "German" Jew or Eastern Jew, as far as he was concerned, all that counted was "race."

The Specter of Jewish World Rule

During pogroms in Russia in 1903, unfathomable atrocities and massacres were committed against Jews in Kishinev. In mortal fear, hundreds of thousands of people once again fled across the borders. Money was collected in Western Europe to provide at least temporarily for the hungry and homeless, and also to aid Galicia, which did not have enough resources to deal with the situation. The anti-Semites berated the donors as Jew lackeys. The donations, they charged, were only going to be handed over to the "Russian Revolution" anyway.[52] Therefore the donors were "supporters of the Jewish murderers and revolutionaries."[53]

In all of Western Europe the fear of further floods of immigrants from Russia was fanned systematically. After all, more than five million Jews lived in the czarist empire, more than in all other countries combined. In comparison: there were more than two million Jews in Austro-Hungary—approximately 850,000 in Hungary, another 850,000 in Galicia, more than 100,000 in Bukovina, and some 200,000 in Vienna. There were altogether fewer than 600,000 Jews in the German Reich, 400,000 of them in Prussia. France had only approximately 100,000 Jews, Italy, some 35,000, and Spain, 25,000.[54]

The anti-Semites painted a nightmarish picture of the Russian Revolution of 1905. They accused the Jews of pulling the wires of the revolution and of trying to provoke a revolution in Western Europe as well, with the support of the Social Democrats, in order to establish "Jewish world rule."

A coincidental encounter provided fodder for these theories: in Austria, the news about the czar's manifesto of October 1905 happened to explode like a bomb during the Social Democrats' party convention. Dr. Wilhelm Ellenbogen was standing at the rostrum, when his fellow party members broke out into shouts of joy, yelling: "Hail to the Russian Revolution! Hail to universal suffrage!" Ellenbogen interrupted his speech and solemnly read the czar's manifesto, which granted freedom of the press and the rights of assembly and of convening the Duma, tying these events to demands he put to the Austrian government: "In Russia, the frightened czar has already gone so far as to grant universal suffrage, and our oh-so comfortable dynasty is supposed to lag behind Russia? . . . We no longer want to be the prototype of the black-robed land, the land of tutelage, the land of backwardness, of camarilla. Suffrage is an existential issue to us." He reminded the deputies of the proletariat's weapon, "the paralyzation of all production, of mass strike," and said: "When push comes to shove, the comfortable and prudent proletariat of Austria will be able to speak Russian too."[55] According to the minutes, this prompted "tumultuous applause."

When at the end of November 1905 the Social Democrats organized a mass rally in Vienna for universal, equal suffrage, the Christian Socials under Lueger held a counterdemonstration in the city hall's Volkshalle, whose tenor was: "Down with Jewish terrorism!" The *Deutsches Volksblatt* wrote: "Who leads Social Democracy? The Jews Adler and Ellenbogen! Who assists them in public? The entire Jewish press! And who provides the money for it? Jewish high finance!—Just as the Jews are the incendiaries and agitators in Russia, so they are here at home."[56]

Before a gathering of constituents, Lueger alluded to the latest Jewish pogroms in southern Russia, which cost several thousands of lives, shouting, "I am warning especially the Jews in Vienna not to go as far as their Russian brethren in faith and not to get too involved with the Social Democratic revolutionaries. I am warning them most emphatically; what happened in Russia, might happen here. We in Vienna are anti-Semites, but we certainly weren't made to commit murder and manslaughter. Yet should the Jews threaten our fatherland, we will know no mercy either. I do want to put out a warning of these sad consequences." At this point "demonstrative applause" broke out "which lasted for minutes."[57]

This speech greatly upset the liberals, who responded with a parliamentary interpellation against Lueger's "inflammatory and incendiary political speech," which contained "direct, open, and brutal calls to excesses, violence, pillaging, theft, and murder against citizens who have equal protection under the federal constitution." This speech was all the more dangerous as it originated from the "chief of such a large city," who should really tend to peace among the populace rather than incite the citizens against one another.[58]

Lueger reinforced his opinion during the debate on the interpellation: "When I look at the leaders of the Social Democratic Party, anybody who can distinguish different races must admit that the leaders of Social Democracy are exclusively Jews. (Cheers and applause.) It may be that here and there one of them is baptized, but surely there are bona fide Jews among them too, and the one who is supposedly baptized, Dr. Adler, is recognizable." Lueger then went on to portray himself as a peaceful man, saying he even had "very often protected the Jews against my party's will": "I can only say, you rarely have a party where the most mellow one is the leader."[59] In March 1906 the Christian Socials submitted another petition for restricting the immigration of Russian Jews in order "to protect the native, Christian resident population from such an invasion."[60]

When Hitler arrived in Vienna in 1907, the topic of the Russian Jews was as hot as before, particularly after the publication of a fiercely anti-Semitic book that the Christian Socials promoted vigorously: *The Revolution in Russia* by Rudolf Vrba. It argued that the pogroms and massacres of Russian Jews were nothing but part of a Christian battle of defense against the Jewish threat: "The Russian with a strong national sense defends himself desperately against the clutches of the Jewish tentacles."[61] "The 'Mandelstams and Silberfarbs' have thrown the torch of sedition into the Czar's gigantic Empire: therefore the blood that was shed during the revolution is now first and foremost spilled on the heads of the Jews."[62]

This book, which with its many statistics and quotes leaves the impression of being a precise documentary account, equated Jews and Social Democrats and conjured up the dangers of a Jewish world conspiracy. It argued that if the Russian Jews obtained equal civil rights on top of everything else, then—"just as in certain constitutional states which we don't have to mention"—the "peoples, upper and lower classes, [would be] exploited and sucked dry, and constitutional governments [would be] forced into total moral and high-financial dependence on them."[63] "For the Jews don't want 'equality' but complete domination."[64]

Vrba wrote that there was no persecution of the Jews, only persecution of Christians, against which Christians had to defend themselves: "One shouldn't confront us with the little anti-Semitism in this world as proof against this assertion. . . . If there has perhaps been a minor exception in Kishinev and not only Christians but Jews too became victims, this has been atoned and made up for by decades of prison sentences."[65]

Later on Hitler would use similar arguments when he denied the existence of the persecution of the Jews, saying, for example, in 1923: *The Jew strives for absolute power in the country of restrictions against the Jews but not of their persecution, for in the past 200 years there have been no more persecutions of the Jews, only one continuing persecution of Christians!*[66]

The *Deutsches Volksblatt* in particular, which Hitler read, fanned the fear of the Russian Jews. In 1908, for example, it published an editorial warning, penned by a Romanian university professor from Yassy. The "invasion" of the Russian Jews, the professor wrote, who "ruin peoples and destroy states," had gone so far "that all national property has fallen into Jewish hands." In 1849, he said, 72 percent of the people in Yassy had still been Romanian, 8 percent of various nationalities, and 20 percent Jewish; but now only 45.5 percent were Romanian, 4.5 of other nationalities, and 50 percent Jewish. The professor continued: "If we let the Jews destroy the middle class, if we deliver our cities to these alien perpetrators, then we are lost. Therefore a healthy solution to the Jewish problem is a veritably existential issue for our nation. It is a question of to be or not to be, of defending our life, and of the highest goods of national security and national future. Woe unto the nation that doesn't have the strength to fend off the alien invasion but apathetically watches

Auch ein Turmkraxler.

"Another tower climber." Warning by the Christian Socials against the alleged threat of Jewish rule in Vienna. The Eastern Jew sits down on top of City Hall and throws down the old Viennese "city hall man."

as legions of cunning Jews penetrate all areas of public life, tear the bread out of the nation's mouth, and economically subjugate it."[67]

Reasoning that the rule of Russian Jews and revolutionaries was a threat first to Romania, but then to Austro-Hungary as well, all anti-Semitic parties called for strict defense measures. The Social Democrats, however continued to express their solidarity with the goals of the Russian Revolution and protested against the 1905 repealing of democratic rights, the dissolution of the Duma, and political tortures and massacres against Jews. In 1911 Leon Trotsky, the Russian revolutionary who had escaped from Siberia, appeared as a speaker at the Social Democratic party convention. Between 1907 and 1914 Trotsky lived in Vienna with his wife and children, worked there as a newspaper correspondent, edited the Russian *Pravda* for workers, and was on friendly terms with Vienna's Social Democrats. In his speech he praised the solidarity of Austria's Social Democracy with the Russian Revolution, saying: "The Russian workers were enthusiastic mainly about two speeches, that of Comrade Adler's powerful indictment in Austria's first parliament of universal suffrage against the sentencing of our second Duma party group, and of Comrade Ellenbogen's glowing speech in the delegation concerning the torture of political prisoners. I recall these two speeches with gratitude."[68] Because Adler, Ellenbogen, and Trotsky were Jewish, the anti-Semites had new "proof" of their assertion regarding the attempted "Jewish world rule" with the help of international Social Democracy and the "Jewish press."

The third supporter on the road to the coming world revolution supposedly were the "money Jews." The *Brigittenauer Bezirks-Nachrichten* commented on some 300 international economic experts, who had convened according to news reports[69]: "These 300 men are from the tribe of Judah and bequeath their right to rule within their families. They are the 300 kings of our time, who rule in actuality, pushing the old monarchs down to the mere level of sham princes." The German nation, the paper said, was ruined and "denationalized."

The Jews were allegedly planning "the establishment of an international alliance of banks with its seat in Washington" and would soon "publicly dictate its laws to the world": "High finance is destined to become the successor to empires and kingdoms, and with a lot more authority at that, since their authority will rule not only one country but the whole world." The local newspaper, with which Hitler was very familiar, drew this conclusion: "We all struggle and get incensed, and even have fights with one another when we get worked up, while the Jew turns the wheel of history, laughing scornfully."[70] Hitler the politician turned the myth about the Jewish revolution into a keystone of his propaganda, usually in connection with the Russian Revolution of 1917—for instance, in a 1942 speech: *We know the theoretical principle and the cruel truth about the aims of this global scourge. It is called rule of the proletariat, and it means dicatorship of the Jews! It implies the extermination of the peoples' national leadership and intelligentsia, and the Jewish-international criminals' exclusive domination over the proletariat, which will then be without leaders and thus defenseless through its own fault. What had happened in Russia to such a horrifying extent, the extermination of countless millions of leaders, was supposed to continue in Germany.*[71]

At any rate, after 1918 and 1919, the young politician put his finger on the pulse of his time when he announced the fight against the alleged cause of all misery, "the Jew": *If the Jew and his Marxist creed are victorious over the other peoples of the world, his crown will be the funeral wreath of humanity and this planet will move through the ether devoid of men, as it did thousands of years ago. Eternal Nature inexorably avenges the infringement of her commands.* Hence today I believe that I am acting in accordance with the will of the Almighty Creator: by defending myself against the Jew, I am fighting for the work of the Lord.[72] The Germans, he continued, had to learn *to combat poison gas with poison gas. It is our duty to inform all weaklings that this is a question of to be or not to be.*[73]

Was Young Hitler an Anti-Semite?

There can be no doubt that while in Vienna, young Hitler studied anti-Semitism, among other matters. The four politicians who may be called his political models—Schönerer, Lueger, Wolf, and Stein—were radical anti-Semites. Many newspapers which Hitler read in Vienna, and many pamphlets he perused for his self-education, were anti-Semitic. Even when he was already Reich chancellor, Hitler's way of expressing himself had a Viennese ring to it when he elaborated on "the Jews." This proves that he mastered the anti-Semitic vocabulary of his Vienna period with all its characteristic clichés perfectly. Therefore many later observers, such as Albert Speer, initially took Hitler's anti-Semitism "for a somewhat vulgar byproduct, a relic from his days in Vienna . . . and only God knows why he couldn't shed it."[74]

Thus it seems to be clear that Hitler's anti-Semitism developed in a straightforward line, especially if one reads Hitler's description in *Mein Kampf* of how he had become an anti-Semite in Vienna: *For me this was a time of the greatest spiritual upheaval I have ever had to go through. I had ceased to be a weak-kneed cosmopolitan and become an anti-Semite.*[75] Vienna, he said, had significantly contributed to his becoming anti-Semitic: *At the time of this bitter struggle between spiritual education and cold reason, the visual instruction of the Vienna streets had performed invaluable services.*[76]

As the decisive event of his transformation into an anti-Semite, Hitler mentions—in 1924, to be sure, in *Mein Kampf*—an encounter with an Eastern Jew. The *apparition in a black caftan and black hair locks* merely made him wonder: *Is this a Jew? was my first thought. And: Is this a German?* Once again, he says, this experience caused him to read up on the subject: *For a few hellers I bought the first anti-Semitic pamphlets of my life.* What happened then, he continues, was what may be called a radical anti-Semite's typical obsession: *Since I had begun to concern myself with this question and to take cognizance of the Jews, Vienna appeared to me in a different light than before. Wherever I went, I began to see Jews, and the more I saw, the more sharply they became distinguished in my eyes from the rest of humanity.*[77] The upshot of this dramatic development, Hitler claims, was the realization regarding Social Democracy's Jewish character: *When I recognized the Jew as the leader of the Social Democracy, the scales dropped from my eyes. A long soul struggle had reached its conclusion.*[78]

Of course, *Mein Kampf* must not be read as an autobiography in the sense of its author dealing with his own past, or as a confession in which he worked through his experiences. The book is clearly a work of political propaganda, in which a power-hungry politician on the rise buttresses his political slogans and builds them up through a fitting life story to form a weltanschauung. In *Mein Kampf* Hitler created an organically grown anti-Semitic career for himself with politically convenient anti-Semitic images in its key scenes. Thus the book must also be read as the developmental history of a Germanic leader who found the right when he was young.

However, reality, as it emerges from the reports of Viennese eyewitnesses, has little to do with the myths *Mein Kampf* purports. Apart from the special case of August Kubizek, no anti-Semitic remark by the young Hitler has been documented.

Reinhold Hanisch, clearly an anti-Semite, was incredulous when he heard that Hitler, of all people, was an extreme, anti-Semitic politician in the thirties. After all, Hanisch and Hitler had their falling out in the men's hostel in 1910 because Hitler turned entirely to his Jewish friends Josef Neumann and Siegfried Löffner. In the thirties, in his anger Hanisch revealed Hitler's youth as anything but anti-Semitic in order to discredit Hitler as a politician.

Hanisch is by no means alone in his assertions. Anonymous from Brünn also wrote, in 1912: "Hitler got along extremely well with Jews. He once said they were an intelligent people that stuck together more than the Germans." Rudolf Häusler, the colleague in the men's hostel, was at a loss when his daughter questioned him about the anti-Semitism of his then twenty-three- to twenty-four-year-old friend Adolf. Häusler told her that he had not noticed anything of the kind in Vienna. Yet he knew that in Munich, Hitler had thought he had been cheated by a Jewish junk dealer, which might have been a reason for Hitler's subsequent anti-Semitism—surely no conclusive proof.[79]

The Viennese eyewitnesses remembered unanimously that Hitler's dealings with Jews had been quite natural. For example, Jakob Wasserberg from Galicia, who ran a small brandy store at 20 Webgasse, close to

Stumpergasse, related that the young man had frequently had breakfast with him: "Mr. Wasserberg, a tea and a *Laberl.*" (A *Laberl* is a cookie.)[80]

It is worthy of note that among all the stories of his sufferings in Vienna, Hitler never mentioned a bad experience with a Jew. Let us briefly recapitulate young Hitler's encounters with Jews in Linz and Vienna: Even when he was Reich chancellor, Hitler expressed his gratitude to his Jewish family doctor in Linz, Dr. Eduard Bloch, who attended to his mother until she died. In his American exile Dr. Bloch clearly stressed that young Hitler had certainly not been an anti-Semite in Linz: "He had not yet begun to hate the Jews."[81] The theory that Hitler's anti-Semitism goes back to a Jewish professor who had flunked him at the academy exam is as untenable as the sensational story about Hitler's getting infected with syphilis by a Jewish prostitute in Leopoldstadt. When in 1908 anti-Semitic smear campaigns at the Vienna Opera were raging against former director Gustav Mahler, Hitler continued to admire Mahler as a Wagner interpreter. Accompanied by Kubizek, nineteen-year-old Hitler witnessed the family life and culture of an educated Jewish middle-class family during musicmaking in the house of the Jahodas; he was deeply impressed and did not utter the slightest anti-Semitic remark.

Furthermore, he had every reason to be grateful to Jewish benefactors. When he was homeless in 1909—and probably earlier and later as well—he profited from Jewish social institutions in many ways, from public *Wärmestuben* to soup kitchens and Jewish citizens' donations to the homeless shelter in Meidling and the men's hostel in Brigittenau.

In the men's hostel, Hitler had mainly Jewish friends, which made Hanisch very angry. His best friend, the religious Jew Neumann, a trained copper polisher, gave him a coat when he had nothing to wear and lent him money. Hitler disappeared with him from the men's hostel for a week. Hanisch's comment: "Neumann was a good-hearted man who liked Hitler very much and whom Hitler of course highly esteemed." Hitler also discussed issues concerning anti-Semitism and Zionism with Neumann—by no means contemptuously as he did with the Social Democratic colleagues in the men's hostel, but jokingly, in a friendly way. He even went so far as to defend Heine, who was under anti-Semitic attack, to quote Lessing's "Parable of the Ring," and to acknowledge the achievements of Jewish composers, such as Mendelssohn and Offenbach.

Siegfried Löffner from Moravia, a Jewish colleague at the men's hostel, even dragged Hitler's archenemy, Hanisch, to the police to report him for defrauding Hitler. The Jewish locksmith Simon Robinson from Galicia, who received a small invalid's pension, helped Hitler out financially. Karl Honisch mentions an additional Jewish acquaintance in the men's hostel in 1913, Rudolf Redlich from Moravia. It would be erroneous to assume that a particularly large percentage of men at the hostel had been Jewish. According to statistics, 8 to 10 percent were Jewish—which corresponded to the median Jewish population in Vienna. From Hitler's later remark on his Vienna years we may conclude that Hanisch was not the only anti-Semite there: "Many workers with whom he had associated, he said, had been decidedly anti-Semitic."[82]

Hitler sold his paintings almost exclusively to Jewish dealers: Morgenstern, Landsberger, and Altenberg. Hanisch writes: "The Christian dealers . . . didn't pay any better than the Jews. Besides, they only bought more material when they had disposed of the first shipment, while the Jewish dealers continued to buy whether they had sold anything or not." When the NSDAP archive searched for early Hitler paintings in 1938, they still found unsold pieces both in Morgenstern's and Altenberg's stores, after more than twenty-five years. Hanisch writes: "Hitler often said that it was only with the Jews that one could do business, because only they were willing to take chances." Frame manufacturer Jakob Altenberg from Galicia could not remember any anti-Semitic statements by Hitler.[83] Hitler had close personal contact with Samuel Morgenstern, who procured private customers for the young man, for example, Jewish lawyer Dr. Josef Feingold, who in turn sponsored Hitler.

Young Hitler's exceptional contacts with Jews may also be an indication that he considered the Jews to be "something better." As Kubizek reports, in the Opera's standing room he had the opportunity to observe the Jews' particularly great cultural interest. Hitler was familiar with the different figures for Christian and Jewish students at the universities, as well as the popular jokes about the "intelligent," "intellectual" Jews who easily got the better of the "nice"Christians.

In the men's hostel he expressed his approval of Jewish tradition, which had managed to preserve the purity of the "Jewish race" for thousands of years. It should be remembered that in the work of List and Lanz von Liebenfels it is not the alien race that is dangerous and ruinous, but only the mixing of races, which decreases the value of the Aryan "noble people" and therefore should be avoided at all cost. As late as 1930 Hitler talked extensively about the Jews' ability to preserve their race by way of religion and strict rules, among them, the prohibition of marriages with non-Jews. Hitler directly continued List's theories when he told Wagener: *Through Moses the Jewish people received a rule for life and living one's life that was elevated to a religion which was entirely tailored toward the essence of one's race, and simply and clearly, without dogmas and dubious rules of faith, soberly and absolutely realistically contains what served the future and self-preservation of the children of Israel. Everything is geared toward the well-being of one's own people, nothing toward consideration of others.* After further explanations, Hitler arrived at the conclusion that *we . . . no doubt have to recognize with admiration this incredible strength* of the Jews' preservation of their race.[84]

Hitler adopted Jewish "purity of race" as nothing less than a model for his own weltanschauung regarding the necessity of the racial purity of Aryans.

It was only as a politician that Hitler portrayed the Jews as "parasites" who robbed Aryans of their strength through their intellectual impact, democracy, Social Democracy, the press, capital, parliamentarianism, modern art, pornography, pacifism, and much more. Around 1930 Hitler said to Wagener: *This is precisely the parasitic instinct, which nonparasitic plants don't have. A special talent! A sixth sense! A business sense—of sadistic origin, to be sure, but the superiority of parasites!*[85] If the "host people" didn't put up a sufficient defense, Hitler said, the Jews would survive as the fittest: *And the last ones, alas, who will still practice usury when the end has come for mankind, will be the Jews, despite everything.* And: *Was it possible that the earth had been promised as a reward to that people?*[86] In Hitler the politician, who liked to present himself as the savior of the German people, all the theories of a duel between races about "to be or not to be," which he had read and took for the truth, became an anti-Semitic syndrome.

Only in his Spandau diaries does Speer reach the conclusion that "the hatred of the Jews was Hitler's motor and core," "sometimes it now even seems to me as if everything else had only been garnish for this, the actual driving force." One argument for this theory would be that toward the end of the war, Hitler "was ready even to risk his plans of conquest for the sake of his extermination mania."[87]

How much all of Hitler's thinking circled around "the Jews," is revealed in his "Political Testament," dictated on April 29, 1945, at 4:00 A.M., shortly before his suicide. It ends with the order *to painstakingly follow the racial laws and to mercilessly resist the global poisoner of all peoples, international Jewry.*[88]

However, the crucial question as to when anti-Semitism became Hitler's central issue and core of his weltanschauung cannot be answered by looking at his years in Linz and Vienna. This development took place in later years. At any rate, when Hitler became a politician and started addressing the public in Munich in 1919, he already employed agressive anti-Semitic slogans. Thus this great turning point must have occurred during the years of the World War, and particularly in the years of upheaval, in 1918–19, when Hitler decided to become a politician.

That time was especially susceptible to those theories with which Hitler had become intimately familiar in Vienna. Again the cliché about a "Jewish world revolution" as the beginning of a forthcoming "Jewish world rule," which was set off in Russia, was bandied about. This time, however—in contrast to 1905—the Russian Revolution was victorious: in 1917 the Bolsheviks toppled the czar from his throne and usurped power. One year later the revolution broke out in Germany and Austro-Hungary. The Hohenzollerns as well as the Hapsburgs lost their power. The Social Democrats, the "November criminals," took over the government. This was followed by the "disgraceful victory of Versailles," forced upon the losers of World War I by "international powers"—which, according to anti-Semitic propaganda, was the work of "the Jews" and humiliated Germany. Hunger and despair, rootlessness and lack of orientation ruled. In addition, legions of immigrants and refugees arrived, among them, many Eastern Jews.

As in all times of hardship, anti-Semitism served public speakers as an effective slogan, as it fell on fertile ground. Radical politicians whose roots were "at the bottom," "with the people," recognized their chance. At that time of confusion, Hitler, who was now thirty years old and had nothing to lose since he didn't have anything, not even a job, grasped his opportunity. Now he could apply all that he had learned in Vienna, the motto being: "The Jews are to blame for everything."

He was encouraged and supported mainly by his "paternal friend," the writer Dietrich Eckart, to whom he erected a remarkable monument at the end of *Mein Kampf*.[89] Eckart was a link to Hitler's Vienna years in that he was a member of the Thule Society, which in turn was connected with the List Society and List's secret order HAO. The early artificial image of Hitler as Germany's future leader who as a modern-day Messiah faced the public at the age of thirty can probably also be attributed to Eckart. Hitler described his decision dramatically in *Mein Kampf*: when he was in the military hospital of Pasewalk in Pomerania, almost blind from a gas injury, the news of the November revolution and Emperor William's II abdication arrived. His immediate response was to blame "the Jew": *There is no making pacts with Jews; there can only be the hard: either–or. I, for my part, decided to go into politics.*[90]

After having become familiar with Hitler's constant efforts at creating an artificial persona after the fact and his persistent obfuscating of his early biography (where the event in question probably happened much less heroically), I would like to point out this version's great similarity with Guido von List's tale of his awakening. After all, List too could "see" again after having been temporarily blind, and in this state allegedly "received" the revelation of the secret of the runes. As he signaled to "those in the know," the sudden realization, in a state of blindness, that he wanted to become a politician, made Hitler appear to be a "chosen one," a "man of Providence," a "strong one from above."

Two Examples

THE JAHODA FAMILY

In Vienna, Hitler did not merely encounter Jews of the lower classes, but also had sporadic glimpses into the lives of well-to-do, educated, middle-class Jews. For in 1908, August Kubizek, who earned some money as a viola player at private evening performances, occasionally took him along to such concerts, for example, to the house of a "family of a well-to-do factory owner at Heiligenstädter Strasse, Dr. Jahoda." We can clearly identify this Dr. Jahoda.[91]

To be sure, in Vienna's address register, the 1910 *Lehmann*, no Jehuda is listed at Heiligenstädter Strasse, but at 86 Grinzinger Strasse. According to old street numbers, this address is the corner building to Heiligenstädter Strasse.[92] That it was in fact this house and this family whom Kubizek mentioned, was confirmed by Dr. Rudolf Jahuda's niece, Professor Marie Jahoda, born in 1907, a sociologist living in England.[93] She, too, knew the address of her uncle's house only as "Heiligenstädter Strasse," where she and her parents and siblings were frequent visitors. Thanks to her, we have the following information.

The house, a beautiful old villa that no longer exists, was in the large, parklike area at the lower end of Rothschild Park in Heiligenstadt, on a very small hill. It was inhabited by Dr. Rudolf Jahoda, a chemist, with his family and his mentally retarded brother Edmund.[94]

Jahoda, director of a chemical factory, born in Vienna in 1862, was forty-six years old in 1908, when Hitler was a guest in his house. According to Marie Jahoda's description, her uncle was a slender, sensitive, quiet man of medium height, with melancholy features and a gray goatee. His wife, Pina, was an Italian Catholic, short and somewhat deformed, with beautiful eyes, and warmhearted. The two had two little daughters who were baptized by the Catholic church: Klara, born in 1902, and Adele, born in 1903.

The Jahoda family may be regarded as a model of the well-to-do circles of assimilated Jews in the Vienna around 1900 who were keenly interested in the arts. Rudolf Jahoda's father had immigrated to Vienna as a Bohemian Jew, and worked there as a printer. He had not become prosperous, but he made enough money to afford to send two of his five sons, Rudolf and Emil, to college and graduate school. According to his niece Marie, Dr. Emil Jahoda, chief doctor of the Francis Joseph Hospital's department of surgery, was the star of the family: elegant, sophisticated, and the heartthrob of his female patients.

The two youngest brothers, Georg and Karl—Marie's father—went into printing and became well-to-do and highly respected. Georg Jahuda printed the *Fackel*, and was in close contact with and a good friend of Karl Kraus, the periodical's editor. The greater Jahuda family belonged to the circle of Kraus's open admirers.

All five brothers distanced themselves from Judaism and, according to Marie Jahuda, were agnostics. Before he married, Rudolf Jahuda officially left his Jewish faith and indicated at the official register that he had no denomination.

Rudolf Jahuda's wealth came from one of his numerous chemical patents, a glow paint that enjoyed great popularity. However, a combination of its radioactive composition and additional chemical experiments caused bad burns and scars on his right hand. Still, Rudolf Jahuda was an accomplished pianist. He was proud to have been a former student of Johannes Brahms, and aside from Brahms, he loved Chopin, Schubert, Beethoven, and Mozart. His wife Pina was a violinist who preferred eighteenth-century Italian music.

On a certain day each week, the Jahodas arranged a private evening of musicmaking, where all brothers and their wives and children got together, as well as cousins and additional relatives. In the large wood-paneled salon, which simultaneously served as a library, Rudolf and Pina Jahoda first played one or two sonatas for piano and violin. Then all of them had dinner together in the adjoining dining room, where the housewive displayed her mastery of culinary art with Italian specialties. After dinner and some lively conversation, the evening concluded with a final piece of music.

In addition, the Jahodas frequently hired music students to augment their repertoire and play trios or quartets. That is how the violist Kubizek came to visit their house. Apparently Kubizek raved to his friend about these evenings: "It was a circle of people with great understanding of the arts and a highly developed taste, a truly sophisticated conviviality of the sort that was possible only in Vienna."[95] Kubizek asked if he could bring a friend. Thus nineteen-year-old Hitler entered the Jahodas' house.

Kubizek reports: "He did like it tremendously. What impressed him most was the library, which Dr. Jahoda had arranged and which served Adolf as a reliable measure of judging the people assembled there. He was less comfortable with having to confine himself to being a passive listener all evening, even though it was he who had imposed that role on himself. On our way back he told me that he had felt very comfortable with those people, but since he was not a musician, he hadn't been able to participate in the conversation." Furthermore, he had felt uneasy because of his poor clothes.[96]

In this cultivated circle young Hitler was shy and inhibited, unable to utter a word. Whatever he may have known about Richard Wagner, he had nothing to contribute in this circle of music connoisseurs, and he turned out to be uninteresting—which of course is hardly surprising for a nineteen-year-old. At least, he did meet, probably for the first time, an upper-middle-class Jewish family—and had not one critical word to say about them.

A postscript on the family's further destiny: Pina Jahoda died early, and Rudolf Jahoda lost his fortune during World War I and inflation, and had to sell his house to boot. He died impoverished in 1924 of cancer, probably caused by the radioactive glow paint.[97] His daughter Klara, a doctor in a Berlin children's home in the 1930s, emigrated via Austria to England, where she found support and shelter with her cousin Marie Jahoda, who, an active Social Democrat, had left Vienna earlier, while Austria was still a corporative state. Because Klara's Viennese doctorate was not recognized in England, she worked for a long time as a housekeeper, until she completed her second degree and obtained a position as a school doctor in Bristol.

Adele Jahoda, who had attended Vienna's School of Arts and Crafts under Dean Alfred Roller, married the composer and violinist Karl Rankl, a disciple of Schönberg, whom she met at her parents' private concerts. The two of them also emigrated to England, where she barely made do for herself and her unemployed husband by arts-and-craft work. Rankl later became musical director of London's Covent Garden Opera. Both daughters of Rudolf Jahoda died in England without any children.

Three of Rudolf Jahoda's brothers had numerous children, who had remarkably successful careers—not in Austria, but in their forced emigration. These include several musicians and numerous scientists, among them many woman university professors.

MR. AND MRS. MORGENSTERN

The Jewish glazier Samuel Morgenstern was the most loyal buyer of Hitler's paintings. In this case, Hitler did not rely on an agent but always delivered his paintings personally. Peter Jahn, who called on Morgenstern between 1937 and 1939 to search for Hitler paintings at the NSDAP's direction, stresses that their relationship was extremely friendly and Morgenstern certainly did not cheat the poor painter. In his deposition he said: "Morgenstern was the first person to pay a good price for the paintings, which is how their business contact was established."[98]

Samuel Morgenstern was born in Budapest in 1875. In 1903 he opened his glazier store with a workshop in the back at 4 Liechtensteinstrasse near downtown Vienna, quite close to Sigmund Freud's practice and apartment. In 1904 he married Emma Pragan, a Jew from Vienna four years his junior. In 1911 their only child, a son, was born. That same year Morgenstern bought an estate in Strebersdorf near Vienna for five thousand kronen, and in May 1914 another piece of land, in Groß Jedlersdorf, for ten times that amount.[99] Within a few years he worked his way up from nothing.

In a deposition he made from memory in 1937, Morgenstern stated that Hitler had come to his store for the first time in 1911 or 1912, offering him three paintings, historical views in the style of Rudolf von Alt. Morgenstern had also sold pictures in his frame and glazier store, "since in my experience it is easier to sell frames if they contain pictures."[100]

Thanks to Morgenstern's fastidiously kept customer database, many owners of Hitler's paintings could later be located. It turned out that most of them were Jewish—in other words, Morgenstern's regular clientele—and lived in the elegant new tenement buildings around Liechtensteinerstrasse.[101] One of Morgenstern's main customers was the lawyer Dr. Josef Feingold, according to the person who interviewed him in May 1938, "apparently not entirely Aryan, but certainly leaving the impression of being respectable, a war veteran."[102] He had his law offices downtown, near Stephansplatz, and supported a number of young painters sent by Morgenstern. He bought a series of old views of Vienna by Hitler, which he had framed by Morgenstern in the style of Biedermeier.[103]

When the former postcard painter took possession of Austria in March 1938 as leader of the "Greater German Empire," Mr. and Mrs. Morgenstern's destiny made an about-face too. In the fall of 1938 their stores, fully stocked warehouse, and workshop were "Aryanized" and taken over by a National Socialist. The "purchase price," which was set at 620 marks, was never paid.[104] Because Morgenstern also lost his commercial license, he was no longer allowed to work. Thus the couple—sixty-three and fifty-nine years old, respectively—had no income whatever, and what is more: they could not leave the country, because they did not have the money either for the trip or for the obligatory "Reich flight tax," or for the required visa.

In this desperate situation Samuel Morgenstern saw only one way out: asking the Führer personally for help, just as Dr. Bloch in Linz did around that time. Considering that Hitler immediately responded to Bloch's request, Morgenstern's hope for the Führer to intervene and save his life was certainly not absurd, as long as the letter reached Hitler.

Morgenstern wrote his cry for help on a typewriter, addressing it to "His Excellency the Reich Chancellor and Führer of the German Reich Adolf Hitler" in Berchtesgaden:

Vienna, 10 August 1939

Excellency!

I humbly ask your indulgence for daring to write to you, Mr. Reich Chancellor, and submitting a request.

For thirty-five years, I had my own business as a glazier and frame manufacturer in Vienna, at 9 Liechtensteinerstrasse, and in the years before the war Mr. Chancellor was frequently in my store and had the opportunity to judge me to be a correct and honest man.

I have no police record and for eight years served as a noncommissioned officer in the Austrian army and was on the Romanian front, plus my industrial association twice gave me a diploma for running an exemplary company.

On November 10 my store was closed [this word is underlined twice; in the margin there is a remark in a different handwriting: "Jew!"] in the course of the legal measures and my commercial license was revoked at the same time which made me totally indigent since to this day I have not received from the Department of Property the slightest compensation for my store which was worth Reichsmark 7,000 and was Aryanized on 24 November 1938.

I am sixty-four, my wife is sixty years old, we have for many months depended on welware and intend to emigrate and to look for work abroad.

It is my most humble request to Your Excellency to please direct the Department of Property to give me in return for handing over to the State my unmortgaged estate in the XXIst District which according to an official estimate is valued at Reichsmark 4,000, a small compensation in the form of foreign currency so I have the necessary disembarkation money and my wife and I can live modestly until we have found work.

Please have my application checked and please approve it.

Faithfully yours,

Samuel Morgenstern Glazier

Vienna, 9.4 Liechtensteinerstrasse[105]

However, getting a letter to Hitler was difficult, particularly in August 1939, shortly before the outbreak of the war. Hitler even mentioned this difficulty to Kubizek, whose letter was months late in reaching him: "Writing to him directly, he said, was not advisable, as he often never even saw mail addressed to him, because it first had to be sorted to relieve him in his work."[106]

Precisely traceable by postmarks and without the eagerly waiting sender's having any idea about this, Morgenstern's letter went on the following journey: mailed in Vienna on August 11, it arrived in Hitler's secretary's office at the Obersalzberg in Berchtesgaden on August 12 and was forwarded from there to the "Führer's Chancellery" in Berlin on August 14, where it was opened on August 15. This is where the marginal note "Jew!" must have been added. In any case, the secretary's office did not hand the letter to Hitler but returned it to Vienna on August 19—however, not to the sender but to the Finance Ministry, where it was filed away and forgotten for the next fifty-six years.

The invasion of Poland began on September 1, 1939, and with it World War II. The Morgensterns waited fruitlessly for help from Hitler, but a short time later their house was taken from them. They had to relocate to a kind of Jewish ghetto in Leopoldstadt. From there, on October 28, 1941, they were deported to the Litzmannstadt ghetto in the Reich district of Wartheland.[107] The deportation order was stamped, in red ink, "To Poland."[108]

Litzmannstadt, named for a German general of World War I, the former Lodz in the former Hapsburg crown colony of Galicia, had with 233,000 inhabitants one of the largest Jewish populations in the world. After the first resettlements another 160,000 Jews were forced into this ghetto. There they lived in poor hygienic conditions, making textiles, shoes, and furniture for the German army and German industries.[109]

The Morgensterns were among 25,000 Jews deported to Litzmannstadt from Berlin, Vienna, Prague, Frankfurt, Cologne, Hamburg, Düsseldorf, and Luxembourg. Five thousand Gypsies from Burgenland were also relocated there; they were shortly sent to Auschwitz. The Western Jews, who spoke Polish and Yiddish, stayed in the ghetto, where they lived uneasily with the unfamiliar Eastern Jews; there was often conflict between the two groups, which, of course, was intended. These internal quarrels among ghetto inhabitants, fanned by their painfully cramped situation, constant hunger, and physical exhaustion through excruciatingly hard work, was meant to rob them of their human dignity. Especially the lack of hygiene proved to be a highly effective means of "corroborating" the old anti-Semitic prejudice about the "filthy Jews." One of the survivors from Lodz, Leon Zelman, has reported details: "The latrines were constantly plugged. People pulled carts loaded with excrement through the streets, passing wagons filled with corpses to which horses had not been put either, but half-starved Jews. Pulling excrement carts . . . equaled a death sentence, because the human draft animals invariably caught infections by breathing in the fecal vapors. . . . In the summer, swarms of mosquitoes came down on the ghetto, spreading epidemics."[110]

We do not know what happened to the Morgensterns there. Samuel Morgenstern died of exhaustion in the ghetto of Litzmannstadt in August 1943. He was sixty-eight years old. He was buried in the ghetto cemetery.[111] As an eyewitness, Emma's brother-in-law Wilhelm Abeles, a former glazier in Vienna, was to report later on, his wife was with him until the end.[112]

In August 1943, when the Russian army was advancing, the ghetto was vacated. The remaining 65,000 people, weakened by hunger and diseases, were deported to Auschwitz. Among them was Abeles, but he survived. Before he was deported, he saw Emma Morgenstern in Litzmannstadt for the last time. There are no other surviving witnesses.

Emma Morgenstern must have been deported to Auschwitz by August 1944, for on August 30 only a "cleaning-up commando" of six hundred men and a few people in hiding remained in the ghetto.[113] Most new arrivals—above all, old women unable to work—were immediately sent to the gas chamber.

As a Vienna court would later determine, Emma Morgenstern could not have lived through the end of the war in 1945. In appoval of her brother's application, retired Major Max Pragan, she was declared dead in December 1946.[114]

11
Young Hitler and Women

Inhibitions and Escapes

The sparse eyewitness reports on Hitler's years in Linz and Vienna all agree on one point: his relations to women consisted mainly of dreams, self-protection, and anxiety. There were no actual relationships. It is strange that no development in this area is discernible during Hitler's years in Vienna. He had no pertinent experiences, and not even a serious crush between the ages of eighteen and twenty-four. It is in this domain that it becomes clear to what degree the life of this strange man from the men's hostel did not unfold in exchange and confrontation with experiences and human encounters, but was determined by phrases he had read and that served him as a substitute for reality—which he tried to overcome.

Kubizek, who of all witnesses was personally closest to Hitler and with whom he shared a room for a few months, remarked that "in this sinful Babel of Vienna, where even prostitution is artistically glorified and celebrated, [he was] truly an unusual person!"[1] "In his self-imposed asceticism" he had looked at women "with alert and critical sympathy, but strictly without any personal involvement," and "everything that became a personal experience for other men of his age" had turned into an issue for him "on which he elaborated in such a dispassionate and detached way as if he himself were entirely outside of these issues."[2]

Therefore, when Hitler says in 1942, *During my youth in Vienna I also met many beautiful women,*[3] this must not be misconstrued as late pride of his wild years in Vienna, but rather the way Kubizek explains it: eighteen- or nineteen-year-old Hitler had certainly had an eye for beautiful women, "but always as if one looked at a beautiful picture, without any secret sexual thoughts."[4] It should be noted that Kubizek made this statement after 1945, and without implying any moral judgment.

Kubizek also says that Hitler was never seduced, which he illustrates by describing the following episode. When they were looking for an apartment in 1908, they entered some elegant house, where "smartly dressed maids" led them into a "very elegantly furnished room with a luxurious double bed": "We immediately realized that this was too distinguished for us. Yet the 'madam' was already standing in the door, a perfect lady, no longer quite young, but very elegant. She wore a silk robe, and her delicate slippers were furred. She greeted us smiling, looked at Adolf and then at me, and offered us a seat."

The lady, Kubizek continues, had suggested that not he but only Hitler move into her house: "While she explained all this to Adolf in a very lively manner, she made some erratic movement, and the cord which held her robe together came undone. 'Oh, I'm sorry, gentlemen!' she immediately cried and closed her robe again. Yet that one moment had been enough to show us that she didn't wear more than tiny pants under her silk robe. Adolf blushed crimson, got up, grabbed my arm, and said: 'Come, Gustl!' I don't remember how we left the apartment. I only recall the one word Adolf angrily uttered when we were finally in the street again: 'What a Potiphar.' "[5]

Hitler's fear of being touched is also revealed in his efforts to avoid the Opera's "Olympus," the standing room on the fourth gallery that was so popular with students. For there—in contrast to the standing room on the ground floor—women were admitted as well.[6]

According to Kubizek, Hitler never received any mail or visitors during the entire time they lived together. He also demanded that his friend not get involved with girls and, according to Kubizek, "never [would have] allowed any such dalliance." "Any step in that direction would have necessarily meant the end of our friendship."[7] Not even the young women who studied piano with Kubizek were allowed to enter the room at Stumpergasse. Kubizek relates that once a female student had called on Kubizek before an exam to ask his advice. Afterward Hitler had attacked him viciously: "He angrily wanted to know whether our room, which was cluttered up anyway because of the grand piano, that monstrosity, was now also to become a place for a rendezvous with that musical woman scum. It was difficult for me to convince him that the poor girl wasn't suffering from love sickness but only exam jitters. This resulted in a detailed lecture on the absurdity of women going to school. . . . I was crouched on the piano chair, silent, while he angrily walked three steps back and three steps forth, releasing his indignation sternly in harsh turns of phrase directed at the door or the piano."[8]

Kubizek does not remember "a single situation where he was able to let go of himself with regard to the opposite sex. At the same time I can absolutely confirm that both physically and sexually, Adolf was entirely normal."[9]

According to Kubizek, Hitler had certainly not had any homosexual leanings. To illustrate this, he describes the advances of a rich, older homosexual, whom nineteen-year-old Hitler had indignantly rejected, saying homosexuality had to be "fought as a perverse phenomenon, by any means possible." Hitler said he kept "such people away from himself with a downright anxious conscientiousness" and turned "against this and other sexual perversions in the big city with nausea and disgust," and he had also rejected "self-gratification, so prevalent among young people."[10] Neither is there the slightest indication that Hitler displayed homosexual tendencies during his years in the men's hostel, which Reinhold Hanisch certainly would not have failed to mention.

Rudolf Häusler, who was four years younger than Hitler and shared a room with him in Munich in 1913–14, does not allude anywhere to a more than friendly relationship between the two of them either. Häusler's daughter "simply cannot imagine this" with her father, who did anything but scorn women. However, she is also aware that he never would have told her anything like that.[11]

Hanisch reports that in the men's hostel, there was once an exchange of experiences with women. Young Hitler too contributed to the conversation by talking about Stefanie—something that had happened before 1910, in Linz. When asked why he had not tried to make contact with her, he replied that the girl had been the daughter of a high government official, whereas he was only the son of a minor civil servant.[12] As the culmination of his experiences with women, Hanisch tells us, Hitler had also given them an example of how he had demonstrated self-control: One summer he met a milkmaid in the country—in other words, in Waldviertel. He liked her and she liked him too. "Once, when he was alone with her, she behaved rather foolishly. But Hitler suddenly thought

Stefanie in Linz

of the eventual consequences and ran away, like the chaste Joseph, knock-ing over a big pot of fresh milk."

Hanisch, the vagrant who knew all the tricks of the trade, judged: "Hitler had very little respect for the female sex, but very austere ideas about relations between men and women. He often said, if men only wanted to, they could adopt a strictly moral way of living," in other words, abstain from sex. Besides, Hanisch said, his poverty and poor clothes prevented him from having anything to do with women.

There is another statement regarding the period in the men's hostel, which has become known only recently. It was made by the daughter of Hitler's frame merchant, Adele Altenberg. She reports that when she was fourteen years old, she sometimes helped out in the store, where she met young Hitler as he was delivering his paintings. The young man had been so shy that he had not even looked at her and "kept his gaze fixed on the ground."[13]

Finally, there are statements by Hitler's colleague Häusler, whom he did not meet until 1913. Hitler told him about his "girlfriend" in Linz as well. Häusler found it strange that on Christmas 1913—when he was already in Munich—Hitler placed an anonymous ad in Linz's local news-paper to send his "girlfriend" his best wishes.[14] However, Hitler appar-ently did not know that Stefanie was already married to an officer.

Through Häusler we can establish with great certainty the identity of that mysterious Emilie who is known as Hitler's alleged first lover in Vienna, in the following context: In her memoirs Hitler's secretary, Christa Schroeder, suggests that as far as the topic "Women around Hitler" is concerned, from the moment he "decided to become a politician"—that is to say, in 1918—Hitler abstained from all sexual activities. From now on "gratification [took place] in his head." "Everything was platonic!" Christa Schroeder said, and even his relationship with Eva Braun had been "a sham relationship." Yet before he became a politician—in Vienna, for example—Hitler did have lovers. Mrs. Schroeder substantiates her claim by recalling that once she had said Emilie was an ugly name, but Hitler had contradicted her, remarking, "Don't say that. Emilie is a beautiful name, that was the name of my first lover!"[15]

This Emilie, who was never before identified, was probably Rudolf Häusler's younger sister. In February 1913, when her brother met twenty-three-year-old Hitler in the men's hostel and frequently took him home, Emilie Häusler, called "Milli," born on May 4, 1895,[16] was seventeen years old. According to her niece Marianne Koppler, Milli was an extremely shy, sensitive, and often sickly girl who suffered from her extremely strict, tyrannical father's ways. She was not pretty, played (like many well-bred daughters of middle-class families) some piano, did a little handicraft, helped her mother with the housekeeping, and among the five Häusler children was the "cipherly," inconspicuous, and quiet one, and gave the impression of being fearful and in need of protection.[17]

The girl admired her brother's friend. At any rate, Mrs. Koppler states that Milli asked him to draw something for her scrapbook. Hitler did not comply right then and there, but promised he would bring her a drawing on his next visit, which he did. The picture, which was done with colored pencils, had the size of a postcard and—according to Häusler's daughter, who saw the picture as a child—represented a historic German with helmet, shield, and spear, standing in front of an oak tree. In the trunk, which was in the center of the drawing, was a sort of plaque with the conspicuous initials "A. H." Milli proudly put this card in her scrapbook.

Along with Hitler's two letters to Ida Häusler, this picture ended up "in Berlin" in the 1930s. Hitler probably managed to get hold of the originals. Perhaps they passed his private secretary's hands and he spoke with her about Emilie. Yet if he really called Milli his "lover" or Mrs. Schroeder only drew the wrong conclusion, cannot be ascertained.

After looking closely at the Häusler family relations, however, one thing is certain: Milli can hardly have been Hitler's "lover." According to her niece, the girl would never have been allowed to leave the house without a chaperon. Furthermore, there was mutual trust between Milli's mother and young Hitler. He surely did not want to annoy the only person in Vienna who helped him. Thus the Viennese "lover" Emilie must also be counted among Hitler's platonic relationships.

Double Standards

Before World War I, Vienna was a swinging and—in contrast to, say, Linz—downright depraved city with great sexual permissiveness. This permissiveness was tied to one's social status: it was practiced by aristocrats and artists, but also by the lower classes, to which Hitler of course belonged as a resident of a Viennese men's hostel. Whether farm hands and farm girls in the country, or unmarried workers and maids in the city, morals were loose.

One social group in Vienna was exempt from this sexual permissiveness, or, to be more exact, the wives of this social group: the middle class and all those who aspired to be part of the middle class. Bourgeois moral conventions, closely tied to the Catholic code, demanded from girls and women strict abstinence outside of marriage. In this regard social pressure was so strong that young women had a chance of marrying well only if they were virgins, and "fallen girls" or women who had even given birth out of wedlock had forfeited their opportunities in life. Therefore middle-class girls had to be protected from sex at all cost.

Young men, on the other hand, were allowed to, and even had to gain experiences in that area in order to "sow their wild oats," as it was called, to free themselves of the vice of allegedly nervewracking masturbation, and to prepare for marriage. Yet because they did not have the chance to have a romantic and physical relationship with girls of their own class, they were permitted—despite the public display of prudishness—to go clandestinely to prostitutes, basically as a necessity of health and "hygiene." In 1912 a scholarly Viennese periodical asked young doctors about the first women they had ever slept with: only 4 percent named a young woman who was a potential spouse, 17 percent a maid or a waitress, and 75 percent a prostitute.[18] Prostitution was accordingly widespread.

Hitler's contemporary Stefan Zweig reports that before 1914, Vienna's sidewalks had been "so cluttered with working girls that it was more difficult to avoid them than to find them. . . . At that time women's goods were openly offered at any price and hour of the day, and a man really didn't have to invest more time and energy in buying himself a woman for a quarter of an hour, an hour, or a night, than in getting himself a pack of cigarettes or a newspaper." According to Zweig, prostitution was supposed to "channel the nuisance of extramarital sex": "In a sense it represented the dark cellar vault over which the magnificent building of bourgeois society rose with an unblemished, clean and shining facade."[19]

Syphilis was rampant and the fear of infection ever-present. No social class was exempt from the disease. Hans Makart, the "painter prince" whom Hitler admired so much, died of syphilis. So did the last emperor's father, Archduke Otto. Statistically, one or even two out of ten men were infected. Zweig wrote: "In addition to the fear of infection, there was the horror of the uncomfortable and humiliating cures of the time. For weeks and weeks, mercury was rubbed into the syphilitic's body, which in turn made your teeth fall out and led to other health damages; the unfortunate victim of bad luck thus felt not only spiritually but also physically contaminated."[20]

The fact that most bourgeois men around 1900 had their first sexual encounters with prostitutes and sex was accompanied by the fear of infection, fundamentally influenced their image of woman and contributed to the general contempt for them.

There are no reliable data on prostitution in Vienna around 1900. All that is known is the minuscule percentage of those "controlled" by the vice squad, who were at least eighteen years of age and checked twice a week: in 1908 there were 1,516 of them in Vienna, a figure that remained approximately constant and was more than twice as high as it is today. According to official statistics on 1912, 29 pregnancies and 249 infections with syphilis were diagnosed during these checkups.[21] In other words, every year approximately one out of six prostitutes was infected and no longer allowed to practice her trade. This typically meant that she disappeared in the huge army of the "clandestine ones."

The number of "clandestine ones" was several times the number of those who were examined. The police checked neither the expensive and notorious VIP call girls, who appeared at the racecourses and in the theaters with their customers, nor the occasional hooker in the flophouses. Girls under eighteen and the numerous prostitutes who were already infected and ill were arrested now and then during a raid, but once they were released after being briefly held in custody, they continued to solicit.

Chaste for the German People

Hitler displayed solid knowledge of prostitution and syphilis. One evening in May 1908, after attending Frank Wedekind's scandalous play *Spring's Awakening* in the theater, the nineteen-year-old took his friend Kubizek to the old, rundown, red-light district by the Spittelberg: "Come, Gustl. We really do have to look at the 'cesspool of iniquity' once."

Kubizek describes the small houses and the girls in front of the lit windows: "As a sign that a deal was made, the light was turned off." Kubizek continues: "I remember how one of these girls found it necessary to take off her shirt or rather to change it just as we were passing her window, another girl fiddled with her stockings and displayed her bare legs. I was genuinely glad when we were done running the exciting gauntlet and had finally reached Westbahnstrasse, but I was silent, while Adolf fumed about the whores' seductive skills."

At home, Kubizek reports, Hitler gave him a lecture, "as cool and dispassionate as if he were explaining his stand on fighting tuberculosis or the issue of cremation." These "conventions on the market of commercial love," he said, existed because "man had in himself the need for sexual gratification, while the pertinent girl merely thought of making a living. . . . In reality, the 'flames of life' had long since been extinguished in these poor creatures."[22]

According to Kubizek, Hitler also elaborated on the history of brothels, called for the prohibition of prostitution, and as a means against this "disgrace for every nation" proposed governmental support of early marriages, in connection with a free dowry for poor girls, marriage loans, and an increase of starting salaries: "This salary is raised with each child and lowered once the children no longer need to be cared for."[23] Incidentally, the Pan-Germans had such plans in order to secure the health of young German men and thus the "race."

Kubizek states that his friend's moral views "were not based on experience but on intellectual realizations,"[24] but it would be more precise to say that the young man gained his "realizations" mainly from the Pan-Germans' moral teachings. In *Unadulterated German Words* we read: "Nothing is as exceedingly advantageous to young people as exceedingly long abstinence. Every muscle becomes tight, the eye begins to glow, the mind is quick, the memory fresh, imagination vivid, determination great and firm, and out of a sense of strength one sees the whole world as if through a multicolored prism." The "slight nervous disorders" celibacy entailed had to be accepted. At any rate, the *Unadulterated German Words* explained, it was by no means hazardous to one's health to remain chaste until one had reached the age of approximately twenty-five.

"Desire" had to be suppressed "through will power, by avoiding stimulating food and beverages (alcohol), as well as by a proper diet and a natural way of life." This would give one "increased energy, of which, as experience shows, particularly one's mental capacities, especially one's will power, profit. Thus, as has been proven thousands of times, sexual abstinence is the absolutely necessary basis for maximum physical or mental performance." Food "which stimulates the genitals" should be avoided: "This includes, first of all, meat. . . . To believe that only meat gives you strength is a fallacy." A vegetarian diet, on the other hand, was "a powerful obstacle to degeneration."[25]

The misogynist Jörg Lanz von Liebenfels also warned young men against corrupting themselves by dealing with women, especially prostitutes—not for moral but exclusively "racial" reasons. Young men, he argued, had the duty to keep the Germanic race pure and strong, and should not expose themselves to potential infection. Prostitutes were usually "racially inferior women," and the "German man" had to entirely leave them to their "racially inferior" customers, until they both would perish: "The superior race, he said, had no way of getting rid of the billions of inferior, hopelessly degenerated bastards if they couldn't be wiped off the earth by prostitution and syphilis! It will be the fire of hell, in which they will howl and gnash their teeth, into which all those shall be thrown who don't wear the superior race's wedding gown." Syphilis was "the worm that won't die, that keeps gnawing in one's bones and marrow up to the third and fourth generation, and that bores on until that thin branch falls off the tree of mankind. . . . That is the iron stylus, which crosses out unworthy and impure clans and peoples in the book of life."[26]

Kubizek mentions Hitler's main motive for being sexually abstinent: "As he often told me, he was afraid of infection."[27] Apparently he was not to lose this fear even later on, as a thirteen-page passage in *Mein Kampf* on syphilis shows.

Vienna's Pan-Germans considered syphilis such a devastating disease mainly because it impaired the health and the ability to bear children for several generations. "German man" was obliged to safeguard the Germans' predominance over other peoples, beyond one's own generation. On one hand this could be accomplished through "purity of blood and race"—in other words, the German man was forbidden to associate with Jews, Slavs, or other people of "mixed parentage"—but on the other hand also by being healthy and able to procreate ("quantity" and "quality"). With its high risk of infection, prostitution endangered the highest good: the "welfare of the German people."

Hitler the politician carried this Pan-German maxim to the extreme: *If I do want to believe in a divine commandment, it can only be: preserving one's species!* According to this opinion, it was only logical for Reich chancellor Hitler to establish brothels for "members of inferior races," as he expected this to accelerate their disintegration.

The Women's Movement

In Catholic Austria the women's movement had a particularly difficult time trying to change women's traditional role. It did not succeed politically but faced a wall of opponents who defended the order that nature had allegedly established.

Fully supported by Vienna's governing Christian Social Party, the church painted the ideal image of woman: the silent and diligent wife and mother serving church, state and, above all, her husband, and sacrificing and spending herself in the process. All prominent positions in church, politics, and society were held by men. Thus Father Heinrich Abel, a prominent Jesuit and friend of Lueger, preached only to men, as he wanted a "vigorous, manly Christendom." Once, when Catholic women occupied in protest a pilgrimage church before the arrival of a "men's pilgrimage," Father Abel cracked one of his popular men's jokes: he had someone get the key to the church, locked the women in, and preached to his men in the open air in front of the church, "greatly cheered" by the thousand amused male pilgrims. The women, locked in, had to wait inside the church until the men were finished with their service.[28]

Most Catholic women obeyed their priest and the Christian Social Party, and fought the allegedly immoral "women's lib movement." The Pan-Germans, to whom Hitler was politically close, also denounced "the degenerate women's emancipation fit": "The women's movement is the first sign of decadence. The decline of states and peoples has always started with the rule of manly women and effeminate men." An emancipated woman, they argued, was "androgynous—anti-German and filled with the Jewish spirit."[29]

Franz Stein's *Hammer* opined that the emancipation of women was the "beginning of one gigantic chaos . . . an intermingling of races which leads to degeneration and threatens to destroy all sound humanity."[30] Emancipation was "an immeasurable degradation of woman." Instead, women should entirely dedicate themselves to their German people: "You are the true priestesses of patriotic love. Carry out the duties of your sublime office! . . . Our fatherland's inner greatness and unity, and even its outer strength, utterly depend on you."[31]

In 1906 a Pan-German author established "Folkish Guidelines for Our Future" in the pamphlet *Ostara*. He suggested that in order to remind women of their duties, a "period of service for young girls" should be established, "where they learn how to conform to others, be quiet, and obey." "Man should stop seeing in woman only the animal of the opposite sex and practicing double standards. . . . We have to stop overemphasizing sexuality."[32]

The basic message was to preserve the old-established gender roles at any cost: man was supposed to be sensible and strong, and woman weak, devoted, and emotional. In 1935 Hitler said before the NS Women's Organization: *There used to be a time when Liberalism fought for the "emancipation" of women, yet the faces of German women and German girls were without hope, dispirited, and sad. And today? Today we see innumerable beaming and laughing faces.* National Socialism, he continued, had given woman the *real* man, the *brave, courageous, and determined man. . . . No German generation will ultimately be happier than ours.*[33]

However, there was one issue on which the Pan-Germans and the women's lib movement did agree on and on which both disagreed with the "Clericals" and conservatives: they promoted a healthy, natural way of living for women, approved of women going into sports—which the Catholic church still largely rejected as unchaste—particularly gymnastics, and they opposed the women's fashion of the day, because it was constraining and unhealthy, especially corsets. To quote the Pan-German "Yearbook for German Women and Girls": "Away with corset, knitted stockings, and embroidery frame, and out into the open air so you can steel your body by moving about. . . . A short walk when the body is squeezed together and absurd shoes cripple your feet is enough only to keep a doll healthy."[34]

Lanz von Liebenfels recommended for every "blonde" "a loose hairdo falling across the forehead, with a knot down by the lower neck," so she could "show the beauty of her long wavy hair, her long head, and her long face to their best advantage. . . . Especially if she is forced to be in dubious company, she shouldn't be shy about fitting cut and color of her clothes to her tall body, full bust, and supple hips and thighs."[35]

In this very vein—"German" also having to imply "beautiful" and "healthy"—Hitler berates in *Mein Kampf* our *foppish fashions* and demands *physical beauty* not only of girls, but also young men, saying *the most beautiful bodies should find one another, and so help to give the nation new beauty.*[36]

Women at Universities and Women's Suffrage

According to the *Unadulterated German Words*, everything was sacrificed to the "modern education craze," even "familial happiness and the welfare of the entire people." Woman should remember her tasks in the kitchen: "We have put the health of our people, which depends far more on pots and pans than is generally assumed, into the hands and minds of our housewives."[37]

What was entirely ignored was that around 1900, approximately 40 percent of all women were wage earners, almost all of them as untrained home and factory workers. They certainly did not have enough money to consider motherhood as their main job. Among the middle class too, women made very little money as homeworkers, mainly by knitting, embroidering, and sewing. Lack of professional training and complex social and moral obstacles made it entirely impossible for women to choose a profession commensurate with their talents.

The Dual Monarchy was backward even when it came to admitting women to universities. For while, say, the University of Zurich admitted women as early as 1863, this step took the eight universities in Cisleithania—Vienna, Graz, Innsbruck, and the German and Czech universities in Prague, Cracow, Lemberg, and Czernowitz—until 1897, and even then it applied only to the humanities. In 1900 medicine and pharmacology were added, and law in 1919. However, because the first women's high school was not established until 1903, women even then went to college only very gradually: young women had to prepare at home for earning their high school diploma and approval of their college application.

From the beginning there was an unexpected phenomenon in Cisleithania: there was a higher percentage of Jewish woman students, on all educational levels. In the academic year 1908–09, of the 2,510 students at secondary schools for girls in Lower Austria, including Vienna, 44.5 percent were Catholic—somewhat more than half of the Catholic share of approximately 80 percent of the population; 11.6 percent were Protestants, which was almost twice as many as the Protestant 6 percent share of the population; 40.7 percent of all woman students, however, were "Israelites,"[38] which was four to five times as much as the Jewish share of the population. This peculiarity was even more pronounced when it came to high schools and universities, inasmuch as fewer and fewer Catholic women tried to get a higher education.

The figures for Cisleithania are even more distinct: In 1912–13 there were altogether thirty-two high schools for girls, three of them in Lower Austria including Vienna, four in Bohemia, yet in poor Galicia of all provinces, twenty-one (the schools were smaller, however).[39] Usually the students were not Polish but Jewish girls whose native tongue was Yiddish. In their thirst for an education they later went to Vienna to go to college.

Reunion weiblicher Berufe.

"Reunion of professional women." "Come on in! Here you can see the
first woman apothecary, the first aviatrix, the first woman athlete, the first
woman band leader, the first woman lawyer, and the lady without belly!"
As an unmistakable hint, a Jewess is sitting at the cashier. (*Kikeriki*)

In 1906–07, 51.2 percent of all female medical students in Vienna were
religious Jews, and in 1908–09, 68.3 percent.[40]

The Catholic church's traditional opposition to education plays a
part here, as well as its specific moral objections to the study of medicine. The church argued that it jeopardized the girls' morality, led them
away from faith, and promoted unchastity: after all, a woman student of
medicine might see strange naked men, which was bound to deter potential husbands. Under these circumstances, a young woman from a
Catholic family faced difficulties, for in wanting to go to school, she
typically had to flout her family's wishes. In Jewish families, however,
education and erudition had always been considered very important.
Children were not prevented from going to school but were instead
strongly encouraged to pursue their goals, no matter how poor they were.
In those days, Jewish boys and girls were typically allowed to get an equally good education.

These well-educated women then became more involved in women's
liberation. Politically they favored the Social Democrats, who supported
women's rights the most and, in addition, were neither anti-Semitic nor
antieducation. Therefore the battle for women's rights was considered a
Jewish, Social Democratic, immoral, and degenerate battle.

The Pan-German "Yearbook for German Women and Girls" constantly admonished women to preserve traditional female virtues: "The
German house is still German woman's stronghold. Yet many an inimical

power is fighting for it; admittance is denied the fresh Jew, but not Jewish freshness; its words find admittance via the press, and drop by drop the poison penetrates the hearts, the poison of a non-German outlook on life."[41] *Der Hammer*, the periodical whose purpose it was to fight Social Democracy, viewed the women's movement as part of "Jewish modernism": "Social Democracy uses the women's movement to more effectively fight the national state and bourgeois culture."[42]

For the sake of comparison, here is what Reich chancellor Hitler said at the conference of the NS Women's Organization in Nuremberg in 1934: *The term women's liberation is only a term invented by the Jewish intellect, and its content is characterized by the same spirit. In the truly good times of German life German woman never had to liberate herself.*[43] Among women there was a need for *fighters who don't look at the rights some Jewish intellectualism is deceptively suggesting to them, but who look at the duties with which nature burdens all of us.*[44]

When the Social Democrats held a "Woman's Day" in Vienna in 1912, where they called for women's suffrage, the Christian Social *Brigittenauer Bezirks-Nachrichten* derided them by saying that more than half of the "woman proletarians" represented there had been "older and younger Jewesses who looked quite unproletarian." Neither did one have to look far to encounter the charge of "immorality" and "free love." The newspaper proceeded to prove the absurdity of women's rights by mentioning none other than "the used-up female individuals whom you run into in the labor districts wherever you go. In eighty out of one hundred cases these are the victims of the 'more sublime relationship between the two sexes' which Marx predicted and which assigns women the role of the working animals' slaves."[45]

In 1912 Stein's *Hammer* challenged its readers to join the "German League Against Women's Liberation" and called for "keeping traditional order and tried and true customs, according to which the active and the passive right to vote for state assemblies as well as communities and legislatures have to remain restricted to men. We believe that according to their entire nature, women are not destined to fight those fights that today automatically accompany the right to vote." Women's suffrage would not result in anything but "even more political parties, even more candidates, and more election abuses" anyway. Again the *Hammer* charged that feminists were largely members of the chosen people, "which isn't aiming for equal rights but for predominance." The conclusion: "German woman is too good for this."[46]

Jokes about feminists pepped up the atmosphere during political

Ein Erfolg des roten „Frauentages".

One of the red "Woman's Day" successes. Viktor Adler as a pioneer of women's suffrage in a caricature in the Christian Social *Kikeriki*.

gatherings. Lueger, Wolf, Stein, and Schönerer knew this, and so did Hitler the politician, who liked to work pertinent derisive comments into his speeches, to the great amusement of his audiences.

During a private talk, Hitler explained that he employed this tactic quite consciously against self-confident Social Democratic oppositional woman speakers: "He said he had always ridiculed women in the Marxist camp who contributed to discussions by mentioning holes in their stockings or claiming their children had lice or something to that effect. Since women couldn't be convinced by reason, but on the other hand one couldn't have them removed by security without turning the mood of the assembled group against oneself, this was the best way of dealing with them."[47]

The Cult of the German Mother

The goal of female education must invariably be the future mother.[48] This quote from *Mein Kampf* is entirely in line with general public opinion in Vienna—and elsewhere—around 1900. In mixed-language areas the role of the mother was always specially emphasized. There women were sublimely important as "protectors of folkish purity," and they were urged to give their "people" as many children as possible.

It was the policy of all nationalities in the multiethnic empire to aim for as high a "folkish" birthrate as possible. Pointing out their high birthrate, the Slavs demanded more political rights, whereas their low birthrate served the Germans as a reason to appeal to the "German woman" to be prepared to make sacrifices for her people and to bear more children.

In Parliament, for example, Christian Social deputy Hermann Bielohlawek complained: "German women no longer bear children. Our civilized nation has regressed to a level of one or two children per family. And the gentlemen Slavs—please excuse the expression—still produce them as if in factories. (Amusement.) In that case, of course, there will be more Czechs than Germans. But you can't expect the government to do things it can't do."[49]

And to quote the *Unadulterated German Words*: "Folkish circles are right in pointing out woman's significant role in training our children in regard to our national concerns." And: "We need woman's cooperation in achieving our high goal of physically and mentally enlarging and strengthening our people." And: "We best get at our youth via their mothers. There is a tremendous amount of work that would have to be done in this respect, in associations for young males and females, from preschool to the sports arena to the apprenticeship workshop. And women will supply us with a large number of national workers."[50]

Part of the issue was raising young men to be soldiers. Under the title "A Genuine German Woman and Mother," the Pan-German "Yearbook for German Women and Girls" praised a heroic mother who had urged her soldier sons before a battle: "My love for you will be requited if you are the first ones during the attack and the last ones during retreat!" The "Yearbook" 's comment: "Would that all women raised their sons in the essential and Pan-German spirit—even during the quiet days of peace—so that at times of national hardship an army of enthusiastic soldiers will protect German land and German folkdom."[51]

Hitler had the following to say about this before the National Socialist Women's Organization: *What men contribute in heroic courage on the battlefield, women contribute in constant patient dedication, constant patient suffering and forbearance. Every child she bears is a battle she endures for the life and death of her people. And, in Mein Kampf:*[52] *Marriage cannot be an end in itself, but must serve the one higher goal, the increase and preservation of the species and the race. This alone is its meaning and its task.*[53]

In return for their service to the German people the Führer gave German mothers with the most children the Mother's Cross: in bronze for four or five children, in silver for six or seven, and in gold for eight or more.

Hitler witnessed the great political effect of the display of love for one's mother in his idol, Vienna's mayor Karl Lueger. Women adored "handsome Karl," but he remained single and practiced a public cult of his mother. Everyone in Vienna knew that as a widow Lueger's mother had made ends meet for her family with a tobacconist's store and that she had worshipped her only son, who went to college.

In Reverend Franz Stauracz's biography of Lueger, which appeared in 1907 and with which young Hitler was surely familiar, Lueger's mother receives effusive praise: "She loved him with maternal tenderness; she cherished him, her only son, all her life with a pride full of hope, and he cherished his mother in return, thinking of her with moving piety to this day." Lueger even insisted on including a picture of his mother in the official mayor's portrait at city hall: "That way she shall live on, together with him, in the memory of the people, and he who mentions her name, shall never forget that Dr. Lueger could become who he is only under his mother's influence: a great man in difficult times, *a man of Providence*."[54]

Twice a year the mayor visited his parents' grave with a large entourage, including many journalists. He left the impression that no woman could ever jeopardize his virtue, and in public he appeared only in the company of his sisters Rosa and Hildegard, who kept house for him. When he became ill, nuns joined them as nurses.

However, this did not mean that there were no women in Lueger's life. Yet his lovers had to remain in the background and never appeared beside the mayor in public. He refused to get married, reasoning with his lover, the painter Marianne Beskiba, who was pushing him: "I still want to achieve something, and for that I need the women, and you know how horrible jealousy is."[55] "The women," these were above all the members of the Christian Association of Women, his "Amazon Corps." Marianne Beskiba writes: "He flattered women by suggesting to them how supremely powerful they were over their husbands—'a smart woman can achieve anything, she'll always have her will; simply influence men, then everything will work out.' This drove women, whom 'handsome Karl' had made recognize their dignity and power, to veritable ecstasy. Countless gatherings took place, and in the end 'He' would appear as the pièce de résistance, welcomed by frenetic applause."[56]

Whenever someone publicly addressed the issue of his not being married, Lueger always gave the famous, much-applauded reply—he had no time for a personal life, let alone a family. For he only belonged to "my Viennese." Only one year after his death, the astonished public learned that Lueger had never married out of careful political deliberation: Marianne Beskiba expressed her disappointment and anger about the tremendous poverty in which she had to live in a self-published book of memoirs, which included facsimiles of unambiguous, highly erotic letters by Lueger that left no doubt as to the nature of their relationship. This created a huge scandal, of which Hitler was bound to have taken notice.

In any case, Hitler did witness in Vienna women's euphoric, even hysterical sacrificial acts for a charismatic politician. Later on he was to manage just as brilliantly to assign to women this very same part so they would serve his political purposes. In order to win over "his" women, he flattered them, yet he always accepted them merely as servants, never as partners.

It is impossible to overlook the parallels between Lueger's political style and that of Reich chancellor Hitler. If the former allegedly only belonged to the Viennese, Hitler was later to formulate: *My lover is Germany*.[57] And he too would use a sort of Amazon Corps as an argument when he said, *jokingly, one couldn't even imagine what the women and girls in the NS movement would do if he got married. He would immediately lose in popularity*. And he *seriously* stressed *that he couldn't even think of getting married, because he belonged to the whole people and the reconstruction dedicated to this people. Without a doubt, he said, he was not born to enjoy life, but to shape it*.[58] While he was alive, Germans did not know there was an Eva Braun in his life.

As for Lueger, so for Hitler there was only one woman worthy of his reverence: his mother. She played an important, and even dominating role in his life. During World War I he carried her crumpled little photograph in his chest pocket. Later on he had portraits of her painted in oil after this photo. All eyewitnesses reported that the picture of his mother was the only personal picture that was ever in any of his bedrooms, and it always hung in a prominent place.[59]

Klara Hitler had died shortly before Christmas, and so Hitler made that holiday her annual memorial day. His servant Karl-Wilhelm Krause reported about the years 1934 to 1936 that Hitler did not allow a Christmas tree in his house, would always withdraw from Christmas Eve to Boxing Day, and have food and newspapers put in front of his door, explaining, as Krause probably embellished romantically, and in any case not quite correctly, "My mother died on a Christmas Eve under the Christmas tree."[60]

It is worthy of note that he spent these lonely days of mourning for his mother in the room where his niece Geli Raubal died; she had shot herself in 1931 at the age of twenty-three after a fight with him. Geli (Angelika) was the child with whom Hitler's half-sister Angela Raubal was pregnant when Mother died, and who was born shortly after Klara Hitler's funeral in Linz on January 4, 1908. Hitler the politician took his nineteen-year-old niece into his household, just as his father Alois had taken in his sixteen-year-old niece Klara Pölzl from Waldviertel. In this relationship—definitely the most emotional one Hitler ever had with a woman—his mother thus played an important role that can certainly not be explained only rationally.

In public, Hitler the politician particularly liked to stress that his mother's true significance was in him, her son: *Compared to all those educated, intellectual women, my mother certainly was only a little woman . . . but she has given the German people a great son.*[61] When he made Klara Hitler's birthday, August 12, the "day of honor for the German mother," this public mother cult was mainly part of the Führer cult.

12
Before the Great War

The Last Year at the Men's Hostel

We have no fewer than three reports independent of each other, from Hitler's last year in Vienna, 1912–13, written by his hostel coresidents Anonymous from Brünn, Karl Honisch, and Rudolf Häusler. Anonymous, who met Hitler in the spring of 1912, reports about the twenty-three-year-old's appearance: "The upper half of his body was covered almost down to his knees by a bicycle coat of indeterminate color, perhaps gray or yellow. He had an old, gray, soft hat whose ribbon was missing." He wore his hair down to his shoulders, and his beard was unruly. "In response to my question of why he never took off his coat, even though he was sitting in a well-heated room, he confessed with embarrassment that unfortunately he didn't have a shirt either. The elbows in his coat and the bottom of his pants were one single hole as well." The soles of his shoes were worn through and had been replaced by paper, so that in the wintertime he could not possibly go out into the street. Hitler had been so sparing with food that Anonymous sometimes gave him some bread, butter, or a few pieces of ham fat from the butcher.

At the time, Anonymous reports, Hitler had sat in the hostel's reading room all day painting pictures: "He copied from an old little book which at the time middle-class pupils received as a memento." No doubt this was the richly illustrated booklet *Vienna for the Past Sixty Years*, which the City of Vienna gave away to all Viennese pupils and municipal shelters in 1908, the anniversary year. It contained Vienna's most famous buildings and views. The similarity to Hitler's paintings is indeed remarkable.

According to Anonymous, Hitler received 2 to 3.60 kronen at the most for his pictures per piece—significantly less than when he was working with Reinhold Hanisch. A retiree sold two to three of the paintings per week.[1] When these figures are added up, Hitler's monthly income was between twenty and forty kronen, an amount on which it was impossible to live, especially not now that he no longer received an orphan's allowance.

Hitler confessed to Anonymous that he had "really gone to the Academy of Arts only for a few semesters and then dropped out": "on the one hand, because he did too much political work in students' associations, and on the other, because he lacked the money for continuing his studies." These statements clearly sound like Hitler and his fantasy about the student who was persecuted because he was political. He explained to Anonymous why he dropped out of school in a similar manner: that he was by no means asked to leave because of his poor achievements, but for political reasons, because he had endorsed Georg Schönerer's "Away from Rome" movement. So even that early Hitler tried to rewrite his personal history, to turn himself into a resistance fighter, and to prove what sacrifices he had made for his political conviction—which is reminiscent of his story about the altercation with the construction workers.

At any rate, during that time things were anything but peaceful around Hitler. One colleague had reported him to the police because he had falsely assumed the title of "art school graduate." His old special enemy Hanisch had also reappeared. His friends lived in the men's hostel, and that is where he settled again for the winter, from November 28, 1912, to March 29, 1913, under the assumed name Friedrich Walter.[2] He had some regular income from his work for the frame factory Altenberg. Hitler supplied that company as well, so there was cause for conflict. Frequently the two "artists" also must have inevitably run into each other during their work in the hostel's reading room. Hanisch was most likely doing much better than Hitler financially at that time.

The general social situation in Vienna had deteriorated. Owing to inflation, even the men's hostel was now no longer fully occupied—only

95.41 percent rather than 100 percent. It recorded "a fluctuation of guests that has never happened before to such an extent." Compared to 1912, the rate of medical assistance administered at the hostel increased almost twofold. That indicates that many afforded going to the hostel only when they were ill and there was no room at the hospital. In order to make up for the additional cost, both model shelters in Vienna increased the price for one week to three kronen in 1914.[3]

Eyewitness Honisch, who met Hitler in early 1913, reports that contrary to most other shelter residents, Hitler had had "an even, extremely proper lifestyle" and was extremely frugal. He had worked diligently and every day painted a watercolor of about 14 x 18 inches. Often he executed popular motifs "a dozen times in a row" and received three to five kronen per painting—which confirms Anonymous's statement.

Honisch, who did not write his report until the 1930s, was commissioned by the NSDAP archive and therefore had to portray Hitler in as positive a light as possible, described the reading room as the meeting place of the men's hostel's "intelligentsia": "A relatively small circle of about fifteen to twenty people, who pretty much kept to themselves—there were men with graduate degrees who had somehow been ruined, retired officers next to business employees, men with small pensions, and others. Since I was an office clerk by profession, I was naturally drawn to that circle, where I soon felt at home. There were people with solid knowledge in their special fields, and there were also quite a number of eccentrics, of course."

He says that Hitler had "very much enjoyed" eagerly participating in the political discussions, which "often lasted for hours," and he developed "an incredible temper." Initially he usually had sat over his work, and listened to the others. "But if finally the opinions he heard really rubbed him the wrong way, he all of a sudden had to contradict. It then frequently happened that he would jump up from his chair, throw brush or pencil across the table, and explained his views in an extremely hot-tempered way, not even shying away from strong expressions; his eyes were ablaze, and again and again he threw back his head to throw back his hair, which kept falling over his forehead." According to Honisch, there were two topics which incensed him most of all: "These were the Reds and the Jesuits."

Honisch continued: "It frequently happened that he stopped short in the middle of his speech and sat down again with a resigned hand gesture, and continued working on his drawing, as if he wanted to say: Everything I say is wasted on you, you don't understand anyway."[4]

Karl May in Vienna

According to Anonymous, Hitler rarely went out in the spring of 1912. He was all the more surprised when on March 22 Hitler asked him "to lend him my second pair of shoes for a few hours. When I inquired what he intended to do, he told me happily that Karl May was giving a lecture in Vienna, and he had to be there." Posters announced the topic of Karl May's lecture all over the city: "Up into the World of the Noble Man." Hitler, in his borrowed shoes, set out for the long walk from Brigittenau to the Sofie Halls in the Third District. With an audience of approximately three thousand, the evening was completely sold out. May's appearance was such a special event because the seventy-year-old author was surrounded by scandal. Some time before, journalists had revealed that when he was young, he had spent a considerable amount of time in jail and prison for fraud and theft—and that he had never seen all those distant countries he so vividly described in his books. As elsewhere, there were heated discussions between fans and critics of May in the men's hostel. Hitler defended his idol, saying it was mean to use May's past to attack a great writer. Those who did were hyenas and scoundrels.

May's lecture was a tribute to the peace movement, to which he had dedicated his book *And Peace on Earth,* and an expression of his admiration for pacifist Bertha von Suttner. The sixty-eight-year-old woman, who sat in the front row as a guest of honor, acknowledged May as a "brother in spirit in matters of peace," defended him against all charges, and pronounced her solidarity with him: "we intellectual workers, who are holding the ladder on which mankind is supposed to climb 'noble-mankind.' "[5]

The title of the lecture was vintage Suttner. As a convicted Darwinist, she believed in the progress of humankind toward a state of nobility and goodness, peace and overcoming all wars, as if in a law of nature. As far as she was concerned, the "noble human beings," who had found the right way in working toward peace, had to lead the others, convince them, and thus accelerate progress toward the arrival of justice and peace.[6]

May conjured up the coming world of peace in his fairy tale about the star Sitara: "There cannot be three or even five different human races and five continents,* but only two continents with one single race, which however is divided into good and bad, having sublime and low thoughts, striving upward and downward. Physique, color of skin, etc., do not matter

---

*The German-speaking countries count only five continents: Africa, America, Asia, Australia, and Europe. (*Translator's note*)

at all and don't in the least affect a human being's worth or lack of worth. In Ardistan, there are the low and ignoble creatures, and in Djinnistan, the sublime and noble ones. Both are connected by the narrow, upward-moving strip of Märdistan with its forest of Kulub, where the 'Lake of Pain' and the spirits' smithy are.''

May said that man's goal must be to leave dark Ardistan, to fight his way to Djinnistan, and to become a "noble man." May referred to himself as an example: he too had been born "in darkest Ardistan" to poor parents. "Despite all my earthly sorrows, I am an unbelievably happy man. I have worked my way up from the abyss, hundreds and thousands of people keep kicking me back, and yet, I love them all, all of them."[7] In conclusion, May paid tribute to his "mistress" Bertha von Suttner, read from her latest novel, "Humankind's Noble Thoughts," and expressed his solidarity with her in her fight for world peace.

Despite the unusual topic, the audience, which had probably expected to hear stories about Winnetou,* was so enthusiastic that May was celebrated even after he had left the building. According to Suttner, they made "a demonstration of personal reverence, in protest against the malicious smear campaign that had been waged against him."[8]

The response of Vienna's liberal press to the lecturer and his audience, however, was derogatory: "What was particularly interesting was the lecture evening's audience. Petit bourgeois and suburban women and men, small white-collar workers, adolescents of both sexes, and even boys. Every one of them is bound to have a subscription to a public lending library and to have read all sixty volumes of Karl May's works, the fantastic travel stories and novels, whose authenticity has been doubted so often and which have even been the object of long, bitter legal suits. . . . May is a seventy-year-old gentleman; a gaunt, old-fashioned figure, with a half-bureaucratic and half-pedagogical head, which is surrounded by short white curls. He alternately puts a pince-nez made of horn or glasses in front of his cheerful blue eyes."

This article continued by saying the lecture had "really tried the patience of those in the audience who are not enthusiastic readers of May": "May explains his weltanschauung in a rather unstructured and erratic manner. He says he has always striven upward, toward a freer, spiritual world of noblepeople. He alternately calls himself a soul, a drop of water, and—his favorite—a mental-spiritual aviatrix, and now and

---

*Winnetou, chief of the Apaches, was the main protagonist of several of May's most popular novels, known to virtually every reader in the German-speaking countries. (*Translator's note*)

then reaches under the table for one of the numerous volumes of his collected works to read more or less philosophical observations, fairy tales, parables, and poems. The strangest thing about what he says is his seriousness, his bathetic and genuine enthusiasm, which has something of a religious kind of enthusiasm about it."[9]

In any case, according to Anonymous, young Hitler was "absolutely enthusiastic about both the lecture and Karl May personally." During discussions at the men's hostel he called him a "magnificent, perfect human being, since he was absolutely singular at describing countries and people from the most remote continents truthfully." When his colleagues argued that May had never seen the scenes of his novels, Hitler responded "that this spoke even more in favor of May's genius, because his descriptions are true to nature, and much more realistic than those of all other explorers and travelers."

The controversy about Winnetou's father became even more when May suddenly died ten days after his Vienna lecture. "Up into the World of the Noblepeople" thus became his legacy. Anonymous reports that May's death "deeply upset" young Hitler, who "was genuinely very sorry about it."

Even as Reich chancellor he is supposed to have taken the time to read all of May's works.[10] Despite a paper shortage in 1943, he had 300,000 copies of *Winnetou* printed for the soldiers in the field[11]—even though the undeniable fact that May's heroes belonged to a "foreign race," as they were "Redskins," native Americans.

Albert Speer wrote that May's books "uplifted him [Hitler] inside, the same effect philosophical books have on others, or the Bible on older people." Speer claims that May served Hitler "as proof for all kinds of things": "that is wasn't necessary to know the desert to orchestrate troop movements in Africa; that someone with imagination and intuitive understanding of others, who was as entirely alien as the Beduins or Indians were to May, could still know more about them, their soul, their customs, and ways of living than an anthropsychologist or some geographer who had studied everything on location. Karl May, he said, proved that one doesn't need to travel to know the world."

Speer recommended that especially when studying Hitler as commander in chief, historians pay attention to May's influence, in particular to the figure of Winnetou: Hitler had looked at him as "the prime example of a military leader" and "the model of a noble human being." Hitler had maintained that in this "heroic figure" young people could learn "the right concepts of noblemindedness."[12]

Pacifism and Armament

Even May could not make Hitler feel enthusiastic about pacifism, any more than he could most Viennese prior to 1914. During that time of frantic armament and constant Balkan crises the pacifists were considered fools, traitors against the fatherland, and "Jew lackeys." Austro-Hungary's pioneer of pacifism, Bertha von Suttner, author of the bestselling novel *Put the Weapons Down!*, winner of the Nobel Peace Prize in 1905, and a tireless fighter for mutual understanding, was considered ridiculous and provided popular material for the caricaturists. When Suttner's combatant Hermann Fried also received the Nobel Peace Prize in December 1911, the Viennese press all but entirely ignored it. If Fried was mentioned, it was only because he was Jewish, thus supposedly proving the theory that "the Jews" were pacifists, had no sense of fatherland, and were mercenaries of "international Jewry."[13] Baroness Suttner, who was born as Countess Kinsky, the founder of Austria's, Germany's, and Hungary's Association for Peace, was considered a "Jew lackey," for she had also for years been involved in the Association for the Defense against Anti-Semitism.

The *Brigittenauer Bezirks-Nachrichten* claimed that the pacifists were being paid by international high finance, the "mammonarchy," which cunningly tried to made itself the "ruler over war and peace": "It threatens to refuse granting loans for any war and thus to force peoples into eternal peace. This sounds rather conciliatory, but this peace could easily turn into a graveyard peace where the castrated peoples have to do slave work for the new despots in eternal servitude. The peoples' honor and liberty will have been forfeited for good."[14]

The German writer Adolf Harpf, with whom Hitler was well familiar, wrote in the *Ostara* series about "The Time of Eternal Peace, an Apologia of War as a Refresher of Culture and of Races," polemicizing against "our modern international peace giddiness," the "disgusting murmurs of peace by the modern international mixers of peoples," and "the bloodless ideals of the general decline of peoples in internationalism." The international peace of which the pacifists were dreaming was an "infinitely sad golden time of general decay out of 'laziness' . . . a time of general weariness of life, of a general, voluntary death resulting from a weariness of culture and life." The "moral driving force in the cultural man of our race" would thus make way for a "dime-a-dozen uniform structure."[15]

All of Europe, preparing for the apparently unavoidable "war of the future," supported patriotism and war readiness as much as possible. War flags were embroidered, collections for the Navy Club were made, the soldier's profession was glorified, and enemies were berated. Hardly anyone dared pledge allegiance to the "furies of peace." Against this, in a speech in Munich in 1929 Hitler remarked that wars *have at all times taken place to relieve the tension of a situation. This whole idea about global disarmament, however, is not an idea of peace but of preparation for war. In the old days wars were prepared by armament, and today, by getting one of the enemies to disarm.*[17] In connection with the Pan-Europe movement of Count Richard Coudenhove-Kalergi, who was also close to the peace movement, Hitler said: *It is the rootless spirit of the former residential capital of Vienna, that city mixing Orient and Occident, which is speaking to us.*[18]

Of all the parties, only the Social Democrats tried to fight the growing war craze. In October 1912, shortly after the outbreak of the first Balkan War, the International Socialist Bureau in Brussels followed Viktor Adler's suggestion and published a manifesto against the war, calling on the workers of all countries to "oppose" the war plans "with all their might."[19] On November 10 the Social Democrats organized a rally in Vienna against spreading the Balkan conflict. Wilhelm Ellenbogen pointed out: "We are not in the least interested in who shall rule in Sandshak, in Kosovo, in Albania, or in Macedonia. Austria's concerns in the Balkan don't require armed interference in that chaos, but only good trade treaties with the Balkan nations."[20] Adler also appeared next to French pacifist Jean Jaurès during the extraordinary Socialist Congress in Basel. He argued that even a victorious war would bring vast misery and mean "the beginning of the end of Austria as a state": "Austria has nothing left to conquer in the world without being shattered—a danger that is already alarmingly close."[21]

However, like the pacifists, the Social Democrats were charged with being mercenaries of the Jews, of ruining nations through their resistance to war, and thus of playing into the hands of the "global Jewish conspiracy." Along with inflation and social misery, armament grew dramatically. Between 1899 and 1909 the annual Austro-Hungarian military budget increased from 1.5 to 2.3 billion kronen. The annexation of Bosnia swallowed up 167 million, and reparations to Turkey 54 million. In 1909 battleships cost approximately 235 million kronen, and to this was added a large amount for cruisers and a fleet of torpedo boats.[22] In April 1910, the government had to take out a loan of 220 million kronen.[23]

The Airplane as a New Weapon

After 1900 all of Europe, including Vienna, became fascinated with the new "flying machines." Newspapers started new columns to report new developments and events in aviation. From a postcard depicting a blimp, which he sent to August Kubizek in the summer of 1908, we know that Hitler too was interested in aeronautics.[24] On July 1, 1908, aviation pioneer Ferdinand Count von Zeppelin went on his famous twelve-hour flight over Switzerland. The newspapers in Europe celebrated him as a hero.

Only a few weeks later, on August 4, an explosion destroyed another blimp on the ground. The cause of the sensational accident was widely discussed in Vienna, and the dailies argued about the pros and cons of blimp construction. When Hitler talked about Zeppelin's lack of success in 1942, this was probably a result of these discussions: "He said that the principle of only that being good which was in accordance with a natural process, also applied to aeronautics. Therefore the blimp was a completely insane construction. Its design was based on the principle of 'lighter than air'; the fact alone, he said, that nature had equipped not a single bird with a bladder, as we are well familiar with from fishes, proved that this principle was false." Therefore, Hitler said, he refused to ever fly in a blimp, whereas he was not afraid of airplanes even when the weather was bad.[25] Indeed, Hitler was the first politician to take advantage of airplanes, particularly during election campaigns. He liked to give the impression of being omnipresent when he appeared at several distant locations on the same day.

Hitler's interest in aeronautics is well documented. In March 1909, Viennese poured into an "airplane exhibit" on the Ring. In October, 300,000 spectators, among them the emperor, witnessed French aviation pioneer Louis Blériot's exhibition flight on the outskirts of Vienna. In March 1910 the airship *Etrich-Taube* set out on a flight from Vienna to Vienna Neustadt. The biggest sensation in aviation was the competition flight of eleven airplanes from Berlin to Vienna in June 1912. Some of the participants lost their way; others were forced to make emergency landings, were caught in thunderstorms, or crashed. The winner took five hours and thirty-nine minutes.

A third dimension of warfare was developed in the military in addition to army and navy: the air force. Dropping bombs was practiced with sandbags at the new military airport in Vienna. The pacifists' urgent pleas to place the new weapon under the control of the court in The

Hague turned out to be futile. All European countries worked more or less clandestinely on the military development and testing of airships. During the 1911 war in Tripoli bombs were for the first time dropped from the air. Pointing out that the enemy already had a secret air force, and claiming it was planning an attack, the military requested and received ever increasing amounts for its air force.

Writers painted horror pictures of what modern aeronautics meant, especially in regard to warfare. For example, in 1908 *Pall Mall Magazine* published an article containing "war fantasies" about a German attack on the defenseless American fleet.[26] In 1912 the *Neues Wiener Journal* published an article that depicted a German air raid on Paris: "The moment war is declared, all these airplanes will take off at a signal and, supported by the favorable wind they have waited for, set course for Paris at a speed of 100 mph. It will only take them a few hours to reach the Eiffel Tower, and in half an hour at most they will have dropped 10,000 kilograms of explosive materials on our capital. Each device carries forty kilograms of these explosive materials."[27] Articles like this almost always concluded with an urgent plea to expand the national "army of the air" as quickly as possible in the face of this threat.

Chaos in the Balkans

Unimpressed by warnings, the world kept playing with fire: after Austro-Hungary had annexed Bosnia and Herzegovina, Italy too took part of the crumbling Turkish empire by force, attacking the Turkish province of Libya without discussing this with its partners in the Triple Alliance.

The war in Tripoli lasted more than a year and tickled the Balkan princes' greed. Montenegro, Serbia, Bulgaria, and Greece formed the Balkan League. Adopting the motto "The Balkans for the Balkan people," they declared war on Turkey on October 8, 1912, with the aim of dividing the country's European part among themselves. Thus the First Balkan War started. The major powers involved in the Balkans, Austro-Hungary and Russia, were on the alert. Only three days after the war started, the Austro-Hungarian army requested an additional eighty-two million kronen in armament loans, which were granted against Social Democratic opposition.

Turkey was quickly defeated. However, the victors soon began to quibble about dividing up the loot, particularly the areas to be allocated to the newly founded state of Albania. Prince Nikita of Montenegro requested Skutari, which had been given to Albania, and occupied it. He would not be deterred even when an international fleet under British command turned up at the coast of Montenegro some time later. The headline of a Viennese newspaper read, "The Unbelievable Has Happened! Montenegro has audacity to throw gauntlet to all of Europe."[28]

Yet this Balkan prince was extremely deft at protecting himself; he married off his two daughters to the thrones of Russia and Italy. As late as 1943, Hitler would entertain his audience with Viennese stories about Nikita, the "ram thief": *To be sure, he said, in civilian life it would certainly be very difficult to marry a daughter if Dad has stolen rams and been in jail countless times; in courtly life, however, that's not a disgrace but an honor: there princes are hot on the princesses. To think that good old Nikita had been nothing indeed but a scoundrel who had fled Austria, who had committed nothing but one blackmail after another, and who always played the two against each other, Italy and Austria.*[29]

The prince revealed the superpowers' impotence and helplessness. Calls for "keepers of orders" and a forceful intervention in the Balkans by Austro-Hungary became louder and louder. The Dual Monarchy had shown enough patience, the argument ran, particularly with Serbia, and should not longer let itself be made a fool of.

Franz Ferdinand, the successor to the throne, a fierce opponent of Serbia, Hungary, and Italy, worked on plans to politically "clean up" the Balkans for Austro-Hungary's sake. He aimed toward restructuring the monarchy's dualism into a trialism, with a relatively independent Southern Slavic empire under the sovereignty of the Hapsburgs. This empire was supposed to attract all Southern Slavs in the Balkans, thus counteracting the Kingdom of Serbia's attempts to unite all Southern Slavs under its own scepter. The heavily mixed countries of Bosnia and Herzegovina were the main bone of contention between Austro-Hungary and Serbia.

At home, this plan met with the opposition not only of the Hungarians, who were not willing to accept such a loss of power, but also of many other nationalities in the multiethnic empire. Since 1867 there had clearly been discrimination against the Czechs, who had for centuries been the Dual Monarchy's third-strongest power. Now they had reason to demand independence. The Poles demanded a similar status for themselves. The Italians would have liked to take the chance to pledge their allegiance to Italy. And so forth. Once again it turned out that the slightest change in the Dual Monarchy's jeopardized the overall, complex structure.

What Hitler said in *Mein Kampf* expressed general public opinion: *Austria was then like an old mosaic; the cement, binding the various little stones together, had grown old and begun to crumble; as long as the work of art is not touched, it can continue to give a show of existence, but as soon as it receives a blow, it breaks into a thousand fragments.*[30]

Plans for a Preventive War

Ever since the annexation crisis of 1908, rumors had been bandied about in Vienna about the Dual Monarchy's alleged need to wage a preventive war, particularly against Serbia. Austro-Hungarian general chief of staff Franz Conrad von Hötzendorf worked diligently on such plans and gained more and more supporters, even outside the army. His argument was that Russia was rearming fast. The sooner and more surprisingly Austro-Hungary attacked, he said, the more the danger of a "big" war would be decreased. Among the many civilian supporters of a preventive strike were many who hoped to calm things down domestically, particularly the various national battles. The major part of the army—certainly its German-speaking part—was on Conrad's side anyway. The government went ahead with armament at great speed and expense. "Serbia has to die" became a ubiquitous slogan in Vienna.

In 1909 a prominent Viennese military newspaper published its lead article under the headline: "Before the War": "The hour has come. War is unavoidable. Never was a war more just. And never before has our belief in a victorious outcome been grounded more firmly. We are being forced into the war: Russia is forcing us. Italy is forcing us. Serbia and Montenegro are forcing us, and Turkey is forcing us." And: "The army is waiting for the tasks ahead, full of joyful anticipation. . . . We are entering the battle knowing that the Empire's future depends on us. . . . Our blood is boiling, we can hardly restrain ourselves. *Call us, Emperor!*"[31] Yet the old emperor was reluctant. In 1909 he was still able to preserve peace.

Conrad, who thought Austro-Hungary surrounded by enemies, also advocated an allegedly necessary preventive war against the monarchy's unpopular ally, Italy—in 1907, then again in 1909, and particularly during the Tripoli war. Popular opinion in Vienna held that Rome was only waiting for the monarchy to fall apart so that it could annex Trieste, Terentino, and South Tyrol. Many considered the Triple Alliance somewhat of a handicap; as Hitler wrote in *Mein Kampf*: *That anyone even for a moment should have dared to believe in the possibility of . . . the miracle that Italy would fight side by side with Austria . . . could be nothing but incomprehensible to anyone who was not stricken with diplomatic blindness.*[32] The old emperor opposed all preventive war plans. Indeed, treacherously attacking an ally to whom he officially always pledged loyalty, fundamentally violated Franz Josef's sense of legal ethics. He fired Conrad in 1911. At Crown Prince Franz Ferdinand's request, however, Conrad resumed his office in 1912, without having changed his opinion on Serbia, Italy, and the preventive war.

Later on Hitler, who as a politician was interested in good relations with Italy, dealt extensively with the heavily burdened relations between Austro-Hungary and Italy and exhibited sympathy for Italy's lack of love for the Hapsburg Empire: *Sooner would Italy have turned into a volcano than a government to send even a single Italian to the battlefield for the fanatically hated Habsburg state, except as an enemy. More than once in Vienna I saw outbursts of the passionate contempt and bottomless hatred with which the Italian was "devoted" to the Austrian state. The sins of the House of Habsburg against Italian freedom and independence in the course of the centuries was too great to be forgotten, even if the will to forget them had been present. And it was not present; neither in the people nor in the Italian government. At that* time Italy had had only two possibilities: *either alliance or war. By choosing the first, the Italians were able to prepare, undisturbed, for the second.*[33] In other words, Hitler too presumed that Italy was only waiting for the right moment to break the alliance and start a war against Austro-Hungary— exactly as Conrad had surmised.

Many personal letters and diary entries of the time document that all social groups were increasingly prepared to go to war. Even the emperor's forty-year-old daughter, Archduchess Marie Valerie, entered in her diary: "Continuing rumors about war. . . . Would it be wrong to think that a great upheaval such a war would entail would also have its positive aspects . . . that it would build up character, such as is lacking today?"[34]

The Pan-Germans, too, were hoping that war would break out soon, albeit for different reasons. They expected a war to lead quickly to the collapse of the multiethnic monarchy, and therefore, to German-Austria's annexation to the German Reich. The Pan-Germans considered the Double Alliance between Germany and Austro-Hungary a mistake: clueless about what was really going on in the Hapsburg Monarchy, Berlin was being pushed toward the abyss. The *Alldeutsches Tagblatt* constantly appealed to Berlin to leave the Hapsburg empire to its unavoidable decline and not to watch calmly "as directly by its national borders ten million Germans are being destroyed as a nation, which is creating a powerful state inimical to Germans."[35]

Hitler took the same view throughout his life, with identical arguments: Berlin, he said, *had no idea about what was going on inside their ally's country,*[36] and in his opinion should have withdrawn its allegiance to Austro-Hungary: *I solemnly confess that if Germany had been a National*

Socialist state at the time, as a statesman I would have dropped Austria. I would not have led millions into battle in order to save a political cadaver.[37] He believed that the war should have taken place much sooner: *But this was the curse of German as well as Austrian diplomacy, that it had always striven to postpone the inevitable reckoning, until it was forced to strike at the most unfavorable hour.*[38]

What with all his criticism of the Hapsburg monarchy, Hitler always made one exception, a general for whom he expressed his respect: Franz Conrad von Hötzendorf—clearly in part because of the latter's plans for a preventive war and the termination of Austro-Hungary's allegiance in the Triple Alliance in favor of strict power policies. In 1941 Hitler said in a monologue about commanding the army in World War I: *The most sophisticated military leader in the World War was perhaps Conrad von Hötzendorf. He clearly recognized what was politically and militarily necessary, all he was lacking was the proper instrument.*[39] The "instrument" Hitler was referring to was the Austro-Hungarian army.

On March 12, 1939, Hero Memorial Day, the Führer of the Greater German Empire put down three wreaths as a sign of his admiration: at Hindenburg's grave in Tannenberg, at Ludendorff's grave in Tutzing, and at Conrad von Hötzendorf's grave in Hietzing Cemetery in Vienna.[40]

In view of his thorough knowledge of military history, we may believe Hitler when he wrote in a letter in 1921, *Since my twenty-second year I most eagerly devoured writings on military history, and through all those years never failed to study very intensively general world history.*[41]

His knowledge distinctly reveals Pan-German writings. It was mainly in the field of German and German-Austrian history, as Professor Poetsch had taught it in his Linz high school, but also in what was dealt with in Pan-German history groups in Vienna: battles and strategies, from the Cherusci to the Liberation Wars, from 1848 to the culmination of German-national military history, the German army's victory over France in 1870–71, the necessary basis for the foundation of the "Second" German Empire.

According to Anonymous from Brünn, Hitler owned only a single book in 1912: the two-volume *History of the Franco-German War of 1870–1871*, presumably a "faithfully guarded treasure" mainly because as his father's favorite book it was a memento and a symbol of father and son's joint admiration for the German national Reich as created by Bismarck.

Anonymous writes: "Hitler very much liked to talk about that war's people and issues, and exhibited extensive knowledge. He had the same admiration and knowledge for the war of 1866.* He knew all the commanders of the war and admired Moltke and, above all, Bismarck the most. The latter was his greatest idol." According to Anonymous, young Hitler only excluded one Hohenzollern from those he admired, quite in accordance with the Schönerians—Wilhelm II: *That political baby dared fire Bismarck! Yet all his power was the work of Bismarck.* As Hanisch reports, Hitler dismissed Wilhelm as *a conceited babbler who poses for monuments.*

Later on Hitler liked to use his great factual knowledge to buttress what he wanted to prove with fitting historical examples. In a conversation with Hungary's governor Miklós Horthy during the disastrous situation after Stalingrad he recalled the battle of Königgrätz: *In war, he said, one always knew how bad off oneself was, but never how difficult the enemy's situation was. . . . If the loser had known how troubled the other side was, it would have persevered and been victorious.* He illustrated this by saying that in Königgrätz Prussia had been in an extremely critical situation around 4:00 P.M. *But the Austrians had noticed nothing about it, and so ultimately the Prussians' stronger nerves had prevailed. Around six P.M. Moltke could light his famous cigar, since the crisis was over. These observations, Hitler said, were also pertinent now.*[42]

Yet as we can see from long passages in *Mein Kampf* and *Das zweite Buch,* Hitler was thoroughly familiar not only with the course of battles but also with the content and problems of the treaties of the Double and Triple Alliance. To him, a preventive war against an ally was never a moral issue, but always merely a matter of strategy and power politics.

Attempt to Dodge the Draft

In order to increase the strength of the Austro-Hungarian army in the face of the constant danger of war, the government prevailed in establishing new draft laws in 1912. This law eased the draftees' obligations by shortening the period of active duty to two years, with ten years of reserve duty. However, the number of draftees was drastically increased. Until then, 103,100 men had been drafted, but in 1912, the figure was 136,000 men; in 1913, 154,000; and in 1914, 159,000, the majority of them from the empire's western half.[43] The law had been preceded by months of debates—in the men's hostel as well, as Anonymous reports.

*The war between the Prussian-Italian alliance against Austria that led to the end of the German Confederation. The battle of Königgrätz marked Austria's decisive victory. (*Translator's note*)

According to an old tradition, the Germans were clearly in a privileged position in the Austro-Hungarian army. Of 17,552 active officers in Cisleithnia in 1900, 14,581—83.1 percent—were German; in the ranks, only 36.7 percent were German. Even in the war year 1915, 761 of 1,000 officers were German, 568 of 1,000 reserve officers, but in the ranks, only 248 of 1,000.[44] The Pan-Germans called these privileges an excessive "blood tax" imposed by the multiethnic empire. The Pan-German newspapers constantly published reports about grievances in the Austro-Hungarian army and about the German recruits' sufferings in the multinational "Moloch the Military." Every father was bound to be "filled with fear and horror when his son has the misfortune of paying the blood tax."[45] The country was facing a war "which has to be waged not only with the Austrian Germans' money, but also with their blood, for one wouldn't dare use the Czech regiments, and the Polish ones stay at home, they have to be treated gently."[46] The Pan-Germans called on their followers to refuse the "un-German" state this "blood tax," "this acrid, utterly burdensome tax of constantly sacrificing to the Army the strongest and most beautiful years of every single fellow German."[47]

Hitler mentions the German soldier's role in the Austro-Hungarian Army in Mein Kampf: *Military service alone cast him far beyond the narrow boundaries of his homeland. The German-Austrian recruit might join a German regiment, but the regiment itself might well be in Herzegovina, Vienna, or Galicia.*[48] Obviously, Hitler did not want to serve in Galicia, Bosnia, or any other non-German crown province.

In any case, he tried as hard as he could to avoid military service. In the fall of 1909 all men born the same year as he, 1889, were called in newspapers and on posters to register for the draft in the spring of 1910. The draft list was kept in the young men's native towns—in Hitler's case, Linz. Yet there we find the same entry three times before 1913: "Unexcused absence, as he couldn't be located."[49]

Later Hitler would justify himself by claiming that he had done his duty at the conscription office in Vienna's city hall not in the fall of 1909, but in February 1910. Yet the city hall official had sent him to the district where he lived at the time, Brigittenau. *There I requested that I be allowed to report for military service in Vienna, had to sign a deposition or application and pay one krone, and never again heard a word about the matter.*[50]

We cannot check this statement, for such a document never surfaced—and Hitler was never summoned in Vienna. In any case, he was careful not to try this a second time, during the obligatory post-callups in 1911 and 1912. However, we do have to note that during all that time, except during the period when he was homeless, Hitler was officially registered. The authorities could have found him if they had wanted to.

Yet Hitler's plans to emigrate reveal that he had indeed no intention of serving in the Austro-Hungarian military. There was only one major obstacle that kept him from acting on his plans: his paternal inheritance, which he urgently needed, was not going to be handed over to him until his twenty-fourth birthday, on April 20, 1913.

Even long before that, Hitler was ready to leave for Munich. He diligently studied its architectural history, and had for years—for example, in 1910 to Hanisch and Neumann, and in 1912 to Anonymous— talked enthusiastically about Germany in general and Munich, which he was to call *the most German of all German cities*,[51] in particular. Anonymous reports: "He was full of praise for that city and never forgot to mention its great galleries, beer parlors, radishes, etc." Hitler had been dismissive of Austria: "He said that all they ever did there was to suppress talent out of envious competition and through its bureaucracy. Whenever a new talent arrived, Austrian bureaucracy had immediately smothered it. In Austria, he said, they put problems in the way of anyone with talent so he would be in trouble. All talented people and all inventors in Austria had found recognition only abroad, that's where they found fame and honor. In Austria—Hitler always said Clostria—patronage and a distinguished background was all that counted." "Clostria" was an anticlerical term the Schönerians liked to use.[52]

By comparison, Anonymous reports that Hitler praised *American freedom of competition* and *Northern German preciseness*. He had always complained: *If only I could soon get a better wardrobe. I can't wait any longer until I can finally rid myself of the dust of this country, especially since I might have to go to the military call-up. But under no circumstances do I want to serve in the Austrian Army.*

Rudolf Häusler

On February 4, 1913, a nineteen-year-old pharmaceutical apprentice moved into the men's hostel. Rudolf Häusler was from a Viennese middle-class family. His father was a "chief commissioner for fiscal supervision" at the customs office in Sievering, and his older brother was going to college. Rudolf was the black sheep of the family. Due to a gross prank, he had been expelled from school, and on his eighteenth birthday his tyrannical father threw him out of the house to boot. Since that time he had lived in various shelters in Vienna.[53]

He met Hitler, who was four years his senior and whom he described as a quiet, diligent man wearing conspicuously old-fashioned clothes, in the reading room of the men's hostel at Meldemannstrasse. As usual, Hitler was sitting and painting, and because Häusler also liked to paint, they started talking to each other. Gradually the older of the two began to look after the younger one, who was handicapped by bad eyesight and a thick pince-nez. Hitler, whom his protégé soon started calling "Adi," had sympathy for "Rudi"'s story, which was very much like his own. Häusler too had to suffer from his strict, dominant father, who even had the same profession as Alois Hitler.

Häusler had close ties to his mother as well. Because his father had forbidden him to enter his house, he would surreptitiously visit his mother whenever his father was not home. As a sign that he could come, Ida Häusler put a light in a certain window of the apartment. She provided him with everything he needed, particularly food and clothing.

Soon Häusler took his friend Adi along to Döblinger Sommergasse to visit his mother and three younger siblings. Ida Häusler, who was fifty at the time, a self-confident, educated woman from a good family, was glad that her unruly son had found a well-bred older friend, trusted Hitler, and was supportive of their friendship. Furthermore, she generously invited the obviously destitute young man to eat with them. Häusler's seventeen-year-old sister Milli soon had a crush on Adi, who liked the comfortable, clean bourgeois atmosphere which resembled that of his former home in Linz. Father Häusler remained invisible.

Rudolf Häusler was to tell his family again and again that he had learned a great deal from Adi. He had talked to him about the books he was reading and, above all, opened up the work of Richard Wagner for him. In his only written statement about his relationship with Hitler, Häusler said in 1939 that Hitler took him under his care, "enlightened me politically, and thus laid the foundation for my political and general education."[54] The nineteen-year-old apparently saw in the twenty-three-year-old a sort of father substitute. Hitler once again had an audience for his oratory exercises.

Later on Häusler also liked to tell about his first visit to the opera, when his friend Adi took him along to Wagner's *Tristan and Isolde*. It was the somewhat modified and shortened Mahler/Roller production, and the main cast was still the same as during Hitler's first Viennese *Tristan* on 8 May 1906: Erik Schmedes sang Tristan, and Anna Bahr-Mildenberg sang Isolde.[55]

According to Häusler, they had stood in line at 2:00 P.M. and then spent the long evening in the standing room. Hitler had been very excited

Rudolf Häusler

Ida Häusler

that night and during the performance also kept explaining to him the various musical motifs. Häusler, however, barely made it through the evening, for he was not only exceedingly tired but also extremely hungry. According to the playbill, the performance lasted from 7:00 until 11:30 P.M., and so the two did not return to the men's hostel until long past midnight. Still, Hitler's attempts at educating Häusler turned him into a lifelong lover of Wagner.

In Häusler's presence, young Hitler also raved about Germany. His departure date was getting closer and closer, and Hitler persuaded his friend to join him on his move to Munich, just as he had persuaded his Linz friend Kubizek to accompany him to Vienna. And just as he had convinced Kubizek's reluctant parents at the time, he now convinced Ida Häusler. Rudi had just finished his pharmaceutical apprenticeship and also wanted to go to Germany, a country that sounded so fascinating in his friend's descriptions.

On May 16, 1913, the Austrian District Court Linz decreed that the paternal inheritance be disbursed to the "artist" Adolf Hitler in Vienna, Meldemannstrasse, with the remark: "The cash amount will be sent by mail."[56] With interest, the 652 kronen per annum in 1903 had increased to 819 kronen and 98 heller, which was a considerable amount of money.

Hitler accompanied Rudi on his farewell visit to his mother, who gave her son plenty of clothes and linen. Hitler promised her to take care of Rudi in Munich. On May 24, 1913, Hitler and Häusler properly notified their police precinct that they were moving, without, however, indi-

Registration slip

cating where they were going. Hitler's new registration file has the entry "unknown" as his new place of residence. The next day Honisch and other colleagues from the men's hostel accompanied the two emigrants on part of the way to the Western Railway Station. *I had set foot in this town while still half a boy and I left it a man, grown quiet and grave*, Hitler writes in *Mein Kampf*.[57] Departing from Vienna, he had significantly less luggage than when he had arrived. At that time Kubizek had mentioned four heavy suitcases with many books, but now, Honisch tells us, he only had "one small briefcase." Among other things, this must have contained some watercolors with views of Vienna, those pictures Hitler had painted with particular care and did not sell but kept all his life.[58]

Before his departure, Hitler got himself a completely new wardrobe. Honisch still mentioned Hitler's "worn-out" suit in the men's hostel, but shortly later Hitler's landlords in Munich met a well-dressed, clean-cut young man, whom they immediately accepted as a tenant. The tailor Popp and his wife report that Hitler had not had a single worn-out piece of clothing at the time, and that his suits, coats, and underwear had been tidy and taken care of.[59]

In short, Hitler left Vienna the way he had arrived: as a neat young bourgeois who had inherited money from his father and now wanted to become an architect in Munich, the city of his dreams. *I was very happy going to Munich; I wanted to study for another three years; I planned to go to Heilmann & Littmann as a draftsman at twenty-eight; I would participate in the first competition, and then, I told myself, people would realize, This guy's good. I had privately participated in all competitions at the time, and when the designs for the Berlin Opera were published, my heartbeat started racing when I had to admit to myself, Much worse than your own designs! I had made theater my specialty.*[60] In *Mein Kampf* Hitler writes about Munich: *A German city! What a difference from Vienna! I grew sick to my stomach when I even thought back on this Babylon of races.*[61]

Hitler and Häusler shared a room in the apartment of tailor Popp at 34 Schleißheimer Strasse. When they registered with the police, Häusler produced his Viennese residence certificate.[62] Hitler, however, falsely stated he had no nationality. He doubtless did so to escape being reported to Austria and avoid proceedings against him there for evading the draft. He stated "artist" as his profession, which he later changed to "writer according to passport."[63]

Later Häusler would say that the early days in Munich had been very difficult. Hitler's money was quickly spent. Neither of the two men found a job. Again Hitler had to paint postcard pictures. Deft and energetic, Häusler tried to sell them, but the income was minimal. So they were frequently hungry and accepted any job, no matter how small. For example, they painted signs for a nearby dairy in return for milk and bread: "Curdled Milk," "Closed," "I'll be back soon," and the like. Häusler, who was good at building things, tried to make picture frames.

Soon their contact with Vienna and their fellow residents in the men's hostel petered out. Honisch says: "Two or three times, there was a letter or a postcard from Munich. Then I didn't hear from him for a long time."

Ida Häusler, who had waited for word from her son for quite some time, finally turned to Hitler, asking him to tell her how her son was. He responded with a two-page letter to calm her down. In the fragment of this letter which has survived as a photograph—the bottom part of the first page—we read: *tried extremely hard to find just a halfway decent job, this will certainly be no harder for him here, but rather, easier. Opportunities in the German Reich with its almost fifty cities with over one hundred thousand people and its gigantic global trade are surely infinitely better than in Austria. I dare say he shouldn't feel sorry to be here even if he couldn't work his way up, for in that case he'd be even worse off in Austria. But I don't believe that at all. In a country*[64]

This fragment also tells us how much Hitler's handwriting developed

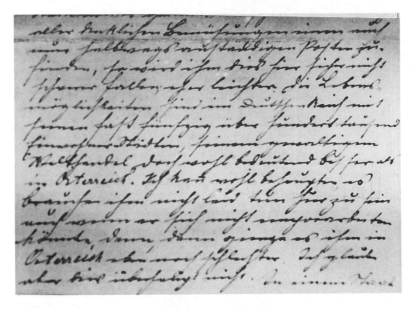

Fragment that has been preserved of Hitler's 1913 letter to Ida Häusler
from Munich

during his Vienna years. His spelling was now correct, which was probably
a consequence of his voracious reading.

The two of them discovered Munich together. Later on Häusler
would laugh when he told the story of how they once sat in the 'Bürger-
bräu' tavern, overhearing people at the table next to them berating Austria. Incensed, Hitler jumped to his feet, angrily interrupted their conversation, and defended Austria. Häusler, who was perfectly familiar with
Hitler's tirades against Austria, was flabbergasted. When he asked his
friend why he had suddenly changed his opinion, Hitler curtly replied
that as an Austrian, he was entitled to criticize his country, but a foreigner
who had no idea what he was talking about was not.

Hitler often had a similar reaction later on, when his audience was
overly ignorant of the complicated state of affairs in the multiethnic empire. For example, in 1942 he said: *People from the Old Empire haven't got
the slightest idea about nationalities; they grew up surrounded by a cloud of
stupidity. No idea about the problem with Austria! They haven't understood
that it is not a state in the sense we use the word, but a conglomerate! Austria
didn't have divisions, Austria had Czechs, Croats, Serbs! Blessed ignorance,
everything's in vain here.*[65]

Häusler was much more self-confident and self-motivated than Kubizek had been. He increasingly rebelled against his older friend's bossiness, particularly against his hot temper and pigheadedness. He also turned out to be less and less willing to listen to Hitler's agitated monologues all night. Häusler was to tell his family that it had been extremely difficult to interrupt Hitler's wet flood of words. He, Häusler, had at first tried to stop him by saying, "Come on, Adi, stop spitting! Otherwise I'll get an umbrella!"

In 1952, neighbors in Munich told the journalist Thomas Orr, who was the first to mention Hitler's previously unknown friend Häusler in the *Neue Revue*, about frequent arguments between the two men. Häusler, they said, had wanted to sleep at night, "while Hitler often let the kerosene lamp burn until three or four in the morning, sitting over fat volumes." They had also quarreled about politics, for Häusler had been a socialist.[66] His daughter reports that when the sixty-year-old Häusler got hold of the magazine in Vienna, he became angry, swearing that he would continue to keep silent about his relationship with Hitler, particularly toward journalists. Häusler said he had not at all been a socialist but a German-national, like his political mentor Adi.

In January 1914 Hitler was in an extremely difficult situation: the Austro-Hungarian authorities had caught up with the draft evader. On January 12, 1914, an official letter from Linz ordered him to immediately report for a callup. Noncompliance might result in severe punishment in the form of a jail sentence of four weeks to one year and a fine of up to two thousand kronen.

Hitler wrote a long letter back, justifying himself and swearing that he was innocent. He described his years of suffering in Vienna and his decency: *Despite the greatest hardships, in an often more than dubious environment, I have always kept my name clean, have no legal record and a pure conscience, with the sole exception of that missed military call-up, of which I wasn't even aware at the time.* He cited financial reasons for requesting to be allowed to appear not in Linz but in Salzburg, which was closer by.[67] His request was granted, and so in mid-February Hitler went to Salzburg. He was examined on February 15, 1914, and declared unfit owing to physical weakness. Thus he escaped military service in the Austro-Hungarian army and evaded legal proceedings for draft dodging.

The same day Hitler was in Salzburg to face the recruiting board, Häusler took advantage of Adi's absence and, after sharing a room with him for almost nine months, moved out. He took his own room, where no one robbed him of his sleep by giving him political lectures. Hitler could not help but accept this decision. Still, Häusler remained nearby, and for a while even lived in the same house and on the same floor.[68] He continued to sell Hitler's paintings and got by doing odd jobs.

The assassination of Hapsburg's sucessor to the throne at the end of June 1914 in Sarajevo did nothing to revive Hitler's patriotism for Austria. On the contrary, he felt satisfied, later saying that *it was the hand of the goddess of eternal justice and inexorable retribution which caused Archduke Franz Ferdinand, the most mortal enemy of Austrian-Germanism, to fall by the bullets which he himself had helped to mold. For had he not been the patron of Austria's Slavization from above!*[69] Hanisch reports that like the Schönerians, young Hitler hated this Hapsburg prince, whose succession to the throne would *cause the Germans' decline in Austria.*[70]

Hitler hoped for a major war and Austro-Hungary's downfall as *the beginning of the redemption of the German nation.*[71] And: *My own position on the conflict was . . . not that Austria was fighting for some Serbian satisfaction, but that Germany was fighting for her existence, the German nation for life or death, freedom and future.*[72]

On August 3, 1914, he enlisted as a volunteer in the German Army. He explained this step in Mein Kampf: *I had left Austria primarily for political reasons; what was more natural than that, now the struggle had begun, I should really begin to take account of this conviction. I did not want to fight for the Habsburg state, but was ready at any time to die for my people and for the Reich which embodied it.*[73] Häusler, however, returned to Vienna on August 3 to enlist in the Austro-Hungarian Army. This broke off the contact between the two men.

Because Hitler was fighting in the army of allied Germany, he did not have to comply with the draft into the Austrian *landsturm* a short while later. In 1932 Austria's War Archive and other federal authorities examined this matter thoroughly. The result of the examination was that Hitler could indeed not be called a draft dodger, inasmuch as he had no pertinent prior record.[74]

When the issue of his citizenship was discussed in 1924, Hitler had a public declaration printed, dated Landsberg, October 16, 1924: *The loss of my Austrian citizenship is not painful to me, as I never felt as an Austrian citizen but always as a German only. . . . It was this mentality that made me draw the ultimate conclusion and do military service in the German Army.*[75]

On April 7, 1925, Hitler, not quite thirty-six years old, applied for release from his Austrian citizenship, which was granted on April 30, 1925, for a fee of 7.5 shillings.[76] He was now a stateless person. Hitler did not become a German citizen until 1932, one year before he "took power." He carefully held on to his legal residence certificate, issued in Linz on February 21, 1906, as well as his old Austrian passport.[77]

A Political Career Considered Impossible

Häusler and Hanisch, Dr. Bloch, Kubizek and Samuel Morgenstern, his former fellow residents in the men's hostel, and his schoolmates in Linz were astonished by Hitler's political career in Germany, which began in 1919. Not one of them would have considered anything like that possible. His former colleagues understood even less why the same person who had once gotten along with Jews especially well was now all of a sudden supposed to be a leading German anti-Semite.

As they knew, Adolf Hitler was not particularly conspicuous in the gray army of casual laborers and the unemployed; he had no special talent, no tendency toward crime or the demonic. Young Hitler was a physically weak eccentric who avoided regular work, became engrossed in strange theories about the creation of the world, and idolized the "German people." He was a "quarrelsome fellow" with a hot temper who always had to be right and during discussions talked until the others were finished off.

What was most conspicuous about him were his mental rigidity, his inflexibility and inhibition, his fear of women, and his inability to be merry and have a good time with others. His admirer Kubizek said: "Being carefree and letting himself go . . . no, he could never do that." And: "He hated the typical Viennese from the bottom of his heart. He couldn't even stand their mellifluous, really very melodious way of speaking. Above all, however, he hated the Viennese way of always yielding and their dull indifference, their way of forever blundering along and living from one day to the next without a care in the world. Personally he was entirely the opposite in that respect."[78]

If one applies the criteria of the artistic and intellectual Vienna of the turn of the century, a man like Hitler was uninteresting. There was nothing ingenious about him. He was square and had the same common taste as the "little people," boasting that his father had been a civil servant. He had no original ideas, was not creative, not witty, and when he talked, he used phrases he had read elsewhere. Karl Kraus's much-quoted remark that when thinking of Hitler nothing occurred to him illustrates the general complete puzzlement about the career of this Austrian, of all people, in Germany. There were worlds between the Viennese fin-de-siècle and the "artist" Adolf Hitler.

Neither did anyone notice the "compelling force" of Hitler's blue eyes, which later became proverbial, or any other power of suggestion in him. It seems likely that Hitler, who had had oratory training with an actor, who practiced his gestures in front of a mirror and had them photographed so he could improve them, also practiced the supposedly irresistible suggestive power of his eyes. He wanted his interlocutor to interpret a look into his eyes as a transfer of power and used this quite deliberately as a weapon. It is difficult to decide whether it was pure irony or whether he was also partly serious when he said on January 27, 1945, before a meeting with the Norwegian head of government, *I still have some unpleasant work to do today. I have to "hypnotize" Quisling today.*[79]

To these deliberately developed skills must have been added a considerable degree of autosuggestion, a fanatical belief in himself—plus a perfect, painstakingly practiced way of staging himself within a theatrical set with all the theater magic available, light effects and music, flags and torches, and all of this underscored by and enveloped in a mood of religious solemnity. This must have added up to the impression of Hitler as a man of suggestive power—the German people's savior.

In any case, Hitler's career cannot be derived, let alone understood, from his situation in Vienna. This Austrian had a career only in the Weimar Republic. He returned to Austria in March 1938 as German Reich chancellor.

The "Führer" liked to emphasize with ardor how difficult it had been *to set out as a lonesome wanderer on the path from nothing to the top of the German nation*—as he put it on September 12, 1936, at a Hitler Youth celebration. The following day, before a combat formation of the NSDAP, he said: *That is the miracle of our time, that you have found me among so many millions! And that I have found you, that is Germany's good fortune!*[80]

Later on Hitler would glorify what he had got out of Vienna and taken with him into his new life: *Yet Vienna was and remained for me the hardest, though most thorough, school of my life. . . . In it I obtained the foundations for a philosophy in general and a political view in particular which later I only needed to supplement in detail, but which never left me.*

Hitler wrote this much-quoted sentence in connection with his sufferings in Vienna: *Only he who has felt in his own skin what it means to be a German, deprived of the right to belong to his cherished fatherland, can measure the deep longing which burns at all times in the hearts of children separated from their mother country.*[81]

In addition to his exaggerated, boundless love of "Germandom" and his dismissal of non-German peoples, Hitler also took along his contempt for parliamentarianism, democracy, equality before the law, and international organizations, for none of these could be brought into agreement with Germany's superior rank. He took along all sorts of theories he had read, which hardly anyone took as seriously and literally as he did: for example, the theory of the disastrous mixing of races and the purity of blood that had to be regained as a prerequisite for Germanic world rule, that could only be achieved by fighting the Jews, who were aspiring to the identical goal.

He had his decisive political experiences in Vienna: Dr. Karl Lueger taught him the tactics of a people's tribune who moves the masses to emotional outbursts, who sacrifices himself for his followers, the "little people," and increases their sense of self-worth by isolating a minority and relinquishing them to scorn. In his personal life the people's tribune is modest, lives simply, and has no family. Like a priest, he devoted himself entirely to his people.

Georg Schönerer taught Hitler the national goal of a pan-Germany that was finally also to comprise the Austrian Germans, in other words, that aspired to the annexation of the German parts of Austria, including the Sudetenland.

Franz Stein gave him the opportunity to study the aggressiveness of extraparlamentary opposition and the political goal of snatching the German workers away from the "international" Social Democrats and of returning them into the "community of the German people."

Karl Hermann Wolf taught him the tireless fight for Germandom. This is also where he must have realized how helplessly a huge machinery of power can be in the hands of a fanatical, terroristic minority. The warning example of the Hapsburg monarchy's warring German-national parties, however, also made Hitler recognize the necessity to overcome social as well as political boundaries within the "noble people" if he wanted to have any chance of success.

Hitler took along a great deal of detailed knowledge, facts and figures, whether it was the length and width of the Danube, the Ring Boulevard architects' years of birth and death, detailed designs of historical buildings with their exact measurements, the works of Wagner, tricky details of stagecraft, the battle plans of Königgrätz, or Germanic heroic legends— but also the Schönerians' "Heil" greeting, the List disciples' swastika, the Germanic cult, the idea of breeding, as well as Karl Iro's proposal to control the Gypsies by tattooing numbers on their lower arms, and many other things.

Yet it was fragments of his readings with which he left Vienna in 1913, a grab-bag that was preserved inside an excellent memory. It was only in Germany that all these pieces fell into place, as in a magnetic field, to form a weltanschauung on the basis of ethnic anti-Semitism.

Hitler the politician appeared in public expressly not with a party program but as the leader of a movement, as a herald of his weltanschauung. He wanted to arouse *in the hearts* of his *supporters the holy conviction that with* his movement *political life was to be given, not to a new* election slogan, *but to a new* philosophy *of fundamental significance.*[82]

He thus made National Socialism an aggressive community of faith with the goal of Germanic world rule by a strong Aryan race whose basis was to be formed by selective breeding and to be purified through the elimination of "non-German elements." Thirty years after Vienna's fin-de-siècle, the confused ideas of German-folkish sectarians combined with one political power in a Germany that was shaken by crises. It was a combination that turned into dangerous ammunition which wreaked havoc on the world.

NOTES

Chapter 1

1. Hermann Giesler, *Ein anderer Hitler* (A different Hitler), 2d ed. (Leoni, 1977), pp. 48 and 96ff.

2. Adolf Hitler, *Monologe im Führerhauptquartier 1941–1944* (Monologues in the Führer's headquarters 1941–1944), ed. Werner Jochmann (Hamburg, 1980), p. 405, entry of 25 June 1943.

3. Giesler, *Ein anderer Hitler*, p. 216.

4. Hitler, *Monologe*, 1 October 1941; Albert Speer, *Spandauer Tagebücher* (Berlin, 1975), p. 258. (Cf. *Inside the Walls of Spandau: The Prison Diaries of Albert Speer*, tr. Richard and Clara Winston [New York, 1976].)

5. Linz OÖLA, "Politische Akten" (Upper Austrian Provincial Archive Linz, political files), box 49. District Director Eigruber's minutes, written down from memory, of speeches by Hitler, 1941–1943; all other details on the Linz development project were taken from this source as well.

6. Hitler, *Monologe*, 27 April 1942.

7. For more details, see Evan Burr Bukey, *Hitler's Hometown: Linz, Austria, 1908–1945*, (Bloomington, 1986), and Ingo Sarley, *Hitlers Linz: Die Stadtplanung von Linz an der Donau 1938–1945*, Ph.D. diss., Technical University of Graz, 1985.

8. *Adolf Hitlers drei Testamente* (Adolf Hitler's three testaments), ed. Gert Sudholt (Leoni, n.d.).

9. Klaus Backes, *Hitler und die bildenden Künste* (Hitler and the visual arts) (Cologne, 1988), p. 103.

10. Goebbels, *Tagebücher* (Diaries), pt. 1, vol. 4, p. 652, 17 May 1941.

11. Eigruber's minutes.

12. Henry Picker, *Hitlers Tischgespräche im Führerhauptquartier* (Hitler's talks at dinner at the Führer's headquarters) (Frankfurt, 1951), pp. 244 ff., 26 April 1942.

13. Giesler, *Ein anderer Hitler*, p. 99.

14. Albert Speer, *Erinnerungen* (Frankfurt/1969), p. 113. (Cf. *Inside the Third Reich: Memoirs*, tr. Richard and Clara Winston [New York, 1970].)

15. Speer, *Tagebücher*, p. 142.

16. Goebbels, *Tagebücher*, pt. 1, vol. 4, p. 537, 13 March 1941.

17. Picker, p. 339, 29 May 1942.

18. *NWB-Kalender für das Jahr 1909*, p. 38.

19. MK, p. 3.

20. Franz Jetzinger, *Hitlers Jugend* (Hitler's youth) (Vienna, 1956), p. 81, quotes an eyewitness according to whom Johanna was a "hunchbacked retard."

21. Washington NA, *Hitler Source Book*, interview with William Patrick Hitler in New York on 9 October 1943.

22. *MK*, p. 123.

23. Hitler, *Monologe*, p. 324, 3 August 1942.

24. *Hitler aus nächster Nähe: Aufzeichnungen eines Vertrauten 1929–1932* (Hitler from up close: Notes of a confidant 1929–1932), ed. H. A. Turner (Berlin, 1978), quoted in Wagener, p. 425. In 1939 Hitler bought the badly rundown school, renovated it, and turned it into the home of the Hitler Youth.

25. *MK*, p. 6.

26. Albert Zoller, *Hitler privat* (Hitler in private) (Düsseldorf, 1949), p. 190.

27. Hitler to his aide Engel, in *Heeresadjutant bei Hitler 1938–1943: Aufzeichnungen des Majors Engel* (Hitler's aide-de-camp 1938–1943: Major Engel's notes), ed. Hildegard von Kotze (Stuttgart, 1974), p. 22.

28. Jetzinger, *Hitlers Jugend*, p. 69.

29. Goebbels, *Tagebücher*, pt. 1, vol. 3, p. 488, 22 July 1938.

30. Eberhard Jäckel and Axel Kuhn, *Hitler: Sämtliche Aufzeichnungen 1905–1924* (Complete notes 1905–1924) (Stuttgart, 1980), p. 1038, in a letter to Fritz Seidl, 16 October 1923.

31. *MK*, pp. 157ff.

32. Jetzinger, *Hitlers Jugend*, p. 92.

33. Christa Schroeder, *Er war mein Chef* (He was my boss) (Munich, 1985), p. 64.

34. Erwin A. Schmiedl, "Österreicher im Burenkrieg" (Austrians in the Boer War), Ph.D. diss., University of Vienna 1980, pp. 117ff.

35. *MK*, p. 158.

36. Jäckel and Kuhn, *Hitler*, p. 885, speech in Munich on 13 April 1923.

37. Eleonore Kandl, *Hitler's Österreichbild* (Hitler's image of Austria), Ph.D. diss., University of Vienna, 1963, p. xxxix, statement by Commanda.

38. *WSMZ*, 18 September 1933.

39. *MK*, p. 6.

40. Jetzinger, *Hitlers Jugend*, p. 72.

41. Alfred Zerlik, "Adolf Hitler in den Schulprotokollen der Realschule" (Adolf Hitler in the school records of his high school), *Jahresbericht des Bundesrealgymnasiums Linz*, 1974–75, pp. 36ff.

42. Jetzinger, *Hitlers Jugend*, p. 105.

43. Hitler, *Monologe*, p. 281.

44. Speer, *Tagebücher*, p. 259.

45. Kandl, *Hitlers Österreichbild*, p. xxxix, statement by Commanda.

46. Picker, *Hitlers Tischgespräche*, p. 277, 10 May 1942.

47. Munich, IfZ. ED 100, p. 42.

48. *MK*, p. 8.

49. Goebbels, *Tagebücher*, pt. 1, vol. 2, p. 681, 9 August 1932.

50. Hans Frank, *Im Angesicht des Galgens* (Facing the gallows) (Munich, 1953), p. 332.

51. Statement by Josef Mayrhofer Jr. in the film by Georg Stefan Toller and Axel Corti, *Ein junger Mann aus dem Innviertel* (A young man from the Inn district).

52. *WSMZ*, 18 September 1933.

53. *MK*, p. 51.

54. *MK*, pp. 12ff.

55. Kandl, *Hitlers Österreichbild*, p. xxviii, statement by Anton Estermann.

56. *MK*, pp. 14f.

57. Kandl, *Hitlers Österreichbild*, pp. xxiiiff., statement by engineer Josef Keplinger.

58. Ibid., pp. 25ff.

59. Ibid., p. 33, quotes Poetsch, "Vortragszyklus über das Nibelungenlied" (Lecture cycle on the Song of the Nibelungs).

60. Max Domarus, *Hitler: Reden und Proklamationen 1932–1945* (Hitler: Speeches and proclamations 1932–1945) (Munich, 1965), p. 836, speech of 25 March 1938 in Königsberg, similarly on 2 April 1938 in Munich; also sung in connection with World War I, for example, Hitler, *Reden*, pt. 3, vol. 1, p., 213.

61. Hitler, *Monologe*, p. 185, 8–9 January 1942. For other pranks at school see Schroeder, pp. 61ff.

62. Kandl, *Hitlers Österreichbild*, p. 71.

63. *MK*, p. 13.

64. *MK*, p. 15.

65. Jetzinger, *Hitlers Jugend*, p. 108.

66. Brian McGuiness, *Wittgensteins frühe Jahre* (Wittgenstein's early years) (Frankfurt, 1988), pp. 97ff.

67. Kandl, *Hitlers Österreichbild*, p. xxxi, statement by Estermann.

68. Linz StA, "Rechenschafts-Bericht des Gemeinderates für 1903" (City council's statement of account for 1903).

69. *MK*, p. 51.

70. Michael John, "Die jüdische Bevölkerung in Linz" (Linz's Jewish population), in *HJ der Stadt Linz 1991* (Linz, 1992), p. 115.

71. Harry Slapnicka, *Oberösterreich unter Kaiser Franz Joseph* (Upper Austria under Emperor Franz Josef) (Linz, 1982), p. 296.

72. Linz StA, archivist Ferdinand Krackowizer's handwritten diary.

73. *Linzer Fliegende*, 24 November 1907.

74. Kandl, *Hitlers Österreichbild*, pp. xxixff., statement by Estermann.

75. Ibid., p. xxiv, statement by Keplinger.

76. Speer, *Spandauer Tagebücher*, p. 112.

77. Hitler, *Reden*, pt. 3, vol. 2, p. 248, statement before the District Court Munich on 7 May 1929.

78. Linz StA, "Rechenschafts-Bericht des Gemeindesrates für 193."

79. Harry Slapnicka, "Linz, Oberösterreich und die 'Tschechische Frage'" (Linz, Upper Austria, and the "Czech question"), in *HJ der Stadt Linz*, 1977, pp. 209ff.

80. Kandl, p. 57, statement by Keplinger. S.a. interview in the film by Troller and Corti (see n. 51).

81. Coblenz BA NS 26/65/84, copy from the Leonding death register.

82. Jetzinger, *Hitlers Jugend*, p. 73.

83. Ibid., p. 70.

84. Schroeder, *Er war mein Chef*, p. 63.

85. Goebbels, *Tagebücher*, pt. 1, vol. 3, p. 447, 3 June 1938.

86. Hitler, *Monologe*, p. 64, 21 September 1941. Given similarly in the notes of

standard bearer F. Werner Koeppen, who was also present. IfZ Munich Fa 514, p. 23, and *MK*, p. 158.

87. Jetzinger, *Hitlers Jugend*, p. 116.

88. Hitler, *Monologe*, p. 288, 20–21 February 1942.

89. Ibid., p. 377, 29 August 1942.

90. *MK*, p. 18.

91. Bradley F. Smith, *Adolf Hitler: His Family, Childhood and Youth* (Stanford, 1967), pp. 97ff.

92. This reference and the following in Eduard Bloch (as told to J. D. Radcliff), "My Patient, Hitler," in *Collier's*, 15 and 22 March 1941.

93. Ernst Koref, *Die Gezeiten meines Lebens* (The tides of my life), (Vienna, 1980), p. 225.

94. Bloch, "My Patient, Hitler."

95. Jetzinger, *Hitlers Jugend*, pp. 125ff.

96. *MK*, pp. 18 and 21.

97. Hitler, *Monologe*, p. 190, 8–9 January 1942.

98. Helga Embacher, "Von liberal zu national: Das Linzer Vereinswesen 1848–1938" (From liberal to national: Associations in Linz 1848–1938), in *HJ der Stadt Linz 1991*, (Linz, 1992), pp. 83ff.

99. *Linzer Fliegende*, 22 July ("Julmond") 1907.

100. Krackowizer, 16 October 1907.

101. Coblenz BA. NS 26/17a, "Notizen für die Kartei" (Notes for the card index), 8 December 1938.

102. Hitler, *Reden*, vol. 3, pt. 2, p. 249. Statement before the district court in Munich on 7 May 1929.

103. Gerhart Marckhgott, " 'Von der Hohlheit des gemächlichen Lebens': Neues Material über die Familie Hitler in Linz" ("About the hollowness of comfortable life": New sources on the Hitler family in Linz), in *Jahrbuch des Oberösterreichischen Musealvereins*, vol. 138/i (Linz, 1993), pp. 273ff.

104. Krackowizer, 3 January 1905.

105. Jetzinger, *Hitlers Jugend*, pp. 131ff.

106. Coblenz BA. NS 26/17a, report by Renato Bleibtreu of 1 November 1938.

107. According to the kind statement by Kubizek's daughter-in-law, Mrs. Margarete Kubizek, September 1994.

108. August Kubizek, *Adolf Hitler, Mein Jugenfrennd* (Adolf Hitler, my childhood friend) (Graz, 1953), pp. 133–42.

109. Martin Gregor-Dellin, *Richard Wagner: Sein Leben—Sein Werk—Sein Jahrhundert* (Richard Wagner: His life—his work—his century) (Munich, 1991), p. 130.

110. According to the statement by Kubizek's widow Paula in the film by Troller and Corti (see n. 51).

111. Kubizek, *Adolf Hitler*, p. 36.

112. Linz OÖLA, "Materialien Jetzinger," letter by Kubizek of 28 June 1949.

113. Kubizek, *Adolf Hitler*, p. 23.

114. Ibid., p. 35.

115. Linz OÖLA, "Materialien Jetzinger," letter by Kubizek of 28 June 1949.

116. Jetzinger, *Hitlers Jugend*, pp. 143ff., dates the beginning of the one-sided love affair to November 1906 in order to disprove Kubizek; at that time the academic year ended at Easter.

117. Linz OLA, "Materialien Jetzinger," letters by Kubizek of 28 and 19 June 1949; Kubizek, *Adolf Hitler*, pp. 76–89.

118. *SJSW* for 1907 (Vienna, 1909).

119. *SJSW* for 1908 (Vienna, 1910), p. 206.

120. Krackowizer, 29 March 1905.

121. Coblenz BA. NS 26/17a. Statement of profession according to Gustav Hitler's baptism certificate of 1885 and Vienna StLA Meldearchiv (registration archive).

122. Kubizek, *Adolf Hitler*, p. 175.

123. *MK*, p. 19.

124. Kubizek, *Adolf Hitler*, pp. 146–49, with reproductions, original spelling in Jetzinger, *Hitlers Jugend*, p. 152.

125. *MK*, p. 19.

126. Vienna ThM, programs of the double monarchy's court theaters.

127. The claim that Hitler attended the Austrian premiere of Richard Strauss's *Salomé* in Graz (Erich Alban Berg, *Alban Berg* [Frankfurt, 1976], p. 18) is incorrect.

128. Kubizek, *Adolf Hitler*, p. 145.

129. All events listed were taken from Krackowizer, May through October 1906.

130. Personal report by Mrs. Marlene Exner, Hitler's cook at the Wolf Entrenchment, to the author in 1993.

131. Coblenz BA. NS 26/65, statement by Josef Wendt/Pewratsky of 17 November 1938. According to the instruction book, lessons lasted from 2 October 1906 until 31 January 1907.

132. Coblenz BA NS 26/65/38.

133. Linz OÖLA, *Einschreibbuch der Familie Hitler aus dem Jahr 1908* (The Hitler family's registration book for 1908): "Paid Haniaunt interest for May and August K175 H[eller]70," and underneath: Kronen "49.21" and "48.71"; in that context, see Marckghott, "Von der Hohlheit," p. 272.

134. Linz StA, *Adreßbuch der Städte Linz und Urfahr 1909.*

135. Coblenz BA, NS 26/65. The cashbook was first interpreted by Rudolf Binion in his book ". . . *daß ihr mich gefunden habt." Hitler und die Deutschen* (". . . that you have found me": Hitler and the Germans) (Stuttgart, 1978), pp. 14ff.

136. *MK*, pp. 20ff.

137. Jetzinger, p. 144. Interview with Mrs. Stefanie Rabatsch in the film by Troller and Corti. The extremely primitive portrait drawing with letter to a Miss Agnes in Linz (Billy Price, *Adolf Hitler als Maler und Zeichner*, [Zug, 1983], p. 63; Jäckel and Kuhn, *Hitler*, p. 1255) of 4 March 1908 is a forgery by Kujau.

138. Jetzinger, *Hitlers Jugend*, p. 143.

139. Vienna StLA, Registrar's Office. The address 29 Stumpergasse can be attributed to an error by Kubizek.

140. Kubizek, *Adolf Hitler*, pp. 310 and 187.

141. Ibid., p. 187.

142. *SJSW* for 1908 (Vienna, 1910): "Die Mieten in städtischen Zinshäusern" (Rents in the city's apartment houses). Compared to other tenement buildings, these tended to be cheaper rather than more expensive.

143. Ibid., p. 502.

144. Oskar Kokoschka, *Mein Leben* (My life) (Munich, 1971), p. 49.

145. *SJSW* for 1908, (Vienna, 1908), p. 380.

146. *MK*, p. 19. The examination works Price lists as numbers 40–43 are probably

fakes (Günther Picker, *Der Fall Kujau* (The Kujau case), (Frankfurt, 1992), p. 18), as is the commentary printed in Price, p. 105, and Jäckel *Adolf Hitler als Maler*, and Kuhn, *Hitler*, p. 1054.

147. According to Vienna's address book of 1910, the school was at 11 Gurkgasse. The Academy for Visual Art's classification lists plus figures for teachers and students taken from *SJSW für das Jahr 1908* (Vienna, 1910).

148. For the complete text of the tasks, see Werner Maser, *Adolf Hitler* (Munich, 1971), p. 76.

149. Vienna AHBK, with sincere thanks to the archivist, Mr. Ferdinand Gutschi.

150. Ludwig Walther Regele, "Akademieaspirant Hitler und Alois Delug" (Candidate for the Academy Adolf Hitler and Alois Delug), in *Katalog Alois Delug*, ed. Museumsverein Bozen, 1990, p. 41.

151. J. Sidney Jones, *Hitlers Weg begann in Wien* (Hitler's path began in Vienna) (Wiesbaden, 1980), p. 317, erroneously states that that four of the seven Academy professors had been Jewish.

152. Heinz Schöny, *Wiener Künstlerahnen* (Ancestors of Viennese artists), vol. 2 (Vienna, 1975), pp. 147ff.

153. *MK*, p. 20.

154. The Andersen mentioned in Goebbels's diary of 7 and 8 October 1928, who had just died, is not identical with R. C. Andersen, who did not die until 1969. Elke Fröhlich's interim register, Munich, 1987, needs to be corrected on that point.

155. Picker, *Hitlers Tischgespräche*, p. 267, 10 May 1942.

156. Ibid., p. 149, 27 March 1942. See also Kubizek, *Adolf Hitler*, p. 199.

157. Munich IfZ ED 100, p. 43.

158. Coblenz BA NS 26/65, copy of Dr. Bloch's cashbook.

159. Kubizek, *Adolf Hitler*, pp. 166ff.

160. Coblenz BA NS 26/65, Dr. Bloch's cashbook.

161. Bloch, "My Patient, Hitler," 15 and 22 March 1941. These memoirs by Bloch, printed in exile, are absolutely consistent with those Bloch wrote on 7 November 1938 for the NSDAP's party archive (Coblenz BA, NS 26/65). Quotes henceforth are from the issues of *Collier's*.

162. Kubizek, *Adolf Hitler*, p. 152.

163. According to Linz dailies, Krackowizer, and Kubizek, *Adolf Hitler*, p. 170. Marlis Steinert's claim (Hitler [Munich, 1994], p. 37) that there had been heavy snow flurries on that day and that for that reason Hitler had developed "an aversion to snow in later years" is an example of false facts leading to false hypotheses.

164. Kubizek, *Adolf Hitler*, pp. 169ff.

165. The drawings "Father's Gravestone" and "Leonding Church," published in Price, *Adolf Hitler als Maler*, pp. 50–52, are by Kujau, as is the letter of 4 August 1907 to mother and sister, published in Jäckel and Kuhn, *Hitler*, p. 1253.

166. *MK*, p. 204.

167. Coblenz BA NS 26/65/39.

168. Ibid.

169. This hypothesis was put forth by Rudolph Binion.

170. In her letter to *Spiegel* magazine (no. 7/1978) Mrs. Kren also vehemently contradicted Rudolph Binion's charges against Dr. Bloch that he had tortured Hitler's mother through false and overly expensive treatment. Mrs. Kren emphasized how much young Hitler had granted her father "all permissible alleviations" after 1938.

171. Coblenz BA NS 26/17a, "Notizen für die Kartei" (Notes for the index card file), 8 December 1938. The two autographs, which were still among Bloch's possessions, were confiscated in 1938 without compensation (ibid.).

172. Coblenz BA NS 26/65, 7 November 1938, similarly in a letter to Renato Bleibtreu of 16 November 1938 and in *Collier's.*

173. Ibid.

174. Jetzinger, *Hitlers Jugend,* pp. 182ff.

175. Krackowizer.

176. Jäckel and Kuhn, *Hitler,* p. 525, letter, Munich, 29 November 1921.

177. Maser, *Adolf Hitler,* p. 81.

178. Coblenz BA. NS 26/174, copy of the article "A. Hitler in Urfahr" in *Mitteilungen des deutschvölkischen Turnvereins Urfahr,* ser. 67, March, vol. 12.

179. Copies of the letters in IfZ Munich (F 19/19). The correspondence was found in 1941 among the estate of Johanna Motloch and confiscated by the Gestapo (letter of the Principal Stapo Office Vienna to the Reich Main Security Office in Berlin of 30 December 1941). After showing Hitler copies of the letters, Bormann wrote to Himmler on 14 October 1942: "The Führer was very touched by the memory of these events, which he was of course familiar with" (Coblenz BA, NS 19/1261).

180. Evidently the wrong date, 1909, can be attributed to the young man's excitement. The postmark clearly shows that the letter was sent on 11 February 1908 and arrived in Vienna on 12 February 1908.

181. Jetzinger, *Hitlers Jugend,* p. 187.

182. Ibid, p. 190.

183. Linz OÖLA, "Materialien Jetzinger," letter by Kubizek of 24 June 1949.

184. Kubizek, *Adolf Hitler,* pp. 182ff.

185. Linz StA, "Einschreibbuch der Familie Hitler ab 12.2.1908." According to the 1909 address book of the towns of Linz and Urfahr, Johanna Pölzl was registered in Linz as late as 1909. She returned to Waldviertel no later than in the summer of 1910, when she was sick. Paula moved to Angela Raubal's, who had meanwhile become a widow.

186. Munich, IfZ ED 100, 44. Interview of Paula Hitler by the Americans in Berchtesgaden on 16 May 1945.

187. For example: Oscar Robert Achenbach, *Aus Adolf Hitlers Heimat* (From Adolf Hitler's homeland) (Munich, 1933), pp. 6ff. The standard work is *Die alte Heimat, Beschreibung des Waldviertels um Döllersheim* (The old *Heimat,* description of Waldviertel around Döllersheim), ed. Deutsche Ansiedlungsgesellschaft (German Settlers Society) (Berlin, 1942).

188. See Frank, *Ahnentafeln* (Family trees); Werner Maser, *Frühgeschichte der NSDAP* (Early history of the NSDAP), unrevised reprint (Düsseldorf, 1994), p. 51.

189. Franz Jetzinger, *Hitlers Jugend* (Vienna, 1956), p. 20.

190. Ibid., pp. 45ff.

191. The original is at the district court of Krems's notary office archive; a facsimile and first interpretations of the complicated affair were published in Karl Merinsky, *Das Ende des Zweiten Weltkrieges und die Besatzungszeit im Raum von Zwettl in Niederösterreich* (The end of World War II and the time of occupation in the area around Zwettl in Lower Austria), Ph.D. diss., University of Vienna, 1966.

192. Ibid., Appendix 21.

193. For an inquiry with the bishopric in Sankt Pölten, 1876, and correspondence

between the bishopric and the ministry, see Merinsky, Appendix 22 A–D. See also (Appendix 23,) an expert legal opinion by Professor Winfried Kralik of Vienna University.

194. August Kubizek, *Adolf Hitler* (Graz, 1956), p. 59.

195. Bradley F. Smith, *Adolf Hitler* (Stanford, 1967), p. 31.

196. Munich IfZ ED 100, p. 42; questioning of Paula Hitler in Berchtesgaden, 26 May 1945.

197. Archive Senftenegg Castle, Lower Austria.

198. *WSMB*, 8 April 1932.

199. *Monatsblatt der Heraldisch-Genealogischen Gesellschaft "ADLER* (The Heraldic-Genealogical Society EAGLE's monthly), vol. xi, nos. 16–17, May 1932, pp. 146–48.

200. Archive Senftenegg Castle, Lower Austria.

201. Ibid.

202. Ibid., Frank's typescript.

203. Munich BHStA; clippings in the Rehse collection.

204. Karl Friedrich von Frank, "Adolf Hitler," in *Ahnentafeln berühmter Deutscher: Neue Folge* (Genealogical trees of famous Germans: New series) (Leipzig, 1933).

205. Konrad Heiden, *Hitler: Das Leben eines Diktators* (Hitler: A dictator's life) (Zurich, 1936), p. 14, as well as that title's subsequent editions up to *Der Fuehrer: Hitler's Rise to Power*, which was published in Boston in 1944 (pp. 40ff.).

206. Rudolf Koppensteiner, "Die Ahnentafel des Führers" (The Führer's family tree), in *Ahnentafeln berühmter Deutscher* (Family trees of famous Germans), (Leipzig, 1937).

207. Parish of Rastenfeld, typescript: Rev. Johannes Müllner, *Die entweihte Heimat: Die Sakralbauten auf dem Gebiet des Truppenübungsplatzes Döllersheim einst und jetzt* (Desecrated *Heimat*: Sacred buildings in the military maneuver area of Döllersheim, then and now), 1982, p. 12; with profuse thanks to Count Philipp Thurn-Valsassina, Rastenberg.

208. Beatrice Heiber and Helmut Heiber, *Die Rückseite des Hakenkreuzes* (The flip side of the swastika) (Munich, 1993), p. 63.

209. Ibid., p. 61, BA R43 II 266.

210. Müllner, *Der entweihte Heimat*, p. 7.

211. Today Döllersheim's early parish registers, including those from 1837, are in the diocese archive of St. Pölten.

212. Hitler, *Monologe*, p. 357, 21 August 1942.

213. Hans Frank, *Im Angesicht des Galgens* (Facing the gallows) (Munich, 1953), pp. 330ff. I refrain from going into obvious mixups on the part of Frank so as to avoid further confusion.

214. Nikolaus von Preradovich, "Adolf Hitler—Mischling zweiten Grades?" (Adolf Hitler—of second-generation mixed parentage?) in *Deutsche Monatshefte*, April 1989, pp. 6ff.

215. *Paris-Soir*, 5 August 1939, pp. 4ff.: Patrick Hitler, "Mon Oncle Adolf." This was already mentioned in Werner Maser, *Adolf Hitler* (Munich, 1971), p. 19.

216. Washington NA, "Hitler Source Book," interview with William Patrick Hitler on 10 September 1943 in New York.

217. *Look Magazine*, January 1939.

218. See *New York Herald Tribune*, 25 June 1941, "Irish Wife of Der Führer's Half-Brother Glad to Do Her Bit to Defeat Nazis."

219. Washington NA, "Hitler Source Book."

220. *The Memoirs of Bridget Hitler*, ed. Michael Unger (London, 1979).

221. Jetzinger, *Hitler Jugend*, p. 32.

222. This information was obtained through the good offices of the Bibliothèque Nationale in Paris.

223. Preradovich, "Adolf Hitler"; of no informational value is Anton Adalbert Klein, "Hitlers dunkler Punkt in Graz" (Hitler's dark spot in Graz), in *HJStG* (Graz 1970), pp. 7–30.

224. Werner Maser, *Adolf Hitler*, pp. 24ff. and 44ff.

225. Kubizek, *Adolf Hitler*, pp. 319ff.

226. Ibid., p. 322.

227. Ibid., p. 325.

228. Ibid., pp. 328ff. Kubizek's three sons became teachers and musicians. Augustin Kubizek is a well-known choir conductor and composer.

229. Ibid., p. 338.

230. Ibid., p. 343.

231. Ibid, p. 345ff.

232. Coblenz BA, Neue Reichskanzlei R43 II, letter by Eigruber to the Reich governor of the Upper Danube, Linz, 3 May 1943. Approval by the Reich minister of finance in Berlin, 28 June 1943: "Promotion of a local civil servant."

233. Eigruber protocols (see Chapter 1, n. 5), p. 577, 3 May 1943.

234. Linz OÖLA, "Jetzinger-Materialien," letter by Kubizek of 19 June 1949.

235. Linz OÖLA, "Jetzinger-Materialien," Kubizek, *Erinnerungen*, vol. 2, *Vienna*, p. 22.

236. Ibid., p. 43.

237. Ibid., p. 47.

238. Jetzinger is wrong in claiming (p. 134) that this first draft consisted only of two thin notepads "which would hardly fill fifteen printed pages." In Jetzinger's own files in the OÖLA Linz the Vienna part of Kubizek's first draft alone amounts to fifty single-spaced typed pages. Assuming that the Linz part was just as long as the Vienna part, this leads to the conclusion that the whole draft was at least 150 pages long.

239. A. Joachimsthaler, *Korrektur einer Biographie: Adolf Hitler 1908–1920* (Revising a biography: Adolf Hitler 1908–1920) (Munich, 1989), p. 260.

240. Linz OÖLA, "Jetzinger-Materialien," letter by Kubizek of 24 June 1949.

241. Ibid.

242. Kubizek, *Adolf Hitler*, pp. 298ff.

243. Ibid., p. 349.

244. Ibid., p. 301.

245. Jetzinger, *Hitlers Jugend*, pp. 137ff.

246. Ibid., p. 136.

247. Kubizek, *Adolf Hitler*, p. 75.

248. Jetzinger, p. 141.

249. Bradley F. Smith, *Adolf Hitler* (Stanford, 1967), p. 112.

250. Erich Fromm, *The Anatomy of Human Destructiveness* (New York, 1992).

251. Joachim C. Fest, *Hitler* (New York, 1973).

252. Jetzinger, *Hitlers Jugend*, p. 129.

253. Jetzinger, p. 126. Facsimile of the document "Ausfolgung des in der gemeinschaftlichen Waisenkasse erliegenden Vermögens" (Handing over of the funds kept in the joint orphans' account) 1913, without commentary, in Werner Maser, *Frühgeschichte der NSDAP* (Early history of the NSDAP) (Düsseldorf, 1994), pp. 80ff.

254. Jetzinger, pp. 231ff.

255. Maser, p. 81.

256. The book by Hugo Rabitsch, *Jugend-Erinnerungen eines zeitgenössischen Linzer Realschülers* (The memoirs of the youth of a contemporary schoolmate in Linz) (Munich, 1938), is completely uninformative; the author neither knew young Hitler nor contributed anything to his biography.

Chapter 2

1. Alfred E. Frauenfeld, *Der Weg zur Bühne* (The path to the stage) (Berlin, 1940), pp. 273ff.

2. Hitler, *Monologe*, p. 200, 15–16 January 1942.

3. Henry Picker, *Hitlers Tischgespräche* (Frankfurt, 1951), p. 276, 10 May 1942.

4. Berlin BA, *Bericht Alfred Rollers über seine Reise nach Bayreuth und Berlin im Februar 1934* (Alfred Roller's report about his trip to Bayreuth and Berlin in February 1934).

5. Frauenfeld's report was also confirmed to the author by Roller's oldest son, Professor Dietrich Roller, in March 1994. The drawings published in Price (nos. 115–121), which Hitler was said to have showed to Roller and Panholzer for evaluation, are forgeries by Kujau.

6. August Kubizek, *Adolf Hitler, Mein Jugendfreund* (graz, 1953), pp. 187 and 191.

7. Ibid., p. 188.

8. Despite her not quite "Aryan" background, Hitler later transferred his admiration for Leo Slezak onto his daughter Gretel. The 1932 portraits of Gretel and their accompanying text that are published as no. 11 in Price, as well as the remarkably simple portrait of Wagner, allegedly drawn for Kubizek, and the reproduction of Hans Sachs's hymn (Price, no. 56, Jäckel/Kuhn, p. 1254) are fakes by Kujau.

9. Kubizek, p. 234. Later witnesses confirm Hitler's excellent knowledge of Wagner, for example: Ernst Hanfstaengl, *Zwischen Weißem und Braunem Haus: Memoiren eines politischen Auenseiters* (Between the white and the brown house: Memoirs of a political outsider) (Munich, 1970), p. 55.

10. Josef Goebbels, *Tagebücher* (Munich, 1993), pt. 1, vol. 2, p. 731, 19 November 1935.

11. Kubizek, p. 233.

12. Ibid., p. 101.

13. Hitler, *Monologe*, p. 294, 22–23 February 1942.

14. Kubizek, pp. 230ff.

15. Kubizek reports that "each night one could observe pedestrians starting to run in the streets of Vienna so they would be able to reach the doors of their buildings before the ten o'clock cut-off time." See Linz OÖLA, "Jetzinger-Materialien," Kubizek, 1st draft, p. 19.

16. Munich IfZ, F 19/19.

17. IWEB, 26 February 1908.

18. Picker, p. 251, Berghof, 30 April 1942, and statement by Professor Otto Strasser to the author in 1994.

19. *AdT*, 20 June 1908.

20. Kubizek, 1st draft, p. 31.

21. Kubizek, p. 229.

22. Kubizek, 1st draft, p. 24.

23. Munich IfZ, ZS 2242.

24. Kubizek, p. 239.

25. Kubizek, 1st draft, pp. 43ff.

26. Kubizek, p. 246.

27. According to Schirach in a conversation with Speer. Speer, *Tagebücher*, pp. 154ff. Sketches for *Turandot, Julius Caesar,* and *Lohengrin* in Albert Zoller, *Hitler privat* (Hitler in private) (Düsseldorf, 1949), nos. 5–7.

28. Kubizek, 1st draft, pp. 32ff.

29. Hitler, *Monologe*, p. 198, 13–14 January 1942.

30. Kubizek, 1st draft, p. 32.

31. Ibid., p. 38.

32. Hermann Giesler, *Ein anderer Hitler* (Leoni, 1977), p. 242.

33. Hitler, *Reden* (Speeches), vol. 3, pt. 2, p. 146, 3 April 1929.

34. Albert Speer, *Erinnerungen* (Frankfurt, 1969), p. 54, similarly in *Monologe*, pp. 198f.

35. MK, p. 77.

36. Speer, p. 54, see also Hanisch.

37. Linz OÖLA, "Jetzinger-Materialien," memoirs by Wilhelm Hagmüller.

38. Goebbels, *Tagebücher*, 31 August 1940.

39. Kubizek, 1st draft, p. 5.

40. Kubizek, pp. 206ff.

41. Ibid., p. 221.

42. Ibid., pp. 195ff.

43. Kubizek, 1st draft, p. 4.

44. Coblenz BA, NS 26/36; copy of the transcript of a conversation on 12 March 1944 on the Obersalzberg Mountain.

45. Speer, p. 89.

46. Giesler, p. 242; see also Speer, p. 89.

47. Giesler, p. 242.

48. Picker, p. 283, 13 May 1942.

49. Kubizek, p. 222.

50. Ibid., p. 228.

51. Kubizek, 1st draft, p. 12.

52. Heinrich Hoffmann, *Hitler wie ich ihn sah* (Hitler as I saw him) (Munich, 1974), p. 29.

53. Oskar Kokoschka, *Mein Leben* (My life) (Munich, 1971), p. 60.

54. Hitler, *Monologe*, pp. 386ff.

55. Kokoschka, p. 55.

56. Ibid., pp. 65ff.

57. Picker, p. 146, 27 March 1942.

58. Quoted from the speech for the 1935 party convention by Klaus Backes, *Hitler und die bildenden Künste* (Hitler and the visual arts) (Cologne, 1977), p. 52.

59. Kubizek, p. 227.

60. ÖNB ThM, Burgtheater's performance schedule.

61. Kubizek, pp. 227ff.

62. Willi Reich, *Alban Berg: Leben und Werk* (Alban Berg: Life and work) (Munich, 1985), p. 21.

63. Catalog of the Richard Strauss exhibit, Austrian National Library in Vienna, 1964, p. 149.

64. Nike Wagner, *Geist und Geschlecht: Karl Kraus und die Erotik der Wiener Moderne* (Mind and sex: Karl Kraus and the eroticism of Viennese modernism) (Frankfurt, 1982), p. 165.

65. UDW Ostermond, 1908, p. 27.

66. P. Heinrich Abel SJ, *Zurück zum praktischen Christentum!* (Back to a practical Christianity!) (Vienna, 1895), p. 97.

67. Richard von Krafft-Ebing, *Psychopathia sexualis* (Munich, 1984).

68. *AdT*, 24 June 1908, "Das Tschechentum in Wien" (Czechdom in Vienna).

69. Kubizek, p. 115.

70. Ibid., p. 293.

71. Wagner, *Gesammelte Werke* (Collected Works), vol. 8, p. 111.

72. Hans Tietze, *Die Juden Wiens* (Vienna's Jews) (Vienna, 1933), p. 206.

73. *AdT*, 18 April 1908.

74. Ibid.

75. Ibid., 28 March 1909.

76. Kubizek, 1st draft, pp. 23 and 34ff.

77. Ibid., pp. 37ff.

78. Picker, pp. 146ff., 27 March 1942.

79. Hitler, *Reden*, vol. 3, pt. 2, Munich, 1994, pp. 177ff. Speech of 9 April 1929 at NSDAP convention in Munich.

80. *Heeresadjutant bei Hitler 1938–1943: Aufzeichnungen des Majors Engel* (Hitler's aide-de-camp 1938–1943: Major Engel's notes), ed. Hildegard von Kotze (Stuttgart, 1974), p. 46, June 1939.

81. Domarus, p. 442, speech in Hamburg, 17 August 1934.

82. Otto Dietrich, *12 Jahre mit Hitler* (Twelve years with Hitler) (Munich, 1955), p. 157.

83. MK, pp. 254f.

84. *Meyers Konversations-Lexikon* (Meyer's encyclopedia) (Leipzig, 1888).

85. Max Nordau, *Entartung*, vol. 2 (Berlin, 1893), p. 498.

86. Ibid., pp. 469, 471, 493.

87. Ibid., pp. 504ff.

88. Ibid., p. 505.

89. Ibid., vol. 1, pp. 267, 281, and 282.

90. Ibid., vol. 2, p. 501.

91. Guido List, *Der Unbesiegbare* (The invincible) (Vienna, 1898), p. 29.

92. F. Siebert, *Alldeutsches zur Frauenbewegung* (Pan-German thoughts on the women's movement) (Ostermond, 1911).

93. *Deutsche Hochschulstimmen aus der Ostmark* (German voices from Ostmark universities), 12 December 1909, "Zur Rassenästhetik" (On racial aesthetics).

94. *Der deutsche Eisenbahner* (The German railway worker), 10 and 20 November 1908, "Zur Judenfrage" (Concerning the Jewish question).

95. UDW Ostermond, 1908, p. 25, Theodor Fritsch, "Frauen-Frage II" (Women's question II).

96. Hitler, *Monologe*, pp. 128ff., 5 November 1941.

97. Domarus, p. 709; speech at the opening of the "House of German Art" in Munich, 13 July 1937.

Chapter 3

1. Henry Picker, *Hitlers Tischgespräche* (Frankfurt, 1993) pp. 339ff., 29 May 1942.

2. Hitler, *Monologe*, pp. 74ff., 1 October 1941.

3. Ibid., pp. 264ff., 4 February 1942.

4. Picker, p. 339, 29 May 1942.

5. Hitler, *Monologe*, pp. 404ff., 25 June 1943.

6. Joseph Goebbels, *Tagebücher* (Munich, 1993), pt. 2, vol. 7, p. 608, 21 March 1943.

7. Ibid., vol. 8, p. 540, 25 June 1943.

8. Ibid., vol. 15, p. 692.

9. Hitler, *Monologe*, pp. 74ff., 1 October 1941.

10. Goebbels apparently misspelled a word, writing "schlechten" (bad) instead of "schlichten" (simple). The emperor, who saw himself as a "vir simplex et iustus," was typically characterized as "simple." Goebbels, *Tagebücher*, pt. 1, vol. 3, p. 612, 17 October 1939.

11. Stefan Zweig, *Die Welt von gestern* (The world of yesterday) (Hamburg, 1965), p. 33.

12. Felix Somary, *Erinnerungen aus meinem Leben* (Zurich, n.d.), pp. 28ff.

13. *MK*, p. 159.

14. Hitler, *Monologe*, p. 304, 27 February 1942.

15. August Kubizek, *Adolf Hitler, Mein Jugend freund* (Graz, 1953), p. 201.

16. Kubizek, 1st draft, p. 14.

17. Albert Baron von Margutti, *Kaiser Franz Joseph* (Vienna, 1924), pp. 190ff.

18. Ibid., p. 174.

19. Hitler, *Monologe*, pp. 390ff., 5 September 1942.

20. Heinrich Hoffmann, *Hitler, wie ich ihn sah* (Hitler, the way I saw him) (Munich, 1974), p. 162.

21. Hitler, *Monologe*, p. 380, 1 September 1942.

22. Koeppen transcript, pp. 39ff., 5 October 1941.

23. Margutti, pp. 228ff.

24. Bonn PA, Austria 86, no. 1, Secret; report by the German ambassador in St. Petersburg to Reich Chancellor von Bülow.

25. Franz Brandl, *Kaiser, Politiker und Menschen: Erinnerungen eines Wiener Polizeipräsidenten* (Emperors, politicians, and human beings: Memoirs of a police president in Vienna) (Vienna, 1936), p. 170.

26. Elisabeth Grossegger, *Der Kaiserhuldigungsfestzug* (The parade in the emperor's honor) (Vienna, 1992), p. 30.

27. An anonymous letter to Mayor Lueger, ibid., p. 25.

28. *Budapesti Hirlap*, 31 May 1908, front-page article: "Opposition and Patriotism" (in Hungarian).

29. *DVB*, 7 April 1908, p. 10.

30. StP HdA, 10 April 1908.

31. *DVB*, 8 April 1908, p. 9.

32. Grossegger, p. 164.

33. *Zweites Buch*, p. 312 and *MK*, p. 130.

34. In the newspapers on 11 June 1908, for example, *ODR*.

35. *NWB*, 14 June 1908.

36. *NIK*, 13 October 1909, Count Wilczek's testimony during the trial.

37. *ODR*, 14 June 1908.

38. Grossegger, p. 160.

39. *NWB*, 14 June 1908.

40. Grossegger, p. 167.

41. Peter Urbanitsch, "Die Deutschen in Österreich" (The Germans in Austria), in *Die Habsburgsmonarchie 1848–1918* (The Hapsburg monarchy 1848–1918), vol. 3 (Vienna, 1980), p. 77.

42. *Die Fackel*, 10 June 1908.

43. Adolf Loos, *Sämtliche schriften* (complete works), vol. 1: *Ornament und verbrechen* (ornament and crime) (Vienna, 1963).

44. *Simplicissimus*, 15 June 1908, cartoonist Eduard Thöny.

45. StP HdA, 20 June 1908.

46. Brigitte Hamann, *Bertha von Suttner: Ein Leben für den Frieden* (Munich, 1986), p. 466.

47. *IWE*, 12 June 1908. About this topic in general, see Wolfgang Hartmann, *Der historische Festzug* (The historic parade) (Munich, 1976).

48. Bonn PA, "Österreich 1" (Austria 1), Tschirschky to Bülow, 9 December 1908, "Ganz vertraulich" (Absolutely confidential).

49. *NIK*, 11 December 1908.

50. *AdT*, 18 January 1909, "Der deutsche Standpunkt in der bosnischen Frage" (The German standpoint regarding the Bosnian question).

51. Ibid., 6 January 1909, as one example for many.

52. StP HdA, 17 December 1908, pp. 8129ff.

53. Bonn PA, "Österreich 101," Ratibow to Bülow, 10 December 1908.

54. *NWT*, 2 December 1908.

55. StP HdA, 17 December 1908, p. 8162.

56. *Die Große Politik der Europäischen Kabinette 1871–1914* (The European parliaments' larger policies 1871–1914), vol. 26, pt. 2 (Berlin, 1925), p. 722.

57. Washington NA, American Embassy no. 853, Vienna, 15 May 1909.

58. Jäckel/Kuhn, p. 330, 6 March 1921.

59. *MK*, p. 141.

60. Ibid., p. 16.

61. Ibid., p. 128.

62. Picker, p. 392, 29 June 1942.

63. Ibid., p. 319, 20 May 1942.

64. Goebbels, *Tagebücher*, pt. 2, vol. 7, p. 515, 9 March 1943.

65. Frank, p. 422.

66. Hitler, *Monologe*, p. 335, 9 August 1942.

67. Ibid., p. 374, 29 August 1942.

68. Domarus, pp. 524f., speech in Nuremberg on 10 September 1935.

69. Pichl, *Georg Schönerer*, vol. 6, p. 532.

70. Harald Arjuna Grävell von Jostenoode, "Die Reichskleinodien zurück nach dem Reich!" (The imperial insignia back to the Reich!) in *Ostara*, July 1906, pp. 3–6.

71. *Mein Kampf*, p. 13.

72. Donarus, p. 732, speech in Nuremberg on 13 September 1937.

73. *AdT*, 20 March 1908.

74. For example, *AZ*, 9 March 1908, "Die Märztage der Arbeiter" (The workers' days in March).

75. Reinhold Hanisch, "I Was Hitler's Buddy," *The New Republic*, 19 April 1939.
76. Domarus, p. 841, speech in Frankfurt on 30 March 1938; and VB, 1 April 1938.
77. See also *Mein Kampf*, p. 72.
78. Hitler, *Monologe*, p. 123, 2 November 1941.
79. August Kubizek, *Adolf Hitler, Mein Jugend Freund* (Graz, 1953), pp. 307ff.
80. VB, 16 March 1938.

Chapter 4

1. MK, p. 75.
2. Fritz Freund, *Das österreichische Abgeordnetenhaus* (Austria's House of Representatives) (Vienna, 1907).
3. Walter Kleindel, *Österreich: Daten zur Geschichte und Kultur* (Austria: Facts on its history and culture) (Vienna, 1979), p. 295.
4. StP HdA, 16 December 1907, pp. 3511ff.
5. Information kindly provided by Günter Schefbeck, Ph.D., Director of the Parliamentary Archive in Vienna.
6. Anonymous, *Wien und die Wiener: Schilderungen eines fahrenden Gesellen* (Vienna and the Viennese: A journeyman's portraits) (Berlin, 1893), p. 137.
7. MK, p. 75.
8. August Kubizek, *Adolf Hitler, Mein Jugendfreund* (Graz, 1953), p. 289.
9. MK, p. 76.
10. Ibid., p. 77.
11. Kubizek, p. 223.
12. Ibid., p. 291.
13. Ibid., p. 290.
14. *IKZ*, 5 December 1908.
15. Albert Baron von Margutte, *Kaiser Franz Joseph* (Vienna, 1924), p. 218.
16. Richard Charmatz, *Österreichs äußere und innere Politik von 1895 bis 1914* (Austria's foreign and domestic policy from 1895 to 1914) (Vienna, 1918), pp. 81ff.
17. *Prager Tagblatt*, evening edition, 3 February 1909.
18. Ibid., 5 February 1909.
19. *IKZ*, 6 February 1909.
20. *Prager Tagblatt*, 5 February 1909.
21. *Die Friedens-Warte*, February 1909, pp. 30ff.
22. W. Ellenbogen, "Volksparlament und Geschäftsordnung" (Democratic parliament and standing orders), in *Der Kampf*, 1 February 1909, pp. 196–202.
23. Freund.
24. Joseph Schleicher, *Erlebnisse und Erinnerungen* (Events and memories), vol. 6, (Vienna, n.d)., p. 55.
25. Ibid., p. 93.
26. Ibid., vol. 4, p. 19.
27. Bonn PA, "Österreich 91," Tschirschky to Bülow, 18 March 1909.
28. *IKZ*, 15 November 1909.
29. *Der Hammer*, p. 15. Heuerts 1907, "Unsere nationale Zukunft" (Our national future).
30. StP HdA, 26 November 1909, p. 486.
31. MK, p. 74.

32. Ibid., p. 92.

33. Ibid., p. 146.

34. Hitler, *Monologe*, p. 374, 29 August 1942.

35. Rep. Karl Iro's speech on 2 June 1908 in the Reichsrat, printed on the title page of *AdT*, 4 June 1908.

36. *MK*, p. 104.

37. Ibid., p. 102.

38. Ibid., p. 38.

39. Koeppen, p. 374, dinner with Heydrich on 2 October 1941.

40. StP, HdA, 5 June 1908, pp. 9833ff.

41. *MK*, pp. 78 and 92.

42. Ibid., p. 78.

43. Ibid., p. 84.

44. Ibid., p. 87.

45. Ibid., p. 80.

46. Ibid., pp. 90 and 89.

47. Hitler, *Reden, Schriften* (Speeches, writings), vol. 3/i (Munich, 1994), p. 197. Speech at an NSDAP assembly in Munich on 29 October 1928.

Chapter 5

1. Franz Jetzinger, *Hitlers Jugend* (Vienna, 1956), Kubizek is the first one to mention all these missives, but he does not copy them correctly. I am deliberately not quoting the dates given either by Kubizek or Jetzinger, inasmuch as they cannot be verified without the originals.

2. Ibid., pp. 204ff.

3. Ibid., p. 205.

4. Ibid., p. 202.

5. Linz OÖLA, "Hitler-Materialien, Einschreibbuch"; in this context see also Gerhart Marckhgott, " ' . . . Von der Hohlheit des gemächlichen Lebens': Neues Material über die Familie Hitler in Linz" (". . . About the hollowness of comfortable life": New material on the Hitler family in Linz), in *Jahrbuch des Oberösterreichischen Musealvereins* (Yearbook of the Upper Austrian Museum Association), vol. 138/i (Linz, 1993), p. 112.

6. Jetzinger, p. 206.

7. Ibid., p. 275.

8. Hitler, *Monologe*, p. 115, 29 October 1941.

9. August Kubizek, *Adolf Hitler, Mein Jugendfreund* (Graz, 1953), pp. 314ff.

10. Jetzinger, p. 165.

11. OÖLA Linz, Archive of the Museum Association, entry in the register. Senior Archive Councillor Georg Heilingsetzer kindly provided this clue.

12. *MK*, p. 21.

13. Hitler, *Monologe*, p. 72, 27–28 September 1941.

14. Vienna, AHBK, notes in the classification lists of 1907 and 1908.

15. *Wiener Adreßbuch* (Lehmann, 1908).

16. Jetzinger, p. 210, unjustly accuses Kubizek of lying when he claims that at the time in question there had been no rallies at all in Vienna. In fact, there were a number of very different rallies between February and July 1908, and even details of the one by the unemployed of 26 February 1908 are in agreement with what Kubizek reports.

17. *Neues Wiener Abendblatt*, 27 February 1908.

18. Kubizek, pp. 294ff.

19. Ibid., pp. 295ff.

20. *AdT*, 20 September 1910.

21. *DVP*, 19 January 1908.

22. *Kikeriki*, 1910, no. 51.

23. *AZ*, 3 June 1910, p. 5.

24. Michael John, *Wohnverhältnisse sozialer Unterschichten im Wien Kaiser Franz Josephs* (Living conditions in Emperor Francis Joseph's Vienna) (Vienna, 1984), p. 15.

25. Kubizek, p. 210.

26. Ibid., p. 205.

27. Ibid., p. 210.

28. Ibid., p. 216.

29. "15. Jahresbericht der Kaiser Franz Joseph Jubiläumsstiftung für . . . 1910" (15th annual report of the Emperor Francis Joseph anniversary foundation for . . . 1910), Vienna, 1911, p. 149.

30. Julius Deutsch, *Ein weiter Weg* (A long way) (Vienna, 1960), pp. 37ff.

31. Hitler, *Monologe*, p. 379, 1 September 1942.

32. Henry Picker, *Hitlers Tischgespräche* (Frankfurt, 1951), p. 343, 30 May 1942.

33. G. M. Gilbert, *Nürnberger Tagebuch* (Nuremberg diary) (Frankfurt, 1962), p. 279.

34.. Coblenz BA, NS 26/17a.

35. For example, *NWB*, 20 March 1938.

36. *Wie die Ostmark ihre Befreiung erlebte* (How the Ostmark experienced its liberation), ed. Heinrich Hoffmann (n. p., n. d.) (1940), p. 15.

37. According to information supplied by the district museum in Alsergrund, all that is known is that during the years of National Socialism people claimed that Hitler had once lived there, without anyone knowing him at the time.

38. *MK*, p. 39.

39. Ibid., p. 25.

40. Eberhard Jäckel and Axel Kuhn, *Adolf Hitler, Sämtliche Aufzeichnungen, 1905–1924* (Stuttgart, 1980), pp. 525ff., 20 November 1921.

41. Max Domarus, *Hitler, Reden u. Proklamationen 1932–1945* (Munich, 1962), p. 267, 10 May 1933.

42. Max Winter, *Höhlenbewohner in Wien: Brigittenauer Wohn- und Sittenbilder aus der Luegerzeit* (Cave dwellers in Vienna: Portraits of the living conditions and customs from the Lueger era) (Vienna, 1927), pp. 16ff.

43. Bradley F. Smith, *Adolf Hitler: His Family, Childhood, and Youth* (Stanford, 1967), p. 93.

44. *MK*, p. 356.

45. Ibid., p. 40.

46. Ibid., p. 41.

47. *BBN*, 11 April 1912, p. 7.

48. Ibid., 4 April 1912, p. 1: "Die Sünden der Sozialdemokratie" (Social Democracy's sins).

49. In all Viennese newspapers. The quote is from *NWT*, 19 and 20 May 1913.

50. This information was kindly provided in September 1995 by Privy Councillor Kugler, director of the Art Historical Museum's picture collection.

51. Otto Thomae, *Die Propaganda-Maschinerie* (The propaganda machinery) (Berlin, 1978), p. 161.

52. Jetzinger, p. 263.

53. *IKZ*, 17 February 1906.

54. *BBN*, 11 April 1912, "Sozialdemokratie und Großkapital" (Social Democracy and big business). See also *BBN*, 21 July 1912, "Die Sozialdemokratie als Jugendschutz-truppe" (Social Democracy as organized guards of the young), listing dozens of names.

55. Jetzinger, p. 220.

56. *Wiener Bilder* (Images of Vienna), 21 November 1906.

57. *SJSW für 1908*, Vienna, 1910, p. 840.

58. Emil Kläger, *Durch die Quartiere der Not und des Verbrechens* (Through the quarters of hardship and crime) (Vienna, 1908), pp. 98ff.

59. *IWB*, 25 December 1910, "Im Asyl for Obdachlose" (In the homeless shelter).

60. Kläger, pp. 101ff.

61. *MK*, p. 24.

62. Ibid., p. 30.

63. Winter, pp. 47, 49, and 70.

64. Kläger, pp. 140ff.

65. Kubizek, p. 203.

66. Ibid., p. 210.

67. Ibid., p. 310.

68. *MK*, pp. 32ff.

69. *IWE*, 18 January 1908.

70. *SJSW für 1908* (Vienna, 1910), p. 855.

71. *MK*, pp. 23f.

72. Hitler, *Monologe*, p. 126, "Führerhauptquartier" (Führer's headquarters), 5 November 1941.

73. Max Winter, *Im unterirdischen Wien: Großstadtdokumente* (In subterranean Vienna: Documents from a metropolis), vol. 13 (Berlin, n.d.), p. 58.

74. Otruba, p. 236.

75. *AZ*, 9 April 1910, p. 4.

76. *NNZ*, 26 February 1909.

77. *Ostara*, no. 18, December 1907, pp. 6ff., 9, and 15.

78. *Blätter für das Armenwesen der Stadt Wien* (Publications on the charity organizations of the City of Vienna) (Vienna, 1912), pp. 5ff.

79. *IKZ*, 14 July 1910.

80. StP HdA, 15 December 1908, p. 8012.

81. *AZ*, 7 April 1910, "Revolution vor dem Asyl" (Revolution in front of the shelter).

82. Vienna StLA, Registrar's Office.

83. Smith, p. 163.

84. Unless otherwise noted, Hanisch is always quoted from *The New Republic*, 5, 12, and 19 April 1939, throughout.

85. *AZ*, 5 April 1910, p. 5.

Chapter 6

1. *SJSW für 1911* (Vienna, 1913), p. 45.

2. *10. Jahresbericht der Kaiser Franz Joseph I. Jubiläumsstiftung . . . über das Jahr 1905* (Tenth annual report of the Emperor Franz Josef I Anniversary Foundation . . . for 1905) (Vienna, 1906), p. 8.

3. *SJSW für 1908* (Vienna, 1910), p. 206.

4. *10. Jahresbericht*, p. 13.

5. The result of an inquiry with the present hostel administration was that copies of this first library or files regarding its contents no longer exist. In the last ninety years the hostel was repeatedly remodeled. A new library is only now being put together.

6. *9. Jahresbericht . . . über das Jahr 1904* (Vienna, 1905), pp. 1–10.

7. *15. Jahresbericht . . . über das Jahr 1910* (Vienna, 1911), pp. 1–16.

8. *16. Jahresbericht . . . über das Jahr 1911* (Vienna, 1912), p. 10. Because we have only statistics about the shelter at Wurlitzergasse but not about the one at Meldemann-strasse but the two are very similar, figures are quoted for the shelter at Wurlitzergasse.

9. AZ, 16 August 1909.

10. Vienna StLA, Registration Office.

11. *16. Jahresbericht*, p. 6.

12. Wagener, p. 462.

13. Billy Price, *Adolf Hitler als Maler und Zeichner* (Zug, 1983), nos. 128 and 129. Because this book combines a mixture of originals and fakes, one needs to be careful. All pictures from the source "USA 2" are admitted forgeries by Konrad Kujau. A scholarly examination of the old forgeries, particularly those by Reinhold Hanisch, is still waiting to be done. Many of them are included in Price.

14. On Adele Heller-Binder, née Altenberg, who emigrated to London, see Maurice Samuelson, "Post von Hitler" (Mail from Hitler), in *Die Presse*, Vienna, 14 May 1994, "Spectrum IV."

15. Coblenz BA, NS 26/36, copy of the record of a conversation on the Obersalzberg of 12 March 1944.

16. Coblenz BA, NS 26/24.

17. Vienna StLA, Registration Office. These facts are also quoted in A. Joachims-thaler, *Korrektur einer Biographie: Adolf Hitler 1908–1920* (Munich, 1989), pp. 67ff.

18. According to the Austrian Film Archive, shooting of the film was completed in 1915. The best-selling novel by Bernhard Kellermann on which the movie is based did not appear until 1913 either. When Albert Speer mentions that Hitler frequently "raved about Kellermann's *Tunnel*, also the story of a demagogue, as one of the great reading experiences of his youth," this must have happened during Hitler's period in Munich. Speer, *Tagebücher*, p. 460.

19. Jäckel/Kuhn, p. 889; VB, 15–16 April 1923.

20. Details in Brigitte Hamann, *The Reluctant Empress*.

21. Hitler, *Monologe*, p. 317, 11–12 March 1942.

22. Otto Dietrich, *12 Jahre mit Hitler* (Twelve years with Hitler) (Munich, 1955), p. 164: "Hitler read a great deal, mostly late at night, when he had retired and couldn't sleep."

23. MK, p. 34.

24. Felix Salten, *Wurstelprater* (Vienna, 1973), pp. 72, 76, and 81.

25. August Kubizek, pp. 203 *Adolf Hitler, Mien Jugundfreund* (Graz, 1953), ff.

26. Price, nos. 92, 111 and 123. However, without the originals it is ultimately impossible to decide which pictures are genuine and which ones forged.

27. Samuelson.

28. This is the picture listed as no. 248 in Price with the notice "from the estate of Franz Feiler, Innsbruck," which in 1946 became the property of Minister Rodolfo Siviero in Florence and during the 1984 exhibition "Hitler's Watercolors" in Florence was displayed as no. 4. See Hermann Weiß, *Die Hitler zugeschriebenen Aquarelle im Nachlaß Siviero/ Florenz* (The watercolors ascribed to Hitler in the Siviero estate Florence) (Florence, 1984), pp. 73ff.

29. Joachimsthaler, p. 72.

30. Franz Jetzinger, *Hitlers Jugend* (Vienna, 1956), p. 224.

31. Coblenz BA, NS 26/64, statement of May 1933.

32. Anonymous from Brünn, in *Moravsky ilustrovany spravodaj*, 1935, no. 40, pp. 10ff. (in Czech).

33. According to a statement by Mrs. Senta Altenberg, after the Anschluss there still were two unsold pictures by Hitler in the warehouse, which the family had to sell to the NSDAP's main archive for a small amount. Owing to his Aryan wife, Jakob Altenberg escaped deportation. With the exception of one, his stores were "Aryanized," and, aside from a minuscule pension, his money confiscated. He died in Vienna in 1944.

34. Samuelson, "Post von Hitler."

35. This information was kindly provided by Father Bertrand Baumann of the Chapter in Zwettl.

36. Jetzinger, pp. 226ff.

37. Munich IfZ, Paula Hitler ED 100.

38. Bonn BA PA, Austria 91, 22 June 1911.

39. Washington NA, "Diplomatic Report from Vienna," 22 July 1911.

40. See, for example, his enthusiastic article "Richard Wagner," in *Österreichischer Arbeiter-Kalender* (Austrian worker's almanac), 1908, pp. 53–58.

41. Robert Ehrhart, *Im Dienste des alten Österreich* (In the service of old Austria) (Vienna, 1958), p. 227.

42. *Die Zeit*, 14 June 1911, p. 3.

43. Ibid., pp. 3 and 7; see also AZ, 14 June 1911, p. 6.

44. AZ, 23 April 1914.

45. MK, p. 41.

46. *NIK*, 19 September 1911.

47. *DVB*, 18 September 1911.

48. *Wiener Bilder*, 20 September 1911.

49. MK, p. 41.

50. Ibid., p. 61.

51. *BBN*, 10 November 1912, p. 3.

52. Ibid., 4 April 1912, "Die Sünden der Sozialdemokratie" (The sins of Social Democracy).

53. Ibid., 11 April 1912, "Sozialdemokratie und Großkapital" (Social Democracy and big business).

54. *BBN*, pp. 4ff.

55. Jäckel/Kuhn, pp. 404ff., Munich, 22 May 1920.

56. Otto Strasser, *Aufbau des deutschen Sozialismus* (The development of Socialism in Germany) (Prague, 1936), p. 122.

57. *MK*, p. 30.

58. Ibid., p. 62.

59. Ibid., p. 68.

60. Kubizek, p. 296.

61. Ibid., pp. 203.

62. Ibid., pp. 296ff.

63. Wagener, p. 348.

64. Jäckel/Kuhn, p. 165, Munich, 27 July 1920.

65. *The New Republic*, 5, 12, and 19 April 1939. Grateful acknowledgment is made to the Library of Congress in Washington, D.C., for its assistance. Heiden's estate—he died in 1966—contains no documents on the years before 1945 and no letters or other clues on Hanisch either. A smaller part of Heiden's estate, particularly about his youth, is in Zurich's Zentralbibliothek (central library).

66. Konrad Heiden, *Adolf Hitler*, 2 vols. (Zurich, 1936–1937).

67. Coblenz BA, NS 26/64. The value of Hanisch's two-page report "Meine Begegnung mit Hitler" (My encounter with Hitler), dated May 1933, as a historical source is essentially the same as that of the much more detailed text published in *The New Republic*. It should be emphasized that the claim that this text was a commissioned work for the party archive is absolutely false.

68. Feiler, b. 1914, d. 1992 in Aldrans (Tyrol).

69. Coblenz BA, NS 26/64.

70. Probably all of the flower paintings Price published are by Hanisch.

71. Coblenz BA, NS 26/64, Hanisch to Feiler.

72. Maurice Samuelson, "Post von Hitler" (Mail from Hitler), in *Die Presse*, 14 May 1994.

73. Reference to this booklet is found in Bradley F. Smith, *Adolf Hitler: His Family, Childhood and Youth* (Stanford, 1967), p. 163.

74. Coblenz BA, NS 26/64.

75. Feiler's statement according to *Reichspost*, 6 July 1933.

76. For example, *Reichspost*, 6 July 1933.

77. Rudolf Olden, *Hitler* (New York, 1936).

78. Coblenz BA, NS 26/64, Hanisch to Feiler.

79. Smith, pp. 163ff.

80. Vienna StLA, Registration Office.

81. Vienna StLA, coroner's file on Hanisch. The file gives Hanisch's date of death as February 2, 1937. It also notes naively that Hanisch hanged himself "after Austria was taken over." Coblenz BA, NS 19/51/11.

82. Werner Maser, *Adolf Hitler* (Munich, 1971), p. 89, erroneously interprets this date as that of Hanisch's death and draws false conclusions from this, which in turn is liberally spread in the literature on Hitler.

83. Coblenz BA, NS 26/64.

84. Coblenz BA, NS 19 new, no. 2411; also Berlin BA, folders 4874–4941.

85. No. 40, pp. 10ff.

86. Coblenz BA, NS 26/17a, Hanisch records, 12 May 1939.

87. Vienna StLA, Registration Office. Inquiries with Brünn's Registration Office yielded no results.

88. Vienna StLA, Registration Office.

89. Facsimiles of the two registration slips are in Joachimsthaler, pp. 17ff.; his

information here is supplemented by the statements by Häusler's daughter Marianne Koppler.

90. First documented in Joachimsthaler, pp. 80 ff and 258.

91. Berlin BA, Personal Files, and Marianne Koppler.

92. Vienna AdR, District Files, no. 345. According to this source, he was several times—the last in 1944—refused NSDAP party membership, for which he had applied, on account of an incident in 1937: at the time Häusler, as lessee of the tavern Bischofs-koppe in Czechoslovakia, was said to have made two of his waiters lure a German citizen into his tavern, who was then arrested by the Czech police and ultimately received a stiff sentence.

93. Josef Greiner, *Sein Kampf und Sieg: Eine Erinnerung an Adolf Hitler* (Vienna, 1938), p. 135.

94. Ibid., pp. 72ff.

95. Ibid., p. 75.

96. Ibid., pp. 76ff.

97. Ibid., pp. 54–67.

98. Ibid., pp. 66 and 130.

99. Maser, p. 377.

100. Greiner, p. 342.

101. Ibid, pp. 283–98.

102. Vienna AdR, BMdI no. 52.043-2/56; here also similar party documents as in the BA in Berlin.

103. Munich IfZ, MS. 82, Franz Jetzinger, "Das Hitler-Buch Greiners" (Greiner's Hitler book).

104. In the archive of Amalthea-Verlag in Vienna.

105. Greiner, p. 29.

106. Munich IfZ, MS. 82, Jetzinger, pp. 30 and 68.

107. Berlin BA. Application for NSDA membership, 1 March 1940, response on 26 May 1940, quoted previously in Joachimsthaler, p. 76.

108. Joseph Wulf, *Literatur und Dichtung im Dritten Reich* (Literature and poetry in the Third Reich) (Gütersloh, 1973), 354 and passim.

109. Heinrich Hoffmann, *Hitler, wie ich ihn sah* (Munich, 1974), pp. 29ff.

110. Henriette von Schirach, *Der Preis der Herrlichkeit* (What price magnificence) (Wiesbaden, 1956), p. 220.

111. Marco Pozzetto, *Max Fabiani: Ein Architekt der Moderne* (Max Fabiani: A modernist architect) (Vienna, 1983), p. 16.

112. *La Nazione*, Florence, 2 June 1966, quoted in Pozzetto, p. 30.

113. *The Memoirs of Bridget Hitler*, ed. Michael Unger, (London, 1979), pp. 22ff.

114. Rosa Albach-Retty, *So kurz sind hundert Jahre* (That's how short one hundred years are) (Munich, 1979), pp. 171ff.

Chapter 7

1. MK, p. 22.

2. August Kubizek, *Adolf Hitler, Mein Jugendfreund* (Graz, 1953), p. 226.

3. MK, p. 85.

4. Wagener, p. 149.

5. MK, p. 35.

6. Kubizek, p. 225.

7. Albert Zoller, *Hitler privat* (Hitler in private) (Düsseldorf, 1949), p. 40.

8. Ibid., pp. 40ff.

9. Houston Stewart Chamberlain, *Die Grundlagen des 19. Jahrhunderts* (Munich, 1899), vol. 1, pp. 278ff. (Cf. *The Foundations of the Nineteenth Century,* 1911.)

10. *Wiener Deutsches Tagblatt,* 10 September 1907.

11 *UDW,* "Ostermond" (April) 1908, p. 25, "Frauen-Frage" (Women's question).

12. Florian Albrecht, "Der Kampf gegen das Deutschtum in der Ostmark" (The fight against Germandom in the Ostmark), pamphlet of the *Alldeutsches Tagblatt,* Vienna, 1908, pp. 4f., 7, 12, 15, and 16.

13. Vienna AVA, N. Pichl, box 74, flier "Der Verein Südmark und seine Gegner" (The Südmark Association and its opponents).

14. *AdT,* "Ostermond," April 1908, "Bismarck und Schönerer."

15. Harals Arjuna Grävell van Jostenoode, "Germanisches Zwölftafelgesetz" (Germanic twelve tablet law), in *Ostara* (Vienna, 1906), p. 7.

16. Johannes Balzli, *Guido v. List: Der Wiederentdecker Uralter Arischer Weisheit* (Guido von List: Rediscoverer of Ancient Aryan Wisdom) (Leipzig, 1917), pp. 53ff.

17. UDW, "Hornung," February 1909/2022 n.N., H. C. Heinrich Mayer, "Die Rita der Ariogermanen von Guido List" (Guido List's Rita of the Aryo-Germans), pp. 201–8.

18. Guido List, *Die Armanenschaft der Ario-Germanen,* vol. 2 (Vienna, 1911), p. 86.

19. AA, vol. 2, p. 71.

20. Kubizek, p. 226.

21. List, *Armanenschaft,* p. 107.

22. Guido List, *Übergang vom Wuotanstum zum Christentum* (Transition from Wodandom to Christendom) (Lenzmond, 1911), p. 106.

23. "Guido von List und die Bodenrechtsfrage" (Guido von List and the legal issue of land ownership), UDW, "Lenzmond," March 1911, pp. 234–37.

24. Guido List, *Die Bilderschrift der Ario-Germanen* (The Aryo-Germans' hieroglyphics) (Vienna, 1910), pp. 7ff.

25. Linz OÖLA, "Materialien Jetzinger," letter by Kubizek, 6 May 1949.

26. Jäckel/Kuhn, p. 186.

27. *MK,* pp. 496f.

28. Reginald H. Phelps, "Die Hitler-Bibliothek" (Hitler's library), in *Deutsche Rundschau,* vol. 80 (1954), p. 925. The books are in the Library of Congress in Washington, D.C.

29. Nicholas Goodrick-Clarke, *The Occult Roots of Nazism* (London, 1992), p. 199.

30. Elsa Schmidt-Falk to Prof. Wilfried Daim; the information was kindly provided by Prof. Daim.

31. Allusions to Wannieck in the publications of the List Society.

32. Vienna, Private Archive Daim.

33. Jäckel/Kuhn, pp. 187 and 186, Hofbräuhaus in Munich on 13 August 1920.

34. List, *Die Namen der Völkerstämme Germaniens und deren Deutung* (The names of Germania's tribes and their interpretation) (Vienna, 1909), p. 5.

35. *MK,* p. 383.

36. Domarus, p. 533, speech in Nuremberg, 14 September 1935.

37. Hitler, *Reden,* vol. 3, pt. 2, pp. 487 and 480. Speech at the NSDAP assembly in Munich, 29 November 1923.

38. Jäckel/Kuhn, pp. 908ff., Munich, 20 April 1923.

39. Gerhard Bredel, *Der Führer über die Juden* (The Führer on the Jews) (Munich, 1943), p. 64.

40. Guido List, *Der Wiederaufbau von Carnuntum* (The reconstruction of Carnuntum) (Vienna, 1900).

41. All these statements by Elsa Schmidt-Falk were taken from the minutes that Prof. Wilfried Daim took from memory of their conversation in Rosenheim on 22 February 1995.

42. "Spruchkammerakten" (tribunal files), writ of Elsa Schmidt-Falk, 25 March 1947, were made by Dr. Hans Brunschlik from Ottobrunn in Bavaria.

43. Elsa Schmidt-Falk, born in Budapest in 1897, grew up in Vienna and was an NSDAP member and wife of an SA leader since 1933. According to Munich's tribunal in 1947, she had a half-time job as director of the Department of Family Research in the NSDAP's Munich-North executive district committee and assistant adviser for genealogy in the National Socialist women's organization. Both were honorary positions. Presumably her difficulties with the district leadership mentioned during the trial, which resulted in her acquittal, had something to do with her inability to produce a certificate of Aryan descent.

44. Guido List, *Der Unbesiegbare* (The invincible) (Vienna, 1898), p. 23.

45. Ibid., p. 12.

46. Ibid., p. 7.

47. Ibid., pp. 9ff.

48. Ibid., pp. 19ff.

49. Fritz Wiedemann, *Der Mann, der Feldherr werden wollte* (The man who wanted to become general) (Velbert, 1964), p. 205.

50. MK, p. 68.

51. Domarus, p. 606, speech in Munich, 14 March 1936.

52. Ibid., p. 700, speech in Regensburg, 6 June 1937.

53. Ibid., p. 704, speech in Würzburg, 27 June 1937.

54. Otto Dietrich, *12 Jahre mit Hitler* (12 years with Hitler) (Munich, 1955), p. 58.

55. List (see n. 3), p. 179.

56. Gustave Le Bon, *Psychologie der Massen*, (Leipzig, 1908), p. 84. (Cf. *Psychology of the Masses*.) See also Alfred Stein, "Hitler und Gustave le Bon," in *Geschichte in Wissenschaft und Unterricht* (History in research and in the classroom) (Stuttgart, 1955), pp. 362–68.

57. Domarus, pp. 568f., speech in Berlin, 25 January 1936.

58. Ekkehard Hieronimus, *Lanz von Liebenfels: Eine Bibliographie* (Toppenstedt, 1991), p. 12.

59. Guido List, *Die Bilderschrift der Ario-Germanen*, p. 285 and ill. 376.

60. According to the registration office, the Hoffenreich family was Catholic, but a relative, Georg Fischer, stated that according to the Third Reich's racial laws it was "non-Aryan."

61. Vienna StLA, "Meldeakten" (registration files).

62. AdT, 1 April 1908, "Bismarck und Schönerer."

63. See, for example, *Katholizismus wider Jesuitismus* (Catholicism versus Jesuitism) (Frankfurt, 1903), p. 84.

64. AdT, 17 January 1909.

65. Ibid., 30 January 1909.

66. Ibid., 17 January 1909.

67. J. Lanz-Liebenfels, "Charakterbeurteilung nach der Schädelform" (Judging character by the shape of the skull), in *Ostara*, 1910, p. 7.

68. Hieronimus, pp. 36ff.

69. Lanz von Liebenfels, "Die geheime Prostitution der 'Anständigen' " (The clandestine prostitution of the "decent people"), in *Deutsche Hochschul-Stimmen aus der Ostmark* (German voices from universities in the *Ostmark*), 23 April 1910, pp. 4ff.

70. J. Lanz-Liebenfels, "Über das Wesen der Rasse" (On the nature of race), in *Deutsche Hochschul-Stimmen aus der Ostmark*, 15 January 1910.

71. J. Lanz-Liebenfels, "Der Gefangene von Potsdam" (The prisoner of Potsdam), in *AdT*, 17 August 1911, pp. 1ff.

72. J. Lanz-Liebenfels, "Die rassenwirtschaftliche Lösung des sexuellen Problems" (The eugenic solution to the sexual problem), in *Ostara*, 1909, p. 1.

73. J. Lanz-Liebenfels, "Die Komik der Frauenrechtlerei, eine heitere Chronik der Weiberwirtschaft" (The comic aspect of women's rights, an amusing chronicle), in *Ostara*, no. 44, Rodaun, 1911, p. 2.

74. J. Lanz-Liebenfels, "Die Blonden als Schöpfer der Sprachen" (Blond people as the creators of languages), in *Ostara*, 1911.

75. Daim, p. 151.

76 *Die Fackel*, 20 October 1913, pp. 6ff.

77. Washington, Library of Congress, Hitler Library, according to its inventory on microfilm at Munich's IfZ. The original German title is *Das Buch der Psalmen teutsch: Das Gebetbuch der Ariosophen, Rassenmystiker und Antisemiten.*

78. Peter Emil Becker, *Zur Geschichte der Rassenhygiene: Wege ins Dritte Reich* (On the history of eugenics: Paths toward the Third Reich) (Stuttgart, 1988), p. 384.

79. F. Dietrich, *Jörg Lanz von Liebenfels—60 Jahre* (Vienna, 1932), p. 143.

80. Vienna, private archive Fischer; written document by Luigi Hoffenreich, dated 3 August 1966, concerning his father Ludwig Hoffenreich and Georg Lanz.

81. Daim, pp. 27ff.

82. Ibid., p. 279.

83. Dr. Brunschlik's letter of 12 January 1995 in Vienna, private archive Daim.

84. This is the title of Daim's book (*Der Mann, der Hitler die Ideen gab*).

85. MK, p. 325.

86. Jäckel/Kuhn, p. 531, 16 December 1921.

87. MK, pp. 359–64.

88. "Die Verfälschung des Rassegedankens durch Geheimlehren," Munich IfZ, MA 744, pilot issue of the newspaper *Leib und Leben*.

89. Reinhard Spitzy, *So haben wir das Reich verspielt* (Munich, 1986), p. 131.

90. Wagener, p. 466.

91. Th. Newest (Hans Goldzier), *Einige Weltprobleme*, pt. 7: "Abgründe der Wissenschaft" (The abysses of science) (Vienna, 1911), p. 9.

92. Th. Newest, *Weltprobleme*, pt. 6: "Vom Zweck und Ursprung des organischen Lebens" (On the purpose and origin of organic life) (Vienna, 1908), pp. 136ff.

93. Ibid., p. 138.

94. Munich IfZ, ED 60/2, Otto Wagener, pt. 9, p. 528.

95. Newest, pp. 141ff. and 192.

96. Wagener, p. 468.

97. *Hörbiger's Glazial-Kosmogonie: Eine neue Entwicklungsgeschichte des Weltalls und des Sonnensystems* (Hörbiger's glacial cosmogony: A new history and evolution of

the universe and the solar system), ed. Philipp Fauth (Kaiserslautern, 1913), pp. vii and xi.

98. Rudolf John Gorsleben, "Welteislehre und Edda: Der Schlüssel zu Weltgeschehen" (World ice theory and Edda: The key to world events), in *Zeitschrift für Freunde der Welteislehre* (Periodical for friends of the world ice theory), 1926, pp. 209ff.

99. Hitler, *Monologe*, pp. 233, 25–26 January 1942.

100. Egon Friedell, *Kulturgeschichte der Neuzeit*, 1st edition 1927ff., new ed. (Munich, 1974), pp. 1500ff.

101. Hitler, *Monologe*, p. 233, 25–26 January 1942.

102. Ibid., pp. 285ff., 20–21 February 1942.

103. Linz OÖLA, "Politische Akten," box 49, "Protokolle des Gauleiters Eigruber über Vorträge bei Hitler 1941–43," 27 April 1942 in Munich.

104. Brigitte Nagel, "Die Welteislehre: Ihre Geschichte und ihre Bedeutung im Dritten Reich" (The world ice theory: Its history and significance in the Third Reich), in *Medizin, Naturwissenschaft, Technik und Nationalsozialismus*, ed. Christoph Meinel and Peter Voswinckel (Stuttgart, 1994), pp. 166–72.

105. Otto Strasser, *Der Aufbau des deutschen Sozialismus*, 2nd ed. (Prague, 1936), p. 132.

106. This information was kindly provided by Hörbiger's granddaughter Elisabeth Orth.

107. Otto Weininger, *Geschlecht und Charakter*, 3d ed. (Vienna, 1905) p. 418.

108. Ibid., pp. 451ff.

109. Ibid., p. 454.

110. Ibid., pp. 428ff.

111. Jacques Le Rider, "Otto Weininger als Anti-Freud," in *Katalog Traum und Wirklichkeit* (Catalog Dream and reality) (Vienna, 1985), pp. 248ff.

112. Weininger, p. 320.

113. Ibid., pp. 403ff.

114. Ibid., p. 112.

115. Ibid., p. 411.

116. Ibid., pp. 460ff.

117. Arthur Trebitsch, *Geist und Judentum* (The Jews and the mind) (Vienna, 1919), p. 209.

118. *Die Fackel*, 17 October 1903.

119. *Monologe*, p. 148, 1–2 December 1941.

120. Frank, p. 313.

121. Jäckel/Kuhn, p. 199, 13 August 1920.

122. Richard Wagner, "Das Kunstwerk der Zukunft," in *Gesammelte Werke*, p. 157.

123. Walter Warlimont, *Im Hauptquartier der deutschen Wehrmacht 1939 bis 1945* (In the headquarters of the German Army 1939–1945) (Frankfurt, 1964), p. 401.

124. NNZ, 1909, no. 4, p. 9.

126. Arthur Trebitsch, *Geist und Judentum* (The Jews and the mind) (Vienna, 1919), p. 174.

126. *Die Fackel*, 8 May 1913, pp. 44ff.

127. Roderich Müller-Guttenbrunn, *Der brennende Mensch: Das geistige Vermächtnis von Arthur Trebitsch* (Burning man: Arthur Trebitsch's intellectual legacy) (Leipzig, 1930), p. 132.

128. Ibid., p. 189.

129. Trebitsch, pp. 238ff.

130. Theodor Lessing, *Der jüdische Selbsthaß* (Jewish self-hatred) (Berlin, 1930), pp. 119ff.; a more recent publication on the topic is Sander L. Gilman, *Jüdischer Selbsthaß: Antisemitismus und die verborgene Sprache der Juden* (Frankfurt, 1993).

131. Müller-Guttenbrunn, pp. 322ff.

132. Munich IfZ, ED 209/34, N. Heiden, manuscript, p. 17.

133. Dietrich Eckart, *Der Bolschewismus von Moses bis Lenin* (Munich, 1925), pp. 34 and 51.

134. Friedrich Heer, *Der Glaube des Adolf Hitler* (Adolf Hitler's belief) (Munich, 1968), pp. 167ff., based on a letter by Baron Falk von Gagern to Heer dated 10 January 1968. The baron, born in 1912, confirmed in December 1995 that his father Friedrich had been a close friend of Trebitsch, that Trebitsch had still been in Munich in 1926, and that afterward he had made extemely critical remarks about Hitler's surroundings, in particular about Georg Strasser. He had called these people dangerous because they were "entirely under Jewish influence."

135. Chamberlain, vol. 1, pp. viiiff.

136. Speer, *Tagebücher*, p. 95.

137. MK, p. 337.

138. Ibid., p. 183.

139. Jäckel/Kuhn, p. 887, speech in Munich, 15 April 1923.

140. Goebbels, *Tagebücher*, pt. 2, vol. 7 (Munich, 1993), pp. 295ff., 8 February 1943.

Chapter 8

1. MK, p. 98.

2. AdT, 21 June 1909.

3. Vienna AAK, special issue, 100th birthday, 1942.

4. Eduard Pichl, ed., *Georg Schönerer* (Vienna, 1912), vol. 1, p. 70, speech on 18 December 1878.

5. Vienna NöLA, N. Mescerny von Tsoor/Schönerer, box 20, Zwettl, 7 January 1879.

6. Ibid., Ottenschlag, 6 January 1879.

7. Ibid., Vienna, 14 January 1879.

8. Anonymous, *Wien und die Wiener: Schilderungen eines fahrenden Gesellen* (Vienna and the Viennese: A journeyman's portraits) (Berlin, 1893), p. 135.

9. Pichl, vol. 1, p. 162.

10. Ibid., vol. 2, pp. 240ff.

11. Ibid., vol. 4, pp. 586ff.

12. AdT, 5 December 1909.

13. *Die Judenfrage als Rassen-, Sitten-und Kulturfrage.* StP HDA, 12 February 1884.

14. N. Stein, "Flugblatt mit antisemitischen Zitaten berühmter Männer" (Flier with anti-Semitic quotes from famous men).

15. Pichl, vol. 2, p. 2, 28 April 1887.

16. Eduard Frauenfeld on Schönerer in *Wiener Neueste Nachrichten*, 26 September 1942, p. 2.

17. Arthur Schnitzler, *Jugend in Wien* (Munich, 1971) p. 138. (Cf. *My Youth in Vienna*, Tr. Catherine Hutter, New York: Holt, Rinehart & Winston, 1970.)

18. *AdT*, 11 April 1908, p. 1: "Ein bedeutsames Gedenkfest" (A significant anniversary celebration).

19. In 1898 in Bodenbach; Pichl, vol. 6, p. 198.

20. Pichl, vol. 6, p. 196.

21. Georg Schönerer, "Die deutsche Selstentmannung" (German self-castration), speech in the Reichsrat on 5 November 1906.

22. Quoted in A. Ciller, *Deutscher Sozialismus in den Sudentenländern und der Ostmark* (German socialism in the Sudeten districts and the Ostmark), 2nd ed. (Hamburg, 1943), p. 53.

23. Deutsche Hochschul-Stimmen aus der Ostmark, 1 January 1940, p. 8.

24. Viktor Lischka in *AdT* on the occasion of Karl Iro's expulsion in 1913; Pichl, vol. 5, p. 332.

25. Pichl, vol. 2, p. 429.

26. Ibid., p. 31.

27. Vienna AAK, cue "Schönerer": copy of an essay by Eduard Pichl, "Schönerer und Wien," 1942.

28. Georg Ritter von Schönerer, "Rede über die Presse" (Speech on the press), 24 February 1888, special issue, Vienna, 1888.

29. Josef Scheicher, *Erlebuisse und Erinnerungen* (Vienna, n.d.), vol. 4, p. 371.

30. Brigitte Hamann, *Rudolf: Kronprinz und Rebell* (Rudolf: Crown prince and rebel) (Vienna, 1978), pp. 408ff.

31. *NWT*, 24 November 1897.

32. An appeal by Schönerer from November 1898; *UDW*, 16 "Nebelungs" (November) 1898, quoted frequently, see also *AdT*, 17 "Hartungs" (January) 1909.

33. Pichl, vol. 4, p 93.

34. *AdT*, 17 "Hartungs" (January) 1909.

35. Pichl, vol. 5, p. 385.

36. Walter Ferber, *Die Vorgeschichte der NSDAP in Österreich* (The NSDAP's prehistory in Austria) (Constanz, 1954), pp. 22ff.

37. Pichl, vol. 6, p. 195.

38. *MK*, p. 117.

39. Ibid., p. 122.

40. Kubizek, 1st draft, pp. 42ff.

41. Hitler to Fritz Schäffer, 1 December 1929, in Hitler, *Reden*, vol. 3, pt. 2, p. 510.

42. *MK*, pp. 107ff.

43. *MK*, pp. 95ff.

44. Ibid., p. 98.

45. Ibid., p. 91.

46. Jäckel/Kuhn, p. 999, speech on 5 September 1923 in Munich.

47. *MK*, p. 117.

48. Helmut Heiber, *Walter Frank und sein Reichsinstitut für Geschichte des neuen Deutschlands* (Walter Frank and his Reich institute of the history of the new Germany) (Stuttgart, 1966), p. 356. The first four volumes appeared up until 1923 under the author's pseudonym, "Herwig."

49. Harald Tichy, *Franz Stein ein großdeutscher Kämpfer* (Franz Stein, a Greater-German fighter) (Krems, 1942), pp. 13ff.

50. E. Stein, private property.

51. E. Stein, flier for the exhibition.

52. *AdT*, 1 April 1888.

53. The situation regarding sources on Stein is desolate. There is virtually no literature on him. His estate was split into many different pieces in the eighties. The author succeeded only in finding a fraction of it with a secondhand dealer in Vienna—personal papers, a few letters, and photographs. These sources are quoted as E. Stein (see note 50).

54. Pichl, vol. 6, p. 230.

55. E. Stein, typescript of notes, no date, pp. 11ff.

56. *MK*, pp. 11f.

57. Frequently quoted in the *Hammer* and the *"Hammer* Yearbook."

58. Quoted in Alois Ciller, *Deutscher Sozialismus in den Sudetenländern und der Ostmark* (German Socialism in the Sudeten area and the Ostmark) (Hamburg, 1943), p. 62.

59. Speech on 7 December 1905, published in *AdT*, 10 December 1905, and in special reprints.

60. Ibid.

61. Pichl, vol. 5, p. 192, speech of 27 April 1906.

62. Vienna AVA, E. Pichl, box 75; Franz Stein, "Die Unterschiede zwischen den Anschauungen der deutschvölkischen und sozialdemokratischen Arbeiterschaft: Nachruck der Rede im sudetendeutschen Gablonz" (The differences between the views of the German-folkish and the Social Demoratic workers: Reprint of the speech in the Sudeten German Gablonz), 1899.

63. AZ, 18 March 1908.

64. *Hammer-Jahrbuch 1913*, p. 113.

65. *Der Hammer*, 15 "Nebelungs" (November) 1909.

66. Picker, p. 206, 8 April 1942.

67. Ciller, p. 30.

68. Ibid., p. 78.

69. Andrew G. Whiteside, "Nationaler Sozialismus in Österreich vor 1918," in VjZg, 1961, pp. 340ff.

70. Reginald H. Phelps, "Die Hitler-Bibliothek" (Hitler's library), in *Deutsche Rundschau* (Baden-Baden), 1954, p. 928.

71. Vienna AdR, Bürckel correspondence 99/183.

72. Coblenz BA, NS10, 14 April 1937.

73. Berlin BA, personal files Stein; also in E. Stein.

74. *NWT*, 24 July 1943.

75. *NWT*, 18 June 1941, quoted in Clemens Weber, "Karl Hermann Wolf," Ph.D. diss., University of Vienna 1975, p. 357.

76. Coblenz BA, NS 26/64, "Meine Begegnung mit Hitler" (My encounter with Hitler).

77. *VB*, 18 June 1941.

78. Max Domarus, *Hitler, Reden und Proklamationen, 1932–1945* (Munich, 1962), p. 1724.

79. *Deutsche Wacht* (German guard), 8 August 1886, quoted in Weber, p. 23.

80. Max von Millenkovich-Morold, *Vom Abend zum Morgen: Aus dem alten Österreich ins neue Deutschland* (From evening to morning: From old Austria to the new Germany) (Leipzig, 1940), p. 145.

81. Robert Ehrhart, *Im Dienste des alten Österreich* (In the service of old Austria) (Vienna, 1958), p. 85.

82. Weber, p. 133.

83. *ODR*, 13 July 1897; Weber, p. 132.

84. Ehrhart, p. 85.

85. Friedrich Austerlitz, *Von Schwarzrotgold bis Schwarzgelb* (From black-red-gold to black-yellow) (Vienna, 1911), p. 10.

86. Engelbert Pernerstorfer, "Von Schönerer bis Wolf" (From Schönerer to Wolf), in *Der Kampf*, 1 June 1911.

87. *DVB* for Galicia, 2 December 1910, pp. 1f.

88. *NWT*, 13 May 1913.

89. Weber, pp. 233ff.

90. *AZ*, 16 October 1908, p. 3.

91. Quoted in Pulzer, p. 174.

92. Prelate Scheicher in the Lower Austrian parliament on 28 April 1893; StP NöL, p. 444.

93. *DVB für Galizien*, 24 November 1909, pp. 1f.

94. StP HdA, 363rd session, 11 December 1905, pp. 32869–73.

95. Session of HdA on 4 November 1897; Weber, p. 105.

96. *ODR*, 28 January 1894, "Gründet deutschnationale Tischgesellschaften!" (Found German-national Table Societies!).

97. Ibid., 31 May 1908. The two publications' original titles are "Die Nationalitätenfrage und die Sozialdemokratie" and "Nationale oder internationale Gewerkschaft."

98. Call by the club "German National Comrades" (Deutsche Volksgenossen); private property.

99. *NWJ*, 2 December 1908.

100. StP HdA, 22 January 1909, pp. 8446ff.

101. *AdT*, 23 February 1908.

102. *NIK*, 24 November 1908.

103. Stefan Zweig, *Die Welt von gestern* (Hamburg, 1965), pp. 68f. (Cf. *The World of Yesterday: An Autobiography by Stefan Zweig* [New York: Viking, 1943].)

104. *MK*, p. 55.

105. Franz Stauracz, *Dr. Karl Lueger: 10 Jahre Bürgermeister* (Vienna, 1907), p. 189.

106. *MK*, pp. 54ff.

107. Ibid., p. 55.

108. Hitler, *Monologe*, p. 153, 17 December 1941.

109. *DVB*, 4 July 1908, p. 1, "Wien und die Tschechen" (Vienna and the Czechs).

110. *AZ*, 11 March 1910, Austerlitz, "Nachruf Lueger" (Lueger obituary).

111. Hitler, *Monologe*, p. 153, 17 December 1941.

112. *MK*, p. 69.

113. Ibid., p. 121.

114. Hitler, *Monologe*, p. 153, 17 December 1941.

115. Picker, p. 300.

116. Erich Graf Kielmansegg, *Kaiserhaus, Staatsmänner und Politiker* (Imperial family, statesmen, and politicians) (Vienna, 1966), p. 390.

117. Hitler, *Reden*, vol. 3, pt. 2, p. 146, speech on 3 April 1929.

118. Kielmansegg, p. 391.

119. Scheicher, vol. 4, p. 410.

120. Ibid., p. 414.

121. Ibid., p. 417.

122. Austerlitz in *AZ*, 11 March 1910.

123. *MK*, p. 100.

124. Statistics in *IWE*, 4 January 1908.

125. Stauracz (see n. 2), p. 77.

126. *Monologe*, p. 153, 17 December 1941.

127. *WSMZ*, 6 April 1908.

128. *NIK*, 12 September 1908.

129. Ibid., 29 November 1908.

130. Ibid., 27 October 1908.

131. Henry Picker, *Hitlers Tischgespräche* (Frankfurt, 1951), p. 300, 15 April 1942.

132. Kielmansegg, p. 365.

133. *MK*, p. 119.

134. Coblenz BA, R 18/5018, Franz Stein, "Schönerer und Lueger."

135. StP HdA, 13 February 1890, pp. 13385 and 13388.

136. Paul von Pacher on 15 October 1896, quoted in Weber, p. 103.

137. Friedrich Funder, *Vom Gestern ins Heute* (From yesterday to today) (Vienna, 1952), p. 145.

138. *NFP*, 2 April 1895.

139. Felix Salten, *Das österreichische Antlitz* (Austria's face) (Berlin, 1909), pp. 135ff.

140. Ibid., p. 137.

141. Hugo von Hofmannsthal, *Buch der Freunde* (Leipzig, 1922), p. 74.

142. Marianne Beskiba, *Aus meinen Erinnerungen an Dr. Karl Lueger* (From my memories of Dr. Karl Lueger) (Vienna, n.d.), pp. 6ff.

143. Salten, pp. 132ff.

144. Max von Millenkovich-Morol, *Vom Abend bis zum Morgen* (From evening till morning) (Leipzig, 1940), pp. 227f.

145. Felix Salten, in *NFP*, 19 September 1926 "Denkmalenthüllung in Wien" (Uncovering a monument in Vienna).

146. *MK*, p. 107.

147. Ibid., p. 99.

148. Ibid., p. 180.

149. StP HdA, 13 February 1890, p. 13391.

150. Kielmansegg, p. 401.

151. StP NöL, 28 April 1893, p. 447, Rep. Ernst Schneider.

152. Dr. Karl Lueger, *Reden* (Speeches), delivered in Vienna on 20 July 1899, St. Pölten, 1899, pp. 25ff.

153. StP HdA, 26 May 1894, pp. 14622ff.

154. Salten, p. 132.

155. StP HdA, 6 May 1898.

156. Rudolf Kuppe, *Karl Lueger und seine Zeit* (Karl Lueger and his times) (Vienna, 1933), pp. 216ff.

157. An example is quoted in Kolin, in *WSMZ*, 21 April 1913, p. 4.

158. StP HdA, 13 February 1890, pp. 13386–93.

159. Ibid.

160. Scheicher, vol. 5, pp. 141ff.

161. Ibid., vol. 4, p. 153.

162. Felix Braun, *Das Licht der Welt* (The light of the world) (Vienna, 1949), p. 135.

163. *Bukowinaer Volksblatt*, 12 July 1908, quoted by Dr. Straucher, StP HdA, 15 July 1908, pp. 11788ff.

164. Kielmansegg, p. 382.

165. Sigmund Mayer, *Die Wiener Juden* (The Viennese Jews) (Vienna, 1917), p. 475.

166. Sigmund Mayer, *Ein jüdischer Kaufmann* (A Jewish merchant) (Leipzig, 1911), pp. 198ff and 296.

167. Arthur Schnitzler, *Jugend in Wien* (Munich, 1971), p. 129. (Cf. A.S., *My Youth in Vienna*, tr. Catherine Hutter, New York: Holt, Rinehart and Winston, 1970.) It is worthy of note that to this day there is no scholarly-critical German-language biography of Lueger. Richard S. Geehr, *Mayor of Fin de Siècle Vienna* (Detroit, 1990), which is based on historical sources, has not been translated into German.

168. Hitler, *Monologe*, pp. 152ff., 17 December 1941.

169. MK, pp. 120ff.

170. *Gemeindezeitung* (Parish newspaper), 8 January 1889, quoted in Brigitte Hamann, *Rudolf*, p. 413.

171. MK, p. 100.

172. Ibid., p. 119.

173. Kielmansegg, p. 386.

174. P. Heinrich Abel, SJ, *Wetterleuchten: Metereologische Schwankungen in der religiös-politischen Atmosphäre Österreichs* (Summer lightning: Metereological fluctuations in Austria's religious-political atmosphere) (Vienna, 1909).

175. Peter G. Pulzer, *Die Entstehung des politischen Antisemitismus in Deutschland und Österreich (1867–1914)* (The beginning of anti-Semitism in Germany and Austria 1867–1914) (Gütersloh, 1966), p. 58.

176. P. Abel, SJ, *Wiener Männerwallfahrten nach Mariazell* (Viennese men's pilgrimages to Mariazell) (Vienna, 1907), p. 219, ceremonial address July 1906.

177. Geehr, pp. 291ff.

178. *Ein Leben für Kunst und Volksbildung: Erinnerungen Eduard Leischings* (A life for the arts and popular education: Eduard Leisching's memoirs), ed. Robert Kann and Peter Leisching (Vienna, 1978), pp. 66ff. and 138.

179. Joseph Scheicher, *Aus dem Jahre 1920: Ein Traum* (St. Pölten, 1900), p. 63.

180. Ibid., p. 76.

181. Ibid., p. 88.

182. Ibid., p. 41.

183. Ibid., pp. 61ff.

184. *DVB*, 8 December 1905, p. 8.

185. *WSMZ*, 6 April 1908.

186. *MK*, p. 98.

187. *Reden* (St. Pölten, 1899), p. 32.

188. *IKZ*, 31 January 1909.

189. Kielmansegg, p. 380, see also p. 403.

190. See, e.g., *AZ*, 18 June 1911, p. 21.

191. *DVB*, 1 June 1911, p. 4.

192. *BBN*, 21 July 1912, p. 5.

193. *SJSW für 1908*, Vienna, 1910, p. 832.

194. Hitler, *Monologe*, pp. 73ff., 1 October 1941.

195. Kokoschka, p. 59.

196. Monika Glettler, *Die Wiener Tschechen um 1900* (The Czechs in Vienna around 1900) (Vienna, 1972), pp. 293ff.

197. *Reichspost*, 19 October 1909, p. 2.

198. Quoted in Glettner, p. 311.

199. MK, p. 55.

200. Bonn PA, Austria 70, Tschirschky to Bülow, 11 February 1909.

201 Franz Stauracz, Dr. Karl Lueger: Zehn Jahre Bürgermeister (Vienna, 1907).

202. Bonn PA, Austria 86, no. 2, 15 March 1910.

203. MK, p. 121.

204. AZ, 11 March 1910.

205. MK, p. 122.

206. Ibid., p. 101.

207. Ibid., pp. 97f.

208. Hitler, Monologe, p. 153, 17 December 1941.

209. Kubizek, p. 114.

210. Ibid., p. 297.

211. MK, p. 118.

212. Goebbels, Tagebücher, pt. 2, vol. 3 (Munich, 1994), p. 473, 15 March 1942.

Chapter 9

1. Peter Urbanitsch, Die Deutschen in Österreich (The Germans in Austria) (Vienna, 1980), p. 54.

2. Friedrich Prinz, Geschichte Böhmens 1848–1948 (History of Bohemia 1848–1948) (Frankfurt, 1991), p. 221.

3. Bonn AA PA, Austria 70, "Strictly confidential," Brockendorff-Rantzau, 26 August 1909.

4. Urbanitsch, figure 1.

5. MK, p. 93.

6. Anton Schubert, Das Deutschtum im Wirtschaftshaushalte Österreichs (Germandom in Austria's economic budget), pt. 2 (Reichenberg, 1906), p. 235.

7. UDW, 19 March and 1 April 1908.

8. Koeppen, p. 34. It should read "Austrian" in that Hitler was clearly referring to Cisleithania, without Hungary.

9. According to Henry Picker, Hitlers Tischgespräche (Frankfurt, 1951), p. 198, 5 April 1942, "of 1,880 court officials . . . 1,630 were Czech and only 170 German."

10. Quoted in Michael John and Albert Lichtblau, Schmelztiegel Wien einst und jetzt (Melting pot Vienna, then and now) (Vienna, 1990), p. 19.

11. Gustav Otruba et al., Die Herkunft der Wiener Bevölkerung (Vienna, 1957), p. 237.

12. Eduard Sueß, Erinnerungen (Memoirs), (Leipzig, 1916), p. 38.

13. Monika Glettler, Die Wiener Tschechen um 1900 (Viennese Czechs around 1900) (Vienna, 1972), pp. 41ff.

14. AdT, 17 August 1909.

15. BBN, 28 July 1912, p. 2: "Der deutsche Charakter Wiens bedroht" (Vienna's German character endangered).

16. IKZ, 22 August 1909.

17. AdT, 17 June 1908.

18. Ibid., 16 January 1909, "Der deutsche Charakter Wiens" (Vienna's German character).

19. Vienna AVA, MdI police headquarters Lower Austria 1909–1910, box 22, no. 2824/7, 13 August 1909.

20. StP NÖL, 9 October 1909.

21. StP HdA, 26 November 1909, p. 493.

22. *Prager Tagblatt*, 25 September 1909.

23. *Reichspost*, 9 October 1909.

24. *IKZ*, 12 August 1909.

25. *AZ*, 13 August 1909.

26. *IKZ*, 14 August 1909.

27. Ibid., 13 August 1909.

28. *AdT*, 17 August 1909.

29. *VB*, 10 April 1938, insert, pp. 10ff.

30. Glettler, p. 298.

31. *DVB*, 19 January 1911, p. 1.

32. *NFP*, 9 August 1909; *AdT*, 10 August 1909.

33. *DVB für Galizien*, 1 July 1910, p. 4.

34. Glettler, p. 302.

35. StP NÖL, 16 September 190, p. 308. Karl Seitz, who delivered the speech, was mayor of Vienna from 1923 to 1934.

36. *Nowa Reforma*, 9 October 1909, quoted in *DVB für Galizien*, 5 November 1909, p. 1.

37. *IKZ*, 8 October 1909.

38. The whole intricate matter is documented in Glettler, pp. 338ff.

39. Ludwig Brügel, *Geschichte der österreichischen Sozialdemokratie* (History of Austrian Social Democracy), vol. 5 (Vienna, 1925), p. 41.

40. *BBN*, 7 March 1912, pp. 1–3.

41. Hans Mommsen, *Die Sozialdemokratie und die Nationalitätenfrage im habsburgischen Vielvölkerstaat* (Social Democracy and the issue of nationalities in the multiethnic Hapsburg empire) (Vienna, 1963), p. 413.

42. Viktor Adler, *Briefwechsel mit August Bebel und Karl Kautsky* (Correspondence with August Bebel and Karl Kautsky) (Vienna, 1954), p. 352, 1 June 1901.

43. Quoted from Kautsky's estate in Mommsen, p. 110, 15 August 1911.

44. *Geschichte des Sozialismus* (History of Socialism), ed. Jacques Droz, vol. 4, (Frankfurt, 1975), p. 124.

45. *Der Hammer*, 16 February 1909.

46. Hermann Bahr's letter in Brigitte Hamann, *Bertha von Suttner: Ein Leben für den Frieden* (Munich, 1986), pp. 473f. (Cf. *Bertha von Suttner: A Life for Peace*, tr. Ann Dubsky, [Syracuse, 1996].)

47. StP HdA, 4 February 1909, pp. 8583ff.

48. Ibid., 17 December 1908, pp. 8183ff.

49. *Deutsche Hochschul-Stimmen aus der Ostmark* (German voices from universities in the Ostmark), 27 November 1909, p. 4.

50. *AdT*, 10 August 1910, p. 3.

51. This information was kindly provided by Karl Prince Schwarzenberg.

52. Hitler, *Monologe*, p. 216, 22 January 1942.

53. Heiber, pp. 228ff., Bormann to Lammers, 28 January 1941.

54. *MK*, p. 109.

55. Urbanitsch, p. 67.

56. *Deutsche Hochschul-Stimmen aus der Ostmark*, 20 November 1909.
57. Kubizek, pp. 297ff.
58. Ibid., p. 188.
59. Hitler, *Monologe*, pp. 227ff., 25 January 1942.
60. Koeppen, p. 43, 6 October 1941.
61. Hitler, *Monologe*, p. 216, Wolf Entrenchment, 22 January 1942.
62. MK, pp. 388ff.
63. Koeppen, 6 October 1941.
64. Heiber, p. 219; according to a report to the Foreign Office, 5 October 1940.
65. Picker, pp. 321ff., 20 May 1942.
66. Koeppen, p. 31, 1 October 1941.
67. Hitler, *Monologe*, p. 405, 25 June 1943.

Chapter 10

1. *DVB*, 17 September 1895, p. 7.
2. Peter Urbanitsch, *Die Deutschen in Österreich* (Vienna, 1980), p. 57.
3. Rudolf Vrba, *Die Revolution in Rußland* (Prague, 1906), vol. 1, p. 316.
4. Jakob Wassermann, *Mein Weg als Deutscher und Jude* (My path as a German and Jew) (Berlin, 1921), pp. 102ff.
5. Leo Goldhammer, *Die Juden Wiens: Eine statistische Studie* (Vienna's Jews: A statistical study) (Vienna, 1927), pp. 37ff.
6. Jakob Thon, *Die Juden in Österreich* (The Jews in Austria), ed. Bureau für Statistik der Juden (Office of Jewish Statistics) (Berlin, 1908), p. 102.
7. Goldhammer, p. 40.
8. Hans Tietze, *Die Juden Wiens* (Vienna, 1933), p. 212.
9. R. Granichstaedten-Cerva, J. Mentschl, and G. Otruba, *Altösterreichische Unternehmer* (Entrepreneurs in the former Austria) (Vienna, 1969), pp. 40ff.
10. Hermann Bahr, *Austriaca* (Vienna, 1911), p. 123.
11. Alfred Roller, *Die Bildnisse Gustav Mahlers* (The portraits of Gustav Mahler), Leipzig, 1922, p. 25.
12. Goldhammer, pp. 17f.
13. StP HdA, 20 June 1908.
14. *NNZ*, 15 January 1909.
15. Theodor Billroth, *Über das Lehren und Lernen der medizinischen Wissenschaften an den Universitäten der deutschen Nation* (On the teaching and study of the medical sciences at the universities of The German nation) (Vienna, 1876), pp. 153ff.
16. E. Stein, collection of quotes for the preparation of the 1942 Schönerer exhibit.
17. Klaus Hödl, *Als Bettler in die Leopoldstadt* (To Leopoldstadt as a beggar) (Vienna, 1994), p. 39.
18. *NWJ*, 2 December 1908, p. 3.
19. Entry in the archduchess's diary of 28 July 1887, quoted in Brigitte Hamann, *Rudolf: Kronprinz und Rebell* (Vienna, 1978), pp. 404ff.
20. *BBN*, 22 December 1912, p. 1.
21. Anonymous, *Wien und die Wiener: Schilderungen eines fahrenden Gesellen* (Berlin, 1893), p. 128.
22. MK, p. 56.
23. *Jahrbuch für deutsche Frauen und Mädchen*, ed. Karl Iro (Vienna, 1904), p. 78.

24. Sigmund Mayer, *Ein jüdischer Kaufmann* (A Jewish merchant) (Leipzig, 1911), p. 343.

25. Hödl, p. 68.

26. Anna Staudacher, "Die Aktion 'Girondo': Zur Geschichte des internationalen Mädchenhandels in Österreich-Ungarn um 1885" (Operation "Girondo": On the history of the international white slave trade in Austro-Hungary around 1885), in *Das Weib existiert nicht für sich* (Woman doesn't exist for herself), ed. Heide Dienst and Edith Saurer (Vienna, 1990), pp. 97ff.

27. Josef Schank, *Der Mädchenhandel und seine Bekämpfung* (The white slave trade and the fight against it) (Vienna, 1904), p. 71.

28. Quoted in Hödl, p. 68.

29. *NNZ*, 1 January 1909.

30. Bertha Pappenheim and Sara Rabinowitsch, *Zur Lage der jüdischen Bevölkerung in Galizien: Reise-Eindrücke und Vorschläge zur Besserung der Verhältnisse* (On the situation of the Jewish population in Galicia: Travel impressions and suggestions for improving conditions) (Franfurt/1904).

31. Mayer, pp. 326ff.

32. *MK*, p. 59.

33. StP HdA, 20 June 1908, p. 6119.

34. Ibid., 20 June 1908, quoted in Brigitte Hamann, "Der Verein zur Abwehr des Antisemitismus" (The Association for the Defense of Anti-Semitism), in *Die Macht der Bilder: Katalog* (The power of pictures: catalog), ed. Jewish Museum of the City of Vienna (Vienna, 1995), pp. 253ff.

35. *Reden*, vol. 3, pt. 2, p. 520. Letter to Fritz Schäffer, *Völkischer Beobachter*, 7 December 1929 and note.

36. StP HdA, 91, 20 June 1908, p. 6127.

37. *NNZ*, 3 July 1908.

38. Hödl, p. 121.

39 Wassermann, pp. 107ff.

40. Ibid., p. 119.

41. Josph Roth, *Juden auf Wanderschaft* (Wandering Jews) (Cologne, 1976), pp. 75ff.: "Vorrede zur neuen Auflage" (Preface to the new edition).

42. Max Nordau, "Der Zionismus und seine Gegner" (Zionism and its opponents), in *Die Welt*, Vienna, 20 May 1898, p. 1.

43. Wassermann, p. 110.

44. Roth, p. 17.

45. Max Nordau, "Zionismus und Antisemitismus," in *Die Welt*, July 1899, no. 30, p. 4.

46. Nordau, pp. 1f.

47. Gerald Stourzh, "Die Gleichberechtigung der Volksstämme als Verfassungsprinzip 1848–1918" (The emancipation of folkish tribes as a constitutional principle 1848–1918), in Urbanitsch, p. 1037.

48. Nordau.

49. Karl Kraus, *Eine Krone für Zion* (Vienna, 1898).

50 Nordau.

51. *MK*, p. 57.

52. Vrba, p. 338.

53. Ibid., p. 344.

54. Ibid., pp. 314ff.

55. Helga Riesinger, "Leben und Werk des österreichischen Politikers Wilhelm Ellenbogen" (Life and work of the Austrian politician Wilhelm Ellenbogen), Ph.D. diss. University of Vienna, 1969, pp. 32ff.

56. *DVB*, 6 December 1905, p. 1.

57. Ibid., 6 December 1905, p. 6.

58. Ibid., 8 December 1905, p. 2.

59. Ibid., 8 December 1908, p. 3.

60. StP HdA, 27 March 1906, pp. 35688ff.

61. Vrba, p. 216.

62. Ibid., p. 328.

63. Ibid., p. 210.

64. Ibid., p. 222.

65. Ibid., p. 330.

66. According to VB, 15/16 April 1923, Jäckel, p. 888.

67. *DVB*, 9 January 1908, p. 1.

68. Ludwig Brügel, *Geschichte der österreichischen Sozialdemokratie* (History of Austria's Social Democracy), vol. 5 (Vienna, 1925), p. 97.

69. Walther Rathenau in *NFP*, 25 December 1909.

70. *BBN*, 10 May 1912, pp. 4ff.

71. Domarus, p. 1868, 26 April 1942, during the last session of the Greater German Reichstag.

72. MK, p. 65.

73. Ibid., p. 44.

74. Speer, *Tagebücher* (Diaries), p. 530.

75. MK, p. 64.

76. Ibid., p. 55.

77. Ibid,. p. 56.

78. Ibid., p. 60.

79. Statement by Marianne Koppler.

80. This information was kindly provided by Professor Albert Hackl, whose family owned the Biedermeier house at 20 Webgasse. According to the registration office, Jakob Wassermann, a Jewish saloonkeeper, was born in Komorawitz, Galicia, in 1866. He lived at Webgasse until 1941. In January 1943 the seventy-six-year-old was deported to Theresienstadt. The date of his death is unknown.

81. Dr. Eduard Bloch, as told to J. D. Ratcliff, "My Patient Hitler," pt. 2, *Colliers*, 22 March 1941, p. 69.

82. Speer, p. 112.

83. Smith, p. 150.

84. Wagener, p. 343.

85. Ibid., p. 144.

86. MK, p. 64.

87. Speer, *Tagebücher*, p. 531.

88. *Adolf Hitler's drei Testamente*, ed. Gert Sudholt (Leoni, n.d.), p. 10.

89. MK, p. 687.

90. Ibid., p. 206.

91. August Kubizek, *Adolf Hitler, Mein Jugendfreund* (Graz, 1953), pp. 285ff. Due to the frequent occurrence of their names, the families Graf and Grieser, whom Kubizek also mentions, could not be identified.

92. Vienna StLA, maps of Heiligenstadt and land registry.

93. Professor Marie Jahoda's statements were made during a conversation with the author in Sussex in 1994. I would like to express my gratitude to her for her hospitality.

94. Vienna StLA, register.

95. Kubizek, p. 285.

96. Ibid., p. 286.

97. Vienna StLA. According to the official report on his estate, he had nothing to bequeath.

98. Munich BHStA, "People" collection, 12.659.

99. Vienna AdR MfF, Administration of Property, Aryanization Morgenstern.

100. Munich BDStA, "People" collection 12.659, deposition from memory on 24 March 1937 to Dr. Arthur Kulka, Esq.

101. The wife of the upholsterer Pichler also knew that Hitler supplied mainly Jews. When in its search for more Hitler paintings the NSDAP's Central Archive asked for her help in 1938, she pointed out how difficult this would be: "It is just very awkward that the present owners are most likely Jews" (Coblenz BA, NS 26/20).

102. According to the Registration Office, Dr. Feingold was born in Vienna in 1878, Jewish, married. According to Lehmann's residence listing of 1910 he still lived in Leopoldstadt at the time (5 Kleine Schiffgasse), and his law office was at 5 Rauhensteingasse. Before his emigration to France in 1938 he lived in the Third District, at 6/1/9 Beatrixgasse.

103. When the search for Hitler's paintings began in the 1930s, Feingold no longer had any: after the downsizing of his offices, he said, he had no longer had any use for them and given them away as presents—four alone to his hairdresser's daughter, who sympathized with the National Socialists. According to the hairdresser Mock's report to the NSDAP archive in 1936, these were views of the old Schönbrunn gate, the Ratzenstadl, Auersperg Palace, and the old Burgtheater, all signed "A. Hitler" (Coblenz BA, NS 26/28). Feingold did not tell his curious interviewer anything about young Hitler. According to the Registration Office, he left Vienna on 4 August 1938, heading for France.

104. Vienna AdR FMin, Administration of Property, Gew. 2,755, box 216, Aryanization files Samuel Morgenstern.

105. Ibid.

106. Kubizek, p. 329.

107. Vienna AStW, Registration Office.

108. Vienna AdR Fmin, Department of Property.

109. Oskar Rosenfeld, *Wozu noch Welt: Aufzeichnungen aus dem Getto Lodz* (Why still a world: Notes from the ghetto in Lodz) (Frankfurt/1994), pp. 19ff.

110. *MK*, pp. 59ff.

111. Vienna StLA, report on Samuel Morgenstern's death certificate by the court, 29 November 1945.

112. Vienna StLA, report for Emma Morgenstern's death certificate by the court.

113. Lucjan Dobroszycki, "Die Juden von Wien im Getto von Lodz 1941–1944" (Vienna's Jews in the ghetto of Lodz), in *Jüdisches Echo*, Vienna, 1984, pp. 133ff.

114. Vienna StLA, Pronouncement of Death of Emma Morgenstern.

Chapter 11

1. August Kubizek, *Adolf Hitler, Mein Jugendfreund* (Graz, 1953), p. 278.

2. Ibid., p. 275.

3. Hitler, *Monologe*, p. 231, 25–26 January 1942.

4. Kubizek according to Franz Jetzinger, *Hitlers Jugend* (Vienna, 1956), p. 239.

5. Kubizek, pp. 189ff. In Kubizek's first draft, this episode is much more compressed and told with more reserve.

6. Ibid., p. 230.

7. Ibid., p. 285.

8. Ibid., pp. 194ff.

9. Ibid., p. 276.

10. Ibid., p. 284.

11. Statement by Marianne Koppler.

12. Reinhold Hanisch, *I Was Hitler's Buddy*, in *The New Republic*, 19 April 1939, p. 297.

13. Maurice Samuelson, "Post von Hitler," in *Die Presse*, 14 May 1994.

14. Statement by Marianne Koppler.

15. Schroeder, pp. 152–56.

16. Vienna StLA, Registration Office.

17. Statements by Marianne Koppler.

18. Maser, p. 310.

19. Stefan Zweig, *Die Welt von Gestern* (Hamburg, 1965), pp. 84ff.

20. Ibid., p. 89.

21. H. Montane, *Die Prostitution in Wien* (Vienna, 1925), pp. 170ff.

22. Kubizek, pp. 282ff.

23. Linz OÖLA, Jetzinger files, letter by Kubizek of 6 May 1949.

24. Kubizek, p. 278.

25. E. Peters, "Ist die Prostitution eine gesundheitliche Notwendigkeit?" (Is prostitution necesssary for health maintenance?), in *UDW*, "Brachmond" (June) 1911, no. 3, pp. 47ff.

26. Lanz-Liebenfels, "Die geheime Prostitution der 'Anständigen' " (The secret prostitution of the "decent ones"), pt. 2, in *Deutsche Hochschul-Stimmen aus der Ostmark*, 30 "Ostermond" (April) 1910, pp. 3ff.

27. Kubizek, p. 286.

28. Friedrich Funder, *Vom Gestern ins Heute* (Vienna, 1952), p. 111.

29. *UDW*, "Ostermond" (April) 1909, no. 1, p. 15.

30. *Der Hammer*, 1 "Herbstmond" (September) 1908, "Frauenarbeit!—Männerarbeit!" (Woman's work!—Man's work!).

31. "Die Frauen und die Politik" (Women and politics), in *Der Hammer*, 1 "Heuerts" (July) 1912, pp. 97ff.

32. Harald Arjuna Grävell van Jostenoode, "Völkische Richtlinien für unsere Zukunft," in *Ostara*, July 1906, p. 11.

33. Domarus, pp. 531ff., speech in Nuremberg of 13 September 1935.

34. *Jahrbuch für deutsche Frauen und Mädchen*, ed. Karl Iro (Vienna, 1904), p. 76: "Über Mädchen-Turnen" (On girls' gymnastics); see also p. 94: "Fort mit dem Korsett!" (Away with the corset!).

35. Jörg Lanz von Liebenfels, "Rassenbewußtlose und rassenbewußte Lebens-und Liebeskunst, ein Brevier für die reife blonde Jugend" (Race-unconscious and race-

conscious art of living and loving, a breviary for mature, blond youth), in *Ostara*, Rodaun, 1912.

36. *MK*, p. 412.

37. "Ein Wörtlein zur deutschen Mädchenerziehung" (A brief word on the education of German girls), in *UDW*, "Hartung" (January) 1911, vol. 10, pp. 190ff.

38. *Die Zeit*, 15 June 1911, p. 3.

39. Waltraud Heindl, "Zur Entwicklung des Frauenstudiums in Österreich" (On the development of women's college education in Austria), in *Durch Erkenntnis zu Freiheit und Glück* (Through knowledge to freedom and happiness), ed. Waltraud Heindl and Marina Tichy (Vienna, 1990), pp. 17–26.

40. Waltraud Heindl, "Die konfessionellen Verhältnisse: Jüdische und katholische Studentinnen" (Denominational ratios: Jewish and Catholic woman students), ibid., p. 140.

41. Uto von Melzer, "Deutsches Frauenleben" (A German woman's life), in *Jahrbuch*, p. 75.

42. *Der Hammer*, 1 "Heuerts" (July) 1912, pp. 99ff.

43. Domarus, p. 450, speech of 5 September 1934.

44. Ibid., p. 451, 8 September 1934.

45. *BBN*, 1 June 1912, p. 3.

46. A. Lichtenstettiner, "Ein Beitrag zur Frauenwahlrechtsfrage" (A contribution to the issue of women's suffrage), in *Der Hammer*, 15 June 1912, cover story, pp. 1ff.

47. Picker, pp. 205ff., 8 April 1942.

48. *MK*, p. 414.

49. *AZ*, 4 June 1908, p. 4.

50. F. Siebert, "Alldeutsches zur Frauenbewegung" (Pan-German thoughts on the women's movement), in *UDW*, "Ostermond" (April) 1911, pp. 1ff.

51. *Jahrbuch für deutsche Frauen und Mädchen*, ed. Karl Iro, Vienna, 1904, p. 82.

52. Domarus, p. 451, Speech before the NS Women's Organization in Nuremberg on 8 September 1934.

53. *MK.*, p. 252.

54. Stauracz, pp. 5ff.

55. Marianne Beskiba, *Aus meinen Erinnerungen an Dr. Karl Lueger* (From my memories of Dr. Karl Lueger), self-published (Vienna, 1911), p. 77.

56. Ibid., pp. 24ff.

57. Schroeder, p. 152.

58. Hans Severus Ziegler, *Adolf Hitler aus dem Erleben dargestellt* (Adolf Hitler, portrayed by people who knew him) (Göttingen, 1965), p. 10.

59. See, e.g., Hitler's valet, Karl-Wilhelm Krause, *Zehn Jahre Tag und Nacht* (Ten years, day and night), (Hamburg, 1949), p. 35; Friedelind Wagner, *Nacht über Bayreuth* (Night over Bayreuth) (Cologne, 1946), p. 195; and others.

60. Krause, ibid., pp. 52ff.

61. Hitler, *Monologe*, p. 316, 10–11 March 1942.

Chapter 12

1. Anonymous, "Mein Freund Hitler," in *Moravský ilustrovaný spravodaj*, 1935, no. 40 (in Czech).

2. Vienna StLA, Registration Office.

3. *18. Jahresbericht . . . für 1913*, Vienna, 1914, pp. 3 and 6.

4. Karl Honisch, "Protokoll" (Statement); Coblenz BA NS26/17a.

5. Hansotto Hatzig, "Bertha von Suttner und Karl May," in *Jahrbuch der Karl-May-Gesellschaft 1971*, p. 252.

6. Hamann, *Suttner*, pp. 485ff.

7. Ekkehard Bartsch, "Karl Mays Wiener Rede" (Karl May's Vienna speech), in *Jahrbuch der Karl-May-Gesellschaft 1970*, pp. 50ff. and 55ff.

8. Bertha von Suttner, "Einige Worte über Karl May" (A few words about Karl May), in *Die Zeit*, 5 April 1912.

9. *NFP*, 23 March 1912.

10. Otto Dietrich, *Zwölf Jahre mit Hitler* (Twelve years with Hitler) (Munich, 1955), p. 164.

11. Hans Severus Ziegler, *Adolf Hitler aus dem Erleben dargestellt* (Göttingen, 1965), p. 77.

12. Speer, pp. 523ff.

13. Brigitte Hamann, "Bertha von Suttner und Alfred Hermann Fried," in *The Nobel Peace Prize and the Laureates: The Meaning and Acceptance of the Nobel Peace Prize in the Prize Winners' Countries*, ed. Karl Holl and Anne C. Kjelling (Frankfurt, 1994), pp. 83–93.

14 *BBN*, 10 May 1912.

15. Adolf Harpf, "Die Zeit des ewigen Friedens, eine Apologie des Krieges als Kultur- und Rassenauffrischer," in *Ostara*, Vienna, 1908, pp. 4ff., 7, and 11.

16. *MK*, p. 396.

17. Hitler, *Reden Schriften Anordnungen Februar 1925 bis Januar 1933* (Speeches, writings, orders, February 1925 to January 1933), vol. 3, pt. 2, p. 195, 29 October 1929.

18. *Zweites Buch*, p. 132.

19. Ludwig Brügel, *Geschichte der österreichischen Sozialdemokratie* (The history of Social Democracy in Austria), vol. 5 (Vienna, 1925), p. 119.

20. Helga Riesinger, "Leben und Werk des österreichischen Politikers Wilhelm Ellenbogen" (Life and work of the Austrian politician Wilhelm Ellenbogen), Ph.D. diss., University of Vienna, 1969, p. 74.

21. Brügel, p. 121.

22. *DVB für Galizien*, 8 October 1909, p. 4.

23. Charmatz, pp. 107ff.

24. Kubizek, p. 307, reads "7-19-1909," Jetzinger, p. 205, "8-19-1909."

25. Picker, p. 347, 2 June 1942.

26. *DVB*, 2 July 1908, "Kriegsphantasien" (War fantasies).

27. *NWJ*, 3 March 1912, "Der Luftkoller" (War madness), translated from the newspaper *Excelsior* and with a commentary by Bertha von Suttner.

28. *WSMZ*, 7 April 1913.

29. *Lagebesprechungen im Führerhauptquartier* (Discussions of the situation at general headquarters), ed. Helmut Heiber (Munich, 1963), pp. 235ff., 20 May 1943.

30. *MK*, p. 124.

31. *Danzer's Armee-Zeitung*, 7 January 1909.

32. *MK*, pp. 128ff.

33. Ibid., p. 130.

34. Munich BHStA, Hss. N. Sexau, copy of 21 March 1909.

35. *AdT*, 3 May 1912.

36. *Zweites Buch*, p. 91.

37. Hitler, *Reden*, vol. 3, pt. 2, p. 254, before the Munich District Court on 7 May 1929.

38. *MK*, p. 160.

39. Hitler, *Monologe*, p. 77, 10–11 October 1941.

40. Domarus, p. 1090.

41. Jäckel/Kuhn, p. 526, letter of 29 November 1921.

42. *Staatsmänner und Diplomaten bei Hitler* (Statesmen and diplomats visit Hitler), ed. Andreas Hillgruber, pt. 2 (Frankfurt, 1970), p. 260, conversation with Horthy on April 17, 1943.

43. *Hammer-Jahrbuch 1913*, pp. 134ff.

44. Urbanitsch, pp. 109ff.

45. *AdT*, 10 "Hornungs" (February) 1909, "Leiden eines k.u.k. Soldaten" (Sufferings of an Austro-Hungarian soldier).

46. Ibid., 28 March 1909.

47. (Anton Schubert,) *Das Deutschtum im Wirtschaftshaushalte Österreichs* (German-dom in Austria's budget), pt. 2: *Die Abgabenleistungen der Deutschen in Österreich an den Staat* (German taxes to the state of Austria) (Reichenberg, 1906), p. 209.

48. *MK*, p. 70.

49. The entire matter was documented for the first time in Jetzinger, pp. 254 ff.

50. Jäckel/Kuhn, p. 54, letter dated 21 January 1914 from Munich to the Linz magistrate. This was confirmed by the investigation of Vienna's federal police administration by order of the Federal Chancellery of 13 March 1932; Coblenz BA, NS 26/18.

51. Hitler, *Reden*, vol. 3, pt. 2, p. 150, Munich, 3 April 1929.

52. See, e.g., *AdT*, no. 227, March 1908, "Aus dem Schuldbuche des Zölibats" (From celibacy's debt register).

53. Vienna StLA, registration files Häusler. All of Häusler's statements quoted here were told to the author by his daughter Marianne Koppler on 21 January 1996. I am indebted to Professor Peter Csendes for his expedient help when it looked like my rather intricate search for Häusler's daughter was going nowhere.

54. From Häusler's answers to the DAF questionnaire of 9 October 1939, quoted in Joachimsthaler, p. 81.

55. *Wien ThM Hofoper*, program of May 1913. It was most likely the performance on Monday, 5 May 1913.

56. Facsimile in Werner Maser, *Sturm auf die Republik* (Storming the republic) (Düsseldorf, 1994), pp. 81ff. The document is from the estate of Hitler's housekeeper Anny Winter, who in 1945 took possession of the contents of Hitler's desk in Munich. Her estate was auctioned in 1971. (See Maser, p. 546, n. 12.)

57. *MK*, p. 125.

58. In 1945 these paintings were among those personal effects that were stored at the Berghof and then transported to Bozen in six trucks, accompanied by Mrs. Bormann and her twelve children. When Mrs. Bormann died in Bozen in 1946, the paintings disappeared (Munich IfZ, ZS 2238). In 1984, eighteen pictures resurfaced in Florence at an exhibition of the estate of Italian minister Siviero.

59. Maser, p. 92.

60. *Monologe*, p. 115, 29 October 1941.

61. *MK*, p. 126.

62. Joachimsthaler, p. 18.

63. Coblenz BA, NS 26/17a.

64. Private archive Marianne Koppler.

65. Hitler, *Monologe*, 25 January 1942, p. 227.

66. Joachimsthaler, p. 80. Josef Popp mentioned his second subtenant—without, however, mentioning Häusler's name—to Maser (p. 118), but not until 1966. He said that every night the two of them had had political discussions, and the second subtenant had moved out because he could stand it no longer.

67. Jetzinger, p. 258, with a reprint of the request of 19 January 1914.

68. Joachimsthaler, p. 81.

69. *MK*, p. 15.

70. Hanisch.

71. *MK*, p. 124.

72. Ibid., p. 162.

73. Ibid., p. 163.

74. Vienna AdR, BMfI Zl. 204.787-33/68. Copy of the file from the Austrian War Archive, MS Allg. 483. The matter was looked into because Hitler had started legal proceedings for libel against two reporters who had called him a draft dodger.

75. Munich BHStA, Collection Rehse, no. 1124.

76. A copy of the application is reprinted in Jetzinger, p. 273.

77. Munich BHStA, E. Hitler.

78. Kubizek, pp. 43 and 203.

79. *Lagebesprechungen*, p. 862.

80. Domarus, pp. 641 and 643.

81. *MK*, pp. 124ff.

82. Ibid., p. 373.

SELECTED BIBLIOGRAPHY

Anonymous. "Mein Freund Hitler" (My friend Hitler). In *Moravsky ilustrovany zpravodaj* no. 40 (1935), pp. 10 ff.

Binion, Rudolph. *". . . dass ihr mich gefunden habt." Hitler und die Deutschen* ("That you have found me": Hitler and the Germans). Stuttgart, 1978.

Bloch, Eduard. "My Patient Hitler." *Collier's*, March 15 and 22, 1941.

Daim, Wilfried. *Der Mann, der Hitler die Ideen gab. Jörg Lanz von Liebenfels* (The man who gave Hitler ideas: Jörg Lanz von Liebenfels). New edition. Vienna, 1994.

Domarus, Max, ed. *Hitler, Reden und Proklamationen, 1932–1945* (Hitler, Speeches and Proclamations, 1932–1945). Munich, 1962.

Frank, Hans. *Im Angesicht des Galgens* (Facing the gallows). Munich, 1953.

Giesler, Hermann. *Ein anderer Hitler* (A different Hitler). Leoni, 1977.

Glettler, Monika. *Die Wiener Tschechen um 1900. Strukturanalyse einer nationaler Minderheit in der Grossstadt* (The Viennese Czechs around 1900: Stuctural Analysis of an Ethnic Minority in the Capital). Vienna, 1972.

Goebbels, Joseph. *Die Tagebücher von Joseph Goebbels* (The diaries of Joseph Goebbels). Edited by Elke Fröhlich. 4 volumes. Munich, 1987.

Hamann, Brigitte. *Rudolf. Kronprinz und Rebell* (Rudolf: crown prince and rebel). Vienna, 1978.

————. *Bertha von Suttner. Ein Leben für die Frieden* (Bertha von Suttner: A life for peace). Munich, 1986.

Hanisch, Reinhold. "I Was Hitler's Buddy." *The New Republic*, April 5, 12, and 19, 1939.

Heiber, Beatrice and Helmut. *Die Rückseite des Hakenkreuzes* (The other side of the swastika). Munich, 1993.

Heiden, Konrad. *Adolf Hitler*. 2 volumes. Zürich, 1936–37.

Hitler, Adolf. *Reden, Schriften, Anordnungen* (Speeches, writings, mandates). Munich, 1993.

————. *Monologe in Führerhauptquartier, 1941–1944* (Monologues in the Führer's headquarters, 1941–1944). Edited by Werner Jochmann. Hamburg, 1980.

Jäckel, Eberhard, and Kuhn, Axel, eds. *Hitler. Sämtliche Aufzeichnungen, 1905–1924* (Hitler: Collected sketches, 1905–1924). Stuttgart, 1980.

Jetzinger, Franz. *Hitlers Jugend* (Hitler's youth). Vienna, 1956.

Joachimsthaler, A. *Korrektur einer Biographie: Adolf Hitler, 1908–1920* (Correction of a biography: Adolf Hitler, 1908–1920). Munich, 1989.

Kandl, Eleonore. Hitlers Österreichbild. Ph.D. dissertation. Vienna, 1963.

Kielmansegg, Erich Graf. *Kaiserhaus, Staatsmänner und Politiker* (Palace, statesmen, and politicians). Vienna, 1966.

Kokoschka, Oskar. *Mein Leben* (My life). Munich, 1971.

Kubizek, August. *Adolf Hitler, Mein Jugendfreund* (Adolf Hitler, my boyhood friend). Graz, 1953.

Maser, Werner. *Adolf Hitler*. Munich, 1971.

Mommsen, Hans. *Die Sozialdemokratie und die Nationaltätenfrage in habsburgischen Vielvölkerstaat, 1867–1907* (Social Democracy and the question of nationalities in the Habsburg multiethnic empire, 1867–1907). Vienna, 1963.

Otruba, Gustav, et al. "Die Herkunft der Wiener Bevölkerung" (The origins of the Viennese population). In *Jahrbuch des Vereins der Geschichte der Stadt Wien*, vol. 13. Vienna, 1957.

Pichl, Eduard. *Georg Schönerer*. 6 volumes. Vienna and Oldenburg, 1912–1938.

Picker, Henry. *Hitlers Tischgespräche im Führerhauptquartier* (Hitler's table talk in the Führer's headquarters). Frankfurt and Berlin, 1951. (New edition, 1993.)

Price, Billy. *Adolf Hitler als Maler und Zeichner* (Adolf Hitler as painter and sketch artist). Zug, 1983.

Pulzer, Peter G. J. *Die Entstehung des politischen Antisemitismus in Deutschland und Österreich, 1867–1914* (The establishment of political anti-Semitism in Germany and Austria, 1867–1914). Gütersloh, 1966.

Salten, Felix. *Das österreichische Antlitz* (The face of Austria). Berlin, 1909.

Scheicher, Joseph. *Erlebnisse und Erinnerungen* (Experiences and Memories). 6 volumes. Vienna, n.d.

Schroeder, Christa. *Er war mein Chef* (He was my boss). Munich, 1985.

Smith, Bradley F. *Adolf Hitler: His Family, Childhood and Youth*. Stanford, 1967.

Somary, Felix. *Erinnerungen aus meinem Leben* (Memoirs from my life). Zürich, 1955.

Speer, Albert. *Erinnerungen* (Memoirs). Frankfurt, 1969.

———. *Spandau Tagebücher* (Spandau diaries). Berlin, 1975.

Turner, H. A., ed. *Hitler als nächster Nähe* (Hitler as next-door neighbor). Berlin, 1978.

Urbanitsch, Peter. "Die Deutschen in Österreich" (The Germans in Austria). In Adam Wandruszka and Peter Urbanitsch, eds., *Die Habsburgmonarchie 1848–1918*, vol. 3, *Die Völker des Reiches*, pp. 33–153. Vienna, 1980.

Vrba, Rudolph. *Die Revolution in Russland* (The Revolution in Russia). Prague, 1906.

Wasserman, Jakob. *Mein Weg als Deutscher und Jude* (My path as a German and Jew). Berlin, 1921.

Weininger, Otto. *Geschlecht und Charakter* (Kind and character). Vienna, n.d.

Zweig, Stefan. *Die Welt von Gestern* (The world of yesterday). Hamburg, 1965.

INDEX

J

Jahn, Peter, 356
Jahoda family, 349, 353–55
Jaurès, Jean, 386
Jerusalem: King of, 88
Jesuits, 164, 217, 232, 248, 250, 251, 252, 292, 302, 369, 381
Jetzinger, Franz, 52, 55–59, 194
Jewish Modernism, 78–82, 286, 373
Jewish press, 129, 246–48, 251, 254, 274, 279–80, 281, 343, 346
Jews: anti-Semitism among, 338; assimilation of, 227, 326, 328–29, 337, 338, 339–40, 354; in Austria, 16; as "beggars," 286, 330–31, 337; and Catholicism, 291–95, 327, 329; children as, 334; citizenship of, 89; civil rights for, 212, 286, 326, 344; and class system, 327; as communists/Marxists, 294, 296, 347; definition of, 290; as degenerates, 83–84; deportation of, 358–59; divisiveness among, 338; Eastern, 286, 326, 329–35, 337–41, 345, 347–48, 352, 359; education of, 293–94, 327–28, 329, 335, 337, 371, 372; emancipation of, 229, 293, 326, 327, 331; expropriation of property of, 286, 356, 357; and Franz Josef II, 112, 113; as friends of Aryans, 243; German fraternities expel, 272–73; as German nationalists, 161, 242, 268; and German People's Party, 12; and German School Association, 249; in Great Britain, 279; and growing hatred of foreigners, 151; as heroes of Hitler, 23; historical background of, 325–30; Hitler's ancestors as, 46–47, 49–52; as Hitler's associates, 164, 166, 167, 171, 181–82, 185, 191, 215, 322, 348–50; Hitler's paintings sold to, 350, 356; Hitler's views about, 166,

324; Hungarian, 290; and intermarriage, 328–29; labor leaders as, 180–82; language of, 340; leadership of, 258; in Leopoldstadt, 307; as liberals, 281, 291, 293, 329; in Linz, 15–16; in men's hostel, 164; migration of, 330–35, 341–42, 343, 344–45; and myth about Hitler as syphilitic, 197; as pacifists, 385; in parliament, 329, 335; parliamentary debates about, 335–37; as part of Austro-Hungarian Empire, 89, 91, 240; as peddlers, 332–33; persecution of, 343–44; as philanthropists, 145, 158, 166, 337, 349; Polish, 258; and politics, 329; and race theories, 203, 207, 208–9, 212, 219, 220, 221, 222, 224; religious, 326, 337, 338, 372; and ritual murder, 287–88; snake as symbol of, 263; as students, 272, 273, 350; Viennese population of, 89, 326; voting rights of, 346; wealth of, 328; and Weininger's identity crisis, 227–30; Western, 272, 337–41, 358–59; as white slave traders, 332, 333–35; women as, 286, 333–35, 371, 372; world rule by, 331, 341–47, 352. *See also* Anti-Semitism; Jewish Modernism; Social Democrats; Zionism/Zionists; *specific part of Austro-Hungarian Empire or specific person*
Joachim Fest, 58
Jostenoode, Harald Arjune Grävell von, 109, 110, 205–6

K

Kafka, Franz, 230
Kainz, Josef, 75
Kalmus & Co., 31
Karlskirche, 162, 198
Kasimir, Knight of Obertynski, 90